Studies in Fuzziness and Soft Computing 279

Editor-in-Chief

For further volumes:
http://www.springer.com/series/2941

Zeshui Xu

Intuitionistic Fuzzy Aggregation and Clustering

Springer

Zeshui Xu
College of Sciences
PLA University of Science
and Technology
Nanjing
People's Republic of China

ISSN 1434-9922 ISSN 1860-0808 (electronic)
ISBN 978-3-642-28405-2 ISBN 978-3-642-28406-9 (eBook)
DOI 10.1007/978-3-642-28406-9
Springer Heidelberg New York Dordrecht London

Library of Congress Control Number: 2012953466

Printed on acid-free paper

Springer is part of Springer Science+Business Media (www.springer.com)

Preface

The concept of intuitionistic fuzzy set (IFS) was originally introduced by Atanassov (1983) to extend the concept of the traditional fuzzy set. Each element in an IFS is expressed by an ordered pair which is called an intuitionistic fuzzy value (IFV) (or intuitionistic fuzzy number (IFN)), and each IFV is characterized by a membership degree, a nonmembership degree, and a hesitancy degree. The sum of the membership degree, the nonmembership degree, and the hesitancy degree of each IFV is equal to one. IFVs can describe the fuzzy characters of things comprehensively, and thus are a powerful and effective tool in expressing uncertain or fuzzy information in actual applications. Recently, a lot of research work has been done on the aggregation and cluster analysis. Since 2006, my research group has been focusing on the investigation of these interesting and important topics, and achieved fruitful research results which have been published in some well-known peer-reviewed professional journals.

This book offers a systematic introduction to the latest research work of my group on information aggregation and cluster analysis under intuitionistic fuzzy environments, including the various algorithms for clustering intuitionistic fuzzy information and the intuitionistic fuzzy aggregation techniques, and their applications in multi-attribute decision making, such as supply chain management, military system performance evaluation, project management, venture capital, information system selection, building materials classification, and operational plan assessment, and so on. We organized this book as below:

Chapter 1 introduces the intuitionistic fuzzy aggregation techniques. We first give a survey of the existing methods for ranking IFVs, and then introduce various operational laws of IFVs. On the basis of these ranking methods and operational laws, we present varieties of the intuitionistic fuzzy power aggregation operators, the intuitionistic fuzzy geometric Bonferroni means, the intuitionistic fuzzy aggregation operators based on Archimedean t-conorm and t-norm, the generalized intuitionistic fuzzy aggregation operators based on Hamacher t-conorm and t-norm, the generalized intuitionistic fuzzy point aggregation operators, and their generalizations in interval-valued intuitionistic fuzzy environments and the applications in multi-attribute decision making.

Chapter 2 introduces the clustering algorithms of IFSs. The chapter first defines the concept of intuitionistic fuzzy similarity degree, and constructs the intuitionistic fuzzy similarity matrix and the intuitionistic fuzzy equivalence matrix. Then, the chapter defines the compound operational law of intuitionistic fuzzy similarity matrix, and gives an approach to transforming the intuitionistic fuzzy similarity matrices into the intuitionistic fuzzy equivalence matrices. After that, the chapter defines the λ-cutting matrices of the intuitionistic fuzzy similarity matrix and the intuitionistic fuzzy equivalence matrix, based on which an approach is presented for clustering IFSs. Moreover, the chapter defines the concept of association and equivalent association matrix, and introduces some methods for calculating the association coefficients of IFSs. Then, based on the association matrix, the chapter introduces a clustering algorithm for IFSs, and extends the algorithm to cluster interval-valued IFSs. Additionally, some other clustering algorithms, such as the intuitionistic fuzzy hierarchical clustering algorithms, the intuitionistic fuzzy orthogonal clustering algorithm, the intuitionistic fuzzy C-means clustering algorithms, the intuitionistic fuzzy minimum spanning tree (MST) clustering algorithm, the intuitionistic fuzzy clustering algorithm based on Boole matrix and association measure, the intuitionistic fuzzy netting clustering method, and the direct cluster analysis based on intuitionistic fuzzy implication are also introduced.

This book can be used as a reference for researchers and practitioners working in the fields of fuzzy mathematics, operations research, information science, management science and engineering, and so on. It can also be used as a textbook for postgraduate and senior undergraduate students.

This work was supported by the National Natural Science Foundation of China under Grant 71071161.

Nanjing, April 2012 Zeshui Xu

Contents

Chapter 1
Intuitionistic Fuzzy Aggregation Techniques

Intuitionistic fuzzy set (IFS), introduced by Atanassov (1983, 1986), is the generalization of Zadeh's fuzzy set (Zadeh 1965). IFS is characterized by a membership function and a non-membership function, and thus can depict the fuzzy character of data more comprehensively than Zadeh's fuzzy set which is only characterized by a membership function. For example, if a girl wants to find a boyfriend, and evaluates the boy from five aspects, she may feel satisfied with three aspects, unsatisfied with one aspect and uncertain with one aspect of the boy. In such a case, fuzzy sets can only reflect the satisfied aspect, which loses some uncertain information, while IFSs can describe all the satisfied, unsatisfied and uncertain information. In a variety of voting events, in addition to the support and the objection, there is usually the abstention which indicates the hesitation or the indeterminacy of the voter to the object. IFSs are more suitable to deal with these cases than fuzzy sets. The core of an IFS is intuitionistic fuzzy values (IFVs) (Xu and Yager 2006; Xu 2007), each of which is composed of a membership degree, a non-membership degree, and a hesitancy degree. IFVs are a powerful tool to depict uncertain or fuzzy information. In many fields, such as decision making, cluster analysis, and information retrieval, etc., information aggregation is an essential process. Therefore, how to aggregate IFVs is an interesting and important research topic, which has received great attention from researchers and a lot of intuitionistic fuzzy aggregation techniques have been developed (Xu and Yager 2006, 2009, 2011; Xu 2007, 2010; Xu and Chen 2007b; Boran et al. 2009; Tan and Chen 2010; Xu and Cai 2010a, b; Zhao et al. 2010; Beliakov et al. 2011; Xu and Xia 2011). Xu and Cai (2010b, 2012) provided a survey of these intuitionistic fuzzy aggregation techniques, and their applications in various fields. Recently, Xia and Xu (2010) developed various generalized intuitionistic fuzzy point aggregation operators, which can control the certainty degrees of the aggregated arguments with some parameters. Xu (2011) gave a series of intuitionistic fuzzy power aggregation operators, whose weighting vectors depend upon the input arguments and allow the values being aggregated to support and reinforce each other. Xia et al. (2012a, b) proposed a geometric Bonferroni mean, based on which they defined the intuitionistic fuzzy geometric Bonferroni means and their generalized versions. Based on Archimedean

Z. Xu, *Intuitionistic Fuzzy Aggregation and Clustering*, Studies in Fuzziness and Soft Computing 279, DOI: 10.1007/978-3-642-28406-9_1,

t-conorm and t-norm, Xia and Xu (2011), and Xia et al. (2012c) presented some intuitionistic fuzzy aggregation operators and their generalizations. In this chapter, we shall introduce these newly developed aggregation operators for IFVs, and their applications in decision making.

1.1 Rankings of Intuitionistic Fuzzy Values

1.1.1 Intuitionistic Fuzzy Values

Atanassov (1986) introduced the concept of intuitionistic fuzzy set (IFS):

Definition 1.1 (Atanassov 1986) Let X be a fixed set, then

$$A = \{\langle x, \mu_A(x), v_A(x)\rangle | x \in X\} \tag{1.1}$$

is called an intuitionistic fuzzy set (IFS), which assigns to each element x a membership degree $\mu_A(x)$ and a non-membership degree $v_A(x)$, with the conditions $\mu_A(x), v_A(x) \geq 0$ and $0 \leq \mu_A(x) + v_A(x) \leq 1, \forall x \in X$. Furthermore, $\pi_A(x) = 1 - \mu_A(x) - v_A(x)$ $(\forall x \in X)$ is called a hesitancy degree or an intuitionistic index of x to A. $A^c = \{\langle x, v_A(x), \mu_A(x)\rangle | x \in X\}$ is called the complement of A.

In the special case $\pi_A(x) = 0$, i.e., $\mu_A(x) + v_A(x) = 1$, the IFS A reduces to a fuzzy set (Zadeh 1965).

Xu and Yager (2006) called each triple $(\mu_A(x), v_A(x), \pi_A(x))$ an intuitionistic fuzzy value (IFV) (or an intuitionistic fuzzy number (IFN)), and for convenience, denoted an IFV by $\alpha = (\mu_\alpha, v_\alpha, \pi_\alpha)$, where

$$\mu_\alpha, v_\alpha \geq 0, \quad \mu_\alpha + v_\alpha \leq 1, \quad \pi_\alpha = 1 - \mu_\alpha - v_\alpha \tag{1.2}$$

Each IFV has a physical interpretation, for example, if $\alpha = (0.6, 0.3, 0.1)$, then $\mu_\alpha = 0.6$, $v_\alpha = 0.3$ and $\pi_\alpha = 0.1$, which can be interpreted as "the vote for resolution is 6 in favor, 3 against, and 1 abstention".

1.1.2 Methods for Ranking IFVs

In the process of applying IFVs to practical problems, one key step is to rank IFVs. Clearly, there are two basic principles we should follow in ranking IFVs: the first is that the IFV which has the larger membership degree and the smaller non-membership degree should be given priority; the second is that the IFV which has a smaller hesitancy degree should be ranked first. When we use these two principles to rank IFVs, the first one is top-priority. If it is not applicable individually, then we shall consider the two principles synthetically (Zhang and Xu 2012). According to the first principle we can easily get that $\alpha^* = (1, 0, 0)$ is the largest IFV and $\alpha_* = (0, 1, 0)$ is the smallest one.

Let $\alpha_i = (\mu_{\alpha_i}, v_{\alpha_i}, \pi_{\alpha_i})$ $(i = 1, 2)$ be any two IFVs, then we also have the following conclusions:

(1) If $\mu_{\alpha_1} \geq \mu_{\alpha_2}$ and $v_{\alpha_1} < v_{\alpha_2}$, then $\alpha_1 > \alpha_2$.
(2) If $\mu_{\alpha_1} < \mu_{\alpha_2}$ and $v_{\alpha_1} \geq v_{\alpha_2}$, then $\alpha_1 < \alpha_2$.
(3) If $\mu_{\alpha_1} = \mu_{\alpha_2}$ and $v_{\alpha_1} = v_{\alpha_2}$, then $\alpha_1 = \alpha_2$.

However, besides the comparisons (1)–(3) above, there are also other situations left, for example, if $\mu_{\alpha_1} < \mu_{\alpha_2}$ and $v_{\alpha_1} < v_{\alpha_2}$, then the IFVs do not satisfy the first principle, which IFV should be ranked first? Zhang and Xu (2012) gave a survey of the existing results related to this issue.

1.1.2.1 The Method for Ranking IFVs by Using the Score Function

Chen and Tan (1994) introduced the concept of the score function S. Let $\alpha = (\mu_\alpha, v_\alpha, \pi_\alpha)$ be an IFV, then the score function of α is defined as:

$$S(\alpha) = \mu_\alpha - v_\alpha \tag{1.3}$$

Now we give an example to illustrate the results derived by using the score function:

Example 1.1 (Zhang and Xu 2012) Let $\alpha_1 = (0.4, 0.3, 0.3)$, $\alpha_2 = (0.3, 0.1, 0.6)$ and $\alpha_3 = (0.3, 0.2, 0.5)$ be three IFVs, the score values derived by Eq. (1.3) are as follows, respectively:

$$S(\alpha_1) = 0.4 - 0.3 = 0.1, \quad S(\alpha_2) = 0.3 - 0.1 = 0.2, \quad S(\alpha_3) = 0.3 - 0.2 = 0.1$$

and then $S(\alpha_1) = S(\alpha_3) < S(\alpha_2)$.

According to Chen and Tan (1994)'s method, we can infer that $\alpha_1 = \alpha_3 < \alpha_2$.

The result is counterintuitive because that α_1 and α_3 are not the same. So only the score function is not enough in ranking IFVs as they have the same score value.

For this reason, Hong and Choi (2000) proposed the accuracy function H:

$$H(\alpha) = \mu_\alpha + v_\alpha \tag{1.4}$$

and Li and Rao (2001) defined another score function S':

$$S'(\alpha) = 1 - v_\alpha \tag{1.5}$$

By using Eqs. (1.3) and (1.4), Xu and Yager (2006), and Xu (2007) gave the following method for ranking IFVs:

(1) If $S(\alpha_i) > S(\alpha_j)$, then α_i is larger than α_j.
(2) If $S(\alpha_i) = S(\alpha_j)$, then

  (a) If $H(\alpha_i) = H(\alpha_j)$, then $\alpha_i = \alpha_j$;
  (b) If $H(\alpha_i) > H(\alpha_j)$, then $\alpha_i > \alpha_j$.

Instead of the method above, Li and Rao (2001) gave another ranking technique by replacing the accuracy function (1.4) with the score function (1.5).

Then let's redo Example 1.1, we calculate the accuracy values and the score values, respectively:

$$H(\alpha_1) = 0.4 + 0.3 = 0.7, \quad H(\alpha_3) = 0.3 + 0.2 = 0.5$$

$$S'(\alpha_1) = 1 - 0.3 = 0.7, \quad S'(\alpha_3) = 1 - 0.2 = 0.8$$

then $H(\alpha_1) > H(\alpha_3)$ and $S'(\alpha_1) < S'(\alpha_3)$.

We find that the two methods have different results. Hong and Choi (2000)'s method emphasizes the amount of information that an IFV contains, but Li and Rao (2001)'s method is inclined to choose the IFV which has the smaller non-membership degree.

Although the methods above can be used to rank all IFVs, sometimes it cannot satisfy our requirements. Let's see an example:

Example 1.2 (Zhang and Xu 2012) Suppose that there are two major state-funded projects y_1 and y_2, and a decision maker wants to select one of them by voting. The results of the voting are expressed by IFVs, the membership degree represents the proportion of the voters who agree to a project, the non-membership degree means the proportion of the voters who against the project, and the hesitation degree denotes the proportion of the abstainers. The results are listed as below:

(1) y_1: $(0.6, 0.15, 0.25)$—60 % in favor, 15 % against, and 25 % abstain.
(2) y_2: $(0.5, 0, 0.5)$—50 % in favor, 0 % against, and 50 % abstain.

In real situations, a decision maker may choose the first project because there are more people who support and believe that the project can be carried out better. But if we use the ranking methods based on the score function, it will produce the opposite result.

1.1.2.2 The Method for Ranking IFVs by Using the Positive Ideal Point

Bustince and Burillo (1995) introduced the distance between two IFSs $A_i = \{\langle x, \mu_{A_i}(x), \nu_{A_i}(x)\rangle | x \in X\}$ $(i = 1, 2)$ as follows:

$$d_1(A_1, A_2) = \frac{1}{2n} \sum_{j=1}^{n} (|\mu_{A_1}(x_j) - \mu_{A_2}(x_j)| + |v_{A_1}(x_j) - v_{A_2}(x_j)|) \tag{1.6}$$

Szmidt and Kacprzyk (2000) extended Eq. (1.6) by adding the hesitancy degrees:

$$\begin{aligned} d_2(A_1, A_2) = \frac{1}{2n} \sum_{j=1}^{n} (&|\mu_{A_1}(x_j) - \mu_{A_2}(x_j)| + |v_{A_1}(x_j) - v_{A_2}(x_j)| \\ &+ |\pi_{A_1}(x_j) - \pi_{A_2}(x_j)|) \end{aligned} \tag{1.7}$$

Motivated by Eqs. (1.6) and (1.7), respectively, we can calculate the distances between the IFV α and the positive ideal point (i.e., the largest IFV) α^* (Xu and Yager 2008):

$$\begin{aligned} d_1(\alpha, \alpha^*) &= \frac{1}{2}(|\mu_\alpha - 1| + |v_\alpha - 0|) \\ &= \frac{1}{2}(1 - \mu_\alpha + v_\alpha) \\ &= \frac{1}{2}(1 - (\mu_\alpha - v_\alpha)) \\ &= \frac{1}{2}(1 - S(\alpha)) \end{aligned} \tag{1.8}$$

$$\begin{aligned} d_2(\alpha, \alpha^*) &= \frac{1}{2}(|\mu_\alpha - 1| + |v_\alpha - 0| + |\pi_\alpha - 0|) \\ &= \frac{1}{2}(1 - \mu_\alpha + v_\alpha + \pi_\alpha) \\ &= \frac{1}{2}(1 - \mu_\alpha + v_\alpha + 1 - \mu_\alpha - v_\alpha) \\ &= 1 - \mu_\alpha \end{aligned} \tag{1.9}$$

We can infer from Eq. (1.8) that it has the similar result with Chen and Tan (1994)'s method, which may produce the same score values even if the two IFVs are different; while we can infer from Eq. (1.9) that the result only relies on the value of μ_α, so it produces the loss of information and cannot distinguish the IFVs which have the same membership degrees and the different non-membership degrees.

Later, Szmidt and Kacprzyk (2009a, b, 2010) further improved the distance measure Eq. (1.9) by considering the hesitancy degrees simultaneously:

$$\begin{aligned} L(\alpha) &= \frac{1}{2}(1 + \pi_\alpha)\, d_2(\alpha, \alpha^*) \\ &= \frac{1}{2}(1 + \pi_\alpha)\, (1 - \mu_\alpha) \end{aligned} \tag{1.10}$$

Obviously, the distance measure (1.9) takes into account all three parameters of IFVs. Szmidt and Kacprzyk (2000) showed that the third parameter cannot be omitted when calculating distance between two IFVs. From Eq. (1.10), we can know that the IFV which has the smaller membership degree and the larger hesitancy degree has the larger value of $L(\alpha)$. In general, the lower $L(\alpha)$, the better α in the sense of the amount and reliability of information (Szmidit and Kacprzyk 2009a, b, 2010). Especially, from Eq. (1.10), we can see that if $L(\alpha) = 0$, then we get the largest IFV $\alpha^* = (1, 0, 0)$; if $L(\alpha) = 1$, then we get the "smallest" IFV $\alpha'_* = (0,0,1)$ in the sense of the reliability of the information (we have no information at all, which means the situation with 100 % lack of knowledge, clearly, this result is very different from the smallest IFVs $\alpha_* = (0,1,0)$ derived by the other ranking methods), and the "quality" measured by the distance from $\alpha^* = (1,0,0)$ (here, the distance is the biggest).

In addition, in some situations, the formula Eq. (1.10) is also not enough in ranking IFVs. Let's see an example below:

Example 1.3 (Zhang and Xu 2012) Let $\alpha_1 = (0.2,0.3,0.5)$ and $\alpha_2 = (0,0.8,0.2)$ be two IFVs. Obviously, the IFVs α_1 and α_2 are intuitively different. But by Eq. (1.10), we have

$$L(\alpha_1) = \frac{1}{2}(1 + 0.5) \times 0.8 = 0.6, \quad L(\alpha_2) = \frac{1}{2}(1 + 0.2) \times 1 = 0.6$$

then $L(\alpha_1) = L(\alpha_2)$, and thus, in this case the formula (1.10) cannot distinguish the IFVs α_1 and α_2.

1.1.2.3 The Method for Ranking IFVs by Using the Intuitionistic Fuzzy Point Operators

Liu and Wang (2007) proposed a new score function by using the intuitionistic fuzzy point operators (Atanassov 1999; Burillo and Bustince 1996):

$$J_n(\alpha) = \mu_\alpha + \sigma\pi_\alpha + \sigma(1 - \sigma - \theta)\pi_\alpha + \cdots + \sigma(1 - \sigma - \theta)^{n-1}\pi_\alpha, \quad n = 1, 2, \ldots \tag{1.11}$$

$$J_\infty(\alpha) = \mu_\alpha + \frac{\sigma}{\sigma + \theta}\pi_\alpha \tag{1.12}$$

where $\sigma, \theta \in [0, 1]$ and $\sigma + \theta \leq 1$. In this way, the larger the value of $J_n(\alpha)$, the more priority should be given in ranking. From Eqs. (1.11) and (1.12), we can infer that the hesitancy degree of the IFV α is divided into three parts: $\sigma\pi_\alpha$, $\theta\pi_\alpha$ and $(1 - \sigma - \theta)\pi_\alpha$, where $\sigma\pi_\alpha$ matches μ_α, $\theta\pi_\alpha$ matches v_α, and $(1 - \sigma - \theta)\pi_\alpha$ is uncertain. In particular, if $\sigma + \theta = 1$, then the IFV α reduces to a fuzzy value $\mu_\alpha + \sigma\pi_\alpha$. In practical applications, the decision maker can choose the suitable parameters σ and θ according to the actual demands.

1.1.2.4 The Method for Ranking IFVs by Using the Similarity Measure and the Accuracy Degree

Szmidt and Kacprzyk (2004) proposed a similarity measure of IFSs:

$$\vartheta_1(A_1, A_2) = \frac{d(A_1, A_2)}{d(A_1, A_2^c)} \tag{1.13}$$

where the distances $d(A_1, A_2)$ and $d(A_1, A_2^c)$ can be calculated by using Eq. (1.6) or Eq. (1.7).

Eq. (1.13) not only considers the distance between two IFSs but also reflects if the compared IFSs are more similar or more dissimilar to each other. However, in practical applications, it is generally expected that the degree of similarity would describe to what extent the IFSs are similar, so the most similar IFSs should have the largest degree of similarity (Hwang and Yoon 1981), which cannot be reflected by Eq. (1.13). To solve this issue, Xu and Yager (2009) improved Szmidt and Kacprzyk (2004)'s result according to Hwang and Yoon (1981)'s idea of technique for order preference by similarity to ideal solution (TOPSIS) and developed the following similarity measure:

$$\vartheta_2(A_1, A_2) = 1 - \frac{d(A_1, A_2)}{d(A_1, A_2) + d(A_1, A_2^c)} = \frac{d(A_1, A_2^c)}{d(A_1, A_2) + d(A_1, A_2^c)} \tag{1.14}$$

The similarity measure (1.14) can not only overcome the disadvantages of Eq. (1.13), but also examine if the compared values are more similar or more dissimilar to each other so as to avoid drawing conclusions about strong similarity between two IFSs on the basis of the small distances between these sets (Xu and Yager 2009).

Motivated by Eq. (1.14) and the idea of positive ideal point, Zhang and Xu (2012) proposed a new method for ranking IFVs. First we give the definition of similarity function ϑ:

Definition 1.2 (Zhang and Xu 2012) Let $\alpha = (\mu_\alpha, \nu_\alpha, \pi_\alpha)$ be an IFV, then the similarity function ϑ about this IFV is defined as:

$$\begin{aligned}
\vartheta(\alpha) &= 1 - \frac{d_2(\alpha, (1,0,0))}{d_2(\alpha, (1,0,0)) + d_2(\alpha, (0,1,0))} \\
&= 1 - \frac{\frac{1}{2}(|\mu_\alpha - 1| + |\nu_\alpha - 0| + |\pi_\alpha - 0|)}{\frac{1}{2}(|\mu_\alpha - 1| + |\nu_\alpha - 0| + |\pi_\alpha - 0|) + \frac{1}{2}(|\mu_\alpha - 0| + |\nu_\alpha - 1| + |\pi_\alpha - 0|)} \\
&= 1 - \frac{1 - \mu_\alpha + \nu_\alpha + \pi_\alpha}{2 + 2\pi_\alpha} \\
&= \frac{1 + \pi_\alpha + \mu_\alpha - \nu_\alpha}{2 + 2\pi_\alpha}
\end{aligned}$$

$$= \frac{1 - v_\alpha}{1 + \pi_\alpha} = 1 - \frac{1 - \mu_\alpha}{1 + \pi_\alpha} \tag{1.15}$$

where $0 \leq \vartheta(\alpha) \leq 1$. We call $\vartheta(\alpha)$ the ϑ value of the IFV. When $\alpha = \alpha^* = (1,0,0)$, it gets the maximum ϑ value: $\vartheta(\alpha) = 1$; and when $\alpha = \alpha_* = (0,1,0)$, it gets the minimum ϑ value: $\vartheta(\alpha) = 0$.

From Eq. (1.15), we can easily conclude that (Zhang and Xu 2012):

(1) If two IFVs have the same hesitancy degree, then the IFV which has the smaller non-membership degree or the larger membership degree should be ranked first.
(2) If two IFVs have the same non-membership degree, then the IFV which has the smaller hesitancy degree should be ranked first.
(3) If two IFVs have the same membership degree, then the IFV which has the larger hesitancy degree should be ranked first.

When we use Eq. (1.15) to rank IFVs, the derived result is in accordance with the first principle introduced at the beginning of Sect. 1.1.2, i.e., the IFV which has the larger membership degree and the smaller non-membership degree should be given priority. Let's prove it below:

Proof Let $\alpha_1 = (\mu_{\alpha_1}, v_{\alpha_1}, \pi_{\alpha_1})$ and $\alpha_2 = (\mu_{\alpha_2}, v_{\alpha_2}, \pi_{\alpha_2})$ be two IFVs, and suppose that $\mu_{\alpha_1} > \mu_{\alpha_2}$ and $v_{\alpha_1} < v_{\alpha_2}$, then by Eq. (1.15), we get

$$\vartheta(\alpha_1) = \frac{1 - v_{\alpha_1}}{2 - \mu_{\alpha_1} - v_{\alpha_1}}, \quad \vartheta(\alpha_2) = \frac{1 - v_{\alpha_2}}{2 - \mu_{\alpha_2} - v_{\alpha_2}}$$

Let $\mu_{\alpha_1} - \mu_{\alpha_2} = \Delta_1$ and $v_{\alpha_2} - v_{\alpha_1} = \Delta_2$, then we have

$$\vartheta(\alpha_1) = \frac{1 - v_{\alpha_1}}{2 - \mu_{\alpha_1} - v_{\alpha_1}} > \frac{1 - v_{\alpha_1}}{2 - (\mu_{\alpha_1} - \Delta_1) - v_{\alpha_1}} = \frac{1 - v_{\alpha_1}}{2 - \mu_{\alpha_2} - v_{\alpha_1}}$$
$$\Rightarrow \vartheta(\alpha_1) > \frac{1 - v_{\alpha_1}}{2 - \mu_{\alpha_2} - v_{\alpha_1}}$$

and similarly,

$$\vartheta(\alpha_2) = \frac{1 - v_{\alpha_2}}{2 - \mu_{\alpha_2} - v_{\alpha_2}} = 1 - \frac{1 - \mu_{\alpha_2}}{2 - \mu_{\alpha_2} - v_{\alpha_2}} < 1 - \frac{1 - \mu_{\alpha_2}}{2 - \mu_{\alpha_2} - (v_{\alpha_2} - \Delta_2)}$$
$$= 1 - \frac{1 - \mu_{\alpha_2}}{2 - \mu_{\alpha_2} - v_{\alpha_1}} = \frac{1 - v_{\alpha_1}}{2 - \mu_{\alpha_2} - v_{\alpha_1}}$$
$$\Rightarrow \vartheta(\alpha_2) < \frac{1 - v_{\alpha_1}}{2 - \mu_{\alpha_2} - v_{\alpha_1}}$$

Thus, we can obtain

$$\vartheta(\alpha_2) < \frac{1 - v_{\alpha_1}}{2 - \mu_{\alpha_2} - v_{\alpha_1}} < \vartheta(\alpha_1) \Rightarrow \vartheta(\alpha_1) > \vartheta(\alpha_2)$$

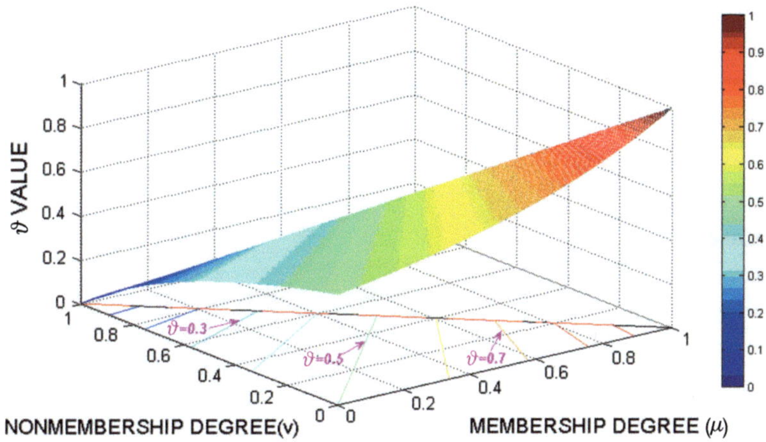

Fig. 1.1 The results derived by Eq. (1.15) and their contours

But sometimes we will face the situations where the considered two IFVs have the same value derived by Eq. (1.15), which can be shown in Fig. 1.1 (Zhang and Xu 2012).

In the bottom of Fig. 1.1, we have given the contours of the results derived by Eq. (1.15), from which we can get the following conclusions:

Theorem 1.1 (Zhang and Xu 2012)

(1) If the membership degree of an IFV is the same as the non-membership degree, then the ϑ value is $\frac{1}{2}$.
(2) If the membership degree of an IFV is larger than the non-membership degree, then the ϑ value is larger than $\frac{1}{2}$.
(3) If the membership degree of an IFV is smaller than the non-membership degree, then the ϑ value is smaller than $\frac{1}{2}$.

Proof Let $\alpha = (\mu_\alpha, v_\alpha, \pi_\alpha)$ be an IFV, then we calculate the ϑ value of α:

$$\vartheta(\alpha) = \frac{1 - v_\alpha}{1 + \pi_\alpha} = \frac{1 - v_\alpha}{1 + (1 - \mu_\alpha - v_\alpha)} = \frac{1 - v_\alpha}{(1 - \mu_\alpha) + (1 - v_\alpha)}$$

which should be discussed in three cases:

Case 1 $\mu_\alpha = v_\alpha$

$$\Rightarrow \frac{1 - v_\alpha}{(1 - \mu_\alpha) + (1 - v_\alpha)} = \frac{1 - v_\alpha}{(1 - v_\alpha) + (1 - v_\alpha)} = \frac{1}{2}$$

$$\Rightarrow \quad \vartheta(\alpha) = \frac{1}{2}$$

Case 2 $\mu_\alpha > v_\alpha$

$$\Rightarrow \frac{1-v_\alpha}{(1-\mu_\alpha)+(1-v_\alpha)} > \frac{1-v_\alpha}{(1-v_\alpha)+(1-v_\alpha)} = \frac{1}{2}$$
$$\Rightarrow \vartheta(\alpha) > \frac{1}{2}$$

Case 3 $\mu_\alpha < v_\alpha$

$$\Rightarrow \frac{1-v_\alpha}{(1-\mu_\alpha)+(1-v_\alpha)} < \frac{1-v_\alpha}{(1-v_\alpha)+(1-v_\alpha)} = \frac{1}{2}$$
$$\Rightarrow \vartheta(\alpha) < \frac{1}{2}$$

In fact, for each value derived by Eq. (1.15), its membership degree μ_α and non-membership degree v_α change in specific ranges, which we can see from the contours. In the following, we shall demonstrate it:

Let $\alpha = (\mu_\alpha, v_\alpha, \pi_\alpha)$ be an IFV, then

(1) If $\vartheta(\alpha) \leq 0.5$, then

(a) When $\pi_\alpha = 0$, μ_α and v_α get the maximums, i.e.,

$$\pi_\alpha = 0 \Rightarrow \mu_\alpha + v_\alpha = 1$$

and

$$\vartheta(\alpha) = \frac{1-v_\alpha}{1+\pi_\alpha} = 1 - v_\alpha \Rightarrow v_\alpha = 1 - \vartheta(\alpha) \Rightarrow \mu_\alpha = \vartheta(\alpha)$$

(b) When $\mu_\alpha = 0$, v_α gets the minimum, i.e.,

$$\vartheta(\alpha) = \frac{1-v_\alpha}{1+\pi_\alpha} = \frac{1-v_\alpha}{1+1-\mu_\alpha-v_\alpha} = \frac{1-v_\alpha}{2-v_\alpha} \Rightarrow v_\alpha = \frac{1-2\vartheta(\alpha)}{1-\vartheta(\alpha)}$$

then the ranges of μ_α and v_α are as follows, respectively:

$$0 \leq \mu_\alpha \leq \vartheta(\alpha), \quad \frac{1-2\vartheta(\alpha)}{1-\vartheta(\alpha)} \leq v_\alpha \leq 1 - \vartheta(\alpha)$$

(2) If $0.5 < \vartheta(\alpha) \leq 1$, then

(a) When $\pi_\alpha = 0$, μ_α and v_α get the maximums, i.e., $\mu_\alpha = \vartheta(\alpha)$ and $v_\alpha = 1 - \vartheta(\alpha)$;

(b) When $v_\alpha = 0$, μ_α gets the minimum, i.e.,

$$\vartheta(\alpha) = \frac{1-v_\alpha}{1+\pi_\alpha} = \frac{1-v_\alpha}{1+1-\mu_\alpha-v_\alpha} = \frac{1}{2-\mu_\alpha} \Rightarrow \mu_\alpha = \frac{2\vartheta(\alpha)-1}{\vartheta(\alpha)}$$

then the ranges of μ_α and v_α are as follows, respectively:

$$\frac{2\vartheta(\alpha)-1}{\vartheta(\alpha)} \leq \mu_\alpha \leq \vartheta(\alpha), \quad 0 \leq v_\alpha \leq 1-\vartheta(\alpha)$$

Based on the analysis above, in what follows, we introduce a new method for ranking IFVs (Zhang and Xu 2012):

Let $\alpha_i = (\mu_{\alpha_i}, v_{\alpha_i}, \pi_{\alpha_i})$ $(i = 1, 2, \ldots, n)$ be a collection of IFVs, then we rank these IFVs according to the following steps:

Step 1 Calculate the ϑ values of the IFVs α_i $(i = 1, 2, \ldots, n)$ using Eq. (1.15).

Step 2 Rank the IFVs α_i $(i = 1, 2, \ldots, n)$ according to the order of the ϑ values, and the IFV with the larger ϑ value should be ranked first. If there exist some IFVs with the same ϑ value, then go to Step 3.

Step 3 Calculate the accuracy degrees of these IFVs using Eq. (1.4), and then rank the IFVs according to the following principles:

(1) If $\vartheta(\alpha_i) > \vartheta(\alpha_j)$, then $\alpha_i > \alpha_j$.
(2) If $\vartheta(\alpha_i) = \vartheta(\alpha_j)$, then

$$\begin{aligned}
&\text{(a) If } H(\alpha_i) > H(\alpha_j), && \text{then } \alpha_i > \alpha_j;\\
&\text{(b) If } H(\alpha_i) < H(\alpha_j), && \text{then } \alpha_i < \alpha_j;\\
&\text{(c) If } H(\alpha_i) = H(\alpha_j), && \text{then } \alpha_i = \alpha_j,
\end{aligned} \tag{1.16}$$

which are in accordance with the basic principles introduced at the beginning of Sect. 1.1.2.

In the following, we give an example to illustrate the method above and compare it with all the existing ones:

Example 1.4 (Zhang and Xu 2012) Let $\alpha_1 = (0.6,0.1,0.3)$, $\alpha_2 = (0.6,0.15,0.25)$, $\alpha_3 = (0.5,0,0.5)$, $\alpha_4 = (0.2,0.3,0.5)$, and $\alpha_5 = (0,0.8,0.2)$ be five IFVs. Here, we rank them using all the methods discussed previously. The derived results are listed in Table 1.1 (Zhang and Xu 2012).

According to the data in Table 1.1, we can get the following ranking results:

(i) By the formulas (1.3) and (1.4), we get $\alpha_1 > \alpha_3 > \alpha_2 > \alpha_4 > \alpha_5$.

Table 1.1 The results derived by the existing methods

α_i	$S(\alpha_i)$	$H(\alpha_i)$	$S'(\alpha_i)$	$d_1(\alpha_i, \alpha^*)$	$d_2(\alpha_i, \alpha^*)$	$L(\alpha_i)$	$J(\alpha_i)$	$\vartheta(\alpha_i)$
(0.6,0.1,0.3)	0.5	0.7	0.9	0.25	0.4	0.26	6/7	9/13
(0.6,0.15,0.25)	0.45	0.75	0.85	0.275	0.4	0.25	0.8	17/25
(0.5,0,0.5)	0.5	0.5	1	0.25	0.5	0.375	1	2/3
(0.2,0.3,0.5)	−0.1	0.5	0.7	0.55	0.8	0.6	0.4	7/15
(0,0.8,0.2)	−0.8	0.8	0.2	0.9	1	0.6	0	1/6

Note 1. In the process of calculating $J(\alpha_i)$, we choose $\sigma = \dfrac{\mu_\alpha}{\mu_\alpha + v_\alpha}$ and $\theta = \dfrac{v_\alpha}{\mu_\alpha + v_\alpha}$

(ii) By the formulas (1.3) and (1.5), we get $\alpha_3 > \alpha_1 > \alpha_2 > \alpha_4 > \alpha_5$.
(iii) By the formula (1.8), we get $\alpha_3 = \alpha_1 > \alpha_2 > \alpha_4 > \alpha_5$.
(iv) By the formula (1.9), we get $\alpha_1 = \alpha_2 > \alpha_3 > \alpha_4 > \alpha_5$.
(v) By the formula (1.10), we get $\alpha_2 > \alpha_1 > \alpha_3 > \alpha_4 = \alpha_5$.
(vi) By the formula (1.11), we get $\alpha_3 > \alpha_1 > \alpha_2 > \alpha_4 > \alpha_5$.
(vii) By the formula (1.16), we get $\alpha_1 > \alpha_2 > \alpha_3 > \alpha_4 > \alpha_5$.

From the results above, we can see that the derived rankings in both (ii) and (vi) are the same, but all the other methods get different rankings. However, if we choose other values of σ and θ, then the results in (ii) and (vi) may be different. Now let's give a detailed analysis on the results in (i)–(vii). The rankings in (iii), (iv) and (v) are mainly based on the distance measures of IFVs, the used methods sometimes cannot distinguish IFVs. The used methods in (i) and (ii) focus on the differences between the membership degrees and the non-membership degrees, and consider these differences as a main factor in ranking IFVs. The used method in (vi) tries to decrease the uncertainty of an IFV by dividing its hesitancy degree into three parts, and uses the method of limit to turn an IFV into a fuzzy value. The different divisions may lead to different ranking results, in actual applications, the decision maker sometimes cannot give a precise division of the hesitancy degree because of the complexity and uncertainty of objective thing and the fuzziness of human thought. Zhang and Xu (2012)'s method in (vii) focuses on the similarity measure between an IFV and the positive ideal point, by using this method, we can solve lots of problems such as described in Example 1.2. In short, different methods may produce different results, and thus, we should choose appropriate ones in accordance with the actual demands.

1.1.3 The Application of Ranking IFVs Using the Similarity Measure and the Accuracy Degree in Multi-Attribute Decision Making

In the above subsection, we have introduced Zhang and Xu (2012)'s method for ranking IFVs. In what follows, we shall demonstrate how to use the method to solve a multi-attribute decision making problem through an illustrative example (Zhang and Xu 2012).

In modern warfare, the status of communication command is very important, and it plays a key role in campaign's success and failure. So in order to improve the capacity of communication jamming, a military unit decides to equip with a communication jamming system. According to the consultations with different suppliers, there are four possible systems (alternatives) y_j $(j = 1, 2, 3, 4)$ to choose from. Then the leaders of the military unit invite three experts e_k $(k = 1, 2, 3)$ to evaluate these systems so as to choose the most reasonable one. Based on the expertise and experiences of these experts, the leaders give the weight vector of these experts as

$\eta = (0.4,0.3,0.3)^T$. For a comprehensive assessment, the experts e_k $(k = 1, 2, 3)$ decide to evaluate the systems y_j $(j = 1, 2, 3, 4)$ from four layers:

(1) G_1: Reconnaissance capability. It is very useful for a communication jamming system, because when we want to jam enemy's communication system, we should first find them. This capability can be reflected in four aspects:

G_{11}: Search capability;
G_{12}: Intercept capability;
G_{13}: Parameter measurements capability;
G_{14}: Recognition capability.

(2) G_2: Command and control capability. This capability is a bridge of connecting the system and the user, from which we can operate the system. It contains three factors:

G_{21}: Information processing capability;
G_{22}: Situation display capability;
G_{23}: Reaction time.

(3) G_3: Jamming capability. This capability is very important, due to that if a communication jamming system doesn't have powerful jamming capability, it cannot destroy enemy's communication system. There also have three factors about this capability:

G_{31}: Jamming power;
G_{32}: The capability of frequency-aiming;
G_{33}: The coverage of frequency domain.

(4) G_4: Survival capability. It reflects the resistance against enemy's destroy. It can be shown in four aspects:

G_{41}: Mobility;
G_{42}: Hidden performance;
G_{43}: Invulnerability;
G_{44}: Reliability and maintainability.

The experts e_k $(k = 1, 2, 3)$ evaluate the systems y_j $(j = 1, 2, 3, 4)$ through the above factors (attributes). Each evaluation value given by the kth expert over the jth system under ith attribute of the lth layer is represented by an IFV $r_{l,i}^{(k,j)} = (\mu_{r_{l,i}^{(k,j)}}, \nu_{r_{l,i}^{(k,j)}}, \pi_{r_{l,i}^{(k,j)}})$, and all the IFVs given by kth expert about the jth system are contained in the intuitionistic fuzzy matrix $R^{(k,j)}$, shown as follows (Zhang and Xu 2012):

$$R^{(1,1)} = \begin{pmatrix} (0.6,0.3,0.1) & (0.7,0.2,0.1) & (0.7,0.1,0.2) & (0.7,0.1,0.2) \\ (0.7,0.2,0.1) & (0.6,0.2,0.2) & (0.8,0.1,0.1) & \text{--} \\ (0.8,0.2,0) & (0.8,0.1,0.1) & (0.7,0.1,0.2) & \text{--} \\ (0.6,0.1,0.3) & (0.7,0.1,0.2) & (0.6,0.2,0.2) & (0.7,0.2,0.1) \end{pmatrix}$$

$$R^{(1,2)} = \begin{pmatrix} (0.6,0.3,0.1) & (0.6,0.2,0.2) & (0.6,0.1,0.3) & (0.7,0.1,0.2) \\ (0.7,0.2,0.1) & (0.6,0.2,0.2) & (0.6,0.1,0.3) & -- \\ (0.7,0.3,0) & (0.7,0.1,0.2) & (0.7,0.2,0.1) & -- \\ (0.5,0.2,0.3) & (0.6,0.1,0.3) & (0.6,0.2,0.2) & (0.7,0.2,0.1) \end{pmatrix}$$

$$R^{(1,3)} = \begin{pmatrix} (0.6,0.3,0.1) & (0.6,0.2,0.2) & (0.6,0.1,0.3) & (0.7,0.1,0.2) \\ (0.8,0.2,0) & (0.7,0.2,0.1) & (0.8,0.1,0.1) & -- \\ (0.7,0.3,0) & (0.6,0.1,0.3) & (0.6,0.2,0.2) & -- \\ (0.6,0.2,0.2) & (0.6,0.1,0.3) & (0.6,0.1,0.3) & (0.6,0.2,0.2) \end{pmatrix}$$

$$R^{(1,4)} = \begin{pmatrix} (0.6,0.3,0.1) & (0.6,0.2,0.2) & (0.6,0.1,0.3) & (0.7,0.1,0.2) \\ (0.6,0.2,0.2) & (0.7,0.2,0.1) & (0.6,0.1,0.3) & -- \\ (0.7,0.3,0) & (0.6,0.1,0.3) & (0.6,0.2,0.2) & -- \\ (0.7,0.2,0.1) & (0.8,0.1,0.1) & (0.8,0.1,0.1) & (0.7,0.2,0.1) \end{pmatrix}$$

$$R^{(2,1)} = \begin{pmatrix} (0.5,0.2,0.3) & (0.7,0.2,0.1) & (0.7,0.1,0.2) & (0.7,0.1,0.2) \\ (0.7,0.2,0.1) & (0.6,0.2,0.2) & (0.8,0.1,0.1) & -- \\ (0.9,0.1,0) & (0.8,0.1,0.1) & (0.7,0.1,0.2) & -- \\ (0.6,0.1,0.3) & (0.7,0.1,0.2) & (0.6,0.2,0.2) & (0.6,0.2,0.2) \end{pmatrix}$$

$$R^{(2,2)} = \begin{pmatrix} (0.5,0.2,0.3) & (0.6,0.3,0.1) & (0.7,0.2,0.1) & (0.6,0.1,0.3) \\ (0.6,0.2,0.2) & (0.5,0.1,0.4) & (0.6,0.1,0.3) & -- \\ (0.6,0.4,0) & (0.6,0.1,0.3) & (0.7,0.2,0.1) & -- \\ (0.6,0.2,0.2) & (0.6,0.2,0.2) & (0.6,0.2,0.2) & (0.6,0.2,0.2) \end{pmatrix}$$

$$R^{(2,3)} = \begin{pmatrix} (0.6,0.3,0.1) & (0.7,0.2,0.1) & (0.6,0.1,0.3) & (0.6,0.1,0.3) \\ (0.8,0.1,0.1) & (0.8,0.2,0) & (0.8,0.2,0) & -- \\ (0.6,0.4,0) & (0.6,0.1,0.3) & (0.6,0.2,0.2) & -- \\ (0.5,0.1,0.4) & (0.6,0.2,0.2) & (0.6,0.1,0.3) & (0.6,0.2,0.2) \end{pmatrix}$$

$$R^{(2,4)} = \begin{pmatrix} (0.6,0.3,0.1) & (0.6,0.2,0.2) & (0.6,0.1,0.3) & (0.7,0.1,0.2) \\ (0.6,0.2,0.2) & (0.7,0.2,0.1) & (0.6,0.1,0.3) & -- \\ (0.7,0.3,0) & (0.6,0.1,0.3) & (0.6,0.2,0.2) & -- \\ (0.8,0.1,0.1) & (0.7,0.1,0.2) & (0.8,0.1,0.1) & (0.8,0.1,0.1) \end{pmatrix}$$

$$R^{(3,1)} = \begin{pmatrix} (0.6,0.3,0.1) & (0.6,0.1,0.3) & (0.7,0.1,0.2) & (0.7,0.2,0.1) \\ (0.6,0.3,0.1) & (0.7,0.2,0.1) & (0.8,0.1,0.2) & -- \\ (0.8,0.2,0) & (0.8,0.1,0.1) & (0.7,0.1,0.2) & -- \\ (0.6,0.1,0.3) & (0.7,0.1,0.2) & (0.6,0.2,0.2) & (0.7,0.2,0.1) \end{pmatrix}$$

$$R^{(3,2)} = \begin{pmatrix} (0.6,0.3,0.1) & (0.6,0.2,0.2) & (0.6,0.1,0.3) & (0.7,0.1,0.2) \\ (0.7,0.2,0.1) & (0.6,0.2,0.2) & (0.6,0.1,0.3) & -- \\ (0.6,0.4,0) & (0.7,0.1,0.2) & (0.7,0.2,0.1) & -- \\ (0.5,0.2,0.3) & (0.6,0.1,0.3) & (0.6,0.2,0.2) & (0.7,0.2,0.1) \end{pmatrix}$$

$$R^{(3,3)} = \begin{pmatrix} (0.6,0.3,0.1) & (0.6,0.2,0.2) & (0.6,0.1,0.3) & (0.7,0.1,0.2) \\ (0.8,0.1,0.1) & (0.8,0.1,0.1) & (0.8,0.1,0.1) & -- \\ (0.7,0.3,0) & (0.6,0.1,0.3) & (0.7,0.2,0.1) & -- \\ (0.6,0.2,0.2) & (0.6,0.2,0.2) & (0.7,0.2,0.1) & (0.6,0.2,0.2) \end{pmatrix}$$

$$R^{(3,4)} = \begin{pmatrix} (0.5,0.1,0.4) & (0.6,0.2,0.2) & (0.8,0.1,0.1) & (0.5,0.4,0.1) \\ (0.6,0.3,0.1) & (0.6,0.2,0.2) & (0.7,0.2,0.1) & \text{--} \\ (0.6,0.4,0) & (0.7,0.1,0.2) & (0.6,0.1,0.3) & \text{--} \\ (0.8,0.1,0.1) & (0.7,0.1,0.2) & (0.7,0.2,0.1) & (0.7,0.1,0.2) \end{pmatrix}$$

where "--" means that there are no elements for the second and the third layers each of which has only three attributes.

Below we shall use Zhang and Xu (2012)'s method to aggregate the given information: We first analyze the importance of the considered attributes. Here we adopt the method introduced by Xu (2006) to construct the reciprocal judgment matrix J_l corresponding to the attributes in the lth layer, $l = 1, 2, 3, 4$, and then construct the reciprocal judgment matrix J of the layers in this system. After that, we use Xu (2006)'s model to get the weight vectors w_l $(l = 1, 2, 3, 4)$ of the attributes in the lth layer and the weight vector w of the layers as follows, respectively:

$$w = (0.2,0.3,0.4,0.1)^T, \quad w_1 = (0.3,0.3,0.2,0.2)^T, \quad w_2 = (0.5,0.2,0.3)^T$$
$$w_3 = (0.4,0.4,0.2)^T, \quad w_4 = (0.4,0.2,0.2,0.2)^T$$

Then we aggregate the information on the attributes in each layer by calculating the membership degree $\mu_l^{(k)}(y_j)$, the non-membership degree $v_l^{(k)}(y_j)$ and the hesitancy degree $\pi_l^{(k)}(y_j)$ corresponding to the lth layer of the system y_j and the expert e_k:

$$\mu_1^{(1)}(y_1) = \sum_{j=1}^{4} \mu_{r_{1,j}^{(1,1)}} w_{1,j} = 0.6 \times 0.3 + 0.7 \times 0.3 + 0.7 \times 0.2 + 0.7 \times 0.2 = 0.67$$

$$v_1^{(1)}(y_1) = \sum_{j=1}^{4} v_{r_{1,j}^{(1,1)}} w_{1,j} = 0.3 \times 0.3 + 0.2 \times 0.3 + 0.1 \times 0.2 + 0.1 \times 0.2 = 0.19$$

$$\pi_1^{(1)}(y_1) = 1 - \mu_1^{(1)}(y_1) - v_1^{(1)}(y_1) = 1 - 0.67 - 0.19 = 0.14$$

Similarly, we can get the membership degrees, the non-membership degrees and the hesitancy degrees of the other layers, and all the aggregated results corresponding to the expert e_k are contained in the intuitionistic fuzzy matrix $R^{(k)}$, listed as follows (Zhang and Xu 2012):

$$R^{(1)} = \begin{pmatrix} (0.67,0.19,0.14) & (0.71,0.17,0.12) & (0.78,0.14,0.08) & (0.64,0.14,0.22) \\ (0.62,0.19,0.19) & (0.65,0.17,0.18) & (0.70,0.20,0.10) & (0.58,0.18,0.24) \\ (0.62,0.19,0.19) & (0.78,0.17,0.05) & (0.64,0.20,0.16) & (0.60,0.16,0.24) \\ (0.62,0.19,0.19) & (0.62,0.17,0.21) & (0.64,0.20,0.16) & (0.74,0.16,0.10) \end{pmatrix}$$

$$R^{(2)} = \begin{pmatrix} (0.64,0.16,0.20) & (0.71,0.17,0.12) & (0.82,0.10,0.08) & (0.62,0.14,0.24) \\ (0.59,0.21,0.20) & (0.58,0.15,0.27) & (0.62,0.24,0.14) & (0.60,0.20,0.20) \\ (0.63,0.19,0.18) & (0.80,0.15,0.05) & (0.60,0.24,0.16) & (0.56,0.14,0.30) \\ (0.62,0.19,0.19) & (0.62,0.17,0.21) & (0.64,0.20,0.16) & (0.78,0.10,0.12) \end{pmatrix}$$

$$R^{(3)} = \begin{pmatrix} (0.64,0.19,0.17) & (0.68,0.10,0.22) & (0.78,0.20,0.02) & (0.64,0.20,0.16) \\ (0.62,0.19,0.19) & (0.65,0.17,0.18) & (0.66,0.24,0.10) & (0.58,0.18,0.24) \\ (0.62,0.19,0.19) & (0.80,0.10,0.10) & (0.66,0.20,0.14) & (0.62,0.20,0.18) \\ (0.59,0.19,0.22) & (0.63,0.25,0.12) & (0.64,0.22,0.14) & (0.74,0.12,0.14) \end{pmatrix}$$

Also we aggregate the information of the four layers and get the membership degree $\mu^{(k)}(y_j)$, the non-membership degree $v^{(k)}(y_j)$ and the hesitancy degree $\pi^{(k)}(y_j)$ of the system y_j with respect to the expert e_k:

$$\mu^{(1)}(y_1) = \sum_{i=1}^{4} \mu_i^{(1)}(y_1)w_i = 0.67 \times 0.2 + 0.71 \times 0.3 + 0.78 \times 0.4 + 0.64 \times 0.1 = 0.7230$$

$$v^{(1)}(y_1) = \sum_{i=1}^{4} v_i^{(1)}(y_1)w_i = 0.19 \times 0.2 + 0.17 \times 0.3 + 0.14 \times 0.4 + 0.14 \times 0.1 = 0.1590$$

$$\pi_1^{(1)}(y_1) = 1 - \mu_1^{(1)}(y_1) - v_1^{(1)}(y_1) = 1 - 0.7230 - 0.1590 = 0.1180$$

In a similar way, we can calculate the values of the rest systems, which are all represented in the intuitionistic fuzzy matrices $F^{(k)}$ $(k = 1, 2, 3)$ (Zhang and Xu 2012):

$$F^{(1)} = \begin{pmatrix} (0.7230,0.1590,0.1180) \\ (0.6570,0.1870,0.1560) \\ (0.6740,0.1850,0.1410) \\ (0.6400,0.1850,0.1750) \end{pmatrix}, \quad F^{(2)} = \begin{pmatrix} (0.7310,0.1370,0.1320) \\ (0.6000,0.2030,0.1970) \\ (0.6620,0.1930,0.1450) \\ (0.6440,0.1790,0.1770) \end{pmatrix}$$

$$F^{(3)} = \begin{pmatrix} (0.7080,0.1680,0.1240) \\ (0.6410,0.2030,0.1560) \\ (0.6900,0.1680,0.1420) \\ (0.6370,0.2130,0.1500) \end{pmatrix}$$

and then calculate the total membership degree $\mu(y_j)$, the total non-membership degree $v(y_j)$ and the total hesitancy degree of the system y_j according to the weights of the experts:

$$\mu(y_1) = \sum_{k=1}^{3} \mu^{(k)}(y_1)\eta_k = 0.723 \times 0.4 + 0.731 \times 0.3 + 0.708 \times 0.3 = 0.7209$$

$$v(y_1) = \sum_{k=1}^{3} v^{(k)}(y_1)\eta_k = 0.159 \times 0.4 + 0.137 \times 0.3 + 0.168 \times 0.3 = 0.1551$$

$$\pi(y_1) = 1 - \mu(y_1) - v(y_1) = 1 - 0.7209 - 0.1551 = 0.1240$$

After that, we get the comprehensive evaluation value $z(y_j)$ of the system y_j:

$$z(y_1) = (0.7209,0.1551,0.1240), \quad z(y_2) = (0.6351,0.1966,0.1683)$$
$$z(y_3) = (0.6752,0.1823,0.1425), \quad z(y_4) = (0.6403,0.1916,0.1681)$$

Using Eq. (1.15), we can calculate $\vartheta(z(y_j))$ $(j = 1, 2, 3, 4)$ as:

$$\vartheta(z(y_1)) = 0.7517, \quad \vartheta(z(y_2)) = 0.6877$$
$$\vartheta(z(y_3)) = 0.7157, \quad \vartheta(z(y_4)) = 0.6921$$

and thus,

$$\vartheta(z(y_1)) > \vartheta(z(y_3)) > \vartheta(z(y_4)) > \vartheta(z(y_2))$$

by which we get the ranking of the systems y_l $(l = 1, 2, 3, 4)$:

$$y_1 \succ y_3 \succ y_4 \succ y_2$$

where "$\succ$" denotes "be superior to". Therefore, the most desirable systems is y_1.

From the results above, we can see that the first system has the higher Jamming capability which is the most important capability of a jamming system, and its other capabilities are not bad. As a result, the comprehensive evaluation value of this system is the largest one; while the second system doesn't have particular capability, and all of its capabilities are rather mediocre, so its comprehensive evaluation result is very bad, and thus ranks the last. This ranking of the systems is basically in accordance with our intuition.

1.2 Intuitionistic Fuzzy Power Aggregation Operators

1.2.1 Power Aggregation Operators

Information aggregation is a process that fuses data from various resources by using a proper aggregation technique. In order to develop a tool to aid and provide more versatility in the data aggregation process, Yager (2001) introduced a power average (PA) operator to aggregate a collection of negative real numbers a_i $(i = 1, 2, \ldots, n)$, defined as follows:

$$PA(a_1, a_2, \ldots, a_n) = \frac{\sum_{i=1}^{n} (1 + T(a_i))a_i}{\sum_{i=1}^{n} (1 + T(a_i))} \tag{1.17}$$

where $T(a_i) = \sum_{\substack{j=1 \\ j \neq i}}^{n} Sup(a_i, a_j)$, and $Sup(a_i, a_j)$ is the support for a_i from a_j, which satisfies the following properties:

(1) $Sup(a_i, a_j) \in [0, 1]$.
(2) $Sup(a_i, a_j) = Sup(a_j, a_i)$.
(3) $Sup(a_i, a_j) \geq Sup(a_s, a_t)$, if $|a_i - a_j| < |a_s - a_t|$.

Based on the PA operator and the geometric mean, Xu and Yager (2010) further defined a power geometric (PG) operator:

$$PG(a_1, a_2, \ldots, a_n) = \prod_{i=1}^{n} a_i^{\frac{1+T(a_i)}{\sum_{i=1}^{n}(1+T(a_i))}} \tag{1.18}$$

Obviously, the PA and PG operators are a nonlinear weighted aggregation tool, whose weighting vectors depend upon the input data and allow the values being aggregated to support and reinforce each other, that is, the closer two values a_i and a_j, the more similar they are, and the more they support each other.

1.2.2 Some Operational Laws of IFVs

Xu and Yager (2006), and Xu (2007) introduced some operational laws of IFVs as follows:

Definition 1.3 (Xu and Yager 2006; Xu 2007) Let $\alpha_i = (\mu_{\alpha_i}, v_{\alpha_i}, \pi_{\alpha_i})$ $(i = 1, 2)$ be any two IFVs, then

(1) $\alpha_1 \oplus \alpha_2 = (\mu_{\alpha_1} + \mu_{\alpha_2} - \mu_{\alpha_1}\mu_{\alpha_2}, v_{\alpha_1}v_{\alpha_2}, (1-\mu_{\alpha_1})(1-\mu_{\alpha_2}) - v_{\alpha_1}v_{\alpha_2})$.
(2) $\alpha_1 \otimes \alpha_2 = (\mu_{\alpha_1}\mu_{\alpha_2}, v_{\alpha_1} + v_{\alpha_2} - v_{\alpha_1}v_{\alpha_2}, (1-v_{\alpha_1})(1-v_{\alpha_2}) - \mu_{\alpha_1}\mu_{\alpha_2})$.
(3) $\lambda\alpha_1 = (1-(1-\mu_{\alpha_1})^{\lambda}, v_{\alpha_1}^{\lambda}, (1-\mu_{\alpha_1})^{\lambda} - v_{\alpha_1}^{\lambda}), \lambda > 0$.
(4) $\alpha_1^{\lambda} = (\mu_{\alpha_1}^{\lambda}, 1-(1-v_{\alpha_1})^{\lambda}, (1-v_{\alpha_1})^{\lambda} - \mu_{\alpha_1}^{\lambda}), \lambda > 0$.

All the results of the above operations are also IFVs and the following are all right.

Theorem 1.2 (Xu 2011)

(1) If $\lambda_1 > \lambda_2$, then $\lambda_1\alpha \geq \lambda_2\alpha, \alpha^{1-\lambda_1} \geq \alpha^{1-\lambda_2}, 0 < \lambda_1, \lambda_2 \leq 1$.
(2) If $\mu_{\alpha_1} \geq \mu_{\alpha_2}, v_{\alpha_1} \leq v_{\alpha_2}$, then $\lambda\alpha_1 \geq \lambda\alpha_2, \alpha_1^{\lambda} \geq \alpha_2^{\lambda}, 0 < \lambda \leq 1$.
(3) If $\mu_{\alpha_1} \geq \mu_{\alpha_3}, \mu_{\alpha_2} \geq \mu_{\alpha_4}, v_{\alpha_1} \leq v_{\alpha_3}, v_{\alpha_2} \leq v_{\alpha_4}$, then $\alpha_1 \oplus \alpha_3 \geq \alpha_2 \oplus \alpha_4, \alpha_1 \otimes \alpha_3 \geq \alpha_2 \otimes \alpha_4$.

Proof (1) If $\lambda_1 > \lambda_2$, then

$$1-(1-\mu_{\alpha})^{\lambda_1} \geq 1-(1-\mu_{\alpha})^{\lambda_2}, \quad v_{\alpha}^{\lambda_1} \leq v_{\alpha}^{\lambda_2} \tag{1.19}$$

therefore,

$$1 - (1 - \mu_{\alpha})^{\lambda_1} - v_{\alpha}^{\lambda_1} \geq 1 - (1 - \mu_{\alpha})^{\lambda_2} - v_{\alpha}^{\lambda_2} \tag{1.20}$$

which implies $\lambda_1\alpha \geq \lambda_2\alpha$, similarly, we can prove that $\alpha^{1-\lambda_1} \geq \alpha^{1-\lambda_2}$, with the condition $0 < \lambda_1, \lambda_2 \leq 1$.

(2) If $\mu_{\alpha_1} \geq \mu_{\alpha_2}, v_{\alpha_1} \leq v_{\alpha_2}$, then

$$1 - (1 - \mu_{\alpha_1})^{\lambda} - v_{\alpha_1}^{\lambda} \geq 1 - (1 - \mu_{\alpha_2})^{\lambda} - v_{\alpha_2}^{\lambda} \tag{1.21}$$

and

$$\mu_{\alpha_1}^{\lambda} - (1 - (1 - v_{\alpha_1})^{\lambda}) \geq \mu_{\alpha_2}^{\lambda} - (1 - (1 - v_{\alpha_2})^{\lambda}) \tag{1.22}$$

thus $\lambda\alpha_1 \geq \lambda\alpha_2$ and $\alpha_1^{\lambda} \geq \alpha_2^{\lambda}$.

(3) If $\mu_{\alpha_1} \geq \mu_{\alpha_3}, \mu_{\alpha_2} \geq \mu_{\alpha_4}, v_{\alpha_1} \leq v_{\alpha_3}$ and $v_{\alpha_2} \leq v_{\alpha_4}$, then

$$\begin{aligned}\mu_{\alpha_1} + \mu_{\alpha_2} - \mu_{\alpha_1}\mu_{\alpha_2} - v_{\alpha_1}v_{\alpha_2} &= 1 - (1 - \mu_{\alpha_1})(1 - \mu_{\alpha_2}) - v_{\alpha_1}v_{\alpha_2} \\ &\geq 1 - (1 - \mu_{\alpha_3})(1 - \mu_{\alpha_4}) - v_{\alpha_3}v_{\alpha_4} \\ &= \mu_{\alpha_3} + \mu_{\alpha_4} - \mu_{\alpha_3}\mu_{\alpha_4} - v_{\alpha_3}v_{\alpha_4}\end{aligned} \tag{1.23}$$

and

$$\begin{aligned}\mu_{\alpha_1}\mu_{\alpha_2} - (v_{\alpha_1} + v_{\alpha_2} - v_{\alpha_1}v_{\alpha_2}) &= \mu_{\alpha_1}\mu_{\alpha_2} - 1 + (1 - v_{\alpha_1})(1 - v_{\alpha_2}) \\ &\geq \mu_{\alpha_3}\mu_{\alpha_4} - 1 + (1 - v_{\alpha_3})(1 - v_{\alpha_4}) \\ &= \mu_{\alpha_1}\mu_{\alpha_2} - (v_{\alpha_3} + v_{\alpha_4} - v_{\alpha_3}v_{\alpha_4})\end{aligned} \tag{1.24}$$

thus, $\alpha_1 \oplus \alpha_3 \geq \alpha_2 \oplus \alpha_4$ and $\alpha_1 \otimes \alpha_3 \geq \alpha_2 \otimes \alpha_4$.

Moreover, the relations of the operational laws above are given as below:

Theorem 1.3 (Xu and Yager 2006; Xu 2007)

(1) $\alpha_1 \oplus \alpha_2 = \alpha_2 \oplus \alpha_1$.
(2) $\alpha_1 \otimes \alpha_2 = \alpha_2 \otimes \alpha_1$.
(3) $\lambda(\alpha_1 \oplus \alpha_2) = \lambda\alpha_1 \oplus \lambda\alpha_2, \lambda > 0$.
(4) $(\alpha_1 \otimes \alpha_2)^{\lambda} = \alpha_1^{\lambda} \otimes \alpha_2^{\lambda}, \lambda > 0$.
(5) $\lambda_1\alpha \oplus \lambda_2\alpha = (\lambda_1 + \lambda_2)\alpha, \lambda > 0$.
(6) $\alpha^{\lambda_1} \otimes \alpha^{\lambda_2} = \alpha^{\lambda_1+\lambda_2}, \lambda > 0$.

Based on the ranking method given by Xu and Yager (2006), and Definition 1.3, Xu (2011) developed a series of intuitionistic fuzzy power aggregation operators, which allow the input data values to support each other in the aggregation process. In what follows, we shall give a detailed introduction to them.

1.2.3 Power Aggregation Operators for IFVs

Let $\alpha_i = (\mu_{\alpha_i}, v_{\alpha_i}, \pi_{\alpha_i})$ $(i = 1, 2, \ldots, n)$ be a collection of IFVs, and $w = (w_1, w_2, \ldots, w_n)^T$ the weight vector of α_i $(i = 1, 2, \ldots, n)$, where $w_i \geq 0, i = 1, 2, \ldots, n$, and $\sum_{i=1}^n w_i = 1$, then Xu (2011) defined an intuitionistic fuzzy power weighted average (IFPWA) operator as follows:

$$IFPWA(\alpha_1, \alpha_2, \ldots, \alpha_n) = \frac{(w_1(1 + T(\alpha_1))\alpha_1) \oplus (w_2(1 + T(\alpha_2))\alpha_2) \oplus \cdots \oplus (w_n(1 + T(\alpha_n))\alpha_n)}{\sum_{i=1}^n w_i(1 + T(\alpha_i))} \tag{1.25}$$

By Definition 1.3, Eq. (1.25) can be transformed into the following form by using mathematical induction on n:

$$IFPWA(\alpha_1, \alpha_2, \ldots, \alpha_n) = \left(1 - \prod_{j=1}^n (1 - \mu_{\alpha_j})^{\frac{w_j(1+T(\alpha_j))}{\sum_{i=1}^n w_i(1+T(\alpha_i))}}, \prod_{j=1}^n (v_{\alpha_j})^{\frac{w_j(1+T(\alpha_j))}{\sum_{i=1}^n w_i(1+T(\alpha_i))}}, \prod_{j=1}^n (1 - \mu_{\alpha_j})^{\frac{w_j(1+T(\alpha_j))}{\sum_{i=1}^n w_i(1+T(\alpha_i))}} - \prod_{j=1}^n (v_{\alpha_j})^{\frac{w_j(1+T(\alpha_j))}{\sum_{i=1}^n w_i(1+T(\alpha_i))}}\right) \tag{1.26}$$

where

$$T(\alpha_i) = \sum_{\substack{j=1 \\ j \neq i}}^n w_j Sup(\alpha_i, \alpha_j) \tag{1.27}$$

and $Sup(\alpha_i, \alpha_j)$ is the support for α_i from α_j, with the following conditions:

(1) $Sup(\alpha_i, \alpha_j) \in [0, 1]$.
(2) $Sup(\alpha_i, \alpha_j) = Sup(\alpha_j, \alpha_i)$.
(3) $Sup(\alpha_i, \alpha_j) \geq Sup(\alpha_s, \alpha_t)$, if $d(\alpha_i, \alpha_j) < d(\alpha_s, \alpha_t)$, where d is a distance measure, such as the normalized Hamming distance or the normalized Euclidean distance (Szmidt and Kacprzyk 2000; Narukawa and Torra 2006; Xu and Yager 2008), where

(a) The normalized Hamming distance for IFVs:

$$d_H(\alpha_i, \alpha_j) = \frac{1}{2}\left(\left|\mu_{\alpha_i} - \mu_{\alpha_j}\right| + \left|v_{\alpha_i} - v_{\alpha_j}\right| + \left|\pi_{\alpha_i} - \pi_{\alpha_j}\right|\right) \tag{1.28}$$

(b) The normalized Euclidean distance for IFVs:

$$d_E(\alpha_i, \alpha_j) = \sqrt{\frac{1}{2}\left((\mu_{\alpha_i} - \mu_{\alpha_j})^2 + (v_{\alpha_i} - v_{\alpha_j})^2 + (\pi_{\alpha_i} - \pi_{\alpha_j})^2\right)} \tag{1.29}$$

Especially, if $w = (1/n, 1/n, \ldots, 1/n)^T$, then the IFPWA operator (1.25) reduces to an intuitionistic fuzzy power average (IFPA) operator:

$$\begin{aligned} & IFPA(\alpha_1, \alpha_2, \ldots, \alpha_n) \\ & = \frac{((1 + T(\alpha_1))\alpha_1) \oplus ((1 + T(\alpha_2))\alpha_2) \oplus \cdots \oplus ((1 + T(\alpha_n))\alpha_n)}{\sum_{i=1}^{n} (1 + T(\alpha_i))} \\ & = \left(1 - \prod_{j=1}^{n} (1 - \mu_{\alpha_j})^{\frac{(1+T(\alpha_j))}{\sum_{i=1}^{n}(1+T(\alpha_i))}}, \prod_{j=1}^{n} (\nu_{\alpha_j})^{\frac{(1+T(\alpha_j))}{\sum_{i=1}^{n}(1+T(\alpha_i))}}, \right. \\ & \left. \prod_{j=1}^{n} (1 - \mu_{\alpha_j})^{\frac{(1+T(\alpha_j))}{\sum_{i=1}^{n}(1+T(\alpha_i))}} - \prod_{j=1}^{n} (\nu_{\alpha_j})^{\frac{(1+T(\alpha_j))}{\sum_{i=1}^{n}(1+T(\alpha_i))}} \right) \end{aligned} \tag{1.30}$$

where

$$T(\alpha_i) = \frac{1}{n} \sum_{\substack{j=1 \\ j \neq i}}^{n} Sup(\alpha_i, \alpha_j) \tag{1.31}$$

Let $(\alpha_1, \alpha_2, \ldots, \alpha_n)$ be a vector of n IFVs, then it can be easily proven that the IFPWA operator has the following desirable properties (Xu 2011):

Theorem 1.4 (Commutativity) Let $(\alpha_1', \alpha_2', \ldots, \alpha_n')$ be any permutation of $(\alpha_1, \alpha_2, \ldots, \alpha_n)$, then

$$IFPWA(\alpha_1, \alpha_2, \ldots, \alpha_n) = IFPWA(\alpha_1', \alpha_2', \ldots, \alpha_n') \tag{1.32}$$

Theorem 1.5 (Idempotency) If $\alpha_j = \alpha$, for all j, then

$$IFPWA(\alpha_1, \alpha_2, \ldots, \alpha_n) = \alpha \tag{1.33}$$

Theorem 1.6 (Boundedness)

$$\alpha^- \leq IFPWA(\alpha_1, \alpha_2, \ldots, \alpha_n) \leq \alpha^+ \tag{1.34}$$

where

$$\alpha^- = \left(\min_j\{\mu_{\alpha_j}\}, \max_j\{\nu_{\alpha_j}\}, 1 - \min_j\{\mu_{\alpha_j}\} - \max_j\{\nu_{\alpha_j}\}\right) \tag{1.35}$$

$$\alpha^+ = \left(\max_j\{\mu_{\alpha_j}\}, \min_j\{\nu_{\alpha_j}\}, 1 - \max_j\{\mu_{\alpha_j}\} - \min_j\{\nu_{\alpha_j}\}\right) \tag{1.36}$$

Based on the IFPWA operator (1.25) and the geometric mean, Xu (2011) defined an intuitionistic fuzzy power weighted geometric (IFPWG) operator:

$$IFPWG(\alpha_1,\alpha_2,\ldots,\alpha_n) = (\alpha_1)^{\frac{1}{n-1}\left(1-\frac{w_1(1+T(\alpha_1))}{\sum_{i=1}^n w_i(1+T(\alpha_i))}\right)} \otimes (\alpha_2)^{\frac{1}{n-1}\left(1-\frac{w_2(1+T(\alpha_2))}{\sum_{i=1}^n w_i(1+T(\alpha_i))}\right)} \otimes \cdots \otimes (\alpha_n)^{\frac{1}{n-1}\left(1-\frac{w_n(1+T(\alpha_n))}{\sum_{i=1}^n w_i(1+T(\alpha_i))}\right)} \tag{1.37}$$

which can be transformed into the following form by using mathematical induction on n:

$$IFPWG(\alpha_1,\alpha_2,\ldots,\alpha_n) = \left(\prod_{j=1}^n (\mu_{\alpha_j})^{\frac{1}{n-1}\left(1-\frac{w_j(1+T(\alpha_j))}{\sum_{i=1}^n w_i(1+T(\alpha_i))}\right)}, 1-\prod_{j=1}^n (1-\nu_{\alpha_j})^{\frac{1}{n-1}\left(1-\frac{w_j(1+T(\alpha_j))}{\sum_{i=1}^n w_i(1+T(\alpha_i))}\right)}, \prod_{j=1}^n (1-\nu_{\alpha_j})^{\frac{1}{n-1}\left(1-\frac{w_j(1+T(\alpha_j))}{\sum_{i=1}^n w_i(1+T(\alpha_i))}\right)} - \prod_{j=1}^n (\mu_{\alpha_j})^{\frac{1}{n-1}\left(1-\frac{w_j(1+T(\alpha_j))}{\sum_{i=1}^n w_i(1+T(\alpha_i))}\right)}\right) \tag{1.38}$$

with the condition (1.27).

Especially, if $w = (1/n, 1/n, \ldots, 1/n)^T$, then the IFPWG operator (1.37) reduces to an intuitionistic fuzzy power geometric (IFPG) operator:

$$\begin{aligned} IFPG(\alpha_1,\alpha_2,\ldots,\alpha_n) &= (\alpha_1)^{\frac{1}{n-1}\left(1-\frac{1+T(\alpha_1)}{\sum_{i=1}^n (1+T(\alpha_i))}\right)} \otimes (\alpha_2)^{\frac{1}{n-1}\left(1-\frac{1+T(\alpha_2)}{\sum_{i=1}^n (1+T(\alpha_i))}\right)} \otimes \cdots \otimes (\alpha_n)^{\frac{1}{n-1}\left(1-\frac{1+T(\alpha_n)}{\sum_{i=1}^n (1+T(\alpha_i))}\right)} \\ &= \left(\prod_{j=1}^n (\mu_{\alpha_j})^{\frac{1}{n-1}\left(1-\frac{1+T(\alpha_j)}{\sum_{i=1}^n (1+T(\alpha_i))}\right)}, 1-\prod_{j=1}^n (1-\nu_{\alpha_j})^{\frac{1}{n-1}\left(1-\frac{1+T(\alpha_j)}{\sum_{i=1}^n (1+T(\alpha_i))}\right)}, \prod_{j=1}^n (1-\nu_{\alpha_j})^{\frac{1}{n-1}\left(1-\frac{1+T(\alpha_j)}{\sum_{i=1}^n (1+T(\alpha_i))}\right)} - \prod_{j=1}^n (\mu_{\alpha_j})^{\frac{1}{n-1}\left(1-\frac{1+T(\alpha_j)}{\sum_{i=1}^n (1+T(\alpha_i))}\right)}\right) \end{aligned} \tag{1.39}$$

with the condition (1.31).

Similar to the IFPWA operator, the IFPWG operator has the following three properties (Xu 2011):

Theorem 1.7 (Commutativity) Let $(\alpha_1', \alpha_2', \ldots, \alpha_n')$ be any permutation of $(\alpha_1, \alpha_2, \ldots, \alpha_n)$, then

$$IFPWG(\alpha_1,\alpha_2,\ldots,\alpha_n) = IFPWG(\alpha_1',\alpha_2',\ldots,\alpha_n') \tag{1.40}$$

Theorem 1.8 (Idempotency) If $\alpha_j = \alpha$, for all j, then

$$IFPWG(\alpha_1, \alpha_2, \ldots, \alpha_n) = \alpha \tag{1.41}$$

Theorem 1.9 (Boundedness) Let α^- and α^+ be given by Eqs. (1.35) and (1.36), then

$$\alpha^- \leq IFPWG(\alpha_1, \alpha_2, \ldots, \alpha_n) \leq \alpha^+ \tag{1.42}$$

The fundamental characteristic of both the IFPWA and IFPWG operators is that they weight all the given IFVs themselves, and the weighting vectors depend upon the input arguments and allow the values being aggregated to support and reinforce each other. However, in many group decision making problems, such as personnel evaluation, diving games, etc., we need to rearrange all the given arguments in descending (or ascending) order, and then weight the ordered positions of the input arguments so as to relieve the influence of unfair arguments on the decision result by assigning low weights to those "false" or "biased" ones. As a result, motivated by the idea of Yager (1988, 2001)'s ordered weighted average, Xu (2011) introduced an intuitionistic fuzzy power ordered weighted average (IFPOWA) operator:

$$IFPOWA(\alpha_1, \alpha_2, \ldots, \alpha_n) = \omega_1 \alpha_{index(1)} \oplus \omega_2 \alpha_{index(2)} \oplus \cdots \oplus \omega_n \alpha_{index(n)} \tag{1.43}$$

which can be further expressed as:

$$\begin{aligned} & IFPOWA(\alpha_1, \alpha_2, \ldots, \alpha_n) \\ & = \left(1 - \prod_{j=1}^{n} (1 - \mu_{\alpha_{index(j)}})^{\omega_j}, \prod_{j=1}^{n} (v_{\alpha_{index(j)}})^{\omega_j}, \prod_{j=1}^{n} (1 - \mu_{\alpha_{index(j)}})^{\omega_j} \right. \\ & \quad \left. - \prod_{j=1}^{n} (v_{\alpha_{index(j)}})^{\omega_j} \right) \end{aligned} \tag{1.44}$$

where *index* is an indexing function such that $index(i)$ is the index of the ith largest of the IFVs $\alpha_j = (\mu_{\alpha_j}, v_{\alpha_j}, \pi_{\alpha_j})$ $(j = 1, 2 \ldots, n)$, and thus, $\alpha_{index(i)}$ is the ith largest of the IFVs $\alpha_j (j = 1, 2, \ldots, n)$. ω_i $(i = 1, 2, \ldots, n)$ are a collection of weights such that

$$\begin{gathered} \omega_i = g\left(\frac{D_i}{TV}\right) - g\left(\frac{D_{i-1}}{TV}\right), \quad D_i = \sum_{j=1}^{i} V_{index(j)} \quad TV = \sum_{i=1}^{n} V_{index(i)} \\ V_{index(j)} = 1 + T(\alpha_{index(j)}) \end{gathered} \tag{1.45}$$

and $T(\alpha_{index(j)})$ denotes the support of the jth largest IFV $\alpha_{index(j)}$ by all the other IFVs, i.e.,

$$T(\alpha_{index(j)}) = \sum_{\substack{i=1 \\ i \neq j}}^{n} Sup\left(\alpha_{index(j)}, \alpha_{index(i)}\right) \tag{1.46}$$

where $Sup\left(\alpha_{index(j)}, \alpha_{index(i)}\right)$ indicates the support of ith largest IFV $\alpha_{index(i)}$ for the jth largest IFV $\alpha_{index(j)}$, and g:[0, 1] $\rightarrow$ [0, 1] is a basic unit-interval monotonic (BUM) function, having the properties:

(1) $g(0) = 0$.
(2) $g(1) = 1$.
(3) $g(x) \geq g(y)$, if $x > y$.

Especially, if $g(x) = x$, then the IFPOWA operator (1.43) reduces to the IFPA operator (1.30).

Furthermore, based on the IFPOWA operator (1.44) and the geometric mean, Xu (2011) defined an intuitionistic fuzzy power ordered weighted geometric (IFPOWG) operator:

$$\begin{aligned} & IFPOWG(\alpha_1, \alpha_2, \ldots, \alpha_n) \\ & = (\alpha_{index(1)})^{\frac{1-\omega_1}{n-1}} \otimes (\alpha_{index(2)})^{\frac{1-\omega_2}{n-1}} \otimes \cdots \otimes (\alpha_{index(n)})^{\frac{1-\omega_n}{n-1}} \end{aligned} \tag{1.47}$$

which can be further expressed as:

$$\begin{aligned} IFPOWG(\alpha_1, \alpha_2, \ldots, \alpha_n) = & \left(\prod_{j=1}^{n} (\mu_{\alpha_{index(j)}})^{\frac{1-\omega_j}{n-1}}, 1 - \prod_{j=1}^{n} (1 - \nu_{\alpha_{index(j)}})^{\frac{1-\omega_j}{n-1}}, \right. \\ & \left. \prod_{j=1}^{n} (1 - \nu_{\alpha_{index(j)}})^{\frac{1-\omega_j}{n-1}} - \prod_{j=1}^{n} (\mu_{\alpha_{index(j)}})^{\frac{1-\omega_j}{n-1}} \right) \end{aligned} \tag{1.48}$$

where ω_i $(i = 1, 2, \ldots, n)$ are a collection of weights satisfying the conditions (1.45) and (1.46). Especially, if $g(x) = x$, then the IFPOWG operator (1.47) reduces to the IFPG operator (1.39).

Clearly, the weighting vectors of both the IFPWA and IFPWG operators not only depend upon the input arguments and allow the values being aggregated to support and reinforce each other, but also emphasize the ordered positions of all the given arguments. Furthermore, the IFPWA and IFPWG operators have also the properties: commutativity, idempotency and boundedness.

1.2.4 Approaches to Multi-Attribute Group Decision Making with Intuitionistic Fuzzy Information

Xu (2011) utilized the intuitionistic fuzzy power aggregation operators to multi-attribute group decision making with intuitionistic fuzzy information:

For a multi-attribute group decision making problem with intuitionistic fuzzy information, let $Y = \{y_1, y_2, \ldots, y_n\}$ be a set of n alternatives, $G=\{G_1, G_2, \ldots, G_m\}$ a set of m attributes, whose weight vector is $w = (w_1, w_2, \ldots, w_m)^T$, with $w_i \geq 0, i = 1, 2, \ldots, m$, and $\sum_{i=1}^{m} w_i = 1$, and let $E = \{e_1, e_2, \ldots, e_s\}$ be a set of s experts, whose weight vector is $\eta = (\eta_1, \eta_2, \ldots, \eta_s)^T$, with $\eta_k \geq 0, k = 1, 2, \ldots, s$, and $\sum_{k=1}^{s} \eta_k = 1$. Let $B^{(k)} = (b_{ij}^{(k)})_{m\times n}$ be an intuitionistic fuzzy decision matrix, where $b_{ij}^{(k)} = (t_{ij}^{(k)}, f_{ij}^{(k)}, \pi_{ij}^{(k)})$ is an attribute value provided by the expert e_k, denoted by an IFV, where $t_{ij}^{(k)}$ indicates the degree that the alternative y_j satisfies the attribute G_i, while $f_{ij}^{(k)}$ indicates the degree that the alternative y_j does not satisfy the attribute G_i, and $\pi_{ij}^{(k)}$ indicates the uncertainty degree of the alternative y_j to the attribute G_i, such that

$$t_{ij}^{(k)} \in [0, 1], \quad f_{ij}^{(k)} \in [0, 1], \quad t_{ij}^{(k)} + f_{ij}^{(k)} \leq 1, \quad \pi_{ij}^{(k)} = 1 - t_{ij}^{(k)} - f_{ij}^{(k)},$$
$$i = 1, 2, \ldots, m; \quad j = 1, 2, \ldots, n \tag{1.49}$$

If all the attributes G_i $(i = 1, 2, \ldots, m)$ are of the same type, then the attribute values do not need normalization. Whereas, there are generally benefit attributes (i.e., the bigger the attribute values the better) and cost attributes (i.e., the smaller the attribute values the better) in multi-attribute decision making. In such cases, we may transform the attribute values of cost type into the attribute values of benefit type, then $B^{(k)} = (b_{ij}^{(k)})_{m\times n}$ can be transformed into the intuitionistic fuzzy decision matrix $R^{(k)} = (r_{ij}^{(k)})_{m\times n}$, where

$$r_{ij}^{(k)} = (\mu_{ij}^{(k)}, v_{ij}^{(k)}, \pi_{ij}^{(k)}) = \begin{cases} b_{ij}^{(k)}, & \text{for benefit attribute } G_i \\ \left(b_{ij}^{(k)}\right)^{c}, & \text{for cost attribute } G_i \end{cases}, \quad j = 1, 2, \ldots, n \tag{1.50}$$

where $\left(b_{ij}^{(k)}\right)^{c}$ is the complement of $b_{ij}^{(k)}$, such that $\left(b_{ij}^{(k)}\right)^{c} = (f_{ij}^{(k)}, t_{ij}^{(k)}, \pi_{ij}^{(k)})$, clearly, $\pi_{ij}^{(k)} = 1 - t_{ij}^{(k)} - f_{ij}^{(k)} = 1 - \mu_{ij}^{(k)} - v_{ij}^{(k)}$.

Then, we can utilize the IFPWA (or IFPWG) operator to develop an approach to multi-attribute group decision making with intuitionistic fuzzy information, which involves the following steps (Xu 2011):

Approach 1.1

Step 1 Calculate the supports:

$$Sup\left(r_{ij}^{(k)}, r_{ij}^{(l)}\right) = 1 - d(r_{ij}^{(k)}, r_{ij}^{(l)}), \quad k, l = 1, 2, \ldots, s \tag{1.51}$$

which satisfy the support conditions (1)–(3) in Sect. 1.2.3. Here, without loss of generality, we calculate $d(r_{ij}^{(k)}, r_{ij}^{(l)})$ with the normalized Hamming distance (1.28):

$$d(r_{ij}^{(k)}, r_{ij}^{(l)}) = \frac{1}{2}\left(\left|\mu_{ij}^{(k)} - \mu_{ij}^{(l)}\right| + \left|v_{ij}^{(k)} - v_{ij}^{(l)}\right| + \left|\pi_{ij}^{(k)} - \pi_{ij}^{(l)}\right|\right), \quad k, l = 1, 2, \ldots, s \tag{1.52}$$

Step 2 Utilize the weights η_k $(k = 1, 2, \ldots, s)$ of the experts e_k $(k = 1, 2, \ldots, s)$ to calculate the weighted support $T(r_{ij}^{(k)})$ of the IFV $r_{ij}^{(k)}$ by the other IFVs $r_{ij}^{(l)}$ $(l = 1, 2, \ldots, s$, and $l \neq k)$:

$$T(r_{ij}^{(k)}) = \sum_{\substack{l=1 \\ l \neq k}}^{s} \eta_l Sup\left(r_{ij}^{(k)}, r_{ij}^{(l)}\right) \tag{1.53}$$

and calculate the weights $\xi_{ij}^{(k)}$ $(k = 1, 2, \ldots, s)$ associated with the IFVs $r_{ij}^{(k)}$ $(k = 1, 2, \ldots, s)$:

$$\xi_{ij}^{(k)} = \frac{\eta_k\left(1 + T(r_{ij}^{(k)})\right)}{\sum_{k=1}^{s} \eta_k\left(1 + T(r_{ij}^{(k)})\right)}, \quad k = 1, 2, \ldots, s \tag{1.54}$$

where $\xi_{ij}^{(k)} \geq 0$, $k = 1, 2, \ldots, s$, and $\sum_{k=1}^{s} \xi_{ij}^{(k)} = 1$.

Step 3 Utilize the IFPWA operator (1.26):

$$\begin{aligned} r_{ij} &= IFPWA(r_{ij}^{(1)}, r_{ij}^{(2)}, \ldots, r_{ij}^{(s)}) \\ &= \left(1 - \prod_{k=1}^{s} (1 - \mu_{ij}^{(k)})^{\frac{\eta_k(1+T(r_{ij}^{(k)}))}{\sum_{k=1}^{s}\eta_k(1+T(r_{ij}^{(k)}))}}, \prod_{j=1}^{s} (v_{ij}^{(k)})^{\frac{\eta_k(1+T(r_{ij}^{(k)}))}{\sum_{k=1}^{s}\eta_k(1+T(r_{ij}^{(k)}))}}, \right. \\ &\quad \left. \prod_{k=1}^{s} (1 - \mu_{ij}^{(k)})^{\frac{\eta_k(1+T(r_{ij}^{(k)}))}{\sum_{k=1}^{s}\eta_k(1+T(r_{ij}^{(k)}))}} - \prod_{k=1}^{s} (v_{ij}^{(k)})^{\frac{\eta_k(1+T(r_{ij}^{(k)}))}{\sum_{k=1}^{s}\eta_k(1+T(r_{ij}^{(k)}))}}\right) \end{aligned} \tag{1.55}$$

or the IFPWG operator (1.38):

$$
\begin{aligned}
r_{ij} &= IFPWG(r_{ij}^{(1)}, r_{ij}^{(2)}, \ldots, r_{ij}^{(s)}) \\
&= \left(\prod_{k=1}^{s} (\mu_{ij}^{(k)})^{\frac{1}{s-1}\left(1 - \frac{\eta_k(1+T(r_{ij}^{(k)}))}{\sum_{k=1}^{s}\eta_k(1+T(r_{ij}^{(k)}))}\right)}, 1 - \prod_{j=1}^{s} (1 - v_{ij}^{(k)})^{\frac{1}{s-1}\left(1 - \frac{\eta_k(1+T(r_{ij}^{(k)}))}{\sum_{k=1}^{s}\eta_k(1+T(r_{ij}^{(k)}))}\right)}, \right. \\
&\left. \prod_{k=1}^{s} (1 - v_{ij}^{(k)})^{\frac{1}{s-1}\left(1 - \frac{\eta_k(1+T(r_{ij}^{(k)}))}{\sum_{k=1}^{s}\eta_k(1+T(r_{ij}^{(k)}))}\right)} - \prod_{k=1}^{s} (\mu_{ij}^{(k)})^{\frac{1}{s-1}\left(1 - \frac{\eta_k(1+T(r_{ij}^{(k)}))}{\sum_{k=1}^{s}\eta_k(1+T(r_{ij}^{(k)}))}\right)} \right)
\end{aligned}
\tag{1.56}
$$

to aggregate all the individual intuitionistic fuzzy decision matrices $R^{(k)} = (r_{ij}^{(k)})_{m\times n}$ $(k = 1, 2, \ldots, s)$ into the collective intuitionistic fuzzy decision matrix $R = (r_{ij})_{m\times n}$, where $r_{ij} = (\mu_{ij}, v_{ij}, \pi_{ij})$, $i = 1, 2, \ldots, m;\ j = 1, 2, \ldots, n$.

Step 4 To get the overall preference value r_j corresponding to the alternative y_j, we aggregate all the preference values r_{ij} $(i = 1, 2, \ldots, m)$ in the *j*th column of R by using the intuitionistic fuzzy weighted average (IFWA) operator (Xu 2007):

$$
\begin{aligned}
r_j &= IFWA(r_{1j}, r_{2j}, \ldots, r_{mj}), \\
&= \left(1 - \prod_{i=1}^{m} (1-\mu_{ij})^{w_i}, \prod_{i=1}^{m} (v_{ij})^{w_i}, \prod_{i=1}^{m} (1-\mu_{ij})^{w_i} - \prod_{i=1}^{m} (v_{ij})^{w_i}\right), \\
&\qquad j = 1, 2, \ldots, n
\end{aligned}
\tag{1.57}
$$

or the following aggregation operator:

$$
\begin{aligned}
r_j &= IFWG(r_{1j}, r_{2j}, \ldots, r_{mj}) \\
&= \left(\prod_{i=1}^{m} (\mu_{ij})^{\frac{1-w_i}{m-1}}, 1 - \prod_{i=1}^{m} (1-v_{ij})^{\frac{1-w_i}{m-1}}, \prod_{i=1}^{m} (1-v_{ij})^{\frac{1-w_i}{m-1}} - \prod_{i=1}^{m} (\mu_{ij})^{\frac{1-w_i}{m-1}}\right), \\
&\qquad j = 1, 2, \ldots, n
\end{aligned}
\tag{1.58}
$$

which is defined based on the intuitionistic fuzzy weighted geometric (IFWG) operator (Xu and Yager 2006).

Step 5 Rank r_j $(j = 1, 2, \ldots, n)$ in descending order by using the ranking method described in Sect. 1.1.2.

Step 6 Rank all the alternatives y_j $(j = 1, 2, \ldots, n)$ and select the best one in accordance with the ranking of r_j $(j = 1, 2, \ldots, n)$.

If the information about the weights of experts is unknown, then we utilize the IFPOWA (or IFPWG) operator to develop an approach to multi-attribute group decision making with intuitionistic fuzzy information, which can be described as follows (Xu 2011):

Approach 1.2
Step 1 Calculate

$$\begin{aligned} Sup\left(r_{ij}^{index(k)}, r_{ij}^{index(l)}\right) &= 1 - d\left(r_{ij}^{index(k)}, r_{ij}^{index(l)}\right) \\ &= 1 - \frac{1}{2}\left(\left|\mu_{ij}^{index(k)} - \mu_{ij}^{index(l)}\right| + \left|v_{ij}^{index(k)} - v_{ij}^{index(l)}\right| \right. \\ &\quad \left. + \left|\pi_{ij}^{index(k)} - \pi_{ij}^{index(l)}\right|\right) \end{aligned} \tag{1.59}$$

which indicates the support of the lth largest IFV $r_{ij}^{index(l)}$ for the kth largest IFV $r_{ij}^{index(k)}$ of $r_{ij}^{(t)}$ $(t = 1, 2, \ldots, s)$.

Step 2 Calculate the support $T\left(r_{ij}^{index(k)}\right)$ of the kth largest IFV $r_{ij}^{index(k)}$ by the other IFVs $r_{ij}^{(l)}$ $(l = 1, 2, \ldots, s$, and $l \neq k)$:

$$T\left(r_{ij}^{index(k)}\right) = \sum_{\substack{l=1 \\ l \neq k}}^{s} Sup\left(r_{ij}^{index(k)}, r_{ij}^{index(l)}\right) \tag{1.60}$$

and utilize Eq. (1.45) to calculate the weight $\omega_{ij}^{(k)}$ associated with the kth largest IFV $r_{ij}^{index(k)}$, where

$$\begin{aligned} &\omega_{ij}^{(k)} = g\left(\frac{D_{ij}^{(k)}}{TV_{ij}}\right) - g\left(\frac{D_{ij}^{(k-1)}}{TV_{ij}}\right) \quad D_{ij}^{(k)} = \sum_{l=1}^{k} V_{ij}^{index(l)} \\ &TV_{ij} = \sum_{l=1}^{s} V_{ij}^{index(l)}, \; V_{ij}^{index(l)} = 1 + T\left(r_{ij}^{index(l)}\right) \end{aligned} \tag{1.61}$$

where $\omega_{ij}^{(k)} \geq 0, k = 1, 2, \ldots, s$, and $\sum_{k=1}^{s} \omega_{ij}^{(k)} = 1$.

Step 3 Utilize the IFPOWA operator (1.44):

$$\begin{aligned} &IFPOWA(r_{ij}^{(1)}, r_{ij}^{(2)}, \ldots, r_{ij}^{(s)}) \\ &= \left(1 - \prod_{k=1}^{s} (1 - \mu_{ij}^{index(k)})^{\omega_{ij}^{(k)}}, \prod_{k=1}^{s} (v_{ij}^{index(k)})^{\omega_{ij}^{(k)}}, \prod_{k=1}^{s} (1 - \mu_{ij}^{index(k)})^{\omega_{ij}^{(k)}} \right. \\ &\quad \left. - \prod_{k=1}^{s} (v_{ij}^{index(k)})^{\omega_{ij}^{(k)}}\right) \end{aligned} \tag{1.62}$$

or the IFPOWG operator (1.48):

$$IFPOWG(r_{ij}^{(1)}, r_{ij}^{(2)}, \ldots, r_{ij}^{(s)})$$
$$= \left(\prod_{k=1}^{s} (\mu_{ij}^{index(k)})^{\frac{1-\omega_{ij}^{(k)}}{s-1}}, 1 - \prod_{k=1}^{s} (1 - \nu_{ij}^{index(k)})^{\frac{1-\omega_{ij}^{(k)}}{s-1}}, \right.$$
$$\left. \prod_{k=1}^{s} (1 - \nu_{ij}^{index(k)})^{\frac{1-\omega_{ij}^{(k)}}{s-1}} - \prod_{k=1}^{s} (\mu_{ij}^{index(k)})^{\frac{1-\omega_{ij}^{(k)}}{s-1}} \right) \tag{1.63}$$

to aggregate all the individual intuitionistic fuzzy decision matrices $R^{(k)} = (r_{ij}^{(k)})_{m \times n}$ $(k = 1, 2, \ldots, s)$ into the collective intuitionistic fuzzy decision matrix $R = (r_{ij})_{m \times n}$, where $r_{ij} = (\mu_{ij}, \nu_{ij}, \pi_{ij})$, $i = 1, 2, \ldots, m$; $j = 1, 2, \ldots, n$.

Step 4 See Approach 1.1.

Step 5 See Approach 1.1.

We have introduced two approaches to dealing with multi-attribute group decision making problems under two different intuitionistic fuzzy situations (i.e., (1) the weights of experts are known; and (2) the information about the weights of experts are completely unknown). Both the approaches can take into account sufficiently the information about the relationships among the arguments being aggregated, and can reduce the influence of outlier arguments on the decision result by assigning lower weights to those outliers and thus can make the decision result more reflective of the total collection of arguments.

1.2.5 Practical Example

Xu (2011) considered a software selection problem in which the alternatives are the software packages to be selected and the criteria are those attributes under consideration (adapted from Wang and Lee 2009). A computer center in a university desires to select a new information system in order to improve work productivity. After preliminary screening, four alternatives y_j $(j = 1, 2, 3, 4)$ have remained in the candidate list. There are three experts e_k $(k = 1, 2, 3)$ from a committee, whose weight vector is $\eta = (0.4, 0.3, 0.3)^T$. There are four attributes to be considered: (1) Costs of hardware/software investment (G_1); (2) Contribution to organization performance (G_2); (3) Effort to transform from current systems (G_3); and (4) Outsourcing software developer reliability (G_4). The weight vector of the attributes G_i $(i = 1, 2, 3, 4)$ is $w = (0.30, 0.25, 0.25, 0.2)^T$. The experts e_k $(k = 1, 2, 3)$ evaluate the software packages y_j $(j = 1, 2, 3, 4)$ with respect to the attributes G_i $(i = 1, 2, 3, 4)$, and construct the following three intuitionistic fuzzy decision matrices $B^{(k)} = (b_{ij}^{(k)})_{4 \times 4}$ $(k = 1, 2, 3)$ (see Tables 1.2, 1.3, 1.4) (Xu 2011).

Among the considered attributes, G_1 is of cost type, and G_i $(i = 2, 3, 4)$ are of benefit type, i.e., the attributes have two different types, and thus, we need to transform the attribute values of cost type into the attribute values of benefit type by using

Table 1.2 Intuitionistic fuzzy decision matrix $B^{(1)}$

	y_1	y_2	y_3	y_4
G_1	(0.5,0.4,0.1)	(0.4,0.5,0.1)	(0.8,0.2,0.0)	(0.5,0.3,0.2)
G_2	(0.5,0.5,0.0)	(0.6,0.4,0.0)	(0.7,0.3,0.0)	(0.6,0.2,0.2)
G_3	(0.7,0.3,0.0)	(0.2,0.5,0.3)	(0.4,0.6,0.0)	(0.5,0.1,0.4)
G_4	(0.3,0.6,0.1)	(0.5,0.3,0.2)	(0.5,0.2,0.3)	(0.8,0.1,0.1)

Table 1.3 Intuitionistic fuzzy decision matrix $B^{(2)}$

	y_1	y_2	y_3	y_4
G_1	(0.6,0.3,0.1)	(0.3,0.4,0.3)	(0.9,0.1,0.0)	(0.6,0.2,0.2)
G_2	(0.3,0.5,0.2)	(0.5,0.3,0.2)	(0.5,0.2,0.3)	(0.7,0.3,0.0)
G_3	(0.5,0.2,0.3)	(0.2,0.6,0.2)	(0.4,0.4,0.2)	(0.4,0.2,0.4)
G_4	(0.4,0.5,0.1)	(0.6,0.4,0.0)	(0.4,0.6,0.0)	(0.7,0.1,0.2)

Table 1.4 Intuitionistic fuzzy decision matrix $B^{(3)}$

	y_1	y_2	y_3	y_4
G_1	(0.4,0.5,0.1)	(0.4,0.6,0.0)	(0.7,0.3,0.0)	(0.7,0.2,0.1)
G_2	(0.5,0.4,0.1)	(0.7,0.3,0.0)	(0.6,0.4,0.0)	(0.5,0.3,0.2)
G_3	(0.6,0.2,0.2)	(0.3,0.5,0.2)	(0.3,0.5,0.2)	(0.9,0.1,0.0)
G_4	(0.3,0.5,0.2)	(0.5,0.5,0.0)	(0.6,0.2,0.2)	(0.6,0.4,0.0)

Table 1.5 Intuitionistic fuzzy decision matrix $R^{(1)}$

	y_1	y_2	y_3	y_4
G_1	(0.4,0.5,0.1)	(0.5,0.4,0.1)	(0.2,0.8,0.0)	(0.3,0.5,0.2)
G_2	(0.5,0.5,0.0)	(0.6,0.4,0.0)	(0.7,0.3,0.0)	(0.6,0.2,0.2)
G_3	(0.7,0.3,0.0)	(0.2,0.5,0.3)	(0.4,0.6,0.0)	(0.5,0.1,0.4)
G_4	(0.3,0.6,0.1)	(0.5,0.3,0.2)	(0.5,0.2,0.3)	(0.8,0.1,0.1)

Eq. (1.50), then $B^{(k)} = (b_{ij}^{(k)})_{4\times4}$ $(k = 1, 2, 3)$ are transformed into $R^{(k)} = (r_{ij}^{(k)})_{4\times4}$ $(k = 1, 2, 3)$ (see Tables 1.5, 1.6, 1.7) (Xu 2011).

Considering that the weights of the experts are known, here, we utilize Approach 1.1 to select the software packages:

Step 1 Utilize Eqs. (1.51)–(1.54) to calculate the weights $\xi_{ij}^{(k)}$ $(i, j = 1, 2, 3, 4;$ $k = 1, 2, 3)$ associated with the attribute values $r_{ij}^{(k)}$ $(i, j = 1, 2, 3, 4;\ k = 1, 2, 3)$, which are contained in the matrices $\Delta_k = (\xi_{ij}^{(k)})_{4\times4}$ $(k = 1, 2, 3)$ respectively:

Table 1.6 Intuitionistic fuzzy decision matrix $R^{(2)}$

	y_1	y_2	y_3	y_4
G_1	(0.3,0.6,0.1)	(0.4,0.3,0.3)	(0.1,0.9,0.0)	(0.2,0.6,0.2)
G_2	(0.3,0.5,0.2)	(0.5,0.3,0.2)	(0.5,0.2,0.3)	(0.7,0.3,0.0)
G_3	(0.5,0.2,0.3)	(0.2,0.6,0.2)	(0.4,0.4,0.2)	(0.4,0.2,0.4)
G_4	(0.4,0.5,0.1)	(0.6,0.4,0.0)	(0.4,0.3,0.3)	(0.7,0.1,0.2)

Table 1.7 Intuitionistic fuzzy decision matrix $R^{(3)}$

	y_1	y_2	y_3	y_4
G_1	(0.5,0.4,0.1)	(0.6,0.4,0.0)	(0.3,0.7,0.0)	(0.2,0.7,0.1)
G_2	(0.5,0.4,0.1)	(0.7,0.3,0.0)	(0.6,0.4,0.0)	(0.5,0.3,0.2)
G_3	(0.6,0.2,0.2)	(0.3,0.5,0.2)	(0.3,0.5,0.2)	(0.9,0.1,0.0)
G_4	(0.3,0.5,0.2)	(0.5,0.5,0.0)	(0.6,0.2,0.2)	(0.6,0.4,0.0)

$$\Delta_1 = \begin{pmatrix} 0.3909 & 0.3937 & 0.3909 & 0.3847 \\ 0.3892 & 0.3892 & 0.3921 & 0.3892 \\ 0.3811 & 0.3864 & 0.3829 & 0.4000 \\ 0.3864 & 0.3829 & 0.3909 & 0.3921 \end{pmatrix}$$

$$\Delta_2 = \begin{pmatrix} 0.3046 & 0.2992 & 0.3046 & 0.3115 \\ 0.3015 & 0.3015 & 0.2960 & 0.3015 \\ 0.3055 & 0.3068 & 0.3085 & 0.3124 \\ 0.3068 & 0.3085 & 0.3046 & 0.3119 \end{pmatrix}$$

$$\Delta_3 = \begin{pmatrix} 0.3046 & 0.3070 & 0.3046 & 0.3038 \\ 0.3093 & 0.3093 & 0.3119 & 0.3093 \\ 0.3134 & 0.3068 & 0.3085 & 0.2876 \\ 0.3068 & 0.3085 & 0.3046 & 0.2960 \end{pmatrix}$$

Step 2 Utilize the IFPWA operator (1.26) to aggregate all the individual intuitionistic fuzzy decision matrices $R^{(k)} = (r_{ij}^{(k)})_{4\times 4}$ $(k = 1, 2, 3)$ into the collective intuitionistic fuzzy decision matrix $R = (r_{ij})_{4\times 4}$:

$$R = \begin{pmatrix} (0.4052,0.4938,0.1010) & (0.5069,0.3670,0.1261) & (0.2038,0.7962,0.0000) \\ (0.4466,0.4667,0.0867) & (0.6086,0.3355,0.0559) & (0.6183,0.2910,0.0907) \\ (0.6162,0.2334,0.1504) & (0.2321,0.5288,0.2391) & (0.3707,0.5005,0.1288) \\ (0.3323,0.5365,0.1312) & (0.5332,0.3838,0.0830) & (0.5062,0.2263,0.2675) \end{pmatrix.$$
$$\begin{matrix} (0.2401,0.5862,0.1737) \\ (0.6070,0.2562,0.1368) \\ (0.6668,0.1242,0.2090) \\ (0.7214,0.1507,0.1279) \end{matrix}\Bigg)$$

Step 3 Aggregate all the preference values r_{ij} $(j = 1, 2, 3, 4)$ in the jth column of R by using the IFWA operator (1.57), and get the overall preference value r_j corresponding to the alternative y_j:

$$r_1 = (0.4642,0.4105,0.1253), \quad r_2 = (0.4857,0.3967,0.1176)$$
$$r_3 = (0.4322,0.4286,0.1392), \quad r_4 = (0.5710,0.2464,0.1826)$$

Step 4 By Eq. (1.3), we calculate the scores of r_j $(j = 1, 2, 3, 4)$ respectively:

Table 1.8 Fuzzy decision matrix $F^{(1)}$

	y_1	y_2	y_3	y_4
G_1	0.4	0.5	0.2	0.3
G_2	0.5	0.6	0.7	0.6
G_3	0.7	0.2	0.4	0.5
G_4	0.3	0.5	0.5	0.8

Table 1.9 Fuzzy decision matrix $F^{(2)}$

	y_1	y_2	y_3	y_4
G_1	0.3	0.4	0.1	0.2
G_2	0.3	0.5	0.5	0.7
G_3	0.5	0.2	0.4	0.4
G_4	0.4	0.6	0.4	0.7

Table 1.10 Fuzzy decision matrix $F^{(3)}$

	y_1	y_2	y_3	y_4
G_1	0.5	0.6	0.3	0.2
G_2	0.5	0.7	0.6	0.5
G_3	0.6	0.3	0.3	0.9
G_4	0.3	0.5	0.6	0.6

$$S(r_1) = 0.4642 - 0.4105 = 0.0537, \quad S(r_2) = 0.4857 - 0.3967 = 0.0890$$
$$S(r_3) = 0.4322 - 0.4286 = 0.0036, \quad S(r_4) = 0.5710 - 0.2464 = 0.3246$$

Since $S(r_4) > S(r_2) > S(r_1) > S(r_3)$, then by Xu and Yager (2006)'s ranking method, we have $r_4 > r_2 > r_1 > r_3$, and thus, $y_4 \succ y_2 \succ y_1 \succ y_3$. Therefore, y_4 is the best software package.

In the illustrative example, if we use fuzzy sets, each of which is characterized only by a membership information, to express the experts' evaluations, then Tables 1.5, 1.6 and 1.7 can be written as Tables 1.8, 1.9 and 1.10 (Xu 2011).

To get the optimal alternative, the following steps are involved (Xu 2011):

Step 1 Utilize Eqs. (1.51)–(1.54) to calculate the weights $\xi_{ij}^{(k)}$ $(i, j = 1, 2, 3, 4;$ $k = 1, 2, 3)$ associated with the attribute values $r_{ij}^{(k)}$ $(i, j = 1, 2, 3, 4; k = 1, 2, 3)$, which are contained in the matrices $\Delta_k = (\xi_{ij}^{(k)})_{4\times 4}$ $(k = 1, 2, 3)$ respectively (here we assume that all the non-membership degrees and the hesitancy degrees are zero):

$$\Delta_1 = \begin{pmatrix} 0.3911 & 0.3911 & 0.3911 & 0.4046 \\ 0.3911 & 0.3911 & 0.4000 & 0.3911 \\ 0.4000 & 0.3954 & 0.3954 & 0.3802 \\ 0.3954 & 0.3954 & 0.3911 & 0.4000 \end{pmatrix}$$

$$\Delta_2 = \begin{pmatrix} 0.3044 & 0.3044 & 0.3044 & 0.2977 \\ 0.3155 & 0.3044 & 0.3055 & 0.3044 \\ 0.3055 & 0.2965 & 0.2965 & 0.2950 \\ 0.3081 & 0.3081 & 0.3044 & 0.2950 \end{pmatrix}$$

$$\Delta_3 = \begin{pmatrix} 0.3044 & 0.3044 & 0.3044 & 0.2977 \\ 0.2934 & 0.3044 & 0.2945 & 0.3044 \\ 0.2945 & 0.3081 & 0.3081 & 0.3248 \\ 0.2965 & 0.2965 & 0.3044 & 0.3055 \end{pmatrix}$$

Step 2 Utilize the PA operator (1.17) to aggregate all the individual fuzzy decision matrices $F^{(k)} = (F_{ij}^{(k)})_{4\times4}$ $(k = 1, 2, 3)$ into the collective fuzzy decision matrix $F = (F_{ij})_{4\times4}$:

$$F = \begin{pmatrix} 0.4000 & 0.5000 & 0.2000 & 0.2405 \\ 0.4369 & 0.6000 & 0.6094 & 0.6000 \\ 0.6094 & 0.2308 & 0.3692 & 0.6004 \\ 0.3308 & 0.5308 & 0.5000 & 0.7094 \end{pmatrix}$$

Step 3 Aggregate all the preference values F_{ij} $(j = 1, 2, 3, 4)$ in the jth column of F by using the well-known weighted averaging (WA) operator (Harsanyi 1955), and get the overall preference value F_j corresponding to the alternative y_j:

$$F_1 = 0.3431, \quad F_2 = 0.5534, \quad F_3 = 0.4529, \quad F_4 = 0.4988$$

Since $F_4 > F_2 > F_1 > F_3$, and thus, $y_2 \succ y_4 \succ y_3 \succ y_1$.

It is noted that the rankings of the alternatives are very different in such two cases, this is because that all the non-membership information and the hesitancy information are lost in the second case, and thus, the final results obtained in the second case are obviously less reasonable than those when the experts' evaluations are expressed in IFVs comprehensively.

In the next section, we shall extend the aggregation operators and the decision making approaches introduced in this section to interval-valued intuitionistic fuzzy environments.

1.3 Interval-Valued Intuitionistic Fuzzy Power Aggregation Operators

1.3.1 Interval-Valued Intuitionistic Fuzzy Values

Atanassov and Gargov (1989) extended IFS to interval-valued intuitionistic fuzzy environments, and defined an interval-valued intuitionistic fuzzy set (IVIFS), shown as:

$$\tilde{A} = \{\langle x, \tilde{\mu}_{\tilde{A}}(x), \tilde{v}_{\tilde{A}}(x)\rangle | x \in X\} \tag{1.64}$$

where $\tilde{\mu}_{\tilde{A}}(x) = [\mu^-_{\tilde{A}}(x), \mu^+_{\tilde{A}}(x)]$ and $\tilde{v}_{\tilde{A}}(x) = [v^-_{\tilde{A}}(x), v^+_{\tilde{A}}(x)]$ are interval ranges, and each triple $(\tilde{\mu}_{\tilde{A}}(x), \tilde{v}_{\tilde{A}}(x), \tilde{\pi}_{\tilde{A}}(x))$ in $\tilde{A}$ is called an interval-valued intuitionistic fuzzy value (IVIFV) or called an interval-valued intuitionistic fuzzy number (IVIFN) (Xu and Chen 2007b), where $\tilde{\pi}_{\tilde{A}}(x) = [\pi^-_{\tilde{A}}(x), \pi^+_{\tilde{A}}(x)], \pi^-_{\tilde{A}}(x) = 1 - \mu^+_{\tilde{A}}(x) - v^+_{\tilde{A}}(x)$ and $\pi^+_{\tilde{A}}(x) = 1 - \mu^-_{\tilde{A}}(x) - v^-_{\tilde{A}}(x)$, for all $x \in X$. For convenience, we denote an IVIFV by $\tilde{\alpha} = (\tilde{\mu}_{\tilde{\alpha}}, \tilde{v}_{\tilde{\alpha}}, \tilde{\pi}_{\tilde{\alpha}})$, where $\tilde{\mu}_{\tilde{\alpha}}, \tilde{v}_{\tilde{\alpha}}$ and $\tilde{\pi}_{\tilde{\alpha}}$ are the membership degree range, the non-membership degree range and the hesitancy degree (or the uncertainty degree) range respectively, and satisfy

$$\begin{aligned} &\tilde{\mu}_{\tilde{\alpha}} = [\mu^-_{\tilde{\alpha}}, \mu^+_{\tilde{\alpha}}] \subset [0, 1], \quad \tilde{v}_{\tilde{\alpha}} = [v^-_{\tilde{\alpha}}, v^+_{\tilde{\alpha}}] \subset [0, 1], \quad \mu^+_{\tilde{\alpha}} + v^+_{\tilde{\alpha}} \leq 1, \\ &\tilde{\pi}_{\tilde{\alpha}} = [\pi^-_{\tilde{\alpha}}, \pi^+_{\tilde{\alpha}}] \subset [0, 1], \quad \pi^-_{\tilde{\alpha}} = 1 - \mu^+_{\tilde{\alpha}} - v^+_{\tilde{\alpha}}, \quad \pi^+_{\tilde{\alpha}} = 1 - \mu^-_{\tilde{\alpha}} - v^-_{\tilde{\alpha}} \end{aligned} \tag{1.65}$$

Similar to the comparison method of IFVs, Xu and Chen (2007b) defined the score function and the accuracy degree of IVIFS $\tilde{\alpha}$ as follows:

$$S(\tilde{\alpha}) = \frac{1}{2}(\mu^-_{\tilde{\alpha}} - v^-_{\tilde{\alpha}} + \mu^+_{\tilde{\alpha}} - v^+_{\tilde{\alpha}}) \tag{1.66}$$

$$H(\tilde{\alpha}_i) = \frac{1}{2}(\mu^-_{\tilde{\alpha}} + v^-_{\tilde{\alpha}} + \mu^+_{\tilde{\alpha}} + v^+_{\tilde{\alpha}}) \tag{1.67}$$

and they gave the following definition to compare two IVIFVs:

Definition 1.4 (Xu and Chen 2007b) Let $\tilde{\alpha}_i = (\tilde{\mu}_{\tilde{\alpha}_i}, \tilde{v}_{\tilde{\alpha}_i}, \tilde{\pi}_{\tilde{\alpha}_i})$ $(i = 1, 2)$ be any two IVIFVs, $S(\tilde{\alpha}_i)$ $(i = 1, 2)$ and $H(\tilde{\alpha}_i)$ $(i = 1, 2)$ the scores and accuracy degrees of $\tilde{\alpha}_i$ $(i = 1, 2)$ respectively, then

(1) If $S(\tilde{\alpha}_1) > S(\tilde{\alpha}_2)$, then $\tilde{\alpha}_1$ is larger than $\tilde{\alpha}_2$, denoted by $\tilde{\alpha}_1 > \tilde{\alpha}_2$.
(2) If $S(\tilde{\alpha}_1) = S(\tilde{\alpha}_2)$, then

  (a) If $H(\tilde{\alpha}_1) = H(\tilde{\alpha}_2)$, then there is no difference between $\tilde{\alpha}_1$ and $\tilde{\alpha}_2$, denoted by $\tilde{\alpha}_1 \sim \tilde{\alpha}_2$.
  (b) If $H(\tilde{\alpha}_1) > H(\tilde{\alpha}_2)$, then $\tilde{\alpha}_1$ is larger than $\tilde{\alpha}_2$, denoted by $\tilde{\alpha}_1 > \tilde{\alpha}_2$.

Later, Wang et al. (2009) gave another two indices called the membership uncertainty index:

$$g_1(\tilde{\alpha}) = \mu^+_{\tilde{\alpha}} + v^-_{\tilde{\alpha}} - \mu^-_{\tilde{\alpha}} - v^+_{\tilde{\alpha}} \tag{1.68}$$

and the hesitation uncertainty index:

$$g_2(\tilde{\alpha}) = \mu^+_{\tilde{\alpha}} + v^+_{\tilde{\alpha}} - \mu^-_{\tilde{\alpha}} - v^-_{\tilde{\alpha}} \tag{1.69}$$

respectively to supplement the ranking procedure in Definition 1.4. In the case where $S(\tilde{\alpha}_1) = S(\tilde{\alpha}_2)$ and $H(\tilde{\alpha}_1) = H(\tilde{\alpha}_2)$, one can further consider these two indices:

(1) If $g_1(\tilde{\alpha}_1) < g_1(\tilde{\alpha}_2)$, then $\tilde{\alpha}_1$ is larger than $\tilde{\alpha}_2$, denoted by $\tilde{\alpha}_1 > \tilde{\alpha}_2$.

(2) If $g_1(\tilde{\alpha}_1) = g_2(\tilde{\alpha}_2)$, then

(a) If $g_2(\tilde{\alpha}_1) < g_2(\tilde{\alpha}_2)$, then $\tilde{\alpha}_1$ is larger than $\tilde{\alpha}_2$, denoted by $\tilde{\alpha}_1 > \tilde{\alpha}_2$;
(b) If $g_2(\tilde{\alpha}_1) = g_2(\tilde{\alpha}_2)$, then $\tilde{\alpha}_1$ is equal to $\tilde{\alpha}_2$, denoted by $\tilde{\alpha}_1 = \tilde{\alpha}_2$.

Xu (2011) extended Definition 1.3 to interval-valued intuitionistic fuzzy environments:

Definition 1.5 (Xu 2011) Let $\tilde{\alpha}_i = (\tilde{\mu}_{\tilde{\alpha}_i}, \tilde{v}_{\tilde{\alpha}_i}, \tilde{\pi}_{\tilde{\alpha}_i}) = ([\mu^-_{\tilde{\alpha}_i}, \mu^+_{\tilde{\alpha}_i}], [v^-_{\tilde{\alpha}_i}, v^+_{\tilde{\alpha}_i}], [\pi^-_{\tilde{\alpha}_i}, \pi^+_{\tilde{\alpha}_i}])$ $(i = 1, 2)$ be two IVIFVs, then

(1)
$$\tilde{\alpha}_1 \oplus \tilde{\alpha}_2 = ([\mu^-_{\tilde{\alpha}_1} + \mu^-_{\tilde{\alpha}_2} - \mu^-_{\tilde{\alpha}_1}\mu^-_{\tilde{\alpha}_2}, \mu^+_{\tilde{\alpha}_1} + \mu^+_{\tilde{\alpha}_2} - \mu^+_{\tilde{\alpha}_1}\mu^+_{\tilde{\alpha}_2}], [v^-_{\tilde{\alpha}_1}v^-_{\tilde{\alpha}_2}, v^+_{\tilde{\alpha}_1}v^+_{\tilde{\alpha}_2}],$$
$$[(1 - \mu^+_{\tilde{\alpha}_1})(1 - \mu^+_{\tilde{\alpha}_2}) - v^+_{\tilde{\alpha}_1}v^+_{\tilde{\alpha}_2}, (1 - \mu^-_{\tilde{\alpha}_1})(1 - \mu^-_{\tilde{\alpha}_2}) - v^-_{\tilde{\alpha}_1}v^-_{\tilde{\alpha}_2}]).$$

(2)
$$\tilde{\alpha}_1 \otimes \tilde{\alpha}_2 = ([\mu^-_{\tilde{\alpha}_1}\mu^-_{\tilde{\alpha}_2}, \mu^+_{\tilde{\alpha}_1}\mu^+_{\tilde{\alpha}_2}], [v^-_{\tilde{\alpha}_1} + v^-_{\tilde{\alpha}_2} - v^-_{\tilde{\alpha}_1}v^-_{\tilde{\alpha}_2}, v^+_{\tilde{\alpha}_1} + v^+_{\tilde{\alpha}_2} - v^+_{\tilde{\alpha}_1}v^+_{\tilde{\alpha}_2}],$$
$$[(1 - v^+_{\tilde{\alpha}_1})(1 - v^+_{\tilde{\alpha}_2}) - \mu^+_{\tilde{\alpha}_1}\mu^+_{\tilde{\alpha}_2}, (1 - v^-_{\tilde{\alpha}_1})(1 - v^-_{\tilde{\alpha}_2}) - \mu^-_{\tilde{\alpha}_1}\mu^-_{\tilde{\alpha}_2}].$$

(3)
$$\lambda\tilde{\alpha}_1 = ([1 - (1 - \mu^-_{\tilde{\alpha}_1})^\lambda, 1 - (1 - \mu^+_{\tilde{\alpha}_1})^\lambda], [(v^-_{\tilde{\alpha}_1})^\lambda, (v^+_{\tilde{\alpha}_1})^\lambda],$$
$$[(1 - \mu^+_{\tilde{\alpha}_1})^\lambda - (v^+_{\tilde{\alpha}_1})^\lambda, (1 - \mu^-_{\tilde{\alpha}_1})^\lambda - (v^-_{\tilde{\alpha}_1})^\lambda]), \quad \lambda > 0.$$

(4)
$$\tilde{\alpha}_1^\lambda = ([(\mu^-_{\tilde{\alpha}_1})^\lambda, (\mu^+_{\tilde{\alpha}_1})^\lambda], [1 - (1 - v^-_{\tilde{\alpha}_1})^\lambda, 1 - (1 - v^+_{\tilde{\alpha}_1})^\lambda],$$
$$[(1 - v^+_{\tilde{\alpha}_1})^\lambda - (\mu^+_{\tilde{\alpha}_1})^\lambda, (1 - v^-_{\tilde{\alpha}_1})^\lambda - (\mu^-_{\tilde{\alpha}_1})^\lambda]), \quad \lambda > 0.$$

All the results of the above operations are also IVIFVs, and similar to Theorem 1.2, the following are all right:

Theorem 1.10 (Xu 2011)

(1) If $\lambda_1 > \lambda_2$, then $\lambda_1\tilde{\alpha} \geq \lambda_2\tilde{\alpha}, \tilde{\alpha}^{1-\lambda_1} \geq \tilde{\alpha}^{1-\lambda_2}, 0 < \lambda_1, \lambda_2 \leq 1$.
(2) If $\mu_{\tilde{\alpha}_1} \geq \mu_{\tilde{\alpha}_2}, v_{\tilde{\alpha}_1} \leq v_{\tilde{\alpha}_2}$, then $\lambda\tilde{\alpha}_1 \geq \lambda\tilde{\alpha}_2, \tilde{\alpha}_1^\lambda \geq \tilde{\alpha}_2^\lambda, 0 < \lambda \leq 1$.
(3) If $\mu_{\tilde{\alpha}_1} \geq \mu_{\tilde{\alpha}_3}, \mu_{\tilde{\alpha}_2} \geq \mu_{\tilde{\alpha}_4}, v_{\tilde{\alpha}_1} \leq v_{\tilde{\alpha}_3}, v_{\tilde{\alpha}_2} \leq v_{\tilde{\alpha}_4}$, then $\tilde{\alpha}_1 \oplus \tilde{\alpha}_3 \geq \tilde{\alpha}_2 \oplus \tilde{\alpha}_4, \tilde{\alpha}_1 \otimes \tilde{\alpha}_3 \geq \tilde{\alpha}_2 \otimes \tilde{\alpha}_4$.

1.3.2 Power Aggregation Operators for IVIFVs

On the basis of Definitions 1.4 and 1.5, Xu (2011) extended all the operators developed in Sect. 1.2.3 to aggregate interval-valued intuitionistic fuzzy information.

Let $\tilde{\alpha}_i = (\tilde{\mu}_{\tilde{\alpha}_i}, \tilde{v}_{\tilde{\alpha}_i}, \tilde{\pi}_{\tilde{\alpha}_i})$ $(i = 1, 2, \ldots, n)$ be a collection of IVIFVs, and $w = (w_1, w_2, \ldots, w_n)^T$ the weight vector of $\tilde{\alpha}_i$ $(i = 1, 2, \ldots, n)$, where $w_i \geq 0$, $i = 1, 2, \ldots, n$, and $\sum_{i=1}^n w_i = 1$, then Xu (2011) defined an interval-valued intuitionistic fuzzy power weighted average (IVIFPWA) operator:

$$IVIFPWA(\tilde{\alpha}_1, \tilde{\alpha}_2, \ldots, \tilde{\alpha}_n) = \frac{(w_1(1 + T(\tilde{\alpha}_1))\tilde{\alpha}_1) \oplus (w_2(1 + T(\tilde{\alpha}_2))\tilde{\alpha}_2) \oplus \cdots \oplus (w_n(1 + T(\tilde{\alpha}_n))\tilde{\alpha}_n)}{\sum_{i=1}^n w_i(1 + T(\tilde{\alpha}_i))} \tag{1.70}$$

which can be transformed into the following form:

$$\begin{aligned} IVIFPWA(\tilde{\alpha}_1, \tilde{\alpha}_2, \ldots, \tilde{\alpha}_n) = \Bigg(& \left[1 - \prod_{j=1}^n (1 - \mu^-_{\tilde{\alpha}_j})^{\frac{w_j(1+T(\tilde{\alpha}_j))}{\sum_{i=1}^n w_i(1+T(\tilde{\alpha}_i))}}, 1 - \prod_{j=1}^n (1 - \mu^+_{\tilde{\alpha}_j})^{\frac{w_j(1+T(\tilde{\alpha}_j))}{\sum_{i=1}^n w_i(1+T(\tilde{\alpha}_i))}}\right], \\ & \left[\prod_{j=1}^n (v^-_{\tilde{\alpha}_j})^{\frac{w_j(1+T(\tilde{\alpha}_j))}{\sum_{i=1}^n w_i(1+T(\tilde{\alpha}_i))}}, \prod_{j=1}^n (v^+_{\tilde{\alpha}_j})^{\frac{w_j(1+T(\tilde{\alpha}_j))}{\sum_{i=1}^n w_i(1+T(\tilde{\alpha}_i))}}\right], \\ & \left[\prod_{j=1}^n (1 - \mu^+_{\tilde{\alpha}_j})^{\frac{w_j(1+T(\tilde{\alpha}_j))}{\sum_{i=1}^n w_i(1+T(\tilde{\alpha}_i))}} - \prod_{j=1}^n (v^+_{\tilde{\alpha}_j})^{\frac{w_j(1+T(\tilde{\alpha}_j))}{\sum_{i=1}^n w_i(1+T(\tilde{\alpha}_i))}}, \right. \\ & \left. \prod_{j=1}^n (1 - \mu^-_{\tilde{\alpha}_j})^{\frac{w_j(1+T(\tilde{\alpha}_j))}{\sum_{i=1}^n w_i(1+T(\tilde{\alpha}_i))}} - \prod_{j=1}^n (v^-_{\tilde{\alpha}_j})^{\frac{w_j(1+T(\tilde{\alpha}_j))}{\sum_{i=1}^n w_i(1+T(\tilde{\alpha}_i))}}\right]\Bigg) \end{aligned} \tag{1.71}$$

where

$$T(\tilde{\alpha}_i) = \sum_{\substack{j=1 \\ j \neq i}}^n w_j Sup(\tilde{\alpha}_i, \tilde{\alpha}_j) \tag{1.72}$$

and $Sup(\tilde{\alpha}_i, \tilde{\alpha}_j)$ is the support for $\tilde{\alpha}_i$ from $\tilde{\alpha}_j$, with the following conditions:

(1) $Sup(\tilde{\alpha}_i, \tilde{\alpha}_j) \in [0, 1]$.
(2) $Sup(\tilde{\alpha}_i, \tilde{\alpha}_j) = Sup(\tilde{\alpha}_j, \tilde{\alpha}_i)$.

(3) $Sup(\tilde{\alpha}_i, \tilde{\alpha}_j) \geq Sup(\tilde{\alpha}_s, \tilde{\alpha}_t)$, if $d(\tilde{\alpha}_i, \tilde{\alpha}_j) < d(\tilde{\alpha}_s, \tilde{\alpha}_t)$, where d is a distance measure, such as the normalized Hamming distance or the normalized Euclidean distance, where

(a) The normalized Hamming distance for IVIFVs:

$$d_H(\tilde{\alpha}_i, \tilde{\alpha}_j) = \frac{1}{4}\left(\left|\mu^-_{\alpha_i} - \mu^-_{\alpha_j}\right| + \left|\mu^+_{\alpha_i} - \mu^+_{\alpha_j}\right| + \left|v^-_{\alpha_i} - v^-_{\alpha_j}\right| + \left|v^+_{\alpha_i} - v^+_{\alpha_j}\right| + \left|\pi^-_{\alpha_i} - \pi^-_{\alpha_j}\right| + \left|\pi^+_{\alpha_i} - \pi^+_{\alpha_j}\right|\right) \tag{1.73}$$

(b) The normalized Euclidean distance for IVIFVs:

$$d_E(\tilde{\alpha}_i, \tilde{\alpha}_j) = \sqrt{\frac{1}{4}\left((\mu^-_{\alpha_i} - \mu^-_{\alpha_j})^2 + (\mu^+_{\alpha_i} - \mu^+_{\alpha_j})^2 + (v^-_{\alpha_i} - v^-_{\alpha_j})^2 + (v^+_{\alpha_i} - v^+_{\alpha_j})^2 + (\pi^-_{\alpha_i} - \pi^-_{\alpha_j})^2 + (\pi^+_{\alpha_i} - \pi^+_{\alpha_j})^2\right)} \tag{1.74}$$

Especially, if $w = (1/n, 1/n, \ldots, 1/n)^T$, then the IVIFPWA operator (1.71) reduces to an interval-valued intuitionistic fuzzy power average (IVIFPA) operator:

$$\begin{aligned} &IVIFPA(\tilde{\alpha}_1, \tilde{\alpha}_2, \ldots, \tilde{\alpha}_n) \\ &= \frac{\big((1 + T(\tilde{\alpha}_1))\tilde{\alpha}_1\big) \oplus \big((1 + T(\tilde{\alpha}_2))\tilde{\alpha}_2\big) \oplus \cdots \oplus \big((1 + T(\tilde{\alpha}_n))\tilde{\alpha}_n\big)}{\sum_{i=1}^n (1 + T(\tilde{\alpha}_i))} \\ &= \left(\left[1 - \prod_{j=1}^n (1 - \mu^-_{\tilde{\alpha}_j})^{\frac{(1+T(\tilde{\alpha}_j))}{\sum_{i=1}^n (1+T(\tilde{\alpha}_i))}}, 1 - \prod_{j=1}^n (1 - \mu^+_{\tilde{\alpha}_j})^{\frac{(1+T(\tilde{\alpha}_j))}{\sum_{i=1}^n (1+T(\tilde{\alpha}_i))}}\right],\right. \\ &\left[\prod_{j=1}^n (v^-_{\tilde{\alpha}_j})^{\frac{(1+T(\tilde{\alpha}_j))}{\sum_{i=1}^n (1+T(\tilde{\alpha}_i))}}, \prod_{j=1}^n (v^+_{\tilde{\alpha}_j})^{\frac{(1+T(\tilde{\alpha}_j))}{\sum_{i=1}^n (1+T(\tilde{\alpha}_i))}}\right], \\ &\left[\prod_{j=1}^n (1 - \mu^+_{\tilde{\alpha}_j})^{\frac{(1+T(\tilde{\alpha}_j))}{\sum_{i=1}^n (1+T(\tilde{\alpha}_i))}} - \prod_{j=1}^n (v^+_{\tilde{\alpha}_j})^{\frac{(1+T(\tilde{\alpha}_j))}{\sum_{i=1}^n (1+T(\tilde{\alpha}_i))}},\right. \\ &\left.\left.\prod_{j=1}^n (1 - \mu^-_{\tilde{\alpha}_j})^{\frac{(1+T(\tilde{\alpha}_j))}{\sum_{i=1}^n (1+T(\tilde{\alpha}_i))}} - \prod_{j=1}^n (v^-_{\tilde{\alpha}_j})^{\frac{(1+T(\tilde{\alpha}_j))}{\sum_{i=1}^n (1+T(\tilde{\alpha}_i))}}\right]\right) \end{aligned} \tag{1.75}$$

where

$$T(\tilde{\alpha}_i) = \frac{1}{n}\sum_{\substack{j=1 \\ j \neq i}}^n Sup(\tilde{\alpha}_i, \tilde{\alpha}_j) \tag{1.76}$$

Based on the IVIFPWA operator (1.71) and the geometric mean, Xu (2011) introduced an interval-valued intuitionistic fuzzy power weighted geometric (IVIFPWG) operator:

$$
\begin{aligned}
&IVIFPWG(\tilde{\alpha}_1, \tilde{\alpha}_2, \ldots, \tilde{\alpha}_n) \\
&= (\tilde{\alpha}_1)^{\frac{1}{n-1}\left(1-\frac{w_1(1+T(\tilde{\alpha}_1))}{\sum_{i=1}^n w_i(1+T(\tilde{\alpha}_i))}\right)} \otimes (\tilde{\alpha}_2)^{\frac{1}{n-1}\left(1-\frac{w_2(1+T(\tilde{\alpha}_2))}{\sum_{i=1}^n w_i(1+T(\tilde{\alpha}_i))}\right)} \\
&\otimes \cdots \otimes (\tilde{\alpha}_n)^{\frac{1}{n-1}\left(1-\frac{w_n(1+T(\tilde{\alpha}_n))}{\sum_{i=1}^n w_i(1+T(\tilde{\alpha}_i))}\right)}
\end{aligned} \tag{1.77}
$$

which can be transformed into Eq. (1.78) by using mathematical induction on n:

$$
\begin{aligned}
&IVIFPWG(\tilde{\alpha}_1, \tilde{\alpha}_2, \ldots, \tilde{\alpha}_n) \\
&= \left(\left[\prod_{j=1}^n (\mu_{\tilde{\alpha}_j}^-)^{\frac{1}{n-1}\left(1-\frac{w_j(1+T(\tilde{\alpha}_j))}{\sum_{i=1}^n w_i(1+T(\tilde{\alpha}_i))}\right)}, \prod_{j=1}^n (\mu_{\tilde{\alpha}_j}^+)^{\frac{1}{n-1}\left(1-\frac{w_j(1+T(\tilde{\alpha}_j))}{\sum_{i=1}^n w_i(1+T(\tilde{\alpha}_i))}\right)} \right], \right. \\
&\left[1 - \prod_{j=1}^n (1 - \nu_{\tilde{\alpha}_j}^-)^{\frac{1}{n-1}\left(1-\frac{w_j(1+T(\tilde{\alpha}_j))}{\sum_{i=1}^n w_i(1+T(\tilde{\alpha}_i))}\right)}, \right. \\
&\left. 1 - \prod_{j=1}^n (1 - \nu_{\tilde{\alpha}_j}^+)^{\frac{1}{n-1}\left(1-\frac{w_j(1+T(\tilde{\alpha}_j))}{\sum_{i=1}^n w_i(1+T(\tilde{\alpha}_i))}\right)} \right], \\
&\left[\prod_{j=1}^n (1 - \nu_{\tilde{\alpha}_j}^+)^{\frac{1}{n-1}\left(1-\frac{w_j(1+T(\tilde{\alpha}_j))}{\sum_{i=1}^n w_i(1+T(\tilde{\alpha}_i))}\right)} - \prod_{j=1}^n (\mu_{\tilde{\alpha}_j}^+)^{\frac{1}{n-1}\left(1-\frac{w_j(1+T(\tilde{\alpha}_j))}{\sum_{i=1}^n w_i(1+T(\tilde{\alpha}_i))}\right)}, \right. \\
&\left.\left. \prod_{j=1}^n (1 - \nu_{\tilde{\alpha}_j}^-)^{\frac{1}{n-1}\left(1-\frac{w_j(1+T(\tilde{\alpha}_j))}{\sum_{i=1}^n w_i(1+T(\tilde{\alpha}_i))}\right)} - \prod_{j=1}^n (\mu_{\tilde{\alpha}_j}^-)^{\frac{1}{n-1}\left(1-\frac{w_j(1+T(\tilde{\alpha}_j))}{\sum_{i=1}^n w_i(1+T(\tilde{\alpha}_i))}\right)} \right] \right)
\end{aligned} \tag{1.78}
$$

with the condition (1.72).

Especially, if $w = (1/n, 1/n, \ldots, 1/n)^T$, then the IVIFPWG operator (1.78) reduces to an interval-valued intuitionistic fuzzy power geometric (IVIFPG) operator:

$$
\begin{aligned}
&IVIFPG(\tilde{\alpha}_1, \tilde{\alpha}_2, \ldots, \tilde{\alpha}_n) \\
&= (\tilde{\alpha}_1)^{\frac{1}{n-1}\left(1-\frac{1+T(\tilde{\alpha}_1)}{\sum_{i=1}^n (1+T(\tilde{\alpha}_i))}\right)} \otimes (\tilde{\alpha}_2)^{\frac{1}{n-1}\left(1-\frac{1+T(\tilde{\alpha}_2)}{\sum_{i=1}^n (1+T(\tilde{\alpha}_i))}\right)} \\
&\otimes \cdots \otimes (\tilde{\alpha}_n)^{\frac{1}{n-1}\left(1-\frac{1+T(\tilde{\alpha}_n)}{\sum_{i=1}^n (1+T(\tilde{\alpha}_i))}\right)} \\
&= \left(\left[\prod_{j=1}^n (\mu_{\tilde{\alpha}_j}^-)^{\frac{1}{n-1}\left(1-\frac{(1+T(\tilde{\alpha}_j))}{\sum_{i=1}^n (1+T(\tilde{\alpha}_i))}\right)}, \prod_{j=1}^n (\mu_{\tilde{\alpha}_j}^+)^{\frac{1}{n-1}\left(1-\frac{(1+T(\tilde{\alpha}_j))}{\sum_{i=1}^n (1+T(\tilde{\alpha}_i))}\right)} \right], \right. \\
&\left[1 - \prod_{j=1}^n (1 - \nu_{\tilde{\alpha}_j}^-)^{\frac{1}{n-1}\left(1-\frac{(1+T(\tilde{\alpha}_j))}{\sum_{i=1}^n (1+T(\tilde{\alpha}_i))}\right)}, \right.
\end{aligned}
$$

$$1-\prod_{j=1}^{n}(1-v_{\tilde{\alpha}_j}^{+})^{\frac{1}{n-1}\left(1-\frac{(1+T(\tilde{\alpha}_j))}{\sum_{i=1}^{n}(1+T(\tilde{\alpha}_i))}\right)}\Bigg],$$

$$\Bigg[\prod_{j=1}^{n}(1-v_{\tilde{\alpha}_j}^{+})^{\frac{1}{n-1}\left(1-\frac{(1+T(\tilde{\alpha}_j))}{\sum_{i=1}^{n}(1+T(\tilde{\alpha}_i))}\right)}-\prod_{j=1}^{n}(\mu_{\tilde{\alpha}_j}^{+})^{\frac{1}{n-1}\left(1-\frac{(1+T(\tilde{\alpha}_j))}{\sum_{i=1}^{n}(1+T(\tilde{\alpha}_i))}\right)},$$

$$\prod_{j=1}^{n}(1-v_{\tilde{\alpha}_j}^{-})^{\frac{1}{n-1}\left(1-\frac{(1+T(\tilde{\alpha}_j))}{\sum_{i=1}^{n}(1+T(\tilde{\alpha}_i))}\right)}-\prod_{j=1}^{n}(\mu_{\tilde{\alpha}_j}^{-})^{\frac{1}{n-1}\left(1-\frac{(1+T(\tilde{\alpha}_j))}{\sum_{i=1}^{n}(1+T(\tilde{\alpha}_i))}\right)}\Bigg]\Bigg) \tag{1.79}$$

with the condition (1.76).

Similar to the IFPOWA operator (1.43), Xu (2011) defined an interval-valued intuitionistic fuzzy power ordered weighted average (IVIFPOWA) operator as follows:

$$IVIFPOWA(\tilde{\alpha}_1,\tilde{\alpha}_2,\ldots,\tilde{\alpha}_n)=\omega_1\tilde{\alpha}_{index(1)}\oplus\omega_2\tilde{\alpha}_{index(2)}\oplus\cdots\oplus\omega_n\tilde{\alpha}_{index(n)} \tag{1.80}$$

which can be further expressed as:

$$IVIFPOWA(\tilde{\alpha}_1,\tilde{\alpha}_2,\ldots,\tilde{\alpha}_n)$$
$$=\left(\left[1-\prod_{j=1}^{n}(1-\mu_{\tilde{\alpha}_{index(j)}}^{-})^{\omega_j},1-\prod_{j=1}^{n}(1-\mu_{\tilde{\alpha}_{index(j)}}^{+})^{\omega_j}\right],\right.$$
$$\left.\left[\prod_{j=1}^{n}(v_{\tilde{\alpha}_{index(j)}}^{-})^{\omega_j},\prod_{j=1}^{n}(v_{\tilde{\alpha}_{index(j)}}^{+})^{\omega_j}\right]\right) \tag{1.81}$$

where $\tilde{\alpha}_j=(\tilde{\mu}_{\tilde{\alpha}_j},\tilde{v}_{\tilde{\alpha}_j},\tilde{\pi}_{\tilde{\alpha}_j})$ $(j=1,2\ldots,n)$ are a collection of IVIFVs, and $\tilde{\alpha}_{index(i)}$ is the ith largest of the IVIFVs $\tilde{\alpha}_j$ $(j=1,2,\ldots,n)$. ω_i $(i=1,2,\ldots,n)$ are a collection of weights such that

$$\omega_i=g\left(\frac{D_i}{TV}\right)-g\left(\frac{D_{i-1}}{TV}\right),\quad D_i=\sum_{j=1}^{i}V_{index(j)},\quad TV=\sum_{i=1}^{n}V_{index(i)}$$
$$V_{index(j)}=1+T(\tilde{\alpha}_{index(j)}) \tag{1.82}$$

and $T(\tilde{\alpha}_{index(j)})$ denotes the support of the jth largest IVIFV $\tilde{\alpha}_{index(j)}$ by all the other IVIFVs, i.e.,

$$T(\tilde{\alpha}_{index(j)})=\sum_{\substack{i=1\\ i\neq j}}^{n}Sup\left(\tilde{\alpha}_{index(j)},\tilde{\alpha}_{index(i)}\right) \tag{1.83}$$

where $Sup\left(\tilde{\alpha}_{index(j)}, \tilde{\alpha}_{index(i)}\right)$ indicates the support of ith largest IVIFV $\tilde{\alpha}_{index(i)}$ for the jth largest IVIFV $\tilde{\alpha}_{index(j)}$, and $g: [0, 1] \to [0, 1]$ is a BUM function.

Especially, if $g(x) = x$, then the IVIFPOWA operator (1.80) reduces to the IVIFPA operator (1.75).

Then based on the IVIFPOWA operator (1.80) and the geometric mean, Xu (2011) defined an interval-valued intuitionistic fuzzy power ordered weighted geometric (IVIFPOWG) operator:

$$\begin{aligned} & IVIFPOWG(\tilde{\alpha}_1, \tilde{\alpha}_2, \ldots, \tilde{\alpha}_n) \\ & = (\tilde{\alpha}_{index(1)})^{\frac{1-\omega_1}{n-1}} \otimes (\tilde{\alpha}_{index(2)})^{\frac{1-\omega_2}{n-1}} \otimes \cdots \otimes (\tilde{\alpha}_{index(n)})^{\frac{1-\omega_n}{n-1}} \end{aligned} \tag{1.84}$$

which can be further expressed as:

$$\begin{aligned} & IVIFPOWG(\tilde{\alpha}_1, \tilde{\alpha}_2, \ldots, \tilde{\alpha}_n) \\ & = \left(\left[\prod_{j=1}^{n} (\mu^-_{\tilde{\alpha}_{index(j)}})^{\frac{1-\omega_j}{n-1}}, \prod_{j=1}^{n} (\mu^+_{\tilde{\alpha}_{index(j)}})^{\frac{1-\omega_j}{n-1}} \right], \right. \\ & \left[1 - \prod_{j=1}^{n} (1 - v^-_{\tilde{\alpha}_{index(j)}})^{\frac{1-\omega_j}{n-1}}, 1 - \prod_{j=1}^{n} (1 - v^+_{\tilde{\alpha}_{index(j)}})^{\frac{1-\omega_j}{n-1}} \right], \\ & \left[\prod_{j=1}^{n} (1 - v^+_{\tilde{\alpha}_{index(j)}})^{\frac{1-\omega_j}{n-1}} - \prod_{j=1}^{n} (\mu^+_{\tilde{\alpha}_{index(j)}})^{\frac{1-\omega_j}{n-1}}, \prod_{j=1}^{n} (1 - v^-_{\tilde{\alpha}_{index(j)}})^{\frac{1-\omega_j}{n-1}} \right. \\ & \left. \left. - \prod_{j=1}^{n} (\mu^-_{\tilde{\alpha}_{index(j)}})^{\frac{1-\omega_j}{n-1}} \right] \right) \end{aligned} \tag{1.85}$$

where $\omega_i (i = 1, 2, \ldots, n)$ are a collection of weights satisfying the conditions (1.82) and (1.83). Especially, if $g(x) = x$, then the IVIFPOWG operator (1.84) reduces to the IVIFPG operator (1.79).

Let $(\tilde{\alpha}_1, \tilde{\alpha}_2, \ldots, \tilde{\alpha}_n)$ be a vector of n IVIFVs, then all the IVIFPWA, IVIFPWG, IVIFPOWA and IVIFPOWG operators have the following properties (Xu 2011):

Theorem 1.11 (Commutativity) Assume that $(\tilde{\alpha}'_1, \tilde{\alpha}'_2, \ldots, \tilde{\alpha}'_n)$ is any permutation of $(\tilde{\alpha}_1, \tilde{\alpha}_2, \ldots, \tilde{\alpha}_n)$, then

$$IVIFPWA(\tilde{\alpha}_1, \tilde{\alpha}_2, \ldots, \tilde{\alpha}_n) = IVIFPWA(\tilde{\alpha}'_1, \tilde{\alpha}'_2, \ldots, \tilde{\alpha}'_n) \tag{1.86}$$

$$IVIFPWG(\tilde{\alpha}_1, \tilde{\alpha}_2, \ldots, \tilde{\alpha}_n) = IVIFPWG(\tilde{\alpha}'_1, \tilde{\alpha}'_2, \ldots, \tilde{\alpha}'_n) \tag{1.87}$$

$$IVIFPOWA(\tilde{\alpha}_1, \tilde{\alpha}_2, \ldots, \tilde{\alpha}_n) = IVIFPOWA(\tilde{\alpha}'_1, \tilde{\alpha}'_2, \ldots, \tilde{\alpha}'_n) \tag{1.88}$$

$$IVIFPOWG(\tilde{\alpha}_1, \tilde{\alpha}_2, \ldots, \tilde{\alpha}_n) = IVIFPOWG(\tilde{\alpha}'_1, \tilde{\alpha}'_2, \ldots, \tilde{\alpha}'_n) \tag{1.89}$$

Theorem 1.12 (Boundedness) Let $\tilde{\alpha}_j$ $(j = 1, 2 \ldots, n)$ be a collection of IVIFVs, then

$$\tilde{\alpha}^- \leq IVIFPWA(\tilde{\alpha}_1, \tilde{\alpha}_2, \ldots, \tilde{\alpha}_n) \leq \tilde{\alpha}^+ \tag{1.90}$$

$$\tilde{\alpha}^- \leq IVIFPWG(\tilde{\alpha}_1, \tilde{\alpha}_2, \ldots, \tilde{\alpha}_n) \leq \tilde{\alpha}^+ \tag{1.91}$$

$$\tilde{\alpha}^- \leq IVIFPOWA(\tilde{\alpha}_1, \tilde{\alpha}_2, \ldots, \tilde{\alpha}_n) \leq \tilde{\alpha}^+ \tag{1.92}$$

$$\tilde{\alpha}^- \leq IVIFPOWG(\tilde{\alpha}_1, \tilde{\alpha}_2, \ldots, \tilde{\alpha}_n) \leq \tilde{\alpha}^+ \tag{1.93}$$

where

$$\tilde{\alpha}^- = \Big([\min_j\{\mu^-_{\tilde{\alpha}_j}\}, \min_j\{\mu^+_{\tilde{\alpha}_j}\}], [\max_j\{v^-_{\tilde{\alpha}_j}\}, \max_j\{v^+_{\tilde{\alpha}_j}\}], [1 - \min_j\{\mu^+_{\tilde{\alpha}_j}\} - \max_j\{v^+_{\tilde{\alpha}_j}\}],$$
$$[1 - \min_j\{\mu^-_{\tilde{\alpha}_j}\} - \max_j\{v^-_{\tilde{\alpha}_j}\}] \Big) \tag{1.94}$$

$$\tilde{\alpha}^+ = \Big([\max_j\{\mu^-_{\tilde{\alpha}_j}\}, \max_j\{\mu^+_{\tilde{\alpha}_j}\}], [\min_j\{v^-_{\tilde{\alpha}_j}\}, \min_j\{v^+_{\tilde{\alpha}_j}\}],$$
$$[1 - \max_j\{\mu^+_{\tilde{\alpha}_j}\} - \min_j\{v^+_{\tilde{\alpha}_j}\}], [1 - \max_j\{\mu^-_{\tilde{\alpha}_j}\} - \min_j\{v^-_{\tilde{\alpha}_j}\}] \Big) \tag{1.95}$$

1.3.3 Approaches to Multi-Attribute Group Decision Making with Interval-Valued Intuitionistic Fuzzy Information

In the following, we investigate the application of the interval-valued intuitionistic fuzzy power aggregation operators to multi-attribute group decision making with interval-valued intuitionistic fuzzy information:

For a multi-attribute group decision making problem with interval-valued intuitionistic fuzzy information, suppose that Y, G and E are defined as in Sect. 1.2.4. Let $\tilde{B}^{(k)} = (\tilde{b}_{ij}^{(k)})_{m \times n}$ be an interval-valued intuitionistic fuzzy decision matrix, where $\tilde{b}_{ij}^{(k)} = (\tilde{t}_{ij}^{(k)}, \tilde{f}_{ij}^{(k)}, \tilde{\pi}_{ij}^{(k)})$ is an attribute value provided by the expert e_k, denoted by an IVIFV, where $\tilde{t}_{ij}^{(k)} = [t_{ij}^{-(k)}, t_{ij}^{+(k)}]$ indicates the degree range that the alternative y_j satisfies the attribute G_i, while $\tilde{f}_{ij}^{(k)} = [f_{ij}^{-(k)}, f_{ij}^{+(k)}]$ indicates the degree range that the alternative y_j does not satisfy the attribute G_i, and $\tilde{\pi}_{ij}^{(k)} = [\pi_{ij}^{-(k)}, \pi_{ij}^{+(k)}]$ indicates the degree range of uncertainty of the alternative y_j to the attribute G_i, such that

$$\tilde{t}_{ij}^{(k)} = [t_{ij}^{-(k)}, t_{ij}^{+(k)}] \subseteq [0,1], \quad \tilde{f}_{ij}^{(k)} = [f_{ij}^{-(k)}, f_{ij}^{+(k)}] \subseteq [0,1], \quad t_{ij}^{+(k)} + f_{ij}^{+(k)} \leq 1,$$
$$\pi_{ij}^{-(k)} = 1 - t_{ij}^{+(k)} - f_{ij}^{+(k)}, \quad \pi_{ij}^{+(k)} = 1 - t_{ij}^{-(k)} - f_{ij}^{-(k)},$$
$$i = 1, 2, \ldots, m; \quad j = 1, 2, \ldots, n \tag{1.96}$$

In general, there are benefit attributes and cost attributes in multi-attribute decision making, and all the attribute values need to be transformed into the same type. Without loss of generality, here, we transform the attribute values of cost type into the attribute values of benefit type, i.e., transform $\tilde{B}^{(k)} = (\tilde{b}_{ij}^{(k)})_{m\times n}$ into the interval-valued intuitionistic fuzzy decision matrix $\tilde{R}^{(k)} = (\tilde{r}_{ij}^{(k)})_{m\times n}$, where

$$\tilde{r}_{ij}^{(k)} = (\tilde{\mu}_{ij}^{(k)}, \tilde{v}_{ij}^{(k)}, \tilde{\pi}_{ij}^{(k)}) = \begin{cases} \tilde{b}_{ij}^{(k)}, & \textit{for benefit attribute } G_i \\ \left(\tilde{b}_{ij}^{(k)}\right)^{c}, & \textit{for cost attribute } G_i \end{cases}, \quad j = 1, 2, \ldots, n \tag{1.97}$$

where $\left(\tilde{b}_{ij}^{(k)}\right)^{c}$ is the complement of $\tilde{b}_{ij}^{(k)}$, such that $\left(\tilde{b}_{ij}^{(k)}\right)^{c} = (\tilde{f}_{ij}^{(k)}, \tilde{t}_{ij}^{(k)}, \tilde{\pi}_{ij}^{(k)})$, where

$$\tilde{\pi}_{ij}^{(k)} = [\pi_{ij}^{-(k)}, \pi_{ij}^{+(k)}], \quad \pi_{ij}^{-(k)} = 1 - t_{ij}^{+(k)} - f_{ij}^{+(k)} = 1 - \mu_{ij}^{+(k)} - v_{ij}^{+(k)},$$
$$\pi_{ij}^{+(k)} = 1 - t_{ij}^{-(k)} - f_{ij}^{-(k)} = 1 - \mu_{ij}^{-(k)} - v_{ij}^{-(k)} \tag{1.98}$$

Then, we can utilize the IVIFPWA (or IVIFPWG) operator to develop an approach to multi-attribute group decision making with interval-valued intuitionistic fuzzy information, which involves the following steps (Xu 2011):

Approach 1.3

Step 1 Calculate the supports:

$$Sup\left(\tilde{r}_{ij}^{(k)}, \tilde{r}_{ij}^{(l)}\right) = 1 - d\left(\tilde{r}_{ij}^{(k)}, \tilde{r}_{ij}^{(l)}\right), \quad l = 1, 2, \ldots, s \tag{1.99}$$

which satisfy the support conditions (1)–(3) in Sect. 1.3.2. Without loss of generality, here we let

$$d\left(\tilde{r}_{ij}^{(k)}, \tilde{r}_{ij}^{(l)}\right) = \frac{1}{4}\left(\left|\mu_{ij}^{-(k)} - \mu_{ij}^{-(l)}\right| + \left|\mu_{ij}^{+(k)} - \mu_{ij}^{+(l)}\right| + \left|v_{ij}^{-(k)} - v_{ij}^{-(l)}\right|\right.$$
$$\left. + \left|v_{ij}^{+(k)} - v_{ij}^{+(l)}\right| + \left|\pi_{ij}^{-(k)} - \pi_{ij}^{-(l)}\right| + \left|\pi_{ij}^{+(k)} - \pi_{ij}^{+(l)}\right|\right),$$
$$l = 1, 2, \ldots, s \tag{1.100}$$

Step 2 Utilize the weights η_k $(k = 1, 2, \ldots, s)$ of the experts e_k $(k = 1, 2, \ldots, q)$ to calculate the weighted support $T(\tilde{r}_{ij}^{(k)})$ of the IVIFV $\tilde{r}_{ij}^{(k)}$ by the other IVIFVs $\tilde{r}_{ij}^{(l)}$ $(l = 1, 2, \ldots, s$ and $l \neq k)$:

$$T(\tilde{r}_{ij}^{(k)}) = \sum_{\substack{l=1 \\ l \neq k}}^{s} \eta_l Sup\left(\tilde{r}_{ij}^{(k)}, \tilde{r}_{ij}^{(l)}\right) \tag{1.101}$$

and calculate the weights $\xi_{ij}^{(k)}$ $(k = 1, 2, \ldots, s)$ associated with the IVIFVs $\tilde{r}_{ij}^{(k)}$ $(k = 1, 2, \ldots, s)$:

$$\xi_{ij}^{(k)} = \frac{\eta_k \left(1 + T(\tilde{r}_{ij}^{(k)})\right)}{\sum_{k=1}^{s} \eta_k \left(1 + T(\tilde{r}_{ij}^{(k)})\right)}, \quad k = 1, 2, \ldots, s \tag{1.102}$$

where $\xi_{ij}^{(k)} \geq 0, k = 1, 2, \ldots, s$, and $\sum_{k=1}^{s} \xi_{ij}^{(k)} = 1$.

Step 3 Utilize the IVIFPWA operator (1.71):

$$\begin{aligned}
\tilde{r}_{ij} &= IVIFPWA(\tilde{r}_{ij}^{(1)}, \tilde{r}_{ij}^{(2)}, \ldots, \tilde{r}_{ij}^{(s)}) \\
&= \left(\left[1 - \prod_{k=1}^{s} (1 - \mu_{ij}^{-(k)})^{\xi_{ij}^{(k)}}, 1 - \prod_{k=1}^{s} (1 - \mu_{ij}^{+(k)})^{\xi_{ij}^{(k)}}\right],\right. \\
&\quad \left[\prod_{k=1}^{s} (v_{ij}^{-(k)})^{\xi_{ij}^{(k)}}, \prod_{k=1}^{s} (v_{ij}^{+(k)})^{\xi_{ij}^{(k)}}\right], \\
&\quad \left.\left[\prod_{k=1}^{s} (1 - \mu_{ij}^{+(k)})^{\xi_{ij}^{(k)}} - \prod_{k=1}^{s} (v_{ij}^{+(k)})^{\xi_{ij}^{(k)}}, \prod_{k=1}^{s} (1 - \mu_{ij}^{-(k)})^{\xi_{ij}^{(k)}} - \prod_{k=1}^{s} (v_{ij}^{-(k)})^{\xi_{ij}^{(k)}}\right]\right) \\
&= \left(\left[1 - \prod_{k=1}^{s} (1 - \mu_{ij}^{-(k)})^{\frac{\eta_k(1+T(\tilde{r}_{ij}^{(k)}))}{\sum_{k=1}^{s} \eta_k(1+T(\tilde{r}_{ij}^{(k)}))}}, 1 - \prod_{k=1}^{s} (1 - \mu_{ij}^{+(k)})^{\frac{\eta_k(1+T(\tilde{r}_{ij}^{(k)}))}{\sum_{k=1}^{s} \eta_k(1+T(\tilde{r}_{ij}^{(k)}))}}\right],\right. \\
&\quad \left[\prod_{k=1}^{s} (v_{ij}^{-(k)})^{\frac{\eta_k(1+T(\tilde{r}_{ij}^{(k)}))}{\sum_{k=1}^{s} \eta_k(1+T(\tilde{r}_{ij}^{(k)}))}}, \prod_{j=1}^{s} (v_{ij}^{+(k)})^{\frac{\eta_k(1+T(\tilde{r}_{ij}^{(k)}))}{\sum_{i=1}^{s} \eta_i(1+T(\tilde{r}_{ij}^{(k)}))}}\right], \\
&\quad \left[\prod_{k=1}^{s} (1 - \mu_{ij}^{+(k)})^{\frac{\eta_k(1+T(\tilde{r}_{ij}^{(k)}))}{\sum_{i=1}^{s} \eta_i(1+T(\tilde{r}_{ij}^{(k)}))}} - \prod_{k=1}^{s} (v_{ij}^{+(k)})^{\frac{\eta_k(1+T(\tilde{r}_{ij}^{(k)}))}{\sum_{k=1}^{s} \eta_k(1+T(\tilde{r}_{ij}^{(k)}))}},\right. \\
&\quad \left.\left.\prod_{k=1}^{s} (1 - \mu_{ij}^{-(k)})^{\frac{\eta_k(1+T(\tilde{r}_{ij}^{(k)}))}{\sum_{k=1}^{s} \eta_k(1+T(\tilde{r}_{ij}^{(k)}))}} - \prod_{k=1}^{s} (v_{ij}^{-(k)})^{\frac{\eta_k(1+T(\tilde{r}_{ij}^{(k)}))}{\sum_{k=1}^{s} \eta_k(1+T(\tilde{r}_{ij}^{(k)}))}}\right]\right)
\end{aligned} \tag{1.103}$$

or the IVIFPWG operator (1.78):

$$\tilde{r}_{ij} = IVIFPWG(\tilde{r}_{ij}^{(1)}, \tilde{r}_{ij}^{(2)}, \ldots, \tilde{r}_{ij}^{(s)})$$
$$= \left(\left[\prod_{k=1}^{s} (\mu_{\tilde{r}_{ij}}^{-(k)})^{\frac{1-\xi_{ij}^{(k)}}{s-1}}, \prod_{k=1}^{s} (\mu_{\tilde{r}_{ij}}^{+(k)})^{\frac{1-\xi_{ij}^{(k)}}{s-1}}\right],\right.$$
$$\left[1-\prod_{k=1}^{s} (1-v_{\tilde{r}_{ij}}^{-(k)})^{\frac{1-\xi_{ij}^{(k)}}{s-1}}, 1-\prod_{k=1}^{s} (1-v_{\tilde{r}_{ij}}^{+(k)})^{\frac{1-\xi_{ij}^{(k)}}{s-1}}\right],$$
$$\left[\prod_{k=1}^{s} (1-v_{\tilde{r}_{ij}}^{+(k)})^{\frac{1-\xi_{ij}^{(k)}}{s-1}} - \prod_{k=1}^{s} (\mu_{\tilde{r}_{ij}}^{+(k)})^{\frac{1-\xi_{ij}^{(k)}}{s-1}},\right.$$
$$\left.\left.\prod_{k=1}^{s} (1-v_{\tilde{r}_{ij}}^{-(k)})^{\frac{1-\xi_{ij}^{(k)}}{s-1}} - \prod_{k=1}^{s} (\mu_{\tilde{r}_{ij}}^{-(k)})^{\frac{1-\xi_{ij}^{(k)}}{s-1}}\right]\right)$$
$$= \left(\left[\prod_{k=1}^{s} (\mu_{\tilde{r}_{ij}}^{-(k)})^{\frac{1}{s-1}\left(1-\frac{\eta_k(1+T(\tilde{r}_{ij}^{(k)}))}{\sum_{k=1}^{s}\eta_k(1+T(\tilde{r}_{ij}^{(k)}))}\right)}, \prod_{k=1}^{s} (\mu_{\tilde{r}_{ij}}^{+(k)})^{\frac{1}{s-1}\left(1-\frac{\eta_k(1+T(\tilde{r}_{ij}^{(k)}))}{\sum_{k=1}^{s}\eta_k(1+T(\tilde{r}_{ij}^{(k)}))}\right)}\right],\right.$$
$$\left[1-\prod_{k=1}^{s} (1-v_{\tilde{r}_{ij}}^{-(k)})^{\frac{1}{s-1}\left(1-\frac{\eta_k(1+T(\tilde{r}_{ij}^{(k)}))}{\sum_{k=1}^{s}\eta_k(1+T(\tilde{r}_{ij}^{(k)}))}\right)},\right.$$
$$\left.1-\prod_{k=1}^{s} (1-v_{\tilde{r}_{ij}}^{+(k)})^{\frac{1}{s-1}\left(1-\frac{\eta_k(1+T(\tilde{r}_{ij}^{(k)}))}{\sum_{k=1}^{s}\eta_k(1+T(\tilde{r}_{ij}^{(k)}))}\right)}\right],$$
$$\left[\prod_{k=1}^{s} (1-v_{\tilde{r}_{ij}}^{+(k)})^{\frac{1}{s-1}\left(1-\frac{\eta_k(1+T(\tilde{r}_{ij}^{(k)}))}{\sum_{k=1}^{s}\eta_k(1+T(\tilde{r}_{ij}^{(k)}))}\right)} - \prod_{k=1}^{s} (\mu_{\tilde{r}_{ij}}^{+(k)})^{\frac{1}{s-1}\left(1-\frac{\eta_k(1+T(\tilde{r}_{ij}^{(k)}))}{\sum_{k=1}^{s}\eta_k(1+T(\tilde{r}_{ij}^{(k)}))}\right)},\right.$$
$$\left.\left.\prod_{k=1}^{s} (1-v_{\tilde{r}_{ij}}^{-(k)})^{\frac{1}{s-1}\left(1-\frac{\eta_k(1+T(\tilde{r}_{ij}^{(k)}))}{\sum_{k=1}^{s}\eta_k(1+T(\tilde{r}_{ij}^{(k)}))}\right)} - \prod_{k=1}^{s} (\mu_{\tilde{r}_{ij}}^{-(k)})^{\frac{1}{s-1}\left(1-\frac{\eta_k(1+T(\tilde{r}_{ij}^{(k)}))}{\sum_{k=1}^{s}\eta_k(1+T(\tilde{r}_{ij}^{(k)}))}\right)}\right]\right) \tag{1.104}$$

to aggregate all the individual interval-valued intuitionistic fuzzy decision matrices $\tilde{R}^{(k)} = (\tilde{r}_{ij}^{(k)})_{m\times n}$ $(k = 1, 2, \ldots, s)$ into the collective interval-valued intuitionistic fuzzy decision matrix $\tilde{R} = (\tilde{r}_{ij})_{m\times n}$, where

$$\tilde{r}_{ij} = (\tilde{\mu}_{ij}, \tilde{v}_{ij}) = \left([\mu_{ij}^{-}, \mu_{ij}^{+}], [v_{ij}^{-}, v_{ij}^{+}], [\pi_{ij}^{-}, \pi_{ij}^{+}]\right),$$
$$i = 1, 2, \ldots, m; \quad j = 1, 2, \ldots, n \tag{1.105}$$

Step 4 To get the overall preference value $\tilde{r}_j$ corresponding to the alternative y_j, we aggregate all the preference values $\tilde{r}_{ij}$ $(j = 1, 2, \ldots, n)$ in the jth column of $\tilde{R}$ by using the interval-valued intuitionistic fuzzy weighted average (IVIFWA) operator (Xu and Cai 2009):

$$\begin{aligned}\tilde{r}_j &= IVIFWA(\tilde{r}_{1j}, \tilde{r}_{2j}, \ldots, \tilde{r}_{mj})\\ &= \left(\left[1-\prod_{i=1}^{m}(1-\mu_{ij}^{-})^{w_i}, 1-\prod_{i=1}^{m}(1-\mu_{ij}^{+})^{w_i} \right], \left[\prod_{i=1}^{m}(v_{ij}^{-})^{w_i}, \prod_{i=1}^{m}(v_{ij}^{+})^{w_i} \right], \right.\\ &\left. \left[\prod_{i=1}^{m}(1-\mu_{ij}^{+})^{w_i} - \prod_{i=1}^{m}(v_{ij}^{+})^{w_i}, \prod_{i=1}^{m}(1-\mu_{ij}^{-})^{w_i} - \prod_{i=1}^{m}(v_{ij}^{-})^{w_i} \right] \right),\\ & \qquad j = 1, 2, \ldots, n \end{aligned} \tag{1.106}$$

or the interval-valued intuitionistic fuzzy weighted geometric (IVIFWG) operator (Xu and Cai 2009):

$$\begin{aligned}\tilde{r}_j &= IVIFWG(\tilde{r}_{1j}, \tilde{r}_{2j}, \ldots, \tilde{r}_{mj})\\ &= \left(\left[\prod_{i=1}^{m}(\mu_{ij}^{-})^{\frac{1-w_i}{m-1}}, \prod_{i=1}^{m}(\mu_{ij}^{+})^{\frac{1-w_i}{m-1}} \right], \left[1-\prod_{i=1}^{m}(1-v_{ij}^{-})^{\frac{1-w_i}{m-1}}, 1-\prod_{i=1}^{m}(1-v_{ij}^{+})^{\frac{1-w_i}{m-1}} \right], \right.\\ &\left. \left[\prod_{i=1}^{m}(1-v_{ij}^{+})^{\frac{1-w_i}{m-1}} - \prod_{i=1}^{m}(\mu_{ij}^{+})^{\frac{1-w_i}{m-1}}, \prod_{i=1}^{m}(1-v_{ij}^{-})^{\frac{1-w_i}{m-1}} - \prod_{i-1}^{m}(\mu_{ij}^{-})^{\frac{1-w_i}{m-1}} \right] \right),\\ & \qquad j = 1, 2, \ldots, n \end{aligned} \tag{1.107}$$

Step 5 Rank $\tilde{r}_j$ $(j = 1, 2, \ldots, n)$ in descending order by using the ranking method described in Definition 1.4.

Step 6 Rank all the alternatives y_j $(j = 1, 2, \ldots, n)$ and select the best one in accordance with the ranking of $\tilde{r}_j$ $(j = 1, 2, \ldots, n)$.

In the case where the information about the weights of experts is unknown, we can utilize the IVIFPOWA (or IVIFPWG) operator to develop an approach to multi-attribute group decision making with interval-valued intuitionistic fuzzy information, which can be described as follows (Xu 2011):

Approach 1.4

Step 1 Calculate

$$\begin{aligned} & Sup\left(\tilde{r}_{ij}^{index(k)}, \tilde{r}_{ij}^{index(l)}\right)\\ &= 1 - d\left(\tilde{r}_{ij}^{index(k)}, \tilde{r}_{ij}^{index(l)}\right)\\ &= 1 - \frac{1}{4}\left(\left| \mu_{ij}^{-(index(k))} - \mu_{ij}^{-(index(l))} \right| + \left| \mu_{ij}^{+(index(k))} - \mu_{ij}^{+(index(l))} \right| \right.\\ &+ \left| v_{ij}^{-(index(k))} - v_{ij}^{-(index(l))} \right| + \left| v_{ij}^{+(index(k))} - v_{ij}^{+(index(l))} \right|\\ &\left. + \left| \pi_{ij}^{-(index(k))} - \pi_{ij}^{-(index(l))} \right| + \left| \pi_{ij}^{+(index(k))} - \pi_{ij}^{+(index(l))} \right| \right) \end{aligned} \tag{1.108}$$

which indicates the support of the lth largest IVIFV $\tilde{r}_{ij}^{index(l)}$ for the kth largest IVIFV $\tilde{r}_{ij}^{index(k)}$ of $\tilde{r}_{ij}^{(t)}$ $(t = 1, 2, \ldots, s)$.

Step 2 Calculate the support $T\left(\tilde{r}_{ij}^{index(k)}\right)$ of the kth largest IVIFV $\tilde{r}_{ij}^{index(k)}$ by the other IVIFVs $\tilde{r}_{ij}^{(l)}$ ($l = 1, 2, \ldots, s$, and $l \neq k$):

$$T\left(\tilde{r}_{ij}^{index(k)}\right) = \sum_{\substack{l=1 \\ l \neq k}}^{s} Sup\left(\tilde{r}_{ij}^{index(k)}, \tilde{r}_{ij}^{index(l)}\right) \tag{1.109}$$

and utilize Eq. (1.82) to calculate the weight $\omega_{ij}^{(k)}$ associated with the kth largest IVIFV $\tilde{r}_{ij}^{index(k)}$, where

$$\omega_{ij}^{(k)} = g\left(\frac{D_{ij}^{(k)}}{TV_{ij}}\right) - g\left(\frac{D_{ij}^{(k-1)}}{TV_{ij}}\right),\ D_{ij}^{(k)} = \sum_{l=1}^{k} V_{ij}^{index(l)},\ TV_{ij} = \sum_{l=1}^{s} V_{ij}^{index(l)}$$
$$V_{ij}^{index(l)} = 1 + T\left(\tilde{r}_{ij}^{index(l)}\right) \tag{1.110}$$

where $\omega_{ij}^{(k)} \geq 0$, $k = 1, 2, \ldots, s$, and $\sum_{k=1}^{s} \omega_{ij}^{(k)} = 1$.

Step 3 Utilize the IVIFPOWA operator (1.81):

$$\begin{aligned} & IVIFPOWA(\tilde{r}_{ij}^{(1)}, \tilde{r}_{ij}^{(2)}, \ldots, \tilde{r}_{ij}^{(s)}) \\ & = \left(\left[1 - \prod_{k=1}^{s}(1 - \mu_{ij}^{-(index(k))})^{\omega_{ij}^{(k)}}, 1 - \prod_{k=1}^{s}(1 - \mu_{ij}^{+(index(k))})^{\omega_{ij}^{(k)}}\right],\right. \\ & \quad \left[\prod_{k=1}^{s}(v_{ij}^{-(index(k))})^{\omega_{ij}^{(k)}}, \prod_{k=1}^{s}(v_{ij}^{+(index(k))})^{\omega_{ij}^{(k)}}\right], \\ & \quad \left[\prod_{k=1}^{s}(1 - \mu_{ij}^{+(index(k))})^{\omega_{ij}^{(k)}} - \prod_{k=1}^{s}(v_{ij}^{+(index(k))})^{\omega_{ij}^{(k)}},\right. \\ & \quad \left.\left.\prod_{k=1}^{s}(1 - \mu_{ij}^{-(index(k))})^{\omega_{ij}^{(k)}} - \prod_{k=1}^{s}(v_{ij}^{-(index(k))})^{\omega_{ij}^{(k)}}\right]\right) \end{aligned} \tag{1.111}$$

or the IVIFPOWG operator (1.85):

$$\begin{aligned} & IVIFPOWG(\tilde{r}_{ij}^{(1)}, \tilde{r}_{ij}^{(2)}, \ldots, \tilde{r}_{ij}^{(s)}) \\ & = \left(\left[\prod_{k=1}^{s}(\mu_{ij}^{-(index(k))})^{\frac{1-\omega_{ij}^{(k)}}{s-1}}, \prod_{k=1}^{s}(\mu_{ij}^{+(index(k))})^{\frac{1-\omega_{ij}^{(k)}}{s-1}}\right],\right. \\ & \quad \left[1 - \prod_{k=1}^{s}(1 - v_{ij}^{-(index(k))})^{\frac{1-\omega_{ij}^{(k)}}{s-1}}, 1 - \prod_{k=1}^{s}(1 - v_{ij}^{+(index(k))})^{\frac{1-\omega_{ij}^{(k)}}{s-1}}\right], \end{aligned}$$

$$\left[\prod_{k=1}^{s}(1-\nu_{ij}^{+(index(k))})^{\frac{1-\omega_{ij}^{(k)}}{s-1}}-\prod_{k=1}^{s}(\mu_{ij}^{+(index(k))})^{\frac{1-\omega_{ij}^{(k)}}{s-1}},\right.$$
$$\left.\prod_{k=1}^{s}(1-\nu_{ij}^{-(index(k))})^{\frac{1-\omega_{ij}^{(k)}}{s-1}}-\prod_{k=1}^{s}(\mu_{ij}^{-(index(k))})^{\frac{1-\omega_{ij}^{(k)}}{s-1}}\right]\Bigg) \quad (1.112)$$

to aggregate all the individual interval-valued intuitionistic fuzzy decision matrices $\tilde{R}^{(k)}=(\tilde{r}_{ij}^{(k)})_{m\times n}$ $(k=1,2,\ldots,s)$ into the collective interval-valued intuitionistic fuzzy decision matrix $\tilde{R}=(\tilde{r}_{ij})_{m\times n}$.

Step 4 See Approach 1.3.

Step 5 See Approach 1.3.

Clearly, Approaches 1.3 and 1.4 are the extensions of Approaches 1.1 and 1.2 in interval-valued intuitionistic fuzzy environments, and thus, they have similar characteristics.

In the case where the evaluation values given by the experts are expressed with IVIFVs in the example of Sect. 1.2.5, we can utilize Approach 1.3 to solve the problem, here omitted for brevity.

1.4 Intuitionistic Fuzzy Geometric Bonferroni Means

The Bonferroni mean was originally introduced by Bonferroni (1950) and then generalized by Yager (2009). The desirable characteristic of the Bonferroni mean is its capability to capture the interrelationship between input arguments. Xu and Yager (2011) further applied the Bonferroni mean to intuitionstic fuzzy environments and introduced the intuitionistic fuzzy Bonferroni mean and the weighted Bonferroni mean. Xia et al. (2012a) developed a geometric Bonferroni mean based on the Bonferroni mean and the geometric mean and further extended it to intuitionistic fuzzy environments.

1.4.1 Geometric Bonferroni Mean

The Bonferroni mean, introduced by Bonferroni (1950), can be defined as follows:

Definition 1.6 (Bonferroni 1950) Let a_i $(i=1,2,\ldots,n)$ be a collection of crisp data, where $a_i\geq 0$, for all i, and $p,q\geq 0$, then

$$BM^{p,q}(a_1,a_2,\ldots,a_n)=\left(\frac{1}{n(n-1)}\sum_{\substack{i,j=1\\ i\neq j}}^{n}a_i^p a_j^q\right)^{\frac{1}{p+q}} \quad (1.113)$$

is called a Bonferroni mean.

Especially, if $q = 0$, then by Eq. (1.113), the Bonferroni mean reduces to the generalized mean operator (Dyckhoff and Pedrycz 1984) as follows:

$$BM^{p,0}(a_1, a_2, \ldots, a_n) = \left(\frac{1}{n} \sum_{i=1}^{n} a_i^p \left(\frac{1}{(n-1)} \sum_{\substack{j=1 \\ j \neq i}}^{n} a_j^0 \right) \right)^{\frac{1}{p+0}} = \left(\frac{1}{n} \sum_{i=1}^{n} a_i^p \right)^{\frac{1}{p}} \tag{1.114}$$

If $p = 1$ and $q = 0$, then Eq. (1.113) reduces to the well-known arithmetic average:

$$BM^{1,0}(a_1, a_2, \ldots, a_n) = \frac{1}{n} \sum_{i=1}^{n} a_i \tag{1.115}$$

Based on the usual geometric mean and the Bonferroni mean, Xia et al. (2012a) proposed a geometric Bonferroni mean as follows:

Definition 1.7 (Xia et al. 2012a) Let $p, q > 0$, and a_i $(i = 1, 2, \ldots, n)$ be a collection of non-negative numbers. If

$$GBM^{p,q}(a_1, a_2, \ldots, a_n) = \frac{1}{p+q} \prod_{\substack{i,j=1 \\ i \neq j}}^{n} (pa_i + qa_j)^{\frac{1}{n(n-1)}} \tag{1.116}$$

then we call $GBM^{p,q}$ a geometric Bonferroni mean (GBM).

Obviously, the GBM has the following properties (Xia et al. 2012a):

(1) $GBM^{p,q}(0, 0, \ldots, 0) = 0$.
(2) $GBM^{p,q}(a, a, \ldots, a) = a$, if $a_i = a$, for all i.
(3) $GBM^{p,q}(a_1, a_2, \ldots, a_n) \geq GBM^{p,q}(b_1, b_2, \ldots, b_n)$, i.e., $GBM^{p,q}$ is monotonic, if $a_i \geq b_i$, for all i.
(4) $\min_i\{a_i\} \leq GBM^{p,q}(a_1, a_2, \ldots, a_n) \leq \max_i\{a_i\}$.

Furthermore, if $q = 0$, then by Eq. (1.116), the GBM reduces to the geometric mean:

$$GBM^{p,0}(a_1, a_2, \ldots, a_n) = \frac{1}{p} \prod_{\substack{i,j=1 \\ i \neq j}}^{n} (pa_i)^{\frac{1}{n(n-1)}} = \prod_{i=1}^{n} (a_i)^{\frac{1}{n}} \tag{1.117}$$

1.4.2 Intuitionistic Fuzzy Geometric Bonferroni Mean

Let $\alpha_i = (\mu_{\alpha_i}, v_{\alpha_i}, \pi_{\alpha_i})$ $(i = 1, 2, \ldots, n)$ be a collection of IFVs, based on Eq. (1.116), Xia et al. (2012a) defined a geometric Bonferroni mean for IFVs:

Definition 1.8 (Xia et al. 2012a) For any $p, q > 0$, if

$$IFGBM^{p,q}(\alpha_1, \alpha_2, \ldots, \alpha_n) = \frac{1}{p+q}\left(\underset{\substack{i,j=1\\ i\neq j}}{\overset{n}{\otimes}} \left(p\alpha_i \oplus q\alpha_j\right)^{\frac{1}{n(n-1)}}\right) \tag{1.118}$$

then $IFGBM^{p,q}$ is called an intuitionistic fuzzy geometric Bonferroni mean (IFGBM).

By using the operations and the relations of IFVs given in Sect. 1.2.2, we can derive the following theorem:

Theorem 1.13 (Xia et al. 2012a) Let $p, q > 0$, then the aggregated value by using the IFGBM is also an IFV, and

$$\begin{aligned} &IFGBM^{p,q}(\alpha_1, \alpha_2, \ldots, \alpha_n) \\ &= \left(1 - \left(1 - \prod_{\substack{i,j=1\\ i\neq j}}^{n} \left(1-(1-\mu_{\alpha_i})^p(1-\mu_{\alpha_j})^q\right)^{\frac{1}{n(n-1)}}\right)^{\frac{1}{p+q}},\right. \\ &\left(1 - \prod_{\substack{i,j=1\\ i\neq j}}^{n} \left(1 - v_{\alpha_i}^p v_{\alpha_j}^q\right)^{\frac{1}{n(n-1)}}\right)^{\frac{1}{p+q}}, \left(1 - \prod_{\substack{i,j=1\\ i\neq j}}^{n} \left(1-(1-\mu_{\alpha_i})^p(1-\mu_{\alpha_j})^q\right)^{\frac{1}{n(n-1)}}\right)^{\frac{1}{p+q}} \\ &\left. - \left(1 - \prod_{\substack{i,j=1\\ i\neq j}}^{n} \left(1 - v_{\alpha_i}^p v_{\alpha_j}^q\right)^{\frac{1}{n(n-1)}}\right)^{\frac{1}{p+q}}\right) \end{aligned} \tag{1.119}$$

Proof By the operational laws (1) and (3) described in Definition 1.3, we have

$$p\alpha_i = (1-(1-\mu_{\alpha_i})^p, v_{\alpha_i}^p, (1-\mu_{\alpha_i})^p - v_{\alpha_i}^p) \tag{1.120}$$

$$q\alpha_j = (1-(1-\mu_{\alpha_j})^q, v_{\alpha_j}^q, (1-\mu_{\alpha_j})^q - v_{\alpha_j}^q) \tag{1.121}$$

and then

$$p\alpha_i \oplus q\alpha_j = (1-(1-\mu_{\alpha_i})^p(1-\mu_{\alpha_j})^q, v_{\alpha_i}^p v_{\alpha_j}^q, (1-\mu_{\alpha_i})^p(1-\mu_{\alpha_j})^q - v_{\alpha_i}^p v_{\alpha_j}^q) \tag{1.122}$$

Let

$$\beta_{ij} = (\mu_{\beta_{ij}}, v_{\beta_{ij}}, \pi_{\beta_{ij}}) = p\alpha_i \oplus q\alpha_j$$
$$= \left(1 - (1 - \mu_{\alpha_i})^p (1 - \mu_{\alpha_j})^q, v_{\alpha_i}^p v_{\alpha_j}^q, (1 - \mu_{\alpha_i})^p (1 - \mu_{\alpha_j})^q - v_{\alpha_i}^p v_{\alpha_j}^q\right) \tag{1.123}$$

then

$$IFGBM^{p,q}(\alpha_1, \alpha_2, \ldots, \alpha_n)$$
$$= \frac{1}{p+q}\left(\underset{\substack{i,j=1 \\ i \neq j}}{\overset{n}{\otimes}} (p\alpha_i \oplus q\alpha_j)^{\frac{1}{n(n-1)}}\right) = \frac{1}{p+q}\left(\underset{\substack{i,j=1 \\ i \neq j}}{\overset{n}{\otimes}} \beta_{ij}^{\frac{1}{n(n-1)}}\right) \tag{1.124}$$

Since

$$\underset{\substack{i,j=1 \\ i \neq j}}{\overset{n}{\otimes}} \beta_{ij}^{\frac{1}{n(n-1)}} = \left(\prod_{\substack{i,j=1 \\ i \neq j}}^{n} \mu_{\beta_{ij}}^{\frac{1}{n(n-1)}}, 1 - \prod_{\substack{i,j=1 \\ i \neq j}}^{n} (1 - v_{\beta_{ij}})^{\frac{1}{n(n-1)}}, \right.$$
$$\left. \prod_{\substack{i,j=1 \\ i \neq j}}^{n} (1 - v_{\beta_{ij}})^{\frac{1}{n(n-1)}} - \prod_{\substack{i,j=1 \\ i \neq j}}^{n} \mu_{\beta_{ij}}^{\frac{1}{n(n-1)}}\right) \tag{1.125}$$

which has been proven by Xu and Yager (2006). Then by replacing $\beta_{ij}, \mu_{\beta_{ij}}, v_{\beta_{ij}}$ and $\pi_{\beta_{ij}}$ in Eq. (1.125) with $p\alpha_i \oplus q\alpha_j, 1 - (1 - \mu_{\alpha_i})^p (1 - \mu_{\alpha_j})^q, v_{\alpha_i}^p v_{\alpha_j}^q$ and $(1 - \mu_{\alpha_i})^p (1 - \mu_{\alpha_j})^q - v_{\alpha_i}^p v_{\alpha_j}^q$, respectively, we have

$$\underset{\substack{i,j=1 \\ i \neq j}}{\overset{n}{\otimes}} (p\alpha_i \oplus q\alpha_j)^{\frac{1}{n(n-1)}}$$
$$= \left(\prod_{\substack{i,j=1 \\ i \neq j}}^{n} \left(1 - (1 - \mu_{\alpha_i})^p (1 - \mu_{\alpha_j})^q\right)^{\frac{1}{n(n-1)}}, 1 - \prod_{\substack{i,j=1 \\ i \neq j}}^{n} \left(1 - v_{\alpha_i}^p v_{\alpha_j}^q\right)^{\frac{1}{n(n-1)}}, \right.$$
$$\left. \prod_{\substack{i,j=1 \\ i \neq j}}^{n} \left(1 - v_{\alpha_i}^p v_{\alpha_j}^q\right)^{\frac{1}{n(n-1)}} - \prod_{\substack{i,j=1 \\ i \neq j}}^{n} \left(1 - (1 - \mu_{\alpha_i})^p (1 - \mu_{\alpha_j})^q\right)^{\frac{1}{n(n-1)}}\right) \tag{1.126}$$

Then by Eq. (1.126) and the operational law (3) in Definition 1.3, it yields

$$
\begin{aligned}
& IFGBM^{p,q}(\alpha_1, \alpha_2, \ldots, \alpha_n) \\
&= \frac{1}{p+q} \underset{\substack{i,j=1 \\ i \neq j}}{\overset{n}{\otimes}} \left(p\alpha_i \oplus q\alpha_j\right)^{\frac{1}{n(n-1)}} \\
&= \left(1 - \left(1 - \prod_{\substack{i,j=1 \\ i \neq j}}^{n} \left(1 - (1-\mu_{\alpha_i})^p (1-\mu_{\alpha_j})^q\right)^{\frac{1}{n(n-1)}}\right)^{\frac{1}{p+q}},\right. \\
&\quad \left(1 - \prod_{\substack{i,j=1 \\ i \neq j}}^{n} \left(1 - v_{\alpha_i}^p v_{\alpha_j}^q\right)^{\frac{1}{n(n-1)}}\right)^{\frac{1}{p+q}}, \\
&\quad \left(1 - \prod_{\substack{i,j=1 \\ i \neq j}}^{n} \left(1 - (1-\mu_{\alpha_i})^p (1-\mu_{\alpha_j})^q\right)^{\frac{1}{n(n-1)}}\right)^{\frac{1}{p+q}} \\
&\quad \left.- \left(1 - \prod_{\substack{i,j=1 \\ i \neq j}}^{n} \left(1 - v_{\alpha_i}^p v_{\alpha_j}^q\right)^{\frac{1}{n(n-1)}}\right)^{\frac{1}{p+q}}\right)
\end{aligned} \tag{1.127}
$$

i.e., Eq. (1.119) holds. In addition, since

$$
0 \leq 1 - \left(1 - \prod_{\substack{i,j=1 \\ i \neq j}}^{n} \left(1 - (1-\mu_{\alpha_i})^p (1-\mu_{\alpha_j})^q\right)^{\frac{1}{n(n-1)}}\right)^{\frac{1}{p+q}} \leq 1 \tag{1.128}
$$

$$
0 \leq \left(1 - \prod_{\substack{i,j=1 \\ i \neq j}}^{n} \left(1 - v_{\alpha_i}^p v_{\alpha_j}^q\right)^{\frac{1}{n(n-1)}}\right)^{\frac{1}{p+q}} \leq 1 \tag{1.129}
$$

then

$$
1 - \left(1 - \prod_{\substack{i,j=1 \\ i \neq j}}^{n} \left(1 - (1-\mu_{\alpha_i})^p (1-\mu_{\alpha_j})^q\right)^{\frac{1}{n(n-1)}}\right)^{\frac{1}{p+q}}
$$

$$+\left(1-\prod_{\substack{i,j=1\\ i\neq j}}^{n}\left(1-v_{\alpha_i}^{p}v_{\alpha_j}^{q}\right)^{\frac{1}{n(n-1)}}\right)^{\frac{1}{p+q}}$$

$$\leq 1-\left(1-\prod_{\substack{i,j=1\\ i\neq j}}^{n}\left(1-(1-\mu_{\alpha_i})^{p}(1-\mu_{\alpha_j})^{q}\right)^{\frac{1}{n(n-1)}}\right)^{\frac{1}{p+q}}$$

$$+\left(1-\prod_{\substack{i,j=1\\ i\neq j}}^{n}\left(1-(1-\mu_{\alpha_i})^{p}(1-\mu_{\alpha_j})^{q}\right)^{\frac{1}{n(n-1)}}\right)^{\frac{1}{p+q}}=1 \qquad (1.130)$$

which completes the proof of Theorem 1.13.

Then, in what follows, we introduce some desirable properties of the IFGBM (Xia et al. 2012a):

(1) (Idempotency) If all $\alpha_i (i=1,2,\ldots,n)$ are equal, i.e., $\alpha_i=\alpha=(\mu_\alpha, v_\alpha, \pi_\alpha)$, for all i, then

$$\begin{aligned}
&IFGBM^{p,q}(\alpha_1,\alpha_2,\ldots,\alpha_n)\\
&=IFGB^{p,q}(\alpha,\alpha,\ldots,\alpha)\\
&=\frac{1}{p+q}\left(\underset{\substack{i,j=1\\ i\neq j}}{\overset{n}{\otimes}}(p\alpha\oplus q\alpha)^{\frac{1}{n(n-1)}}\right)=\frac{1}{p+q}\left(\underset{\substack{i,j=1\\ i\neq j}}{\overset{n}{\otimes}}((p+q)\alpha)^{\frac{1}{n(n-1)}}\right)\\
&=\frac{1}{p+q}((p+q)\alpha)^{\frac{n(n-1)}{n(n-1)}}=\alpha
\end{aligned} \qquad (1.131)$$

(2) (Commutativity)

$$IFGBM^{p,q}(\alpha_1,\alpha_2,\ldots,\alpha_n)=IFGBM^{p,q}(\dot{\alpha}_1,\dot{\alpha}_2,\ldots,\dot{\alpha}_n) \qquad (1.132)$$

where $(\dot{\alpha}_1,\dot{\alpha}_2,\ldots,\dot{\alpha}_n)$ is any permutation of $(\alpha_1,\alpha_2,\ldots,\alpha_n)$.

Proof Since $(\dot{\alpha}_1,\dot{\alpha}_2,\ldots,\dot{\alpha}_n)$ is any permutation of $(\alpha_1,\alpha_2,\ldots,\alpha_n)$, then

$$
\begin{aligned}
IFGBM^{p,q}(\alpha_1, \alpha_2, \ldots, \alpha_n) &= \frac{1}{p+q}\left(\underset{\substack{i,j=1 \\ i \neq j}}{\overset{n}{\otimes}} \left(p\alpha_i \oplus q\alpha_j\right)^{\frac{1}{n(n-1)}} \right) \\
&= \frac{1}{p+q}\left(\underset{\substack{i,j=1 \\ i \neq j}}{\overset{n}{\otimes}} \left(p\dot{\alpha}_i \oplus q\dot{\alpha}_j\right)^{\frac{1}{n(n-1)}} \right) \\
&= IFB^{p,q}(\dot{\alpha}_1, \dot{\alpha}_2, \ldots, \dot{\alpha}_n)
\end{aligned} \tag{1.133}
$$

(3) (Monotonicity) Let $\beta_i = (\mu_{\beta_i}, v_{\beta_i}, \pi_{\beta_i})$ $(i = 1, 2, \ldots, n)$ be a collection of IFVs, if $\mu_{\alpha_i} \leq \mu_{\beta_i}$ and $v_{\alpha_i} \geq v_{\beta_i}$, for all i, then

$$
IFGBM^{p,q}(\alpha_1, \alpha_2, \ldots, \alpha_n) \leq IFGBM^{p,q}(\beta_1, \beta_2, \ldots, \beta_n) \tag{1.134}
$$

Proof Since $\mu_{\alpha_i} \leq \mu_{\beta_i}$ and $v_{\alpha_i} \geq v_{\beta_i}$, for all i, then

$$
\begin{cases}
(1-\mu_{\alpha_i})^p(1-\mu_{\alpha_j})^q \geq (1-\mu_{\beta_i})^p(1-\mu_{\beta_j})^q \\
v_{\alpha_i}^p v_{\alpha_j}^q \geq v_{\beta_i}^p v_{\beta_j}^q
\end{cases}
$$

$$
\Rightarrow \begin{cases}
\prod\limits_{\substack{i,j=1 \\ i \neq j}}^{n} \left(1-(1-\mu_{\alpha_i})^p(1-\mu_{\alpha_j})^q\right)^{\frac{1}{n(n-1)}} \\
\leq \prod\limits_{\substack{i,j=1 \\ i \neq j}}^{n} \left(1-(1-\mu_{\beta_i})^p(1-\mu_{\beta_j})^q\right)^{\frac{1}{n(n-1)}} \\
\prod\limits_{\substack{i,j=1 \\ i \neq j}}^{n} \left(1-v_{\alpha_i}^p v_{\alpha_j}^q\right)^{\frac{1}{n(n-1)}} \leq \prod\limits_{\substack{i,j=1 \\ i \neq j}}^{n} \left(1-v_{\beta_i}^p v_{\beta_j}^q\right)^{\frac{1}{n(n-1)}}
\end{cases}
$$

$$
\Rightarrow \begin{cases}
\left(1-\prod\limits_{\substack{i,j=1 \\ i \neq j}}^{n} \left(1-(1-\mu_{\alpha_i})^p(1-\mu_{\alpha_j})^q\right)^{\frac{1}{n(n-1)}}\right)^{\frac{1}{p+q}} \\
\geq \left(1-\prod\limits_{\substack{i,j=1 \\ i \neq j}}^{n} \left(1-(1-\mu_{\beta_i})^p(1-\mu_{\beta_j})^q\right)^{\frac{1}{n(n-1)}}\right)^{\frac{1}{p+q}} \\
1-\prod\limits_{\substack{i,j=1 \\ i \neq j}}^{n} \left(1-v_{\alpha_i}^p v_{\alpha_j}^q\right)^{\frac{1}{n(n-1)}} \geq 1-\prod\limits_{\substack{i,j=1 \\ i \neq j}}^{n} \left(1-v_{\beta_i}^p v_{\beta_j}^q\right)^{\frac{1}{n(n-1)}}
\end{cases}
$$

$$\Rightarrow \begin{cases} 1-\left(1-\prod\limits_{\substack{i,j=1\\ i\neq j}}^{n}\left(1-(1-\mu_{\alpha_i})^p(1-\mu_{\alpha_j})^q\right)^{\frac{1}{n(n-1)}}\right)^{\frac{1}{p+q}} \\ \leq 1-\left(1-\prod\limits_{\substack{i,j=1\\ i\neq j}}^{n}\left(1-(1-\mu_{\beta_i})^p(1-\mu_{\beta_j})^q\right)^{\frac{1}{n(n-1)}}\right)^{\frac{1}{p+q}} \\ \left(1-\prod\limits_{\substack{i,j=1\\ i\neq j}}^{n}\left(1-v_{\alpha_i}^p v_{\alpha_j}^q\right)^{\frac{1}{n(n-1)}}\right)^{\frac{1}{p+q}} \\ \geq \left(1-\prod\limits_{\substack{i,j=1\\ i\neq j}}^{n}\left(1-v_{\beta_i}^p v_{\beta_j}^q\right)^{\frac{1}{n(n-1)}}\right)^{\frac{1}{p+q}} \end{cases}$$

$$\Rightarrow 1-\left(1-\prod_{\substack{i,j=1\\ i\neq j}}^{n}\left(1-(1-\mu_{\alpha_i})^p(1-\mu_{\alpha_j})^q\right)^{\frac{1}{n(n-1)}}\right)^{\frac{1}{p+q}}$$

$$-\left(1-\prod_{\substack{i,j=1\\ i\neq j}}^{n}\left(1-v_{\alpha_i}^p v_{\alpha_j}^q\right)^{\frac{1}{n(n-1)}}\right)^{\frac{1}{p+q}}$$

$$\leq 1-\left(1-\prod_{\substack{i,j=1\\ i\neq j}}^{n}\left(1-(1-\mu_{\beta_i})^p(1-\mu_{\beta_j})^q\right)^{\frac{1}{n(n-1)}}\right)^{\frac{1}{p+q}}$$

$$-\left(1-\prod_{\substack{i,j=1\\ i\neq j}}^{n}\left(1-v_{\beta_i}^p v_{\beta_j}^q\right)^{\frac{1}{n(n-1)}}\right)^{\frac{1}{p+q}} \tag{1.135}$$

which completes the proof.

(4) (Boundedness) Let α^- and α^+ be given by Eqs. (1.35) and (1.36), then

$$\alpha^- \leq IFGBM^{p,q}(\alpha_1, \alpha_2, \ldots, \alpha_n) \leq \alpha^+ \tag{1.136}$$

which can be obtained easily by the monotonicity.

If the values of the parameters p and q change in the IFBGM, then some special cases can be obtained as follows (Xia et al. 2012a):

Case 1 If $q \to 0$, then by Eq. (1.119), we have

$$
\begin{aligned}
& IFGBM^{p,q}(\alpha_1, \alpha_2, \ldots, \alpha_n) \\
&= \frac{1}{p+q}\left(\underset{\substack{i,j=1 \\ i \neq j}}{\overset{n}{\otimes}} \left(p\alpha_i \oplus q\alpha_j\right)^{\frac{1}{n(n-1)}}\right) = \frac{1}{p}\left(\underset{i=1}{\overset{n}{\otimes}} (p\alpha_i)^{\frac{1}{n}}\right) \\
&= \left(1-\left(1-\prod_{i=1}^{n}\left(1-(1-\mu_{\alpha_i})^p\right)^{\frac{1}{n}}\right)^{\frac{1}{p}}, \left(1-\prod_{i=1}^{n}\left(1-v_{\alpha_i}^p\right)^{\frac{1}{n}}\right)^{\frac{1}{p}},\right. \\
&\quad \left.\left(1-\prod_{i=1}^{n}\left(1-(1-\mu_{\alpha_i})^p\right)^{\frac{1}{n}}\right)^{\frac{1}{p}} - \left(1-\prod_{i=1}^{n}\left(1-v_{\alpha_i}^p\right)^{\frac{1}{n}}\right)^{\frac{1}{p}}\right) \\
&= IFGBM^{p,0}(\alpha_1, \alpha_2, \ldots, \alpha_n)
\end{aligned} \tag{1.137}
$$

which is called a generalized intuitionistic fuzzy geometric mean (GIFGM).

Case 2 If $p = 2$ and $q \to 0$, then Eq. (1.119) is transformed as:

$$
\begin{aligned}
& IFGBM^{2,0}(\alpha_1, \alpha_2, \ldots, \alpha_n) = \frac{1}{2}\left(\underset{i=1}{\overset{n}{\otimes}} (2\alpha_i)^{\frac{1}{n}}\right) \\
&= \left(1-\left(1-\prod_{i=1}^{n}\left(1-(1-\mu_{\alpha_i})^2\right)^{\frac{1}{n}}\right)^{\frac{1}{2}}, \left(1-\prod_{i=1}^{n}\left(1-v_{\alpha_i}^2\right)^{\frac{1}{n}}\right)^{\frac{1}{2}},\right. \\
&\quad \left.\left(1-\prod_{i=1}^{n}\left(1-(1-\mu_{\alpha_i})^2\right)^{\frac{1}{n}}\right)^{\frac{1}{2}} - \left(1-\prod_{i=1}^{n}\left(1-v_{\alpha_i}^2\right)^{\frac{1}{n}}\right)^{\frac{1}{2}}\right)
\end{aligned} \tag{1.138}
$$

which is called an intuitionistic fuzzy square geometric mean (IFSGM).

Case 3 If $p = 1$ and $q \to 0$, then Eq. (1.119) reduces to the intuitionistic fuzzy geometric mean (IFGM) (Xu and Yager 2006):

$$
\begin{aligned}
& IFGBM^{1,0}(\alpha_1, \alpha_2, \ldots, \alpha_n) \\
&= \underset{i=1}{\overset{n}{\otimes}} \alpha_i^{\frac{1}{n}} \\
&= \left(\prod_{i=1}^{n} (\mu_{\alpha_i})^{\frac{1}{n}}, 1-\prod_{i=1}^{n} (1-v_{\alpha_i})^{\frac{1}{n}}, \prod_{i=1}^{n} (1-v_{\alpha_i})^{\frac{1}{n}} - \prod_{i=1}^{n} (\mu_{\alpha_i})^{\frac{1}{n}}\right)
\end{aligned} \tag{1.139}
$$

Case 4 If $p = q = 1$, then Eq. (1.119) reduces to the following:

$$
\begin{aligned}
& IFGBM^{1,1}(\alpha_1, \alpha_2, \ldots, \alpha_n) \\
&= \frac{1}{2}\left(\underset{\substack{i,j=1 \\ i \neq j}}{\overset{n}{\otimes}} \left(\alpha_i \oplus \alpha_j\right)^{\frac{1}{n(n-1)}}\right)
\end{aligned}
$$

$$= \left(1-\left(1-\prod_{\substack{i,j=1\\ i\neq j}}^{n}\left(1-(1-\mu_{\alpha_i})(1-\mu_{\alpha_j})\right)^{\frac{1}{n(n-1)}}\right)^{\frac{1}{2}},\right.$$

$$\left(1-\prod_{\substack{i,j=1\\ i\neq j}}^{n}\left(1-\nu_{\alpha_i}\nu_{\alpha_j}\right)^{\frac{1}{n(n-1)}}\right)^{\frac{1}{2}},$$

$$\left(1-\prod_{\substack{i,j=1\\ i\neq j}}^{n}\left(1-(1-\mu_{\alpha_i})(1-\mu_{\alpha_j})\right)^{\frac{1}{n(n-1)}}\right)^{\frac{1}{2}}$$

$$\left.-\left(1-\prod_{\substack{i,j=1\\ i\neq j}}^{n}\left(1-\nu_{\alpha_i}\nu_{\alpha_j}\right)^{\frac{1}{n(n-1)}}\right)^{\frac{1}{2}}\right) \tag{1.140}$$

which is called an intuitionistic fuzzy interrelated square geometric mean (IFISGM).

1.4.3 The Weighted Intuitionistic Fuzzy Geometric Bonferroni Mean and Its Application in Multi-Attribute Decision Making

For a multi-attribute decision making problem. Let Y, G and w be defined as in Sect. 1.2.4. The performance of the alternative y_i with respect to the attribute G_j is measured by an IFV $b_{ij} = (\mu_{ij}, \nu_{ij}, \pi_{ij})$, such that $\mu_{ij} \in [0, 1]$, $\nu_{ij} \in [0, 1]$, $\mu_{ij}+\nu_{ij}+\pi_{ij} = 1$. All b_{ij} $(i = 1, 2, \ldots, n;\ \ j = 1, 2, \ldots, m)$ are contained in an intuitionistic fuzzy decision matrix $B = (b_{ij})_{n\times m}$.

To get the priority of the alternatives, we should aggregate the performance of each alternative, however, it is noted that the IFGBM doesn't consider the importance of the aggregated arguments, but in many practical problems, especially in multi-attribute decision making, the weight vector of the attributes is an important part in the aggregation, to avoid this issue, Xia et al. (2012a) introduced the following definition:

Definition 1.9 (Xia et al. 2012a) Let $w = (w_1, w_2, \ldots, w_n)^T$ be the weight vector of the IFVs α_i $(i = 1, 2, \ldots, n)$, where w_i indicates the importance degree of α_i, satisfying $w_i > 0$ $(i = 1, 2, \ldots, n)$, $\sum_{i=1}^{n} w_i = 1$. If

$$IFGBM_w^{p,q}(\alpha_1, \alpha_2, \ldots, \alpha_n) = \frac{1}{p+q}\left(\underset{\substack{i,j=1\\ i\neq j}}{\overset{n}{\otimes}}\left(p\alpha_i^{w_i} \oplus q\alpha_j^{w_j}\right)^{\frac{1}{n(n-1)}}\right), \quad p,q>0 \tag{1.141}$$

then $IFGBM_w^{p,q}$ is called a weighted intuitionistic fuzzy geometric Bonferroni mean (WIFGBM).

Similar to Theorem 1.13, we have

Theorem 1.14 (Xia et al. 2012a) The aggregated value by using the WIFGBM is also an IFV, and

$$\begin{aligned} & IFGBM_w^{p,q}(\alpha_1, \alpha_2, \ldots, \alpha_n) \\ &= \left(1-\left(1-\prod_{\substack{i,j=1\\ i\neq j}}^{n}\left(1-\left(1-\mu_{\alpha_i}^{w_i}\right)^p\left(1-\mu_{\alpha_j}^{w_j}\right)^q\right)^{\frac{1}{n(n-1)}}\right)^{\frac{1}{p+q}}\right., \\ & \left(1-\prod_{\substack{i,j=1\\ i\neq j}}^{n}\left(1-\left(1-(1-\nu_{\alpha_i})^{w_i}\right)^p\left(1-(1-\nu_{\alpha_j})^{w_j}\right)^q\right)^{\frac{1}{n(n-1)}}\right)^{\frac{1}{p+q}}, \\ & \left(1-\prod_{\substack{i,j=1\\ i\neq j}}^{n}\left(1-\left(1-\mu_{\alpha_i}^{w_i}\right)^p\left(1-\mu_{\alpha_j}^{w_j}\right)^q\right)^{\frac{1}{n(n-1)}}\right)^{\frac{1}{p+q}} \\ & \left.-\left(1-\prod_{\substack{i,j=1\\ i\neq j}}^{n}\left(1-\left(1-(1-\nu_{\alpha_i})^{w_i}\right)^p\left(1-(1-\nu_{\alpha_j})^{w_j}\right)^q\right)^{\frac{1}{n(n-1)}}\right)^{\frac{1}{p+q}}\right) \end{aligned} \tag{1.142}$$

Based on Definition 1.9 and Theorem 1.14, Xia et al. (2012a) developed an approach for multi-attribute decision making under intuitionistic fuzzy environments, which involves the following steps:

Step 1 Transform the intuitionistic fuzzy decision matrix $B = (b_{ij})_{n\times m}$ into the normalized intuitionistic fuzzy decision matrix $R = (r_{ij})_{n\times m}$ by the method given by Xu and Hu (2010), where

$$r_{ij} = (t_{ij}, f_{ij}, \pi_{ij}) = \begin{cases} b_{ij}, & \text{for benefit attribute } G_j \\ b_{ij}^c, & \text{for cost attribute } G_j \end{cases}, \quad i = 1, 2, \ldots, n; \; j = 1, 2, \ldots, m \tag{1.143}$$

where b_{ij}^c is the complement of b_{ij}, such that $b_{ij}^c = (\nu_{ij}, \mu_{ij}, \pi_{ij})$.

Step 2 Aggregate all the performance values $r_{ij}(j = 1, 2, \ldots, m)$ of the ith line, and get the overall performance value r_i corresponding to the alternative y_i by the WIFGBM:

$$\begin{aligned} r_i &= (t_i, f_i, \pi_i) = IFGBM_w^{p,q}(r_{i1}, r_{i2}, \ldots, r_{im}) \\ &= \left(1 - \left(1 - \prod_{\substack{j,k=1 \\ j \neq k}}^{m} \left(1 - \left(1 - \mu_{ij}^{w_j}\right)^p \left(1 - \mu_{ik}^{w_k}\right)^q\right)^{\frac{1}{m(m-1)}} \right)^{\frac{1}{p+q}}, \right. \\ &\quad \left(1 - \prod_{\substack{j,k=1 \\ j \neq k}}^{m} \left(1 - (1 - (1 - \nu_{ij})^{w_j})^p \left(1 - (1 - \nu_{ik})^{w_k}\right)^q\right)^{\frac{1}{m(m-1)}} \right)^{\frac{1}{p+q}}, \\ &\quad \left(1 - \prod_{\substack{j,k=1 \\ j \neq k}}^{m} \left(1 - \left(1 - \mu_{ij}^{w_j}\right)^p \left(1 - \mu_{ik}^{w_k}\right)^q\right)^{\frac{1}{m(m-1)}} \right)^{\frac{1}{p+q}} \\ &\quad \left. - \left(1 - \prod_{\substack{j,k=1 \\ j \neq k}}^{m} \left(1 - (1 - (1 - \nu_{ij})^{w_j})^p \left(1 - (1 - \nu_{ik})^{w_k}\right)^q\right)^{\frac{1}{m(m-1)}} \right)^{\frac{1}{p+q}} \right) \end{aligned} \tag{1.144}$$

where $p, q > 0$.

Step 3 Rank the overall performance values r_i $(i = 1, 2, \ldots, n)$ according to Xu and Yager (2006)'s ranking method, and obtain the priority of the alternatives y_i $(i = 1, 2, \ldots, n)$ according to $r_i (i = 1, 2, \ldots, n)$.

Next, we give an example to illustrate the proposed method:

Example 1.5 (Xia et al. 2012a) A city is planning to build a municipal library. One of the problems facing the city development commissioner is to determine what kind of air-conditioning system should be installed in the library (adapted from Yoon (1989)). The contractor offers five feasible alternatives y_i $(i = 1, 2, 3, 4, 5)$, which might be adapted to the physical structure of the library. Suppose that three attributes: (1) G_1: economic; (2) G_2: functional; and (3) G_3: operational, are taken

Table 1.11 Intuitionistic fuzzy decision matrix B

	G_1	G_2	G_3
y_1	(0.3,0.4,0.3)	(0.7,0.2,0.1)	(0.5,0.3,0.2)
y_2	(0.5,0.2,0.3)	(0.4,0.1,0.5)	(0.7,0.1,0.2)
y_3	(0.4,0.5,0.1)	(0.7,0.2,0.1)	(0.4,0.4,0.2)
y_4	(0.2,0.6,0.2)	(0.8,0.1,0.1)	(0.8,0.2,0.0)
y_5	(0.9,0.1,0.0)	(0.6,0.3,0.1)	(0.2,0.5,0.3)

into consideration in the installation problem, the weight vector of the attributes G_j $(j = 1, 2, 3)$ is $w = (0.3,0.5,0.2)^T$. Assume that the characteristics of the alternatives y_i $(i = 1, 2, 3, 4, 5)$ with respect to the attributes G_j $(j = 1, 2, 3)$ are represented by the IFVs $b_{ij} = (\mu_{ij}, v_{ij}, \pi_{ij})$, and all b_{ij} $(i = 1, 2, 3, 4, 5;\ j = 1, 2, 3)$ are contained in the intuitionistic fuzzy decision matrix $B = (b_{ij})_{5\times3}$ (see Table 1.11) (Xia et al. 2012a).

Step 1 Considering all the attributes G_j $(j = 1, 2, 3)$ are the benefit attributes, the performance values of the alternatives y_i $(i = 1, 2, 3, 4, 5)$ do not need normalization.

Step 2 Utilize the WIFGBM (here we take p = q = 1) to aggregate all the performance values $b_{ij}(j = 1, 2, 3)$ of the ith line, and get the overall performance value b_i corresponding to the alternative y_i:

$$b_1 = (0.8084, 0.1034, 0.0882), \quad b_2 = (0.8101, 0.0438, 0.1461)$$
$$b_3 = (0.8112, 0.1269, 0.0619), \quad b_4 = (0.8561, 0.0915, 0.0524)$$
$$b_5 = (0.8381, 0.1006, 0.0613)$$

Step 3 Calculate the scores of all the alternatives:

$$S(b_1) = 0.7050, \quad S(b_2) = 0.7664, \quad S(b_3) = 0.6843$$
$$S(b_4) = 0.7647, \quad S(b_5) = 0.7375$$

Since

$$S(b_2) > S(b_4) > S(b_5) > S(b_1) > S(b_3)$$

then the ranking of the alternatives y_i $(i = 1, 2, 3, 4, 5)$ is

$$y_2 \succ y_4 \succ y_5 \succ y_1 \succ y_3$$

If we take $p = q = 2$, then by $b_i = (\mu_i, v_i, \pi_i) = IFGBM_w^{2,2}(b_{i1}, b_{i2}, b_{i3})$, we get

$$b_1 = (0.8039, 0.1056, 0.0905), \quad b_2 = (0.7924, 0.0465, 0.1611)$$
$$b_3 = (0.8100, 0.1290, 0.0610), \quad b_4 = (0.8406, 0.0971, 0.0623)$$
$$b_5 = (0.8092, 0.1130, 0.0778)$$

Then we calculate the scores of all the alternatives:

$$S(b_1) = 0.6982, \quad S(b_2) = 0.7459, \quad S(b_3) = 0.6810$$
$$S(b_4) = 0.7435, \quad S(b_5) = 0.6962$$

Since

$$S(b_2) > S(b_4) > S(b_1) > S(b_5) > S(b_3)$$

then

$$y_2 \succ y_4 \succ y_1 \succ y_5 \succ y_3$$

It can be seen that as the values of the parameters p and q change according to the experts' subjective preferences, the rankings of the alternatives are slightly different, which can reflect the experts' risk preferences. If we use the weighted intuitionistic fuzzy Bonferroni mean (WIFBM) given by Xu and Yager (2011) to aggregate the alternative performances, different results can be obtained. To give a detail comparison, we express the scores of alternatives by Figs. 1.2, 1.3, 1.4, 1.5, 1.6, 1.7, 1.8, 1.9, 1.10 and 1.11 (Xia et al. 2012a) as the parameters p and q change between 0 and 10.

Figures 1.2, 1.3, 1.4, 1.5 and 1.6 describe the scores of alternatives obtained by Xia et al. (2012a)'s method, and Figs. 1.7, 1.8, 1.9, 1.10 and 1.11 describe the scores obtained by Xu and Yager (2011)'s method. It is noted that most of the scores obtained by Xia et al. (2012a)'s method are bigger than 0 and most of the ones obtained by Xu

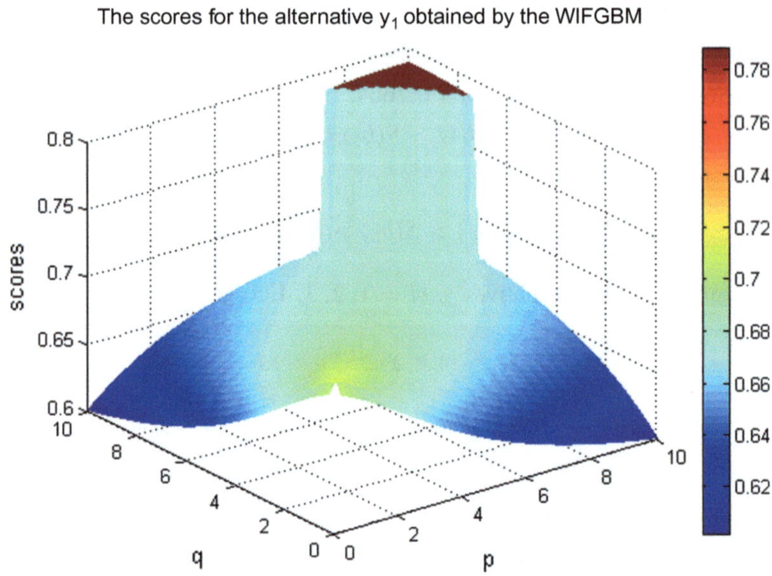

Fig. 1.2 The scores for the alternative y_1 obtained by the WIFGBM

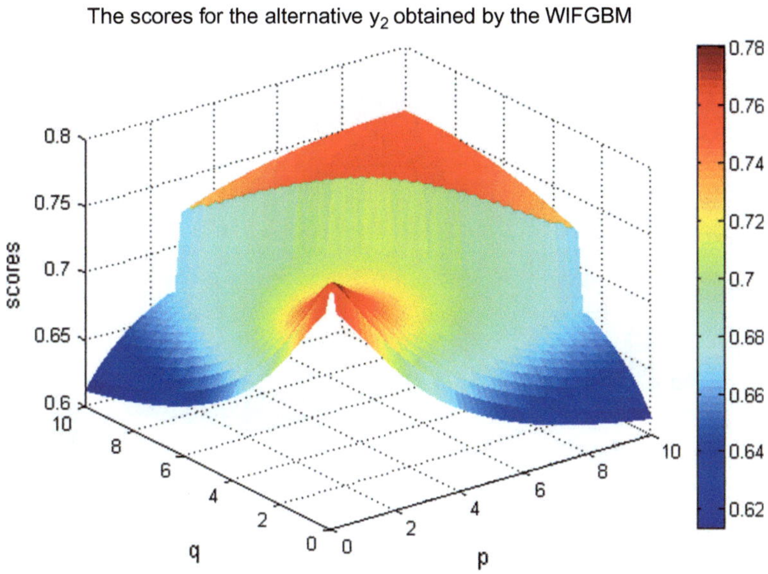

Fig. 1.3 The scores for the alternative y_2 obtained by the WIFGBM

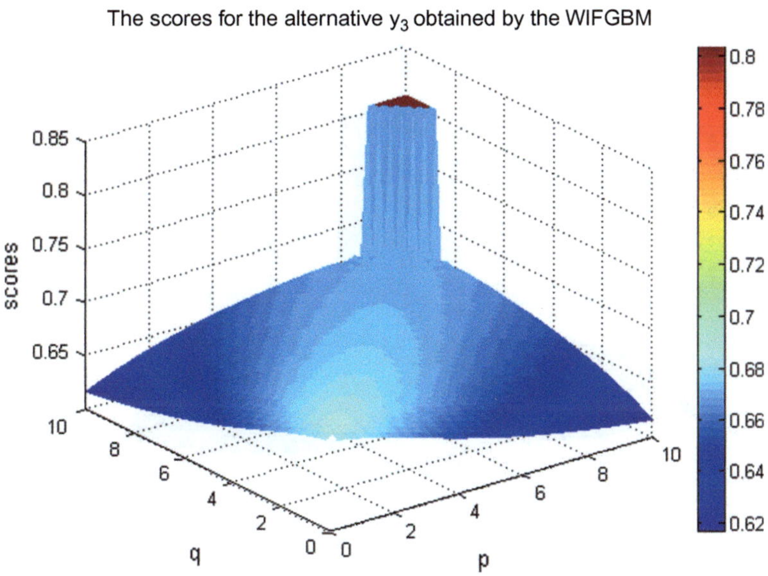

Fig. 1.4 The scores for the alternative y_3 obtained by the WIFGBM

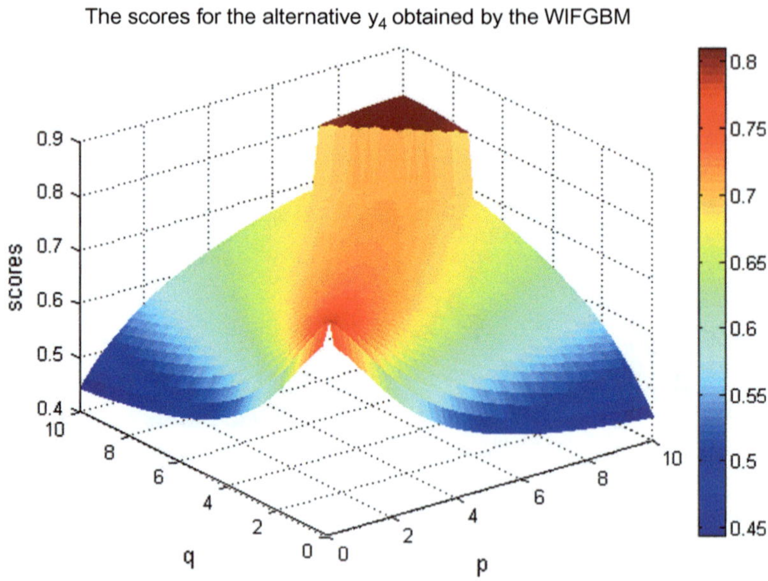

Fig. 1.5 The scores for the alternative y_4 obtained by the WIFGBM

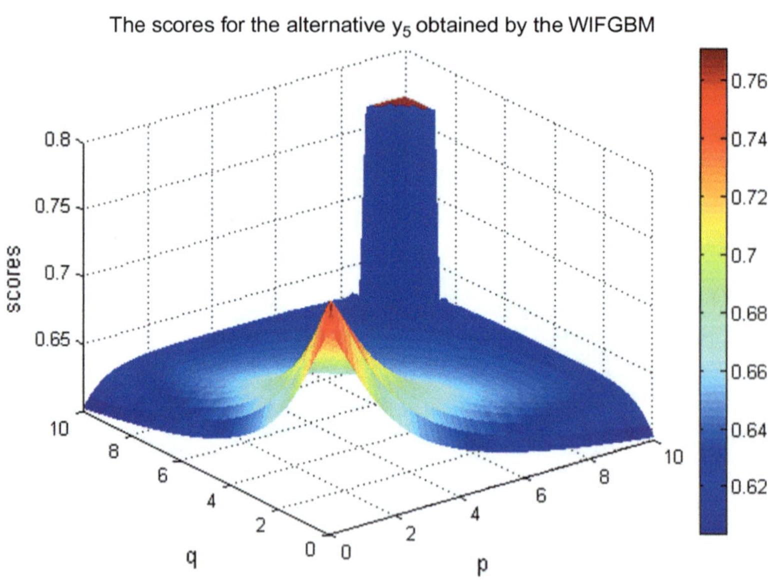

Fig. 1.6 The scores for the alternative y_5 obtained by the WIFGBM

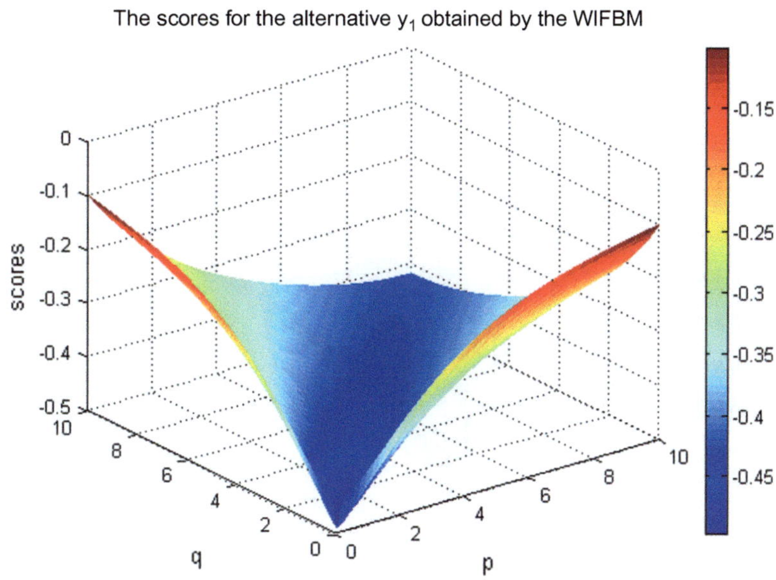

Fig. 1.7 The scores for the alternative y_1 obtained by the WIFBM

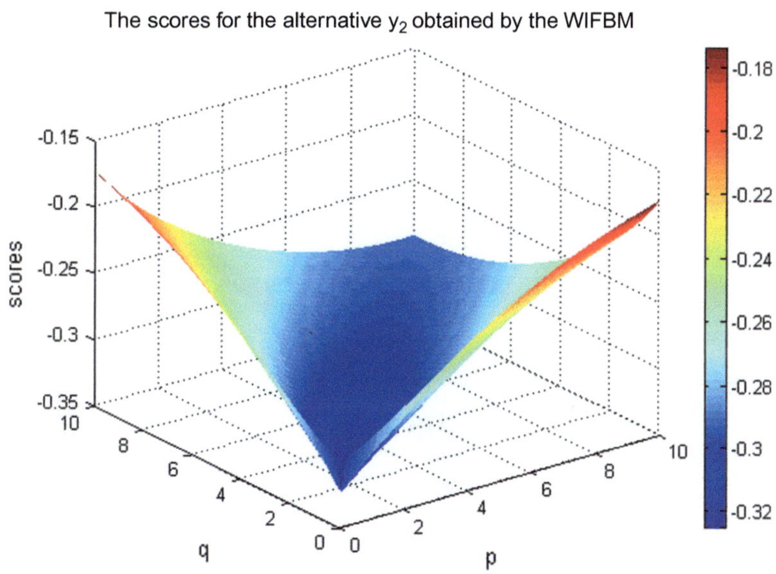

Fig. 1.8 The scores for the alternative y_2 obtained by the WIFBM

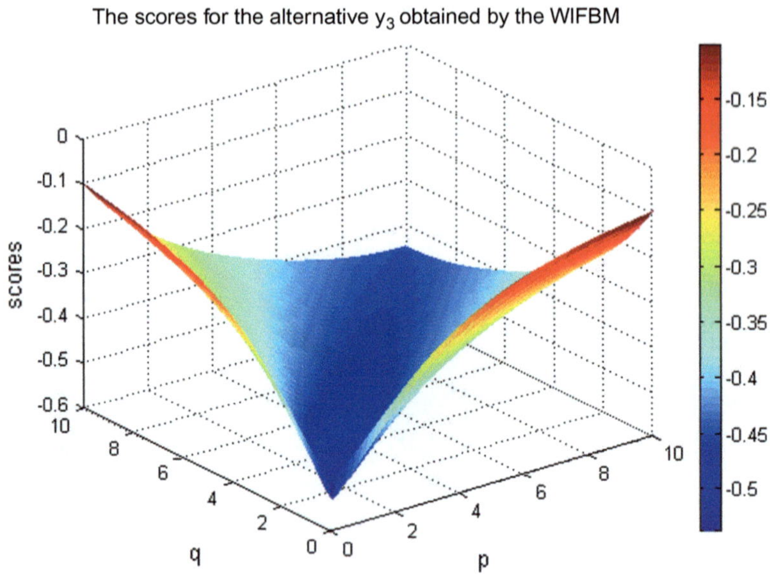

Fig. 1.9 The scores for the alternative y_3 obtained by the WIFBM

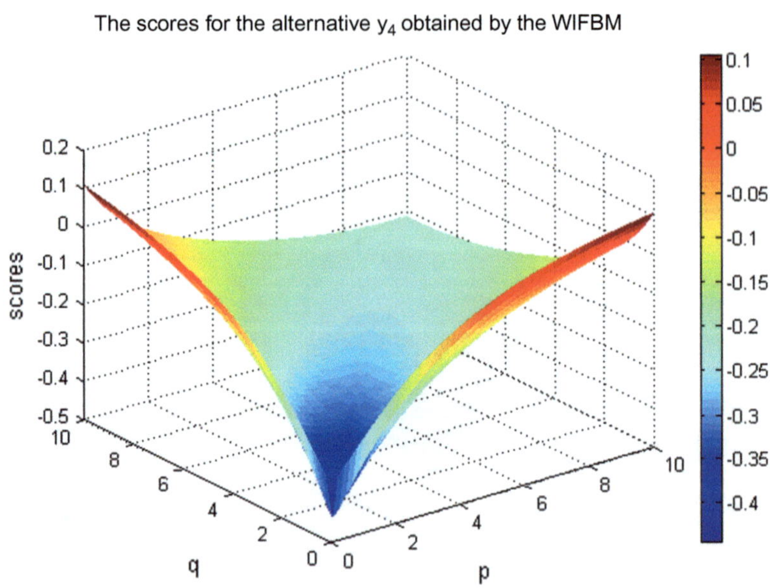

Fig. 1.10 The scores for the alternative y_4 obtained by the WIFBM

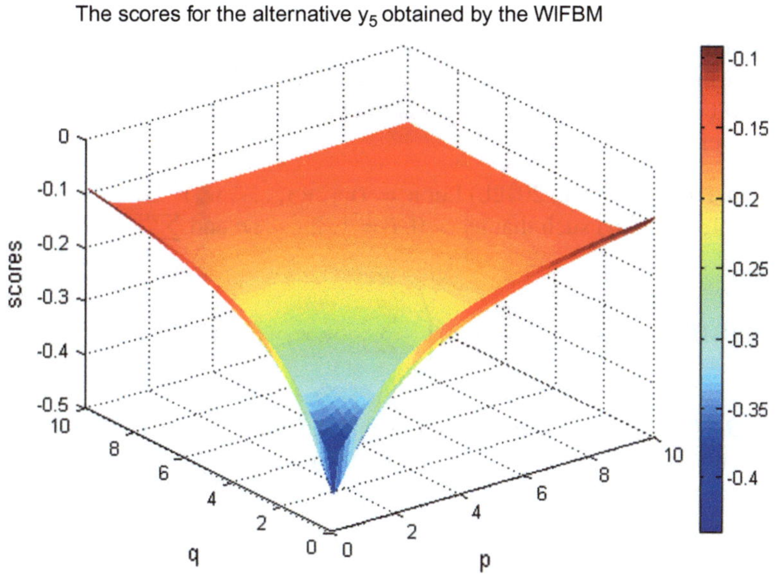

Fig. 1.11 The scores for the alternative y_5 obtained by the WIFBM

and Yager (2011)'s method are smaller than 0, which could indicate that Xia et al. (2012a)'s method is more optimistic, while the one given by Xu and Yager (2011) is more pessimistic. Thus, we can choose the right one according to the practical problem and the experts' risk preferences.

1.5 Generalized Intuitionistic Fuzzy Bonferroni Means

1.5.1 Generalized Bonferroni Means

Let $p, q, r \geq 0$, and $a_i (i = 1, 2, \ldots, n)$ be a collection of nonnegative numbers. Beliakov et al. (2010) further extended the Bonferroni means by considering the correlations of any three aggregated arguments instead of any two:

Definition 1.10 (Beliakov et al. 2010) If

$$GBM^{p,q,r}(a_1, a_2, \ldots, a_n) = \left(\frac{1}{n(n-1)(n-2)} \sum_{\substack{i,j,k=1 \\ i \neq j \neq k}}^{n} a_i^p a_j^q a_k^r \right)^{\frac{1}{p+q+r}} \tag{1.145}$$

then $GBM^{p,q,r}$ is called a generalized Bonferroni mean (GBM).

Especially, if $r = 0$, then the GBM reduces to the Bonferroni mean. However, it is noted that both the Bonferroni mean and the GBM do not consider the situation that $i = j$ or $j = k$ or $i = k$, and the weight vector of the aggregated arguments is not also considered. To overcome this drawback, Xia et al. (2012b) defined the weighted version of the GBM:

Definition 1.11 (Xia et al. 2012b) Let $w = (w_1, w_2, \ldots, w_n)^T$ be the weight vector of a_i $(i = 1, 2, \ldots, n)$ such that $w_i > 0$, $i = 1, 2, \ldots, n$ and $\sum_{i=1}^{n} w_i = 1$. If

$$GWBM^{p,q,r}(a_1, a_2, \ldots, a_n) = \left(\sum_{i,j,k=1}^{n} w_i w_j w_k a_i^p a_j^q a_k^r \right)^{\frac{1}{p+q+r}} \tag{1.146}$$

then $GWBM^{p,q,r}$ is called a generalized weighed Bonferroni mean (GWBM).

Especially, if $w = (1/n, 1/n, \ldots, 1/n)^T$, then the GWBM reduces to the following:

$$RBM^{p,q,r}(a_1, a_2, \ldots, a_n) = \left(\frac{1}{n^3} \sum_{i,j,k=1}^{n} a_i^p a_j^q a_k^r \right)^{\frac{1}{p+q+r}} \tag{1.147}$$

which is called the revised Bonferroni mean (RBM).

Moreover, the GWBM has the following properties:

Theorem 1.15 (Xia et al. 2012b)

(1) $GWBM^{p,q,r}(0, 0, \ldots, 0) = 0$.
(2) $GWBM^{p,q,r}(a, a, \ldots, a) = a$, if $a_i = a$, for all i.
(3) $GWBM^{p,q,r}(a_1, a_2, \ldots, a_n) \geq GWBM^{p,q,r}(b_1, b_2, \ldots, b_n)$, i.e., $GWBM^{p,q,r}$ is monotonic, if $a_i \geq b_i$, for all i.
(4) $\min\{a_i\} \leq GWBM^{p,q,r}(a_1, a_2, \ldots, a_n) \leq \max\{a_i\}$.

Some special cases can be obtained as the change of the parameters (Xia et al. 2012b):

(1) If $r = 0$, then the GWBM reduces to the following:

$$GWBM^{p,q,0}(a_1, a_2, \ldots, a_n) = \left(\sum_{i,j,k=1}^{n} w_i w_j w_k a_i^p a_j^q \right)^{\frac{1}{p+q}}$$

$$= \left(\sum_{i,j=1}^{n} w_i w_j a_i^p a_j^q \sum_{k=1}^{n} w_k \right)^{\frac{1}{p+q}} = \left(\sum_{i,j=1}^{n} w_i w_j a_i^p a_j^q \right)^{\frac{1}{p+q}} \tag{1.148}$$

which we call a weighted Bonferroni mean (WBM).

(2) If $q = 0$ and $r = 0$, then

$$GWBM^{p,0,0}(a_1, a_2, \ldots, a_n) = \left(\sum_{i,j,k=1}^{n} w_i w_j w_k a_i^p \right)^{\frac{1}{p}}$$

$$= \left(\sum_{i=1}^{n} w_i a_i^p \sum_{j=1}^{n} w_j \sum_{k=1}^{n} w_k \right)^{\frac{1}{p}} = \left(\sum_{i=1}^{n} w_i a_i^p \right)^{\frac{1}{p}} \tag{1.149}$$

which is the generalized weighted averaging operator (Yager 2004).

The above aggregation techniques can only deal with the situations where the arguments are represented by exact nonnegative numbers, but are invalid if the aggregation information is given in other forms, such as the IFSs (Atanassov 1983, 1986), which is a widely used tool to deal with uncertainty and fuzziness.

1.5.2 Generalized Intuitionistic Fuzzy Weighted Bonferroni Mean

Let $\alpha_i = (\mu_{\alpha_i}, v_{\alpha_i}, \pi_{\alpha_i})$ $(i = 1, 2, \ldots, n)$ be a collection of IFVs. To aggregate the intuitionistic fuzzy correlated information, Xu and Yager (2011) extended the Bonferroni mean to intuitionistic fuzzy environment and gave the following definition:

Definition 1.12 (Xu and Yager 2011) For any $p, q > 0$, if

$$IFBM^{p,q}(\alpha_1, \alpha_2, \ldots, \alpha_n) = \left(\frac{1}{n(n-1)} \left(\underset{\substack{i,j=1 \\ i \neq j}}{\overset{n}{\oplus}} \left(\alpha_i^p \otimes \alpha_j^q \right) \right) \right)^{\frac{1}{p+q}} \tag{1.150}$$

then $IFBM^{p,q}$ is called an intuitionistic fuzzy Bonferroni mean (IFBM).

Considering the weight vector of the aggregated arguments, the weighted form is also proposed:

Definition 1.13 (Xu and Yager 2011) Let $w = (w_1, w_2, \ldots, w_n)^T$ be the weight vector of α_i $(i = 1, 2, \ldots, n)$, where w_i indicates the importance degree of α_i, satisfying $w_i > 0, i = 1, 2, \ldots, n$ and $\sum_{i=1}^{n} w_i = 1$. If

$$IFWBM^{p,q}(\alpha_1, \alpha_2, \ldots, \alpha_n) = \left(\frac{1}{n(n-1)} \left(\underset{\substack{i,j=1 \\ i \neq j}}{\overset{n}{\oplus}} \left((w_i \alpha_i)^p \otimes (w_j \alpha_j)^q \right) \right) \right)^{\frac{1}{p+q}} \tag{1.151}$$

where $p, q > 0$, then $IFWBM^{p,q}$ is called an intuitionistic fuzzy weighted Bonferroni mean (IFWBM).

However, it is noted that if $w = (1/n, 1/n, \ldots, 1/n)^T$ in Definition 1.13, then the IFWBM cannot reduce to the IFBM given in Definition 1.12. Moreover, both the IFBM and the IFWBM can only deal with the situations where there are correlations between any two aggregated arguments, but not the situations where there exist connections among any three aggregated arguments. To solve this issue, and motivated by Definition 1.11, we define the following:

Definition 1.14 (Xia et al. 2012b) For any $p, q, r > 0$, if

$$GIFWBM^{p,q,r}(\alpha_1, \alpha_2, \ldots, \alpha_n) = \left(\mathop{\oplus}_{i,j,k=1}^{n} w_i w_j w_k \left(\alpha_i^p \otimes \alpha_j^q \otimes \alpha_k^r \right) \right)^{\frac{1}{p+q+r}} \tag{1.152}$$

then $GIFWBM^{p,q,r}$ is called a generalized intuitionistic fuzzy weighted Bonferroni mean (GIFWBM).

Especially, if $r \to 0$, then the GIFWBM reduces to:

$$\begin{aligned} &\lim_{r \to 0} GIFWBM^{p,q,r}(\alpha_1, \alpha_2, \ldots, \alpha_n) \\ &= \left(\mathop{\oplus}_{i,j,k=1}^{n} w_i w_j w_k (\alpha_i^p \otimes \alpha_j^q) \right)^{\frac{1}{p+q}} \\ &= \left(\left(\sum_{k=1}^{n} w_k \right) \mathop{\oplus}_{i,j=1}^{n} w_i w_j (\alpha_i^p \otimes \alpha_j^q) \right)^{\frac{1}{p+q}} = \left(\mathop{\oplus}_{i,j=1}^{n} w_i w_j (\alpha_i^p \otimes \alpha_j^q) \right)^{\frac{1}{p+q}} \end{aligned} \tag{1.153}$$

which is called an intuitionistic fuzzy weighted Bonferroni mean (IFWBM).

Especially, if $q \to 0$ and $r \to 0$, then the GIFWBM reduces to:

$$\begin{aligned} &\lim_{\substack{r \to 0 \\ q \to 0}} GIFWBM^{p,q,r}(\alpha_1, \alpha_2, \ldots, \alpha_n) \\ &= \left(\mathop{\oplus}_{i,j,k=1}^{n} w_i w_j w_k \alpha_i^p \right)^{\frac{1}{p}} \\ &= \left(\sum_{j=1}^{n} w_j \sum_{k=1}^{n} w_k \mathop{\oplus}_{i=1}^{n} w_i \alpha_i^p \right)^{\frac{1}{p}} = \left(\mathop{\oplus}_{i=1}^{n} w_i \alpha_i^p \right)^{\frac{1}{p}} \end{aligned} \tag{1.154}$$

which is the generalized intuitionistic fuzzy weighted mean (GIFWM) (Zhao et al. 2010).

Based on the operational laws of IFVs, we can derive the following theorem:

Theorem 1.16 (Xia et al. 2012b) Let $p, q, r > 0$, then the aggregated value by using the GIFWBM is also an IFV, and

$$
\begin{aligned}
&GIFWBM^{p,q,r}(\alpha_1, \alpha_2, \ldots, \alpha_n) \\
&= \left(\left(1 - \prod_{i,j,k=1}^{n} \left(1 - \mu_{\alpha_i}^p \mu_{\alpha_j}^q \mu_{\alpha_k}^r\right)^{w_i w_j w_k} \right)^{\frac{1}{p+q+r}}, \right. \\
&\quad 1 - \left(1 - \prod_{\substack{i,j,k=1 \\ i \neq j \neq k}}^{n} \left(1 - (1 - \nu_{\alpha_i})^p (1 - \nu_{\alpha_j})^q (1 - \nu_{\alpha_k})^r\right)^{w_i w_j w_k} \right)^{\frac{1}{p+q+r}}, \\
&\quad \left(1 - \prod_{\substack{i,j,k=1 \\ i \neq j \neq k}}^{n} \left(1 - (1 - \nu_{\alpha_i})^p (1 - \nu_{\alpha_j})^q (1 - \nu_{\alpha_k})^r\right)^{w_i w_j w_k} \right)^{\frac{1}{p+q+r}} \\
&\quad \left. - \left(1 - \prod_{i,j,k=1}^{n} \left(1 - \mu_{\alpha_i}^p \mu_{\alpha_j}^q \mu_{\alpha_k}^r\right)^{w_i w_j w_k} \right)^{\frac{1}{p+q+r}} \right) \qquad (1.155)
\end{aligned}
$$

Proof By the operational laws for IFVs, we have

$$\alpha_i^p = (\mu_{\alpha_i}^p, 1 - (1 - \nu_{\alpha_i})^p, (1 - \nu_{\alpha_i})^p - \mu_{\alpha_i}^p) \qquad (1.156)$$

$$\alpha_j^q = (\mu_{\alpha_j}^q, 1 - (1 - \nu_{\alpha_j})^q, (1 - \nu_{\alpha_j})^q - \mu_{\alpha_j}^q) \qquad (1.157)$$

$$\alpha_k^r = (\mu_{\alpha_k}^r, 1 - (1 - \nu_{\alpha_k})^r, (1 - \nu_{\alpha_k})^r - \mu_{\alpha_k}^r) \qquad (1.158)$$

and

$$
\begin{aligned}
\alpha_i^p \otimes \alpha_j^q \otimes \alpha_k^r = &\left(\mu_{\alpha_i}^p \mu_{\alpha_j}^q \mu_{\alpha_k}^r, 1 - (1 - \nu_{\alpha_i})^p (1 - \nu_{\alpha_j})^q (1 - \nu_{\alpha_k})^r, \right. \\
&\left. (1 - \nu_{\alpha_i})^p (1 - \nu_{\alpha_j})^q (1 - \nu_{\alpha_k})^r - \mu_{\alpha_i}^p \mu_{\alpha_j}^q \mu_{\alpha_k}^r \right) \qquad (1.159)
\end{aligned}
$$

then

$$
\begin{aligned}
&\bigoplus_{i,j,k=1}^{n} w_i w_j w_k \left(\alpha_i^p \otimes \alpha_j^q \otimes \alpha_k^r\right) \\
&= \left(1 - \prod_{i,j,k=1}^{n} \left(1 - \mu_{\alpha_i}^p \mu_{\alpha_j}^q \mu_{\alpha_k}^r\right)^{w_i w_j w_k}, \right.
\end{aligned}
$$

$$\prod_{i,j,k=1}^{n} \left(1-(1-\nu_{\alpha_i})^p(1-\nu_{\alpha_j})^q(1-\nu_{\alpha_k})^r\right)^{w_iw_jw_k},$$

$$\left.\prod_{i,j,k=1}^{n} \left(1-\mu_{\alpha_i}^p\mu_{\alpha_j}^q\mu_{\alpha_k}^r\right)^{w_iw_jw_k} - \prod_{i,j,k=1}^{n} \left(1-(1-\nu_{\alpha_i})^p(1-\nu_{\alpha_j})^q(1-\nu_{\alpha_k})^r\right)^{w_iw_jw_k}\right) \tag{1.160}$$

Therefore,

$$\begin{aligned}
&GIFWBM^{p,q,r}(\alpha_1,\alpha_2,\ldots,\alpha_n)\\
&= \left(\bigoplus_{i,j,k=1}^{n} w_iw_jw_k(\alpha_i^p \otimes \alpha_j^q \otimes \alpha_k^r)\right)^{\frac{1}{p+q+r}}\\
&= \left(\left(1-\prod_{i,j,k=1}^{n}\left(1-\mu_{\alpha_i}^p\mu_{\alpha_j}^q\mu_{\alpha_k}^r\right)^{w_iw_jw_k}\right)^{\frac{1}{p+q+r}},\right.\\
&\quad 1-\left(1-\prod_{i,j,k=1}^{n}\left(1-(1-\nu_{\alpha_i})^p(1-\nu_{\alpha_j})^q(1-\nu_{\alpha_k})^r\right)^{w_iw_jw_k}\right)^{\frac{1}{p+q+r}},\\
&\quad \left(1-\prod_{i,j,k=1}^{n}\left(1-(1-\nu_{\alpha_i})^p(1-\nu_{\alpha_j})^q(1-\nu_{\alpha_k})^r\right)^{w_iw_jw_k}\right)^{\frac{1}{p+q+r}}\\
&\quad \left.-\left(1-\prod_{i,j,k=1}^{n}\left(1-\mu_{\alpha_i}^p\mu_{\alpha_j}^q\mu_{\alpha_k}^r\right)^{w_iw_jw_k}\right)^{\frac{1}{p+q+r}}\right)
\end{aligned} \tag{1.161}$$

In addition, since

$$0 \le \left(1-\prod_{i,j,k=1}^{n}\left(1-\mu_{\alpha_i}^p\mu_{\alpha_j}^q\mu_{\alpha_k}^r\right)^{w_iw_jw_k}\right)^{\frac{1}{p+q+r}} \le 1 \tag{1.162}$$

and

$$0 \le 1-\left(1-\prod_{i,j,k=1}^{n}\left(1-(1-\nu_{\alpha_i})^p(1-\nu_{\alpha_j})^q(1-\nu_{\alpha_k})^r\right)^{w_iw_jw_k}\right)^{\frac{1}{p+q+r}} \le 1 \tag{1.163}$$

then we have

$$\left(1-\prod_{i,j,k=1}^{n}\left(1-\mu_{\alpha_i}^{p}\mu_{\alpha_j}^{q}\mu_{\alpha_k}^{r}\right)^{w_iw_jw_k}\right)^{\frac{1}{p+q+r}}$$
$$+\ 1-\left(1-\prod_{i,j,k=1}^{n}\left(1-(1-\nu_{\alpha_i})^{p}(1-\nu_{\alpha_j})^{q}(1-\nu_{\alpha_k})^{r}\right)^{w_iw_jw_k}\right)^{\frac{1}{p+q+r}}$$
$$\leq 1+\left(1-\prod_{i,j,k=1}^{n}\left(1-(1-\nu_{\alpha_i})^{p}(1-\nu_{\alpha_j})^{q}(1-\nu_{\alpha_k})^{r}\right)^{w_iw_jw_k}\right)^{\frac{1}{p+q+r}}$$
$$-\left(1-\prod_{i,j,k=1}^{n}\left(1-(1-\nu_{\alpha_i})^{p}(1-\nu_{\alpha_j})^{q}(1-\nu_{\alpha_k})^{r}\right)^{w_iw_jw_k}\right)^{\frac{1}{p+q+r}}=1 \tag{1.164}$$

which completes the proof of the theorem.

Moreover, the GIFWBM also has the following properties (Xia et al. 2012b):

Theorem 1.17 If all α_i $(i=1,2,\ldots,n)$ are equal, i.e., $\alpha_i=\alpha$, for all i, then

$$GIFWBM^{p,q,r}(\alpha_1,\alpha_2,\ldots,\alpha_n)=GIFWBM^{p,q,r}(\alpha,\alpha,\ldots,\alpha)=\alpha \tag{1.165}$$

Theorem 1.18 Let $\beta_i=(\mu_{\beta_i},\nu_{\beta_i},\pi_{\beta_i})$ $(i=1,2,\ldots,n)$ be a collection of IFVs, if $\mu_{\alpha_i}\leq\mu_{\beta_i}$ and $\nu_{\alpha_i}\geq\nu_{\beta_i}$, for all i, then

$$GIFWBM^{p,q,r}(\alpha_1,\alpha_2,\ldots,\alpha_n)\leq GIFWBM^{p,q,r}(\beta_1,\beta_2,\ldots,\beta_n) \tag{1.166}$$

Proof Since $\mu_{\alpha_i}\leq\mu_{\beta_i}$ and $\nu_{\alpha_i}\geq\nu_{\beta_i}$, for all i, then

$$\mu_{\alpha_i}^{p}\mu_{\alpha_j}^{q}\mu_{\alpha_k}^{r}\leq\mu_{\beta_i}^{p}\mu_{\beta_j}^{q}\mu_{\beta_k}^{r}$$
$$\Rightarrow\prod_{i,j,k=1}^{n}\left(1-\mu_{\alpha_i}^{p}\mu_{\alpha_j}^{q}\mu_{\alpha_k}^{r}\right)^{w_iw_jw_k}\geq\prod_{i,j,k=1}^{n}\left(1-\mu_{\beta_i}^{p}\mu_{\beta_j}^{q}\mu_{\beta_k}^{r}\right)^{w_iw_jw_k}$$
$$\Rightarrow 1-\prod_{i,j,k=1}^{n}\left(1-\mu_{\alpha_i}^{p}\mu_{\alpha_j}^{q}\mu_{\alpha_k}^{r}\right)^{w_iw_jw_k}\leq 1-\prod_{i,j,k=1}^{n}\left(1-\mu_{\beta_i}^{p}\mu_{\beta_j}^{q}\mu_{\beta_k}^{r}\right)^{w_iw_jw_k}$$
$$\Rightarrow\left(1-\prod_{i,j,k=1}^{n}\left(1-\mu_{\alpha_i}^{p}\mu_{\alpha_j}^{q}\mu_{\alpha_k}^{r}\right)^{w_iw_jw_k}\right)^{\frac{1}{p+q+r}}$$
$$\leq\left(1-\prod_{i,j,k=1}^{n}\left(1-\mu_{\beta_i}^{p}\mu_{\beta_j}^{q}\mu_{\beta_k}^{r}\right)^{w_iw_jw_k}\right)^{\frac{1}{p+q+r}} \tag{1.167}$$

and

$$\begin{aligned}
&(1-\nu_{\alpha_i})^p(1-\nu_{\alpha_j})^q(1-\nu_{\alpha_k})^r \leq (1-\nu_{\beta_i})^p(1-\nu_{\beta_j})^q(1-\nu_{\beta_k})^r \\
&\Rightarrow \prod_{i,j,k=1}^{n}\left(1-(1-\nu_{\alpha_i})^p(1-\nu_{\alpha_j})^q(1-\nu_{\alpha_k})^r\right)^{w_iw_jw_k} \\
&\geq \prod_{i,j,k=1}^{n}\left(1-(1-\nu_{\beta_i})^p(1-\nu_{\beta_j})^q(1-\nu_{\beta_k})^r\right)^{w_iw_jw_k} \\
&\Rightarrow \left(1-\prod_{i,j,k=1}^{n}\left(1-(1-\nu_{\alpha_i})^p(1-\nu_{\alpha_j})^q(1-\nu_{\alpha_k})^r\right)^{w_iw_jw_k}\right)^{\frac{1}{p+q+r}} \\
&\geq \left(1-\prod_{i,j,k=1}^{n}\left(1-(1-\nu_{\beta_i})^p(1-\nu_{\beta_j})^q(1-\nu_{\beta_k})^r\right)^{w_iw_jw_k}\right)^{\frac{1}{p+q+r}} \\
&\Rightarrow 1-\left(1-\prod_{i,j,k=1}^{n}\left(1-(1-\nu_{\alpha_i})^p(1-\nu_{\alpha_j})^q(1-\nu_{\alpha_k})^r\right)^{w_iw_jw_k}\right)^{\frac{1}{p+q+r}} \\
&\leq 1-\left(1-\prod_{i,j,k=1}^{n}\left(1-(1-\nu_{\beta_i})^p(1-\nu_{\beta_j})^q(1-\nu_{\beta_k})^r\right)^{w_iw_jw_k}\right)^{\frac{1}{p+q+r}}
\end{aligned} \tag{1.168}$$

Therefore,

$$\begin{aligned}
&\left(1-\prod_{i,j,k=1}^{n}\left(1-\mu_{\alpha_i}^p\mu_{\alpha_j}^q\mu_{\alpha_k}^r\right)^{w_iw_jw_k}\right)^{\frac{1}{p+q+r}} \\
&-\left(1-\left(1-\prod_{i,j,k=1}^{n}\left(1-(1-\nu_{\alpha_i})^p(1-\nu_{\alpha_j})^q(1-\nu_{\alpha_k})^r\right)^{w_iw_jw_k}\right)^{\frac{1}{p+q+r}}\right) \\
&\leq \left(1-\prod_{i,j,k=1}^{n}\left(1-\mu_{\beta_i}^p\mu_{\beta_j}^q\mu_{\beta_k}^r\right)^{w_iw_jw_k}\right)^{\frac{1}{p+q+r}} \\
&-\left(1-\left(1-\prod_{i,j,k=1}^{n}\left(1-(1-\nu_{\beta_i})^p(1-\nu_{\beta_j})^q(1-\nu_{\beta_k})^r\right)^{w_iw_jw_k}\right)^{\frac{1}{p+q+r}}\right)
\end{aligned} \tag{1.169}$$

Let $\alpha = GIFWBM^{p,q,r}(\alpha_1, \alpha_2, \ldots, \alpha_n)$ and $\beta = GIFWBM^{p,q,r}(\beta_1, \beta_2, \ldots, \beta_n)$, and let $S(\alpha)$ and $S(\beta)$ be the scores of α and β, then Eq. (1.169) is equal to $S(\alpha) \le S(\beta)$. Now we discuss the following cases:

Case 1 If $S(\alpha) < S(\beta)$, then by Xu and Yager (2006)'s ranking method, it can be obtained that

$$GIFWBM^{p,q}(\alpha_1, \alpha_2, \ldots, \alpha_n) < GIFWBM^{p,q}(\beta_1, \beta_2, \ldots, \beta_n) \tag{1.170}$$

Case 2 If $S(\alpha) = S(\beta)$, then

$$\begin{aligned}
&\left(1 - \prod_{i,j,k=1}^{n} \left(1 - \mu_{\alpha_i}^{p} \mu_{\alpha_j}^{q} \mu_{\alpha_k}^{r}\right)^{w_i w_j w_k}\right)^{\frac{1}{p+q+r}} \\
&- \left(1 - \left(1 - \prod_{i,j,k=1}^{n} \left(1 - (1 - v_{\alpha_i})^{p}(1 - v_{\alpha_j})^{q}(1 - v_{\alpha_k})^{r}\right)^{w_i w_j w_k}\right)^{\frac{1}{p+q+r}}\right) \\
&= \left(1 - \prod_{i,j,k=1}^{n} \left(1 - \mu_{\beta_i}^{p} \mu_{\beta_j}^{q} \mu_{\beta_k}^{r}\right)^{w_i w_j w_k}\right)^{\frac{1}{p+q+r}} \\
&- \left(1 - \left(1 - \prod_{i,j,k=1}^{n} \left(1 - (1 - v_{\beta_i})^{p}(1 - v_{\beta_j})^{q}(1 - v_{\beta_k})^{r}\right)^{w_i w_j w_k}\right)^{\frac{1}{p+q+r}}\right)
\end{aligned} \tag{1.171}$$

Since $\mu_{\alpha_i} \le \mu_{\beta_i}$ and $v_{\alpha_i} \ge v_{\beta_i}$, for all i, we have

$$\begin{aligned}
&\left(1 - \prod_{i,j,k=1}^{n} \left(1 - \mu_{\alpha_i}^{p} \mu_{\alpha_j}^{q} \mu_{\alpha_k}^{r}\right)^{w_i w_j w_k}\right)^{\frac{1}{p+q+r}} \\
&\quad = \left(1 - \prod_{i,j,k=1}^{n} \left(1 - \mu_{\beta_i}^{p} \mu_{\beta_j}^{q} \mu_{\beta_k}^{r}\right)^{w_i w_j w_k}\right)^{\frac{1}{p+q+r}}
\end{aligned} \tag{1.172}$$

and

$$1 - \left(1 - \prod_{i,j,k=1}^{n} \left(1 - (1 - v_{\alpha_i})^{p}(1 - v_{\alpha_j})^{q}(1 - v_{\alpha_k})^{r}\right)^{w_i w_j w_k}\right)^{\frac{1}{p+q+r}}$$

$$= 1 - \left(1 - \prod_{i,j,k=1}^{n} \left(1 - (1 - \nu_{\beta_i})^p (1 - \nu_{\beta_j})^q (1 - \nu_{\beta_k})^r \right)^{w_i w_j w_k} \right)^{\frac{1}{p+q+r}} \tag{1.173}$$

and thus,

$$\begin{aligned} h_\alpha &= \left(1 - \prod_{i,j,k=1}^{n} \left(1 - \mu_{\alpha_i}^p \mu_{\alpha_j}^q \mu_{\alpha_k}^r \right)^{w_i w_j w_k} \right)^{\frac{1}{p+q+r}} \\ &\quad + \left(1 - \left(1 - \prod_{i,j,k=1}^{n} \left(1 - (1 - \nu_{\alpha_i})^p (1 - \nu_{\alpha_j})^q (1 - \nu_{\alpha_k})^r \right)^{w_i w_j w_k} \right)^{\frac{1}{p+q+r}} \right) \\ &= \left(1 - \prod_{i,j,k=1}^{n} \left(1 - \mu_{\beta_i}^p \mu_{\beta_j}^q \mu_{\beta_k}^r \right)^{w_i w_j w_k} \right)^{\frac{1}{p+q+r}} \\ &\quad + \left(1 - \left(1 - \prod_{i,j,k=1}^{n} \left(1 - (1 - \nu_{\beta_i})^p (1 - \nu_{\beta_j})^q (1 - \nu_{\beta_k})^r \right)^{w_i w_j w_k} \right)^{\frac{1}{p+q+r}} \right) \\ &= h_\beta \end{aligned} \tag{1.174}$$

Then by Xu and Yager (2006)'s ranking method, we get

$$GIFWBM^{p,q,r}(\alpha_1, \alpha_2, \ldots, \alpha_n) = GIFWBM^{p,q,r}(\beta_1, \beta_2, \ldots, \beta_n) \tag{1.175}$$

which completes the proof.

Theorem 1.19 Let $(\dot{\alpha}_1, \dot{\alpha}_2, \ldots, \dot{\alpha}_n)$ be any permutation of $(\alpha_1, \alpha_2, \ldots, \alpha_n)$, then

$$GIFWBM^{p,q,r}(\alpha_1, \alpha_2, \ldots, \alpha_n) = GIFWBM^{p,q,r}(\dot{\alpha}_1, \dot{\alpha}_2, \ldots, \dot{\alpha}_n) \tag{1.176}$$

Theorem 1.20 Let α^- and α^+ be given by Eqs. (1.35) and (1.36), then

$$\alpha^- \leq GIFWBM^{p,q}(\alpha_1, \alpha_2, \ldots, \alpha_n) \leq \alpha^+ \tag{1.177}$$

1.5.3 Generalized Intuitionistic Fuzzy Weighted Bonferroni Geometric Mean

Apparently, the aggregation operators proposed in Sects. 1.5.1 and 1.5.2 are all based on the arithmetic average, which is one of the basic aggregation techniques and focuses on the group opinion, and another fundamental one is the geometric mean, which gives more importance to the individual opinions. In this subsection, we first introduce the generalized weighted Bonferroni geometric mean, based on which, the generalized intuitionistic fuzzy weighted Bonferroni geometric mean is given.

Let $p, q, r \geq 0$, and a_i $(i = 1, 2, \ldots, n)$ be a collection of nonnegative numbers, then

Definition 1.15 (Xia et al. 2012b) Let $w = (w_1, w_2, \ldots, w_n)^T$ be the weight vector of a_i $(i = 1, 2, \ldots, n)$ such that $w_i > 0$, $i = 1, 2, \ldots, n$ and $\sum_{i=1}^{n} w_i = 1$. If

$$GWBGM^{p,q,r}(a_1, a_2, \ldots, a_n) = \frac{1}{p+q+r} \prod_{i,j,k=1}^{n} (pa_i + qa_j + ra_k)^{w_i w_j w_k} \tag{1.178}$$

then $GWBGM^{p,q,r}$ is called a generalized weighted Bonferroni geometric mean (GWBGM), which has the following properties:

Theorem 1.21 (Xia et al. 2012b)

(1) $GWBGM^{p,q,r}(0, 0, \ldots, 0) = 0$.
(2) $GWBGM^{p,q,r}(a, a, \ldots, a) = a$, if $a_i = a$, for all i.
(3) $GWBGM^{p,q,r}(a_1, a_2, \ldots, a_n) \geq GWBGM^{p,q,r}(b_1, b_2, \ldots, b_n)$, i.e., $GWBGM^{p,q,r}$ is monotonic, if $a_i \geq b_i$, for all i.
(4) $\min\{a_i\} \leq GWBGM^{p,q,r}(a_1, a_2, \ldots, a_n) \leq \max\{a_i\}$.

In addition, some special cases can be obtained as the change of the parameters:

(1) If $r = 0$, then the GWBGM reduces to:

$$\begin{aligned} GWBGM^{p,q,0}(a_1, a_2, \ldots, a_n) &= \frac{1}{p+q} \prod_{i,j,k=1}^{n} (pa_i + qa_j)^{w_i w_j w_k} \\ &= \frac{1}{p+q} \prod_{i,j=1}^{n} (pa_i + qa_j)^{w_i w_j} \end{aligned} \tag{1.179}$$

which is called a weighted Bonferroni geometric mean (WBGM).

(2) If $q = 0$ and $r = 0$, then

$$GWBGM^{p,0,0}(a_1, a_2, \ldots, a_n) = \frac{1}{p} \prod_{i,j,k=1}^{n} (pa_i)^{w_i w_j w_k} = \prod_{i=1}^{n} a_i^{w_i} \tag{1.180}$$

which is the usual geometric mean.

Let $p, q, r > 0$ and $\alpha_i = (\mu_{\alpha_i}, v_{\alpha_i}, \pi_{\alpha_i})$ $(i = 1, 2, \ldots, n)$ be a collection of IFVs.

To aggregate the intuitionistic fuzzy information, we further introduce the following:

Definition 1.16 (Xia et al. 2012b) Let $w = (w_1, w_2, \ldots, w_n)^T$ be the weight vector of α_i $(i = 1, 2, \ldots, n)$ such that $w_i > 0, i = 1, 2, \ldots, n$ and $\sum_{i=1}^{n} w_i = 1$. If

$$GIFWBGM^{p,q,r}(\alpha_1, \alpha_2, \ldots, \alpha_n) = \frac{1}{p+q+r}\left(\bigotimes_{i,j,k=1}^{n} \left(p\alpha_i \oplus q\alpha_j \oplus r\alpha_k\right)^{w_i w_j w_k}\right) \tag{1.181}$$

then $GIFWBGM^{p,q,r}$ is called a generalized intuitionistic fuzzy weighted Bonferroni geometric mean (GIFWBGM).

Based on the operational laws of the IFVs, and similar to Theorem 1.16, we can derive the following theorem:

Theorem 1.22 (Xia et al. 2012b) The aggregated value by using the GIFWBGM is also an IFV, and

$$\begin{aligned} & GIFWBGM^{p,q,r}(\alpha_1, \alpha_2, \ldots, \alpha_n) \\ & = \left(1 - \left(1 - \prod_{i,j,k=1}^{n} \left(1 - (1-\mu_{\alpha_i})^p (1-\mu_{\alpha_j})^q (1-\mu_{\alpha_k})^r\right)^{w_i w_j w_k}\right)^{\frac{1}{p+q+r}},\right. \\ & \quad \left.\left(1 - \prod_{i,j,k=1}^{n} \left(1 - v_{\alpha_i}^p v_{\alpha_j}^q v_{\alpha_k}^r\right)^{w_i w_j w_k}\right)^{\frac{1}{p+q+r}}\right) \end{aligned} \tag{1.182}$$

Now let us discuss some desirable properties of the GIFGBM (Xia et al. 2012b):

Theorem 1.23 If all α_i $(i = 1, 2, \ldots, n)$ are equal, i.e., $\alpha_i = \alpha = (\mu_\alpha, v_\alpha, \pi_\alpha)$, for all i, then

$$GIFWBGM^{p,q}(\alpha_1, \alpha_2, \ldots, \alpha_n) = \alpha \tag{1.183}$$

Theorem 1.24 Let $\beta_i = (\mu_{\beta_i}, v_{\beta_i}, \pi_{\beta_i})$ $(i = 1, 2, \ldots, n)$ be a collection of IFVs, if $\mu_{\alpha_i} \le \mu_{\beta_i}$ and $v_{\alpha_i} \ge v_{\beta_i}$, for all i, then

$$GIFWBGM^{p,q}(\alpha_1, \alpha_2, \ldots, \alpha_n) \le GIFWBGM^{p,q}(\beta_1, \beta_2, \ldots, \beta_n) \tag{1.184}$$

Theorem 1.25 Let $(\dot{\alpha}_1, \dot{\alpha}_2, \ldots, \dot{\alpha}_n)$ be any permutation of $(\alpha_1, \alpha_2, \ldots, \alpha_n)$, then

$$GIFWBGM^{p,q}(\alpha_1, \alpha_2, \ldots, \alpha_n) = GIFWBGM^{p,q}(\dot{\alpha}_1, \dot{\alpha}_2, \ldots, \dot{\alpha}_n) \tag{1.185}$$

Theorem 1.26 Let α^- and α^+ be given by Eqs. (1.35) and (1.36), then

$$\alpha^- \le GIFWBGM^{p,q}(\alpha_1, \alpha_2, \ldots, \alpha_n) \le \alpha^+ \tag{1.186}$$

In what follows, we apply the aggregation operators proposed in Sects. 1.5.2 and 1.5.3 to multi-attribute decision making with intuitionistic fuzzy information:

For a multi-attribute decision making problem, let Y, G and w be defined as in Sect. 1.2.4. The performance of the alternative y_i with respect to the attribute G_j is measured by an IFV $b_{ij} = (t_{ij}, f_{ij}, \pi_{ij})$, and all $b_{ij}(i = 1, 2, \ldots, n;$ $j = 1, 2, \ldots, m)$ are contained in the intuitionistic fuzzy decision matrix $B = (b_{ij})_{n\times m}$. Then an approach is given for multi-criteria decision making under intuitionistic fuzzy environments (Xia et al. 2012b):

Step 1 Transform the matrix $B = (b_{ij})_{m\times n}$ into the normalized intuitionistic fuzzy decision matrix $R = (r_{ij})_{n\times m}$ by Xu and Hu (2010)'s method, where

$$r_{ij} = (\mu_{ij}, v_{ij}, \pi_{ij}) = \begin{cases} b_{ij}, & \textit{for benefit attribute } G_j \\ b_{ij}^c, & \textit{for cost attribute } G_j \end{cases}, \quad i = 1, 2, \ldots, m; \quad j = 1, 2, \ldots, n \tag{1.187}$$

where b_{ij}^c is the complement of b_{ij}, such that $b_{ij}^c = (f_{ij}, t_{ij}, \pi_{ij})$.

Step 2 Aggregate all the performance values r_{ij} $(j = 1, 2, \ldots, n)$ of the ith line, and get the overall performance value r_i corresponding to the alternative y_i by the GIFWBM or the GIFWBGM:

$$\begin{aligned} r_i = (\mu_i, v_i, \pi_i) &= GIFWBM_w^{p,q,r}(r_{i1}, r_{i2}, \ldots, r_{in}) \\ &= \left(\bigoplus_{j,k,l=1}^{n} w_j w_k w_l \left(r_{ij}^p \otimes r_{ik}^q \otimes r_{il}^r\right)\right)^{\frac{1}{p+q+r}} \end{aligned} \tag{1.188}$$

or

$$\begin{aligned} r_i = (\mu_i, v_i, \pi_i) &= GIFWBGM_w^{p,q,r}(r_{i1}, r_{i2}, \ldots, r_{in}) \\ &= \frac{1}{p+q+r}\left(\bigotimes_{j,k,l=1}^{n} \left(pr_{ij} \oplus qr_{ik} \oplus rr_{il}\right)^{w_j w_k w_l}\right) \end{aligned} \tag{1.189}$$

where $p, q, r > 0$.

Step 3 Rank the overall performance values r_i $(i = 1, 2, \ldots, m)$ according to Xu and Yager (2006)'s ranking method and obtain the priority of the alternatives y_i $(i = 1, 2, \ldots, m)$ according to r_i $(i = 1, 2, \ldots, m)$.

Next, we give an example to illustrate the proposed approach:

Example 1.6 (Wu and Chen 2011) We know that human resource management is very important during the recruiting and hiring stages of employment. Suppose that the committee of a company intends to choose a project manager from a group of

Table 1.12 Intuitionistic fuzzy decision matrix B

	G_1	G_2	G_3	G_4
y_1	(0.33, 0.33, 0.34)	(0.22, 0.34, 0.44)	(0.23, 0.49, 0.28)	(0.15, 0.57, 0.28)
y_2	(0.24, 0.34, 0.42)	(0.26, 0.40, 0.34)	(0.21, 0.28, 0.51)	(0.44, 0.39, 0.17)
y_3	(0.11, 0.16, 0.73)	(0.19, 0.47, 0.34)	(0.23, 0.31, 0.46)	(0.35, 0.46, 0.19)
y_4	(0.19, 0.38, 0.43)	(0.31, 0.29, 0.40)	(0.44, 0.24, 0.32)	(0.21, 0.25, 0.54)
y_5	(0.37, 0.48, 0.15)	(0.29, 0.39, 0.32)	(0.32, 0.35, 0.33)	(0.34, 0.25, 0.41)
y_6	(0.25, 0.34, 0.41)	(0.24, 0.35, 0.41)	(0.30, 0.28, 0.42)	(0.45, 0.28, 0.27)

candidates. Project management is the application of knowledge, skills, tools, and techniques to the implementation of project activities for the purpose of meeting project requirements. The requirements of a project manager are not only morale, but also proficiency in project management. Suppose that four attributes: (1) G_1 (self-confidence); (2) G_2 (personality); (3) G_3 (past experience); and (4) G_4 (proficiency in project management), are taken into consideration in the selection problem and there exist six candidates y_i $(i = 1, 2, \ldots, 6)$. Assume that the performance of the alternative y_i with respect to the attribute G_j is measured by an IFV $b_{ij} = (\mu_{ij}, v_{ij}, \pi_{ij})$, and then we construct the intuitionistic fuzzy decision matrix $B = (b_{ij})_{6\times4}$ (see Table 1.12) (Xia et al. 2012b).

To get the optimal alternative(s), the following steps are given (Xia et al. 2012b):

Step 1 Considering all the attributes G_j $(j = 1, 2, 3, 4)$ are the benefit attributes, the performance values of the alternatives y_i $(i = 1, 2, \ldots, 6)$ do not need normalization.

Step 2 Aggregate all the performance values r_{ij} $(i = 1, 2, 3, 4;\ j = 1, 2, \ldots, 6)$ of the ith line, and get the overall performance value r_i corresponding to the alternative y_i by the GIFWBM (without of generalization, let $p = q = r = 1$):

$$r_1 = (0.2061, 0.4744, 0.3195), \quad r_2 = (0.3156, 0.3532, 0.3312)$$
$$r_3 = (0.2583, 0.3841, 0.3576), \quad r_4 = (0.2975, 0.2673, 0.4352)$$
$$r_5 = (0.3270, 0.3291, 0.3439), \quad r_6 = (0.3435, 0.2997, 0.3568)$$

Step 3 Calculate the scores of all the alternatives:

$$S(r_1) = -0.2683, \quad S(r_2) = -0.0376, \quad S(r_3) = -0.1259$$
$$S(r_4) = 0.0303, \quad S(r_5) = -0.0021, \quad S(r_6) = 0.0439$$

Since

$$S(r_6) > S(r_4) > S(r_5) > S(r_2) > S(r_3) > S(r_1)$$

then by Xu and Yager (2006)'s ranking method, we get the ranking of the IFVs:

$$r_6 > r_4 > r_5 > r_2 > r_3 > r_1$$

by which we obtain

$$y_6 \succ y_4 \succ y_5 \succ y_2 \succ y_3 \succ y_1$$

In Step 2, if we let $p = q = r = 2$, then we have

$$r_1 = (0.2132, 0.4666, 0.3202), \quad r_2 = (0.3316, 0.3516, 0.3168)$$
$$r_3 = (0.2708, 0.3771, 0.3521), \quad r_4 = (0.3140, 0.2664, 0.4196)$$
$$r_5 = (0.3278, 0.3259, 0.3463), \quad r_5 = (0.3547, 0.2992, 0.3461)$$

Then we calculate the scores of all the alternatives:

$$S(r_1) = -0.2534, \quad S(r_2) = -0.0200, \quad S(r_3) = -0.1064$$
$$S(r_4) = 0.0475, \quad S(r_5) = 0.0019, \quad S(r_6) = 0.0555$$

and thus,

$$y_6 \succ y_4 \succ y_5 \succ y_2 \succ y_3 \succ y_1$$

In Step 2, if we use the GIFWBGM to aggregate the performances of the alternatives (here, we let $p = q = r = 1$), then

$$r_1 = (0.2401, 0.4773, 0.2826), \quad r_2 = (0.3111, 0.3542, 0.3347)$$
$$r_3 = (0.2546, 0.3879, 0.3575), \quad r_4 = (0.2929, 0.2681, 0.4390)$$
$$r_5 = (0.3268, 0.3313, 0.3419), \quad r_6 = (0.3404, 0.3000, 0.3596)$$

from which we calculate the scores of all the alternatives:

$$S(r_1) = -0.2732, \quad S(r_2) = -0.0431, \quad S(r_3) = -0.1333$$
$$S(r_4) = 0.0248, \quad S(r_5) = -0.0045, \quad S(r_6) = 0.0404$$

and thus,

$$y_6 \succ y_4 \succ y_5 \succ y_2 \succ y_3 \succ y_1$$

If we let $p = q = r = 2$, then

$$r_1 = (0.2029, 0.4861, 0.3110), \quad r_2 = (0.3052, 0.3577, 0.3371)$$
$$r_3 = (0.2514, 0.4004, 0.3482), \quad r_4 = (0.2875, 0.2712, 0.4413)$$
$$r_5 = (0.3265, 0.3395, 0.3340), \quad r_5 = (0.3357, 0.3016, 0.3627)$$

and the scores of all the alternatives are:

$$S(r_1) = -0.2832, \quad S(r_2) = -0.0525, \quad S(r_3) = -0.1490$$
$$S(r_4) = 0.0163, \quad S(r_5) = -0.0129, \quad S(r_6) = 0.0341$$

Therefore,

$$y_6 \succ y_4 \succ y_5 \succ y_2 \succ y_3 \succ y_1$$

From the above analysis, the results obtained by Xia et al. (2012b)'s approach are very similar to the ones obtained by Wu and Chen (2011)'s approach, but the former is much simpler. In addition, Xia et al. (2012b)'s approach is more flexible than Wu and Chen (2011)'s one, because it can provide the decision makers (or experts) more choices as the parameters are assigned different values.

1.6 Intuitionistic Fuzzy Aggregation Operators Based on Archimedean t-conorm and t-norm

1.6.1 Intuitionistic Fuzzy Operational Laws Based on t-conorm and t-norm

Definition 1.17 (Klir and Yuan 1995) A function τ: $[0, 1] \times [0, 1] \to [0, 1]$ is called a t-norm if it satisfies the following four conditions:

(1) $\tau(1, x) = x$, for all x.
(2) $\tau(x, y) = \tau(y, x)$, for all x and y.
(3) $\tau(x, \tau(y, z)) = \tau(\tau(x, y), z)$, for all x, y and z.
(4) If $x \leq x'$ and $y \leq y'$, then $\tau(x, y) \leq \tau(x', y')$.

Definition 1.18 (Klir and Yuan 1995) A function $\dot{s}$: $[0, 1] \times [0, 1] \to [0, 1]$ is called a t-conorm if it satisfies the following four conditions:

(1) $\dot{s}(0, x) = x$, for all x.
(2) $\dot{s}(x, y) = \dot{s}(y, x)$, for all x and y.
(3) $\dot{s}(x, \dot{s}(y, z)) = \dot{s}(\dot{s}(x, y), z)$, for all x, y and z.
(4) If $x \leq x'$ and $y \leq y'$, then $\dot{s}(x, y) \leq \dot{s}(x', y')$.

Definition 1.19 (Klir and Yuan 1995) A t-norm function $\tau(x, y)$ is called Archimedean t-norm if it is continuous and $\tau(x, x) < x$ for all $x \in (0, 1)$. An Archimedean t-norm is called strict Archimedean t-norm if it is strictly increasing in each variable for $x, y \in (0, 1)$.

Definition 1.20 (Klir and Yuan 1995) A t-conorm function $\dot{s}(x, y)$ is called Archimedean t-conorm if it is continuous and $\dot{s}(x, x) > x$ for all $x \in (0, 1)$. An Archimedean t-conorm is called strict Archimedean t-conorm if it is strictly increasing in each variable for $x, y \in (0, 1)$.

It is well known (Klement and Mesiar 2005) that a strict Archimedean t-norm is expressed via its additive generator h as $\dot{s}(x, y) = h^{-1}(h(x) + h(y))$, and similarly, applied to its dual t-conorm $T(x, y) = g^{-1}(g(x) + g(y))$ with $h(t) = g(1 - t)$.

We notice that an additive generator of a continuous Archimedean t-norm is a strictly decreasing function g: [0, 1] → 0, 1] such that $g(1) = 0$. If we assign specific forms to the function g, then some well-known t-cornorms and t-norms can be obtained (Xia et al. 2012b):

(1) Let $g(t) = -\log t$, then $h(t) = -\log(1-t)$, $g^{-1}(t) = e^{-t}$, $h^{-1}(t) = 1-e^{-t}$, and Algebraic t-conorm and t-norm (Beliakov et al. 2007) are obtained as follows:

$$\dot{s}_A(x, y) = x + y - xy, \quad \tau_A(x, y) = xy \tag{1.190}$$

(2) Let $g(t) = \log\left(\frac{2-t}{t}\right)$, then

$$h(t) = \log\left(\frac{2-(1-t)}{1-t}\right), \quad g^{-1}(t) = \frac{2}{e^t+1}, \quad h^{-1}(t) = 1 - \frac{2}{e^t+1} \tag{1.191}$$

and we can get Einstein t-conorm and t-norm (Beliakov et al. 2007):

$$\dot{s}_E(x, y) = \frac{x+y}{1+xy}, \quad \tau_E(x, y) = \frac{xy}{1+(1-x)(1-y)} \tag{1.192}$$

(3) Let $g(t) = \log\left(\frac{\gamma+(1-\gamma)t}{t}\right)$, $\gamma \in (0, +\infty)$, then we have

$$h(t) = \log\left(\frac{\gamma+(1-\gamma)1-t)}{1-t}\right), \quad g^{-1}(t) = \frac{\gamma}{e^t+\gamma-1}, \quad h^{-1}(t) = 1 - \frac{\gamma}{e^t+\gamma-1} \tag{1.193}$$

and Hamacher t-conorm and t-norm (Beliakov et al. 2007) are obtained as follows:

$$\dot{s}_H(x, y) = \frac{x+y-xy-(1-\gamma)xy}{1-(1-\gamma)xy}, \quad \gamma \in (0, +\infty) \tag{1.194}$$

$$\tau_H(x, y) = \frac{xy}{\gamma+(1-\gamma)(x+y-xy)}, \quad \gamma \in (0, +\infty) \tag{1.195}$$

Especially, if $\gamma = 1$, then Hamacher t-conorm and t-norm reduce to Algebraic t-conorm and t-norm, respectively; if $\gamma = 2$, then Hamacher t-conorm and t-norm reduce to Einstein t-conorm and t-norm, respectively.

(4) Let $g(t) = \log\left(\frac{\gamma-1}{\gamma^t-1}\right)$, $\gamma \in (1, +\infty)$, then

$$g(t) = \log\left(\frac{\gamma}{(1-\gamma)^t-1}\right), \quad g^{-1}(t) = \frac{\gamma-1+e^{\gamma}}{e^{\gamma}},$$
$$h^{-1}(t) = 1 - \frac{\gamma}{e^t+\gamma-1} \tag{1.196}$$

and get Frank t-conorm and t-norm (Beliakov et al. 2007):

$$\dot{s}_F(x, y) = 1 - \log_\gamma \left(1 + \frac{(\gamma^{1-x} - 1)(\gamma^{1-y} - 1)}{\gamma - 1}\right), \quad \gamma \in (1, +\infty) \tag{1.197}$$

$$\tau_F(x, y) = \log_\gamma \left(1 + \frac{(\gamma^{x} - 1)(\gamma^{y} - 1)}{\gamma - 1}\right), \quad \gamma \in (1, +\infty) \tag{1.198}$$

Especially, if $\gamma \to 1$, then

$$\lim_{\gamma\to 1} g(t) = \lim_{\gamma\to 1} \log\left(\frac{\gamma - 1}{\gamma^t - 1}\right) = \lim_{\gamma\to 1} \log\left(\frac{1}{t\gamma^{t-1} - 1}\right) = -\log t \tag{1.199}$$

which indicates that $\lim_{\gamma\to 1} \dot{s}_F(x, y) = \dot{s}_A(x, y)$ and $\lim_{\gamma\to 1} \tau_F(x, y) = \tau_A(x, y)$.

Considering the relationships among all the three components: $\pi_{\alpha_i} = 1-\mu_{\alpha_i}-v_{\alpha_i}$, we usually denote an IFV $\alpha = (\mu_\alpha, v_\alpha, \pi_\alpha)$ only by its two former components $\alpha = (\mu_\alpha, v_\alpha)$ for brevity. Based on Archimedean t-norm and t-conorm (Klir and Yuan 1995), Beliakov et al. (2011) defined the sum operation on two IFVs $\alpha_i = (\mu_{\alpha_i}, v_{\alpha_i})$ $(i = 1, 2)$:

$$\alpha_1 \oplus \alpha_2 = \left(\dot{s}(\mu_{\alpha_1}, \mu_{\alpha_2}), \tau(v_{\alpha_1}, v_{\alpha_2})\right) \tag{1.200}$$

which can be expressed by the following:

$$\begin{aligned} \alpha_1 \oplus \alpha_2 &= \left(\dot{s}(\mu_{\alpha_1}, \mu_{\alpha_2}), \tau(v_{\alpha_1}, v_{\alpha_2})\right) \\ &= \left(h^{-1}(h(\mu_{\alpha_1}) + h(\mu_{\alpha_2})), g^{-1}(g(v_{\alpha_1}) + g(v_{\alpha_2}))\right) \end{aligned} \tag{1.201}$$

Beliakov et al. (2011) also mentioned that for an IFV $\alpha = (\mu_\alpha, v_\alpha)$, let $\lambda\alpha = (\mu_{\lambda\alpha}, v_{\lambda\alpha})$, then $g(v_{\lambda\alpha}) = \lambda g(v_\alpha)$ and $h(\mu_{\lambda\alpha}) = \lambda h(\mu_\alpha)$.

Let $\alpha_i = (\mu_{\alpha_i}, v_{\alpha_i})$ $(i = 1, 2)$ and $\alpha = (\mu_\alpha, v_\alpha)$ be three IFVs, then with the above analysis, the operations about these IFVs based on Archimedean t-norm and Archimedean t-conorm (Klir and Yuan 1995) can be also expressed as below:

Definition 1.21 (Xia et al. 2012b)

(1) $$\begin{aligned} \alpha_1 \oplus \alpha_2 &= \left(\dot{s}(\mu_{\alpha_1}, \mu_{\alpha_2}), \tau(v_{\alpha_1}, v_{\alpha_2})\right) \\ &= \left(h^{-1}(h(\mu_{\alpha_1}) + h(\mu_{\alpha_2})), g^{-1}(g(v_{\alpha_1}) + g(v_{\alpha_2}))\right). \end{aligned}$$

(2) $$\begin{aligned} \alpha_1 \otimes \alpha_2 &= \left(\tau(\mu_{\alpha_1}, \mu_{\alpha_2}), \dot{s}(v_{\alpha_1}, v_{\alpha_2})\right) \\ &= \left(g^{-1}(g(\mu_{\alpha_1}) + g(\mu_{\alpha_2})), h^{-1}(h(v_{\alpha_1}) + h(v_{\alpha_2}))\right). \end{aligned}$$

(3) $\lambda\alpha = \left(h^{-1}(\lambda h(\mu_\alpha)), g^{-1}(\lambda g(v_\alpha))\right), \lambda > 0.$

(4) $\alpha_\lambda = \left(g^{-1}(\lambda g(\mu_\alpha)), h^{-1}(\lambda h(v_\alpha))\right), \lambda > 0.$

Especially, if $g(t) = -\log(t)$, then the operational laws (1)–(4) can be transformed into the corresponding operational laws (1)–(4) of Definition 1.3, which are the ones based on Algebraic t-conorm and t-norm.

If $g(t) = \log\left(\frac{2-t}{t}\right)$, then

(5) $\alpha_1 \oplus \alpha_2 = \left(\dfrac{\mu_{\alpha_1} + \mu_{\alpha_2}}{1 + \mu_{\alpha_1}\mu_{\alpha_2}}, \dfrac{v_{\alpha_1} v_{\alpha_2}}{1 + (1 - v_{\alpha_1})(1 - v_{\alpha_2})}\right).$

(6) $\alpha_1 \otimes \alpha_2 = \left(\dfrac{\mu_{\alpha_1}\mu_{\alpha_2}}{1 + (1 - \mu_{\alpha_1})(1 - \mu_{\alpha_2})}, \dfrac{v_{\alpha_1} + v_{\alpha_2}}{1 + v_{\alpha_1} v_{\alpha_2}}\right).$

(7) $\lambda\alpha = \left(\dfrac{(1+\mu_\alpha)^\lambda - (1-\mu_\alpha)^\lambda}{(1+\mu_\alpha)^\lambda + (1-\mu_\alpha)^\lambda}, \dfrac{2v_\alpha^\lambda}{(2 - v_\alpha))^\lambda + v_\alpha^\lambda}\right), \quad \lambda > 0.$

(8) $\alpha^\lambda = \left(\dfrac{2\mu_\alpha^\lambda}{(2-\mu_\alpha)^\lambda + \mu_\alpha^\lambda}, \dfrac{(1+v_\alpha)^\lambda - (1-v_\alpha)^\lambda}{(1+v_\alpha)^\lambda + (1-v_\alpha)^\lambda}\right), \quad \lambda > 0,$

where the operational laws (5) and (6) are the ones defined by Wang and Liu (2011) based on Einstein t-conorm and t-norm.

If $g(t) = \log\left(\frac{\gamma + (1-\gamma)t}{t}\right)$, $\gamma \in (0, +\infty)$, then

(9) $$\alpha_1 \oplus \alpha_2 = \left(\frac{\mu_{\alpha_1} + \mu_{\alpha_2} - \mu_{\alpha_1}\mu_{\alpha_2} - (1-\gamma)\mu_{\alpha_1}\mu_{\alpha_2}}{1 - (1-\gamma)\mu_{\alpha_1}\mu_{\alpha_2}}, \frac{v_{\alpha_1} v_{\alpha_2}}{\gamma + (1-\gamma)(v_{\alpha_1} + v_{\alpha_2} - v_{\alpha_1} v_{\alpha_2})}\right).$$

(10) $$\alpha_1 \otimes \alpha_2 = \left(\frac{\mu_{\alpha_1}\mu_{\alpha_2}}{\gamma + (1-\gamma)(\mu_{\alpha_1} + \mu_{\alpha_2} - \mu_{\alpha_1}\mu_{\alpha_2})}, \frac{v_{\alpha_1} + v_{\alpha_2} - v_{\alpha_1} v_{\alpha_2} - (1-\gamma) v_{\alpha_1} v_{\alpha_2}}{1 - (1-\gamma) v_{\alpha_1} v_{\alpha_2}}\right).$$

(11) $$\lambda\alpha = \left(\frac{(1 + (\gamma-1)\mu_\alpha)^\lambda - (1-\mu_\alpha)^\lambda}{(1 + (\gamma-1)\mu_\alpha)^\lambda + (\gamma-1)(1-\mu_\alpha)^\lambda}, \frac{\gamma v_\alpha^\lambda}{(1 + (\gamma-1)(1-v_\alpha))^\lambda + (\gamma-1)v_\alpha^\lambda}\right), \lambda > 0.$$

(12) $$\alpha_\lambda = \left(\frac{\gamma\mu_\alpha^\lambda}{(1 + (\gamma-1)(1-\mu_\alpha))^\lambda + (\gamma-1)\mu_\alpha^\lambda}, \frac{(1 + (\gamma-1)v_\alpha)^\lambda - (1-v_\alpha)^\lambda}{(1 + (\gamma-1)v_\alpha)^\lambda + (\gamma-1)(1-v_\alpha)^\lambda}\right), \lambda > 0,$$

which are the ones defined based on Hammer t-conorm and t-norm.

Especially, if $\gamma = 1$, then the operational laws (9)–(12) reduce to the corresponding operational laws (1)–(4) of Definition 1.3; if $\gamma = 2$, then the operational laws (9)–(12) above reduce to the operational laws (5)–(8).

If $g(t) = \log\left(\frac{\gamma-1}{\gamma^t-1}\right)$, $\gamma \in (1, +\infty)$, then

$$(13)\quad \alpha_1 \oplus \alpha_2 = \left(1 - \log_\gamma\left(1 + \frac{(\gamma^{1-\mu_{\alpha_1}} - 1)\,(\gamma^{1-\mu_{\alpha_2}} - 1)}{\gamma - 1}\right),\right.$$

$$\left.\log_\gamma\left(1 + \frac{(\gamma^{\nu_{\alpha_1}} - 1)\,(\gamma^{\nu_{\alpha_2}} - 1)}{\gamma - 1}\right)\right), \quad \gamma > 1.$$

$$(14)\quad \alpha_1 \otimes \alpha_2 = \left(\log_\gamma\left(1 + \frac{(\gamma^{\mu_{\alpha_1}} - 1)(\gamma^{\mu_{\alpha_2}} - 1)}{\gamma - 1}\right),\right.$$

$$\left.1 - \log_\gamma\left(1 + \frac{(\gamma^{1-\nu_{\alpha_1}} - 1)(\gamma^{1-\nu_{\alpha_2}} - 1)}{\gamma - 1}\right)\right), \quad \gamma > 1.$$

$$(15)\ \lambda\alpha = \left(1 - \log_\gamma\left(1 + \frac{(\gamma^{1-\mu_\alpha} - 1)^\lambda}{(\gamma - 1)^{\lambda-1}}\right), \log_\gamma\left(1 + \frac{(\gamma^{\nu_\alpha} - 1)^\lambda}{(\gamma - 1)^{\lambda-1}}\right)\right), \lambda > 0,\ \gamma > 1.$$

$$(16)\ \alpha^\lambda = \left(\log_\gamma\left(1 + \frac{(\gamma^{\mu_\alpha} - 1)^\lambda}{(\gamma - 1)^{\lambda-1}}\right), 1 - \log_\gamma\left(1 + \frac{(\gamma^{1-\nu_\alpha} - 1)^\lambda}{(\gamma - 1)^{\lambda-1}}\right)\right), \lambda > 0,\ \gamma > 1,$$

which are the ones defined based on Frank t-conorm and t-norm. Especially, if $\gamma = 1$, then the operational laws (13)–(16) reduce to the corresponding operational laws (1)–(4) of Definition 1.3.

Moreover, in what follows, we discuss some relationships of the above operational laws of the IFVs:

Theorem 1.27 (Xia et al. 2012c)

(1) $\alpha_1 \oplus \alpha_2 = \alpha_2 \oplus \alpha_1$.

(2) $\alpha_1 \otimes \alpha_2 = \alpha_2 \otimes \alpha_1$.

(3) $\lambda(\alpha_1 \oplus \alpha_2) = \lambda\alpha_1 \oplus \lambda\alpha_2$.

(4) $(\alpha_1 \otimes \alpha_2)^\lambda = \alpha_1^\lambda \otimes \alpha_2^\lambda$.

(5) $\lambda_1\alpha \oplus \lambda_2\alpha = (\lambda_1 + \lambda_2)\alpha$.

(6) $\alpha^{\lambda_1} \otimes \alpha^{\lambda_2} = \alpha^{\lambda_1+\lambda_2}$.

Proof (1) and (2) are obvious, we prove the others:

$$
\begin{aligned}
(3)\ &\lambda(\alpha_1 \oplus \alpha_2)\\
&= \lambda(h^{-1}(h(\mu_{\alpha_1}) + h(\mu_{\alpha_2})), g^{-1}(g(v_{\alpha_1}) + g(v_{\alpha_2})))\\
&= \left(h^{-1}\left(\lambda h\left(h^{-1}(h(\mu_{\alpha_1}) + h(\mu_{\alpha_2}))\right)\right), g^{-1}\left(\lambda g\left(g^{-1}(g(v_{\alpha_1}) + g(v_{\alpha_2}))\right)\right)\right)\\
&= \left(h^{-1}\left(\lambda\left(h(\mu_{\alpha_1}) + h(\mu_{\alpha_2})\right)\right), g^{-1}\left(\lambda\left(g(v_{\alpha_1}) + g(v_{\alpha_2})\right)\right)\right)
\end{aligned}
$$

$$
\begin{aligned}
\lambda\alpha_1 \oplus \lambda\alpha_2 &= \left(h^{-1}\left(\lambda h(\mu_{\alpha_1})\right), g^{-1}\left(\lambda g(v_{\alpha_1})\right)\right) \oplus \left(h^{-1}\left(\lambda h(\mu_{\alpha_2})\right), g^{-1}\left(\lambda g(v_{\alpha_2})\right)\right)\\
&= \left(h^{-1}\left(h\left(h^{-1}\left(\lambda h(\mu_{\alpha_1})\right)\right) + h\left(h^{-1}\left(\lambda h(\mu_{\alpha_2})\right)\right)\right),\right.\\
&\qquad \left. g^{-1}\left(g\left(g^{-1}\left(\lambda g(v_{\alpha_1})\right)\right) + g\left(g^{-1}\left(\lambda g(v_{\alpha_2})\right)\right)\right)\right)\\
&= \left(h^{-1}\left(\lambda h(\mu_{\alpha_1}) + \lambda h(\mu_{\alpha_2})\right), g^{-1}\left(\lambda g(v_{\alpha_1}) + \lambda g(v_{\alpha_2})\right)\right)\\
&= \lambda(\alpha_1 \oplus \alpha_2).
\end{aligned}
$$

$$
\begin{aligned}
(5)\quad \lambda_1\alpha \oplus \lambda_2\alpha &= \left(h^{-1}\left(\lambda_1 h(\mu_\alpha)\right), g^{-1}\left(\lambda_1 g(v_\alpha)\right)\right) \oplus \left(h^{-1}\left(\lambda_2 h(\mu_\alpha)\right), g^{-1}\left(\lambda_2 g(v_\alpha)\right)\right)\\
&= \left(h^{-1}\left(h\left(h^{-1}\left(\lambda_1 h(\mu_\alpha)\right)\right) + h\left(h^{-1}\left(\lambda_2 h(\mu_\alpha)\right)\right)\right),\right.\\
&\qquad \left. g^{-1}\left(g\left(g^{-1}\left(\lambda_1 g(v_\alpha)\right)\right) + g\left(g^{-1}\left(\lambda_2 g(v_\alpha)\right)\right)\right)\right)\\
&= \left(h^{-1}\left(\lambda_1 h(\mu_\alpha) + \lambda_2 h(\mu_\alpha)\right), g^{-1}\left(\lambda_1 g(v_\alpha) + \lambda_2 g(v_\alpha)\right)\right) = (\lambda_1 + \lambda_2)\alpha.
\end{aligned}
$$

Similarly, (4) and (6) can be proven which completes the proof of the theorem.

Theorem 1.28 (Xia et al. 2012c)

(1) $(\alpha^c)^\lambda = (\lambda\alpha)^c, \lambda > 0.$

(2) $\lambda(\alpha^c) = (\alpha^\lambda)^c, \lambda > 0.$

(3) $\alpha_1^c \oplus \alpha_2^c = (\alpha_1 \otimes \alpha_2)^c.$

(4) $\alpha_1^c \otimes \alpha_2^c = (\alpha_1 \oplus \alpha_2)^c,$

where $\alpha^c = (v_\alpha, \mu_\alpha)$ denotes the complement of the IFV α.

Proof Based on the operations defined in Definition 1.21, we have

(1) $(\alpha^c)^\lambda = \left(g^{-1}\left(\lambda g(v_\alpha)\right), h^{-1}\left(\lambda h(\mu_\alpha)\right)\right) = (\lambda\alpha)^c.$

(2) $\lambda(\alpha^c) = \left(h^{-1}\left(\lambda h(v_\alpha)\right), g^{-1}\left(\lambda g(v_\alpha)\right)\right) = (\alpha^\lambda)^c.$

(3) $\alpha_1^c \oplus \alpha_2^c = \left(h^{-1}\left(h(v_{\alpha_1}) + h(v_{\alpha_2})\right), g^{-1}\left(g(\mu_{\alpha_1}) + g(\mu_{\alpha_2})\right)\right) = (\alpha_1 \otimes \alpha_2)^c.$

(4) $\alpha_1^c \otimes \alpha_2^c = \left(g^{-1}\left(g(v_{\alpha_1}) + g(v_{\alpha_2})\right), h^{-1}\left(h(\mu_{\alpha_1}) + g(\mu_{\alpha_2})\right)\right) = (\alpha_1 \oplus \alpha_2)^c,$

which completes the proof.

1.6.2 Intuitionistic Fuzzy Aggregation Operators Based on Archimedean t-conorm and t-norm

The operational laws defined in Sect. 1.6.1 can be used to aggregate the intuitionistic fuzzy information, which is the focus of this subsection.

Definition 1.22 (Xia et al. 2012c) Let $w = (w_1, w_2, \ldots, w_n)^T$ be the weight vector of the IFVs $\alpha_i = (\mu_{\alpha_i}, v_{\alpha_i})$ $(i = 1, 2, \ldots, n)$, where w_i indicates the importance degree of α_i, satisfying $w_i > 0$ $(i = 1, 2, \ldots, n)$ and $\sum_{i=1}^{n} w_i = 1$, if

$$ATS - IFWA(\alpha_1, \alpha_2, \ldots, \alpha_n) = \mathop{\oplus}_{i=1}^{n} (w_i\alpha_i) \tag{1.202}$$

then ATS-IFWA is called an Archimedean t-conorm and t-norm based intuitionistic fuzzy weighted averaging (ATS-IFWA) operator.

Theorem 1.29 (Xia et al. 2012c) The aggregated value by using the ATS-IFWA operator is also an IFV, and

$$\begin{aligned} ATS - IFWA(\alpha_1, \alpha_2, \ldots, \alpha_n) &= \mathop{\oplus}_{i=1}^{n} w_i\alpha_i \\ &= \left(h^{-1}\left(\sum_{i=1}^{n} w_i h(\mu_{\alpha_i})\right), g^{-1}\left(\sum_{i=1}^{n} w_i g(v_{\alpha_i})\right)\right) \end{aligned} \tag{1.203}$$

which has been investigated by Beliakov et al. (2011), Xu and Yager (2009), Xu and Cai (2010a), and next we give a further study:

Proof By using mathematical induction on n: For $n = 2$, we have

$$\begin{aligned} & ATS - IFWA(\alpha_1, \alpha_2) \\ &= \mathop{\oplus}_{i=1}^{2} w_i\alpha_i = w_1\alpha_1 \oplus w_2\alpha_2 \\ &= \left(h^{-1}\left(h(h^{-1}(w_1 h(\mu_{\alpha_1}))) + h(h^{-1}(w_2 h(\mu_{\alpha_2})))\right),\right. \\ &\quad \left. g^{-1}\left(g(g^{-1}(w_1 g(v_{\alpha_1}))) + g(g^{-1}(w_2 g(v_{\alpha_2})))\right)\right) \\ &= \left(g^{-1}\left(w_1 g(\mu_{\alpha_1}) + w_2 g(\mu_{\alpha_2})\right), h^{-1}\left(w_1 h(v_{\alpha_1}) + w_2 h(v_{\alpha_2})\right)\right) \end{aligned} \tag{1.204}$$

Suppose that Eq. (1.203) holds for $n = k$, that is,

$$ATS - IFWA(\alpha_1, \alpha_2, \ldots, \alpha_k) = \mathop{\oplus}_{i=1}^{k} w_i\alpha_i = w_1\alpha_1 \oplus w_2\alpha_2 \oplus \ldots \oplus w_k\alpha_k$$
$$= \left(h^{-1}\left(\sum_{i=1}^{k} w_i h(\mu_{\alpha_i})\right), g^{-1}\left(\sum_{i=1}^{k} w_i g(v_{\alpha_i})\right)\right) \tag{1.205}$$

then

$$ATS - IFWA(\alpha_1, \alpha_2, \ldots, \alpha_k, \alpha_{k+1})$$
$$= \mathop{\oplus}_{i=1}^{k} w_i\alpha_i \oplus w_{k+1}\alpha_{k+1}$$
$$= \left(h^{-1}\left(\sum_{i=1}^{k} w_i h(\mu_{\alpha_i})\right), g^{-1}\left(\sum_{i=1}^{k} w_i g(v_{\alpha_i})\right)\right)$$
$$\oplus \left(h^{-1}\left(w_{k+1}h(\mu_{\alpha_{k+1}})\right), g^{-1}\left(w_{k+1}g(v_{\alpha_{k+1}})\right)\right)$$
$$= \left(h^{-1}\left(h\left(h^{-1}\left(\sum_{i=1}^{k} w_i h(\mu_{\alpha_i})\right)\right) + h\left(h^{-1}\left(w_{k+1}h(\mu_{\alpha_{k+1}})\right)\right)\right),\right.$$
$$\left. g^{-1}\left(g\left(g^{-1}\left(\sum_{i=1}^{k} w_i g(v_{\alpha_i})\right)\right) + g\left(g^{-1}\left(w_{k+1}g(v_{\alpha_{k+1}})\right)\right)\right)\right)$$
$$= \left(h^{-1}\left(\sum_{i=1}^{k} w_i h(\mu_{\alpha_i}) + w_{k+1}h(\mu_{\alpha_{k+1}})\right), g^{-1}\left(\sum_{i=1}^{k} w_i g(v_{\alpha_i}) + w_{k+1}g(v_{\alpha_{k+1}})\right)\right)$$
$$= \left(h^{-1}\left(\sum_{i=1}^{k+1} w_i h(\mu_{\alpha_i})\right), g^{-1}\left(\sum_{i=1}^{k+1} w_i g(v_{\alpha_i})\right)\right) \tag{1.206}$$

i.e., Eq. (1.203) holds for $n = k + 1$. Thus Eq. (1.203) holds for all n.

In addition, we have known that $h(t) = g(1-t)$, and g: $[0, 1] \to 0, 1]$ is a strictly decreasing function, then $h(t)$ is a strictly increasing function which indicates that

$$0 \leq h^{-1}\left(\sum_{i=1}^{n} w_i h(\mu_{\alpha_i})\right), g^{-1}\left(\sum_{i=1}^{n} w_i g(v_{\alpha_i})\right) \leq 1 \tag{1.207}$$

and

$$h^{-1}\left(\sum_{i=1}^{n} w_i h(\mu_{\alpha_i})\right) + g^{-1}\left(\sum_{i=1}^{n} w_i g(v_{\alpha_i})\right)$$
$$\leq h^{-1}\left(\sum_{i=1}^{n} w_i h(\mu_{\alpha_i})\right) + g^{-1}\left(\sum_{i=1}^{n} w_i g(1 - \mu_{\alpha_i})\right)$$

$$= h^{-1}\left(\sum_{i=1}^{n} w_i h(\mu_{\alpha_i})\right) + 1 - h^{-1}\left(\sum_{i=1}^{n} w_i h(\mu_{\alpha_i})\right) = 1 \qquad (1.208)$$

which completes the proof of Theorem 1.29.

Then we can investigate some desirable properties of the ATS-IFWA operator:

Theorem 1.30 (Xia et al. 2012c) If all α_i $(i = 1, 2, \ldots, n)$ are equal, i.e., $\alpha_i = \alpha = (\mu_\alpha, v_\alpha)$, for all i, then

$$ATS - IFWA(\alpha_1, \alpha_2, \ldots, \alpha_n) = \alpha \qquad (1.209)$$

Proof Let $\alpha_i = \alpha = (\mu_\alpha, v_\alpha)$, we have

$$ATS - IFWA(\alpha_1, \alpha_2, \ldots, \alpha_n) = ATS - IFWA(\alpha, \alpha, \ldots, \alpha) = \bigoplus_{i=1}^{n} w_i\alpha$$

$$= \left(h^{-1}\left(\sum_{i=1}^{n} w_i h(\mu_\alpha)\right), g^{-1}\left(\sum_{i=1}^{n} w_i g(v_\alpha)\right)\right)$$

$$= \left(h^{-1}\left(h(\mu_\alpha)\right), g^{-1}\left(g(v_\alpha)\right)\right) = \alpha \qquad (1.210)$$

Theorem 1.31 (Xia et al. 2012c) Let $\beta_i = (\mu_{\beta_i}, v_{\beta_i})$ $(i = 1, 2, \ldots, n)$ be a collection of IFVs, if $\mu_{\alpha_i} \le \mu_{\beta_i}$ and $v_{\alpha_i} \ge v_{\beta_i}$, for all i, then

$$ATS - IFWA(\alpha_1, \alpha_2, \ldots, \alpha_n) \le ATS - IFWA(\beta_1, \beta_2, \ldots, \beta_n) \qquad (1.211)$$

Proof We have known that $h(t) = g(1 - t)$, and g: [0, 1] $\to$ 0, 1] is a strictly decreasing function, then $h(t)$ is a strictly increasing function. Since $\mu_{\alpha_i} \le \mu_{\beta_i}$ and $v_{\alpha_i} \ge v_{\beta_i}$, then we have

$$h^{-1}\left(\sum_{i=1}^{n} w_i h(\mu_{\alpha_i})\right) \le h^{-1}\left(\sum_{i=1}^{n} w_i h(\mu_{\beta_i})\right) \qquad (1.212)$$

$$g^{-1}\left(\sum_{i=1}^{n} w_i g(v_{\alpha_i})\right) \ge g^{-1}\left(\sum_{i=1}^{n} w_i g(v_{\beta_i})\right) \qquad (1.213)$$

and thus,

$$S(\text{ATS-IFWA}(\alpha_1, \alpha_2, \ldots, \alpha_n)) \le S(\text{ATS-IFWA}(\beta_1, \beta_2, \ldots, \beta_n)) \qquad (1.214)$$

which completes the proof.

Based on Theorem 1.31, the following property can be obtained:

Theorem 1.32 (Xia et al. 2012c) Let α^- and α^+ be given by Eqs. (1.179) and (1.180), then

$$\alpha^- \leq ATS-IFWA(\alpha_1, \alpha_2, \ldots, \alpha_n) \leq \alpha^+ \tag{1.215}$$

Theorem 1.33 (Xia et al. 2012c) Let $w = (w_1, w_2, \ldots, w_n)^T$ be the weight vector of the IFVs $\alpha_i (i = 1, 2, \ldots, n)$, such that $\sum_{i=1}^n w_i = 1$. If $\beta = (\mu_\beta, v_\beta)$ is an IFV, then

$$ATS-IFWA(\alpha_1 \oplus \beta, \alpha_2 \oplus \beta, \ldots, \alpha_n \oplus \beta) = ATS-IFWA(\alpha_1, \alpha_2, \ldots, \alpha_n) \oplus \beta \tag{1.216}$$

Proof Since

$$\alpha_j \oplus \beta = \left(h^{-1}(h(\mu_{\alpha_i}) + h(\mu_\beta)), g^{-1}(g(v_{\alpha_i}) + g(v_\beta))\right) \tag{1.217}$$

then

$$\begin{aligned} &ATS-IFWA(\alpha_1 \oplus \beta, \alpha_2 \oplus \beta, \ldots, \alpha_n \oplus \beta) \\ &= \left(h^{-1}\left(\sum_{i=1}^n w_i h(h^{-1}(h(\mu_{\alpha_i}) + h(\mu_\beta)))\right), g^{-1}\left(\sum_{i=1}^n w_i g(g^{-1}(g(v_{\alpha_i}) + g(v_\beta)))\right)\right) \\ &= \left(h^{-1}\left(\sum_{i=1}^n w_i (h(\mu_{\alpha_i}) + h(\mu_\beta))\right), g^{-1}\left(\sum_{i=1}^n w_i (g(v_{\alpha_i}) + g(v_\beta))\right)\right) \end{aligned} \tag{1.218}$$

and

$$\begin{aligned} &ATS-IFWA(\alpha_1, \alpha_1, \ldots, \alpha_n) \oplus \beta \\ &= \left(h^{-1}\left(\sum_{i=1}^n w_i h(\mu_{\alpha_i})\right), g^{-1}\left(\sum_{i=1}^n w_i g(v_{\alpha_i})\right)\right) \oplus (\mu_\beta, v_\beta) \\ &= \left(h^{-1}\left(h\left(h^{-1}\left(\sum_{i=1}^n w_i h(\mu_{\alpha_i})\right)\right) + h(\mu_\beta)\right),\right. \\ &\qquad \left. g^{-1}\left(g\left(g^{-1}\left(\sum_{i=1}^n w_i g(v_{\alpha_i})\right)\right) + g(v_\beta)\right)\right) \\ &= \left(h^{-1}\left(\sum_{i=1}^n w_i h(\mu_{\alpha_i}) + h(\mu_\beta)\right), g^{-1}\left(\sum_{i=1}^n w_i g(v_{\alpha_i}) + g(v_\beta)\right)\right) \\ &= \left(h^{-1}\left(\sum_{i=1}^n w_i (h(\mu_{\alpha_i}) + h(\mu_\beta))\right), g^{-1}\left(\sum_{i=1}^n w_i (g(v_{\alpha_i}) + g(v_\beta))\right)\right) \end{aligned} \tag{1.219}$$

which completes the proof.

Theorem 1.34 (Xia et al. 2012c) If $r > 0$, then

$$ATS - IFWA(r\alpha_1, r\alpha_2, \ldots, r\alpha_n) = rATS - IFWA(\alpha_1, \alpha_2, \ldots, \alpha_n) \tag{1.220}$$

Proof According to Definition 1.21, we have

$$r\alpha = \left(h^{-1}(rh(\mu_{\alpha_i})), g^{-1}(rg(v_{\alpha_i}))\right) \tag{1.221}$$

then

$$\begin{aligned}
&ATS - IFWA(r\alpha_1, r\alpha_2, \ldots, r\alpha_n)\\
&= \left(h^{-1}\left(\sum_{i=1}^{k+1} w_i h(h^{-1}(rh(\mu_{\alpha_i})))\right), g^{-1}\left(\sum_{i=1}^{k+1} w_i g(g^{-1}(rg(v_{\alpha_i})))\right)\right)\\
&= \left(h^{-1}\left(\sum_{i=1}^{k+1} w_i (rh(\mu_{\alpha_i}))\right), g^{-1}\left(\sum_{i=1}^{k+1} w_i (rg(v_{\alpha_i}))\right)\right)
\end{aligned} \tag{1.222}$$

and

$$\begin{aligned}
&rATS - IFWA(\alpha_1, \alpha_2, \ldots, \alpha_n)\\
&= \left(h^{-1}\left(rh\left(h^{-1}\left(\sum_{i=1}^{n} w_i h(\mu_{\alpha_i})\right)\right)\right), g^{-1}\left(rg\left(g^{-1}\left(\sum_{i=1}^{n} w_i g(v_{\alpha_i})\right)\right)\right)\right)\\
&= \left(h^{-1}\left(r\sum_{i=1}^{n} w_i h(\mu_{\alpha_i})\right), g^{-1}\left(r\sum_{i=1}^{n} w_i g(v_{\alpha_i})\right)\right)
\end{aligned} \tag{1.223}$$

According to Theorems 1.33 and 1.34, we can get the following result easily:

Theorem 1.35 (Xia et al. 2012c) If $r > 0$, and $\beta = (\mu_\beta, v_\beta)$ is an IFV, then

$$ATS - IFWA(r\alpha_1 \oplus \beta, r\alpha_2 \oplus \beta, \ldots, r\alpha_n \oplus \beta) = rATS - IFWA(\alpha_1, \alpha_2, \ldots, \alpha_n) \oplus \beta \tag{1.224}$$

Theorem 1.36 (Xia et al. 2012c) Let $\beta_i = (\mu_{\beta_i}, v_{\beta_i})$ $(i = 1, 2, \ldots, n)$ be a collection of IFVs, and $w = (w_1, w_2, \ldots, w_n)^T$ their weight vector, such that $\sum_{i=1}^n w_i = 1$, then

$$\begin{aligned}
&ATS - IFWA(\alpha_1 \oplus \beta_1, \alpha_2 \oplus \beta_2, \ldots, \alpha_n \oplus \beta_n)\\
&= ATS - IFWA(\alpha_1, \alpha_2, \ldots, \alpha_n) \oplus ATS - IFWA(\beta_1, \beta_2, \ldots, \beta_n)
\end{aligned} \tag{1.225}$$

Proof According to Definition 1.21, we have

$$\alpha_i \oplus \beta_i = \left(h^{-1}(h(\mu_{\alpha_i}) + h(\mu_{\beta_i})), g^{-1}(g(v_{\alpha_i}) + g(v_{\beta_i}))\right) \tag{1.226}$$

then

$$\begin{aligned}
&ATS-IFWA(\alpha_1\oplus\beta_1,\alpha_2\oplus\beta_2,\ldots,\alpha_n\oplus\beta_n)\\
&=\left(h^{-1}\left(\sum_{i=1}^n w_ih(h^{-1}(h(\mu_{\alpha_i})+h(\mu_{\beta_i})))\right),g^{-1}\left(\sum_{i=1}^n w_ig(g^{-1}(g(\nu_{\alpha_i})+g(\nu_{\beta_i})))\right)\right)\\
&=\left(h^{-1}\left(\sum_{i=1}^n w_i(h(\mu_{\alpha_i})+h(\mu_{\beta_i}))\right),g^{-1}\left(\sum_{i=1}^n w_i(g(\nu_{\alpha_i})+g(\nu_{\beta_i}))\right)\right)
\end{aligned}\tag{1.227}$$

and

$$\begin{aligned}
&ATS-IFWA(\alpha_1,\alpha_2,\ldots,\alpha_n)\oplus ATS-IFWA(\beta_1,\beta_2,\ldots,\beta_n)\\
&=\left(h^{-1}\left(\sum_{i=1}^n w_ih(\mu_{\alpha_i})\right),g^{-1}\left(\sum_{i=1}^n w_ig(\nu_{\alpha_i})\right)\right)\\
&\quad\oplus\left(h^{-1}\left(\sum_{i=1}^n w_ih(\mu_{\beta_i})\right),g^{-1}\left(\sum_{i=1}^n w_ig(\nu_{\beta_i})\right)\right)\\
&=\left(h^{-1}\left(h\left(h^{-1}\left(\sum_{i=1}^n w_ih(\mu_{\alpha_i})\right)\right)+h\left(h^{-1}\left(\sum_{i=1}^n w_ih(\mu_{\beta_i})\right)\right)\right),\right.\\
&\quad\left.g^{-1}\left(g\left(g^{-1}\left(\sum_{i=1}^n w_ig(\nu_{\alpha_i})\right)\right)+g\left(g^{-1}\left(\sum_{i=1}^n w_ig(\nu_{\beta_i})\right)\right)\right)\right)\\
&=\left(h^{-1}\left(\sum_{i=1}^n w_ih(\mu_{\alpha_i})+\sum_{i=1}^n w_ih(\mu_{\beta_i})\right),g^{-1}\left(\sum_{i=1}^n w_ig(\nu_{\alpha_i})+\sum_{i=1}^n w_ig(\nu_{\beta_i})\right)\right)
\end{aligned}\tag{1.228}$$

which completes the proof.

If the additive generator g is assigned different forms, then some specific intuitionistic fuzzy aggregation operators can be obtained (Xia et al. 2012c):

Case 1 If $g(t)=-\log(t)$, then the ATS-IFWA operator reduces to the following:

$$IFWA(\alpha_1,\alpha_2,\ldots,\alpha_n)=\left(1-\prod_{i=1}^n(1-\mu_{\alpha_i})^{w_i},\prod_{i=1}^n\nu_{\alpha_i}^{w_i}\right)\tag{1.229}$$

which is the IFWA operator defined by Xu (2007).

Case 2 If $g(t)=\log\left(\frac{2-t}{t}\right)$, then the ATS-IFWA operator reduces to the following:

$$\begin{aligned}
&EIFWA(\alpha_1,\alpha_2,\ldots,\alpha_n)\\
&=\left(\frac{\prod_{i=1}^n(1+\mu_{\alpha_i})^{w_i}-\prod_{i=1}^n(1-\mu_{\alpha_i})^{w_i}}{\prod_{i=1}^n(1+\mu_{\alpha_i})^{w_i}+\prod_{i=1}^n(1-\mu_{\alpha_i})^{w_i}},\frac{2\prod_{i=1}^n\nu_{\alpha_i}^{w_i}}{\prod_{i=1}^n(2-\nu_{\alpha_i})^{w_i}+\prod_{i=1}^n\nu_{\alpha_i}^{w_i}}\right)
\end{aligned}\tag{1.230}$$

which is called an Einstein intuitionistic fuzzy weighted averaging (EIFWA) operator.

Case 3 If $g(t) = \log\left(\frac{\gamma+(1-\gamma)t}{t}\right)$, $\gamma \in (0, +\infty)$, then the ATS-IFWA operator reduces to the following:

$$HIFWA(\alpha_1, \alpha_2, \ldots, \alpha_n) = \left(\frac{\prod_{i=1}^{n}(1+(\gamma-1)\mu_{\alpha_i})^{w_i} - \prod_{i=1}^{n}(1-\mu_{\alpha_i})^{w_i}}{\prod_{i=1}^{n}(1+(\gamma-1)\mu_{\alpha_i})^{w_i} + (\gamma-1)\prod_{i=1}^{n}(1-\mu_{\alpha_i})^{w_i}}, \frac{\gamma\prod_{i=1}^{n}\nu_{\alpha_i}^{w_i}}{\prod_{i=1}^{n}(1+(\gamma-1)(1-\nu_{\alpha_i}))^{w_i} + (\gamma-1)\prod_{i=1}^{n}\nu_{\alpha_i}^{w_i}}\right) \tag{1.231}$$

which is called a Hammer intuitionistic fuzzy weighted averaging (HIFWA) operator. Especially, if $\gamma = 1$, then the HIFWA operator reduces to the IFWA operator; if $\gamma = 2$, then the HIFWA operator reduces to the EIFWA operator.

Case 4 If $g(t) = \log\left(\frac{\gamma-1}{\gamma^t-1}\right)$, $t \in (1, +\infty)$, then the ATS-IFWA operator reduces to the following:

$$\text{FIFWA}(\alpha_1, \alpha_1, \ldots, \alpha_n)$$
$$= \left(1 - \log_\gamma\left(1 + \frac{\prod_{i=1}^{n}(\gamma^{1-\mu_{\alpha_i}} - 1)^{w_i}}{\gamma - 1}\right), \log_\gamma\left(1 + \frac{\prod_{i=1}^{n}(\gamma^{\nu_{\alpha_i}} - 1)^{w_i}}{\gamma - 1}\right)\right) \tag{1.232}$$

which is called a Frank intuitionistic fuzzy weighted averaging (FIFWA) operator. Especially, if $\gamma \to 1$, then the FIFWA operator reduces to the IFWA operator.

Motivated by the geometric mean, the following definition is given:

Definition 1.23 (Xia et al. 2012c) If

$$ATS - IFWG(\alpha_1, \alpha_2, \ldots, \alpha_n) = \underset{i=1}{\overset{n}{\otimes}} \alpha_i^{w_i} \tag{1.233}$$

then ATS-IFWG is called an Archimedean t-cornorm and t-norm based intuitionistic fuzzy geometric (ATS-IFWG) operator.

Based on the operational laws of the IFVs given in Definition 1.21, we can derive the following theorem:

Theorem 1.37 (Xia et al. 2012c) The aggregated value by using the ATS-IFWG operator is also an IFV, and

$$ATS - IFWG(\alpha_1, \alpha_2, \ldots, \alpha_n) = \underset{i=1}{\overset{n}{\otimes}} w_i\alpha_i$$
$$= \left(g^{-1}\left(\sum_{i=1}^{n} w_i g(\mu_{\alpha_i})\right), h^{-1}\left(\sum_{i=1}^{n} w_i h(\nu_{\alpha_i})\right)\right) \tag{1.234}$$

Similarly, we can prove the ATS-IFWG operator also satisfies the properties that the ATS-IFWA operator has, here we will not repeat them. Moreover, if the additive generator g is assigned different forms, then the following intuitionistic fuzzy aggregation operators can be obtained (Xia et al. 2012c):

Case 1 If $g(t) = -\log(t)$, then the ATS-IFWG operator reduces to:

$$\mathrm{IFWG}(\alpha_1, \alpha_2, \ldots, \alpha_n) = \left(\prod_{i=1}^{n} \mu_{\alpha_i}^{w_i}, 1 - \prod_{i=1}^{n} (1 - \nu_{\alpha_i})^{w_i}\right) \tag{1.235}$$

which is the IFWG operator defined by Xu and Yager (2006).

Case 2 If $g(t) = \log\left(\frac{2-t}{t}\right)$, then the ATS-IFWG operator reduces to:

$$EIFWG(\alpha_1, \alpha_2, \ldots, \alpha_n) = \left(\frac{2\prod_{i=1}^{n} \mu_{\alpha_i}^{w_i}}{\prod_{i=1}^{n} (2 - \mu_{\alpha_i})^{w_i} + \prod_{i=1}^{n} \mu_{\alpha_i}^{w_i}}, \frac{\prod_{i=1}^{n} (1 + \nu_{\alpha_i})^{w_i} - \prod_{i=1}^{n} (1 - \nu_{\alpha_i})^{w_i}}{\prod_{i=1}^{n} (1 + \nu_{\alpha_i})^{w_i} + \prod_{i=1}^{n} (1 - \nu_{\alpha_i})^{w_i}}\right) \tag{1.236}$$

which is the Einstein intuitionistic fuzzy weighted geometric (EIFWG) operator defined by Wang and Liu (2011).

Case 3 If $g(t) = \log\left(\frac{\gamma + (1-\gamma)t}{t}\right)$, $\gamma \in (0, +\infty)$, then the ATS-IFWG operator reduces to:

$$HIFWG(\alpha_1, \alpha_2, \ldots, \alpha_n) = \left(\frac{\gamma\prod_{i=1}^{n} \mu_{\alpha_i}^{w_i}}{\prod_{i=1}^{n} (1 + (\gamma - 1)(1 - \mu_{\alpha_i}))^{w_i} + (\gamma - 1)\prod_{i=1}^{n} \mu_{\alpha_i}^{w_i}}, \frac{\prod_{i=1}^{n} (1 + (\gamma - 1)\nu_{\alpha_i})^{w_i} - \prod_{i=1}^{n} (1 - \nu_{\alpha_i})^{w_i}}{\prod_{i=1}^{n} (1 + (\gamma - 1)\nu_{\alpha_i})^{w_i} + (\gamma - 1)\prod_{i=1}^{n} (1 - \nu_{\alpha_i})^{w_i}}\right) \tag{1.237}$$

which is called a Hammer intuitionistic fuzzy weighted geometric (HIFWG) operator. Especially, if $\gamma = 1$, then the HIFWG operator reduces to the IFWA operator; if $\gamma = 2$, then the HIFWG operator reduces to the EIFWG operator.

Case 4 If $g(t) = \log\left(\frac{\gamma - 1}{\gamma^t - 1}\right)$, $t \in (1, +\infty)$, then the ATS-IFWG operator reduces to:

$$FIFWG(\alpha_1, \alpha_1, \ldots, \alpha_n) = \left(\log_\gamma\left(1 + \frac{\prod_{i=1}^{n} (\gamma^{\mu_{\alpha_i}} - 1)^{w_i}}{\gamma - 1}\right), 1 - \log_\gamma\left(1 + \frac{\prod_{i=1}^{n} (\gamma^{1-\nu_{\alpha_i}} - 1)^{w_i}}{\gamma - 1}\right)\right) \tag{1.238}$$

which is called a Frank intuitionistic fuzzy weighted geometric (FIFWG) operator. Especially, if $\gamma \to 1$, then the FIFWG operator reduces to the IFWG operator.

1.6.3 An Approach to Intuitionistic Fuzzy Multi-Attribute Decision Making

For a multi-attribute decision making under intuitionistic fuzzy environment, let Y and G be defined as in Sect. 1.2.4. To evaluate the performance of the alternative y_i under the attribute G_j, the expert is required to provide not only the information that the alternative y_i satisfies the attribute G_j, but also the information that the alternative y_i doesn't satisfy the attribute G_j. These two part information can be expressed by μ_{ij} and v_{ij} which denote the degrees that the alternative y_i satisfies the attribute G_j and doesn't satisfy the attribute G_j, then the performance of the alternative y_i under the attribute G_j can be expressed by an IFV $\alpha_{ij} = (\mu_{ij}, v_{ij})$ with the condition that $0 \leq \mu_{ij}, v_{ij} \leq 1$ and $\mu_{ij} + v_{ij} \leq 1$. When all the performances of the alternatives are provided, the intuitionistic fuzzy decision matrix $B = (b_{ij})_{m\times n} = \left((\mu_{ij}, v_{ij})\right)_{m\times n}$ can be constructed. To obtain the ranking of the alternatives, the following steps can be given (Xia et al. 2012c):

Step 1 Transform the intuitionistic fuzzy decision matrix $B = (b_{ij})_{n\times n}$ into the normalized intuitionistic fuzzy decision matrix $R = (r_{ij})_{n\times n}$, where

$$r_{ij} = \begin{cases} b_{ij}, & \textit{for benefit attribute } G_i \\ b_{ij}^c, & \textit{for cost attribute } G_i \end{cases}, \quad i = 1, 2, \ldots, m, \quad j = 1, 2, \ldots, n \tag{1.239}$$

Step 2 Aggregate the intuitionistic fuzzy values r_i $(i = 1, 2, \ldots, m)$ of the alternatives y_i $(i = 1, 2, \ldots, m)$ by the HIFWA operator:

$$r_i = ATS - IFWA(r_{i1}, r_{i2}, \ldots, r_{in}) = \bigoplus_{j=1}^{n} w_j r_{ij}, \quad i = 1, 2, \ldots, m \tag{1.240}$$

or the HIFWG operator:

$$r_i = ATS - IFWG(r_{i1}, r_{i2}, \ldots, r_{in}) = \bigotimes_{j=1}^{n} r_{ij}^{w_j}, \quad i = 1, 2, \ldots, m \tag{1.241}$$

Step 3 Calculate the scores $S(b_i)$ of b_i by using Xu and Yager (2006)'s ranking method, and obtain the priority of the alternatives according to the ranking of r_i $(i = 1, 2, \ldots, m)$, the bigger the r_i, the better the alternative y_i.

To illustrate the proposed method, we give an example adapted from Chen (2011) as follows:

Example 1.7 The purchasing manager in a small enterprise considers various criteria (or attributes) involving: (1) G_1: financial factors (e.g., economic performance, financial stability); (2) G_2: performance (e.g., delivery, quality, price); (3) G_3: technology (e.g., manufacturing capability, design capability, ability to cope with technology changes); and (4) G_4: organizational culture and strategy (e.g., feeling of trust, internal and external integration of suppliers, compatibility across levels and

Table 1.13 Intuitionistic fuzzy decision matrix B

	G_1	G_2	G_3	G_4
y_1	$(0.60, 0.18)$	$(0.24, 0.44)$	$(0.10, 0.54)$	$(0.45, 0.23)$
y_2	$(0.41, 0.25)$	$(0.49, 0.09)$	$(0.10, 0.39)$	$(0.52, 0.45)$
y_3	$(0.62, 0.18)$	$(0.67, 0.28)$	$(0.36, 0.42)$	$(0.12, 0.67)$
y_4	$(0.21, 0.58)$	$(0.76, 0.22)$	$(0.48, 0.34)$	$(0.15, 0.53)$
y_5	$(0.38, 0.19)$	$(0.65, 0.32)$	$(0.06, 0.29)$	$(0.24, 0.39)$
y_6	$(0.56, 0.12)$	$(0.50, 0.41)$	$(0.21, 0.07)$	$(0.06, 0.28)$

functions of the buyer and the supplier). The set of evaluative criteria is denoted by $G = \{G_1, G_2, G_3, G_4\}$, whose weight vector is $w = (0.34, 0.23, 0.22, 0.21)^T$. There are six suppliers available, and the set of all alternatives is denoted by $Y = \{y_1, y_2, \ldots, y_6\}$. The characteristics of the suppliers y_i $(i = 1, 2, \ldots, 6)$ in terms of the criteria in G are expressed by the intuitionistic fuzzy decision matrix B (see Table 1.13) (Xia et al. 2012c).

To obtain the alternative(s), the following steps are given (Xia et al. 2012c):

Step 1 Considering all the criteria G_j $(j = 1, 2, 3, 4)$ are the benefit criteria, the performance values of the alternatives y_i $(i = 1, 2, \ldots, 6)$ do not need normalization.

Step 2 Aggregate the intuitionistic fuzzy values b_i of the alternative y_i by the HIFWA operator (without loss of generality, let $\gamma = 1$):

$$b_1 = (0.4075{,}0.2964), \quad b_2 = (0.4005{,}0.2466), \quad b_3 = (0.5079{,}0.3163)$$
$$b_4 = (0.4437{,}0.4049), \quad b_5 = (0.3783{,}0.2734), \quad b_2 = (0.3955, 0.1689)$$

Step 3 Calculate the scores $S(b_i)$ of b_i by using Xu and Yager (2006)'s ranking method:

$$S(b_1) = 0.1111, \quad S(b_i) = 0.1539, \quad S(b_3) = 0.1915$$
$$S(b_4) = 0.0388, \quad S(b_5) = 0.1049, \quad S(b_6) = 0.2266$$

Since

$$S(b_6) > S(b_3) > S(b_2) > S(b_1) > S(b_5) > S(b_4)$$

then we can obtain the priority of the alternatives y_i $(i = 1, 2, \ldots, 6)$:

$$y_6 \succ y_3 \succ y_2 \succ y_1 \succ y_5 \succ y_4$$

To investigate the variation trends of the scores and the rankings of the alternatives with the change of the values of the parameter γ, we use the figures to illustrate these issues (Xia et al. 2012c).

Figure 1.12 gives the scores of the alternatives obtained by the HIFWA operator as γ is assigned different values, we can find that the scores for the alternatives decrease as the values of the parameter γ increase from 0 to 10. Figure 1.13 shows the scores

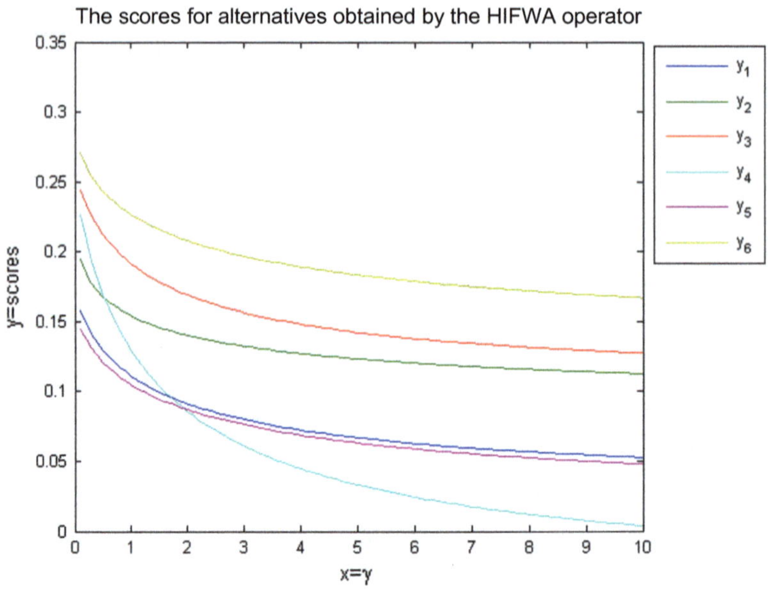

Fig. 1.12 The scores for alternatives obtained by the HIFWA operator

of the alternatives obtained by the HIFWG operator, and as the values of γ increase from 0 to 10, we can find that the scores for the alternatives increase. Figure 1.14 illustrates the deviation values between the scores obtained by the HIFWA operator and the ones obtained by the HIFWG operator. It is noted that the scores obtained by the HIFWA operator are bigger than the ones obtained by the HIFWG operator, and as the values of γ increase, the deviations decrease. Moreover, if $\gamma = 1$, then the scores and the ranking of the alternatives obtained in Fig. 1.12 are the ones obtained by the IFWA operator (Xu 2007), and the results obtained in Fig. 1.13 are just the ones obtained by the IFWG operator (Xu and Yager 2006).

If we use the FIFWA or FIFWG operator instead of the HIFWA or HIFWG operator to aggregate the attribute values for the alternatives, then scores for each alternative can be found in Figs. 1.15 and 1.16 (Xia et al. 2012c), respectively.

Figure 1.15 gives the scores of the alternatives obtained by the FIFWA operator as γ is assigned different values, we can find that the scores for the alternatives decrease as the values of the parameter γ increase from 0 to 100. Figure 1.16 shows the scores of the alternatives obtained by the FIFWG operator, and as the values of γ increase from 0 to 100, we can find that the scores for the alternatives increase. Figure 1.17 (Xia et al. 2012c) illustrates the deviation values between the scores obtained by the FIFWA operator and the ones obtained by the FIFWG operator. It is noted that the scores obtained by the HIFWA operator are bigger than the ones obtained by the HIFWG operator as the values of γ increase.

From the above analysis, we can find that the parameter γ can be considered as a reflection of the decision makers' preferences, as the parameter γ is assigned different values, the scores of the alternatives are different, and the rankings of the

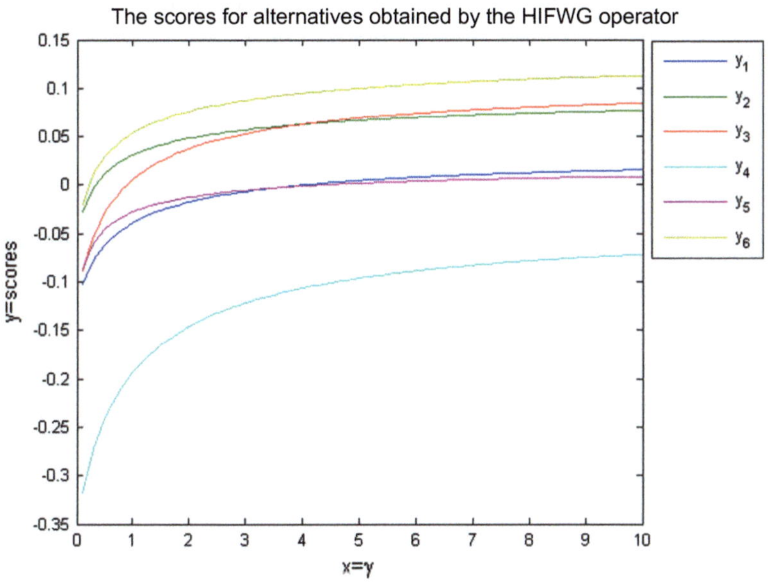

Fig. 1.13 The scores for alternatives obtained by the HIFWG operator

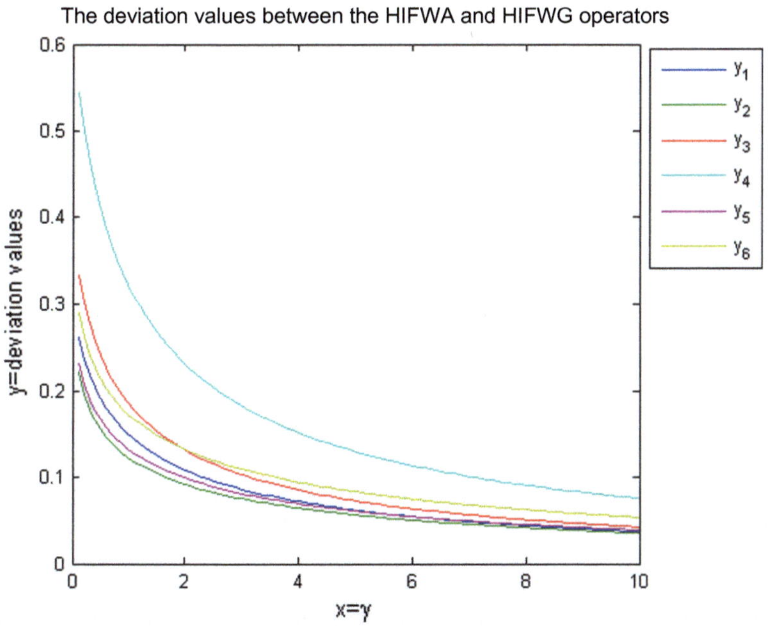

Fig. 1.14 The deviation values for alternatives between the HIFWA and HIFWG operators

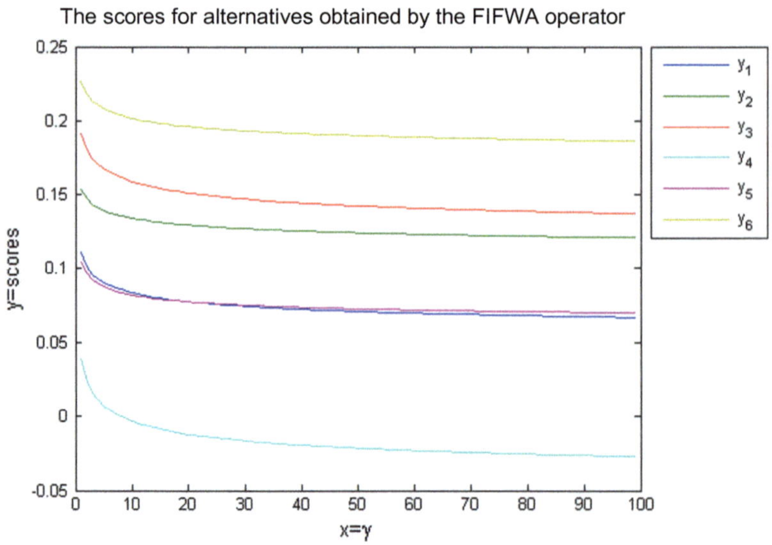

Fig. 1.15 The scores for alternatives obtained by the FIFWA operator

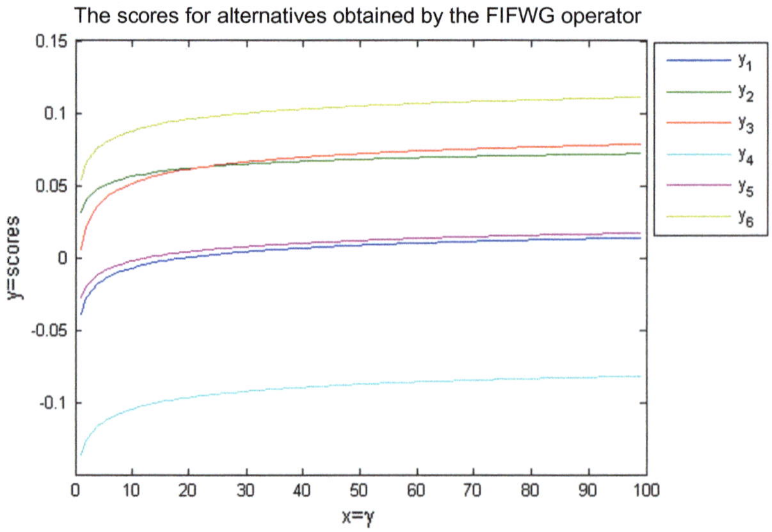

Fig. 1.16 The scores for alternatives obtained by the FIFWG operator

alternatives are also different. Therefore, the proposed aggregation operators with parameters can provide the decision makers more choices and thus are more flexible than the existing ones, because we can choose different values of the parameters according to the different situations. This is an interesting topic and is worthy to be further studied in the future.

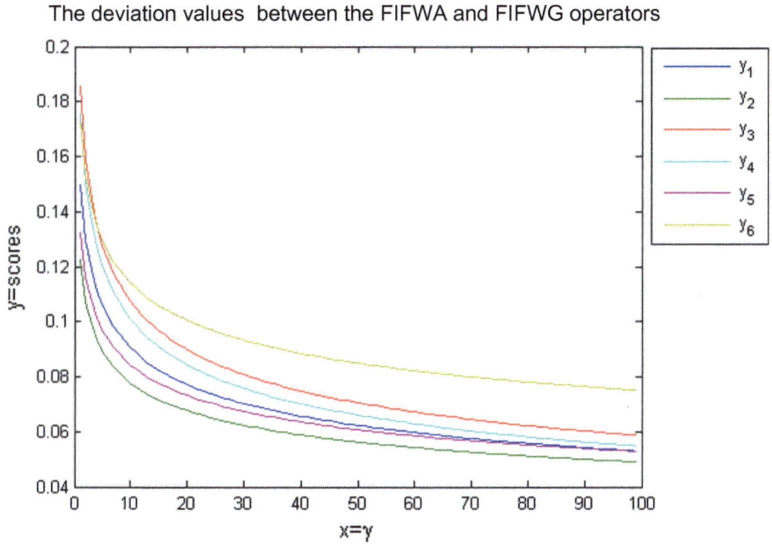

Fig. 1.17 The deviation values for alternatives between the FIFWA and FIFWG operators

1.7 Generalized Intuitionistic Fuzzy Aggregation Operators Based on Hamacher t-conorm and t-norm

Yager (2004) proposed the generalized ordered weighted aggregation operators, which give the aggregated arguments a function and a corresponding reverse function to the arguments after being aggregated, and as the function changes, a family of aggregation operators can be obtained. Based on this useful idea and using the basic operations given in Definition 1.21, in this section, we shall introduce the generalized intuitionistic fuzzy aggregations based on Hamacher t-conorm and t-norm.

Let $\alpha_i = (\mu_{\alpha_i}, v_{\alpha_i})$ $(i = 1, 2, \ldots, n)$ be a collection of IFVs and $w = (w_1, w_2, \ldots, w_n)^T$ the weight vector of α_i $(i = 1, 2, \ldots, n)$, where w_i indicates the importance degree of α_i, satisfying $w_i > 0$ $(i = 1, 2, \ldots, n)$ and $\sum_{i=1}^{n} w_i = 1$. Then based on Eqs. (1.194), (1.195), and Definition 1.21, we define the following:

Definition 1.24 (Xia and Xu 2011) If

$$GHIFWA(\alpha_1, \alpha_2, \ldots, \alpha_n) = \left(\mathop{\oplus}_{i=1}^{n} w_i \alpha_i^{\lambda} \right)^{\frac{1}{\lambda}} \quad (1.242)$$

then *GHIFWA* is called a generalized Hamacher intuitionistic fuzzy averaging (GHIFWA) operator.

Theorem 1.38 (Xia and Xu 2011) The aggregated value by using the GHIFWA operator is also an IFV, and

$$GHIFWA(\alpha_1, \alpha_2, \ldots, \alpha_n) = \left(\frac{\gamma \left(\mu_{1,n}^l - \mu_{1,n}^r\right)^{\frac{1}{\lambda}}}{\left(\mu_{1,n}^l + (\gamma^2 - 1)\mu_{1,n}^r\right)^{\frac{1}{\lambda}} + (\gamma - 1)\left(\mu_{1,n}^l - \mu_{1,n}^r\right)^{\frac{1}{\lambda}}}, \right.$$
$$\left. \frac{\left(v_{1,n}^l + (\gamma^2 - 1)v_{1,n}^r\right)^{\frac{1}{\lambda}} - \left(v_{1,n}^l - v_{1,n}^l\right)^{\frac{1}{\lambda}}}{\left(v_{1,n}^l + (\gamma^2 - 1)v_{1,n}^l\right)^{\frac{1}{\lambda}} + (\gamma - 1)\left(v_{1,n}^l - v_{1,n}^l\right)^{\frac{1}{\lambda}}} \right) \tag{1.243}$$

where

$$\mu_{1,n}^l = \prod_{i=1}^n \left((1 + (\gamma - 1)(1 - \mu_{\alpha_i}))^\lambda + (\gamma^2 - 1)\mu_{\alpha_i}^\lambda\right)^{w_i} \tag{1.244}$$

$$\mu_{1,n}^r = \prod_{i=1}^n \left((1 + (\gamma - 1)(1 - \mu_{\alpha_i}))^\lambda - \mu_{\alpha_i}^\lambda\right)^{w_i} \tag{1.245}$$

$$v_{1,n}^l = \prod_{i=1}^n \left((1 + (\gamma - 1)(1 - v_{\alpha_i}))^\lambda + (\gamma^2 - 1)v_{\alpha_i}^\lambda\right)^{w_i} \tag{1.246}$$

$$v_{1,n}^r = \prod_{i=1}^n \left((1 + (\gamma - 1)(1 - v_{\alpha_i}))^\lambda - v_{\alpha_i}^\lambda\right)^{w_i} \tag{1.247}$$

Proof Let $\beta_i = w_i \alpha_i^\lambda$, then Eq. (1.242) can be written as:

$$GHIFWA(\alpha_1, \alpha_2, \ldots, \alpha_n) = \left(\mathop{\oplus}_{i=1}^n w_i \alpha_i^\lambda\right)^{\frac{1}{\lambda}} = \left(\mathop{\oplus}_{i=1}^n \beta_i\right)^{\frac{1}{\lambda}} \tag{1.248}$$

and we first prove the following equation by using mathematical induction on n:

$$\mathop{\oplus}_{i=1}^n \beta_i = \left(\frac{\prod_{i=1}^n (1 + (\gamma - 1)\mu_{\beta_i}) - \prod_{i=1}^n (1 - \mu_{\beta_i})}{\prod_{i=1}^n (1 + (\gamma - 1)\mu_{\beta_i}) + (\gamma - 1)\prod_{i=1}^n (1 - \mu_{\beta_i})}, \right.$$
$$\left. \frac{\gamma \prod_{i=1}^n v_{\beta_i}}{\prod_{i=1}^n (1 + (\gamma - 1)(1 - v_{\beta_i})) + (\gamma - 1)\prod_{i=1}^n v_{\beta_i}} \right) \tag{1.249}$$

For $n = 2$, Eq. (1.249) holds obviously. Suppose that Eq. (1.249) holds for $n = k$, that is,

$$\mathop{\oplus}\limits_{i=1}^{k}\beta_i=\left(\mu_{\mathop{\oplus}\limits_{i=1}^{k}\beta_i},\nu_{\mathop{\oplus}\limits_{i=1}^{k}\beta_i}\right)$$
$$=\left(\frac{\prod_{i=1}^{k}(1+(\gamma-1)\mu_{\beta_i})-\prod_{i=1}^{k}(1-\mu_{\beta_i})}{\prod_{i=1}^{k}(1+(\gamma-1)\mu_{\beta_i})+(\gamma-1)\prod_{i=1}^{k}(1-\mu_{\beta_i})},\right.$$
$$\left.\frac{\gamma\prod_{i=1}^{k}\nu_{\beta_i}}{\prod_{i=1}^{k}(1+(\gamma-1)(1-\nu_{\beta_i}))+(\gamma-1)\prod_{i=1}^{k}\nu_{\beta_i}}\right) \tag{1.250}$$

Then we prove that Eq. (1.249) holds for $n=k+1$, that is,

$$\left(\mathop{\oplus}\limits_{i=1}^{k}\beta_i\right)\oplus\beta_{k+1}$$
$$=\left(\frac{\left(1+(\gamma-1)\mu_{\mathop{\oplus}\limits_{i=1}^{k}\beta_i}\right)\left(1+(\gamma-1)\mu_{\beta_{k+1}}\right)-\left(1-\mu_{\mathop{\oplus}\limits_{i=1}^{k}\beta_i}\right)\left(1-\mu_{\beta_{k+1}}\right)}{\left(1+(\gamma-1)\mu_{\mathop{\oplus}\limits_{i=1}^{k}\beta_i}\right)\left(1+(\gamma-1)\mu_{\beta_{k+1}}\right)+(\gamma-1)\left(1-\mu_{\mathop{\oplus}\limits_{i=1}^{k}\beta_i}\right)\left(1-\mu_{\beta_{k+1}}\right)},\right.$$
$$\left.\frac{\gamma\nu_{\mathop{\oplus}\limits_{i=1}^{k}\beta_i}\nu_{\beta_{k+1}}}{\left(1+(\gamma-1)\left(1-\nu_{\mathop{\oplus}\limits_{i=1}^{k}\beta_i}\right)\right)\left(1+(\gamma-1)\left(1-\nu_{\beta_{k+1}}\right)\right)+(\gamma-1)\nu_{\mathop{\oplus}\limits_{i=1}^{k}\beta_i}\nu_{\beta_{k+1}}}\right) \tag{1.251}$$

By the operational laws for IFVs, we have

$$\left(1+(\gamma-1)\mu_{\mathop{\oplus}\limits_{i=1}^{k}\beta_i}\right)\left(1+(\gamma-1)\mu_{\beta_{k+1}}\right)$$
$$=\left(1+(\gamma-1)\frac{\prod_{i=1}^{k}(1+(\gamma-1)\mu_{\beta_i})-\prod_{i=1}^{k}(1-\mu_{\beta_i})}{\prod_{i=1}^{k}(1+(\gamma-1)\mu_{\beta_i})+(\gamma-1)\prod_{i=1}^{k}(1-\mu_{\beta_i})}\right)\left(1+(\gamma-1)\mu_{\beta_{k+1}}\right)$$
$$-\left(1-\frac{\prod_{i=1}^{k}(1+(\gamma-1)\mu_{\beta_i})-\prod_{i=1}^{k}(1-\mu_{\beta_i})}{\prod_{i=1}^{k}(1+(\gamma-1)\mu_{\beta_i})+(\gamma-1)\prod_{i=1}^{k}(1-\mu_{\beta_i})}\right)\left(1-\mu_{\beta_{k+1}}\right)$$
$$=\frac{\gamma\prod_{i=1}^{k}(1+(\gamma-1)\mu_{\beta_i})\left(1+(\gamma-1)\mu_{\beta_{k+1}}\right)-\gamma\prod_{i=1}^{k}(1-\mu_{\beta_i})\left(1-\mu_{\beta_{k+1}}\right)}{\prod_{i=1}^{k}(1+(\gamma-1)\mu_{\beta_i})+(\gamma-1)\prod_{i=1}^{k}(1-\mu_{\beta_i})}$$
$$=\frac{\gamma\prod_{i=1}^{k+1}(1+(\gamma-1)\mu_{\beta_i})-\gamma\prod_{i=1}^{k+1}(1-\mu_{\beta_i})}{\prod_{i=1}^{k}(1+(\gamma-1)\mu_{\beta_i})+(\gamma-1)\prod_{i=1}^{k}(1-\mu_{\beta_i})} \tag{1.252}$$

$$\left(1-\mu_{\overset{k}{\underset{i=1}{\oplus}}\beta_i}\right)\left(1-\mu_{\beta_{k+1}}\right)$$
$$=\left(1-\frac{\prod_{i=1}^{k}(1+(\gamma-1)\mu_{\beta_i})-\prod_{i=1}^{k}(1-\mu_{\beta_i})}{\prod_{i=1}^{k}(1+(\gamma-1)\mu_{\beta_i})+(\gamma-1)\prod_{i=1}^{k}(1-\mu_{\beta_i})}\right)\left(1-\mu_{\beta_{k+1}}\right)$$
$$=\frac{\gamma\prod_{i=1}^{k}(1-\mu_{\beta_i})\left(1-\mu_{\beta_{k+1}}\right)}{\prod_{i=1}^{k}(1+(\gamma-1)\mu_{\beta_i})+(\gamma-1)\prod_{i=1}^{k}(1-\mu_{\beta_i})}$$
$$=\frac{\gamma\prod_{i=1}^{k+1}(1-\mu_{\beta_i})}{\prod_{i=1}^{k}(1+(\gamma-1)\mu_{\beta_i})+(\gamma-1)\prod_{i=1}^{k}(1-\mu_{\beta_i})} \tag{1.253}$$

$$v_{\overset{k}{\underset{i=1}{\oplus}}\beta_i}v_{\beta_{k+1}}=\frac{\gamma\prod_{i=1}^{k}v_{\beta_i}}{\prod_{i=1}^{k}(1+(\gamma-1)(1-v_{\beta_i}))+(\gamma-1)\prod_{i=1}^{k}v_{\beta_i}}v_{\beta_{k+1}}$$
$$=\frac{\gamma\prod_{i=1}^{k+1}v_{\beta_i}}{\prod_{i=1}^{k}(1+(\gamma-1)(1-v_{\beta_i}))+(\gamma-1)\prod_{i=1}^{k}v_{\beta_i}} \tag{1.254}$$

and

$$\left(1+(\gamma-1)\left(1-v_{\overset{k}{\underset{i=1}{\oplus}}\beta_i}\right)\right)\left(1+(\gamma-1)\left(1-v_{\beta_{k+1}}\right)\right)$$
$$=\frac{\gamma\prod_{i=1}^{k}(1+(\gamma-1)(1-v_{\beta_i}))\left(1+(\gamma-1)\left(1-v_{\beta_{k+1}}\right)\right)}{\prod_{i=1}^{k}(1+(\gamma-1)(1-v_{\beta_i}))+(\gamma-1)\prod_{i=1}^{k}v_{\beta_i}}$$
$$=\frac{\gamma\prod_{i=1}^{k+1}(1+(\gamma-1)(1-v_{\beta_i}))}{\prod_{i=1}^{k}(1+(\gamma-1)(1-v_{\beta_i}))+(\gamma-1)\prod_{i=1}^{k}v_{\beta_i}} \tag{1.255}$$

Therefore,

$$\left(\overset{k}{\underset{i=1}{\oplus}}\beta_i\right)\oplus\beta_{k+1}$$
$$=\left(\frac{\left(1+(\gamma-1)\mu_{\overset{k}{\underset{i=1}{\oplus}}\beta_i}\right)\left(1+(\gamma-1)\mu_{\beta_{k+1}}\right)-\left(1-\mu_{\overset{k}{\underset{i=1}{\oplus}}\beta_i}\right)\left(1-\mu_{\beta_{k+1}}\right)}{\left(1+(\gamma-1)\mu_{\overset{k}{\underset{i=1}{\oplus}}\beta_i}\right)\left(1+(\gamma-1)\mu_{\beta_{k+1}}\right)+(\gamma-1)\left(1-\mu_{\overset{k}{\underset{i=1}{\oplus}}\beta_i}\right)\left(1-\mu_{\beta_{k+1}}\right)},\right.$$
$$\left.\frac{\gamma v_{\overset{k}{\underset{i=1}{\oplus}}\beta_i}v_{\beta_{k+1}}}{\left(1+(\gamma-1)\left(1-v_{\overset{k}{\underset{i=1}{\oplus}}\beta_i}\right)\right)\left(1+(\gamma-1)\left(1-v_{\beta_{k+1}}\right)\right)+(\gamma-1)v_{\overset{k}{\underset{i=1}{\oplus}}\beta_i}v_{\beta_{k+1}}}\right)$$

$$= \left(\frac{\gamma \prod_{i=1}^{k} (1+(\gamma-1)\mu_{\beta_i})(1+(\gamma-1)\mu_{\beta_{k+1}}) - \gamma \prod_{i=1}^{k} (1-\mu_{\beta_i})(1-\mu_{\beta_{k+1}})}{\gamma \prod_{i=1}^{k} (1+(\gamma-1)\mu_{\beta_i})(1+(\gamma-1)\mu_{\beta_{k+1}})(1+(\gamma-1)\mu_{\beta_{k+1}}) + (\gamma-1)\gamma \prod_{i=1}^{k} (1-\mu_{\beta_i})(1-\mu_{\beta_{k+1}})}, \right.$$

$$\left. \frac{\gamma^2 \prod_{i=1}^{k} \nu_{\beta_i} \nu_{\beta_{k+1}}}{\gamma \prod_{i=1}^{k} (1 + (\gamma-1)(1-\nu_{\beta_i}))\left(1 + (\gamma-1)\left(1-\nu_{\beta_{k+1}}\right)\right) + \gamma(\gamma-1)\prod_{i=1}^{k} \nu_{\beta_i}\nu_{\beta_{k+1}}} \right)$$

$$= \left(\frac{\prod_{i=1}^{k+1} (1+(\gamma-1)\mu_{\beta_i}) - \prod_{i=1}^{k+1} (1-\mu_{\beta_i})}{\prod_{i=1}^{k+1} (1+(\gamma-1)\mu_{\beta_i}) + (\gamma-1)\prod_{i=1}^{k+1} (1-\mu_{\beta_i})}, \frac{\gamma \prod_{i=1}^{k+1} \nu_{\beta_i}}{\prod_{i=1}^{k+1} (1+(\gamma-1)(1-\nu_{\beta_i})) + (\gamma-1)\prod_{i=1}^{k+1} \nu_{\beta_i}} \right) \quad (1.256)$$

which indicates that Eq. (1.251) holds for $n = k + 1$. Thus Eq. (1.249) holds for all n. Since

$$\beta_i = (\mu_{\beta_i}, \nu_{\beta_i}) = w_i \alpha_i^\lambda$$

$$= \left(\frac{\left(1+(\gamma-1)\frac{\gamma\mu_\alpha^\lambda}{(1+(\gamma-1)(1-\mu_\alpha))^\lambda+(\gamma-1)\mu_\alpha^\lambda}\right)^{w_i} - \left(1-\frac{\gamma\mu_\alpha^\lambda}{(1+(\gamma-1)(1-\mu_\alpha))^\lambda+(\gamma-1)\mu_\alpha^\lambda}\right)^{w_i}}{\left(1+(\gamma-1)\frac{\gamma\mu_\alpha^\lambda}{(1+(\gamma-1)(1-\mu_\alpha))^\lambda+(\gamma-1)\mu_\alpha^\lambda}\right)^{w_i} + (\gamma-1)\left(1-\frac{\gamma\mu_\alpha^\lambda}{(1+(\gamma-1)(1-\mu_\alpha))^\lambda+(\gamma-1)\mu_\alpha^\lambda}\right)^{w_i}}, \right.$$

$$\left. \frac{\gamma\left(\frac{(1+(\gamma-1)\nu_\alpha)^\lambda-(1-\nu_\alpha)^\lambda}{(1+(\gamma-1)\nu_\alpha)^\lambda+(\gamma-1)(1-\nu_\alpha)^\lambda}\right)^{w_i}}{\left(1+(\gamma-1)\left(1-\frac{(1+(\gamma-1)\nu_\alpha)^\lambda-(1-\nu_\alpha)^\lambda}{(1+(\gamma-1)\nu_\alpha)^\lambda+(\gamma-1)(1-\nu_\alpha)^\lambda}\right)\right)^{w_i} + (\gamma-1)\left(\frac{(1+(\gamma-1)\nu_\alpha)^\lambda-(1-\nu_\alpha)^\lambda}{(1+(\gamma-1)\nu_\alpha)^\lambda+(\gamma-1)(1-\nu_\alpha)^\lambda}\right)^{w_i}} \right)$$

$$= \left(\frac{\left((1+(\gamma-1)(1-\mu_\alpha))^\lambda+(\gamma^2-1)\mu_\alpha^\lambda\right)^{w_i} - \left((1+(\gamma-1)(1-\mu_\alpha))^\lambda-\mu_\alpha^\lambda\right)^{w_i}}{\left((1+(\gamma-1)(1-\mu_\alpha))^\lambda+(\gamma^2-1)\mu_\alpha^\lambda\right)^{w_i} + (\gamma-1)\left((1+(\gamma-1)(1-\mu_\alpha))^\lambda-\mu_\alpha^\lambda\right)^{w_i}}, \right.$$

$$\left. \frac{\gamma\left((1+(\gamma-1)\nu_\alpha)^\lambda-(1-\nu_\alpha)^\lambda\right)^{w_i}}{\left((1+(\gamma-1)\nu_\alpha)^\lambda+(\gamma^2-1)(1-\nu_\alpha)^\lambda\right)^{w_i} + (\gamma-1)\left((1+(\gamma-1)\nu_\alpha)^\lambda-(1-\nu_\alpha)^\lambda\right)^{w_i}} \right) \quad (1.257)$$

then we have

$$\prod_{i=1}^{n} (1+(\gamma-1)\mu_{\beta_i}) - \prod_{i=1}^{n} (1-\mu_{\beta_i})$$

$$= \prod_{i=1}^{n} \left(1+(\gamma-1)\frac{\left((1+(\gamma-1)(1-\mu_{\alpha_i}))^\lambda+(\gamma^2-1)\mu_{\alpha_i}^\lambda\right)^{w_i} - \left((1+(\gamma-1)(1-\mu_{\alpha_i}))^\lambda-\mu_{\alpha_i}^\lambda\right)^{w_i}}{\left((1+(\gamma-1)(1-\mu_{\alpha_i}))^\lambda+(\gamma^2-1)\mu_{\alpha_i}^\lambda\right)^{w_i} + (\gamma-1)\left((1+(\gamma-1)(1-\mu_{\alpha_i}))^\lambda-\mu_{\alpha_i}^\lambda\right)^{w_i}} \right)$$

$$- \prod_{i=1}^{n} \left(1-\frac{\left((1+(\gamma-1)(1-\mu_{\alpha_i}))^\lambda+(\gamma^2-1)\mu_{\alpha_i}^\lambda\right)^{w_i} - \left((1+(\gamma-1)(1-\mu_{\alpha_i}))^\lambda-\mu_{\alpha_i}^\lambda\right)^{w_i}}{\left((1+(\gamma-1)(1-\mu_{\alpha_i}))^\lambda+(\gamma^2-1)\mu_{\alpha_i}^\lambda\right)^{w_i} + (\gamma-1)\left((1+(\gamma-1)(1-\mu_{\alpha_i}))^\lambda-\mu_{\alpha_i}^\lambda\right)^{w_i}} \right)$$

$$= \frac{\gamma \prod_{i=1}^{n} \left((1+(\gamma-1)(1-\mu_{\alpha_i}))^\lambda+(\gamma^2-1)\mu_{\alpha_i}^\lambda\right)^{w_i} - \gamma \prod_{i=1}^{n} \left((1+(\gamma-1)(1-\mu_{\alpha_i}))^\lambda-\mu_{\alpha_i}^\lambda\right)^{w_i}}{\prod_{i=1}^{n} \left(\left((1+(\gamma-1)(1-\mu_{\alpha_i}))^\lambda+(\gamma^2-1)\mu_{\alpha_i}^\lambda\right)^{w_i} + (\gamma-1)\left((1+(\gamma-1)(1-\mu_{\alpha_i}))^\lambda-\mu_{\alpha_i}^\lambda\right)^{w_i}\right)} \quad (1.258)$$

$$\prod_{i=1}^{k} (1+(\gamma-1)\mu_{\beta_i}) + (\gamma-1)\prod_{i=1}^{k} (1-\mu_{\beta_i})$$

$$= \prod_{i=1}^{n} \left(1+(\gamma-1)\frac{\left((1+(\gamma-1)(1-\mu_{\alpha_i}))^\lambda+(\gamma^2-1)\mu_{\alpha_i}^\lambda\right)^{w_i} - \left((1+(\gamma-1)(1-\mu_{\alpha_i}))^\lambda-\mu_{\alpha_i}^\lambda\right)^{w_i}}{\left((1+(\gamma-1)(1-\mu_{\alpha_i}))^\lambda+(\gamma^2-1)\mu_{\alpha_i}^\lambda\right)^{w_i} + (\gamma-1)\left((1+(\gamma-1)(1-\mu_{\alpha_i}))^\lambda-\mu_{\alpha_i}^\lambda\right)^{w_i}} \right)$$

$$+(\gamma-1)\prod_{i=1}^{n}\left(1-\frac{\left((1+(\gamma-1)(1-\mu_{\alpha_i}))^{\lambda}+(\gamma^2-1)\mu_{\alpha_i}^{\lambda}\right)^{w_i}-\left((1+(\gamma-1)(1-\mu_{\alpha_i}))^{\lambda}-\mu_{\alpha_i}^{\lambda}\right)^{w_i}}{\left((1+(\gamma-1)(1-\mu_{\alpha_i}))^{\lambda}+(\gamma^2-1)\mu_{\alpha_i}^{\lambda}\right)^{w_i}+(\gamma-1)\left((1+(\gamma-1)(1-\mu_{\alpha_i}))^{\lambda}-\mu_{\alpha_i}^{\lambda}\right)^{w_i}}\right)$$

$$=\frac{\gamma\prod_{i=1}^{n}\left((1+(\gamma-1)(1-\mu_{\alpha_i}))^{\lambda}+(\gamma^2-1)\mu_{\alpha_i}^{\lambda}\right)^{w_i}+\gamma(\gamma-1)\prod_{i=1}^{n}\left((1+(\gamma-1)(1-\mu_{\alpha_i}))^{\lambda}-\mu_{\alpha_i}^{\lambda}\right)^{w_i}}{\prod_{i=1}^{n}\left(\left((1+(\gamma-1)(1-\mu_{\alpha_i}))^{\lambda}+(\gamma^2-1)\mu_{\alpha_i}^{\lambda}\right)^{w_i}+(\gamma-1)\left((1+(\gamma-1)(1-\mu_{\alpha_i}))^{\lambda}-\mu_{\alpha_i}^{\lambda}\right)^{w_i}\right)} \tag{1.259}$$

$$\gamma\prod_{i=1}^{n}v_{\beta_i}$$

$$=\frac{\gamma^2\prod_{i=1}^{n}\left((1+(\gamma-1)v_{\alpha_i})^{\lambda}-(1-v_{\alpha_i})^{\lambda}\right)^{w_i}}{\prod_{i=1}^{n}\left(\left((1+(\gamma-1)v_{\alpha_i})^{\lambda}+(\gamma^2-1)(1-v_{\alpha_i})^{\lambda}\right)^{w_i}+(\gamma-1)\left((1+(\gamma-1)v_{\alpha_i})^{\lambda}-(1-v_{\alpha_i})^{\lambda}\right)^{w_i}\right)} \tag{1.260}$$

and

$$\prod_{i=1}^{k}(1+(\gamma-1)(1-v_{\beta_i}))+(\gamma-1)\prod_{i=1}^{k}v_{\beta_i}$$

$$=\prod_{i=1}^{k}\left(1+(\gamma-1)\left(1-\frac{\gamma\left((1+(\gamma-1)v_{\alpha_i})^{\lambda}-(1-v_{\alpha_i})^{\lambda}\right)^{w_i}}{\left((1+(\gamma-1)v_{\alpha_i})^{\lambda}+(\gamma^2-1)(1-v_{\alpha_i})^{\lambda}\right)^{w_i}+(\gamma-1)\left((1+(\gamma-1)v_{\alpha_i})^{\lambda}-(1-v_{\alpha_i})^{\lambda}\right)^{w_i}}\right)\right)$$

$$+(\gamma-1)\prod_{i=1}^{k}\frac{\gamma\left((1+(\gamma-1)v_{\alpha_i})^{\lambda}-(1-v_{\alpha_i})^{\lambda}\right)^{w_i}}{\left((1+(\gamma-1)v_{\alpha_i})^{\lambda}+(\gamma^2-1)(1-v_{\alpha_i})^{\lambda}\right)^{w_i}+(\gamma-1)\left((1+(\gamma-1)v_{\alpha_i})^{\lambda}-(1-v_{\alpha_i})^{\lambda}\right)^{w_i}}$$

$$=\frac{\gamma\prod_{i=1}^{n}\left((1+(\gamma-1)v_{\alpha_i})^{\lambda}+(\gamma^2-1)(1-v_{\alpha_i})^{\lambda}\right)^{w_i}+\gamma(\gamma-1)\prod_{i=1}^{n}\left((1+(\gamma-1)v_{\alpha_i})^{\lambda}-(1-v_{\alpha_i})^{\lambda}\right)^{w_i}}{\prod_{i=1}^{n}\left(\left((1+(\gamma-1)v_{\alpha_i})^{\lambda}+(\gamma^2-1)(1-v_{\alpha_i})^{\lambda}\right)^{w_i}+(\gamma-1)\left((1+(\gamma-1)v_{\alpha_i})^{\lambda}-(1-v_{\alpha_i})^{\lambda}\right)^{w_i}\right)} \tag{1.261}$$

Thus,

$$\mathop{\oplus}_{i=1}^{n}\beta_i=\left(\frac{\prod_{i=1}^{n}\left((1+(\gamma-1)(1-\mu_{\alpha_i}))^{\lambda}+(\gamma^2-1)\mu_{\alpha_i}^{\lambda}\right)^{w_i}-\prod_{i=1}^{n}\left((1+(\gamma-1)(1-\mu_{\alpha_i}))^{\lambda}-\mu_{\alpha_i}^{\lambda}\right)^{w_i}}{\prod_{i=1}^{n}\left((1+(\gamma-1)(1-\mu_{\alpha_i}))^{\lambda}+(\gamma^2-1)\mu_{\alpha_i}^{\lambda}\right)^{w_i}+(\gamma-1)\prod_{i=1}^{n}\left((1+(\gamma-1)(1-\mu_{\alpha_i}))^{\lambda}-\mu_{\alpha_i}^{\lambda}\right)^{w_i}},\right.$$
$$\left.\frac{\gamma\prod_{i=1}^{n}\left((1+(\gamma-1)v_{\alpha_i})^{\lambda}-(1-v_{\alpha_i})^{\lambda}\right)^{w_i}}{\prod_{i=1}^{n}\left((1+(\gamma-1)v_{\alpha_i})^{\lambda}+(\gamma^2-1)(1-v_{\alpha_i})^{\lambda}\right)^{w_i}+(\gamma-1)\prod_{i=1}^{n}\left((1+(\gamma-1)v_{\alpha_i})^{\lambda}-(1-v_{\alpha_i})^{\lambda}\right)^{w_i}}\right) \tag{1.262}$$

Let

$$\mu_{1,n}^{l}=\prod_{i=1}^{n}\left((1+(\gamma-1)(1-\mu_{\alpha_i}))^{\lambda}+(\gamma^2-1)\mu_{\alpha_i}^{\lambda}\right)^{w_i} \tag{1.263}$$

$$\mu_{1,n}^{r}=\prod_{i=1}^{n}\left((1+(\gamma-1)(1-\mu_{\alpha_i}))^{\lambda}-\mu_{\alpha_i}^{\lambda}\right)^{w_i} \tag{1.264}$$

$$v_{1,n}^{l} = \prod_{i=1}^{n} \left((1 + (\gamma - 1)(1 - v_{\alpha_i}))^{\lambda} + (\gamma^2 - 1) v_{\alpha_i}^{\lambda} \right)^{w_i} \tag{1.265}$$

$$v_{1,n}^{r} = \prod_{i=1}^{n} \left((1 + (\gamma - 1)(1 - v_{\alpha_i}))^{\lambda} - v_{\alpha_i}^{\lambda} \right)^{w_i} \tag{1.266}$$

then

$$\overset{k}{\underset{i=1}{\oplus}} \beta_i = \left(\frac{\mu_{1,n}^{l} - \mu_{1,n}^{r}}{\mu_{1,n}^{l} + (\gamma - 1)\mu_{1,n}^{r}}, \frac{\gamma v_{1,n}^{r}}{v_{1,n}^{l} + (\gamma - 1) v_{1,n}^{r}} \right) \tag{1.267}$$

and

$$\begin{aligned}
&\left(\overset{k}{\underset{i=1}{\oplus}} \beta_i \right)^{\frac{1}{\lambda}} \\
&= \left(\frac{\gamma \left(\frac{\mu_{1,n}^{l} - \mu_{1,n}^{r}}{\mu_{1,n}^{l} + (\gamma-1)\mu_{1,n}^{r}} \right)^{\frac{1}{\lambda}}}{\left(1 + (\gamma - 1)\left(1 - \frac{\mu_{1,n}^{l} - \mu_{1,n}^{r}}{\mu_{1,n}^{l} + (\gamma-1)\mu_{1,n}^{r}} \right) \right)^{\frac{1}{\lambda}} + (\gamma - 1)\left(\frac{\mu_{1,n}^{l} - \mu_{1,n}^{r}}{\mu_{1,n}^{l} + (\gamma-1)\mu_{1,n}^{r}} \right)^{\frac{1}{\lambda}}}, \right. \\
&\qquad \left. \frac{\left(1 + (\gamma - 1)\frac{\gamma v_{1,n}^{r}}{v_{1,n}^{l} + (\gamma-1) v_{1,n}^{r}} \right)^{\frac{1}{\lambda}} - \left(1 - \frac{\gamma v_{1,n}^{r}}{v_{1,n}^{l} + (\gamma-1) v_{1,n}^{r}} \right)^{\frac{1}{\lambda}}}{\left(1 + (\gamma - 1)\frac{\gamma v_{1,n}^{r}}{v_{1,n}^{l} + (\gamma-1) v_{1,n}^{r}} \right)^{\frac{1}{\lambda}} + (\gamma - 1)\left(1 - \frac{\gamma v_{1,n}^{r}}{v_{1,n}^{l} + (\gamma-1) v_{1,n}^{r}} \right)^{\frac{1}{\lambda}}} \right) \\
&= \left(\frac{\gamma \left(\mu_{1,n}^{l} - \mu_{1,n}^{r} \right)^{\frac{1}{\lambda}}}{\left(\mu_{1,n}^{l} + (\gamma^2 - 1)\mu_{1,n}^{r} \right)^{\frac{1}{\lambda}} + (\gamma - 1)\left(\mu_{1,n}^{l} - \mu_{1,n}^{r} \right)^{\frac{1}{\lambda}}}, \right. \\
&\qquad \left. \frac{\left(v_{1,n}^{l} + (\gamma^2 - 1) v_{1,n}^{r} \right)^{\frac{1}{\lambda}} - \left(v_{1,n}^{l} - v_{1,n}^{l} \right)^{\frac{1}{\lambda}}}{\left(v_{1,n}^{l} + (\gamma^2 - 1) v_{1,n}^{l} \right)^{\frac{1}{\lambda}} + (\gamma - 1)\left(v_{1,n}^{l} - v_{1,n}^{l} \right)^{\frac{1}{\lambda}}} \right)
\end{aligned} \tag{1.268}$$

which completes the proof.

Then in what follows, we introduce some desirable properties of the GHIFWA operator (Xia and Xu 2011):

Theorem 1.39 If all α_i $(i = 1, 2, \ldots, n)$ are equal, i.e., $\alpha_i = \alpha = (\mu_\alpha, v_\alpha)$, for all i, then

$$GHIFWA(\alpha_1, \alpha_2, \ldots, \alpha_n) = GHIFWA(\alpha, \alpha, \ldots, \alpha) = \left(\mathop{\oplus}_{i=1}^{n} w_i \alpha^\lambda \right)^{\frac{1}{\lambda}} = \alpha \tag{1.269}$$

which is called of idempotency.

Theorem 1.40 Let $\beta_i = (\mu_{\beta_i}, v_{\beta_i})$ $(i = 1, 2, \ldots, n)$ be a collection of IFVs, if $\mu_{\alpha_i} \leq \mu_{\beta_i}$ and $v_{\alpha_i} \geq v_{\beta_i}$, for all i, then

$$GHIFWA(\alpha_1, \alpha_2, \ldots, \alpha_n) \leq GHIFWA(\beta_1, \beta_2, \ldots, \beta_n) \tag{1.270}$$

which is called of monotonicity.

Proof Let $f(x, y) = \frac{x+y-xy-(1-\gamma)xy}{1-(1-\gamma)xy}$, then

$$\begin{aligned} f(x, y)'_x &= \frac{(1-(2-\gamma)y)(1-(1-\gamma)xy)+(x+y-(2-\gamma)xy)(1-\gamma)y}{(1-(1-\gamma)xy)^2} \\ &= \frac{1-(2-\gamma)y-(1-\gamma)xy+(2-\gamma)(1-\gamma)xy^2+(1-\gamma)xy+(1-\gamma)y^2-(2-\gamma)(1-\gamma)xy^2}{(1-(1-\gamma)xy)^2} \\ &= \frac{1-(2-\gamma)y+(1-\gamma)y^2}{(1-(1-\gamma)xy)^2} = \frac{((1-\gamma)y-1)(y-1)}{(1-(1-\gamma)xy)^2} \end{aligned} \tag{1.271}$$

Since $0 < x, y < 1$ and $\gamma > 0$, then $f(x, y)'_x = \frac{((1-\gamma)y-1)(y-1)}{(1-(1-\gamma)xy)^2} > 0$, which indicates that $f(x, y)$ is an increasing function of x. Similarly, we can prove that $f(x, y)$ is also an increasing function of y.

Let $g(x, y) = \frac{xy}{\gamma+(1-\gamma)(x+y-xy)}$, then

$$\begin{aligned} g(x, y)'_x &= \frac{y(\gamma + (1-\gamma)(x+y-xy)) - xy(\gamma + (1-\gamma)(1-y))}{\gamma + (1-\gamma)(x+y-xy)} \\ &= \frac{\gamma y + (1-\gamma)xy + (1-\gamma)y^2 - (1-\gamma)xy^2 - (1-\gamma)xy + (1-\gamma)xy^2}{\gamma + (1-\gamma)(x+y-xy)} \\ &= \frac{\gamma y + (1-\gamma)y^2}{\gamma + (1-\gamma)(x+y-xy)} = \frac{y(\gamma(1-y) + y)}{\gamma + (1-\gamma)(x+y-xy)} > 0 \end{aligned} \tag{1.272}$$

which indicates that $g(x, y)$ is an increasing function of x. Similarly, we can prove that $g(x, y)$ is also an increasing function of y.

Let $h(x) = \frac{(1+(\gamma-1)x)^\lambda-(1-x)^\lambda}{(1+(\gamma-1)x)^\lambda+(\gamma-1)(1-x)^\lambda}$ and $r(x) = \frac{\gamma x^\lambda}{(1+(\gamma-1)x)^\lambda+(\gamma-1)x^\lambda}$,

then

$$h(x)' = \frac{\left(\lambda(\gamma-1)(1+(\gamma-1)x)^{\lambda-1}+\lambda(1-x)^{\lambda-1}\right)\left((1+(\gamma-1)x)^{\lambda}-(\gamma-1)(1-x)^{\lambda}\right)}{\left((1+(\gamma-1)x)^{\lambda}+(\gamma-1)(1-x)^{\lambda}\right)^2}$$
$$-\frac{\left((1+(\gamma-1)x)^{\lambda}-(1-x)^{\lambda}\right)\left(\lambda(\gamma-1)(1+(\gamma-1)x)^{\lambda-1}-\lambda(\gamma-1)(1-x)^{\lambda-1}\right)}{\left((1+(\gamma-1)x)^{\lambda}+(\gamma-1)(1-x)^{\lambda}\right)^2}$$
$$=\frac{\lambda(1-x)^{\lambda-1}(1+(\gamma-1)x)^{\lambda}+\lambda(\gamma-1)^2(1-x)^{\lambda}(1+(\gamma-1)x)^{\lambda-1}}{\left((1+(\gamma-1)x)^{\lambda}+(\gamma-1)(1-x)^{\lambda}\right)^2}$$
$$+\frac{\lambda(\gamma-1)(1-x)^{\lambda}(1+(\gamma-1)x)^{\lambda-1}+\lambda(\gamma-1)(1-x)^{\lambda-1}(1+(\gamma-1)x)^{\lambda}}{\left((1+(\gamma-1)x)^{\lambda}+(\gamma-1)(1-x)^{\lambda}\right)^2}$$
$$=\frac{\lambda\gamma^2(1-x)^{\lambda-1}(1+(\gamma-1)x)^{\lambda-1}}{\left((1+(\gamma-1)x)^{\lambda}-(\gamma-1)(1-x)^{\lambda}\right)^2} > 0 \tag{1.273}$$

and

$$r(x)'$$
$$=\frac{\lambda\gamma x^{\lambda-1}\left((1+(\gamma-1)x)^{\lambda}+(\gamma-1)x^{\lambda}\right)-\gamma x^{\lambda}\left(\lambda(\gamma-1)(1+(\gamma-1)x)^{\lambda-1}-\lambda(\gamma-1)x^{\lambda-1}\right)}{\left((1+(\gamma-1)x)^{\lambda}+(\gamma-1)x^{\lambda}\right)^2}$$
$$=\frac{\lambda\gamma^2 x^{\lambda-1}(1+(\gamma-1)x)^{\lambda-1}}{\left((1+(\gamma-1)x)^{\lambda}+(\gamma-1)x^{\lambda}\right)^2} > 0 \tag{1.274}$$

Therefore, both $h(x)$ and $r(x)$ are the increasing functions of x.

Based on the above analysis, for two collections of IFVs $\alpha_i = (\mu_{\alpha_i}, v_{\alpha_i})$ $(i = 1, 2, \ldots, n)$ and $\beta_i = (\mu_{\beta_i}, v_{\beta_i})$ $(i = 1, 2, \ldots, n)$, if $\mu_{\alpha_i} \leq \mu_{\beta_i}$ and $v_{\alpha_i} \geq v_{\beta_i}$, for all i, we have

$$S(GHIFWA(\alpha_1, \alpha_2, \ldots, \alpha_n)) \leq S(GHIFWA(\beta_1, \beta_2, \ldots, \beta_n)) \tag{1.275}$$

which completes the proof.

Based on the monotonicity, the following property can be obtained:

Theorem 1.41 (Xia and Xu 2011) Let α^- and α^+ be given by Eqs. (1.35) and (1.36), then

$$\alpha^- \leq GHIFWA(\alpha_1, \alpha_2, \ldots, \alpha_n) \leq \alpha^+ \tag{1.276}$$

which is called of boundedness.

As the values of the parameters change, some special cases can be obtained (Xia and Xu 2011):

Case 1 If $\lambda = 1$, then Eq. (1.243) is transformed as:

$$HIFWA(\alpha_1, \alpha_2, \ldots, \alpha_n) = \left(\frac{\prod_{i=1}^{n}(1+(\gamma-1)\mu_{\alpha_i})^{w_i} - \prod_{i=1}^{n}(1-\mu_{\alpha_i})^{w_i}}{\prod_{i=1}^{n}(1+(\gamma-1)\mu_{\alpha_i})^{w_i} + (\gamma-1)\prod_{i=1}^{n}(1-\mu_{\alpha_i})^{w_i}}, \frac{\gamma\prod_{i=1}^{n} v_{\alpha_i}^{w_i}}{\prod_{i=1}^{n}(1+(\gamma-1)(1-v_{\alpha_i}))^{w_i} + (\gamma-1)\prod_{i=1}^{n} v_{\alpha_i}^{w_i}}\right) \tag{1.277}$$

which is the Hamacher intuitionistic fuzzy averaging (HIFWA) operator (Xia et al. 2012c).

Case 2 If $\lambda = 1$ and $\gamma = 1$, then Eq. (1.243) becomes the IFWA operator (Xu 2007):

$$IFWA(\alpha_1, \alpha_2, \ldots, \alpha_n) = \left(1 - \prod_{i=1}^{n}((1-\mu_{\alpha_i})^{w_i}, \prod_{i=1}^{n} v_{\alpha_i}^{w_i}\right) \tag{1.278}$$

Case 3 If $\gamma = 1$, then Eq. (1.243) becomes the generalized intuitionistic fuzzy weighted averaging (GIFWA) operator (Zhao et al. 2010):

$$GIFWA(\alpha_1, \alpha_2, \ldots, \alpha_n) = \left(\left(1 - \prod_{i=1}^{n}((1-\mu_{\alpha_i}^{\lambda})^{w_i}\right)^{\frac{1}{\lambda}}, 1 - \left(1 - \prod_{i=1}^{n}((1-(1-v_{\alpha_i})^{\lambda})^{w_i}\right)^{\frac{1}{\lambda}}\right) \tag{1.279}$$

Case 4 If $\gamma = 2$, then Eq. (1.243) is written as:

$$GEIFWA(\alpha_1, \alpha_2, \ldots, \alpha_n) = \left(\frac{2\left(\mu_{1,n}^{l} - \mu_{1,n}^{r}\right)^{\frac{1}{\lambda}}}{\left(\mu_{1,n}^{l} + 3\mu_{1,n}^{r}\right)^{\frac{1}{\lambda}} + \left(\mu_{1,n}^{l} - \mu_{1,n}^{r}\right)^{\frac{1}{\lambda}}}, \frac{\left(v_{1,n}^{l} + 3v_{1,n}^{r}\right)^{\frac{1}{\lambda}} - \left(v_{1,n}^{l} - v_{1,n}^{r}\right)^{\frac{1}{\lambda}}}{\left(v_{1,n}^{l} + 3v_{1,n}^{l}\right)^{\frac{1}{\lambda}} + \left(v_{1,n}^{l} - v_{1,n}^{r}\right)^{\frac{1}{\lambda}}}\right) \tag{1.280}$$

where

$$\mu_{1,n}^{l} = \prod_{i=1}^{n}((1+(1-\mu_{\alpha_i}))^{\lambda} + 3\mu_{\alpha_i}^{\lambda})^{w_i}, \mu_{1,n}^{r} = \prod_{i=1}^{n}((1+(1-\mu_{\alpha_i}))^{\lambda} - \mu_{\alpha_i}^{\lambda})^{w_i} \tag{1.281}$$

$$v_{1,n}^{l} = \prod_{i=1}^{n}((1+(1-v_{\alpha_i}))^{\lambda} + 3v_{\alpha_i}^{\lambda})^{w_i}, \quad v_{1,n}^{r} = \prod_{i=1}^{n}((1+(1-v_{\alpha_i}))^{\lambda} - v_{\alpha_i}^{\lambda})^{w_i} \tag{1.282}$$

which is called a generalized Einstein intuitionistic fuzzy weighted averaging (GEIFWA) operator.

Case 5 If $\gamma = 2$ and $\lambda = 1$, then Eq. (1.243) is transformed as:

$$EIFWA(\alpha_1, \alpha_2, \ldots, \alpha_n) = \left(\frac{\prod_{i=1}^{n} (1+\mu_{\alpha_i})^{w_i} - \prod_{i=1}^{n} (1-\mu_{\alpha_i})^{w_i}}{\prod_{i=1}^{n} (1+\mu_{\alpha_i})^{w_i} + \prod_{i=1}^{n} (1-\mu_{\alpha_i})^{w_i}}, \frac{2\prod_{i=1}^{n} v_{\alpha_i}^{w_i}}{\prod_{i=1}^{n} (2-v_{\alpha_i}))^{w_i} + \prod_{i=1}^{n} v_{\alpha_i}^{w_i}} \right) \tag{1.283}$$

which is the EIFWA operator (Xia et al. 2012c).

Combining the GHIFWA operator and the geometric mean, then we introduce the following:

Definition 1.25 (Xia and Xu 2011) Let $w = (w_1, w_2, \ldots, w_n)^T$ be the weight vector of the IFVs α_i $(i = 1, 2, \ldots, n)$, where w_i indicates the importance degree of α_i, satisfying $w_i > 0$ $(i = 1, 2, \ldots, n)$ and $\sum_{i=1}^{n} w_i = 1$, if

$$GAIFWG(\alpha_1, \alpha_2, \ldots, \alpha_n) = \frac{1}{\lambda} \left(\bigotimes_{i=1}^{n} \lambda \alpha_i^{w_i} \right) \tag{1.284}$$

then $GAIFWG$ is called a generalized Archimedean intuitionistic fuzzy geometric (GHIFWG) operator.

Similarly, the following theorem can be obtained:

Theorem 1.42 (Xia and Xu 2011) The aggregated value by using the GHIFWG operator is also an IFV, and

$$GHIFWG(\alpha_1, \alpha_2, \ldots, \alpha_n) = \left(\frac{\left(\mu_{1,n}^{l} + (\gamma^2-1)\mu_{1,n}^{r}\right)^{\frac{1}{\lambda}} - \left(\mu_{1,n}^{l} - \mu_{1,n}^{l}\right)^{\frac{1}{\lambda}}}{\left(\mu_{1,n}^{l} + (\gamma^2-1)\mu_{1,n}^{l}\right)^{\frac{1}{\lambda}} + (\gamma-1)\left(\mu_{1,n}^{l} - \mu_{1,n}^{l}\right)^{\frac{1}{\lambda}}}, \frac{\gamma\left(v_{1,n}^{l} - v_{1,n}^{r}\right)^{\frac{1}{\lambda}}}{\left(v_{1,n}^{l} + (\gamma^2-1)v_{1,n}^{r}\right)^{\frac{1}{\lambda}} + (\gamma-1)\left(v_{1,n}^{l} - v_{1,n}^{r}\right)^{\frac{1}{\lambda}}} \right) \tag{1.285}$$

where

$$\mu_{1,n}^{l} = \prod_{i=1}^{n} \left((1 + (\gamma-1)(1-\mu_{\alpha_i}))^{\lambda} + (\gamma^2-1)\mu_{\alpha_i}^{\lambda} \right)^{w_i} \tag{1.286}$$

$$\mu_{1,n}^{r} = \prod_{i=1}^{n} \left((1 + (\gamma-1)(1-\mu_{\alpha_i}))^{\lambda} - \mu_{\alpha_i}^{\lambda} \right)^{w_i} \tag{1.287}$$

$$v_{1,n}^{l}=\prod_{i=1}^{n}\left((1+(\gamma-1)(1-v_{\alpha_i}))^{\lambda}+(\gamma^2-1)v_{\alpha_i}^{\lambda}\right)^{w_i} \tag{1.288}$$

$$v_{1,n}^{r}=\prod_{i=1}^{n}\left((1+(\gamma-1)(1-v_{\alpha_i}))^{\lambda}-v_{\alpha_i}^{\lambda}\right)^{w_i} \tag{1.289}$$

In the same way, we can prove that the GHIFWG operator also satisfies idempotency, monotonicity and boundedness, and some special cases of the GHIFWG operator can be discussed as below (Xia and Xu 2011):

Case 1 If $\lambda = 1$, then Eq. (1.285) reduces to:

$$\begin{aligned}&HIFWG(\alpha_1,\alpha_2,\ldots,\alpha_n)\\&=\left(\frac{\gamma\prod_{i=1}^{n}\mu_{\alpha_i}^{w_i}}{\prod_{i=1}^{n}(1+(\gamma-1)(1-\mu_{\alpha_i}))^{w_i}+(\gamma-1)\prod_{i=1}^{n}\mu_{\alpha_i}^{w_i}},\right.\\&\left.\frac{\prod_{i=1}^{n}(1+(\gamma-1)v_{\alpha_i})^{w_i}-\prod_{i=1}^{n}(1-v_{\alpha_i})^{w_i}}{\prod_{i=1}^{n}(1+(\gamma-1)v_{\alpha_i})^{w_i}+(\gamma-1)\prod_{i=1}^{n}(1-v_{\alpha_i})^{w_i}}\right)\end{aligned} \tag{1.290}$$

which is the Hamacher intuitionistic fuzzy geometric (HIFWG) operator (Xia et al. 2012c).

Case 2 If $\gamma = 1$ and $\lambda = 1$, then Eq. (1.285) is transformed as:

$$IFWG(\alpha_1,\alpha_2,\ldots,\alpha_n)=\left(\prod_{i=1}^{n}\mu_{\alpha_i}^{w_i},1-\prod_{i=1}^{n}\left((1-v_{\alpha_i}\right)^{w_i}\right) \tag{1.291}$$

which is the IFWG operator (Xu and Yager 2006).

Case 3 If $\gamma = 1$, then by Eq. (1.285), we have

$$\begin{aligned}&GHIFWG(\alpha_1,\alpha_2,\ldots,\alpha_n)\\&=\left(1-\left(1-\prod_{i=1}^{n}\left((1-(1-\mu_{\alpha_i})^{\lambda}\right)^{w_i}\right)^{\frac{1}{\lambda}},\left(1-\prod_{i=1}^{n}\left((1-v_{\alpha_i}^{\lambda}\right)^{w_i}\right)^{\frac{1}{\lambda}}\right)\end{aligned} \tag{1.292}$$

which is the generalized intuitionistic fuzzy weighted geometric (GIFWG) operator.

Case 4 If $\gamma = 2$, then Eq. (1.285) is transformed as:

$$\begin{aligned}&GEIFWG(\alpha_1,\alpha_2,\ldots,\alpha_n)\\&=\left(\frac{\left(\mu_{1,n}^{l}+3\mu_{1,n}^{r}\right)^{\frac{1}{\lambda}}-\left(\mu_{1,n}^{l}-\mu_{1,n}^{r}\right)^{\frac{1}{\lambda}}}{\left(\mu_{1,n}^{l}+3\mu_{1,n}^{l}\right)^{\frac{1}{\lambda}}+\left(\mu_{1,n}^{l}-\mu_{1,n}^{r}\right)^{\frac{1}{\lambda}}},\frac{2\left(v_{1,n}^{l}-v_{1,n}^{r}\right)^{\frac{1}{\lambda}}}{\left(v_{1,n}^{l}+3v_{1,n}^{r}\right)^{\frac{1}{\lambda}}+\left(v_{1,n}^{l}-v_{1,n}^{r}\right)^{\frac{1}{\lambda}}}\right)\end{aligned} \tag{1.293}$$

where

$$\mu_{1,n}^{l}=\prod_{i=1}^{n}\left((1+(1-\mu_{\alpha_i}))^{\lambda}+3\mu_{\alpha_i}^{\lambda}\right)^{w_i},\ \mu_{1,n}^{r}=\prod_{i=1}^{n}\left((1+(1-\mu_{\alpha_i}))^{\lambda}-\mu_{\alpha_i}^{\lambda}\right)^{w_i} \tag{1.294}$$

$$\nu_{1,n}^{l}=\prod_{i=1}^{n}\left((1+(1-\nu_{\alpha_i}))^{\lambda}+3\nu_{\alpha_i}^{\lambda}\right)^{w_i},\ \nu_{1,n}^{r}=\prod_{i=1}^{n}\left((1+(1-\nu_{\alpha_i}))^{\lambda}-\nu_{\alpha_i}^{\lambda}\right)^{w_i} \tag{1.295}$$

which is a generalized Einstein intuitionistic fuzzy weighted geometric (GEIFWG) operator.

Case 5 If $\gamma=2$ and $\lambda=1$, then Eq. (1.285) is transformed as:

$$\begin{aligned} &EIFWG(\alpha_1,\alpha_2,\ldots,\alpha_n)\\ &=\left(\frac{2\prod_{i=1}^{n}\mu_{\alpha_i}^{w_i}}{\prod_{i=1}^{n}(2-\mu_{\alpha_i}))^{w_i}+\prod_{i=1}^{n}\mu_{\alpha_i}^{w_i}},\frac{\prod_{i=1}^{n}(1+\nu_{\alpha_i})^{w_i}-\prod_{i=1}^{n}(1-\nu_{\alpha_i})^{w_i}}{\prod_{i=1}^{n}(1+\nu_{\alpha_i})^{w_i}+\prod_{i=1}^{n}(1-\nu_{\alpha_i})^{w_i}}\right)\end{aligned} \tag{1.296}$$

which is the EIFWG operator (Xia et al. 2012c).

In what follows, we apply the GHIFWA and GHIFWG operators to decision making (Xia and Xu 2011):

For a multi-attribute decision making problem, let Y, G and w be as defined previously. The expert provides the performance of the alternative y_i under the attribute G_j denoted by the IFVs $\alpha_{ij}=(\mu_{ij},\nu_{ij})$ $(i=1,2,\ldots,m;\ j=1,2,\ldots,n)$. All the IFVs α_{ij} $(i=1,2,\ldots,m;\ j=1,2,\ldots,n)$ construct the intuitionistic fuzzy decision matrix $B=(b_{ij})_{n\times n}$.

To obtain the alternative(s), the following steps are given (Xia and Xu 2011):

Step 1 Transform the intuitionistic fuzzy decision matrix $B=(b_{ij})_{n\times n}$ into the normalized intuitionistic fuzzy decision matrix $R=(r_{ij})_{n\times n}$, where

$$r_{ij}=\begin{cases} b_{ij}, & for\ benefit\ attribute\ G_i\\ b_{ij}^{c}, & for\ cost\ attribute\ G_i\end{cases},\quad i=1,2,\ldots,m;\quad j=1,2,\ldots,n \tag{1.297}$$

Step 2 Aggregate the intuitionistic fuzzy values r_i of the alternative y_i by the GAIFWA or GHIFWG operator:

$$r_i=GHIFWA(r_{i1},r_{i2},\ldots,r_{in})=\left(\mathop{\oplus}_{j=1}^{n}w_j r_{ij}^{\lambda}\right)^{\frac{1}{\lambda}} \tag{1.298}$$

or

$$r_i=GHIFWG(r_{i1},r_{i2},\ldots,r_{in})=\frac{1}{\lambda}\left(\mathop{\otimes}_{j=1}^{n}\lambda r_{ij}^{w_j}\right) \tag{1.299}$$

Step 3 Calculate the scores $S(r_i)$ of r_i by using Xu and Yager (2006)'s ranking method, and obtain the priority of the alternatives according to the ranking of r_i $(i = 1, 2, \ldots, m)$, the bigger the value r_i, the better the alternative y_i.

Now we utilize Example 1.7 to illustrate the proposed method. To obtain the most preferred supplier(s), the following steps are given:

Step 1 Aggregate the intuitionistic fuzzy values r_i of the supplier y_i by the GHIFWA operator (without loss of generality, let $\gamma = 2$ and $\lambda = 2$):

$$r_1 = (0.4439, 0.2936), \quad r_2 = (0.4231, 0.2475), \quad r_3 = (0.5348, 0.3099)$$
$$r_4 = (0.4904, 0.3971), \quad r_5 = (0.4226, 0.2733), \quad r_6 = (0.4351, 0.1708)$$

Step 2 Calculate the scores $S(r_i)$ of r_i by using Xu and Yager (2006)'s ranking method:

$$S(r_1) = 0.1502, \quad S(r_2) = 0.1756, \quad S(r_3) = 0.2248$$
$$S(r_4) = 0.0933, \quad S(r_5) = 0.1493, \quad S(r_6) = 0.2643$$

Since

$$S(r_6) > S(r_3) > S(r_2) > S(r_1) > S(r_5) > S(r_4)$$

we can obtain the priority of the suppliers $y_i (i = 1, 2, \ldots, 6)$:

$$y_6 \succ y_3 \succ y_2 \succ y_1 \succ y_5 \succ y_4$$

As the parameters λ and γ are assigned different values, the scores of the suppliers obtained are different, and the rankings of the suppliers are also different, some cases can be found in Tables 1.14 and 1.15 (Xia and Xu 2011), when the GHIFWA and GHIFWG operators are used, respectively.

To investigate the variation trends of the scores and the rankings of the suppliers with the change of the values of the parameters λ and γ, we use figures to illustrate these issues. Figures 1.18, 1.19, 1.20, 1.21, 1.22 and 1.23 (Xia and Xu 2011) give the scores of suppliers obtained by the GHIFWA operator as λ and γ are assigned values between 0 and 10.

It is noted that the scores increase as λ increases, but not suitable for γ. Figures 1.24, 1.25, 1.26, 1.27, 1.28, 1.29, 1.30, 1.31, 1.32, 1.33, 1.34 and 1.35 (Xia and Xu 2011) give the scores of suppliers obtained by the GHIFWG operator as λ and γ are assigned values between 0 and 10. It is noted that the scores decrease as λ increases, but not suitable for γ. Therefore, the proposed aggregation operators with parameters can provide the decision makers (or experts) more choices and thus are more flexible than the existing ones, because we can choose different values according to the practical problems, which is worthy to be further studied in the future.

Table 1.14 Scores and rankings for the alternatives based on the GHIFWA operator

	y_1	y_2	y_3	y_4	y_5	y_6	*Rankings*
$\gamma = 0.7$ $\lambda = 0.3$	−0.0881	0.1377	0.1685	0.0077	0.0801	0.2018	$y_6 \succ y_2 \succ y_5 \succ y_3 \succ y_1 \succ y_4$
$\gamma = 1$ $\lambda = 1$	0.1111	0.1539	0.1915	0.0388	0.1049	0.2266	$y_6 \succ y_3 \succ y_2 \succ y_1 \succ y_5 \succ y_4$
$\gamma = 1$ $\lambda = 10$	0.3012	0.2839	0.3621	0.3453	0.3116	0.3773	$y_6 \succ y_3 \succ y_4 \succ y_5 \succ y_1 \succ y_4$
$\gamma = 2$ $\lambda = 1$	0.0910	0.1401	0.1689	0.0083	0.0867	0.2080	$y_6 \succ y_3 \succ y_2 \succ y_1 \succ y_5 \succ y_4$
$\gamma = 3$ $\lambda = 4$	0.2537	0.2341	0.3218	0.2725	0.2584	0.3341	$y_6 \succ y_3 \succ y_4 \succ y_5 \succ y_1 \succ y_4$
$\gamma = 4$ $\lambda = 3$	0.2193	0.2094	0.2900	0.2121	0.2221	0.3100	$y_6 \succ y_3 \succ y_5 \succ y_1 \succ y_4 \succ y_2$
$\gamma = 5$ $\lambda = 5$	0.3017	0.2762	0.3677	0.3611	0.3124	0.3667	$y_3 \succ y_6 \succ y_4 \succ y_5 \succ y_1 \succ y_2$
$\gamma = 10$ $\lambda = 1$	0.0528	0.1128	0.1274	−0.0407	0.0479	0.1669	$y_6 \succ y_3 \succ y_2 \succ y_1 \succ y_5 \succ y_4$
$\gamma = 10$ $\lambda = 10$	0.3679	0.3702	0.4325	0.4688	0.3960	0.4374	$y_4 \succ y_6 \succ y_3 \succ y_5 \succ y_2 \succ y_1$

Table 1.15 Scores and rankings for the alternatives based on the GHIFWG operator

	y_1	y_2	y_3	y_4	y_5	y_6	*Rankings*
$\gamma = 0.7$ $\lambda = 0.3$	−0.0178	0.0506	0.0363	−0.1168	−0.0145	0.0800	$y_6 \succ y_2 \succ y_5 \succ y_3 \succ y_1 \succ y_4$
$\gamma = 1$ $\lambda = 1$	−0.0388	0.0312	0.0058	−0.1368	−0.0278	0.0541	$y_6 \succ y_2 \succ y_3 \succ y_1 \succ y_5 \succ y_4$
$\gamma = 1$ $\lambda = 10$	−0.2678	−0.1815	−0.3392	−0.3065	0.0087	−0.1916	$y_5 \succ y_2 \succ y_6 \succ y_1 \succ y_4 \succ y_3$
$\gamma = 2$ $\lambda = 1$	−0.0175	0.0483	0.0374	−0.1153	−0.0126	0.0761	$y_6 \succ y_2 \succ y_3 \succ y_5 \succ y_1 \succ y_4$
$\gamma = 3$ $\lambda = 4$	−0.1937	−0.1013	−0.2432	−0.2631	−0.1068	−0.1025	$y_2 \succ y_6 \succ y_5 \succ y_1 \succ y_3 \succ y_4$
$\gamma = 4$ $\lambda = 3$	−0.1485	−0.0563	−0.1729	−0.2307	−0.0748	−0.0549	$y_6 \succ y_2 \succ y_5 \succ y_1 \succ y_3 \succ y_4$
$\gamma = 5$ $\lambda = 5$	−0.2584	−0.1717	−0.3442	−0.3072	−0.1555	−0.1635	$y_5 \succ y_6 \succ y_2 \succ y_1 \succ y_4 \succ y_3$
$\gamma = 10$ $\lambda = 1$	0.0155	0.0771	0.0846	−0.0795	0.0087	0.1131	$y_6 \succ y_3 \succ y_2 \succ y_1 \succ y_5 \succ y_4$
$\gamma = 10$ $\lambda = 10$	−0.3714	−0.2840	−0.4779	−0.3723	−0.2666	−0.2855	$y_5 \succ y_2 \succ y_6 \succ y_1 \succ y_4 \succ y_3$

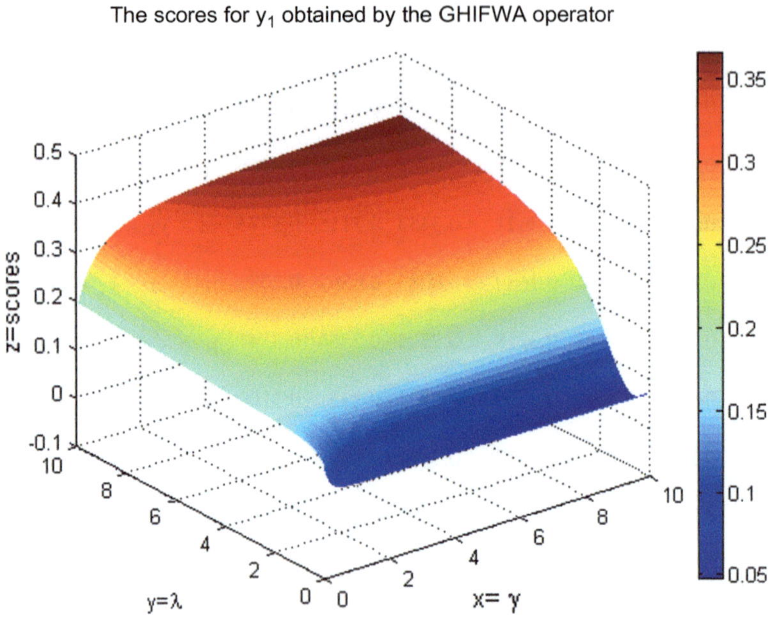

Fig. 1.18 The scores for the supplier y_1 obtained by the GHIFWA operator

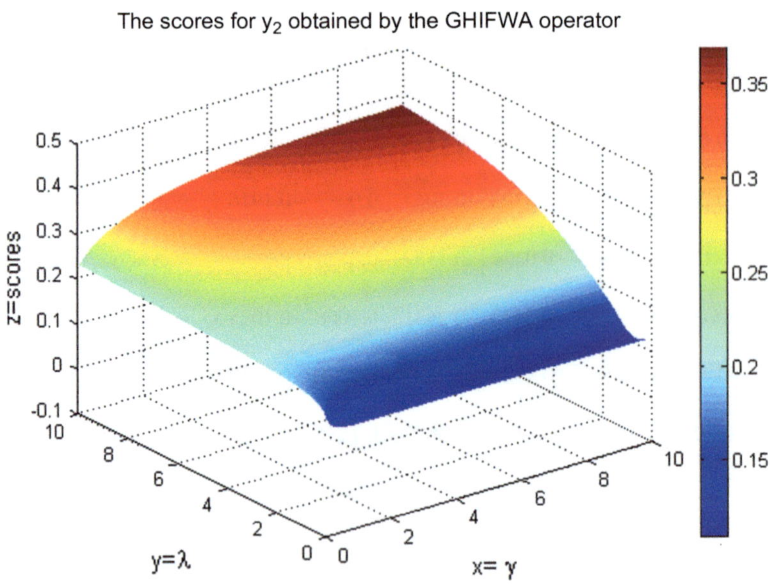

Fig. 1.19 The scores for the supplier y_2 obtained by the GHIFWA operator

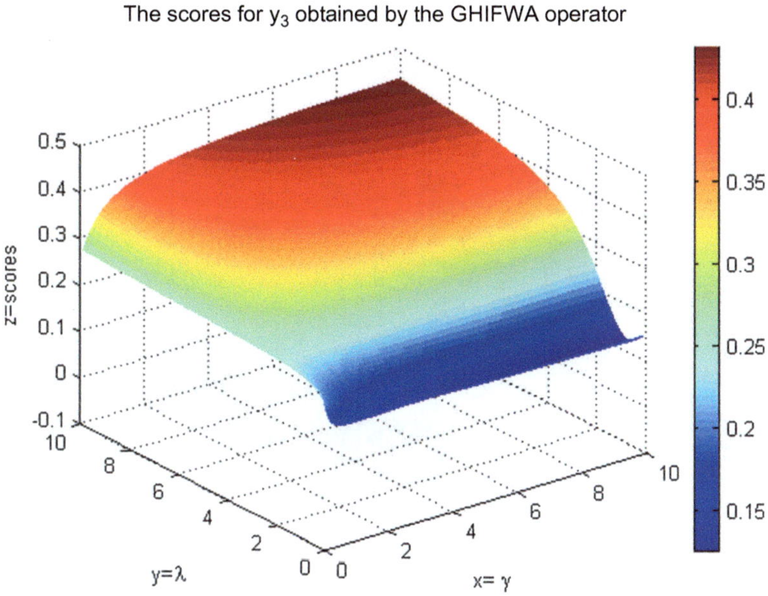

Fig. 1.20 The scores for the supplier y_3 obtained by the GHIFWA operator

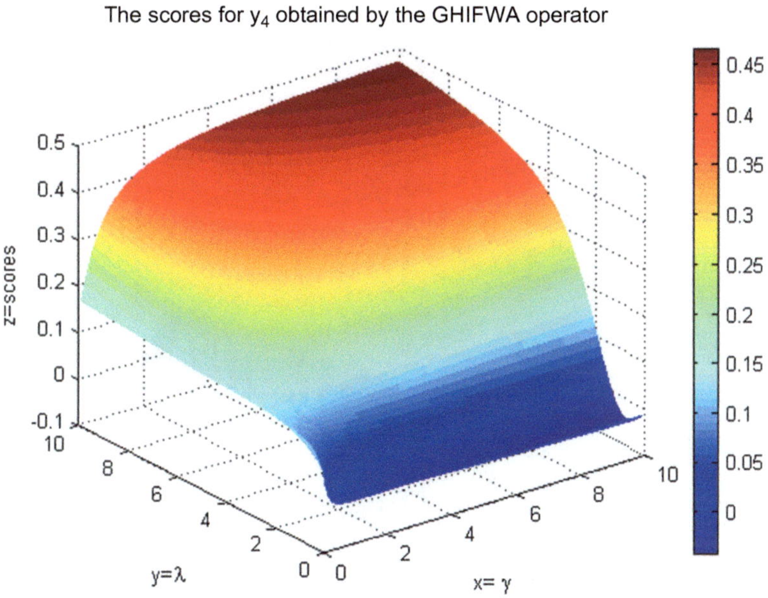

Fig. 1.21 The scores for the supplier y_4 obtained by the GHIFWA operator

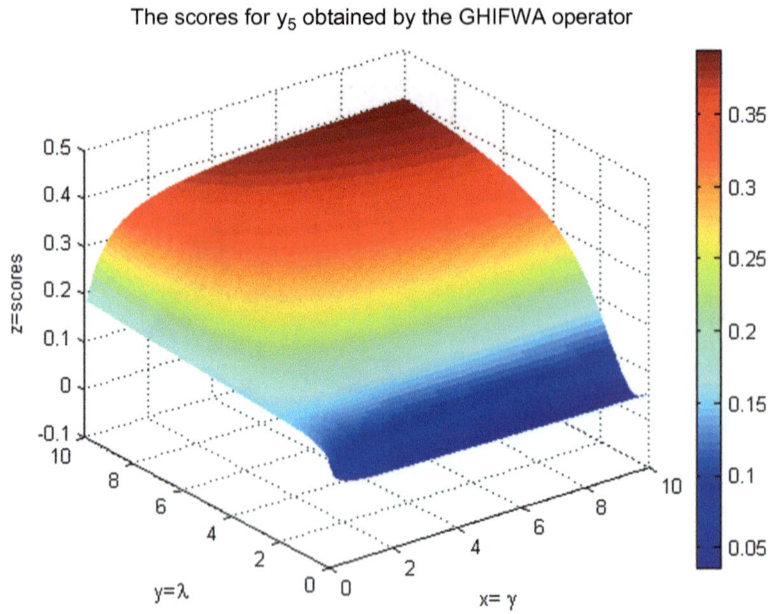

Fig. 1.22 The scores for the supplier y_5 obtained by the GHIFWA operator

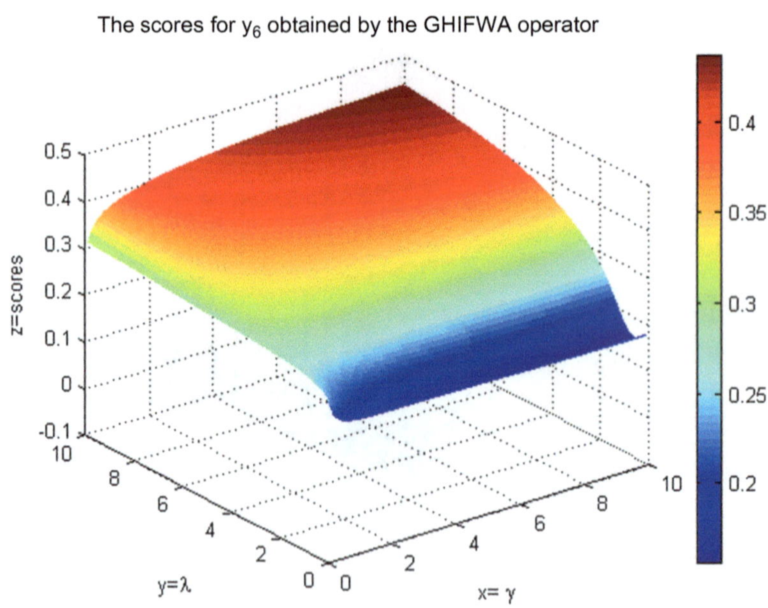

Fig. 1.23 The scores for the supplier y_6 obtained by the GHIFWA operator

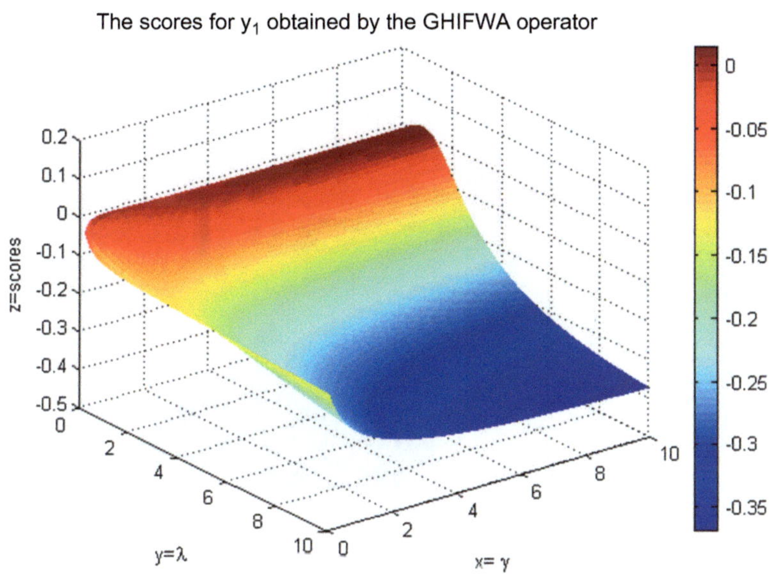

Fig. 1.24 The scores for the supplier y_1 obtained by the GHIFWG operator

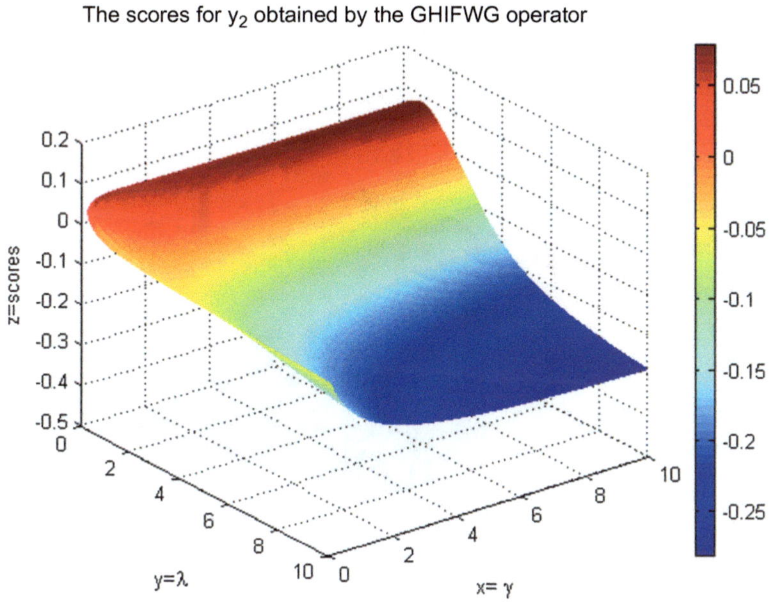

Fig. 1.25 The scores for the supplier y_2 obtained by the GHIFWG operator

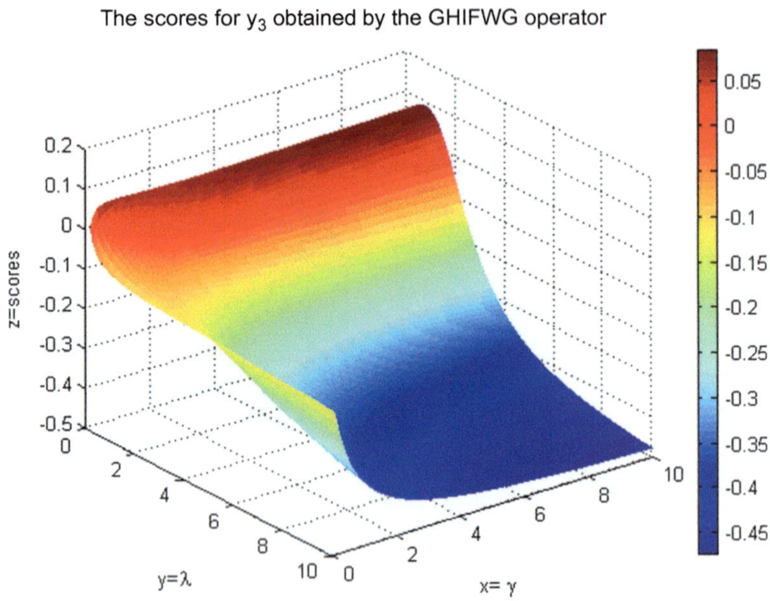

Fig. 1.26 The scores for the supplier y_3 obtained by the GHIFWG operator

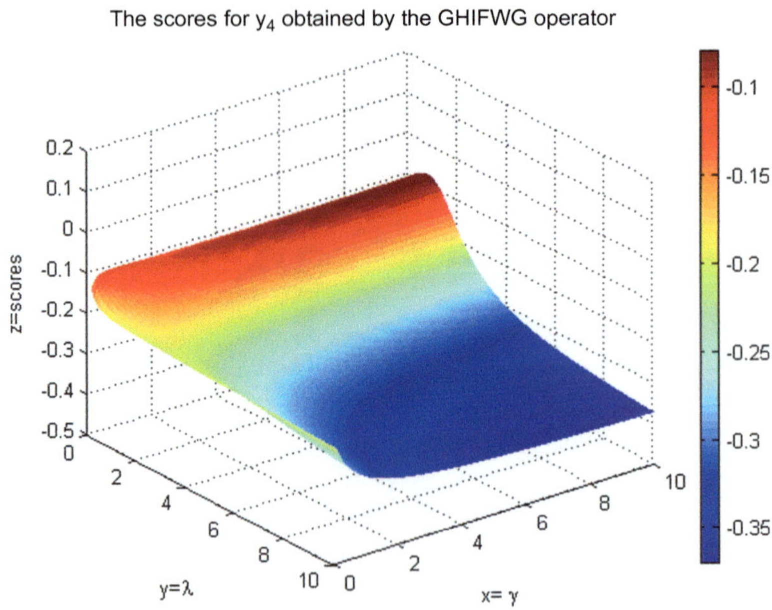

Fig. 1.27 The scores for the supplier y_4 obtained by the GHIFWG operator

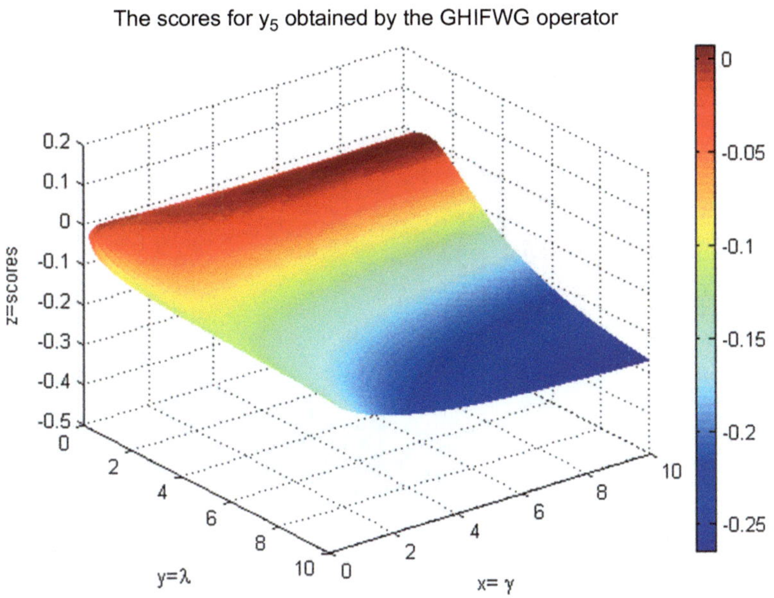

Fig. 1.28 The scores for the supplier y_5 obtained by the GHIFWG operator

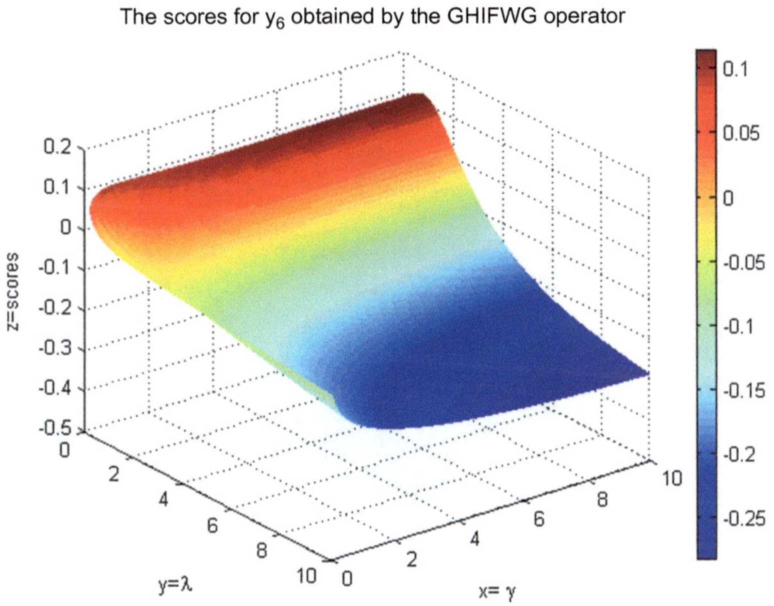

Fig. 1.29 The scores for the supplier y_6 obtained by the GHIFWG operator

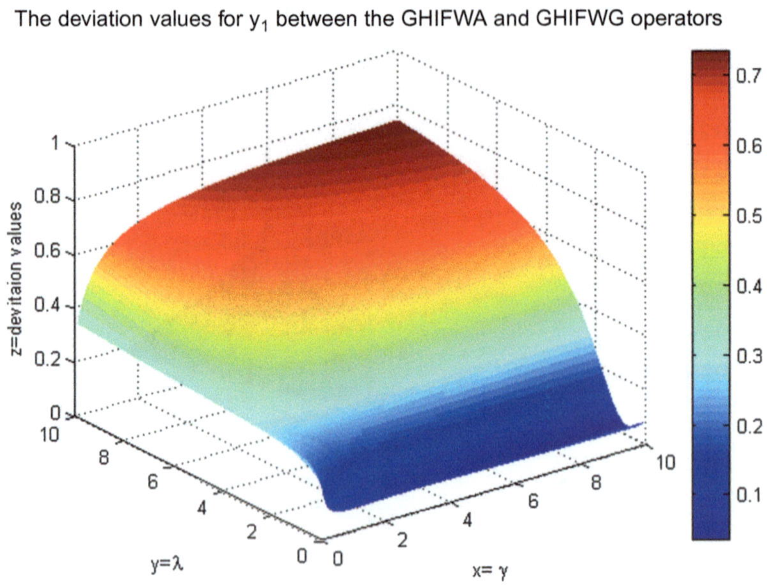

Fig. 1.30 The deviation values for y_1 between the GHIFWA and GHIFWG operators

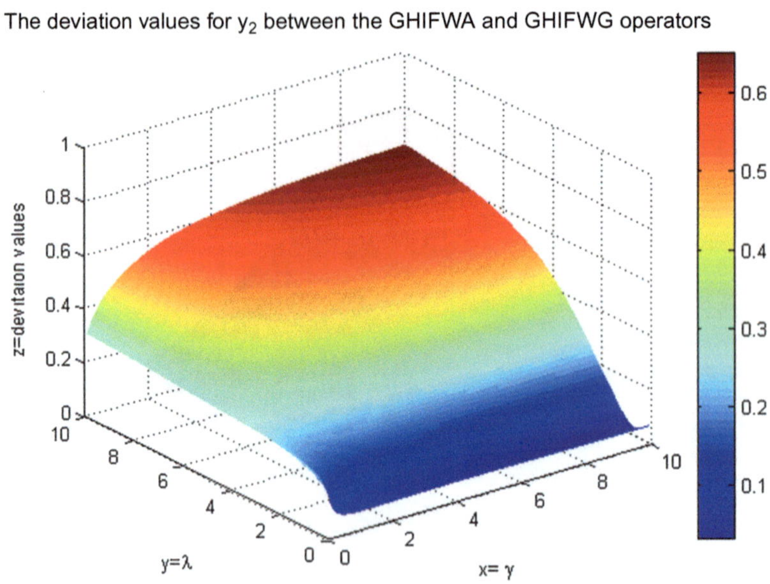

Fig. 1.31 The deviation values for y_2 between the GHIFWA and GHIFWG operators

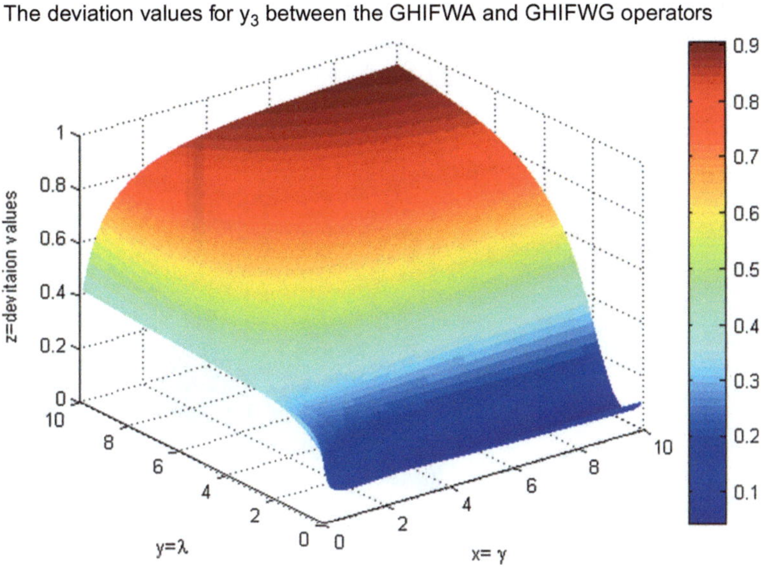

Fig. 1.32 The deviation values for y_3 between the GHIFWA and GHIFWG operators

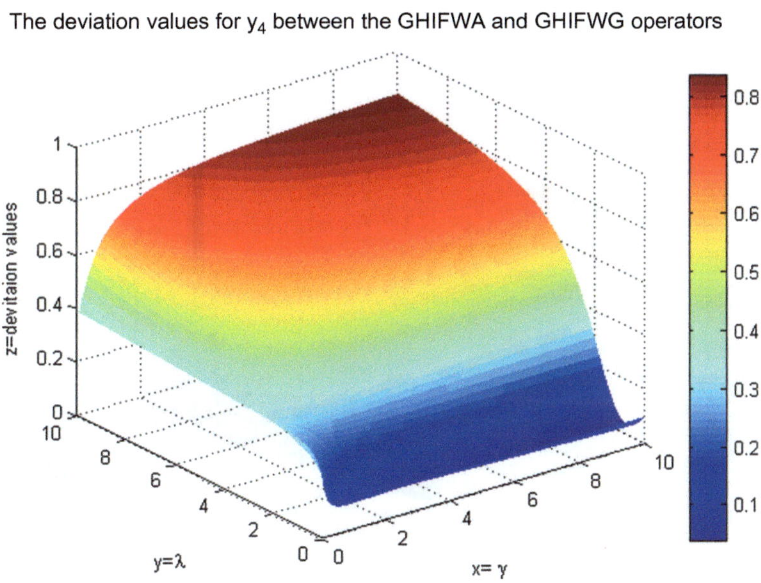

Fig. 1.33 The deviation values for y_4 between the GHIFWA and GHIFWG operators

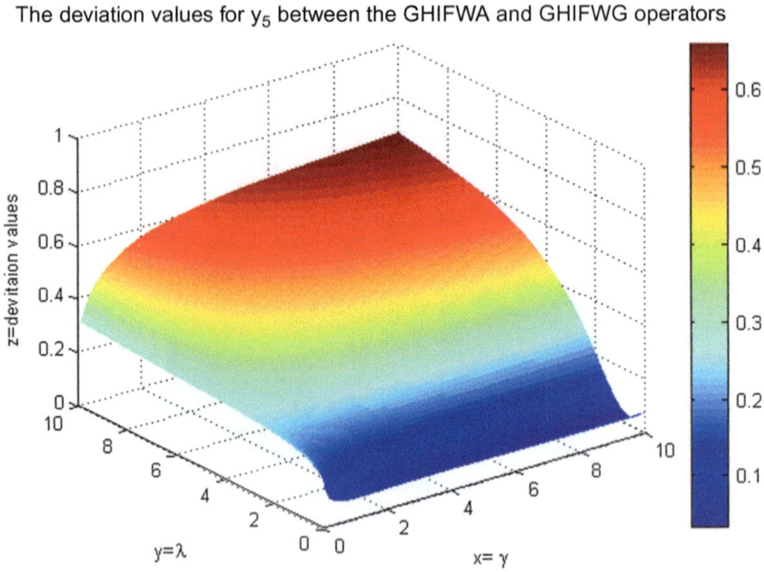

Fig. 1.34 The deviation values for y_5 between the GHIFWA and GHIFWG operators

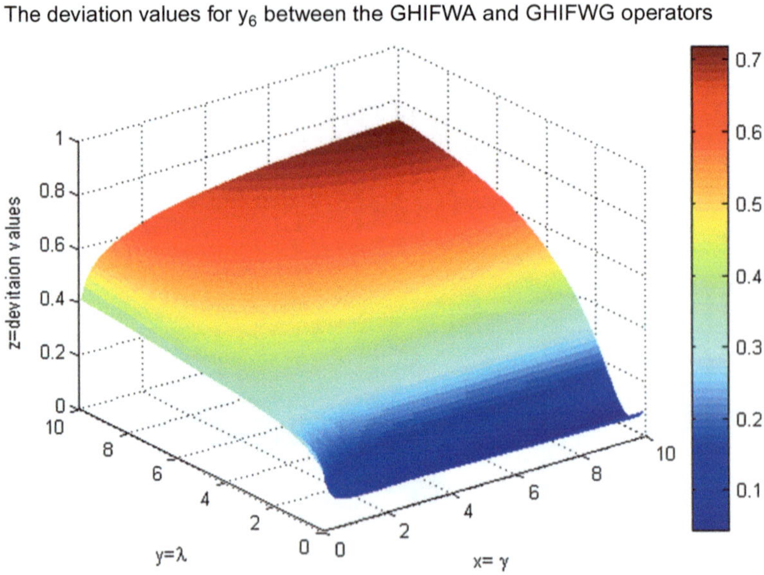

Fig. 1.35 The deviation values for y_6 between the GHIFWA and GHIFWG operators

1.8 Point Operators for Aggregating IFVs

For an IFS $A = \{\langle x, \mu_A(x), v_A(x)\rangle | x \in X\}$, let $\kappa, \lambda \in [0, 1]$, Atanassov (1995) gave the following operators:

(1) $D_\kappa(A) = \{x, \langle \mu_A(x) + \kappa\pi_A(x), v_A(x) + (1-\kappa)\pi_A(x)\rangle | x \in X\}$.

(2) $F_{\kappa,\lambda}(A) = \{x, \langle \mu_A(x) + \kappa\pi_A(x), v_A(x) + \lambda\pi_A(x)\rangle | x \in X\}$, where $\kappa + \lambda \le 1$.

(3) $G_{\kappa,\lambda}(A) = \{x, \langle \kappa\mu_A(x), \lambda v_A(x)\rangle | x \in X\}$.

(4) $H_{\kappa,\lambda}(A) = \{x, \langle \kappa\mu_A(x), v_A(x) + \lambda\pi_A(x)\rangle | x \in X\}$.

(5) $H^*_{\kappa,\lambda}(A) = \{x, \langle \kappa\mu_A(x), v_A(x) + \lambda(1-\kappa\mu_A(x) - v_A(x))\rangle | x \in X\}$.

(6) $J_{\kappa,\lambda}(A) = \{x, \langle \mu_A(x) + \kappa\pi_A(x), \lambda v_A(x)\rangle | x \in X\}$.

(7) $J^*_{\kappa,\lambda}(A) = \{x, \langle \mu_A(x) + \kappa(1-\mu_A(x) - \lambda v_A(x)), \lambda v_A(x)\rangle | x \in X\}$.

(8) $P_{\kappa,\lambda}(A) = \{x, \langle \max(\kappa, \mu_A(x)), \min(\lambda, v_A(x))\rangle | x \in X\}$, where $\kappa + \lambda \le 1$.

(9) $Q_{\kappa,\lambda}(A) = \{x, \langle \min(\kappa, \mu_A(x)), \max(\lambda, v_A(x))\rangle | x \in X\}$, where $\kappa + \lambda \le 1$.

Let IFS(X) be the set of all IFSs on X. For $A \in$ IFS (X), Burillo and Bustince (1996) defined an operator $D_{\kappa_x}(A)$ for each point $x \in X$:

$$D_{\kappa_x}(A) = \{x, \langle \mu_A(x) + \kappa_x\pi_A(x), v_A(x) + (1-\kappa_x)\pi_A(x)\rangle | x \in X\} \quad (1.300)$$

where $\kappa_x \in [0, 1]$.

Then, Liu and Wang (2007) defined an intuitionistic fuzzy point operator for IFSs:

Definition 1.26 (Liu and Wang 2007) Let $A \in$ IFS(X), for each point $x \in X$, taking $\kappa_x, \lambda_x \in [0, 1]$ and $\kappa_x + \lambda_x \le 1$, then an intuitionistic fuzzy point operator $F_{\kappa_x,\lambda_x}(A)$: IFS($X$) $\to$ IFS(X) is as follows:

$$F_{\kappa_x,\lambda_x}(A) = \{x, \langle \mu_A(x) + \kappa_x\pi_A(x), v_A(x) + \lambda_x\pi_A(x)\rangle | x \in X\} \quad (1.301)$$

and if let $F^0_{\kappa_x,\lambda_x}(A) = A$, then

$$F^n_{\kappa_x,\lambda_x}(A) = \left\{x, \left\langle \mu_A(x) + \kappa_x\pi_A(x)\frac{1-(1-\kappa_x-\lambda_x)^n}{\kappa_x+\lambda_x}, \right.\right.$$
$$\left.\left. v_A(x) + \lambda_x\pi_A(x)\frac{1-(1-\kappa_x-\lambda_x)^n}{\kappa_x+\lambda_x}\right\rangle \middle| x \in X\right\} \quad (1.302)$$

Xia and Xu (2010) defined a series of point operators for aggregating IFVs:

Definition 1.27 (Xia and Xu 2010) For an IFV $\alpha = (\mu_\alpha, v_\alpha)$, let $\kappa_\alpha, \lambda_\alpha \in [0, 1]$, we define some point operators as follows:

(1) $D_{\kappa_\alpha,\lambda_\alpha}(\alpha) = (\mu_\alpha + \kappa_\alpha\pi_\alpha, v_\alpha + (1-\kappa_\alpha)\pi_\alpha)$.

(2) $F_{\kappa_\alpha,\lambda_\alpha}(\alpha) = (\mu_\alpha + \kappa_\alpha\pi_\alpha, v_\alpha + \lambda_\alpha\pi_\alpha)$, where $\kappa_\alpha + \lambda_\alpha \le 1$.

(3) $G_{\kappa_\alpha,\lambda_\alpha}(\alpha) = (\kappa_\alpha \mu_\alpha, \lambda_\alpha \nu_\alpha)$.
(4) $H_{\kappa_\alpha,\lambda_\alpha}(\alpha) = (\kappa_\alpha \mu_\alpha, \nu_\alpha + \lambda_\alpha \pi_\alpha)$.
(5) $H^*_{\kappa_\alpha,\lambda_\alpha}(\alpha) = (\kappa_\alpha \mu_\alpha, \nu_\alpha + \lambda_\alpha (1 - \kappa_\alpha \mu_\alpha - \nu_\alpha))$.
(6) $J_{\kappa_\alpha,\lambda_\alpha}(\alpha) = (\mu_\alpha + \kappa_\alpha \pi_\alpha, \lambda_\alpha \nu_\alpha)$.
(7) $J^*_{\kappa_\alpha,\lambda_\alpha}(\alpha) = (\mu_\alpha + \kappa_\alpha (1 - \mu_\alpha - \lambda_\alpha \nu_\alpha), \lambda_\alpha \nu_\alpha)$.
(8) $P_{\kappa_\alpha,\lambda_\alpha}(\alpha) = (\max(\kappa_\alpha, \mu_\alpha), \min(\lambda_\alpha, \nu_\alpha))$, where $\kappa_\alpha + \lambda_\alpha \leq 1$.
(9) $Q_{\kappa_\alpha,\lambda_\alpha}(\alpha) = (\min(\kappa_\alpha, \mu_\alpha), \max(\lambda_\alpha, \nu_\alpha))$, where $\kappa_\alpha + \lambda_\alpha \leq 1$.

Based on Definition 1.27, let

$$\begin{aligned} F^0_{\kappa_x,\lambda_x}(A) &= D^0_{\kappa_x,\lambda_x}(A) = G^0_{\kappa_x,\lambda_x}(A) = H^0_{\kappa_x,\lambda_x}(A) = H^{*,0}_{\kappa_x,\lambda_x}(A) \\ &= J^0_{\kappa_x,\lambda_x}(A) = J^{*,0}_{\kappa_x,\lambda_x}(A) = P^0_{\kappa_x,\lambda_x}(A) = Q^0_{\kappa_x,\lambda_x}(A) = A \end{aligned} \tag{1.303}$$

then we have the following theorem:

Theorem 1.43 (Xia and Xu 2010) Let $\alpha = (\mu_\alpha, \nu_\alpha)$ be an IFV, and n a positive integer, taking $\kappa_\alpha, \lambda_\alpha \in [0, 1]$, then

(1) $D^n_{\kappa_\alpha}(\alpha) = (\mu_\alpha + \kappa_\alpha \pi_\alpha, \nu_\alpha + (1 - \kappa_\alpha)\pi_\alpha)$.

(2) $$F^n_{\kappa_\alpha,\lambda_\alpha}(\alpha) = \left(\mu_\alpha + \kappa_\alpha \pi_\alpha \frac{1 - (1 - \kappa_\alpha - \lambda_\alpha)^n}{\kappa_\alpha + \lambda_\alpha}, \nu_\alpha + \lambda_\alpha \pi_\alpha \frac{1 - (1 - \kappa_\alpha - \lambda_\alpha)^n}{\kappa_\alpha + \lambda_\alpha}\right), \text{ where } \kappa_\alpha + \lambda_\alpha \leq 1.$$

(3) $G^n_{\kappa_\alpha,\lambda_\alpha}(\alpha) = (\kappa^n_\alpha \mu_\alpha, \lambda^n_\alpha \nu_\alpha)$.

(4) $$H^n_{\kappa_\alpha,\lambda_\alpha}(\alpha) = \left(\kappa^n_\alpha \mu_\alpha, \nu_\alpha + (1 - \nu_\alpha)(1 - (1 - \lambda_\alpha)^n) - \mu_\alpha \lambda_\alpha \left(\sum_{t=0}^{n-1} \kappa_\alpha^{n-1-t} (1 - \lambda_\alpha)^t\right)\right).$$

(5) $$H^{*,n}_{\kappa,\lambda}(\alpha) = \left(\kappa^n_\alpha \mu_\alpha, \nu_\alpha + (1 - \nu_\alpha)\left(1 - (1 - \lambda_\alpha)^n\right) - \mu_\alpha \kappa_\alpha \lambda_\alpha \left(\sum_{t=0}^{n-1} \kappa_\alpha^{n-1-t} (1 - \lambda_\alpha)^t\right)\right).$$

(6) $$J_{\kappa_\alpha,\lambda_\alpha}(\alpha) = \left(\mu_\alpha + (1 - \mu_\alpha)\left(1 - (1 - \kappa_\alpha)^n\right) - \nu_\alpha \kappa_\alpha \left(\sum_{t=0}^{n-1} (1 - \kappa_\alpha)^t \lambda_\alpha^{n-1-t}\right), \lambda^n_\alpha \nu_\alpha\right).$$

(7) $J^{*}_{\kappa_\alpha,\lambda_\alpha}(\alpha) = \left(\mu_\alpha + (1-\mu_\alpha)\left(1-(1-\kappa_\alpha)^n\right) - \nu_\alpha\kappa_\alpha\lambda_\alpha \left(\sum_{t=0}^{n-1} (1-\kappa_\alpha)^t \lambda_\alpha^{n-1-t} \right), \lambda_\alpha^n \nu_\alpha \right).$

(8) $P^{n}_{\kappa_\alpha,\lambda_\alpha}(\alpha) = (\max(\kappa_\alpha, \mu_\alpha), \min(\lambda_\alpha, \nu_\alpha))$, where $\kappa_\alpha + \lambda_\alpha \le 1$.

(9) $Q_{\kappa_\alpha,\lambda_\alpha}(\alpha) = (\min(\kappa_\alpha, \mu_\alpha), \max(\lambda_\alpha, \nu_\alpha))$, where $\kappa_\alpha + \lambda_\alpha \le 1$,

which translate one IFV to another IFV.

Proof (1), (3), (8) and (9) are obvious. By the idea of Liu and Wang (2007), we can also easily prove (2). Next, motivated also by the idea of Liu and Wang (2007), we prove (4), (5), (6) and (7) using mathematical induction on n:
(4) For $n = 1$, we have

$$H^{1}_{\kappa_\alpha,\lambda_\alpha}(\alpha) = \left(\mu_{H^{1}_{\kappa_\alpha,\lambda_\alpha}(\alpha)}, \nu_{H^{1}_{\kappa_\alpha,\lambda_\alpha}(\alpha)}\right) = (\kappa_\alpha\mu_\alpha, \nu_\alpha + \lambda_\alpha\pi_\alpha)$$
$$= \left(\kappa_\alpha^1\mu_\alpha, \nu_\alpha + (1-\nu_\alpha)\left(1-(1-\lambda_\alpha)^1\right) - \mu_\alpha\lambda_\alpha \left(\sum_{t=0}^{1-1} \kappa_\alpha^{1-1-t}(1-\lambda_\alpha)^t \right)\right) \tag{1.304}$$

For $n = 2$, we have

$$\mu_{H^{2}_{\kappa_\alpha,\lambda_\alpha}(\alpha)} = \kappa_\alpha^2\mu_\alpha \tag{1.305}$$

$$\begin{aligned}\nu_{H^{2}_{\kappa_\alpha,\lambda_\alpha}(\alpha)} &= \nu_\alpha + \lambda_\alpha\pi_\alpha + \lambda_\alpha(1-\kappa_\alpha\mu_\alpha - \nu_\alpha - \lambda_\alpha\pi_\alpha)\\ &= \nu_\alpha + (1-\nu_\alpha)(\lambda_\alpha + \lambda_\alpha(1-\lambda_\alpha)) - \mu_\alpha\lambda_\alpha(1-\lambda_\alpha+\kappa_\alpha)\\ &= \nu_\alpha + (1-\nu_\alpha)\left(1-(1-\lambda_\alpha)^2\right) - \mu_\alpha\lambda_\alpha\left(\sum_{t=0}^{2-1}\kappa_\alpha^{2-1-t}(1-\lambda_\alpha)^t\right)\end{aligned} \tag{1.306}$$

Suppose that it is true for $n = p$, that is,

$$\mu_{H^{p}_{\kappa,\lambda}(\alpha)} = \kappa_\alpha^p\mu_\alpha \tag{1.307}$$

$$\nu_{H^{p}_{\kappa,\lambda}(\alpha)} = \nu_\alpha + (1-\nu_\alpha)\left(1-(1-\lambda_\alpha)^p\right) - \mu_\alpha\lambda_\alpha\left(\sum_{t=0}^{p-1}\kappa_\alpha^{p-1-t}(1-\lambda_\alpha)^t\right) \tag{1.308}$$

then, when $n = p + 1$, we have

$$\mu_{H^{p+1}_{\kappa_\alpha,\lambda_\alpha}(\alpha)} = \kappa\kappa_\alpha^p\mu_\alpha = \kappa_\alpha^{p+1}\mu_\alpha$$

$$
\begin{aligned}
\nu_{H^{p+1}_{\kappa_\alpha,\lambda_\alpha}}(\alpha) &= \nu_\alpha + (1-\nu_\alpha)\left(1-(1-\lambda_\alpha)^p\right) - \mu_\alpha\lambda_\alpha\left(\sum_{t=0}^{p-1}\kappa_\alpha^{p-1-t}(1-\lambda_\alpha)^t\right) \\
&\quad + \lambda_\alpha\left(1-\kappa_\alpha^p\mu_\alpha - \nu_\alpha - (1-\nu_\alpha)\left(1-(1-\lambda_\alpha)^p\right)\right. \\
&\quad \left. + \mu_\alpha\lambda_\alpha\left(\sum_{t=0}^{p-1}\kappa_\alpha^{p-1-t}(1-\lambda_\alpha)^t\right)\right) \\
&= \nu_\alpha + (1-\nu_\alpha)\left(1-(1-\lambda_\alpha)^p + \lambda_\alpha - \lambda_\alpha\left(1-(1-\lambda_\alpha)^p\right)\right) \\
&\quad - \mu_\alpha\lambda_\alpha\left(\left(\sum_{t=0}^{p-1}\kappa_\alpha^{p-1-t}(1-\lambda_\alpha)^{t+1}\right) + \kappa_\alpha^p\right) \\
&= \nu_\alpha + (1-\nu_\alpha)\left(1-(1-\lambda_\alpha)^{p+1}\right) - \mu_\alpha\lambda_\alpha\left(\sum_{t=0}^{p}\kappa_\alpha^{p-t}(1-\lambda_\alpha)^t\right)
\end{aligned} \tag{1.309}
$$

and thus, (4) holds for $n = p + 1$. Therefore, (4) holds for all n.

(5) For $n = 1$, we have

$$
\begin{aligned}
H^{*,1}_{\kappa_\alpha,\lambda_\alpha}(\alpha) &= \left(\mu_{H^{*,1}_{\kappa_\alpha,\lambda_\alpha}}(\alpha), \nu_{H^{*,1}_{\kappa_\alpha,\lambda_\alpha}}(\alpha)\right) = \left(\kappa_\alpha\mu_\alpha, \nu_\alpha + \lambda_\alpha(1-\kappa_\alpha\mu_\alpha - \nu_\alpha)\right) \\
&= \left(\kappa_\alpha^1\mu_\alpha, \nu_\alpha + (1-\nu_\alpha)\left(1-(1-\lambda_\alpha)^1\right)\right. \\
&\quad \left. - \mu_\alpha\kappa_\alpha\lambda_\alpha\left(\sum_{t=0}^{1-1}\kappa_\alpha^{1-1-t}(1-\lambda_\alpha)^t\right)\right)
\end{aligned} \tag{1.310}
$$

For $n = 2$, we have

$$
\mu_{H^{*,2}_{\kappa_\alpha,\lambda_\alpha}}(\alpha) = \kappa_\alpha^2\mu_\alpha \tag{1.311}
$$

$$
\begin{aligned}
\nu_{H^{*,2}_{\kappa_\alpha,\lambda_\alpha}}(\alpha) &= \nu_\alpha + \lambda_\alpha(1-\kappa_\alpha\mu_\alpha - \nu_\alpha) \\
&\quad + \lambda_\alpha\left(1-\kappa_\alpha^2\mu_\alpha - \nu_\alpha - \lambda_\alpha(1-\kappa_\alpha\mu_\alpha - \nu_\alpha)\right) \\
&= \nu_\alpha + (1-\nu_\alpha)(\lambda_\alpha + \lambda_\alpha(1-\lambda_\alpha)) - \mu_\alpha\kappa_\alpha\lambda_\alpha(1+\kappa_\alpha - \lambda_\alpha) \\
&= \nu_\alpha + (1-\nu_\alpha)\left(1-(1-\lambda_\alpha)^2\right) - \mu_\alpha\kappa_\alpha\lambda_\alpha\left(\sum_{t=0}^{2-1}\kappa_\alpha^{2-1-t}(1-\lambda_\alpha)^t\right)
\end{aligned} \tag{1.312}
$$

Suppose it is true for $n = p$, that is,

$$\mu_{H^{*,p}_{\kappa_\alpha,\lambda_\alpha}(\alpha)} = \kappa_\alpha^p \mu_\alpha \tag{1.313}$$

$$\nu_{H^{*,p}_{\kappa_\alpha,\lambda_\alpha}(\alpha)} = \nu_\alpha + (1-\nu_\alpha)\left(1-(1-\lambda_\alpha)^p\right) - \mu_\alpha\kappa_\alpha\lambda_\alpha\left(\sum_{t=0}^{p-1}\kappa_\alpha^{p-1-t}(1-\lambda_\alpha)^t\right) \tag{1.314}$$

then, when $n = p+1$, we have

$$\mu_{H^{*,p+1}_{\kappa_\alpha,\lambda_\alpha}(\alpha)} = \kappa\kappa_\alpha^p \mu_\alpha = \kappa_\alpha^{p+1}\mu_\alpha \tag{1.315}$$

$$\begin{aligned}
\nu_{H^{*,p+1}_{\kappa_\alpha,\lambda_\alpha}(\alpha)} &= \nu_\alpha + (1-\nu_\alpha)\left(1-(1-\lambda_\alpha)^p\right) - \mu_\alpha\kappa_\alpha\lambda_\alpha\left(\sum_{t=0}^{p-1}\kappa_\alpha^{p-1-t}(1-\lambda_\alpha)^t\right) \\
&\quad + \lambda_\alpha\Bigg(1-\kappa_\alpha^{p+1}\mu_\alpha - \nu_\alpha - (1-\nu_\alpha)\left(1-(1-\lambda_\alpha)^p\right) \\
&\quad + \mu_\alpha\kappa_\alpha\lambda_\alpha\left(\sum_{t=0}^{p-1}\kappa_\alpha^{p-1-t}(1-\lambda_\alpha)^t\right)\Bigg) \\
&= \nu_\alpha + (1-\nu_\alpha)\left(1-\left((1-\lambda_\alpha)^p - \lambda_\alpha(1-\lambda_\alpha)^p\right)\right) \\
&\quad - \mu_\alpha\kappa_\alpha\lambda_\alpha\left(\left(\sum_{t=0}^{p-1}\kappa_\alpha^{p-1-t}(1-\lambda_\alpha)^{t+1}\right) + \kappa_\alpha^p\right) \\
&= \nu_\alpha + (1-\nu_\alpha)\left(1-(1-\lambda_\alpha)^{p+1}\right) - \mu_\alpha\kappa_\alpha\lambda_\alpha\left(\sum_{t=0}^{p}\kappa_\alpha^{p-t}(1-\lambda_\alpha)^t\right)
\end{aligned} \tag{1.316}$$

and thus, (5) holds for $n = p+1$. Therefore, (5) holds for all n.

(6) For $k = 1$, we have

$$\begin{aligned}
J^1_{\kappa_\alpha,\lambda_\alpha}(\alpha) &= (\mu_\alpha + \kappa_\alpha\pi_\alpha, \lambda_\alpha\nu_\alpha) \\
&= \Bigg(\mu_\alpha + (1-\mu_\alpha)\left(1-(1-\kappa_\alpha)^1\right) \\
&\quad - \nu_\alpha\kappa_\alpha\left(\sum_{t=0}^{1-1}\lambda_\alpha^{1-1-t}(1-\kappa_\alpha)^t\right), \lambda_\alpha^1\nu_\alpha\Bigg)
\end{aligned} \tag{1.317}$$

For $k = 2$, we have

$$\begin{aligned}\mu_{J^2_{\kappa_\alpha,\lambda_\alpha}}(\alpha) &= \mu_\alpha + \kappa_\alpha\pi_\alpha + \kappa_\alpha\left(1-\lambda_\alpha\nu_\alpha-\mu_\alpha-\kappa_\alpha\pi_\alpha\right)\\ &= \mu_\alpha + (1-\mu_\alpha)\left(\kappa_\alpha+\kappa_\alpha\left(1-\kappa_\alpha\right)\right) - \nu_\alpha\kappa_\alpha\left(1-\kappa_\alpha+\lambda_\alpha\right)\\ &= \mu_\alpha + (1-\mu_\alpha)\left(1-(1-\kappa_\alpha)^2\right) - \nu_\alpha\kappa_\alpha\left(\sum_{t=0}^{2-1}\lambda_\alpha^{2-1-t}\left(1-\kappa_\alpha\right)^t\right)\end{aligned} \tag{1.318}$$

$$\nu_{J^2_{\kappa_\alpha,\lambda_\alpha}}(\alpha) = \lambda_\alpha^2\nu_\alpha \tag{1.319}$$

Suppose it is true for $n = p$, that is,

$$\mu_{J^p_{\kappa_\alpha,\lambda_\alpha}}(\alpha) = \mu_\alpha + (1-\mu_\alpha)\left(1-(1-\kappa_\alpha)^p\right) - \nu_\alpha\kappa_\alpha\left(\sum_{t=0}^{p-1}\lambda_\alpha^{p-1-t}\left(1-\kappa_\alpha\right)^t\right) \tag{1.320}$$

$$\nu_{J^p_{\kappa_\alpha,\lambda_\alpha}}(\alpha) = \lambda_\alpha^p\nu_\alpha \tag{1.321}$$

then, when $n = p + 1$, we have

$$\begin{aligned}\mu_{J^{p+1}_{\kappa_\alpha,\lambda_\alpha}}(\alpha) &= \mu_\alpha + (1-\mu_\alpha)\left(1-(1-\kappa_\alpha)^p\right) - \nu_\alpha\kappa_\alpha\left(\sum_{t=0}^{p-1}\lambda_\alpha^{p-1-t}\left(1-\kappa_\alpha\right)^t\right)\\ &\quad + \kappa_\alpha\left(1-\lambda_\alpha^p\nu_\alpha-\mu_\alpha-(1-\mu_\alpha)\left(1-(1-\kappa_\alpha)^p\right)\right.\\ &\quad \left.+\nu_\alpha\kappa_\alpha\left(\sum_{t=0}^{p-1}\lambda_\alpha^{p-1-t}\left(1-\kappa_\alpha\right)^t\right)\right)\\ &= \mu_\alpha + (1-\mu_\alpha)\left(1-(1-\kappa_\alpha)^p+\kappa_\alpha-\kappa_\alpha\left(1-(1-\kappa_\alpha)^p\right)\right)\\ &\quad - \nu_\alpha\kappa_\alpha\left(\left(\sum_{t=0}^{p-1}\lambda_\alpha^{p-1-t}\left(1-\kappa_\alpha\right)^{t+1}\right)+\lambda_\alpha^p\right)\\ &= \mu_\alpha + (1-\mu_\alpha)\left(1-(1-\kappa_\alpha)^{p+1}\right) - \nu_\alpha\kappa_\alpha\left(\sum_{t=0}^{p}\lambda_\alpha^{p-t}\left(1-\kappa_\alpha\right)^t\right)\end{aligned} \tag{1.322}$$

$$\nu_{J^{p+1}_{\kappa_\alpha,\lambda_\alpha}}(\alpha) = \lambda\lambda_\alpha^p\nu_\alpha = \lambda_\alpha^{p+1}\nu_\alpha \tag{1.323}$$

and hence, (6) holds for $n = p + 1$. Therefore, (6) holds for all n.
(7) For $n = 1$, we have

$$J^{*,1}_{\kappa_\alpha,\lambda_\alpha}(\alpha) = (\lambda_\alpha \nu_\alpha, \mu_\alpha + \kappa_\alpha (1 - \lambda_\alpha \nu_\alpha - \mu_\alpha))$$
$$= \left(\lambda_\alpha^1 \nu_\alpha, \mu_\alpha + (1 - \mu_\alpha)\left(1 - (1 - \kappa_\alpha)^1\right) - \nu_\alpha \kappa_\alpha \lambda_\alpha \left(\sum_{t=0}^{1-1} \lambda_\alpha^{1-1-t} (1 - \kappa_\alpha)^t \right) \right) \tag{1.324}$$

For $n = 2$, we have

$$\mu_{J^{*,n}_{\kappa_\alpha,\lambda_\alpha}(\alpha)} = \mu_\alpha + \kappa_\alpha (1 - \lambda_\alpha \nu_\alpha - \mu_\alpha) + \kappa_\alpha \left(1 - \lambda_\alpha^2 \nu_\alpha - \mu_\alpha - \kappa_\alpha (1 - \lambda_\alpha \nu_\alpha - \mu_\alpha)\right)$$
$$= \mu_\alpha + (1 - \mu_\alpha)(\kappa_\alpha + \kappa_\alpha (1 - \kappa_\alpha)) - \nu_\alpha \kappa_\alpha \lambda_\alpha (1 + \lambda_\alpha - \kappa_\alpha)$$
$$= \mu_\alpha + (1 - \mu_\alpha)\left(1 - (1 - \kappa_\alpha)^2\right) - \nu_\alpha \kappa_\alpha \lambda_\alpha \left(\sum_{t=0}^{2-1} \lambda_\alpha^{2-1-t} (1 - \kappa_\alpha)^t \right) \tag{1.325}$$

$$\nu_{J^{*,2}_{\kappa_\alpha,\lambda_\alpha}(\alpha)} = \lambda_\alpha^2 \nu_\alpha \tag{1.326}$$

Suppose it is true for $n = p$, that is,

$$\mu_{J^{*,p}_{\kappa_\alpha,\lambda_\alpha}(\alpha)} = \mu_\alpha + (1 - \mu_\alpha)\left(1 - (1 - \kappa_\alpha)^p\right) - \nu_\alpha \kappa_\alpha \lambda_\alpha \left(\sum_{t=0}^{p-1} \lambda_\alpha^{p-1-t} (1 - \kappa_\alpha)^t \right) \tag{1.327}$$

$$\nu_{J^{*,p}_{\kappa_\alpha,\lambda_\alpha}(\alpha)} = \lambda_\alpha^p \nu_\alpha \tag{1.328}$$

then, when $n = p + 1$, we have

$$\mu_{J^{*,p+1}_{\kappa_\alpha,\lambda_\alpha}(\alpha)} = \mu_\alpha + (1 - \mu_\alpha)\left(1 - (1 - \kappa_\alpha)^p\right) - \nu_\alpha \kappa_\alpha \lambda_\alpha \left(\sum_{t=0}^{p-1} \lambda_\alpha^{p-1-t} (1 - \kappa_\alpha)^t \right)$$
$$+ \kappa_\alpha \left(1 - \lambda_\alpha^{p+1} \nu_\alpha - \mu_\alpha - (1 - \mu_\alpha)\left(1 - (1 - \kappa_\alpha)^p\right) + \nu_\alpha \kappa_\alpha \lambda_\alpha \left(\sum_{t=0}^{p-1} \lambda_\alpha^{p-1-t} (1 - \kappa_\alpha)^t \right) \right)$$

$$= \mu_\alpha + (1 - \mu_\alpha)\left(1 - \left((1-\kappa_\alpha)^p - \kappa_\alpha (1-\kappa_\alpha)^p\right)\right)$$
$$- \nu_\alpha \kappa_\alpha \lambda_\alpha \left(\left(\sum_{t=0}^{p-1} \lambda_\alpha^{p-1-t} (1-\kappa_\alpha)^{t+1}\right) + \lambda_\alpha^p\right)$$
$$= \mu_\alpha + (1 - \mu_\alpha)\left(1 - (1-\kappa_\alpha)^{p+1}\right) - \nu_\alpha \kappa_\alpha \lambda_\alpha \left(\sum_{t=0}^{p} \lambda_\alpha^{p-t} (1-\kappa_\alpha)^t\right) \tag{1.329}$$

$$\nu_{J^{*,p+1}_{\kappa_\alpha,\lambda_\alpha}(\alpha)} = \kappa \kappa_\alpha^p \nu_\alpha = \lambda_\alpha^{p+1} \nu_\alpha \tag{1.330}$$

and hence, (7) holds for $n = p + 1$. Therefore, (7) holds for all n.

In addition, by Definition 1.27, we can easily get that intuitionistic fuzzy point operators translate one IFV to another IFV. In the following subsection, we introduce some generalized intuitionistic fuzzy point averaging operators (Xia and Xu 2010) combining the developed point operators with Zhao et al. (2010)'s operators.

1.9 Generalized Point Operators for Aggregating IFVs

Definition 1.28 (Xia and Xu 2010) Let V be the set of all IFVs, $\alpha_j = (\mu_{\alpha_j}, \nu_{\alpha_j})$ $(j = 1, 2, \ldots, m)$ a collection of IFVs, and n a positive integer, taking $\kappa_{\alpha_j}, \lambda_{\alpha_j} \in [0, 1]$, $j = 1, 2, \ldots, m$, $\rho > 0$, and let GIFPWA: $V^m \to V$, if

(1) $GIFPWAD^n_w(\alpha_1, \alpha_2, \ldots, \alpha_m)$

$$= \left(w_1 \left(D^n_{\kappa_{\alpha_1},\lambda_{\alpha_1}}(\alpha_1)\right)^\rho \oplus w_2 \left(D^n_{\kappa_{\alpha_2},\lambda_{\alpha_2}}(\alpha_2)\right)^\rho \oplus \cdots \oplus w_m \left(D^n_{\kappa_{\alpha_m},\lambda_{\alpha_m}}(\alpha_m)\right)^\rho\right)^{\frac{1}{\rho}}.$$

(2) $GIFPWAF^n_w(\alpha_1, \alpha_2, \ldots, \alpha_m)$

$$= \left(w_1 \left(F^n_{\kappa_{\alpha_1},\lambda_{\alpha_1}}(\alpha_1)\right)^\rho \oplus w_2 \left(F^n_{\kappa_{\alpha_2},\lambda_{\alpha_2}}(\alpha_2)\right)^\rho \oplus \cdots \oplus w_m \left(F^n_{\kappa_{\alpha_m},\lambda_{\alpha_m}}(\alpha_m)\right)^\rho\right)^{\frac{1}{\rho}}$$

where $\kappa_{\alpha_j} + \lambda_{\alpha_j} \le 1$, $j = 1, 2, \ldots, m$.

(3) $GIFPWAG^n_w(\alpha_1, \alpha_2, \ldots, \alpha_m)$

$$= \left(w_1 \left(G^n_{\kappa_{\alpha_1},\lambda_{\alpha_1}}(\alpha_1)\right)^\rho \oplus w_2 \left(G^n_{\kappa_{\alpha_2},\lambda_{\alpha_2}}(\alpha_2)\right)^\rho \oplus \cdots \oplus w_m \left(G^n_{\kappa_{\alpha_m},\lambda_{\alpha_m}}(\alpha_m)\right)^\rho\right)^{\frac{1}{\rho}}.$$

(4) $GIFPWAH^n_w(\alpha_1, \alpha_2, \ldots, \alpha_m)$

$$= \left(w_1 \left(H^n_{\kappa_{\alpha_1},\lambda_{\alpha_1}}(\alpha_1)\right)^\rho \oplus w_2 \left(H^n_{\kappa_{\alpha_2},\lambda_{\alpha_2}}(\alpha_2)\right)^\rho \oplus \cdots \oplus w_m \left(H^n_{\kappa_{\alpha_m},\lambda_{\alpha_m}}(\alpha_m)\right)^\rho\right)^{\frac{1}{\rho}}.$$

(5) $GIFPWAH^{*,n}_w(\alpha_1, \alpha_2, \ldots, \alpha_m)$

$$= \left(w_1 \left(H^{*,n}_{\kappa_{\alpha_1},\lambda_{\alpha_1}}(\alpha_1)\right)^\rho \oplus w_2 \left(H^{*,n}_{\kappa_{\alpha_2},\lambda_{\alpha_2}}(\alpha_2)\right)^\rho \oplus \cdots \oplus w_m \left(H^{*,n}_{\kappa_{\alpha_m},\lambda_{\alpha_m}}(\alpha_m)\right)^\rho\right)^{\frac{1}{\rho}}.$$

(6) $GIFPWAJ_w^n(\alpha_1, \alpha_2, \ldots, \alpha_n)$

$$= \left(w_1\left(J^n_{\kappa_{\alpha_1},\lambda_{\alpha_1}}(\alpha_1)\right)^{\rho} \oplus w_2\left(J^n_{\kappa_{\alpha_2},\lambda_{\alpha_2}}(\alpha_2)\right)^{\rho} \oplus \cdots \oplus w_m\left(J^n_{\kappa_{\alpha_m},\lambda_{\alpha_m}}(\alpha_m)\right)^{\rho}\right)^{\frac{1}{\rho}}.$$

(7) $GIFPWAJ_w^{*,n}(\alpha_1, \alpha_2, \ldots, \alpha_n)$

$$= \left(w_1\left(J^{*,n}_{\kappa_{\alpha_1},\lambda_{\alpha_1}}(\alpha_1)\right)^{\rho} \oplus w_2\left(J^{*,n}_{\kappa_{\alpha_2},\lambda_{\alpha_2}}(\alpha_2)\right)^{\rho} \oplus \cdots \oplus w_m\left(J^{*,n}_{\kappa_{\alpha_m},\lambda_{\alpha_m}}(\alpha_m)\right)^{\rho}\right)^{\frac{1}{\rho}}.$$

(8) $GIFPWAP_w^n(\alpha_1, \alpha_2, \ldots, \alpha_n)$

$$= \left(w_1\left(P^n_{\kappa_{\alpha_1},\lambda_{\alpha_1}}(\alpha_1)\right)^{\rho} \oplus w_2\left(P^n_{\kappa_{\alpha_2},\lambda_{\alpha_2}}(\alpha_2)\right)^{\rho} \oplus \cdots \oplus w_m\left(P^n_{\kappa_{\alpha_m},\lambda_{\alpha_m}}(\alpha_m)\right)^{\rho}\right)^{\frac{1}{\rho}}$$

where $\kappa_{\alpha_j} + \lambda_{\alpha_j} \leq 1$, $j = 1, 2, \ldots, m$.

(9) $GIFPWAQ_w^n(\alpha_1, \alpha_2, \ldots, \alpha_n)$

$$= \left(w_1\left(Q^n_{\kappa_{\alpha_1},\lambda_{\alpha_1}}(\alpha_1)\right)^{\rho} \oplus w_2\left(Q^n_{\kappa_{\alpha_2},\lambda_{\alpha_2}}(\alpha_2)\right)^{\rho} \oplus \cdots \oplus w_m\left(Q^n_{\kappa_{\alpha_m},\lambda_{\alpha_m}}(\alpha_m)\right)^{\rho}\right)^{\frac{1}{\rho}}$$

where $\kappa_{\alpha_j} + \lambda_{\alpha_j} \leq 1$, $j = 1, 2, \ldots, m$.

Then, the functions $GIFPWAD_w^n$, $GIFPWAF_w^n$, $GIFPWAG_w^n$, $GIFPWAH_w^n$, $GIFPWAH_w^{*,n}$, $GIFPWAJ_w^n$, $GIFPWAJ_w^{*,n}$, $GIFPWAP_w^n$ and $GIFPWAQ_w^n$ are called the generalized intuitionistic fuzzy point weighted averaging (GIFPWA) operators, where $\rho > 0$, $w = (w_1, w_2, \ldots, w_n)^T$ is a weight vector associated with the GIFPWA operators, with $w_j \geq 0$, $j = 1, 2, \ldots, n$, and $\sum_{j=1}^n w_j = 1$.

Theorem 1.44 (Xia and Xu 2010) The aggregated values by using the GIFPWA operators are also IFVs, and

$$(1)\quad GIFPWAD_w^n(\alpha_1, \alpha_2, \ldots, \alpha_m) = \left(\left(1 - \prod_{j=1}^m \left(1 - \left(\mu_{\alpha_j} + \kappa_{\alpha_j}\pi_{\alpha_j}\right)^{\rho}\right)^{w_j}\right)^{1/\rho}, \right.$$
$$\left. 1 - \left(1 - \prod_{j=1}^m \left(1 - \left(1 - \nu_{\alpha_j} - \left(1 - \kappa_{\alpha_j}\right)\pi_{\alpha_j}\right)^{\rho}\right)^{w_j}\right)^{1/\rho}\right).$$

$$(2)\quad GIFPWAF_w^n(\alpha_1, \alpha_2, \ldots, \alpha_m) = \left(\left(1 - \prod_{j=1}^m \left(1 - \mu^{\rho}_{F^n_{\kappa_{\alpha_j},\lambda_{\alpha_j}}(\alpha)}\right)^{w_j}\right)^{1/\rho}, \right.$$
$$\left. 1 - \left(1 - \prod_{j=1}^m \left(1 - \left(1 - \nu_{F^n_{\kappa_{\alpha_j},\lambda_{\alpha_j}}(\alpha_j)}\right)^{\rho}\right)^{w_j}\right)^{1/\rho}\right)$$

where $\kappa_{\alpha_j} + \lambda_{\alpha_j} \le 1$, $j = 1, 2, \ldots, m$, and

$$\mu_{F^n_{\kappa_{\alpha_j},\lambda_{\alpha_j}}}(\alpha_j) = \mu_{\alpha_j} + \kappa_{\alpha_j}\pi_{\alpha_j}\frac{1-\left(1-\kappa_{\alpha_j}-\lambda_{\alpha_j}\right)^n}{\kappa_{\alpha_j}+\lambda_{\alpha_j}} \tag{1.331}$$

$$v_{F^n_{\kappa_{\alpha_j},\lambda_{\alpha_j}}}(\alpha_j) = v_{\alpha_j} + \lambda_{\alpha_j}\pi_{\alpha_j}\frac{1-\left(1-\kappa_{\alpha_j}-\lambda_{\alpha_j}\right)^n}{\kappa_{\alpha_j}+\lambda_{\alpha_j}} \tag{1.332}$$

(3) $$GIFPWAG^n_w(\alpha_1, \alpha_2, \ldots, \alpha_m) = \left(\left(1-\prod_{j=1}^m\left(1-\left(\kappa^n_{\alpha_j}\mu_{\alpha_j}\right)^\rho\right)^{w_j}\right)^{\frac{1}{\rho}}, 1-\left(1-\prod_{j=1}^m\left(1-\left(1-\lambda^n_{\alpha_j}v_{\alpha_j}\right)^\rho\right)^{w_j}\right)^{\frac{1}{\rho}}\right).$$

(4) $$GIFPWAH^n_w(\alpha_1, \alpha_2, \ldots, \alpha_m) = \left(\left(1-\prod_{j=1}^m\left(1-\left(\kappa^n_{\alpha_j}\mu_{\alpha_j}\right)^\rho\right)^{w_j}\right)^{\frac{1}{\rho}}, 1-\left(1-\prod_{j=1}^m\left(1-\left(1-v_{H^n_{\kappa_{\alpha_j},\lambda_{\alpha_j}}}(\alpha_j)\right)^\rho\right)^{w_j}\right)^{\frac{1}{\rho}}\right).$$

where

$$v_{H^n_{\kappa_{\alpha_j},\lambda_{\alpha_j}}}(\alpha_j) = v_{\alpha_j} + \left(1-v_{\alpha_j}\right)\left(1-\left(1-\lambda_{\alpha_j}\right)^n\right) - \mu_{\alpha_j}\lambda_{\alpha_j}\left(\sum_{t=0}^{n-1}\kappa^{n-1-t}_{\alpha_j}\left(1-\lambda_{\alpha_j}\right)^t\right) \tag{1.333}$$

(5) $$GIFPWAH^{*,n}_w(\alpha_1, \alpha_2, \ldots, \alpha_m) = \left(\left(1-\prod_{j=1}^m\left(1-\left(\kappa^n_{\alpha_j}\mu_{\alpha_j}\right)^\rho\right)^{w_j}\right)^{\frac{1}{\rho}}, 1-\left(1-\prod_{j=1}^m\left(1-\left(1-v_{H^{*,n}_{\kappa_{\alpha_j},\lambda_{\alpha_j}}}(\alpha_j)\right)^\rho\right)^{w_j}\right)^{\frac{1}{\rho}}\right)$$

where

$$\nu_{H^{*,n}_{\kappa_{\alpha_j},\lambda_{\alpha_j}}}(\alpha_j) = \nu_{\alpha_j} + \left(1-\nu_{\alpha j}\right)\left(1-\left(1-\lambda_{\alpha_j}\right)^n\right) - \mu_{\alpha_j}\kappa_{\alpha_j}\lambda_{\alpha_j}\left(\sum_{t=0}^{n-1}\kappa_{\alpha_j}^{n-1-t}\left(1-\lambda_{\alpha_j}\right)^t\right) \tag{1.334}$$

(6) $$GIFPWAJ^n_w(\alpha_1,\alpha_2,\ldots,\alpha_m) = \left(\left(1-\prod_{j=1}^m\left(1-\mu^\rho_{J^n_{\kappa_{\alpha_j},\lambda_{\alpha_j}}}(\alpha_j)\right)^{w_j}\right)^{\frac{1}{\rho}}, 1-\left(1-\prod_{j=1}^m\left(1-\left(1-\lambda^n_{\alpha_j}\nu_{\alpha_j}\right)^\rho\right)^{w_j}\right)^{\frac{1}{\rho}}\right)$$

where

$$\mu_{J^n_{\kappa_{\alpha_j},\lambda_{\alpha_j}}}(\alpha_j) = \mu_{\alpha_j} + \left(1-\mu_{\alpha_j}\right)\left(1-\left(1-\kappa_{\alpha_j}\right)^n\right) - \nu_{\alpha_j}\kappa_{\alpha_j}\left(\sum_{t=0}^{n-1}\lambda_{\alpha_j}^{n-1-t}\left(1-\mu_{\alpha_j}\right)^t\right) \tag{1.335}$$

(7) $$GIFPWAJ^{*,n}_w(\alpha_1,\alpha_2,\ldots,\alpha_m) = \left(\left(1-\prod_{j=1}^m\left(1-\mu^\rho_{J^{*,n}_{\kappa_{\alpha_j},\lambda_{\alpha_j}}}(\alpha_j)\right)^{w_j}\right)^{\frac{1}{\rho}}, 1-\left(1-\prod_{j=1}^m\left(1-\left(1-\lambda^n_{\alpha_j}\nu_{\alpha_j}\right)^\rho\right)^{w_j}\right)^{\frac{1}{\rho}}\right)$$

where

$$\mu_{J^{*,n}_{\kappa_{\alpha_j},\lambda_{\alpha_j}}}(\alpha_j) = \mu_{\alpha_j} + \left(1-\mu_{\alpha_j}\right)\left(1-\left(1-\kappa_{\alpha_j}\right)^n\right) - \nu_{\alpha_j}\kappa_{\alpha_j}\lambda_{\alpha_j}\left(\sum_{t=0}^{n-1}\lambda_{\alpha_j}^{n-1-t}\left(1-\mu_{\alpha_j}\right)^t\right) \tag{1.336}$$

(8) $GIFPWAP_w^n(\alpha_1, \alpha_2, \ldots, \alpha_m) = \left(\left(1 - \prod_{j=1}^{m} \left(1 - \left(\max\left(\kappa_{\alpha_j}, \mu_{\alpha_j}\right)\right)^{\rho}\right)^{w_j}\right)^{\frac{1}{\rho}}, \right.$

$$\left. 1 - \left(1 - \prod_{j=1}^{m} \left(1 - \left(1 - \min\left(\lambda_{\alpha_j}, \nu_{\alpha_j}\right)\right)^{\rho}\right)^{w_j}\right)^{\frac{1}{\rho}} \right)$$

where $\kappa_{\alpha_j} + \lambda_{\alpha_j} \le 1$, $j = 1, 2, \ldots, m$.

(9) $GIFPWAQ_w^n(\alpha_1, \alpha_2, \ldots, \alpha_m) = \left(\left(1 - \prod_{j=1}^{m} \left(1 - \left(\min\left(\kappa_{\alpha_j}, \mu_{\alpha_j}\right)\right)^{\rho}\right)^{w_j}\right)^{\frac{1}{\rho}}, \right.$

$$\left. 1 - \left(1 - \prod_{j=1}^{m} \left(1 - \left(1 - \max\left(\lambda_{\alpha_j}, \nu_{\alpha_j}\right)\right)^{\rho}\right)^{w_j}\right)^{\frac{1}{\rho}} \right)$$

where $\kappa_{\alpha_j} + \lambda_{\alpha_j} \le 1$, $j = 1, 2, \ldots, m$.

Proof Now we prove (2) (the others can be proven similarly). We first prove the following equation by using mathematical induction on m:

$$w_1 \left(F^n_{\kappa_{\alpha_1}, \lambda_{\alpha_1}}(\alpha_1)\right)^{\rho} \oplus w_2 \left(F^n_{\kappa_{\alpha_2}, \lambda_{\alpha_2}}(\alpha_2)\right)^{\rho} \oplus \cdots \oplus w_m \left(F^n_{\kappa_{\alpha_m}, \lambda_{\alpha_m}}(\alpha_m)\right)^{\rho}$$

$$= \left(\left(1 - \prod_{j=1}^{m} \left(1 - \mu^{\rho}_{F^n_{\kappa_{\alpha_j}, \lambda_{\alpha_j}}(\alpha_j)}\right)^{w_j}\right)^{\frac{1}{\rho}}, \right.$$

$$\left. 1 - \left(1 - \prod_{j=1}^{m} \left(1 - \left(1 - \mu_{F^n_{\kappa_{\alpha_j}, \lambda_{\alpha_j}}(\alpha_j)}\right)^{\rho}\right)^{w_j}\right)^{\frac{1}{\rho}} \right) \tag{1.337}$$

where

$$\mu_{F^n_{\kappa_{\alpha_j}, \lambda_{\alpha_j}}(\alpha_j)} = \mu_{\alpha_j} + \kappa_{\alpha_j} \pi_{\alpha_j} \frac{1 - \left(1 - \kappa_{\alpha_j} - \lambda_{\alpha_j}\right)^n}{\kappa_{\alpha_j} + \lambda_{\alpha_j}} \tag{1.338}$$

$$\nu_{F^n_{\kappa_{\alpha_j}, \lambda_{\alpha_j}}(\alpha_j)} = \nu_{\alpha_j} + \lambda_{\alpha_j} \pi_{\alpha_j} \frac{1 - \left(1 - \kappa_{\alpha_j} - \lambda_{\alpha_j}\right)^n}{\kappa_{\alpha_j} + \lambda_{\alpha_j}} \tag{1.339}$$

(1) For $m = 2$: Since

$$\left(F^n_{\kappa\alpha_1,\lambda\alpha_1}(\alpha_1)\right)^\rho = \left(\mu^\rho_{F^n_{\kappa\alpha_1,\lambda\alpha_1}}(\alpha_1), 1-\left(1-\nu_{F^n_{\kappa\alpha_1,\lambda\alpha_1}}(\alpha_1)\right)^\rho\right) \tag{1.340}$$

$$\left(F^n_{\kappa\alpha_2,\lambda\alpha_2}(\alpha_1)\right)^\rho = \left(\mu^\rho_{F^n_{\kappa\alpha_2,\lambda\alpha_2}}(\alpha_2), 1-\left(1-\nu_{F^n_{\kappa\alpha_2,\lambda\alpha_2}}(\alpha_2)\right)^\rho\right) \tag{1.341}$$

then

$$w_1\left(F^n_{\kappa\alpha_1,\lambda\alpha_1}(\alpha_1)\right)^\rho \oplus w_2\left(F^n_{\kappa\alpha_2,\lambda\alpha_2}(\alpha_2)\right)^\rho$$
$$= \left(1-\prod_{j=1}^{2}\left(1-\mu^\rho_{F^n_{\kappa\alpha_1,\lambda\alpha_1}}(\alpha_1)\right)^{w_j}, \prod_{j=1}^{2}\left(1-\left(1-\nu_{F^n_{\kappa\alpha_1,\lambda\alpha_1}}(\alpha_1)\right)^\rho\right)^{w_j}\right) \tag{1.342}$$

(2) If Eq. (1.332) holds for $m = p$, that is,

$$w_1\left(F^n_{\kappa\alpha_1,\lambda\alpha_1}(\alpha_1)\right)^\rho \oplus w_2\left(F^n_{\kappa\alpha_2,\lambda\alpha_2}(\alpha_2)\right)^\rho \oplus \cdots \oplus w_p\left(F^n_{\kappa\alpha_p,\lambda\alpha_p}(\alpha_p)\right)^\rho$$
$$= \left(\left(1-\prod_{j=1}^{p}\left(1-\mu^\rho_{F^n_{\kappa\alpha_j,\lambda\alpha_j}}(\alpha_j)\right)^{w_j}\right)^{\frac{1}{\rho}},\right.$$
$$\left. 1-\left(1-\prod_{j=1}^{p}\left(1-\left(1-\nu_{F^n_{\kappa\alpha_j,\lambda\alpha_j}}(\alpha_j)\right)^\rho\right)^{w_j}\right)^{\frac{1}{\rho}}\right) \tag{1.343}$$

then, when $m = p + 1$, by the operational laws given in Sect. 1.8, we have

$$w_1\left(F^n_{\kappa\alpha_1,\lambda\alpha_1}(\alpha_1)\right)^\rho \oplus w_2\left(F^n_{\kappa\alpha_2,\lambda\alpha_2}(\alpha_2)\right)^\rho \oplus \cdots \oplus w_{p+1}\left(F^n_{\kappa\alpha_{p+1},\lambda\alpha_{p+1}}(\alpha_{p+1})\right)^\rho$$
$$= \left(1-\prod_{j=1}^{p}\left(1-\mu^\rho_{F^n_{\kappa\alpha_j,\lambda\alpha_j}}(\alpha_j)\right)^{w_j}, \prod_{j=1}^{p}\left(1-\left(1-\nu_{F^n_{\kappa\alpha_j,\lambda\alpha_j}}(\alpha_j)\right)^\rho\right)^{w_j}\right)$$
$$\oplus\left(1-\left(1-\mu^\rho_{F^n_{\kappa\alpha_{p+1},\lambda\alpha_{p+1}}}(\alpha_{p+1})\right)^{w_{p+1}}, \left(1-\left(1-\nu_{F^n_{\kappa\alpha_{p+1},\lambda\alpha_{p+1}}}(\alpha_{p+1})\right)^\rho\right)^{w_{p+1}}\right)$$
$$= \left(1-\prod_{j=1}^{p+1}\left(1-\mu^\rho_{F^n_{\kappa\alpha_j,\lambda\alpha_j}}(\alpha_j)\right)^{w_j}, \prod_{j=1}^{p+1}\left(1-\left(1-\nu_{F^n_{\kappa\alpha_j,\lambda\alpha_j}}(\alpha_j)\right)^\rho\right)^{w_j}\right) \tag{1.344}$$

i.e. Eq. (1.337) holds for $m = p + 1$. Thus, Eq. (1.337) holds for all m. Therefore,

$$GIFPWAF_w^n(\alpha_1, \alpha_2, \ldots, \alpha_m)$$
$$= \left(1 - \prod_{j=1}^{m}\left(1 - \mu^{\rho}_{F^n_{\kappa_{\alpha_j}, \lambda_{\alpha_j}}(\alpha_j)}\right)^{w_j}, \prod_{j=1}^{m}\left(1 - \left(1 - \nu_{F^n_{\kappa_{\alpha_j}, \lambda_{\alpha_j}}(\alpha_j)}\right)^{\rho}\right)^{w_j}\right)^{\frac{1}{\rho}}$$
$$= \left(\left(1 - \prod_{j=1}^{m}\left(1 - \mu^{\rho}_{F^n_{\kappa_{\alpha_j}, \lambda_{\alpha_j}}(\alpha_j)}\right)^{w_j}\right)^{\frac{1}{\rho}},\right.$$
$$\left. 1 - \left(1 - \prod_{j=1}^{m}\left(1 - (1 - \nu_{F^n_{\kappa_{\alpha_j}, \lambda_{\alpha_j}}(\alpha_j)})^{\rho}\right)^{w_j}\right)^{\frac{1}{\rho}}\right) \quad (1.345)$$

Moreover, from Definition 1.28 and the operational laws given in Sect. 1.8, we can easily prove that the aggregated values by using the GIFPWA operators are also IFVs.

Theorem 1.45 (Xia and Xu 2010) If all the IFVs $\alpha_j = (\mu_{\alpha_j}, \nu_{\alpha_j})$ $(j = 1, 2, \ldots, m)$ are equal, i.e. $\alpha_j = \alpha$, for all j, then
(1) $GIFPWAD_w^n(\alpha_1, \alpha_2, \ldots, \alpha_m) = D^n_{\kappa_\alpha, \lambda_\alpha}(\alpha)$.

(2) $GIFPWA_w^n(\alpha_1, \alpha_2, \ldots, \alpha_m) = F^n_{\kappa_\alpha, \lambda_\alpha}(\alpha)$, where $\kappa_{\alpha_j} + \lambda_{\alpha_j} \leq 1$, $j = 1, 2, \ldots, m$.

(3) $GIFPWAG_w^n(\alpha_1, \alpha_2, \ldots, \alpha_m) = G^n_{\kappa_\alpha, \lambda_\alpha}(\alpha)$.

(4) $GIFPWAH_w^n(\alpha_1, \alpha_2, \ldots, \alpha_m) = H^n_{\kappa_\alpha, \lambda_\alpha}(\alpha)$.

(5) $GIFPWAH_w^{*,n}(\alpha_1, \alpha_2, \ldots, \alpha_m) = H^{*,n}_{\kappa_\alpha, \lambda_\alpha}(\alpha)$.

(6) $GIFPWAJ_w^n(\alpha_1, \alpha_2, \ldots, \alpha_m) = J^n_{\kappa_\alpha, \lambda_\alpha}(\alpha)$.

(7) $GIFPWAJ_w^{*,n}(\alpha_1, \alpha_2, \ldots, \alpha_m) = J^{*,n}_{\kappa_\alpha, \lambda_\alpha}(\alpha)$.

(8) $GIFPWAP_w^n(\alpha_1, \alpha_2, \ldots, \alpha_m) = P^n_{\kappa_\alpha, \lambda_\alpha}(\alpha)$, where $\kappa_{\alpha_j} + \lambda_{\alpha_j} \leq 1$, $j = 1, 2, \ldots, m$.

(9) $GIFPWAQ_w^n(\alpha_1, \alpha_2, \ldots, \alpha_m) = Q^n_{\kappa_\alpha, \lambda_\alpha}(\alpha)$, where $\kappa_{\alpha_j} + \lambda_{\alpha_j} \leq 1$, $j = 1, 2, \ldots, m$.

Proof We first prove (2), by (2) in Theorem 1.44, we have

$$GIFPWAF_w^n(\alpha_1, \alpha_2, \ldots, \alpha_m)$$
$$= \left(w_1\left(F^n_{\kappa_{\alpha_1}, \lambda_{\alpha_1}}(\alpha_1)\right)^{\rho} \oplus w_2\left(F^n_{\kappa_{\alpha_2}, \lambda_{\alpha_2}}(\alpha_2)\right)^{\rho} \oplus \cdots \oplus w_m\left(F^n_{\kappa_{\alpha_m}, \lambda_{\alpha_m}}(\alpha_m)\right)^{\rho}\right)^{\frac{1}{\rho}}$$
$$= \left(w_1\left(F^n_{\kappa_\alpha, \lambda_\alpha}(\alpha)\right)^{\rho} \oplus w_2\left(F^n_{\kappa_\alpha, \lambda_\alpha}(\alpha)\right)^{\rho} \oplus \cdots \oplus w_m\left(F^n_{\kappa_\alpha, \lambda_\alpha}(\alpha)\right)^{\rho}\right)^{\frac{1}{\rho}}$$

$$= \left((w_1 + w_2 + \cdots + w_n)\left(F^n_{\kappa_\alpha,\lambda_\alpha}(\alpha)\right)^\rho\right)^{\frac{1}{\rho}}$$

$$= \left(\left(F^n_{\kappa_\alpha,\lambda_\alpha}(\alpha)\right)^\rho\right)^{\frac{1}{\rho}} = F^n_{\kappa_\alpha,\lambda_\alpha}(\alpha).$$

Similarly, we can prove the others.

Theorem 1.46 (Xia and Xu 2010)

(1) $\alpha^-_{D_n} \leq GIFPWAD^n_w(\alpha_1, \alpha_2, \ldots, \alpha_m) \leq \alpha^+_{D_n}$.

(2) $\alpha^-_{F_n} \leq GIFPWAF^n_w(\alpha_1, \alpha_2, \ldots, \alpha_m) \leq \alpha^+_{F_n}$, where $\kappa_{\alpha_j} + \lambda_{\alpha_j} \leq 1$, $j = 1, 2, \ldots, m$.

(3) $\alpha^-_{G_n} \leq GIFPWAG^n_w(\alpha_1, \alpha_2, \ldots, \alpha_m) \leq \alpha^+_{G_n}$.

(4) $\alpha^-_{H_n} \leq GIFPWAH^n_w(\alpha_1, \alpha_2, \ldots, \alpha_m) \leq \alpha^+_{H_n}$.

(5) $\alpha^-_{H^*_n} \leq GIFPWAH^{*,n}_w(\alpha_1, \alpha_2, \ldots, \alpha_m) \leq \alpha^+_{H^*_n}$.

(6) $\alpha^-_{J_n} \leq GIFPWAJ^n_w(\alpha_1, \alpha_2, \ldots, \alpha_m) \leq \alpha^+_{J_n}$.

(7) $\alpha^-_{J^*_n} \leq GIFPWAJ^{*,n}_w(\alpha_1, \alpha_2, \ldots, \alpha_m) \leq \alpha^+_{J^*_n}$.

(8) $\alpha^-_{P_n} \leq GIFPWAP^n_w(\alpha_1, \alpha_2, \ldots, \alpha_m) \leq \alpha^+_{P_n}$, where $\kappa_{\alpha_j} + \lambda_{\alpha_j} \leq 1$, $j = 1, 2, \ldots, m$.

(9) $\alpha^-_{Q_n} \leq GIFPWAQ^n_w(\alpha_1, \alpha_2, \ldots, \alpha_m) \leq \alpha^+_{Q_n}$, where $\kappa_{\alpha_j} + \lambda_{\alpha_j} \leq 1$, $j = 1, 2, \ldots, m$, and

$$\alpha^-_{D_n} = \left(\min_j(\mu_{D^n_{\kappa_{\alpha_j},\lambda_{\alpha_j}}(\alpha_j)}), \max_j(\nu_{D^n_{\kappa_{\alpha_j},\lambda_{\alpha_j}}(\alpha_j)})\right)$$

$$\alpha^+_{D_n} = \left(\max_j(\mu_{D^n_{\kappa_{\alpha_j},\lambda_{\alpha_j}}(\alpha_j)}), \min_j(\nu_{D^n_{\kappa_{\alpha_j},\lambda_{\alpha_j}}(\alpha_j)})\right)$$

$$\alpha^-_{F_n} = \left(\min_j(\mu_{F^n_{\kappa_{\alpha_j},\lambda_{\alpha_j}}(\alpha_j)}), \max_j(\nu_{F^n_{\kappa_{\alpha_j},\lambda_{\alpha_j}}(\alpha_j)})\right)$$

$$\alpha^+_{F_n} = \left(\max_j(\mu_{F^n_{\kappa_{\alpha_j},\lambda_{\alpha_j}}(\alpha_j)}), \min_j(\nu_{F^n_{\kappa_{\alpha_j},\lambda_{\alpha_j}}(\alpha_j)})\right)$$

$$\alpha^-_{G_n} = \left(\min_j(\mu_{G^n_{\kappa_{\alpha_j},\lambda_{\alpha_j}}(\alpha_j)}), \max_j(\nu_{G^n_{\kappa_{\alpha_j},\lambda_{\alpha_j}}(\alpha_j)})\right)$$

$$\alpha^+_{G_n} = \left(\max_j(\mu_{G^n_{\kappa_{\alpha_j},\lambda_{\alpha_j}}(\alpha_j)}), \min_j(\nu_{G^n_{\kappa_{\alpha_j},\lambda_{\alpha_j}}(\alpha_j)})\right)$$

$$\alpha^-_{H_n} = \left(\min_j(\mu_{H^n_{\kappa_{\alpha_j},\lambda_{\alpha_j}}(\alpha_j)}), \max_j(\nu_{H^n_{\kappa_{\alpha_j},\lambda_{\alpha_j}}(\alpha_j)})\right)$$

$$\alpha^+_{H_n} = \left(\max_j(\mu_{H^n_{\kappa_{\alpha_j},\lambda_{\alpha_j}}(\alpha_j)}), \min_j(\nu_{H^n_{\kappa_{\alpha_j},\lambda_{\alpha_j}}(\alpha_j)})\right)$$

$$\alpha^-_{H^*_n} = \left(\min_j(\mu_{H^{*,n}_{\kappa_{\alpha_j},\lambda_{\alpha_j}}(\alpha_j)}), \max_j(\nu_{H^{*,n}_{\kappa_{\alpha_j},\lambda_{\alpha_j}}(\alpha_j)})\right)$$

$$\alpha^{+}_{H^*_n} = \left(\max_j(\mu_{H^{*,n}_{\kappa\alpha_j,\lambda\alpha_j}}(\alpha_j)), \min_j(\nu_{H^{*,n}_{\kappa\alpha_j,\lambda\alpha_j}}(\alpha_j))\right)$$

$$\alpha^{-}_{J_n} = \left(\min_j(\mu_{J^n_{\kappa\alpha_j,\lambda\alpha_j}}(\alpha_j)), \max_j(\nu_{J^n_{\kappa\alpha_j,\lambda\alpha_j}}(\alpha_j))\right)$$

$$\alpha^{+}_{J^*_n} = \left(\max_j(\mu_{J^n_{\kappa\alpha_j,\lambda\alpha_j}}(\alpha_j)), \min_j(\nu_{J^n_{\kappa\alpha_j,\lambda\alpha_j}}(\alpha_j))\right)$$

$$\alpha^{-}_{J^*_n} = \left(\min_j(\mu_{J^{*,n}_{\kappa\alpha_j,\lambda\alpha_j}}(\alpha_j)), \max_j(\nu_{J^{*,n}_{\kappa\alpha_j,\lambda\alpha_j}}(\alpha_j))\right)$$

$$\alpha^{+}_{J^*_n} = \left(\max_j(\mu_{J^{*,n}_{\kappa\alpha_j,\lambda\alpha_j}}(\alpha_j)), \min_j(\nu_{J^{*,n}_{\kappa\alpha_j,\lambda\alpha_j}}(\alpha_j))\right)$$

$$\alpha^{-}_{P_n} = \left(\min_j(\mu_{P^n_{\kappa\alpha_j,\lambda\alpha_j}}(\alpha_j)), \max_j(\nu_{P^n_{\kappa\alpha_j,\lambda\alpha_j}}(\alpha_j))\right)$$

$$\alpha^{+}_{P_n} = \left(\max_j(\mu_{P^n_{\kappa\alpha_j,\lambda\alpha_j}}(\alpha_j)), \min_j(\nu_{P^n_{\kappa\alpha_j,\lambda\alpha_j}}(\alpha_j))\right)$$

$$\alpha^{-}_{Q_n} = \left(\min_j(\mu_{Q^n_{\kappa\alpha_j,\lambda\alpha_j}}(\alpha_j)), \max_j(\nu_{Q^n_{\kappa\alpha_j,\lambda\alpha_j}}(\alpha_j))\right)$$

$$\alpha^{+}_{Q_n} = \left(\max_j(\mu_{Q^n_{\kappa\alpha_j,\lambda\alpha_j}}(\alpha_j)), \min_j(\nu_{Q^n_{\kappa\alpha_j,\lambda\alpha_j}}(\alpha_j))\right)$$

Proof We first prove (2), since

$$\min_j\left(\mu_{F^n_{\kappa\alpha_j,\lambda\alpha_j}}(\alpha_j)\right) \le \mu_{F^n_{\kappa\alpha_j,\lambda\alpha_j}}(\alpha_j) \le \max_j\left(\mu_{F^n_{\kappa\alpha_j,\lambda\alpha_j}}(\alpha_j)\right) \tag{1.346}$$

and

$$\min_j\left(\nu_{F^n_{\kappa\alpha_j,\lambda\alpha_j}}(\alpha_j)\right) \le \nu_{F^n_{\kappa\alpha_j,\lambda\alpha_j}}(\alpha_j) \le \max_j\left(\nu_{F^n_{\kappa\alpha_j,\lambda\alpha_j}}(\alpha_j)\right) \tag{1.347}$$

for all j, then

$$\begin{aligned}\prod_{j=1}^{m}\left(1-\mu^{\rho}_{F^n_{\kappa\alpha_j,\lambda\alpha_j}}(\alpha_j)\right)^{w_j} &\ge \prod_{j=1}^{m}\left(1-\left(\max_j\left(\mu_{F^n_{\kappa\alpha_j,\lambda\alpha_j}}(\alpha_j)\right)\right)^{\rho}\right)^{w_j}\\ &= 1-\left(\max_j\left(\mu_{F^n_{\kappa\alpha_j,\lambda\alpha_j}}(\alpha_j)\right)\right)^{\rho}\end{aligned} \tag{1.348}$$

and then

$$\left(1-\prod_{j=1}^{m}\left(1-\mu^{\rho}_{F^n_{\kappa\alpha_j,\lambda\alpha_j}}(\alpha_j)\right)^{w_j}\right)^{\frac{1}{\rho}} \le \max_j\left(\mu_{F^n_{\kappa\alpha_j,\lambda\alpha_j}}(\alpha_j)\right) \tag{1.349}$$

Similarly, we have

$$\left(1-\prod_{j=1}^{m}\left(1-\mu^{\rho}_{F^n_{\kappa\alpha_j,\lambda\alpha_j}}(\alpha_j)\right)^{w_j}\right)^{\frac{1}{\rho}} \geq \min_j\left(\mu_{F^n_{\kappa\alpha_j,\lambda\alpha_j}}(\alpha_j)\right) \tag{1.350}$$

$$\begin{aligned}\prod_{j=1}^{m}\left(1-\left(1-v_{F^n_{\kappa\alpha_j,\lambda\alpha_j}}(\alpha_j)\right)^{\rho}\right)^{w_j} &\leq \prod_{j=1}^{m}\left(1-\left(1-\max_j\left(v_{F^n_{\kappa\alpha_j,\lambda\alpha_j}}(\alpha_j)\right)\right)^{\rho}\right)^{w_j}\\ &= 1-\left(1-\max_j\left(v_{F^n_{\kappa\alpha_j,\lambda\alpha_j}}(\alpha_j)\right)\right)^{\rho}\end{aligned} \tag{1.351}$$

$$1-\prod_{j=1}^{m}\left(1-(1-v_{F^n_{\kappa\alpha_j,\lambda\alpha_j}}(\alpha_j))^{\rho}\right)^{w_j} \geq \left(1-\max_j\left(v_{F^n_{\kappa\alpha_j,\lambda\alpha_j}}(\alpha_j)\right)\right)^{\rho} \tag{1.352}$$

$$\left(1-\prod_{j=1}^{m}\left(1-\left(1-v_{F^n_{\kappa\alpha_j,\lambda\alpha_j}}(\alpha_j)\right)^{\rho}\right)^{w_j}\right)^{\frac{1}{\rho}} \geq 1-\max_j\left(v_{F^n_{\kappa\alpha_j,\lambda\alpha_j}}(\alpha_j)\right) \tag{1.353}$$

$$1-\left(1-\prod_{j=1}^{m}\left(1-\left(1-v_{F^n_{\kappa\alpha_j,\lambda\alpha_j}}(\alpha_j)\right)^{\eta}\right)^{w_j}\right)^{\frac{1}{\rho}} \leq \max_j\left(v_{F^n_{\kappa\alpha_j,\lambda\alpha_j}}(\alpha_j)\right) \tag{1.354}$$

Similarly, we have

$$1-\left(1-\prod_{j=1}^{m}\left(1-\left(1-v_{F^n_{\kappa\alpha_j,\lambda\alpha_j}}(\alpha_j)\right)^{\rho}\right)^{w_j}\right)^{\frac{1}{\rho}} \geq \min_j\left(v_{F^n_{\kappa\alpha_j,\lambda\alpha_j}}(\alpha_j)\right) \tag{1.355}$$

Let

$$GIFPWAF^n_w(\alpha_1,\alpha_2,\ldots,\alpha_n) = \alpha_{F_n} = \left(\mu_{\alpha_{F_n}}, v_{\alpha_{F_n}}\right)$$

then

$$S\left(\alpha_{F_n}\right) = \mu_{\alpha_{F_n}} - v_{\alpha_{F_n}} \leq \max_j\left(\mu_{F^n_{\kappa\alpha_j,\lambda\alpha_j}}(\alpha_j)\right) - \min_j\left(v_{F^n_{\kappa\alpha_j,\lambda\alpha_j}}(\alpha_j)\right) = S\left(\alpha^{+}_{F_n}\right) \tag{1.356}$$

$$S\left(\alpha_{F_n}\right) = \mu_{\alpha_{F_n}} - v_{\alpha_{F_n}} \geq \min_j\left(\mu_{F^n_{\kappa\alpha_j,\lambda\alpha_j}}(\alpha_j)\right) - \max_j\left(v_{F^n_{\kappa\alpha_j,\lambda\alpha_j}}(\alpha_j)\right) = S\left(\alpha^{-}_{F_n}\right) \tag{1.357}$$

If $S\left(\alpha_{F_n}\right) < S\left(\alpha^+_{F_n}\right)$ and $S\left(\alpha_{F_n}\right) > S\left(\alpha^-_{F_n}\right)$, then by using Xu and Yager (2006)'s ranking method, we have

$$\alpha^-_{F_n} < GIFPWAF^n_w(\alpha_1, \alpha_2, \ldots, \alpha_n) < \alpha^+_{F_n} \tag{1.358}$$

If $S\left(\alpha_{F_n}\right) = S\left(\alpha^+_{F_n}\right)$, i.e.,

$$\mu_{\alpha_{F_n}} - \nu_{\alpha_{F_n}} = \max_j \left(\mu_{F^n_{\kappa\alpha_j,\lambda\alpha_j}}(\alpha_j)\right) - \min_j \left(\nu_{F^n_{\kappa\alpha_j,\lambda\alpha_j}}(\alpha_j)\right) \tag{1.359}$$

then by Eqs. (1.349) and (1.355), we have

$$\mu_{\alpha_{F_n}} = \max_j \left(\mu_{F^n_{\kappa\alpha_j,\lambda\alpha_j}}(\alpha_j)\right), \quad \nu_{\alpha_{F_n}} = \min_j \left(\nu_{F^n_{\kappa\alpha_j,\lambda\alpha_j}}(\alpha_j)\right) \tag{1.360}$$

then

$$H\left(\alpha_{F_n}\right) = \mu_{\alpha_{F_n}} + \nu_{\alpha_{F_n}} = \max_j \left(\mu_{F^n_{\kappa\alpha_j,\lambda\alpha_j}}(\alpha_j)\right) + \min_j \left(\nu_{F^n_{\kappa\alpha_j,\lambda\alpha_j}}(\alpha_j)\right) = h\left(\alpha^+_{F_n}\right)$$

So we have

$$GIFPWAF^n_w(\alpha_1, \alpha_2, \ldots, \alpha_m) = \alpha^+_{F_n} \tag{1.361}$$

If $S\left(\alpha_{F_n}\right) = S\left(\alpha^-_{F_n}\right)$, i.e.,

$$\mu_{\alpha_{F_n}} - \nu_{\alpha_{F_n}} = \min_j \left(\mu_{F^n_{\kappa\alpha_j,\lambda\alpha_j}}(\alpha_j)\right) - \max_j \left(\nu_{F^n_{\kappa\alpha_j,\lambda\alpha_j}}(\alpha_j)\right) \tag{1.362}$$

then by Eqs. (1.350) and (1.354), we have

$$\mu_{\alpha_{F_n}} = \min_j \left(\mu_{F^n_{\kappa\alpha_j,\lambda\alpha_j}}(\alpha_j)\right), \quad \nu_{\alpha_{F_n}} = \max_j \left(\nu_{F^n_{\kappa\alpha_j,\lambda\alpha_j}}(\alpha_j)\right) \tag{1.363}$$

hence

$$H\left(\alpha_{F_n}\right) = \mu_{\alpha_{F_n}} + \nu_{\alpha_{F_n}} = \min_j \left(\mu_{F^n_{\kappa\alpha_j,\lambda\alpha_j}}(\alpha_j)\right) + \max_j \left(\nu_{F^n_{\kappa\alpha_j,\lambda\alpha_j}}(\alpha_j)\right) = h\left(\alpha^-_{F_n}\right) \tag{1.364}$$

Thus, it follows that

$$GIFPWAF^n_w(\alpha_1, \alpha_2, \ldots, \alpha_n) = \alpha^-_{F_n} \tag{1.365}$$

and then from Eqs. (1.358), (1.361) and (1.365), we know that (2) always holds.

Theorem 1.47 (Xia and Xu 2010)

(1) If $\mu_{D^n_{\kappa_{\alpha_j},\lambda_{\alpha_j}}}(\alpha_j) \leq \mu_{D^n_{\kappa_{\alpha_j^*},\lambda_{\alpha_j^*}}}(\alpha_j^*)$ and $v_{D^n_{\kappa_{\alpha_j},\lambda_{\alpha_j}}}(\alpha_j) \geq v_{D^n_{\kappa_{\alpha_j^*},\lambda_{\alpha_j^*}}}(\alpha_j^*)$, for all j, then

$$GIFPWAD^n_w(\alpha_1, \alpha_2, \ldots, \alpha_m) \leq GIFPWAD^n_w(\alpha_1^*, \alpha_2^*, \ldots, \alpha_m^*) \quad (1.366)$$

(2) If $\mu_{F^n_{\kappa_{\alpha_j},\lambda_{\alpha_j}}}(\alpha_j) \leq \mu_{F^n_{\kappa_{\alpha_j^*},\lambda_{\alpha_j^*}}}(\alpha_j^*)$ and $v_{F^n_{\kappa_{\alpha_j},\lambda_{\alpha_j}}}(\alpha_j) \geq v_{F^n_{\kappa_{\alpha_j^*},\lambda_{\alpha_j^*}}}(\alpha_j^*)$, for all j, then

$$GIFPWAF^n_w(\alpha_1, \alpha_2, \ldots, \alpha_m) \leq GIFPWAF^n_w(\alpha_1^*, \alpha_2^*, \ldots, \alpha_n^*) \quad (1.367)$$

where $\kappa_{\alpha_j} + \lambda_{\alpha_j} \leq 1$, $j = 1, 2, \ldots, m$.

(3) If $\mu_{G^n_{\kappa_{\alpha_j},\lambda_{\alpha_j}}}(\alpha_j) \leq \mu_{G^n_{\kappa_{\alpha_j^*},\lambda_{\alpha_j^*}}}(\alpha_j^*)$ and $v_{G^n_{\kappa_{\alpha_j},\lambda_{\alpha_j}}}(\alpha_j) \geq v_{G^n_{\kappa_{\alpha_j^*},\lambda_{\alpha_j^*}}}(\alpha_j^*)$, for all j, then

$$GIFPWAG^n_w(\alpha_1, \alpha_2, \ldots, \alpha_m) \leq GIFPWAG^n_w(\alpha_1^*, \alpha_2^*, \ldots, \alpha_m^*) \quad (1.368)$$

(4) If $\mu_{H^n_{\kappa_{\alpha_j},\lambda_{\alpha_j}}}(\alpha_j) \leq \mu_{H^n_{\kappa_{\alpha_j^*},\lambda_{\alpha_j^*}}}(\alpha_j^*)$ and $v_{H^n_{\kappa_{\alpha_j},\lambda_{\alpha_j}}}(\alpha_j) \geq v_{H^n_{\kappa_{\alpha_j^*},\lambda_{\alpha_j^*}}}(\alpha_j^*)$, for all j, then

$$GIFPWAH^n_w(\alpha_1, \alpha_2, \ldots, \alpha_m) \leq GIFPWAH^n_w(\alpha_1^*, \alpha_2^*, \ldots, \alpha_m^*) \quad (1.369)$$

(5) If $\mu_{H^{*,n}_{\kappa_{\alpha_j},\lambda_{\alpha_j}}}(\alpha_j) \leq \mu_{H^{*,n}_{\kappa_{\alpha_j^*},\lambda_{\alpha_j^*}}}(\alpha_j^*)$ and $v_{H^{*,n}_{\kappa_{\alpha_j},\lambda_{\alpha_j}}}(\alpha_j) \geq v_{H^{*,n}_{\kappa_{\alpha_j^*},\lambda_{\alpha_j^*}}}(\alpha_j^*)$, for all j, then

$$GIFPWAH^{*,n}_w(\alpha_1, \alpha_2, \ldots, \alpha_m) \leq GIFPWAH^{*,n}_w(\alpha_1^*, \alpha_2^*, \ldots, \alpha_m^*) \quad (1.370)$$

(6) If $\mu_{J^n_{\kappa_{\alpha_j},\lambda_{\alpha_j}}}(\alpha_j) \leq \mu_{J^n_{\kappa_{\alpha_j^*},\lambda_{\alpha_j^*}}}(\alpha_j^*)$ and $v_{J^n_{\kappa_{\alpha_j},\lambda_{\alpha_j}}}(\alpha_j) \geq v_{J^n_{\kappa_{\alpha_j^*},\lambda_{\alpha_j^*}}}(\alpha_j^*)$, for all j, then

$$GIFPWAJ^n_w(\alpha_1, \alpha_2, \ldots, \alpha_m) \leq GIFPWAJ^n_w(\alpha_1^*, \alpha_2^*, \ldots, \alpha_m^*) \quad (1.371)$$

(7) If $\mu_{J^{*,n}_{\kappa_{\alpha_j},\lambda_{\alpha_j}}}(\alpha_j) \leq \mu_{J^{*,n}_{\kappa_{\alpha_j^*},\lambda_{\alpha_j^*}}}(\alpha_j^*)$ and $v_{J^{*,n}_{\kappa_{\alpha_j},\lambda_{\alpha_j}}}(\alpha_j) \geq v_{J^{*,n}_{\kappa_{\alpha_j^*},\lambda_{\alpha_j^*}}}(\alpha_j^*)$, for all j, then

$$GIFPWAJ^{*,n}_w(\alpha_1, \alpha_2, \ldots, \alpha_m) \leq GIFPWAJ^{*,n}_w(\alpha_1^*, \alpha_2^*, \ldots, \alpha_m^*) \quad (1.372)$$

(8) If $\mu_{P^n_{\kappa_{\alpha_j},\lambda_{\alpha_j}}}(\alpha_j) \leq \mu_{P^n_{\kappa_{\alpha_j^*},\lambda_{\alpha_j^*}}}(\alpha_j^*)$ and $v_{P^n_{\kappa_{\alpha_j},\lambda_{\alpha_j}}}(\alpha_j) \geq v_{P^n_{\kappa_{\alpha_j^*},\lambda_{\alpha_j^*}}}(\alpha_j^*)$, for all j, then

$$GIFPWAP^n_w(\alpha_1, \alpha_2, \ldots, \alpha_m) \leq GIFPWAP^n_w(\alpha_1^*, \alpha_2^*, \ldots, \alpha_m^*) \quad (1.373)$$

where $\kappa_{\alpha_j} + \lambda_{\alpha_j} \leq 1$, $j = 1, 2, \ldots, m$.

(9) If $\mu_{Q^n_{\kappa\alpha_j,\lambda\alpha_j}}(\alpha_j) \leq \mu_{Q^n_{\kappa_{\alpha_j^*},\lambda_{\alpha_j^*}}}(\alpha_j^*)$ and $\nu_{Q^n_{\kappa\alpha_j,\lambda\alpha_j}}(\alpha_j) \geq \nu_{Q^n_{\kappa_{\alpha_j^*},\lambda_{\alpha_j^*}}}(\alpha_j^*)$, for all j, then

$$GIFPWAQ^n_w(\alpha_1,\alpha_2,\ldots,\alpha_m) \leq GIFPWAQ^n_w(\alpha_1^*,\alpha_2^*,\ldots,\alpha_m^*) \tag{1.374}$$

where $\kappa_{\alpha_j} + \lambda_{\alpha_j} \leq 1$, $j = 1, 2, \ldots, m$.

Proof Here, we prove (2), since $\mu_{F^n_{\kappa\alpha_j,\lambda\alpha_j}}(\alpha_j) \leq \mu_{F^n_{\kappa_{\alpha_j^*},\lambda_{\alpha_j^*}}}(\alpha_j^*)$ and $\nu_{F^n_{\kappa\alpha_j,\lambda\alpha_j}}(\alpha_j) \geq \nu_{F^n_{\kappa_{\alpha_j^*},\lambda_{\alpha_j^*}}}(\alpha_j^*)$ for all j, then

$$\prod_{j=1}^{m}\left(1-\mu^{\rho}_{F^n_{\kappa\alpha_j,\lambda\alpha_j}}(\alpha_j)\right)^{w_j} \geq \prod_{j=1}^{m}\left(1-\mu^{\rho}_{F^n_{\kappa_{\alpha_j^*},\lambda_{\alpha_j^*}}}(\alpha_j^*)\right)^{w_j} \tag{1.375}$$

$$1-\prod_{j=1}^{n}\left(1-\mu^{\rho}_{F^n_{\kappa\alpha_j,\lambda\alpha_j}}(\alpha_j)\right)^{w_j} \leq 1-\prod_{j=1}^{n}\left(1-\mu^{\rho}_{F^n_{\kappa_{\alpha_j^*},\lambda_{\alpha_j^*}}}(\alpha_j^*)\right)^{w_j} \tag{1.376}$$

$$\left(1-\prod_{j=1}^{n}\left(1-\mu^{\rho}_{F^n_{\kappa\alpha_j,\lambda\alpha_j}}(\alpha_j)\right)^{w_j}\right)^{\frac{1}{\rho}} \leq \left(1-\prod_{j=1}^{m}\left(1-\mu^{\rho}_{F^n_{\kappa_{\alpha_j^*},\lambda_{\alpha_j^*}}}(\alpha_j^*)\right)^{w_j}\right)^{\frac{1}{\rho}} \tag{1.377}$$

$$\prod_{j=1}^{n}\left(1-(1-\nu_{F^n_{\kappa\alpha_j,\lambda\alpha_j}}(\alpha_j))^{\rho}\right)^{w_j} \geq \prod_{j=1}^{m}\left(1-(1-\nu_{F^n_{\kappa_{\alpha_j^*},\lambda_{\alpha_j^*}}}(\alpha_j^*))^{\rho}\right)^{w_j} \tag{1.378}$$

$$1-\prod_{j=1}^{m}\left(1-(1-\nu_{F^n_{\kappa\alpha_j,\lambda\alpha_j}}(\alpha_j))^{\rho}\right)^{w_j} \leq 1-\prod_{j=1}^{m}\left(1-(1-\nu_{F^n_{\kappa_{\alpha_j^*},\lambda_{\alpha_j^*}}}(\alpha_j^*))^{\rho}\right)^{w_j} \tag{1.379}$$

$$\left(1-\prod_{j=1}^{m}\left(1-(1-\nu_{F^n_{\kappa\alpha_j,\lambda\alpha_j}}(\alpha_j))^{\rho}\right)^{w_j}\right)^{\frac{1}{\rho}} \leq \left(1-\prod_{j=1}^{m}\left(1-(1-\nu_{F^n_{\kappa_{\alpha_j^*},\lambda_{\alpha_j^*}}}(\alpha_j^*))^{\rho}\right)^{w_j}\right)^{\frac{1}{\rho}} \tag{1.380}$$

$$1-\left(1-\prod_{j=1}^{m}\left(1-(1-\nu_{F^n_{\kappa\alpha_j,\lambda\alpha_j}}(\alpha_j))^{\rho}\right)^{w_j}\right)^{\frac{1}{\rho}} \geq 1-\left(1-\prod_{j=1}^{m}\left(1-(1-\nu_{F^n_{\kappa_{\alpha_j^*},\lambda_{\alpha_j^*}}}(\alpha_j^*))^{\rho}\right)^{w_j}\right)^{\frac{1}{\rho}} \tag{1.381}$$

$$\left(1-\prod_{j=1}^{m}\left(1-\mu^{\rho}_{F^n_{\kappa\alpha_j,\lambda\alpha_j}}(\alpha_j)\right)^{w_j}\right)^{\frac{1}{\rho}} - \left(1-\left(1-\prod_{j=1}^{m}\left(1-(1-\nu_{F^n_{\kappa\alpha_j,\lambda\alpha_j}}(\alpha_j))^{\rho}\right)^{w_j}\right)^{\frac{1}{\rho}}\right)$$

$$\leq \left(1-\prod_{j=1}^{m}\left(1-\mu^{\rho}_{F^{n}_{\kappa_{\alpha_j^*},\lambda_{\alpha_j^*}}}(\alpha_j^*)\right)^{w_j}\right)^{\frac{1}{\rho}} - \left(1-\left(1-\prod_{j=1}^{m}\left(1-(1-\nu_{F^{n}_{\kappa_{\alpha_j^*},\lambda_{\alpha_j^*}}}(\alpha_j^*))^{\rho}\right)^{w_j}\right)^{\frac{1}{\rho}}\right) \tag{1.382}$$

Let $\alpha = GIFPWAF^n_w(\alpha_1, \alpha_2, \ldots, \alpha_m)$ and $\alpha^* = GIFPWAF^n_w(\alpha_1^*, \alpha_2^*, \ldots, \alpha_m^*)$, then by Eq. (1.382), we have

$$S(\alpha_{F_n}) \leq S(\alpha^*_{F_n}) \tag{1.383}$$

If $S(\alpha_{F_n}) < S(\alpha^*_{F_n})$, then by using Xu and Yager (2006)'s ranking method, we have

$$GIFPWAF^n_w(\alpha_1, \alpha_2, \ldots, \alpha_m) < GIFPWAF^n_w(\alpha_1^*, \alpha_2^*, \ldots, \alpha_m^*) \tag{1.384}$$

If $S(\alpha_{F_n}) = S(\alpha^*_{F_n})$, then

$$\left(1-\prod_{j=1}^{m}\left(1-\mu^{\rho}_{F^{n}_{\kappa_{\alpha_j},\lambda_{\alpha_j}}}(\alpha_j)\right)^{w_j}\right)^{\frac{1}{\rho}} - \left(1-\left(1-\prod_{j=1}^{m}\left(1-(1-\nu_{F^{n}_{\kappa_{\alpha_j},\lambda_{\alpha_j}}}(\alpha_j))^{\rho}\right)^{w_j}\right)^{\frac{1}{\rho}}\right)$$
$$= \left(1-\prod_{j=1}^{m}\left(1-\mu^{\rho}_{F^{n}_{\kappa_{\alpha_j^*},\lambda_{\alpha_j^*}}}(\alpha_j^*)\right)^{w_j}\right)^{\frac{1}{\rho}} - \left(1-\left(1-\prod_{j=1}^{m}\left(1-(1-\nu_{F^{n}_{\kappa_{\alpha_j^*},\lambda_{\alpha_j^*}}}(\alpha_j^*))^{\rho}\right)^{w_j}\right)^{\frac{1}{\rho}}\right) \tag{1.385}$$

Since $\mu_{F^{n}_{\kappa_{\alpha_j},\lambda_{\alpha_j}}}(\alpha_j) \leq \mu_{F^{n}_{\kappa_{\alpha_j^*},\lambda_{\alpha_j^*}}}(\alpha_j^*)$ and $\nu_{F^{n}_{\kappa_{\alpha_j},\lambda_{\alpha_j}}}(\alpha_j) \geq \nu_{F^{n}_{\kappa_{\alpha_j^*},\lambda_{\alpha_j^*}}}(\alpha_j^*)$, for all j, then

$$\left(1-\prod_{j=1}^{m}\left(1-\mu^{\rho}_{F^{n}_{\kappa_{\alpha_j},\lambda_{\alpha_j}}}(\alpha_j)\right)^{w_j}\right)^{\frac{1}{\rho}} = \left(1-\prod_{j=1}^{m}\left(1-\mu^{\rho}_{F^{n}_{\kappa_{\alpha_j^*},\lambda_{\alpha_j^*}}}(\alpha_j^*)\right)^{w_j}\right)^{\frac{1}{\rho}} \tag{1.386}$$

$$1-\left(1-\prod_{j=1}^{m}\left(1-(1-\nu_{F^{n}_{\kappa_{\alpha_j},\lambda_{\alpha_j}}}(\alpha_j))^{\rho}\right)^{w_j}\right)^{\frac{1}{\rho}}$$
$$= 1-\left(1-\prod_{j=1}^{m}\left(1-(1-\nu_{F^{n}_{\kappa_{\alpha_j^*},\lambda_{\alpha_j^*}}}(\alpha_j^*))^{\rho}\right)^{w_j}\right)^{\frac{1}{\rho}} \tag{1.387}$$

Hence

$$
\begin{aligned}
&H(\alpha_{F_n})\\
&=\left(1-\prod_{j=1}^{m}\left(1-\mu^{\rho}_{F^n_{\kappa\alpha_j,\lambda\alpha_j}}(\alpha_j)\right)^{w_j}\right)^{\frac{1}{\rho}}+\left(1-\left(1-\prod_{j=1}^{m}\left(1-(1-\nu_{F^n_{\kappa\alpha_j,\lambda\alpha_j}}(\alpha_j))^{\rho}\right)^{w_j}\right)^{\frac{1}{\rho}}\right)\\
&=\left(1-\prod_{j=1}^{m}\left(1-\mu^{\rho}_{F^n_{\kappa_{\alpha_j^*},\lambda_{\alpha_j^*}}}(\alpha_j^*)\right)^{w_j}\right)^{\frac{1}{\rho}}+\left(1-\left(1-\prod_{j=1}^{m}\left(1-(1-\nu_{F^n_{\kappa_{\alpha_j^*},\lambda_{\alpha_j^*}}}(\alpha_j^*))^{\rho}\right)^{w_j}\right)^{\frac{1}{\rho}}\right)\\
&=h(\alpha^*_{F_n})
\end{aligned}
\tag{1.388}
$$

thus, we have

$$
GIFPWAF^n_w(\alpha_1,\alpha_2,\ldots,\alpha_m)=GIFPWAF^n_w(\alpha_1^*,\alpha_2^*,\ldots,\alpha_m^*) \tag{1.389}
$$

From Eqs. (1.384) and (1.389), we know that (2) always holds. Similar to the proof of (2), we can prove the others.

We now look at some special cases obtained by using different choices of the parameters n, w and η:

Theorem 1.48 (Xia and Xu 2010)

(1) If $n=0$, then the GIFPWA operators reduce to the following:

$$
GIFWA_w(\alpha_1,\alpha_2,\ldots,\alpha_m)=\left(w_1\alpha_1^{\rho}\oplus w_2\alpha_2^{\rho}\oplus\cdots\oplus w_m\alpha_m^{\rho}\right)^{\frac{1}{\rho}} \tag{1.390}
$$

which is the GIFWA operator (Zhao et al. 2010).

(2) If $\rho=1$ and $n=0$, then the GIFPWA operators reduce to the following:

$$
IFWA_w(\alpha_1,\alpha_2,\ldots,\alpha_m)=w_1\alpha_{\sigma(1)}\oplus w_2\alpha_{\sigma(2)}\oplus\cdots\oplus w_m\alpha_{\sigma(m)} \tag{1.391}
$$

which is the IFWA operator (Xu 2007).

(3) If $\rho\to 0$ and $n=0$, then the GIFPWA operators reduce to the following:

$$
IFWG_w(\alpha_1,\alpha_2,\ldots,\alpha_m)=\alpha_{\sigma(1)}^{w_1}\otimes\alpha_{\sigma(2)}^{w_1}\otimes\cdots\otimes\alpha_{\sigma(m)}^{w_1} \tag{1.392}
$$

which is the IFWG operator (Xu and Yager 2006).

(4) If $\rho\to+\infty$ and $n=0$, then the GIFPWA operators reduce to the following:

$$
IFMAX_w(\alpha_1,\alpha_2,\ldots,\alpha_m)=\max_j(\alpha_j) \tag{1.393}
$$

which is called an intuitionistic fuzzy maximum operator (Chen and Tan 1994).

(5) If $w = (1/m, 1/m, \ldots, 1/m)^T$, $n = 0$ and $\rho = 1$, then the GIFPWA operators reduce to the following:

$$IFA_w(\alpha_1, \alpha_2, \ldots, \alpha_m) = \frac{1}{n}(\alpha_1 \oplus \alpha_2 \oplus \cdots \oplus \alpha_m) \quad (1.394)$$

which is called an intuitionistic fuzzy average operator (Xu 2007).

(6) If $w = (1/m, 1/m, \ldots, 1/m)^T$, $n = 0$ and $\rho \to 0$, then the GIFPWA operators reduces to the following:

$$IFGM_w(\alpha_1, \alpha_2, \ldots, \alpha_m) = (\alpha_1 \otimes \alpha_2 \otimes \cdots \otimes \alpha_m)^{\frac{1}{n}} \quad (1.395)$$

which is the IFGM (Xu and Yager 2006).

Definition 1.29 (Xia and Xu 2010) If
(1) $GIFPOWAD_w^n(\alpha_1, \alpha_2, \ldots, \alpha_m)$

$$= \left(w_1\left(D^n_{\kappa_{\alpha_{\sigma(1)}},\lambda_{\alpha_{\sigma(1)}}}\left(\alpha_{\sigma(1)}\right)\right)^{\rho} \oplus w_2\left(D^n_{\kappa_{\alpha_{\sigma(2)}},\lambda_{\alpha_{\sigma(2)}}}\left(\alpha_{\sigma(2)}\right)\right)^{\rho} \oplus \cdots \oplus w_m\left(D^n_{\kappa_{\alpha_{\sigma(m)}},\lambda_{\alpha_{\sigma(m)}}}\left(\alpha_{\sigma(m)}\right)\right)^{\rho}\right)^{\frac{1}{\rho}}$$

where $D^n_{\kappa_{\alpha_{\sigma(j)}},\lambda_{\alpha_{\sigma(j)}}}\left(\alpha_{\sigma(j)}\right)$ is the jth largest of $D^n_{\kappa_{\alpha_i},\lambda_{\alpha_i}}(\alpha_i)$ $(i = 1, 2, \ldots, m)$.
(2) $GIFPOWAF_w^n(\alpha_1, \alpha_2, \ldots, \alpha_m)$

$$= \left(w_1\left(F^n_{\kappa_{\alpha_{\sigma(1)}},\lambda_{\alpha_{\sigma(1)}}}\left(\alpha_{\sigma(1)}\right)\right)^{\rho} \oplus w_2\left(F^n_{\kappa_{\alpha_{\sigma(2)}},\lambda_{\alpha_{\sigma(2)}}}\left(\alpha_{\sigma(2)}\right)\right)^{\rho} \oplus \cdots \oplus w_m\left(F^n_{\kappa_{\alpha_{\sigma(m)}},\lambda_{\alpha_{\sigma(m)}}}\left(\alpha_{\sigma(m)}\right)\right)^{\rho}\right)^{\frac{1}{\rho}}$$

where $\kappa_{\alpha_{\sigma(j)}} + \lambda_{\alpha_{\sigma(j)}} \leq 1$, $j = 1, 2, \ldots, m$, $F^n_{\kappa_{\alpha_{\sigma(j)}},\lambda_{\alpha_{\sigma(j)}}}\left(\alpha_{\sigma(j)}\right)$ is the jth largest of $F^n_{\kappa_{\alpha_i},\lambda_{\alpha_i}}(\alpha_i)$ $(i = 1, 2, \ldots, m)$.
(3) $GIFPOWAG_w^n(\alpha_1, \alpha_2, \ldots, \alpha_m)$

$$= \left(w_1\left(G^n_{\kappa_{\alpha_{\sigma(1)}},\lambda_{\alpha_{\sigma(1)}}}\left(\alpha_{\sigma(1)}\right)\right)^{\rho} \oplus w_2\left(G^n_{\kappa_{\sigma(2)},\lambda_{\sigma(2)}}\left(\alpha_{\sigma(2)}\right)\right)^{\rho} \oplus \cdots \oplus w_m\left(G^n_{\kappa_{\alpha_{\sigma(m)}},\lambda_{\alpha_{\sigma(m)}}}\left(\alpha_{\sigma(m)}\right)\right)^{\rho}\right)^{\frac{1}{\rho}}$$

where $G^n_{\kappa_{\alpha_{\sigma(j)}},\lambda_{\alpha_{\sigma(j)}}}\left(\alpha_{\sigma(j)}\right)$ is the jth largest of $G^n_{\kappa_{\alpha_i},\lambda_{\alpha_i}}(\alpha_i)$ $(i = 1, 2, \ldots, m)$.

(4) $GIFPOWAH_w^n(\alpha_1, \alpha_2, \ldots, \alpha_m)$

$$= \left(w_1 \left(H^n_{\kappa_{\sigma(1)}, \lambda_{\sigma(1)}} \left(\alpha_{\sigma(1)}\right)\right)^\rho \oplus w_2 \left(H^n_{\kappa_{\sigma(2)}, \lambda_{\sigma(2)}} \left(\alpha_{\sigma(2)}\right)\right)^\rho \oplus \cdots \oplus w_m \left(H^n_{\kappa_{\alpha_{\sigma(m)}}, \lambda_{\alpha_{\sigma(m)}}} (\alpha_m)\right)^\rho\right)^{\frac{1}{\rho}}$$

where $H^n_{\kappa_{\alpha_{\sigma(j)}}, \lambda_{\alpha_{\sigma(j)}}} \left(\alpha_{\sigma(j)}\right)$ is the jth largest of $H^n_{\kappa_{\alpha_i}, \lambda_{\alpha_i}} (\alpha_i)$ $(i = 1, 2, \ldots, m)$.

(5) $GIFPOWAH_w^{*,n}(\alpha_1, \alpha_2, \ldots, \alpha_m)$

$$= \left(w_1 \left(H^{*,n}_{\kappa_{\alpha_{\sigma(1)}}, \lambda_{\alpha_{\sigma(1)}}} \left(\alpha_{\sigma(1)}\right)\right)^\rho \oplus w_2 \left(H^{*,n}_{\kappa_{\alpha_{\sigma(2)}}, \lambda_{\alpha_{\sigma(2)}}} \left(\alpha_{\sigma(2)}\right)\right)^\rho \oplus \cdots \oplus w_m \left(H^{*,n}_{\kappa_{\alpha_{\sigma(m)}}, \lambda_{\alpha_{\sigma(m)}}} \left(\alpha_{\sigma(m)}\right)\right)^\rho\right)^{\frac{1}{\rho}}$$

where $H^{*,n}_{\kappa_{\alpha_{\sigma(j)}}, \lambda_{\alpha_{\sigma(j)}}} \left(\alpha_{\sigma(j)}\right)$ is the jth largest of $H^{*,n}_{\kappa_{\alpha_i}, \lambda_{\alpha_i}} (\alpha_i)$ $(i = 1, 2, \ldots, m)$.

(6) $GIFPOWAJ_w^n(\alpha_1, \alpha_2, \ldots, \alpha_m)$

$$= \left(w_1 \left(J^n_{\kappa_{\alpha_{\sigma(1)}}, \lambda_{\alpha_{\sigma(1)}}} \left(\alpha_{\sigma(1)}\right)\right)^\rho \oplus w_2 \left(J^n_{\kappa_{\alpha_{\sigma(2)}}, \lambda_{\alpha_{\sigma(2)}}} \left(\alpha_{\sigma(2)}\right)\right)^\rho \oplus \cdots \oplus w_m \left(J^n_{\kappa_{\alpha_{\sigma(m)}}, \lambda_{\alpha_{\sigma(m)}}} \left(\alpha_{\sigma(m)}\right)\right)^\rho\right)^{\frac{1}{\rho}}$$

where $J^n_{\kappa_{\alpha_{\sigma(j)}}, \lambda_{\alpha_{\sigma(j)}}} \left(\alpha_{\sigma(j)}\right)$ is the jth largest of $J^n_{\kappa_{\alpha_i}, \lambda_{\alpha_i}} (\alpha_i)$ $(i = 1, 2, \ldots, m)$.

(7) $GIFPOWAJ_w^{*,n}(\alpha_1, \alpha_2, \ldots, \alpha_m)$

$$= \left(w_1 \left(J^{*,n}_{\kappa_{\alpha_{\sigma(1)}}, \lambda_{\alpha_{\sigma(1)}}} \left(\alpha_{\sigma(1)}\right)\right)^\rho \oplus w_2 \left(J^{*,n}_{\kappa_{\alpha_{\sigma(2)}}, \lambda_{\alpha_{\sigma(2)}}} \left(\alpha_{\sigma(2)}\right)\right)^\rho \oplus \cdots \oplus w_m \left(J^{*,n}_{\kappa_{\alpha_{\sigma(m)}}, \lambda_{\alpha_{\sigma(m)}}} \left(\alpha_{\sigma(m)}\right)\right)^\rho\right)^{\frac{1}{\rho}}$$

where $J^{*,n}_{\kappa_{\alpha_{\sigma(j)}}, \lambda_{\alpha_{\sigma(j)}}} \left(\alpha_{\sigma(j)}\right)$ is the jth largest of $J^{*,n}_{\kappa_{\alpha_i}, \lambda_{\alpha_i}} (\alpha_i)$ $(i = 1, 2, \ldots, m)$.

(8) $GIFPOWAP_w^n(\alpha_1, \alpha_2, \ldots, \alpha_m)$

$$= \left(w_1 \left(P^n_{\kappa_{\alpha_{\sigma(1)}}, \lambda_{\alpha_{\sigma(1)}}} \left(\alpha_{\sigma(1)}\right)\right)^\rho \oplus w_2 \left(P^n_{\kappa_{\alpha_{\sigma(2)}}, \lambda_{\alpha_{\sigma(2)}}} \left(\alpha_{\sigma(2)}\right)\right)^\rho \oplus \cdots \oplus w_m \left(P^n_{\kappa_{\alpha_{\sigma(m)}}, \lambda_{\alpha_{\sigma(m)}}} \left(\alpha_{\sigma(m)}\right)\right)^\rho\right)^{\frac{1}{\rho}}$$

where $\kappa_{\alpha_{\sigma(j)}} + \lambda_{\alpha_{\sigma(j)}} \leq 1$, $j = 1, 2, \ldots, m$, $P^n_{\kappa_{\alpha_{\sigma(j)}}, \lambda_{\alpha_{\sigma(j)}}} \left(\alpha_{\sigma(j)}\right)$ is the jth largest of $P^n_{\kappa_{\alpha_i}, \lambda_{\alpha_i}} (\alpha_i)$ $(i = 1, 2, \ldots, m)$.

(9) $GIFPOWAQ_w^n(\alpha_1, \alpha_2, \ldots, \alpha_m)$

$$= \left(w_1 \left(Q^n_{\kappa_{\alpha_{\sigma(1)}}, \lambda_{\alpha_{\sigma(1)}}} \left(\alpha_{\sigma(1)}\right) \right)^\rho \oplus w_2 \left(Q^n_{\kappa_{\alpha_{\sigma(2)}}, \lambda_{\alpha_{\sigma(2)}}} \left(\alpha_{\sigma(2)}\right) \right)^\rho \oplus \cdots \oplus w_m \left(Q^n_{\kappa_{\alpha_{\sigma(m)}}, \lambda_{\alpha_{\sigma(m)}}} \left(\alpha_{\sigma(m)}\right) \right)^\rho \right)^{\frac{1}{\rho}}$$

where $\kappa_{\alpha_{\sigma(j)}} + \lambda_{\alpha_{\sigma(j)}} \leq 1$, $j = 1, 2, \ldots, m$, $Q^n_{\kappa_{\alpha_{\sigma(j)}}, \lambda_{\alpha_{\sigma(j)}}} \left(\alpha_{\sigma(j)}\right)$ is the jth largest of $Q^n_{\kappa_{\alpha_i}, \lambda_{\alpha_i}} (\alpha_i)$ $(i = 1, 2, \ldots, m)$.

Then the functions $GIFPOWAD_w^n$, $GIFPOWAF_w^n$, $GIFPOWAG_w^n$, $GIFPOWAH_w^n$, $GIFPOWAH_w^{*,n}$, $GIFPOWAJ_w^n$, $GIFPOWAJ_w^{*,n}$, $GIFPOWAP_w^n$ and $GIFPOWAQ_w^n$ are called the GIFPOWA operators.

The GIFPOWA operators have some properties similar to those of the GIFPWA operators.

Theorem 1.49 (Xia and Xu 2010) The aggregated value by using the GIFPOWA operators are also IFVs, and

(1) $GIFPOWAD_w^n(\alpha_1, \alpha_2, \ldots, \alpha_m)$

$$= \left(\left(1 - \prod_{j=1}^m \left(1 - \left(\mu_{\alpha_{\sigma(j)}} + \kappa_{\alpha_{\sigma(j)}} \pi_{\alpha_{\sigma(j)}}\right)^\rho\right)^{w_j} \right)^{\frac{1}{\rho}}, \right.$$

$$\left. 1 - \left(1 - \prod_{j=1}^m \left(1 - \left(1 - \nu_{\alpha_{\sigma(j)}} - \left(1 - \kappa_{\alpha_{\sigma(j)}}\right) \pi_{\alpha_{\sigma(j)}}\right)^\rho\right)^{w_j} \right)^{\frac{1}{\rho}} \right)$$

(2) $GIFPOWAF_w^n(\alpha_1, \alpha_2, \ldots, \alpha_m)$

$$= \left(\left(1 - \prod_{j=1}^m \left(1 - \mu^\rho_{F^n_{\kappa_{\alpha_{\sigma(j)}}, \lambda_{\alpha_{\sigma(j)}}}(\alpha_{\sigma(j)})} \right)^{w_j} \right)^{\frac{1}{\rho}}, \right.$$

$$\left. 1 - \left(1 - \prod_{j=1}^m \left(1 - \left(1 - \nu_{F^n_{\kappa_{\alpha_{\sigma(j)}}, \lambda_{\alpha_{\sigma(j)}}}(\alpha_{\sigma(j)})} \right)^\rho \right)^{w_j} \right)^{\frac{1}{\rho}} \right)$$

where $\kappa_{\alpha_{\sigma(j)}} + \lambda_{\alpha_{\sigma(j)}} \leq 1$, $j = 1, 2, \ldots, m$, and

$$\mu_{F^n_{\kappa_{\alpha_{\sigma(j)}},\lambda_{\alpha_{\sigma(j)}}}}(\alpha_{\sigma(j)}) = \mu_{\alpha_{\sigma(j)}} + \kappa_{\alpha_{\sigma(j)}}\pi_{\alpha_{\sigma(j)}}\frac{1-\left(1-\kappa_{\alpha_{\sigma(j)}}-\lambda_{\alpha_{\sigma(j)}}\right)^n}{\kappa_{\alpha_{\sigma(j)}}+\lambda_{\alpha_{\sigma(j)}}} \tag{1.396}$$

$$v_{F^n_{\kappa_{\alpha_{\sigma(j)}},\lambda_{\alpha_{\sigma(j)}}}}(\alpha_{\sigma(j)}) = v_{\alpha_{\sigma(j)}} + \lambda_{\alpha_{\sigma(j)}}\pi_{\alpha_{\sigma(j)}}\frac{1-\left(1-\kappa_{\alpha_{\sigma(j)}}-\lambda_{\alpha_{\sigma(j)}}\right)^n}{\kappa_{\alpha_{\sigma(j)}}+\lambda_{\alpha_{\sigma(j)}}} \tag{1.397}$$

(3) $GIFPOWAG^n_w(\alpha_1,\alpha_2,\ldots,\alpha_n)$

$$= \left(\left(1-\prod_{j=1}^{m}\left(1-\left(\kappa^n_{\alpha_{\sigma(j)}}\mu_{\alpha_{\sigma(j)}}\right)^\rho\right)^{w_j}\right)^{\frac{1}{\rho}},\right.$$
$$\left. 1-\left(1-\prod_{j=1}^{m}\left(1-\left(1-\lambda^n_{\alpha_{\sigma(j)}}v_{\alpha_{\sigma(j)}}\right)^\rho\right)^{w_j}\right)^{\frac{1}{\rho}}\right)$$

(4) $GIFPOWAH^n_w(\alpha_1,\alpha_2,\ldots,\alpha_n)$

$$= \left(\left(1-\prod_{j=1}^{m}\left(1-\left(\kappa^n_{\alpha_{\sigma(j)}}\mu_{\alpha_{\sigma(j)}}\right)^\rho\right)^{w_j}\right)^{\frac{1}{\rho}},\right.$$
$$\left. 1-\left(1-\prod_{j=1}^{m}\left(1-\left(1-v_{H^n_{\kappa_{\alpha_{\sigma(j)}},\lambda_{\alpha_{\sigma(j)}}}}(\alpha_{\sigma(j)})\right)^\rho\right)^{w_j}\right)^{\frac{1}{\rho}}\right)$$

where

$$v_{H^n_{\kappa_{\alpha_{\sigma(j)}},\lambda_{\alpha_{\sigma(j)}}}}(\alpha_{\sigma(j)}) = v_{\alpha_{\sigma(j)}} + \left(1-v_{\alpha_{\sigma(j)}}\right)\left(1-\left(1-\lambda_{\alpha_{\sigma(j)}}\right)^n\right)$$
$$- \mu_{\alpha_{\sigma(j)}}\lambda_{\alpha_{\sigma(j)}}\left(\sum_{t=0}^{n-1}\kappa^{n-1-t}_{\alpha_{\sigma(j)}}\left(1-\lambda_{\alpha_{\sigma(j)}}\right)^n\right) \tag{1.398}$$

(5) $GIFPOWAH^{*,n}_w(\alpha_1,\alpha_2,\ldots,\alpha_n)$

$$= \left(\left(1-\prod_{j=1}^{m}\left(1-\left(\kappa^n_{\alpha_{\sigma(j)}}\mu_{\alpha_{\sigma(j)}}\right)^\rho\right)^{w_j}\right)^{\frac{1}{\rho}},\right.$$
$$\left. 1-\left(1-\prod_{j=1}^{m}\left(1-\left(1-v_{H^{*,n}_{\kappa_{\alpha_{\sigma(j)}},\lambda_{\alpha_{\sigma(j)}}}}(\alpha_{\sigma(j)})\right)^\rho\right)^{w_j}\right)^{\frac{1}{\rho}}\right)$$

where

$$v_{H^{*,n}_{\kappa_{\alpha_{\sigma(j)}},\lambda_{\alpha_{\sigma(j)}}}}(\alpha_{\sigma(j)}) = v_{\alpha_{\sigma(j)}} + \left(1 - v_{\alpha_{\sigma(j)}}\right)\left(1 - \left(1 - \lambda_{\alpha_{\sigma(j)}}\right)^n\right) - \mu_{\alpha_{\sigma(j)}}\kappa_{\alpha_{\sigma(j)}}\lambda_{\alpha_{\sigma(j)}}\left(\sum_{t=0}^{n-1}\kappa_{\alpha_{\sigma(j)}}^{n-1-t}\left(1 - \lambda_{\alpha_{\sigma(j)}}\right)^n\right) \quad (1.399)$$

(6) $GIFPOWAJ^n_w(\alpha_1, \alpha_2, \ldots, \alpha_n)$

$$= \left(\left(1 - \prod_{j=1}^{m}\left(1 - \mu^{\rho}_{J^n_{\kappa_{\alpha_{\sigma(j)}},\lambda_{\alpha_{\sigma(j)}}}}(\alpha_{\sigma(j)})\right)^{w_j}\right)^{\frac{1}{\rho}}, 1 - \left(1 - \prod_{j=1}^{m}\left(1 - \left(1 - \lambda^n_{\alpha_{\sigma(j)}} v_{\alpha_{\sigma(j)}}\right)^{\rho}\right)^{w_j}\right)^{\frac{1}{\rho}}\right)$$

where

$$\mu_{J^n_{\kappa_{\alpha_{\sigma(j)}},\lambda_{\alpha_{\sigma(j)}}}}(\alpha_{\sigma(j)}) = \mu_{\alpha_{\sigma(j)}} + \left(1 - \mu_{\alpha_{\sigma(j)}}\right)\left(1 - \left(1 - \kappa_{\alpha_{\sigma(j)}}\right)^n\right) - v_{\alpha_{\sigma(j)}}\kappa_{\alpha_{\sigma(j)}}\left(\sum_{t=0}^{n-1}\lambda_{\alpha_{\sigma(j)}}^{n-1-t}\left(1 - \kappa_{\alpha_{\sigma(j)}}\right)^n\right) \quad (1.400)$$

(7) $GIFPOWAJ^{*,n}_w(\alpha_1, \alpha_2, \ldots, \alpha_n)$

$$= \left(\left(1 - \prod_{j=1}^{m}\left(1 - \mu^{\eta}_{J^{*,n}_{\kappa_{\alpha_{\sigma(j)}},\lambda_{\alpha_{\sigma(j)}}}}(\alpha_{\sigma(j)})\right)^{w_j}\right)^{\frac{1}{\rho}}, 1 - \left(1 - \prod_{j=1}^{m}\left(1 - \left(1 - \lambda^n_{\alpha_{\sigma(j)}} v_{\alpha_{\sigma(j)}}\right)^{\rho}\right)^{w_j}\right)^{\frac{1}{\rho}}\right)$$

where

$$\mu_{J^{*,n}_{\kappa_{\alpha_{\sigma(j)}},\lambda_{\alpha_{\sigma(j)}}}}(\alpha_{\sigma(j)}) = \mu_{\alpha_{\sigma(j)}} + \left(1 - \mu_{\alpha_{\sigma(j)}}\right)\left(1 - \left(1 - \kappa_{\alpha_{\sigma(j)}}\right)^n\right) - v_{\alpha_{\sigma(j)}}\kappa_{\alpha_{\sigma(j)}}\lambda_{\alpha_{\sigma(j)}}\left(\sum_{t=0}^{n-1}\lambda_{\alpha_{\sigma(j)}}^{n-1-t}\left(1 - \kappa_{\alpha_{\sigma(j)}}\right)^n\right) \quad (1.401)$$

(8) $GIFPOWAP_w^n(\alpha_1, \alpha_2, \ldots, \alpha_n)$

$$= \left(\left(1 - \prod_{j=1}^{m} \left(1 - \left(\max\left(\kappa_{\alpha_{\sigma(j)}}, \mu_{\alpha_{\sigma(j)}}\right)\right)^{\rho}\right)^{w_j} \right)^{\frac{1}{\rho}}, \right.$$

$$\left. 1 - \left(1 - \prod_{j=1}^{m} \left(1 - \left(1 - \min\left(\lambda_{\alpha_{\sigma(j)}}, v_{\alpha_{\sigma(j)}}\right)\right)^{\rho}\right)^{w_j} \right)^{\frac{1}{\rho}} \right)$$

where $\kappa_{\alpha_{\sigma(j)}} + \lambda_{\alpha_{\sigma(j)}} \le 1$, $j = 1, 2, \ldots, m$.

(9) $GIFPOWAQ_w^n(\alpha_1, \alpha_2, \ldots, \alpha_n)$

$$= \left(\left(1 - \prod_{j=1}^{m} \left(1 - \left(\min\left(\kappa_{\alpha_{\sigma(j)}}, \mu_{\alpha_{\sigma(j)}}\right)\right)^{\rho}\right)^{w_j} \right)^{\frac{1}{\rho}}, \right.$$

$$\left. 1 - \left(1 - \prod_{j=1}^{m} \left(1 - \left(1 - \max\left(\lambda_{\alpha_{\sigma(j)}}, v_{\alpha_{\sigma(j)}}\right)\right)^{\rho}\right)^{w_j} \right)^{\frac{1}{\rho}} \right)$$

where $\kappa_{\alpha_{\sigma(j)}} + \lambda_{\alpha_{\sigma(j)}} \le 1$, $j = 1, 2, \ldots, m$.

Theorem 1.50 (Xia and Xu 2010) If all $\alpha_j (j = 1, 2, \ldots, m)$ are equal, i.e. $\alpha_j = \alpha$, for all j, then

(1) $GIFPOWAD_w^n(\alpha_1, \alpha_2, \ldots, \alpha_m) = D^n_{\kappa_\alpha, \lambda_\alpha}(\alpha)$.

(2) $GIFPOWAF_w^n(\alpha_1, \alpha_2, \ldots, \alpha_m) = F^n_{\kappa_\alpha, \lambda_\alpha}(\alpha)$, where $\kappa_{\alpha_j} + \lambda_{\alpha_j} \le 1$, $j = 1, 2, \ldots, m$.

(3) $GIFPOWAG_w^n(\alpha_1, \alpha_2, \ldots, \alpha_m) = G^n_{\kappa_\alpha, \lambda_\alpha}(\alpha)$.

(4) $GIFPOWAH_w^n(\alpha_1, \alpha_2, \ldots, \alpha_m) = H^n_{\kappa_\alpha, \lambda_\alpha}(\alpha)$.

(5) $GIFPOWAH_w^n(\alpha_1, \alpha_2, \ldots, \alpha_m) = H^{*,n}_{\kappa_\alpha, \lambda_\alpha}(\alpha)$.

(6) $GIFPOWAJ_w^n(\alpha_1, \alpha_2, \ldots, \alpha_m) = J^n_{\kappa_\alpha, \lambda_\alpha}(\alpha)$.

(7) $GIFPOWAJ_w^n(\alpha_1, \alpha_2, \ldots, \alpha_m) = J^{*,n}_{\kappa_\alpha, \lambda_\alpha}(\alpha)$.

(8) $GIFPOWAP_w^n(\alpha_1, \alpha_2, \ldots, \alpha_m) = jP^n_{\kappa_\alpha, \lambda_\alpha}(\alpha)$, where $\kappa_{\alpha_j} + \lambda_{\alpha_j} \le 1$, $j = 1, 2, \ldots, m$.

(9) $GIFPOWAQ_w^n(\alpha_1, \alpha_2, \ldots, \alpha_m) = Q^n_{\kappa_\alpha, \lambda_\alpha}(\alpha)$, where $\kappa_{\alpha_j} + \lambda_{\alpha_j} \le 1$, $j = 1, 2, \ldots, m$.

Theorem 1.51 (Xia and Xu 2010)

(1) $\alpha^-_{D_n} \leq GIFPOWAD^n_w(\alpha_1, \alpha_2, \ldots, \alpha_m) \leq \alpha^+_{D_n}$.

(2) $\alpha^-_{F_n} \leq GIFPOWAF^n_w(\alpha_1, \alpha_2, \ldots, \alpha_m) \leq \alpha^+_{F_n}$, where $\kappa_{\alpha_j} + \lambda_{\alpha_j} \leq 1$, $j = 1, 2, \ldots, m$.

(3) $\alpha^-_{G_n} \leq GIFPOWAG^n_w(\alpha_1, \alpha_2, \ldots, \alpha_m) \leq \alpha^+_{G_n}$.

(4) $\alpha^-_{H_n} \leq GIFPOWAH^n_w(\alpha_1, \alpha_2, \ldots, \alpha_m) \leq \alpha^+_{H_n}$.

(5) $\alpha^-_{H^*_n} \leq GIFPOWAH^n_w(\alpha_1, \alpha_2, \ldots, \alpha_m) \leq \alpha^+_{H^*_n}$.

(6) $\alpha^-_{J_n} \leq GIFPOWAJ^n_w(\alpha_1, \alpha_2, \ldots, \alpha_m) \leq \alpha^+_{J_n}$.

(7) $\alpha^-_{J^*_n} \leq GIFPOWAJ^n_w(\alpha_1, \alpha_2, \ldots, \alpha_m) \leq \alpha^+_{J^*_n}$.

(8) $\alpha^-_{P_n} \leq GIFPOWAP^n_w(\alpha_1, \alpha_2, \ldots, \alpha_m) \leq \alpha^+_{P_n}$, where $\kappa_{\alpha_j} + \lambda_{\alpha_j} \leq 1$, $j = 1, 2, \ldots, m$.

(9) $\alpha^-_{Q_n} \leq GIFPOWAQ^n_w(\alpha_1, \alpha_2, \ldots, \alpha_m) \leq \alpha^+_{Q_n}$, where $\kappa_{\alpha_j} + \lambda_{\alpha_j} \leq 1$, $j = 1, 2, \ldots, m$.

Theorem 1.52 (Xia and Xu 2010) Let $\alpha^*_j = (\mu_{\alpha^*_j}, v_{\alpha^*_j})$ $(j = 1, 2, \ldots, m)$ be a collection of IFVs, then

(1) If $\mu_{D^n_{\kappa_{\alpha_j}, \lambda_{\alpha_j}}}(\alpha_j) \leq \mu_{D^n_{\kappa_{\alpha^*_j}, \lambda_{\alpha^*_j}}}(\alpha^*_j)$ and $v_{D^n_{\kappa_{\alpha_j}, \lambda_{\alpha_j}}}(\alpha_j) \geq v_{D^n_{\kappa_{\alpha^*_j}, \lambda_{\alpha^*_j}}}(\alpha^*_j)$, for all j, then

$$GIFPOWAD^n_w(\alpha_1, \alpha_2, \ldots, \alpha_m) \leq GIFPOWAD^n_w(\alpha^*_1, \alpha^*_2, \ldots, \alpha^*_m) \tag{1.402}$$

(2) If $\mu_{F^n_{\kappa_{\alpha_j}, \lambda_{\alpha_j}}}(\alpha_j) \leq \mu_{F^n_{\kappa_{\alpha^*_j}, \lambda_{\alpha^*_j}}}(\alpha^*_j)$ and $v_{F^n_{\kappa_{\alpha_j}, \lambda_{\alpha_j}}}(\alpha_j) \geq v_{F^n_{\kappa_{\alpha^*_j}, \lambda_{\alpha^*_j}}}(\alpha^*_j)$, for all j, then

$$GIFPOWAF^n_w(\alpha_1, \alpha_2, \ldots, \alpha_m) \leq GIFPOWAF^n_w(\alpha^*_1, \alpha^*_2, \ldots, \alpha^*_n) \tag{1.403}$$

where $\kappa_{\alpha_j} + \lambda_{\alpha_j} \leq 1$, $j = 1, 2, \ldots, m$.

(3) If $\mu_{G^n_{\kappa_{\alpha_j}, \lambda_{\alpha_j}}}(\alpha_j) \leq \mu_{G^n_{\kappa_{\alpha^*_j}, \lambda_{\alpha^*_j}}}(\alpha^*_j)$ and $v_{G^n_{\kappa_{\alpha_j}, \lambda_{\alpha_j}}}(\alpha_j) \geq v_{G^n_{\kappa_{\alpha^*_j}, \lambda_{\alpha^*_j}}}(\alpha^*_j)$, for all j, then

$$GIFPOWAG^n_w(\alpha_1, \alpha_2, \ldots, \alpha_m) \leq GIFPOWAG^n_w(\alpha^*_1, \alpha^*_2, \ldots, \alpha^*_m) \tag{1.404}$$

(4) If $\mu_{H^n_{\kappa_{\alpha_j}, \lambda_{\alpha_j}}}(\alpha_j) \leq \mu_{H^n_{\kappa_{\alpha^*_j}, \lambda_{\alpha^*_j}}}(\alpha^*_j)$ and $v_{H^n_{\kappa_{\alpha_j}, \lambda_{\alpha_j}}}(\alpha_j) \geq v_{H^n_{\kappa_{\alpha^*_j}, \lambda_{\alpha^*_j}}}(\alpha^*_j)$, for all j, then

$$GIFPOWAH^n_w(\alpha_1, \alpha_2, \ldots, \alpha_m) \leq GIFPOWAH^n_w(\alpha^*_1, \alpha^*_2, \ldots, \alpha^*_m) \tag{1.405}$$

(5) If $\mu_{H^{*,n}_{\kappa_{\alpha_j}, \lambda_{\alpha_j}}}(\alpha_j) \leq \mu_{H^{*,n}_{\kappa_{\alpha^*_j}, \lambda_{\alpha^*_j}}}(\alpha^*_j)$ and $v_{H^{*,n}_{\kappa_{\alpha_j}, \lambda_{\alpha_j}}}(\alpha_j) \geq v_{H^{*,n}_{\kappa_{\alpha^*_j}, \lambda_{\alpha^*_j}}}(\alpha^*_j)$, for all j, then

$$GIFPOWAH_w^{*,n}(\alpha_1, \alpha_2, \ldots, \alpha_m) \leq GIFPOWAH_w^{*,n}(\alpha_1^*, \alpha_2^*, \ldots, \alpha_m^*) \quad (1.406)$$

(6) If $\mu_{J^n_{\kappa\alpha_j,\lambda\alpha_j}}(\alpha_j) \leq \mu_{J^n_{\kappa_{\alpha_j^*},\lambda_{\alpha_j^*}}}(\alpha_j^*)$ and $v_{J^n_{\kappa\alpha_j,\lambda\alpha_j}}(\alpha_j) \geq v_{J^n_{\kappa_{\alpha_j^*},\lambda_{\alpha_j^*}}}(\alpha_j^*)$, for all j, then

$$GIFPOWAJ_w^n(\alpha_1, \alpha_2, \ldots, \alpha_m) \leq GIFPOWAJ_w^n(\alpha_1^*, \alpha_2^*, \ldots, \alpha_m^*) \quad (1.407)$$

(7) If $\mu_{J^{*,n}_{\kappa\alpha_j,\lambda\alpha_j}}(\alpha_j) \leq \mu_{J^{*,n}_{\kappa_{\alpha_j^*},\lambda_{\alpha_j^*}}}(\alpha_j^*)$ and $v_{J^{*,n}_{\kappa\alpha_j,\lambda\alpha_j}}(\alpha_j) \geq v_{J^{*,n}_{\kappa_{\alpha_j^*},\lambda_{\alpha_j^*}}}(\alpha_j^*)$, for all j, then

$$GIFPOWAJ_w^{*,n}(\alpha_1, \alpha_2, \ldots, \alpha_m) \leq GIFPOWAJ_w^{*,n}(\alpha_1^*, \alpha_2^*, \ldots, \alpha_m^*) \quad (1.408)$$

(8) If $\mu_{P^n_{\kappa\alpha_j,\lambda\alpha_j}}(\alpha_j) \leq \mu_{P^n_{\kappa_{\alpha_j^*},\lambda_{\alpha_j^*}}}(\alpha_j^*)$ and $v_{P^n_{\kappa\alpha_j,\lambda\alpha_j}}(\alpha_j) \geq v_{P^n_{\kappa_{\alpha_j^*},\lambda_{\alpha_j^*}}}(\alpha_j^*)$, for all j, then

$$GIFPOWAP_w^n(\alpha_1, \alpha_2, \ldots, \alpha_m) \leq GIFPOWAP_w^n(\alpha_1^*, \alpha_2^*, \ldots, \alpha_m^*) \quad (1.409)$$

where $\kappa_{\alpha_j} + \lambda_{\alpha_j} \leq 1$, $j = 1, 2, \ldots, m$.
(9) If $\mu_{Q^n_{\kappa\alpha_j,\lambda\alpha_j}}(\alpha_j) \leq \mu_{Q^n_{\kappa_{\alpha_j^*},\lambda_{\alpha_j^*}}}(\alpha_j^*)$ and $v_{Q^n_{\kappa\alpha_j,\lambda\alpha_j}}(\alpha_j) \geq v_{Q^n_{\kappa_{\alpha_j^*},\lambda_{\alpha_j^*}}}(\alpha_j^*)$, for all j, then

$$GIFPOWAQ_w^n(\alpha_1, \alpha_2, \ldots, \alpha_m) \leq GIFPOWAQ_w^n(\alpha_1^*, \alpha_2^*, \ldots, \alpha_m^*) \quad (1.410)$$

where $\kappa_{\alpha_j} + \lambda_{\alpha_j} \leq 1$, $j = 1, 2, \ldots, m$.

Theorem 1.53 (Xia and Xu 2010) Let $(\alpha_1', \alpha_2' \ldots, \alpha_m')^T$ be any permutation of $(\alpha_1, \alpha_2 \ldots, \alpha_m)^T$, then

(1) $GIFPOWAD_w^n(\alpha_1, \alpha_2 \ldots, \alpha_m) = GIFPOWAD_w^n(\alpha_1', \alpha_2' \ldots, \alpha_m')$.

(2) $GIFPOWAF_w^n(\alpha_1, \alpha_2 \ldots, \alpha_m) = GIFPOWAF_w^n(\alpha_1', \alpha_2' \ldots, \alpha_m')$, where $\kappa_{\alpha_j} + \lambda_{\alpha_j} \leq 1$, $j = 1, 2, \ldots, m$.

(3) $GIFPOWAG_w^n(\alpha_1, \alpha_2 \ldots, \alpha_m) = GIFPOWAG_w^n(\alpha_1', \alpha_2' \ldots, \alpha_m')$.

(4) $GIFPOWAH_w^n(\alpha_1, \alpha_2 \ldots, \alpha_m) = GIFPOWAH_w^n(\alpha_1', \alpha_2' \ldots, \alpha_m')$.

(5) $GIFPOWAH_w^{*,n}(\alpha_1, \alpha_2 \ldots, \alpha_m) = GIFPOWAD_w^{*,n}(\alpha_1', \alpha_2' \ldots, \alpha_m')$.

(6) $GIFPOWAJ_w^n(\alpha_1, \alpha_2 \ldots, \alpha_m) = GIFPOWAJ_w^n(\alpha_1', \alpha_2' \ldots, \alpha_m')$.

(7) $GIFPOWAJ_w^{*,n}(\alpha_1, \alpha_2 \ldots, \alpha_m) = GIFPOWAJ_w^{*,n}(\alpha_1', \alpha_2' \ldots, \alpha_m')$.

(8) $GIFPOWAP_w^n(\alpha_1, \alpha_2 \ldots, \alpha_m) = GIFPOWAP_w^n(\alpha_1', \alpha_2' \ldots, \alpha_m')$, where $\kappa_{\alpha_j} + \lambda_{\alpha_j} \leq 1$, $j = 1, 2, \ldots, m$.

(9) $GIFPOWAQ_w^n(\alpha_1, \alpha_2 \ldots, \alpha_n) = GIFPOWAQ_w^n(\alpha_1', \alpha_2' \ldots, \alpha_m')$, where $\kappa_{\alpha_j} + \lambda_{\alpha_j} \leq 1$, $j = 1, 2, \ldots, m$.

We now look at some special cases obtained by using different choices of the parameters n, w and ρ:

Theorem 1.54 (Xia and Xu 2010)

(1) If $n = 0$, then the GIFPOWA operators reduce to the generalized intuitionistic fuzzy ordered weighted average operator (Zhao et al. 2010).
(2) If $\rho = 1$ and $n = 0$, then the GIFPOWA operators reduce to the intuitionistic fuzzy ordered weighted average operator (Xu 2007).
(3) If $\rho \to 0$ and $n = 0$, then the GIFPOWA operators reduce to the intuitionistic fuzzy ordered weighted geometric operator (Xu and Yager 2006).
(4) If $\rho \to +\infty$ and $n = 0$, then the GIFPOWA operators reduce to the intuitionistic fuzzy maximum operator (Chen and Tan 1994).
(5) If $w = (1/m, 1/m, \ldots, 1/m)^T$, $n = 0$, and $\rho = 1$, then the GIFPOWA operators reduce to the intuitionistic fuzzy average operator (Xu 2007).
(6) If $w = (1/m, 1/m, \ldots, 1/m)^T$, $n = 0$, and $\rho \to 0$, then the GIFPOWA operators reduce to the IFGM (Xu and Yager 2006).
(7) If $w = (1, 0, \ldots, 0)^T$ and $n = 0$, then the GIFPOWA operators reduce to the intuitionistic fuzzy maximum operator (Chen and Tan 1994).
(8) If $w = (0, 0, \ldots, 1)^T$ and $n = 0$, then the GIFPOWA operators reduce to the intuitionistic fuzzy minimum operator (Chen and Tan 1994).

The GIFPWA operators weight only the IFVs, while the GIFPOWA operators weight only the ordered positions of the IFVs instead of weighting the IFVs themselves. To overcome this limitation, motivated by the idea of combining the weighted averaging operator and the OWA operators (Torra 1997; Xu and Da 2003), Xia and Xu (2010) developed a generalized intuitionistic fuzzy point hybrid aggregation (GIFPHA) operator, which weights each given IFV and its ordered positions.

Theorem 1.55 (Xia and Xu 2010) The GIFPHA operators of dimension m is a mapping *GIFPHA*: $V^m \to V$, which has an associated vector $w = (w_1, w_2, \ldots, w_m)^T$, with $w_j \geq 0$, $j = 1, 2, \ldots, m$, $\sum_{j=1}^{m} w_j = 1$, such that

(1) $GIFPHAD^n_{w,\omega}(\alpha_1, \alpha_2, \ldots, \alpha_m)$

$$= \left(w_1 \left(D^n_{\kappa_{\dot{\alpha}_{\sigma(1)}}, \lambda_{\dot{\alpha}_{\sigma(1)}}} \left(\dot{\alpha}_{\sigma(1)} \right) \right)^\rho \oplus w_2 \left(D^n_{\kappa_{\dot{\alpha}_{\sigma(2)}}, \lambda_{\dot{\alpha}_{\sigma(2)}}} \left(\dot{\alpha}_{\sigma(2)} \right) \right)^\rho \oplus \cdots \oplus w_m \left(D^n_{\kappa_{\dot{\alpha}_{\sigma(m)}}, \lambda_{\dot{\alpha}_{\sigma(m)}}} \left(\dot{\alpha}_{\sigma(m)} \right) \right)^\rho \right)^{\frac{1}{\rho}}$$

where $D^n_{\kappa_{\dot{\alpha}_{\sigma(j)}}, \lambda_{\alpha_{\sigma(j)}}} \left(\dot{\alpha}_{\sigma(j)} \right)$ is the jth largest of $m\omega_i D^n_{\kappa_{\alpha_i}, \lambda_{\alpha_i}} (\alpha_i)$ $(i = 1, 2, \ldots, m)$.

(2) $GIFPHAF^n_{w,\omega}(\alpha_1, \alpha_2, \ldots, \alpha_m)$

$$= \left(w_1 \left(F^n_{\kappa_{\dot{\alpha}_{\sigma(1)}}, \lambda_{\dot{\alpha}_{\sigma(1)}}} \left(\dot{\alpha}_{\sigma(1)} \right) \right)^\rho \oplus w_2 \left(F^n_{\kappa_{\dot{\alpha}_{\sigma(2)}}, \lambda_{\dot{\alpha}_{\sigma(2)}}} \left(\dot{\alpha}_{\sigma(2)} \right) \right)^\rho \oplus \cdots \oplus w_m \left(F^n_{\kappa_{\dot{\alpha}_{\sigma(m)}}, \lambda_{\dot{\alpha}_{\sigma(m)}}} \left(\dot{\alpha}_{\sigma(m)} \right) \right)^\rho \right)^{\frac{1}{\rho}}$$

where $\kappa_{\dot{\alpha}_{\sigma(j)}} + \lambda_{\dot{\alpha}_{\sigma(j)}} \leq 1$, $j = 1, 2, \ldots, m$, $F^n_{\kappa_{\dot{\alpha}_{\sigma(j)}}, \lambda_{\alpha_{\sigma(j)}}}\left(\dot{\alpha}_{\sigma(j)}\right)$ is the *j*th largest of $m\omega_i F^n_{\kappa_{\alpha_i}, \lambda_{\alpha_i}}(\alpha_i)$ $(i = 1, 2, \ldots, m)$.

(3) $GIFPHAG^n_{w,\omega}(\alpha_1, \alpha_2, \ldots, \alpha_m)$

$$= \left(w_1 \left(G^n_{\kappa_{\dot{\alpha}_{\sigma(1)}}, \lambda_{\dot{\alpha}_{\sigma(1)}}}\left(\dot{\alpha}_{\sigma(1)}\right)\right)^{\rho}_{\sigma(1)} \oplus w_2 \left(G^n_{\kappa_{\dot{\alpha}_{\sigma(2)}}, \lambda_{\dot{\alpha}_{\sigma(2)}}}\left(\dot{\alpha}_{\sigma(2)}\right)\right)^{\rho} \oplus \cdots \oplus w_m \left(G^n_{\kappa_{\dot{\alpha}_{\sigma(m)}}, \lambda_{\dot{\alpha}_{\sigma(m)}}}\left(\dot{\alpha}_{\sigma(m)}\right)\right)^{\rho}\right)^{\frac{1}{\rho}}$$

where $G^n_{\kappa_{\dot{\alpha}_{\sigma(j)}}, \lambda_{\alpha_{\sigma(j)}}}\left(\dot{\alpha}_{\sigma(j)}\right)$ is the *j*th largest of $m\omega_i G^n_{\kappa_{\alpha_i}, \lambda_{\alpha_i}}(\alpha_i)$ $(i = 1, 2, \ldots, m)$.

(4) $GIFPHAH^n_{w,\omega}(\alpha_1, \alpha_2, \ldots, \alpha_m)$

$$\left(w_1 \left(H^n_{\kappa_{\sigma(1)}, \lambda_{\sigma(1)}}\left(\alpha_{\sigma(1)}\right)\right)^{\rho} \oplus w_2 \left(H^n_{\kappa_{\sigma(2)}, \lambda_{\sigma(2)}}\left(\alpha_{\sigma(2)}\right)\right)^{\rho} \oplus \cdots \oplus w_m \left(H^n_{\kappa_{\alpha_{\sigma(m)}}, \lambda_{\alpha_{\sigma(m)}}}\left(\alpha_m\right)\right)^{\rho}\right)^{\frac{1}{\rho}}$$

where $H^n_{\kappa_{\dot{\alpha}_{\sigma(j)}}, \lambda_{\alpha_{\sigma(j)}}}\left(\dot{\alpha}_{\sigma(j)}\right)$ is the *j*th largest of $m\omega_i H^n_{\kappa_{\alpha_i}, \lambda_{\alpha_i}}(\alpha_i)$ $(i = 1, 2, \ldots, m)$.

(5) $GIFPHAH^{*,n}_{w,\omega}(\alpha_1, \alpha_2, \ldots, \alpha_m)$

$$= \left(w_1 \left(H^{*,n}_{\kappa_{\dot{\alpha}_{\sigma(1)}}, \lambda_{\dot{\alpha}_{\sigma(1)}}}\left(\dot{\alpha}_{\sigma(1)}\right)\right)^{\rho} \oplus w_2 \left(H^{*,n}_{\kappa_{\dot{\alpha}_{\sigma(2)}}, \lambda_{\dot{\alpha}_{\sigma(2)}}}\left(\dot{\alpha}_{\sigma(2)}\right)\right)^{\rho} \oplus \cdots \oplus w_m \left(H^{*,n}_{\kappa_{\dot{\alpha}_{\sigma(m)}}, \lambda_{\dot{\alpha}_{\sigma(m)}}}\left(\dot{\alpha}_{\sigma(m)}\right)\right)^{\rho}\right)^{\frac{1}{\rho}}$$

where $H^{*,n}_{\kappa_{\dot{\alpha}_{\sigma(j)}}, \lambda_{\alpha_{\sigma(j)}}}\left(\dot{\alpha}_{\sigma(j)}\right)$ is the *j*th largest of $m\omega_i H^{*,n}_{\kappa_{\alpha_i}, \lambda_{\alpha_i}}(\alpha_i)$ $(i = 1, 2, \ldots, m)$.

(6) $GIFPHAJ^n_{w,\omega}(\alpha_1, \alpha_2, \ldots, \alpha_m)$

$$= \left(w_1 \left(J^n_{\kappa_{\dot{\alpha}_{\sigma(1)}}, \lambda_{\dot{\alpha}_{\sigma(1)}}}\left(\dot{\alpha}_{\sigma(1)}\right)\right)^{\rho} \oplus w_2 \left(J^n_{\kappa_{\dot{\alpha}_{\sigma(2)}}, \lambda_{\dot{\alpha}_{\sigma(2)}}}\left(\dot{\alpha}_{\sigma(2)}\right)\right)^{\rho} \oplus \cdots \oplus w_m \left(J^n_{\kappa_{\dot{\alpha}_{\sigma(m)}}, \lambda_{\dot{\alpha}_{\sigma(m)}}}\left(\dot{\alpha}_{\sigma(m)}\right)\right)^{\rho}\right)^{\frac{1}{\rho}}$$

where $J^n_{\kappa_{\dot{\alpha}_{\sigma(j)}}, \lambda_{\alpha_{\sigma(j)}}}\left(\dot{\alpha}_{\sigma(j)}\right)$ is the *j*th largest of $m\omega_i J^n_{\kappa_{\alpha_i}, \lambda_{\alpha_i}}(\alpha_i)$ $(i = 1, 2, \ldots, m)$.

(7) $GIFPHAJ^{*,n}_{w,\omega}(\alpha_1, \alpha_2, \ldots, \alpha_m)$

$$= \left(w_1 \left(J^{*,n}_{\kappa_{\dot{\alpha}_{\sigma(1)}}, \lambda_{\dot{\alpha}_{\sigma(1)}}}\left(\dot{\alpha}_{\sigma(1)}\right)\right)^{\rho} \oplus w_2 \left(J^{*,n}_{\kappa_{\dot{\alpha}_{\sigma(2)}}, \lambda_{\dot{\alpha}_{\sigma(2)}}}\left(\dot{\alpha}_{\sigma(2)}\right)\right)^{\rho} \oplus \cdots \oplus w_m \left(J^{*,n}_{\kappa_{\dot{\alpha}_{\sigma(m)}}, \lambda_{\dot{\alpha}_{\sigma(m)}}}\left(\dot{\alpha}_{\sigma(m)}\right)\right)^{\rho}\right)^{\frac{1}{\rho}}$$

where $J^{*,n}_{\kappa_{\dot{\alpha}_{\sigma(j)}},\lambda_{\alpha_{\sigma(j)}}}\left(\dot{\alpha}_{\sigma(j)}\right)$ is the *j*th largest of $m\omega_i J^{*,n}_{\kappa_{\alpha_i},\lambda_{\alpha_i}}(\alpha_i)$ $(i = 1, 2, \ldots, m)$.

(8) $GIFPHAP^n_{w,\omega}(\alpha_1, \alpha_2, \ldots, \alpha_m)$

$$= \left(w_1 \left(P^n_{\kappa_{\dot{\alpha}_{\sigma(1)}},\lambda_{\dot{\alpha}_{\sigma(1)}}}\left(\dot{\alpha}_{\sigma(1)}\right)\right)^\rho \oplus w_2 \left(P^n_{\kappa_{\dot{\alpha}_{\sigma(2)}},\lambda_{\dot{\alpha}_{\sigma(2)}}}\left(\dot{\alpha}_{\sigma(2)}\right)\right)^\rho \right.$$
$$\left. \oplus \cdots \oplus w_m \left(P^n_{\kappa_{\dot{\alpha}_{\sigma(m)}},\lambda_{\dot{\alpha}_{\sigma(m)}}}\left(\dot{\alpha}_{\sigma(m)}\right)\right)^\rho \right)^{\frac{1}{\rho}}$$

where $\kappa_{\dot{\alpha}_{\sigma(j)}} + \lambda_{\dot{\alpha}_{\sigma(j)}} \le 1$, $j = 1, 2, \ldots, m$, $P^n_{\kappa_{\dot{\alpha}_{\sigma(j)}},\lambda_{\alpha_{\sigma(j)}}}\left(\dot{\alpha}_{\sigma(j)}\right)$ is the *j*th largest of $m\omega_i P^n_{\kappa_{\alpha_i},\lambda_{\alpha_i}}(\alpha_i)$ $(i = 1, 2, \ldots, m)$.

(9) $GIFPHAQ^n_{w,\omega}(\alpha_1, \alpha_2, \ldots, \alpha_m)$

$$= \left(w_1 \left(Q^n_{\kappa_{\dot{\alpha}_{\sigma(1)}},\lambda_{\dot{\alpha}_{\sigma(1)}}}\left(\dot{\alpha}_{\sigma(1)}\right)\right)^\rho \oplus w_2 \left(Q^n_{\kappa_{\dot{\alpha}_{\sigma(2)}},\lambda_{\dot{\alpha}_{\sigma(2)}}}\left(\dot{\alpha}_{\sigma(2)}\right)\right)^\rho \right.$$
$$\left. \oplus \cdots \oplus w_m \left(Q^n_{\kappa_{\dot{\alpha}_{\sigma(m)}},\lambda_{\dot{\alpha}_{\sigma(m)}}}\left(\dot{\alpha}_{\sigma(m)}\right)\right)^\rho \right)^{\frac{1}{\rho}}$$

where $\kappa_{\dot{\alpha}_{\sigma(j)}} + \lambda_{\dot{\alpha}_{\sigma(j)}} \le 1$, $j = 1, 2, \ldots, m$, $Q^n_{\kappa_{\dot{\alpha}_{\sigma(j)}},\lambda_{\alpha_{\sigma(j)}}}\left(\dot{\alpha}_{\sigma(j)}\right)$ is the *j*th largest of $m\omega_i Q^n_{\kappa_{\alpha_i},\lambda_{\alpha_i}}(\alpha_i)$ $(i = 1, 2, \ldots, m)$.

Let $\dot{\alpha}_{\sigma(j)} = (\mu_{\dot{\alpha}_{\sigma(j)}}, v_{\dot{\alpha}_{\sigma(j)}})$, $j = 1, 2, \ldots, m$, then, similar to Theorem 1.45, we have

Theorem 1.56 (Xia and Xu 2010)

(1) $GIFPHAD^n_{w,\omega}(\alpha_1, \alpha_2, \ldots, \alpha_m)$

$$= \left(\left(1 - \prod_{j=1}^m \left(1 - \left(\mu_{\dot{\alpha}_{\sigma(j)}} + \kappa_{\dot{\alpha}_{\sigma(j)}} \pi_{\dot{\alpha}_{\sigma(j)}}\right)^\rho\right)^{w_j}\right)^{\frac{1}{\rho}}, \right.$$
$$\left. 1 - \left(1 - \prod_{j=1}^m \left(1 - \left(1 - v_{\dot{\alpha}_{\sigma(j)}} - \left(1 - \kappa_{\dot{\alpha}_{\sigma(j)}}\right) \pi_{\dot{\alpha}_{\sigma(j)}}\right)^\rho\right)^{w_j}\right)^{\frac{1}{\rho}}\right)$$

(2) $GIFPHAF^n_{w,\omega}(\alpha_1, \alpha_2, \ldots, \alpha_m)$

$$= \left(\left(1 - \prod_{j=1}^m \left(1 - \mu^\rho_{F^n_{\kappa_{\dot{\alpha}_{\sigma(j)}},\lambda_{\dot{\alpha}_{\sigma(j)}}}\left(\dot{\alpha}_{\sigma(j)}\right)}\right)^{w_j}\right)^{\frac{1}{\rho}}, \right.$$
$$\left. 1 - \left(1 - \prod_{j=1}^m \left(1 - \left(1 - v_{F^n_{\kappa_{\dot{\alpha}_{\sigma(j)}},\lambda_{\dot{\alpha}_{\sigma(j)}}}\left(\dot{\alpha}_{\sigma(j)}\right)}\right)^\rho\right)^{w_j}\right)^{\frac{1}{\rho}}\right)$$

where $\kappa_{\dot{\alpha}_{\sigma(j)}} + \lambda_{\dot{\alpha}_{\sigma(j)}} \leq 1$, $j = 1, 2, \ldots, m$, and

$$\mu_{F^n_{\kappa_{\dot{\alpha}_{\sigma(j)}},\lambda_{\dot{\alpha}_{\sigma(j)}}}}(\dot{\alpha}_{\sigma(j)}) = \mu_{\dot{\alpha}_{\sigma(j)}} + \kappa_{\dot{\alpha}_{\sigma(j)}}\pi_{\dot{\alpha}_{\sigma(j)}}\frac{1-\left(1-\kappa_{\dot{\alpha}_{\sigma(j)}}-\lambda_{\dot{\alpha}_{\sigma(j)}}\right)^n}{\kappa_{\dot{\alpha}_{\sigma(j)}}+\lambda_{\dot{\alpha}_{\sigma(j)}}} \tag{1.411}$$

$$\nu_{F^n_{\kappa_{\dot{\alpha}_{\sigma(j)}},\lambda_{\dot{\alpha}_{\sigma(j)}}}}(\dot{\alpha}_{\sigma(j)}) = \nu_{\dot{\alpha}_{\sigma(j)}} + \lambda_{\dot{\alpha}_{\sigma(j)}}\pi_{\dot{\alpha}_{\sigma(j)}}\frac{1-\left(1-\kappa_{\dot{\alpha}_{\sigma(j)}}-\lambda_{\dot{\alpha}_{\sigma(j)}}\right)^n}{\kappa_{\dot{\alpha}_{\sigma(j)}}+\lambda_{\dot{\alpha}_{\sigma(j)}}} \tag{1.412}$$

(3) $GIFPHAG^n_{w,\omega}(\alpha_1, \alpha_2, \ldots, \alpha_m)$

$$= \left(\left(1 - \prod_{j=1}^{m}\left(1 - \left(\kappa^n_{\dot{\alpha}_{\sigma(j)}}\mu_{\dot{\alpha}_{\sigma(j)}}\right)^{\rho}\right)^{w_j}\right)^{\frac{1}{\rho}},\right.$$
$$\left. 1 - \left(1 - \prod_{j=1}^{m}\left(1 - \left(1 - \lambda^n_{\dot{\alpha}_{\sigma(j)}}\nu_{\dot{\alpha}_{\sigma(j)}}\right)^{\rho}\right)^{w_j}\right)^{\frac{1}{\rho}}\right)$$

(4) $GIFPHAH^n_{w,\omega}(\alpha_1, \alpha_2, \ldots, \alpha_m)$

$$= \left(\left(1 - \prod_{j=1}^{m}\left(1 - \left(\kappa^n_{\dot{\alpha}_{\sigma(j)}}\mu_{\dot{\alpha}_{\sigma(j)}}\right)^{\rho}\right)^{w_j}\right)^{\frac{1}{\rho}},\right.$$
$$\left. 1 - \left(1 - \prod_{j=1}^{m}\left(1 - \left(1 - \nu_{H^n_{\kappa_{\dot{\alpha}_j},\lambda_{\dot{\alpha}_j}}}(\dot{\alpha}_{\sigma(j)})\right)^{\rho}\right)^{w_j}\right)^{\frac{1}{\rho}}\right)$$

where

$$\nu_{H^n_{\kappa_{\dot{\alpha}_j},\lambda_{\dot{\alpha}_j}}}(\dot{\alpha}_{\sigma(j)}) = \nu_{\dot{\alpha}_{\sigma(j)}} + \left(1 - \nu_{\dot{\alpha}_{\sigma(j)}}\right)\left(1 - \left(1 - \lambda_{\dot{\alpha}_{\sigma(j)}}\right)^n\right)$$
$$- \mu_{\dot{\alpha}_{\sigma(j)}}\lambda_{\dot{\alpha}_{\sigma(j)}}\left(\sum_{t=0}^{n-1}\kappa^{n-1-t}_{\dot{\alpha}_{\sigma(j)}}\left(1 - \lambda_{\dot{\alpha}_{\sigma(j)}}\right)^t\right) \tag{1.413}$$

(5) $GIFPHAH^{*,n}_{w,\omega}(\alpha_1, \alpha_2, \ldots, \alpha_m)$

$$= \left(\left(1 - \prod_{j=1}^{m}\left(1 - \left(\kappa^n_{\dot{\alpha}_{\sigma(j)}}\mu_{\dot{\alpha}_{\sigma(j)}}\right)^{\rho}\right)^{w_j}\right)^{\frac{1}{\rho}},\right.$$
$$\left. 1 - \left(1 - \prod_{j=1}^{m}\left(1 - \nu^{\rho}_{H^{*,n}_{\kappa_{\dot{\alpha}_j},\lambda_{\dot{\alpha}_j}}}(\dot{\alpha}_{\sigma(j)})\right)^{w_j}\right)^{\frac{1}{\rho}}\right)$$

where

$$\nu_{H^{*,n}_{\kappa_{\dot{\alpha}_j},\lambda_{\dot{\alpha}_j}}}(\dot{\alpha}_{\sigma(j)}) = \nu_{\dot{\alpha}_{\sigma(j)}} + \left(1-\nu_{\dot{\alpha}_{\sigma(j)}}\right)\left(1-\left(1-\lambda_{\dot{\alpha}_{\sigma(j)}}\right)^n\right) - \mu_{\dot{\alpha}_{\sigma(j)}}\kappa_{\dot{\alpha}_{\sigma(j)}}\lambda_{\dot{\alpha}_{\sigma(j)}}\left(\sum_{t=0}^{n-1}\kappa_{\dot{\alpha}_{\sigma(j)}}^{n-1-t}\left(1-\lambda_{\dot{\alpha}_{\sigma(j)}}\right)^t\right) \quad (1.414)$$

(6) $GIFPHAJ^n_{w,\omega}(\alpha_1,\alpha_2,\ldots,\alpha_m)$

$$= \left(\left(1-\prod_{j=1}^m\left(1-\mu^\rho_{H^n_{\kappa_{\dot{\alpha}_j},\lambda_{\dot{\alpha}_j}}}(\dot{\alpha}_{\sigma(j)})\right)^{w_j}\right)^{\frac{1}{\rho}}, 1-\left(1-\prod_{j=1}^m\left(1-\left(\lambda^n_{\dot{\alpha}_{\sigma(j)}}\nu_{\dot{\alpha}_{\sigma(j)}}\right)^\rho\right)^{w_j}\right)^{\frac{1}{\rho}}\right)$$

where

$$\mu_{H^n_{\kappa_{\dot{\alpha}_j},\lambda_{\dot{\alpha}_j}}}(\dot{\alpha}_{\sigma(j)}) = \mu_{\dot{\alpha}_{\sigma(j)}} + \left(1-\mu_{\dot{\alpha}_{\sigma(j)}}\right)\left(1-\left(1-\kappa_{\dot{\alpha}_{\sigma(j)}}\right)^n\right) - \nu_{\dot{\alpha}_{\sigma(j)}}\kappa_{\dot{\alpha}_{\sigma(j)}}\left(\sum_{t=0}^{n-1}\left(1-\kappa_{\dot{\alpha}_{\sigma(j)}}\right)^t\lambda_{\dot{\alpha}_{\sigma(j)}}^{n-1-t}\right) \quad (1.415)$$

(7) $GIFPHAJ^{*,n}_{w,\omega}(\alpha_1,\alpha_2,\ldots,\alpha_m)$

$$= \left(\left(1-\prod_{j=1}^m\left(1-\mu^\rho_{H^{*,n}_{\kappa_{\dot{\alpha}_j},\lambda_{\dot{\alpha}_j}}}(\dot{\alpha}_{\sigma(j)})\right)^{w_j}\right)^{\frac{1}{\rho}}, 1-\left(1-\prod_{j=1}^m\left(1-\left(\lambda^n_{\dot{\alpha}_{\sigma(j)}}\nu_{\dot{\alpha}_{\sigma(j)}}\right)^\rho\right)^{w_j}\right)^{\frac{1}{\rho}}\right)$$

where

$$\mu_{H^{*,n}_{\kappa_{\dot{\alpha}_j},\lambda_{\dot{\alpha}_j}}}(\dot{\alpha}_{\sigma(j)}) = \mu_{\dot{\alpha}_{\sigma(j)}} + \left(1-\mu_{\dot{\alpha}_{\sigma(j)}}\right)\left(1-\left(1-\kappa_{\dot{\alpha}_{\sigma(j)}}\right)^n\right) - \nu_{\dot{\alpha}_{\sigma(j)}}\kappa_{\dot{\alpha}_{\sigma(j)}}\lambda_{\dot{\alpha}_{\sigma(j)}}\left(\sum_{t=0}^{n-1}\left(1-\kappa_{\dot{\alpha}_{\sigma(j)}}\right)^t\lambda_{\dot{\alpha}_{\sigma(j)}}^{n-1-t}\right) \quad (1.416)$$

(8) $GIFPHAP^n_{w,\omega}(\alpha_1, \alpha_2, \ldots, \alpha_m)$

$$= \left(\left(1 - \prod_{j=1}^{m} \left(1 - \left(\max \left(\kappa_{\dot{\alpha}_{\sigma(j)}}, \mu_{\dot{\alpha}_{\sigma(j)}} \right) \right)^{\rho} \right)^{w_j} \right)^{\frac{1}{\rho}}, \right.$$

$$\left. 1 - \left(1 - \prod_{j=1}^{m} \left(1 - \left(1 - \min \left(\lambda_{\dot{\alpha}_{\sigma(j)}}, \nu_{\dot{\alpha}_{\sigma(j)}} \right) \right)^{\rho} \right)^{w_j} \right)^{\frac{1}{\rho}} \right)$$

where $\kappa_{\dot{\alpha}_{\sigma(j)}} + \lambda_{\dot{\alpha}_{\sigma(j)}} \leq 1$, $j = 1, 2, \ldots, m$.

(9) $GIFPHAQ^n_{w,\omega}(\alpha_1, \alpha_2, \ldots, \alpha_m)$

$$= \left(\left(1 - \prod_{j=1}^{m} \left(1 - \left(\min \left(\kappa_{\dot{\alpha}_{\sigma(j)}}, \mu_{\dot{\alpha}_{\sigma(j)}} \right) \right)^{\rho} \right)^{w_j} \right)^{\frac{1}{\rho}}, \right.$$

$$\left. 1 - \left(1 - \prod_{j=1}^{m} \left(1 - \left(1 - \max \left(\lambda_{\dot{\alpha}_{\sigma(j)}}, \nu_{\dot{\alpha}_{\sigma(j)}} \right) \right)^{\rho} \right)^{w_j} \right)^{\frac{1}{\rho}} \right)$$

where $\kappa_{\dot{\alpha}_{\sigma(j)}} + \lambda_{\dot{\alpha}_{\sigma(j)}} \leq 1$, $j = 1, 2, \ldots, m$.

Theorem 1.57 (Xia and Xu 2010)

(1) If $w = (1/n, 1/n, \ldots, 1/n)^T$ and $n = 0$, then the GIFPHA operators reduce to the GIFWA operators (Zhao et al. 2010).
(2) If $\omega = (1/n, 1/n, \ldots, 1/n)^T$ and $n = 0$, then the GIFPHA operators reduce to the GIFOWA operator (Zhao et al. 2010).
(3) If $\eta = 1$ and $n = 0$, then the GIFPHA operators reduce to the following:

$$IFHA_{w,\omega}(\alpha_1, \alpha_2, \ldots, \alpha_m) = \left(1 - \prod_{j=1}^{m} (1 - \mu_{\dot{\alpha}_{\sigma(j)}})^{w_j}, \prod_{j=1}^{m} \nu_{\dot{\alpha}_{\sigma(j)}}^{w_j} \right) \quad (1.417)$$

which is called an intuitionistic fuzzy hybrid averaging operator (Xu 2007).

Chapter 2
Intuitionistic Fuzzy Clustering Algorithms

Since the fuzzy set theory was introduced (Zadeh 1965), many scholars have investigated the issue how to cluster the fuzzy sets, and a lot of clustering algorithms have been developed for fuzzy sets, such as the fuzzy c-means clustering algorithm (Fan et al. 2004), the maximum tree clustering algorithm (Christopher and Burges 1998), and the net-making clustering method (Wang 1983), etc. However, the studies on clustering problems with intuitionistic fuzzy information are still at an initial stage (Wang et al. 2011, 2012; Xu 2009; Xu and Cai 2012; Xu and Wu 2010; Xu et al. 2008, 2011; Zhang et al. 2007; Zhao et al. 2012a, b). Zhang et al. (2007) first defined the concept of the intuitionistic fuzzy similarity degree and constructed an intuitionistic fuzzy similarity matrix, and then proposed a procedure for deriving an intuitionistic fuzzy equivalence matrix by using the transitive closure of the intuitionistic fuzzy similarity matrix. After that, they presented a clustering technique of IFSs on the basis of the λ-cutting matrix of the interval-valued matrix. Xu et al. (2008) defined the concepts of the association matrix and the equivalent association matrix, they introduced some methods for calculating the association coefficients of IFSs, and used the derived association coefficients to construct an association matrix, from which they derived an equivalent association matrix. Based on the equivalent association matrix, a clustering algorithm for IFSs was developed and extended to cluster interval-valued intuitionistic fuzzy sets (IVIFSs). Xu (2009) introduced an intuitionistic fuzzy hierarchical algorithm for clustering IFSs, which is based on the traditional hierarchical clustering procedure, the intuitionistic fuzzy aggregation operator, and some basic distance measures, such as the Hamming distance, the normalized Hamming distance, the Euclidean distance, and the normalized Euclidean distance, etc. Xu and Wu (2010) developed an intuitionistic fuzzy C-means algorithm to cluster IFSs, which is based on the well-known fuzzy C-means clustering method (Bezdek 1981) and the basic distance measures between IFSs. Then, they extended the algorithm for clustering IVIFSs. Xu et al. (2011) extended the fuzzy closeness degree (Wang 1983) to the intuitionistic fuzzy closeness degree, and defined an intuitionistic fuzzy vector, the inner and outer products of intuitionistic fuzzy vectors. Based on the intuitionistic fuzzy closeness degree, they put forward a new method of constructing intuitionistic fuzzy similarity matrix. Zhao et al. (2012a) developed an

Z. Xu, *Intuitionistic Fuzzy Aggregation and Clustering*, Studies in Fuzziness and Soft Computing 279, DOI: 10.1007/978-3-642-28406-9_2,

intuitionistic fuzzy minimum spanning tree (MST) clustering algorithm to deal with intuitionistic fuzzy information. Zhao et al. (2012b) gave a measure for calculating the association coefficient between IFVs, and presented an algorithm for clustering IFVs. Moreover, they extended the algorithm to cluster IVIFVs. Wang et al. (2011) proposed a formula to derive the intuitionistic fuzzy similarity degree between two IFSs and developed an approach to constructing an intuitionistic fuzzy similarity matrix. Then, they presented a netting method to make cluster analysis of IFSs via intuitionistic fuzzy similarity matrix. Wang et al. (2012) developed an intuitionistic fuzzy implication operator and extended the Lukasiewicz implication operator to intuitionistic fuzzy environments, and then defined an intuitionistic fuzzy triangle product and an intuitionistic fuzzy square product. Furthermore, they used the intuitionistic fuzzy square product to construct an intuitionistic fuzzy similarity matrix, based on which a direct method for intuitionistic fuzzy cluster analysis was given.

Considering their wide range of application prospects of the intuitionistic fuzzy clustering techniques in the fields of medical diagnosis, pattern recognition, etc. (Xu and Cai 2012), in this chapter, we shall give a detailed introduction of the above intuitionistic fuzzy clustering algorithms.

2.1 Clustering Algorithms Based on Intuitionistic Fuzzy Similarity Matrices

Let $\alpha = (\mu_\alpha, v_\alpha)$, $\alpha_1 = (\mu_{\alpha_1}, v_{\alpha_1})$, and $\alpha_2 = (\mu_{\alpha_2}, v_{\alpha_2})$ be three IFVs, Zhang et al. (2007) defined some basic operational laws as below:

(1) $\alpha^c = (v_\alpha, \mu_\alpha)$;
(2) $\alpha_1 \wedge \alpha_2 = (\min\{\mu_{\alpha_1}, \mu_{\alpha_2}\}, \max\{v_{\alpha_1}, v_{\alpha_2}\})$;
(3) $\alpha_1 \vee \alpha_2 = (\max\{\mu_{\alpha_1}, \mu_{\alpha_2}\}, \min\{v_{\alpha_1}, v_{\alpha_2}\})$;

Based on the operational laws above, Zhang et al. (2007) derived the following conclusions:

Theorem 2.1 (Zhang et al. 2007) Let $\alpha_i = (\mu_{\alpha_1}, v_{\alpha_1})$ $(i = 1, 2, 3)$ be the IFVs, then

(1) $(\alpha_1 \vee \alpha_2) \wedge \alpha_3 = (\alpha_1 \wedge \alpha_3) \vee (\alpha_2 \wedge \alpha_3)$.
(2) $(\alpha_1 \wedge \alpha_2) \vee \alpha_3 = (\alpha_1 \vee \alpha_3) \wedge (\alpha_2 \vee \alpha_3)$.
(3) $(\alpha_1 \vee \alpha_2) \vee \alpha_3 = \alpha_1 \vee (\alpha_2 \vee \alpha_3)$.
(4) $(\alpha_1 \wedge \alpha_2) \wedge \alpha_3 = \alpha_1 \wedge (\alpha_2 \wedge \alpha_3)$.

Proof

(1)
$$\begin{aligned}(\alpha_1 \vee \alpha_2) \wedge \alpha_3 &= (\min\{\max\{\mu_{\alpha_1}, \mu_{\alpha_2}\}, \mu_{\alpha_3}\}, \max\{\min\{v_{\alpha_1}, v_{\alpha_2}\}, v_{\alpha_3}\}) \\ &= (\max\{\min\{\mu_{\alpha_1}, \mu_{\alpha_3}\}, \min\{\mu_{\alpha 2,}\mu_{\alpha 3}\}\}, \\ &\quad \min\{\max\{v_{\alpha_1}, v_{\alpha_3}\}, \max\{v_{\alpha_2}, v_{\alpha_3}\}\}) \\ &= (\alpha_1 \vee \alpha_3) \wedge (\alpha_2 \vee \alpha_3)\end{aligned}$$

$$
\begin{aligned}
(2)\quad (\alpha_1 \wedge \alpha_2) \vee \alpha_3 &= (\max\{\min\{\mu_{\alpha_1}, \mu_{\alpha_2}\}, \mu_{\alpha_3}\}, \min\{\max\{v_{\alpha_1}, v_{\alpha_2}\}, v_{\alpha_3}\}) \\
&= (\min\{\max\{\mu_{\alpha_1}, \mu_{\alpha_3}\}, \max\{\mu_{\alpha_2}, \mu_{\alpha_3}\}\}, \\
&\quad \max\{\min\{v_{\alpha_1}, v_{\alpha_3}\}, \min\{v_{\alpha_2}, v_{\alpha_3}\}\}) \\
&= (\alpha_1 \vee \alpha_3) \wedge (\alpha_2 \vee \alpha_3) \\
(3)\quad (\alpha_1 \vee \alpha_2) \vee \alpha_3 &= (\max\{\max\{\mu_{\alpha_1}, \mu_{\alpha_2}\}, \mu_{\alpha_3}\}, \min\{\min\{v_{\alpha_1}, v_{\alpha_2}\}, v_{\alpha_3}\}) \\
&= (\max\{\mu_{\alpha_1}, \mu_{\alpha_2}, \mu_{\alpha_3}\}, \min\{v_{\alpha_1}, v_{\alpha_2}, v_{\alpha_3}\}) \\
&= (\max\{\mu_{\alpha_1}, \max\{\mu_{\alpha_2}, \mu_{\alpha_3}\}, \min\{v_{\alpha_1}, \min\{v_{\alpha_2}, v_{\alpha_3}\}) \\
&= \alpha_1 \vee (\alpha_2 \vee \alpha_3) \\
(4)\quad (\alpha_1 \wedge \alpha_2) \wedge \alpha_3 &= (\min\{\min\{\mu_{\alpha_1}, \mu_{\alpha_2}\}, \mu_{\alpha_3}\}, \max\{\max\{v_{\alpha_1}, v_{\alpha_2}\}, v_{\alpha_3}\}) \\
&= (\min\{\mu_{\alpha_1}, \mu_{\alpha_2}, \mu_{\alpha_3}\}, \max\{v_{\alpha_1}, v_{\alpha_2}, v_{\alpha_3}\}) \\
&= (\min\{\mu_{\alpha_1}, \min\{\mu_{\alpha_2}, \mu_{\alpha_3}\}, \max\{v_{\alpha_1}, \max\{v_{\alpha_2}, v_{\alpha_3}\}) \\
&= \alpha_1 \wedge (\alpha_2 \wedge \alpha_3)
\end{aligned}
$$

which completes the proof.

Let $X = \{x_1, x_2, \ldots, x_n\}$ be a finite universe of discourse, $A_1 = \{\langle x_i, \mu_{A_1}(x_i), v_{A_1}(x_i)\rangle | x_i \in X\}$ and $A_2 = \{\langle x_i, \mu_{A_2}(x_i), v_{A_2}(x_i)\rangle | x_i \in X\}$ be two IFSs. Atanassov (1983, 1986) suggested the inclusion relations between the IFSs as follows:

(1) $A_1 \subseteq A_2$ if and only if $\mu_{A_1}(x_i) \leq \mu_{A_2}(x_i)$ and $v_{A_1}(x_i) \geq v_{A_2}(x_i)$, for any $x_i \in X$;
(2) $A_1 = A_2$ if and only if $A_1 \subseteq A_2$ and $A_1 \supseteq A_2$, i.e., $\mu_{A_1}(x_i) = \mu_{A_2}(x_i)$ and $v_{A_1}(x_i) = v_{A_2}(x_i)$, for any $x_i \in X$.

In fuzzy mathematics, the similarity matrix with reflexivity and symmetry is a common matrix. Zhang et al. (2007) introduced the similarity matrix to the IFS theory, and defined the concept of intuitionistic fuzzy similarity degree:

Definition 2.1 (Zhang et al. 2007) Let $\hat{\vartheta}$: $(\text{IFS}(X))^2 \to \text{IFS}(X)$, where $\text{IFS}(X)$ indicates the set of all IFSs, and let $A_i \in \text{IFS}(X)$ $(i = 1, 2, 3)$. If $\hat{\vartheta}(A_1, A_2)$ satisfies the following properties:

(1) $\hat{\vartheta}(A_1, A_2)$ is an IFV.
(2) $\hat{\vartheta}(A_1, A_2) = (1, 0)$ if and only if $A_1 = A_2$.
(3) $\hat{\vartheta}(A_1, A_2) = \hat{\vartheta}(A_2, A_1)$.

Then $\hat{\vartheta}(A_1, A_2)$ is called an intuitionistic fuzzy similarity degree of A_1 and A_2.

Liu (2005) gave a formula for calculating the similarity degree between A_1 and A_2:

$$
\hat{\vartheta}(A_1, A_2) = 1 - \left[\sum_{i=1}^{n} w_i \left(\beta_1 |\mu_{A_1}(x_i) - \mu_{A_2}(x_i)|^{\lambda} + \beta_2 |v_{A_1}(x_i) - v_{A_2}(x_i)|^{\lambda} \right.\right.
$$

$$
\left.\left. + \ \beta_3 |\pi_{A_1}(x_i) - \pi_{A_2}(x_i)|^{\lambda} \right) \right]^{\frac{1}{\lambda}} \tag{2.1}
$$

where $\lambda \geq 1$, $w = (w_1, w_2, \ldots, w_n)^T$, $w_i \in [0, 1]$, $x_i \in X$, $i = 1, 2, \ldots, n$, and $\sum_{i=1}^n w_i = 1$.

Eq. (2.1) can weight not only the deviation of each IFV, but also the deviations of the corresponding membership degree, the non-membership degree and the hesitancy (indeterminancy) degree. It is more general than the similarity measure:

$$\vartheta'(A_1, A_2) = 1 - \sqrt{\frac{1}{2n}\sum_{j=1}^{n}((\mu_{A_1}(x_j) - \mu_{A_2}(x_j))^2 + (v_{A_1}(x_j) - v_{A_2}(x_j))^2 + (\pi_{A_1}(x_j) - \pi_{A_2}(x_j))^2} \tag{2.2}$$

and thus, Eq. (2.1) is of high flexibility. If we take $\vartheta(A_1, A_2)$ as the function of w, then it is a bounded function. Let

$$d(w) = \sum_{i=1}^{n} w_i|\mu_{A_1}(x_i) - \mu_{A_2}(x_i)|^\lambda + \beta_2|v_{A_1}(x_i) - v_{A_2}(x_i)|^\lambda + \beta_3|\pi_{A_1}(x_i) - \pi_{A_2}(x_i)|^\lambda), \quad \lambda \geq 1 \tag{2.3}$$

then we need to solve the maximum and minimum problem of Eq. (2.1), which can be transformed to solve the maximum and minimum problem of $d(w)$. Since

$$\begin{aligned} d(w) &= \sum_{i=1}^{n} w_i(\beta_1|\mu_{A_1}(x_i) - \mu_{A_2}(x_i)|^\lambda + \beta_2|v_{A_1}(x_i) - v_{A_2}(x_i)|^\lambda \\ &\quad + \beta_3|\pi_{A_1}(x_i) - \pi_{A_2}(x_i)|^\lambda) \\ &\leq \max_i\{\beta_1|\mu_{A_1}(x_i) - \mu_{A_2}(x_i)|^\lambda + \beta_2|v_{A_1}(x_i) - v_{A_2}(x_i)|^\lambda \\ &\quad + \beta_3|\pi_{A_1}(x_i) - \pi_{A_2}(x_i)|^\lambda\}, \quad \lambda \geq 1 \end{aligned} \tag{2.4}$$

There must exist a positive integer k such that

$$\begin{aligned} &\max_i\{\beta_1|\mu_{A_1}(x_i) - \mu_{A_2}(x_i)|^\lambda + \beta_2|v_{A_1}(x_i) - v_{A_2}(x_i)|^\lambda + \beta_3|\pi_{A_1}(x_i) - \pi_{A_2}(x_i)|^\lambda\} \\ &= \beta_1|\mu_{A_1}(x_k) - \mu_{A_2}(x_k)|^\lambda + \beta_2|v_{A_1}(x_k) - v_{A_2}(x_k)|^\lambda + \beta_3|\pi_{A_1}(x_k) \\ &\quad - \pi_{A_2}(x_k)|^\lambda\}, \quad \lambda \geq 1 \end{aligned} \tag{2.5}$$

Hence, when $w_k = 1$ and $w_i = 0$, $i \neq k$, the equality holds. Also since

$$\begin{aligned} d(w) &= \sum_{i=1}^{n} w_i(\beta_1|\mu_{A_1}(x_i) - \mu_{A_2}(x_i)|^\lambda + \beta_2|v_{A_1}(x_i) - v_{A_2}(x_i)|^\lambda \\ &\quad + \beta_3|\pi_{A_1}(x_i) - \pi_{A_2}(x_i)|^\lambda) \end{aligned}$$

$$\geq \min_i\{\beta_1|\mu_{A_1}(x_i) - \mu_{A_2}(x_i)|^\lambda + \beta_2|v_{A_1}(x_i) - v_{A_2}(x_i)|^\lambda + \beta_3|\pi_{A_1}(x_i) - \pi_{A_2}(x_i)|^\lambda\}, \quad \lambda \geq 1 \tag{2.6}$$

There must exist a positive integer s such that

$$\begin{aligned}
&\min_i\{\beta_1|\mu_{A_1}(x_i) - \mu_{A_2}(x_i)|^\lambda + \beta_2|v_{A_1}(x_i) - v_{A_2}(x_i)|^\lambda + \beta_3|\pi_{A_1}(x_i) - \pi_{A_2}(x_i)|^\lambda\} \\
&= \beta_1|\mu_{A_1}(x_s) - \mu_{A_2}(x_s)|^\lambda + \beta_2|v_{A_1}(x_s) - v_{A_2}(x_s)|^\lambda + \beta_3|\pi_{A_1}(x_s) \\
&\quad - \pi_{A_2}(x_s)|^\lambda\}, \quad \lambda \geq 1
\end{aligned} \tag{2.7}$$

As a result, when $w_s = 1$ and $w_i = 0$, $i \neq s$, the equality holds. Let

$$d_*(A_1, A_2) = \min_i\{\beta_1|\mu_{A_1}(x_i) - \mu_{A_2}(x_i)|^\lambda + \beta_2|v_{A_1}(x_i) - v_{A_2}(x_i)|^\lambda + \beta_3|\pi_{A_1}(x_i) - \pi_{A_2}(x_i)|^\lambda\}, \quad \lambda \geq 1 \tag{2.8}$$

$$d^*(A_1, A_2) = \max_i\{\beta_1|\mu_{A_1}(x_i) - \mu_{A_2}(x_i)|^\lambda + \beta_2|v_{A_1}(x_i) - v_{A_2}(x_i)|^\lambda + \beta_3|\pi_{A_1}(x_i) - \pi_{A_2}(x_i)|^\lambda\}, \quad \lambda \geq 1 \tag{2.9}$$

Thus

$$1 - \sqrt[\lambda]{d^*(A_1, A_2)} \leq \vartheta'(A_1, A_2) \leq 1 - \sqrt[\lambda]{d_*(A_1, A_2)}, \lambda \geq 1 \tag{2.10}$$

Based on Eqs. (2.8) and (2.9), Zhang et al. (2007) gave a formula for calculating the similarity degree between two IFSs:

Theorem 2.2 (Zhang et al. 2007) Let A_1 and A_2 be two IFSs. Then

$$\hat{\vartheta}(A_1, A_2) = \left(1 - \sqrt[\lambda]{d^*(A_1, A_2)}, \sqrt[\lambda]{d_*(A_1, A_2)}\right), \lambda \geq 1 \tag{2.11}$$

is called the similarity degree between A_1 and A_2.

Proof (1) We first prove that $\hat{\vartheta}(A_1, A_2)$ is an IFV. Since

$$\begin{aligned}
0 &\leq \beta_1|\mu_{A_1}(x_i) - \mu_{A_2}(x_i)|^\lambda + \beta_2|v_{A_1}(x_i) - v_{A_2}(x_i)|^\lambda + \beta_3|\pi_{A_1}(x_i) - \pi_{A_2}(x_i)|^\lambda \\
&\leq (\beta_1 + \beta_2 + \beta_3)\max\{|\mu_{A_1}(x_i) - \mu_{A_2}(x_i)|^\lambda, |v_{A_1}(x_i) - v_{A_2}(x_i)|^\lambda, \\
&\quad |\pi_{A_1}(x_i) - \pi_{A_2}(x_i)|^\lambda\} \\
&= \max\{|\mu_{A_1}(x_i) - \mu_{A_2}(x_i)|^\lambda, |v_{A_1}(x_i) - v_{A_2}(x_i)|^\lambda, |\pi_{A_1}(x_i) - \pi_{A_2}(x_i)|^\lambda\} \leq 1, \\
&\qquad \lambda \geq 1
\end{aligned}$$

then

$$0 \leq 1 - \sqrt[\lambda]{d^*(A_1, A_2)} \leq 1, 0 \leq \sqrt[\lambda]{d_*(A_1, A_2)} \leq 1, \lambda \geq 1 \tag{2.12}$$

Also since

$$0 \le d_*(A_1, A_2) \le d^*(A_1, A_2) \le 1 \tag{2.13}$$

then

$$0 \le \sqrt[\lambda]{d^*(A_1, A_2)} - \sqrt[\lambda]{d_*(A_1, A_2)} \le 1, \quad \lambda \ge 1 \tag{2.14}$$

i.e.,

$$\begin{aligned} 0 &\le 1 - \sqrt[\lambda]{d^*(A_1, A_2)} + \sqrt[\lambda]{d_*(A_1, A_2)} \\ &= 1 - \left(\sqrt[\lambda]{d^*(A_1, A_2)} - \sqrt[\lambda]{d_*(A_1, A_2)}\right) \le 1, \quad \lambda \ge 1 \end{aligned} \tag{2.15}$$

Thus $\hat{\vartheta}(A_1, A_2)$ is an IFV.

(2) If $\hat{\vartheta}(A_1, A_2) = (1, 0)$, then

$$1 - \sqrt[\lambda]{d^*(A_1, A_2)} = 1, \ \sqrt[\lambda]{d_*(A_1, A_2)} = 0, \quad \lambda \ge 1 \tag{2.16}$$

Also since

$$1 = 1 - \sqrt[\lambda]{d^*(A_1, A_2)} \le \vartheta(A_1, A_2) \le 1 - \sqrt[\lambda]{d_*(A_1, A_2)}, \quad \lambda \ge 1 \tag{2.17}$$

i.e., $\vartheta(A_1, A_2) = 1$, by Eq. (2.1), we get $A_1 = A_2$; otherwise, if $A_1 = A_2$, then by Eqs. (2.8) and (2.9), we have $\hat{\vartheta}(A_1, A_2) = (1, 0)$.

(3) Obviously, we have $\hat{\vartheta}(A_1, A_2) = \hat{\vartheta}(A_2, A_1)$. This completes the proof of the theorem.

Definition 2.2 (Zhang et al. 2007) Let $Z = (z_{ij})_{n \times n}$ be a matrix, if all of its elements z_{ij} $(i, j = 1, 2, \ldots, n)$ are IFVs, then Z is called an intuitionistic fuzzy matrix.

Definition 2.3 (Zhang et al. 2007) Let $Z_1 = (z_{ij}^{(1)})_{n \times n}$ and $Z_2 = (z_{ij}^{(2)})_{n \times n}$ be two intuitionistic fuzzy matrices. If $Z = Z_1 \circ Z_2$, then Z is called the composition matrix of Z_1 and Z_2, where

$$z_{ij} = \bigvee_{k=1}^{n} (z_{ik}^{(1)} \wedge z_{kj}^{(2)}) = (\max_k \{\min\{\mu_{z_{ik}^{(1)}}, \mu_{z_{kj}^{(2)}}\}, \min_k \{\max\{v_{z_{ik}^{(1)}}, v_{z_{kj}^{(2)}}\}\}),$$
$$i, j = 1, 2, \ldots n \tag{2.18}$$

Theorem 2.3 (Zhang et al. 2007) The composition matrix Z of the intuitionistic fuzzy matrix Z_1 and Z_2 is also an intuitionistic fuzzy matrix.

Proof Let $Z_1 = (z_{ij}^{(1)})_{n \times n}$, $Z_2 = (z_{ij}^{(2)})_{n \times n}$ and $Z = (z_{ij})_{n \times n}$. Then by Eq. (2.18), we have

$$\begin{aligned} z_{ij} &= \overset{n}{\underset{k=1}{\vee}} (z_{ik}^{(1)} \wedge z_{kj}^{(2)}) = (\max_k\{\min\{\mu_{z_{ik}^{(1)}}, \mu_{z_{kj}^{(2)}}\}, \min_k\{\max\{\nu_{z_{ik}^{(1)}}, \nu_{z_{kj}^{(2)}}\}\}) \\ &= (\max\{\min\{\mu_{z_{i1}^{(1)}}, \mu_{z_{1j}^{(2)}}\}, \ldots, \min\{\mu_{z_{in}^{(1)}}, \mu_{z_{nj}^{(2)}}\}\}, \\ &\quad \min\{\max\{\nu_{z_{i1}^{(1)}}, \nu_{z_{1j}^{(2)}}\}, \ldots, \max\{\nu_{z_{in}^{(1)}}, \nu_{z_{nj}^{(2)}}\}\}) \end{aligned} \tag{2.19}$$

Since

$$0 \le \max\{\min\{\mu_{z_{i1}^{(1)}}, \mu_{z_{1j}^{(2)}}\}, \ldots, \min\{\mu_{z_{in}^{(1)}}, \mu_{z_{nj}^{(2)}}\}\} \le 1 \tag{2.20}$$

$$0 \le \min\{\max\{\nu_{z_{i1}^{(1)}}, \nu_{z_{1j}^{(2)}}\}, \ldots, \max\{\nu_{z_{in}^{(1)}}, \nu_{z_{nj}^{(2)}}\}\}) \le 1 \tag{2.21}$$

There must exist two positive integers k_1 and k_2 such that

$$\max\{\min\{\mu_{z_{i1}^{(1)}}, \mu_{z_{1j}^{(2)}}\}, \ldots, \min\{\mu_{z_{in}^{(1)}}, \mu_{z_{nj}^{(2)}}\}\} = \min\{\mu_{z_{ik_1}^{(1)}}, \mu_{z_{k_1j}^{(2)}}\} \tag{2.22}$$

$$\min\{\max\{\nu_{z_{i1}^{(1)}}, \nu_{z_{1j}^{(2)}}\}, \ldots, \max\{\nu_{z_{in}^{(1)}}, \nu_{z_{nj}^{(2)}}\}\}) = \max\{\nu_{z_{ik_2}^{(1)}}, \nu_{z_{k_2j}^{(2)}}\} \tag{2.23}$$

Accordingly, we have

$$\begin{aligned} &\max\{\min\{\mu_{z_{i1}^{(1)}}, \mu_{z_{1j}^{(2)}}\}, \ldots, \min\{\mu_{z_{in}^{(1)}}, \mu_{z_{nj}^{(2)}}\}\} + \min\{\max\{\nu_{z_{i1}^{(1)}}, \nu_{z_{1j}^{(2)}}\}, \ldots, \\ &\max\{\nu_{z_{in}^{(1)}}, \nu_{z_{nj}^{(2)}}\}\}) = \min\{\mu_{z_{ik_1}^{(1)}}, \mu_{z_{k_1j}^{(2)}}\} + \max\{\nu_{z_{ik_2}^{(1)}}, \nu_{z_{k_2j}^{(2)}}\} \end{aligned} \tag{2.24}$$

In the case of $k_1 = k_2$, we get

$$\min\{\mu_{z_{ik_1}^{(1)}}, \mu_{z_{k_1j}^{(2)}}\} + \max\{\nu_{z_{ik_1}^{(1)}}, \nu_{z_{k_2j}^{(2)}}\} = \min\{\mu_{z_{ik_1}^{(1)}}, \mu_{z_{k_1j}^{(2)}}\} + \max\{\nu_{z_{ik_1}^{(1)}}, \nu_{z_{k_1j}^{(2)}}\} \le 1 \tag{2.25}$$

Also when $k_1 \neq k_2$, it yields

$$\min\{\mu_{z_{ik_1}^{(1)}}, \mu_{z_{k_1j}^{(2)}}\} + \max\{\nu_{z_{ik_2}^{(1)}}, \nu_{z_{k_2j}^{(2)}}\} \le \min\{\mu_{z_{ik_2}^{(1)}}, \mu_{z_{k2j}^{(2)}}\} + \max\{\nu_{z_{ik_2}^{(1)}}, \nu_{z_{k_2j}^{(2)}}\} \le 1 \tag{2.26}$$

Hence

$$\begin{aligned} &\max\{\min\{\mu_{z_{i1}^{(1)}}, \mu_{z_{1j}^{(2)}}\}, \ldots, \min\{\mu_{z_{in}^{(1)}}, \mu_{z_{nj}^{(2)}}\}\} \\ &\quad + \min\{\max\{\nu_{z_{i1}^{(1)}}, \nu_{z_{1j}^{(2)}}\}, \ldots, \max\{\nu_{z_{in}^{(1)}}, \nu_{z_{nj}^{(2)}}\}\}) \le 1 \end{aligned} \tag{2.27}$$

Consequently, the composition matrix of two intuitionistic fuzzy matrices is also an intuitionistic fuzzy matrix. This completes the proof.

Definition 2.4 (Zhang et al. 2007) If the intuitionistic fuzzy matrix $Z = (z_{ij})_{n\times n}$ satisfies the following condition:

(1) Reflexivity: $z_{ii} = (1, 0), i = 1, 2, \ldots, n$.
(2) Symmetry: $z_{ij} = z_{ji}$, i.e., $\mu_{z_{ij}} = \mu_{z_{ji}}, v_{z_{ij}} = v_{z_{ji}}, i, j = 1, 2, \ldots, n$.

Then Z is called an intuitionistic fuzzy similarity matrix.

Based on Theorem 2.3 and Definition 2.4, we have

Corollary 2.1 (Zhang et al. 2007) The composition matrix of two intuitionistic fuzzy similarity matrices is an intuitionistic fuzzy matrix. However, the composition matrix of two intuitionistic fuzzy similarity matrices may not be an intuitionistic fuzzy similarity matrix. For example, let

$$Z_1 = \begin{bmatrix} (1,0) & (0.2,0.3) & (0.5,0.2) \\ (0.2,0.3) & (1,0) & (0.1,0.7) \\ (0.5,0.2) & (0.1,0.7) & (1,0) \end{bmatrix}$$

$$Z_2 = \begin{bmatrix} (1,0) & (0.4,0.4) & (0.9,0.1) \\ (0.4,0.4) & (1,0) & (0.3,0.3) \\ (0.9,0.1) & (0.3,0.3) & (1,0) \end{bmatrix}$$

Obviously, both Z_1 and Z_2 are intuitionistic fuzzy similarity matrices, but the composition matrix of Z_1 and Z_2 is as follows:

$$Z = Z_1 \circ Z_2 = \begin{bmatrix} (1,0) & (0.4,0.3) & (0.9,0.1) \\ (0.4,0.3) & (1,0) & (0.3,0.3) \\ (0.9,0.1) & (0.4,0.3) & (1,0) \end{bmatrix}$$

where $z_{23} \neq z_{32}$, i.e., Z does not satisfy symmetry property. Thus, Z is not an intuitionistic fuzzy similarity matrix. But when the composition matrix of an intuitionistic fuzzy similarity matrix and itself is an intuitionistic fuzzy similarity matrix:

Theorem 2.4 (Zhang et al. 2007) Let $Z_1 = (z_{ij}^{(1)})_{n \times n}$ be an intuitionistic fuzzy similarity matrix. Then the composition matrix $Z = Z_1 \circ Z_1 = (z_{ij})_{n \times n}$ is also an intuitionistic fuzzy similarity matrix.

Proof (1) Since Z_1 is an intuitionistic fuzzy similarity matrix, by Corollary 2.1, the composition matrix Z of Z_1 and itself is an intuitionistic fuzzy matrix.

(2) Since

$$z_{ii} = \mathop{\vee}_{k=1}^{n} (z_{ik}^{(1)} \wedge z_{ki}^{(1)}) = (\max_k\{\min\{\mu_{z_{ik}^{(1)}}, \mu_{z_{ki}^{(1)}}\}\}, \min_k\{\max\{v_{z_{ik}^{(1)}}, v_{z_{ki}^{(1)}}\}\}) \quad (2.28)$$

then when $k = i$, we have

$$z_{ii}^{(1)} \wedge z_{ii}^{(1)}) = (1, 0) \wedge (1, 0)\} = (1, 0) \quad (2.29)$$

So

$$z_{ii} = \mathop{\vee}_{k=1}^{n} (z_{ik}^{(1)} \wedge z_{ki}^{(1)}) = (1, 0) \quad (2.30)$$

(3) Since Z_1 is an intuitionistic fuzzy similarity matrix, then we have $z_{ik}^{(1)} = z_{ki}^{(1)}$. Thereby

$$\begin{aligned} z_{ji} &= \bigvee_{k=1}^{n} (z_{jk}^{(1)} \wedge z_{ki}^{(1)}) = (\max_k\{\min\{\mu_{z_{jk}^{(1)}}, \mu_{z_{ki}^{(1)}}\}, \min_k\{\max\{\nu_{z_{jk}^{(1)}}, \nu_{z_{ki}^{(1)}}\}\}) \\ &= (\max_k\{\min\{\mu_{z_{jk}^{(1)}}, \mu_{z_{ik}^{(1)}}\}, \min_k\{\max\{\nu_{z_{jk}^{(1)}}, \nu_{z_{ik}^{(1)}}\}\}) \\ &= (\max_k\{\min\{\mu_{z_{ik}^{(1)}}, \mu_{z_{jk}^{(1)}}\}, \min_k\{\max\{\nu_{z_{ik}^{(1)}}, \nu_{z_{jk}^{(1)}}\}\}) \\ &= \bigvee_{k=1}^{n} (z_{ik}^{(1)} \wedge z_{kj}^{(1)}) \\ &= z_{ij} \end{aligned} \tag{2.31}$$

Theorem 2.5 (Zhang et al. 2007) Let $Z_1 = (z_{ij}^{(1)})_{n\times n}$, $Z_2 = (z_{ij}^{(2)})_{n\times n}$ and $Z_3 = (z_{ij}^{(3)})_{n\times n}$ be three intuitionistic fuzzy similarity matrices. Then their composition operation satisfies the associative law:

$$(Z_1 \circ Z_2) \circ Z_3 = Z_1 \circ (Z_2 \circ Z_3) \tag{2.32}$$

Proof Let $(Z_1 \circ Z_2) \circ Z_3 = (z_{it})_{n\times n}$ and $Z_1 \circ (Z_2 \circ Z_3) - (z'_{it})_{n\times n}$. Then by Theorem 2.1, we have

$$\begin{aligned} z_{it} &= \bigvee_{k=1}^{n} \left\{ \left(\bigvee_{j=1}^{n} (z_{ij}^{(1)} \wedge z_{jk}^{(2)}) \right) \wedge z_{kt}^{(3)} \right\} = \bigvee_{k=1}^{n} \left\{ \bigvee_{j=1}^{n} ((z_{ij}^{(1)} \wedge z_{jk}^{(2)}) \wedge z_{kt}^{(3)}) \right\} \\ &= \bigvee_{k=1}^{n} \bigvee_{j=1}^{n} (z_{ij}^{(1)} \wedge (z_{jk}^{(2)} \wedge z_{kt}^{(3)})) = \bigvee_{j=1}^{n} \bigvee_{k=1}^{n} (z_{ij}^{(1)} \wedge (z_{jk}^{(2)} \wedge z_{kt}^{(3)})) \\ &= \bigvee_{j=1}^{n} \left\{ z_{ij}^{(1)} \wedge \left(\bigvee_{k=1}^{n} (z_{jk}^{(2)} \wedge z_{kt}^{(3)}) \right) \right\} \\ &= z'_{it}, \quad i, t = 1, 2, \ldots, n \end{aligned}$$

Hence, Eq. (2.32) holds, which completes the proof.

Corollary 2.2 (Zhang et al. 2007) Let Z be an intuitionistic fuzzy similarity matrix. Then for any positive integers m_1 and m_2, we have

$$Z^{m_1+m_2} = Z^{m_1} \circ Z^{m_2}$$

where Z^{m_1} and Z^{m_2} are the m_1 and m_2 compositions of Z, respectively. Furthermore, Z^{m_1}, Z^{m_2} and their composition matrix $Z^{m_1+m_2}$ are the intuitionistic fuzzy similarity matrix.

Definition 2.5 (Zhang et al. 2007) If the intuitionistic fuzzy matrix $Z = (z_{ij})_{n\times n}$ satisfies the following condition:

(1) Reflexivity: $z_{ii} = (1, 0)$, $i = 1, 2, \ldots, n$.
(2) Symmetry: $z_{ij} = z_{ji}$, i.e., $\mu_{z_{ij}} = \mu_{z_{ji}}$, $\nu_{z_{ij}} = \nu_{z_{ji}}$, $i, j = 1, 2, \ldots, n$.

(3) Transitivity: $Z^2 \subseteq Z$, i.e., $\overset{n}{\underset{k=1}{\vee}} (z_{ik} \wedge z_{kj}) \leq z_{ij}, \quad i, j = 1, 2, \ldots, n.$

Then Z is called an intuitionistic fuzzy equivalence matrix.

In order to save computation, motivated by the idea of Wang (1983), we have the following conclusion:

Theorem 2.6 (Zhang et al. 2007) Let Z be an intuitionistic fuzzy similarity matrix. Then after the finite times of compositions:

$$Z \to Z^2 \to Z^4 \to \cdots \to Z^{2^k} \to \cdots$$

There must exist a positive integer k such that $Z^{2^k} = Z^{2^{(k+1)}}$, and Z^{2^k} is an intuitionistic fuzzy equivalence matrix.

Definition 2.6 (Zhang et al. 2007) Let $Z = (z_{ij})_{n \times n}$ be an intuitionistic fuzzy similarity matrix, where $z_{ij} = (\mu_{z_{ij}}, v_{z_{ij}}), i, j = 1, 2, \ldots, n$. Then $Z_\lambda = ({}_\lambda z_{ij})_{n \times n}$ is called the λ-cutting matrix of Z, where

$$ {}_\lambda z_{ij} = \begin{cases} 0, & \text{if } \lambda > 1 - v_{z_{ij}}, \\ \dfrac{1}{2}, & \text{if } \mu_{z_{ij}} < \lambda \leq 1 - v_{z_{ij}}, \\ 1, & \text{if } \mu_{z_{ij}} \geq \lambda. \end{cases} \tag{2.33}$$

Definition 2.7 (Wang 1983) If the matrix $\dot{Z} = (\dot{z}_{ij})_{n \times n}$ satisfies the following conditions:

(1) Reflexivity: $\dot{z}_{ii} = 1, i = 1, 2, \ldots, n$, and for any $\dot{z}_{ij} \in [0, 1], i, j = 1, 2, \ldots, n$.
(2) Symmetry: $\dot{z}_{ij} = \dot{z}_{ji}$.
(3) Transitivity: $\max_k \{\min\{\dot{z}_{ik}, \dot{z}_{kj}\}\} \leq \dot{z}_{ij}$, for all $i, j = 1, 2, \ldots, n$.

Then $\dot{Z}$ is called a fuzzy equivalence matrix.

Theorem 2.7 (Zhang et al. 2007) $Z = (z_{ij})_{n \times n}$ is an intuitionistic fuzzy equivalence matrix if and only if its λ-cutting matrix $Z_\lambda = ({}_\lambda z_{ij})_{n \times n}$ is a fuzzy equivalence matrix, where $z_{ij} = (\mu_{z_{ij}}, v_{z_{ij}}), i, j = 1, 2, \ldots, n$.

Proof (Necessity)

(1) (Reflexivity) Since $z_{ii} = (1, 0), \lambda \in [0, 1]$, then $\lambda \leq \mu_{z_{ii}} = 1, {}_\lambda z_{ii} = 1$.
(2) (Symmetry) Since $z_{ij} = z_{ji}$, i.e., $\mu_{z_{ij}} = \mu_{z_{ji}}, v_{z_{ij}} = v_{z_{ji}}$, thus ${}_\lambda z_{ij} = {}_\lambda z_{ji}$.
(3) (Transitivity) Since $Z = (z_{ij})_{n \times n}$ is an intuitionistic fuzzy equivalence matrix, we have

$$\max_k \{\min\{\mu_{z_{ik}}, \mu_{z_{kj}}\}\} \leq \mu_{z_{ij}} \tag{2.34}$$

$$\min_k \{\max\{v_{z_{ik}}, v_{z_{kj}}\}\} \leq v_{z_{ij}} \tag{2.35}$$

Also since the intuitionistic fuzzy equivalence matrix $Z = (z_{ij})_{n\times n}$ and the composition matrix of itself is an intuitionistic fuzzy matrix, it yields

$$\max_k\{\min\{\mu_{z_{ik}}, \mu_{z_{kj}}\}\} \geq \min_k\{\max\{v_{z_{ik}}, v_{z_{kj}}\}\} \tag{2.36}$$

(a) When $\lambda \leq \mu_{z_{ij}}$ and ${}_\lambda z_{ij} = 1$, also since

$$\max_k\{\min\{{}_\lambda z_{ik}, {}_\lambda z_{kj}\}\} \in [0, 1] \tag{2.37}$$

then

$$\max_k\{\min\{{}_\lambda z_{ik}, {}_\lambda z_{kj}\}\} \leq {}_\lambda z_{ij} = 1 \tag{2.38}$$

(b) When $1 - v_{z_{ij}} < \lambda$ and ${}_\lambda z_{ij} = 0$, also since

$$\min_k\{\max\{v_{z_{ik}}, v_{z_{kj}}\}\} \geq v_{z_{ij}} > 1 - \lambda \tag{2.39}$$

then, for any k, we have $\max\{v_{z_{ik}}, v_{z_{kj}}\} > 1-\lambda$, i.e., for any k, it can be obtained that

$$\min\{{}_\lambda z_{ik}, {}_\lambda z_{kj}\} = 0 \tag{2.40}$$

Then

$$\max_k\{\min\{{}_\lambda z_{ik}, {}_\lambda z_{kj}\} = 0 \tag{2.41}$$

Thus

$$\max_k\{\min\{{}_\lambda z_{ik}, {}_\lambda z_{kj}\} \leq {}_\lambda z_{ij} \tag{2.42}$$

(c) When $\mu_{z_{ij}} < \lambda \leq 1 - v_{z_{ij}}$, we have ${}_\lambda z_{ij} = 1/2$. In this case, if

$$\min_k\{\max\{v_{z_{ik}}, v_{z_{kj}}\}\} \geq v_{z_{ij}} > 1 - \lambda \tag{2.43}$$

then by (b), we get

$$\max_k\{\min\{{}_\lambda z_{ik}, {}_\lambda z_{kj}\}\} = 0 \tag{2.44}$$

Therefore

$$\max_k\{\min\{{}_\lambda z_{ik}, {}_\lambda z_{kj}\}\} \leq {}_\lambda z_{ij} \tag{2.45}$$

If

$$\max_k\{\min\{\mu_{z_{ik}}, \mu_{z_{kj}}\}\} \leq \lambda \leq 1 - \min_k\{\max\{v_{z_{ik}}, v_{z_{kj}}\}\} \tag{2.46}$$

then

$$\max_k\{\min\{{}_\lambda z_{ik}, {}_\lambda z_{kj}\}\} = \frac{1}{2}, \max_k\{\min\{{}_\lambda z_{ik}, {}_\lambda z_{kj}\}\} = {}_\lambda z_{ij} \tag{2.47}$$

From the known condition, it follows that

$$\max_k\{\min\{\mu_{z_{ik}}, \mu_{z_{kj}}\}\} \leq \mu_{z_{ij}} < \lambda \tag{2.48}$$

which indicates that the case

$$\lambda \leq \max_k\{\min\{\mu_{z_{ik}}, \mu_{z_{kj}}\}\} \tag{2.49}$$

does not exist. Therefore, when $\mu_{z_{ij}} < \lambda \leq 1 - v_{z_{ij}}$, we have

$$\max_k\{\min\{{}_\lambda z_{ik}, {}_\lambda z_{kj}\}\} \leq {}_\lambda z_{ij} \tag{2.50}$$

Hence, $Z_\lambda = ({}_\lambda z_{ij})_{n\times n}$ satisfies the transitivity property.

(Sufficiency)

(1) (Reflexivity) Since ${}_\lambda z_{ii} = 1$, then for any $\lambda \in [0, 1]$, $\lambda \leq \mu_{z_{ii}}$, and then let $\lambda = 1$. Then $z_{ii} = (1, 0)$.

(2) (Symmetry) Since for any i, k, ${}_\lambda z_{ik} = {}_\lambda z_{ki}$, if there exists $z_{ik} \neq z_{ki}$, i.e., $\mu_{z_{ik}} \neq \mu_{z_{ki}}$ or $v_{z_{ij}} \neq v_{z_{ji}}$, without loss of generality, suppose that $\mu_{z_{ij}} < \mu_{z_{ji}}$, and let $\lambda = (\mu_{z_{ij}} + \mu_{z_{ji}})/2$, then $\mu_{z_{ij}} < \lambda < \mu_{z_{ji}}$, ${}_\lambda z_{ik} = 0$ or $1/2$, and ${}_\lambda z_{ki} = 1$, ${}_\lambda z_{ik} \neq {}_\lambda z_{ki}$, which contradicts the known condition. Therefore, $Z = (z_{ij})_{n\times n}$ is symmetry.

(3) (Transitivity) Since for any i, j, we have

$$\max_k\{\min\{{}_\lambda z_{ik}, {}_\lambda z_{kj}\}\} \leq {}_\lambda z_{ij} \tag{2.51}$$

and each element in Z_λ takes its value from $\{0, 1/2, 1\}$. Then

(a) When ${}_\lambda z_{ij} = 1$, for any $\lambda \in [0, 1]$, we have $\mu_{z_{ij}} \geq \lambda$, taking $\lambda = 1$, it can be obtained that $\mu_{z_{ij}} = 1$ and $v_{z_{ij}} = 0$. Consequently,

$$\max_k\{\min\{\mu_{z_{ik}}, \mu_{z_{kj}}\}\} \leq \mu_{z_{ij}}, \min_k\{\max\{v_{z_{ik}}, v_{z_{kj}}\}\} \geq v_{z_{ij}} \tag{2.52}$$

(b) When ${}_\lambda z_{ij} = 1/2$, for any $\lambda \in [0, 1]$, we have $\mu_{z_{ij}} < \lambda \leq 1 - v_{z_{ij}}$. Also since

$$\max_k\{\min\{{}_\lambda z_{ik}, {}_\lambda z_{kj}\}\} \leq \frac{1}{2} \tag{2.53}$$

then

$$\max_k\{\min\{{}_\lambda z_{ik}, {}_\lambda z_{kj}\}\} = 0 \text{ or } \frac{1}{2} \tag{2.54}$$

Thus, for any k, we get

$$\min\{{}_\lambda z_{ik}, {}_\lambda z_{kj}\} = 0 \tag{2.55}$$

or there exists a positive integer s, such that

$$\min\{_\lambda z_{is}, {}_\lambda z_{sj}\} = \frac{1}{2} \tag{2.56}$$

Case 1 If for any k, we have

$$\min\{_\lambda z_{ik}, {}_\lambda z_{kj}\} = 0 \tag{2.57}$$

Then for any $\lambda \in [0, 1]$, it yields

$$\max\{v_{z_{ik}}, v_{z_{kj}}\} > 1 - \lambda \tag{2.58}$$

hence

$$\min_k\{\max\{v_{z_{ik}}, v_{z_{kj}}\}\} \geq v_{z_{ij}} > 1 - \lambda \tag{2.59}$$

Considering the arbitrary of λ, when λ tends to be infinitely small, we get

$$\max_k\{\min\{\mu_{z_{ik}}, \mu_{z_{kj}}\}\} \leq 1 - \min_k\{\max\{v_{z_{ik}}, v_{z_{kj}}\}\} = 0 \tag{2.60}$$

As a result,

$$\max_k\{\min\{\mu_{z_{ik}}, \mu_{z_{kj}}\}\} \leq \mu_{z_{ij}} \tag{2.61}$$

Case 2 If there exists a positive integer k_1, such that

$$\min\{_\lambda z_{ik_1}, {}_\lambda z_{k_1j}\} = \frac{1}{2} \tag{2.62}$$

and for any $k = k_1$, let

$$\min\{_\lambda z_{ik}, {}_\lambda z_{kj}\} = 0 \tag{2.63}$$

Then according to Case 1, we have

$$\min_{k\neq k_1}\{\max\{v_{z_{ik}}, v_{z_{kj}}\}\} \geq v_{z_{ij}} \tag{2.64}$$

$$\max_{k\neq k_1}\{\min\{\mu_{z_{ik}}, \mu_{z_{kj}}\}\} \leq \mu_{z_{ij}} \tag{2.65}$$

and when $k = k_1$, suppose that

$$\min\{\mu_{z_{ik_1}}, \mu_{z_{k_1j}}\} = \mu_{z_{ik_1}}, \mu_{z_{ik_1}} > \mu_{z_{ij}} \tag{2.66}$$

Then let $\lambda = (\mu_{z_{ij}} + \mu_{z_{ik_1}})/2$, and thus, $\mu_{z_{ij}} \leq \lambda \leq \mu_{z_{ik_1}}$. Accordingly,

$$_\lambda z_{ik_1} = {}_\lambda z_{k_1j} = 1, \min\{_\lambda z_{ik_1}, {}_\lambda z_{k_1j}\} = 1 \tag{2.67}$$

$$\max_k\{{}_\lambda z_{ik}, {}_\lambda z_{kj}\} = 1 > {}_\lambda z_{ij} \tag{2.68}$$

which contradicts the known condition. Therefore,

$$\max_{k \neq k_1}\{\min\{\mu_{z_{ik}}, \mu_{z_{kj}}\}\} \leq \mu_{z_{ij}} \tag{2.69}$$

Similarly, we get

$$\min_k\{\max\{\nu_{z_{ik}}, \nu_{z_{kj}}\}\} \geq \nu_{z_{ij}} \tag{2.70}$$

(c) When ${}_\lambda z_{ij} = 0$, i.e., for any $\lambda \in [0, 1]$, we have $1 - \nu_{z_{ij}} < \lambda$. Then by

$$\max_k\{\min\{{}_\lambda z_{ik}, {}_\lambda z_{kj}\}\} \leq {}_\lambda z_{ij} = 0 \tag{2.71}$$

It can be seen that for any k, we get

$$\min\{{}_\lambda z_{ik}, {}_\lambda z_{kj}\} = 0 \tag{2.72}$$

$$\max\{\nu_{z_{ik}}, \nu_{z_{kj}}\} > 1 - \lambda \tag{2.73}$$

Considering the arbitrary of λ, it yields $\mu_{z_{ij}} = 1 - \nu_{z_{ij}} = 0$, and

$$\max_k\{\min\{\mu_{z_{ik}}, \mu_{z_{kj}}\}\} \leq 1 - \min_k\{\max\{\nu_{z_{ik}}, \nu_{z_{kj}}\}\} = 0 \tag{2.74}$$

Thus Z satisfies the transitivity property.

From the above analysis, the sufficiency of Theorem 2.7 holds. The proof is completed.

Definition 2.8 (Zhang et al. 2007) Let $A_i (i = 1, 2, \ldots, n)$ be a collection of IFSs, $Z = (z_{ij})_{n\times n}$ is the intuitionistic fuzzy similarity matrix derived by Eq. (2.11), $Z^* = (z^*_{ij})_{n\times n}$ is the intuitionistic fuzzy equivalence matrix of Z, and ${}_\lambda Z^* = ({}_\lambda z^*_{ij})_{n\times n}$ is the λ-cutting matrix of Z^*. If the corresponding elements in both the ith line (column) and the jth line (column) of ${}_\lambda Z^*$ are equal, then A_i and A_j are classified into one type.

Note: Since λ-cutting matrix ${}_\lambda Z^*$ has the transitivity property, then if A_i and A_k are of the same type, while A_k and A_j are of the same type, then A_i and A_j are of the same type.

On the basis of the above theory, Zhang et al. (2007) introduced a clustering algorithm for IFSs, which involves the following steps:

Algorithm 2.1

Step 1 For a multi-attribute decision making problem, let $Y = \{y_1, y_2, \ldots, y_n\}$ be a finite set of alternatives, and $G = \{G_1, G_2, \ldots, G_m\}$ the set of attributes. Suppose that the characteristic information on the alternative y_i is expressed in IFSs:

$$y_i = \{\langle G_j, \mu_{y_i}(G_j), v_{y_i}(G_j)\rangle \mid G_j \in G\},\ j = 1, 2, \ldots, m \tag{2.75}$$

where $\mu_{y_i}(G_j)$ indicates the degree that the alternative y_i satisfies the attribute G_j, $v_{y_i}(G_j)$ indicates the degree that the alternative y_i does not satisfy the attribute G_j, $\pi_{y_i}(G_j) = 1 - \mu_{y_i}(G_j) - v_{y_i}(G_j)$ indicates the uncertainty degree that the alternative y_i to the attribute G_j. By the intuitionistic fuzzy similarity degree formula (2.11), we establish the intuitionistic fuzzy similarity matrix $Z = (z_{ij})_{n\times n}$, where

$$z_{ij} = \hat{\vartheta}(y_i, y_j) = \left(1 - \sqrt[\lambda]{d^*(y_i, y_j)}, \sqrt[\lambda]{d_*(y_i, y_j)}\right), i, j = 1, 2, \ldots, n \tag{2.76}$$

$$d_*(y_i, y_j) = \min_k \left\{\beta_1|\mu_{y_i}(G_k) - \mu_{y_j}(G_k)|^\lambda + \beta_2|v_{y_i}(G_k) - v_{y_j}(G_k)|^\lambda + \beta_3|\pi_{y_i}(G_k) - \pi_{y_j}(G_k)|^\lambda\right\} \tag{2.77}$$

$$d_*(y_i, y_j) = \min_k \left\{\beta_1|\mu_{y_i}(G_k) - \mu_{y_j}(G_k)|^\lambda + \beta_2|v_{y_i}(G_k) - v_{y_j}(G_k)|^\lambda + \beta_3|\pi_{y_i}(G_k) - \pi_{y_j}(G_k)|^\lambda\right\} \tag{2.78}$$

$$d^*(y_i, y_j) = \max_k \left\{\beta_1|\mu_{y_i}(G_k) - \mu_{y_j}(G_k)|^\lambda + \beta_2|v_{y_i}(G_k) - v_{y_j}(G_k)|^\lambda + \beta_3|\pi_{y_i}(G_k) - \pi_{y_j}(G_k)|^\lambda\right\} \tag{2.79}$$

and $\lambda, \beta_1, \beta_2, \beta_3$ are the predefined parameter, $\lambda \geq 1$, $\beta_i \in [0, 1]$, $i = 1, 2, 3$, and $\sum_{i=1}^3 \beta_i = 1$.

Step 2 Check whether the intuitionistic fuzzy matrix Z is the intuitionistic fuzzy equivalence matrix or not (i.e., check $Z^2 \subseteq Z$ or not); otherwise, do the composition operation: $Z \to Z^2 \to Z^4 \to \cdots \to Z^{2^k} \to \cdots$, until $Z^{2^l} = Z^{2^{l+1}}$. Then Z^{2^l} is the derived intuitionistic fuzzy equivalence matrix. For the sake of convenience, without loss of generality, let $Z^* = (z_{ij}^*)_{n\times n}$ be the derived intuitionistic fuzzy equivalence matrix, where $z_{ij}^* = (\mu_{z_{ij}^*}, v_{z_{ij}^*})$, $i, j = 1, 2, \ldots, n$.

Step 3 For the given confidence level λ, by Eq. (2.33), we calculate the λ-cutting matrix ${}_\lambda Z^* = ({}_\lambda z_{ij}^*)_{n\times n}$ of the intuitionistic fuzzy equivalence matrix Z^*.

Step 4 According to the λ-cutting matrix ${}_\lambda Z^*$ and Definition 2.8, we cluster the given alternatives.

Example 2.1 (Zhang et al. 2007) Consider a car classification problem. There are five new cars $y_i (i = 1, 2, \ldots, 5)$ to be classified in the Guangzhou car market in Guangdong, China, and six attributes: (1) G_1: Fuel economy; (2) G_2: Aerod. Degree; (3) G_3: Price; (4) G_4: Comfort; (5) G_5: Design; and (6) G_6: Safety, are taken into consideration in the classification problem. The characteristics of the ten new cars $y_i (i = 1, 2, \ldots, 5)$ under the six attributes $G_j (j = 1, 2, \ldots, 6)$ are represented by the IFSs, shown in Table 2.1 (Zhang et al. 2007).

Table 2.1 The characteristics of the ten new cars

	G_1	G_2	G_3	G_4	G_5	G_6
y_1	(0.3,0.5)	(0.6,0.1)	(0.4,0.3)	(0.8,0.1)	(0.1,0.6)	(0.5,0.4)
y_2	(0.6,0.3)	(0.5,0.2)	(0.6,0.1)	(0.7,0.1)	(0.3,0.6)	(0.4,0.3)
y_3	(0.4,0.4)	(0.8,0.1)	(0.5,0.1)	(0.6,0.2)	(0.4,0.5)	(0.3,0.2)
y_4	(0.2,0.4)	(0.4,0.1)	(0.9,0)	(0.8,0.1)	(0.2,0.5)	(0.7,0.1)
y_5	(0.5,0.2)	(0.3,0.6)	(0.6,0.3)	(0.7,0.1)	(0.6,0.2)	(0.5,0.3)

Step 1 By Eq. (2.11), we construct the intuitionistic fuzzy similarity matrix (without loss of generality, let $\lambda = 2, \beta_1 = \beta_2 = \beta_3 = 1/3$):

We first calculate

$$1 - \sqrt[\lambda]{d^*(y_1, y_2)} = 1 - \frac{1}{\sqrt{3}}[\max\{|0.3 - 0.6|^2 + |0.5 - 0.3|^2 + |0.2 - 0.1|^2,$$
$$|0.6-0.5|^2 + |0.1-0.2|^2 + |0.3-0.3|^2, |0.4-0.6|^2 + |0.3-0.1|^2 + |0.3-0.3|^2,$$
$$|0.8-0.7|^2 + |0.1-0.1|^2 + |0.1-0.2|^2, |0.1-0.3|^2 + |0.6-0.6|^2 + |0.3-0.1|^2,$$
$$|0.5 - 0.4|^2 + |0.4 - 0.3|^2 + |0.1 - 0.3|^2\}]^{\frac{1}{2}} = 0.78$$

$$\sqrt[\lambda]{d_*(y_1, y_2)} = \frac{1}{\sqrt{3}}[\min\{|0.3 - 0.6|^2 + |0.5 - 0.3|^2 + |0.2 - 0.1|^2,$$
$$|0.6-0.5|^2 + |0.1-0.2|^2 + |0.3-0.3|^2, |0.4-0.6|^2 + |0.3-0.1|^2 + |0.3-0.3|^2,$$
$$|0.8-0.7|^2 + |0.1-0.1|^2 + |0.1-0.2|^2, |0.1-0.3|^2 + |0.6-0.6|^2 + |0.3-0.1|^2,$$
$$|0.5-0.4|^2 + |0.4-0.3|^2 + |0.1-0.3|^2\}]^{\frac{1}{2}} = 0.08$$

Thus, $z_{12} = (0.78, 0.08)$, similarly, we can calculate the other intuitionistic fuzzy similarity degrees, and then get the intuitionistic fuzzy similarity matrix:

$$Z = \begin{pmatrix} (1,0) & (0.78,0.02) & (0.72,0.02) & (0.64,0) & (0.63,0.08) \\ (0.78,0.02) & (1,0) & (0.78,0.08) & (0.71,0.08) & (0.71,0) \\ (0.72,0.08) & (0.78,0.08) & (1,0) & (0.67,0.14) & (0.59,0.08) \\ (0.64,0) & (0.71,0.08) & (0.67,0.14) & (1,0) & (0.63,0.08) \\ (0.63,0.08) & (0.71,0) & (0.59,0.08) & (0.63,0.08) & (1,0) \end{pmatrix}$$

Step 2 Calculate

$$Z^2 = Z \circ Z = \begin{pmatrix} (1,0) & [0.78,0.92] & (0.78,0.08) & (0.71,0) & (0.71,0.08) \\ (0.78,0.08) & (1,0) & (0.78,0.08) & (0.71,0.08) & (0.71,0) \\ (0.78,0.08) & (0.78,0.08) & (1,0) & (0.71,0.08) & (0.71,0.08) \\ (0.71,0) & (0.71,0.08) & (0.71,0.08) & (1,0) & (0.71,0.08) \\ (0.71,0.08) & (0.71,0) & (0.71,0.08) & (0.71,0.08) & (1,0) \end{pmatrix}$$

Since $Z^2 \neq Z$, then Z is not an intuitionistic fuzzy equivalence matrix. Thus we need to calculate

$$Z^4 = Z^2 \circ Z^2$$
$$= \begin{pmatrix} (1,0) & (0.78,0.08) & (0.78,0.08) & (0.71,0) & (0.71,0.08) \\ (0.78,0.08) & (1,0) & (0.78,0.08) & (0.71,0.08) & (0.71,0) \\ (0.78,0.08) & (0.78,0.08) & (1,0) & (0.71,0.08) & (0.71,0.08) \\ (0.71,0) & (0.71,0.08) & (0.71,0.08) & (1,0) & (0.71,0.08) \\ (0.71,0.08) & (0.71,0) & (0.71,0.08) & (0.71,0.08) & (1,0) \end{pmatrix} = Z^2$$

Therefore, Z^2 is an intuitionistic fuzzy equivalence matrix.

Step 3 By Eq. (2.33), we can see that the value of confidence level λ is only related to the membership degree $\mu_{z_{ij}^*}$ and the non-membership degree $v_{z_{ij}^*}$ of the elements $z_{ij}^* = (\mu_{z_{ij}^*}, v_{z_{ij}^*})$ in the intuitionistic fuzzy equivalence matrix $Z^* = Z^2 = (z_{ij}^*)_{5\times 5}$. In general, we can make a detailed discussion by taking $\mu_{z_{ij}^*}$ and $1 - v_{z_{ij}^*}$ corresponding to each element of Z^* as the bounded values of the confidence level λ of the λ-cutting matrix ${}_\lambda Z^*$:

(1) When $\lambda \leq 0.71$, we have

$${}_\lambda Z^* = \begin{pmatrix} 1 & 1 & 1 & 1 & 1 \\ 1 & 1 & 1 & 1 & 1 \\ 1 & 1 & 1 & 1 & 1 \\ 1 & 1 & 1 & 1 & 1 \\ 1 & 1 & 1 & 1 & 1 \end{pmatrix}$$

(2) When $0.71 < \lambda \leq 0.78$, we have

$${}_\lambda Z^* = \begin{pmatrix} 1 & 1 & 1 & \frac{1}{2} & \frac{1}{2} \\ 1 & 1 & 1 & \frac{1}{2} & \frac{1}{2} \\ 1 & 1 & 1 & \frac{1}{2} & \frac{1}{2} \\ \frac{1}{2} & \frac{1}{2} & \frac{1}{2} & 1 & \frac{1}{2} \\ \frac{1}{2} & \frac{1}{2} & \frac{1}{2} & \frac{1}{2} & 1 \end{pmatrix}$$

(3) When $0.78 < \lambda \leq 0.92$, we have

$$
{}_{\lambda}Z^* = \begin{pmatrix} 1 & \frac{1}{2} & \frac{1}{2} & \frac{1}{2} & \frac{1}{2} \\ \frac{1}{2} & 1 & \frac{1}{2} & \frac{1}{2} & \frac{1}{2} \\ \frac{1}{2} & \frac{1}{2} & 1 & \frac{1}{2} & \frac{1}{2} \\ \frac{1}{2} & \frac{1}{2} & \frac{1}{2} & 1 & \frac{1}{2} \\ \frac{1}{2} & \frac{1}{2} & \frac{1}{2} & \frac{1}{2} & 1 \end{pmatrix}
$$

(4) When $0.92 < \lambda \leq 1$, we have

$$
{}_{\lambda}Z^* = \begin{pmatrix} 1 & 0 & 0 & \frac{1}{2} & 0 \\ 0 & 1 & 0 & 0 & \frac{1}{2} \\ 0 & 0 & 1 & 0 & 0 \\ \frac{1}{2} & 0 & 0 & 1 & 0 \\ 0 & \frac{1}{2} & 0 & 0 & 1 \end{pmatrix}
$$

Step 4 According to ${}_{\lambda}Z^*$ and Definition 2.8, we make the following discussions:

(1) If $0 \leq \lambda \leq 0.71$, then the cars y_i $(i = 1, 2, \ldots, 5)$ are classified into one type:

$$\{y_1, y_2, y_3, y_4, y_5\}$$

(2) If $0.71 < \lambda \leq 0.78$, then the cars y_i $(i = 1, 2, \ldots, 5)$ are classified into three types:

$$\{y_1, y_2, y_3\}, \{y_4\}, \{y_5\}$$

(3) If $0.78 < \lambda \leq 1$, then the cars y_i $(i = 1, 2, \ldots, 5)$ are classified into five types:

$$\{y_1\}, \{y_2\}, \{y_3\}, \{y_4\}, \{y_5\}$$

From the above analysis, it can be seen that the clustering of the alternatives (or IFSs) is closely related to the predefined confidence level λ. How to select the confidence level λ is an interesting issue. We suggest the interested readers should refer to the literature (Wang 1983).

2.2 Clustering Algorithms Based on Association Matrices

In the above section, we have introduced an intuitionistic fuzzy clustering algorithm, which is on the basis of the intuitionistic fuzzy similarity matrix. In this clustering technique, all the given intuitionistic fuzzy information is first transformed into the interval-valued fuzzy information. The intuitionistic fuzzy similarity degrees derived by using distance measures are interval numbers, and both the intuitionistic fuzzy similarity matrix and the intuitionistic fuzzy equivalence matrix are also interval-valued matrices. As a result, this clustering technique requires much computational effort and cannot be extended to cluster IVIFSs, and more importantly, it produces the loss of too much information in the process of calculating intuitionistic fuzzy similarity degrees, which implies a lack of precision in the final results. To overcome this drawback, Xu et al. (2008) proposed a straightforward and practical clustering algorithm for IFSs, and extended the algorithm to cluster IVIFSs.

Xu and Chen (2008) gave an overview of the existing association measures for IFSs (or IVIFSs). Based on the association measures, in the following, we introduce the concept of association matrix:

Definition 2.9 (Xu et al. 2008) Let A_j $(j = 1, 2, \ldots, m)$ be m IFSs. Then $C = (c_{ij})_{m\times m}$ is called an association matrix, where $c_{ij} = c(A_i, A_j)$ is the association coefficient of A_i and A_j (which can be derived by one of the intuitionistic fuzzy association measures introduced by Xu and Chen (2008)), and has the following properties:

(1) $0 \le c_{ij} \le 1, i, j = 1, 2, \ldots, m$.
(2) $c_{ij} = 1$ if and only if $A_i = A_j$.
(3) $c_{ij} = c_{ji}, i, j = 1, 2, \ldots, m$.

Definition 2.10 (Xu et al. 2008) Let $C = (c_{ij})_{m\times m}$ be an association matrix. If $C^2 = C \circ C = (\overline{c}_{ij})_{m\times m}$, then C^2 is called the composition matrix of C, where

$$\overline{c}_{ij} = \max_k\{\min\{c_{ik}, c_{kj}\}\}, i, j = 1, 2, \ldots, m \tag{2.80}$$

According to Definition 2.9, we have

Theorem 2.8 (Xu et al. 2008) Let $C = (c_{ij})_{m\times m}$ be an association matrix. Then the composition matrix C^2 is also an association matrix.

Proof (1) Since C is an association matrix, then for any $i, j = 1, 2, \ldots, m$, we have $0 \le c_{ij} \le 1$. Thus

$$0 \le \overline{c}_{ij} = \max_k\{\min\{c_{ik}, c_{kj}\}\} \le 1, i, j = 1, 2, \ldots, m \tag{2.81}$$

(2) Since $c_{ij} = 1$ if and only if $A_i = A_j$, $i, j = 1, 2, \ldots, m$, it yields

$$\overline{c}_{ij} = \max_k \{\min\{c_{ik}, c_{kj}\}\} = 1 \text{ if and only if } A_i = A_k = A_j, k = 1, 2, \ldots, m \quad (2.82)$$

(3) Since $c_{ij} = c_{ji}$, $i, j = 1, 2, \ldots, m$, we get

$$\begin{aligned}\overline{c}_{ij} &= \max_k \{\min\{c_{ik}, c_{kj}\}\} = \max_k \{\min\{c_{ki}, c_{jk}\}\} \\ &= \max_k \{\min\{c_{jk}, c_{ki}\}\} = \overline{c}_{ji}, \ i, j = 1, 2, \ldots, m \end{aligned} \quad (2.83)$$

which completes the proof of the theorem.

According to Theorem 2.8, we can derive the following conclusion:

Theorem 2.9 (Xu et al. 2008) Let $C = (c_{ij})_{m\times m}$ be an association matrix. Then for any positive integer k, we have

$$C^{2^{k+1}} = C^{2^k} \circ C^{2^k} \quad (2.84)$$

where the composition matrix $C^{2^{k+1}}$ is also an association matrix.

Definition 2.11 (Xu et al. 2008) Let $C = (c_{ij})_{m\times m}$ be an association matrix. If $C^2 \subseteq C$, i.e., for any $i, j = 1, 2, \ldots, m$, the following inequality holds:

$$\max_k \{\min\{c_{ik}, c_{kj}\}\} \le c_{ij} \quad (2.85)$$

Thus, C is called an equivalent association matrix.

By the transitivity principle of equivalent matrix (Wang 1983), we can easily prove the following theorem:

Theorem 2.10 (Xu et al. 2008) Let $C = (c_{ij})_{m\times m}$ be an association matrix. Then after the finite times of compositions:

$$C \to C^2 \to C^4 \to \cdots \to C^{2^k} \to \cdots \quad (2.86)$$

there must exist a positive integer k, such that $C^{2^k} = C^{2^{(k+1)}}$, and C^{2^k} is also an equivalent association matrix.

Based on the equivalent association matrix, we give the following useful concept:

Definition 2.12 (Xu et al. 2008) Let $C = (c_{ij})_{m\times m}$ be an equivalent association matrix. Then $C_\lambda = ({}_\lambda c_{ij})_{m\times m}$ is called the λ-cutting matrix of C, where

$${}_\lambda c_{ij} = \begin{cases} 0, & c_{ij} < \lambda, \\ 1, & c_{ij} \ge \lambda, \end{cases}, \ i, j = 1, 2, \ldots, m \quad (2.87)$$

and λ is the confidence level with $\lambda \in [0, 1]$.

From the above theoretical analysis, we introduce an algorithm for clustering IFSs as follows (Xu et al. 2008):

Algorithm 2.2

Step 1 Let $X = \{x_1, x_2, \ldots, x_n\}$ be a discrete universe of discourse, and let $w = (w_1, w_2, \ldots, w_n)^T$ be the weight vector of the elements x_i $(i = 1, 2, \ldots, n)$, with $w_i \in [0, 1]$, $i = 1, 2, \ldots, n$, and $\sum_{i=1}^{n} w_i = 1$. Consider a collection of m IFSs A_j $(j = 1, 2, \ldots, m)$, where

$$A_j = \{\langle x, \mu_{A_j}(x_i), \nu_{A_j}(x_i)\rangle | x_i \in X\} \tag{2.88}$$

with $\pi_{A_j}(x_i) = 1 - \mu_{A_j}(x_i) - \nu_{A_j}(x_i), j = 1, 2, \ldots, m$.

Step 2 Select an intuitionistic fuzzy association measure, such as

$$c(A_i, A_j) = \frac{\sum_{k=1}^{n} w_k(\mu_{A_i}(x_k) \cdot \mu_{A_j}(x_k) + \nu_{A_i}(x_k) \cdot \nu_{A_j}(x_k) + \pi_{A_i}(x_k) \cdot \pi_{A_j}(x_k))}{\max\left(\sum_{k=1}^{n} w_k(\mu_{A_i}^2(x_k) + \nu_{A_i}^2(x_k) + \pi_{A_i}^2(x_k)),\ \sum_{k=1}^{n} w_k(\mu_{A_j}^2(x_k) + \nu_{A_j}^2(x_k) + \pi_{A_j}^2(x_k))\right)} \tag{2.89}$$

to calculate the association coefficients of the IFSs A_i and A_j $(i, j = 1, 2, \ldots, m)$. Then construct an association matrix $C = (c_{ij})_{m\times m}$, where $c_{ij} = c(A_i, A_j)$, $i, j = 1, 2, \ldots, m$.

Step 3 If the association matrix $C = (c_{ij})_{n\times n}$ is an equivalent association matrix, then we construct a λ-cutting matrix $C_\lambda = ({}_\lambda c_{ij})_{m\times m}$ of C by using Eq. (2.87); otherwise, we compose the association matrix C by using Eq. (2.86) to derive an equivalent association matrix $\overline{C}$. Then we construct a λ-cutting matrix $\overline{C}_\lambda = ({}_\lambda \overline{c}_{ij})_{m\times m}$ of $\overline{C}$ by using Eq. (2.87).

Step 4 If all elements of the ith line (column) in C_λ (or $\overline{C}_\lambda$) are the same as the corresponding elements of the jth line (column) in C_λ (or $\overline{C}_\lambda$), then the IFSs A_i and A_j are of the same type. By this principle, we can classify all these m IFSs A_j $(j = 1, 2, \ldots, m)$.

By using the cutting matrix of the equivalent association matrix, Algorithm-IFSC classifies the IFSs under the given confidence levels. Considering that the confidence levels have a close relationship with the elements of equivalent association matrices, in practical applications, people can properly specify the confidence levels according to the elements of the equivalent association matrices and the actual situations, and thus, the algorithm has desirable flexibility and practicability. However, in some cases, people may expect that the algorithm can automatically generate the "optimal" clustering without any interaction with them. In other words, the algorithm should have the ability to set the optimal λ according to cluster structure. To fulfill this requirement, here we use the Separation Index (SI), one of the relative measures for cluster validity, which was introduced by Nasibov and Ulutagay (2007).

For two clusters C_i and C_j, let $\vartheta(C_i, C_j)$ $(i \neq j)$ be the inter-cluster similarity degree of C_i and C_j, and let $\vartheta'(C_i)$ be the intra-cluster similarity degree of C_i. Then the similarity-based SI can be defined as:

$$SI_{sim} = \frac{\max\limits_{i \neq j} \vartheta(C_i, C_j)}{\min\limits_{i} \vartheta'(C_i)} \tag{2.90}$$

where

$$\vartheta(C_i, C_j) = \max_{A \in C_i, B \in C_j} \vartheta(A, B) \tag{2.91}$$

$$\vartheta'(C_i) = \min_{A, B \in C_i} \vartheta(A, B) \tag{2.92}$$

As a relative measure, SI does not depend on the cluster number, but on the structure of clusters. Therefore, the optimal λ can be selected as:

$$\lambda = \arg\min_{\lambda} SI_{sim}(\lambda) \tag{2.93}$$

where $SI_{sim}(\lambda)$ is the SI of the resultant clusters with λ being the confidence level of the equivalent association matrix.

In the following, we shall extend the algorithm for clustering IVIFSs. Before doing so, we first introduce the basic concepts related to IVIFSs:

Atanassov and Gargov (1989) defined the concept of IVIFS:

Definition 2.13 (Atanassov and Gargov 1989) Let X be a fixed set. Then

$$\tilde{A} = \{\langle x, \tilde{\mu}_{\tilde{A}}(x), \tilde{v}_{\tilde{A}}(x)\rangle | x \in X\} \tag{2.94}$$

is called an interval-valued intuitionistic fuzzy set (IVIFS), where $\tilde{\mu}_{\tilde{A}}(x) \subset [0, 1]$ and $\tilde{v}_{\tilde{A}}(x) \subset [0, 1]$, $x \in X$, with the condition:

$$\sup \tilde{\mu}_{\tilde{A}}(x) + \sup \tilde{v}_{\tilde{A}}(x) \leq 1, x \in X \tag{2.95}$$

Clearly, if $\inf \tilde{\mu}_{\tilde{A}}(x) = \sup \tilde{\mu}_{\tilde{A}}(x)$ and $\inf \tilde{v}_{\tilde{A}}(x) = \sup \tilde{v}_{\tilde{A}}(x)$, then the IVIFS $\tilde{A}$ reduces to a traditional IFS.

Atanassov and Gargov (1989) further gave some basic operational laws of IVIFSs:

Definition 2.14 (Atanassov and Gargov 1989) Let $\tilde{A} = \{\langle x, \tilde{\mu}_{\tilde{A}}(x), \tilde{v}_{\tilde{A}}(x)\rangle | x \in X\}$, $\tilde{A}_1 = \{\langle x, \tilde{\mu}_{\tilde{A}_1}(x), \tilde{v}_{\tilde{A}_1}(x)\rangle | x \in X\}$ and $\tilde{A}_2 = \{\langle x, \tilde{\mu}_{\tilde{A}_2}(x), \tilde{v}_{\tilde{A}_2}(x)\rangle | x \in X\}$ be three IVIFSs. Then

(1) $\overline{\tilde{A}} = \{\langle x, \tilde{v}_{\tilde{A}}(x), \tilde{\mu}_{\tilde{A}}(x) | x \in X\}$.

(2) $\tilde{A}_1 \cap \tilde{A}_2 = \{\langle x, [\min\{\inf \tilde{\mu}_{\tilde{A}_1}(x), \inf \tilde{\mu}_{\tilde{A}_2}(x)\}, \min\{\sup \tilde{\mu}_{\tilde{A}_1}(x), \sup \tilde{\mu}_{\tilde{A}_2}(x)\}], [\max\{\inf \tilde{v}_{\tilde{A}_1}(x), \inf \tilde{v}_{\tilde{A}_2}(x)\}, \max\{\sup \tilde{v}_{\tilde{A}_1}(x), \sup \tilde{v}_{\tilde{A}_2}(x)\}]\rangle | x \in X\}$.

(3) $\tilde{A}_1 \cup \tilde{A}_2 = \{\langle x, [\max\{\inf \tilde{\mu}_{\tilde{A}_1}(x), \inf \tilde{\mu}_{\tilde{A}_2}(x)\}, \max\{\sup \tilde{\mu}_{\tilde{A}_1}(x), \sup \tilde{\mu}_{\tilde{A}_2}(x)\}], [\min\{\inf \tilde{v}_{\tilde{A}_1}(x), \inf \tilde{v}_{\tilde{A}_2}(x)\}, \min\{\sup \tilde{v}_{\tilde{A}_1}(x)), \sup \tilde{v}_{\tilde{A}_2}(x)]\}\rangle | x \in X\}$.

(4) $\tilde{A}_1 + \tilde{A}_2 = \{\langle x, [\inf \tilde{\mu}_{\tilde{A}_1}(x) + \inf \tilde{\mu}_{\tilde{A}_2}(x) - \inf \tilde{\mu}_{\tilde{A}_1}(x) \cdot \inf \tilde{\mu}_{\tilde{A}_2}(x), \sup \tilde{\mu}_{\tilde{A}_1}(x) + \sup \tilde{\mu}_{\tilde{A}_2}(x) - \sup \tilde{\mu}_{\tilde{A}_1}(x) \cdot \sup \tilde{\mu}_{\tilde{A}_2}(x)], [\inf \tilde{v}_{\tilde{A}_1}(x) \cdot \inf \tilde{v}_{\tilde{A}_2}(x), \sup \tilde{v}_{\tilde{A}_1}(x) \cdot \sup \tilde{v}_{\tilde{A}_2}(x)]\rangle | x \in X\}$.

(5) $\tilde{A}_1 \cdot \tilde{A}_2 = \{\langle x, [\inf \tilde{\mu}_{\tilde{A}_1}(x) \cdot \inf \tilde{\mu}_{\tilde{A}_2}(x), \sup \tilde{\mu}_{\tilde{A}_1}(x) \cdot \sup \tilde{\mu}_{\tilde{A}_2}(x)], [\inf \tilde{v}_{\tilde{A}_1}(x) + \inf \tilde{v}_{\tilde{A}_2}(x) - \inf \tilde{v}_{\tilde{A}_1}(x). \inf \tilde{v}_{\tilde{A}_2}(x), \sup \tilde{v}_{\tilde{A}_1}(x) + \sup \tilde{v}_{\tilde{A}_2}(x) - \sup \tilde{v}_{\tilde{A}_1}(x) \cdot \sup \tilde{v}_{\tilde{A}_2}(x)]\rangle | x \in X\}$.

Taking into account the needs of the application, Xu and Chen (2007a) further introduced another two operational laws:

(6) $\lambda \tilde{A} = \{\langle x, [1 - (1 - \inf \tilde{\mu}_{\tilde{A}}(x))^{\lambda}, 1 - (1 - \sup \tilde{\mu}_{\tilde{A}}(x))^{\lambda}], [(\inf \tilde{v}_{\tilde{A}}(x))^{\lambda}, (\sup \tilde{v}_{\tilde{A}}(x))^{\lambda}]\rangle | x \in X\}, \lambda > 0$.

(7) $\tilde{A}^{\lambda} = \{\langle x, [(\inf \tilde{\mu}_{\tilde{A}}(x))^{\lambda}, (\sup \tilde{\mu}_{\tilde{A}}(x))^{\lambda}], [1 - (1 - \inf \tilde{v}_{\tilde{A}}(x))^{\lambda}, 1 - (1 - \sup \tilde{v}_{\tilde{A}}(x))^{\lambda}]\rangle | x \in X\}, \lambda > 0$.

Let $X = \{x_1, x_2, \ldots, x_n\}$ be a discrete universe of discourse, $\tilde{A}_1 = \{\langle x_i, \tilde{\mu}_{\tilde{A}_1}(x_i), \tilde{v}_{\tilde{A}_1}(x_i)\rangle | x_i \in X\}$ and $\tilde{A}_2 = \{\langle x_i, \tilde{\mu}_{\tilde{A}_2}(x_i), \tilde{v}_{\tilde{A}_2}(x_i)\rangle | x_i \in X\}$ two IVIFSs, where

$$\tilde{\mu}_{\tilde{A}_1}(x_i) = [\mu^-_{\tilde{A}_1}(x_i), \mu^+_{\tilde{A}_1}(x_i)], \tilde{\mu}_{\tilde{A}_2}(x_i) = [\mu^-_{\tilde{A}_2}(x_i), \mu^+_{\tilde{A}_2}(x_i)] \tag{2.96}$$

$$\tilde{v}_{\tilde{A}_1}(x_i) = [v^-_{\tilde{A}_1}(x_i), v^+_{\tilde{A}_1}(x_i)], \tilde{v}_{\tilde{A}_2}(x_i) = [v^-_{\tilde{A}_2}(x_i), v^+_{\tilde{A}_2}(x_i)] \tag{2.97}$$

Atanassov and Gargov (1989) defined the inclusion relation between two IVIFSs:

(1) $\tilde{A}_1 \subseteq \tilde{A}_2$ if and only if $\mu^+_{\tilde{A}_1}(x_i) \leq \mu^+_{\tilde{A}_2}(x_i)$, $\mu^-_{\tilde{A}_1}(x_i) \leq \mu^-_{\tilde{A}_2}(x_i)$, $v^+_{\tilde{A}_1}(x_i) \geq v^+_{\tilde{A}_2}(x_i)$ and $v^-_{\tilde{A}_1}(x_i) \geq v^-_{\tilde{A}_2}(x_i)$, $x_i \in X$.
(2) $\tilde{A}_1 = \tilde{A}_2$ if and only if $\tilde{A}_1 \subseteq \tilde{A}_2$ 且 $\tilde{A}_1 \supseteq \tilde{A}_2$.

Similar to Definition 2.9, we have

Definition 2.15 (Xu et al. 2008) Let $\tilde{A}_j$ $(j = 1, 2, \ldots, m)$ be m IVIFSs. Then $\dot{C} = (\dot{c}_{ij})_{m \times m}$ is called an association matrix, where $\dot{c}_{ij} = c(\tilde{A}_i, \tilde{A}_j)$ is the association coefficient of $\tilde{A}_i$ and $\tilde{A}_j$ (which can be derived by one of the interval-valued intuitionistic fuzzy association measures introduced by Xu and Chen (2008)), and has the following properties:

(1) $0 \le \dot{c}_{ij} \le 1, i, j = 1, 2, \ldots, m.$
(2) $\dot{c}_{ij} = 1$ if and only if $\tilde{A}_i = \tilde{A}_j$.
(3) $\dot{c}_{ij} = \dot{c}_{ji}, i, j = 1, 2, \ldots, m.$

Based on the association matrix of the IVIFSs, in what follows, we introduce an algorithm for clustering IVIFSs (Xu et al. 2008):

Algorithm 2.3

Step 1 Let $X = \{x_1, x_2, \ldots, x_n\}$ be a discrete universe of discourse, $w = (w_1, w_2, \ldots, w_n)^T$ the weight vector of the elements x_i $(i = 1, 2, \ldots, n)$, with $w_i \in [0, 1]$, $i = 1, 2, \ldots, n$, and $\sum_{i=1}^n w_i = 1$, and let $\tilde{A}_j$ $(j = 1, 2, \ldots, m)$ be a collection of IVIFSs:

$$\tilde{A}_j = \{\langle x_i, \tilde{\mu}_{\tilde{A}_j}(x_i), \tilde{v}_{\tilde{A}_j}(x_i)\rangle | x_i \in X\} \tag{2.98}$$

where

$$\tilde{\mu}_{\tilde{A}_j}(x_i) = [\mu^-_{\tilde{A}_j}(x_i), \mu^+_{\tilde{A}_j}(x_i)] \subset [0, 1], \quad \tilde{v}_{\tilde{A}_j}(x_i) = [v^-_{\tilde{A}_j}(x_i), v^+_{\tilde{A}_j}(x_i)] \subset [0, 1],$$

$$\mu^+_{\tilde{A}_j}(x_i) + v^+_{\tilde{A}_j}(x_i) \le 1, x_i \in X \tag{2.99}$$

Additionally, $\tilde{\pi}_{\tilde{A}_j}(x_i) = [\pi^-_{\tilde{A}_j}(x_i), \pi^+_{\tilde{A}_j}(x_i)] \subset [0, 1], \pi^-_{\tilde{A}_j}(x_i) = 1 - \mu^+_{\tilde{A}_j}(x_i) - 1 - v^+_{\tilde{A}_j}(x_i), \pi^+_{\tilde{A}_j}(x_i) = 1 - \mu^-_{\tilde{A}_j}(x_i) - 1 - v^-_{\tilde{A}_j}(x_i).$

Step 2 Utilize the interval-valued intuitionistic fuzzy association measures:

$$c(\tilde{A}_i, \tilde{A}_j) = \frac{\begin{array}{c}\sum_{k=1}^n w_k\Big(\mu^-_{\tilde{A}_i}(x_k)\cdot\mu^-_{\tilde{A}_j}(x_k) + \mu^+_{\tilde{A}_i}(x_k)\cdot\mu^+_{\tilde{A}_j}(x_k) \\ +v^-_{\tilde{A}_i}(x_k)\cdot v^-_{\tilde{A}_j}(x_k) + v^+_{\tilde{A}_i}(x_k)\cdot v^+_{\tilde{A}_j}(x_k) \\ +\pi^-_{\tilde{A}_i}(x_k)\cdot\pi^-_{\tilde{A}_j}(x_k) + \pi^+_{\tilde{A}_i}(x_k)\cdot\pi^+_{\tilde{A}_j}(x_k)\Big)\end{array}}{\begin{array}{c}\max\Big(\sum_{k=1}^n w_k\Big(\big(\mu^-_{\tilde{A}_i}(x_k)\big)^2 + \big(\mu^+_{\tilde{A}_i}(x_k)\big)^2 + \big(v^-_{\tilde{A}_i}(x_k)\big)^2 \\ +\big(v^+_{\tilde{A}_i}(x_k)\big)^2 + \big(\pi^-_{\tilde{A}_i}(x_k)\big)^2 + \big(\pi^+_{\tilde{A}_i}(x_k)\big)^2\Big), \\ \sum_{k=1}^n w_k\Big(\big(\mu^-_{\tilde{A}_j}(x_k)\big)^2 + \big(\mu^+_{\tilde{A}_j}(x_k)\big)^2 + \big(v^-_{\tilde{A}_j}(x_k)\big)^2 \\ +\big(v^+_{\tilde{A}_j}(x_k)\big)^2 + \big(\pi^-_{\tilde{A}_j}(x_k)\big)^2 + \big(\pi^+_{\tilde{A}_j}(x_k)\big)^2\Big)\Big)\end{array}} \tag{2.100}$$

to calculate the association coefficients of the IVIFSs $\tilde{A}_i$ and $\tilde{A}_j$ $(i, j = 1, 2, \ldots, m)$, and then construct an association $\dot{C} = (\dot{c}_{ij})_{m\times m}$, where $\dot{c}_{ij} = \dot{c}(\tilde{A}_i, \tilde{A}_j)$, $i, j = 1, 2, \ldots, m$.

Step 3 If the association matrix $\dot{C} = (\dot{c}_{ij})_{m\times m}$ is an equivalent association matrix, then we construct a λ-cutting matrix $\dot{C}_\lambda = ({}_\lambda c_{ij})_{m\times m}$ of $\dot{C}$ by using

Eq. (2.87); otherwise, we compose the association matrix $\dot{C}$ by using Eq. (2.86) to derive an equivalent association matrix $\overline{\dot{C}}$, and then construct a λ-cutting matrix $\overline{\dot{C}}_\lambda = ({}_\lambda\overline{c}_{ij})_{m\times m}$ of $\overline{\dot{C}}$ by using Eq. (2.87).

Step 4 If all elements of the ith line (column) in $\dot{C}_\lambda$ (or $\overline{\dot{C}}_\lambda$) are the same as the corresponding elements of the jth line (column) in $\dot{C}_\lambda$ (or $\overline{\dot{C}}_\lambda$), then the IVIFSs $\tilde{A}_i$ and $\tilde{A}_j$ are of the same type. By this principle, we can classify all these m IVIFSs $\tilde{A}_j$ ($j = 1, 2, \ldots, m$).

Example 2.2 (Xu et al. 2008) We conduct experiments on both the real-world and simulated data sets in order to demonstrate the effectiveness of the proposed clustering algorithm for IVIFSs.

Below we first introduce the experimental tool and the experimental data set, respectively:

(1) Experimental tool. In the experiments, we use Algorithm 2.2 as a tool implemented by ourselves in MATLAB. Note that if we let $\pi(x) = 0$, for any $x \in X$, then Algorithm 2.2 reduces to the traditional algorithm for clustering fuzzy sets (denoted by Algorithm-FSC). Therefore, we can use Algorithm 2.2 to compare the performance of both Algorithm 2.2 and Algorithm-FSC.

(2) Experimental data set. We use two kinds of data in our experiments. The car data set contains the information of ten new cars to be classified in the Guangzhou car market in Guangdong, China. Let y_i ($i = 1, 2, \ldots, 10$) be the cars, each of which is described by six attributes: (1) G_1: Fuel economy; (2) G_2: Aerod degree; (3) G_3: Price; (4) G_4: Comfort; (5) G_5: Design; and (6) G_6: Safety. The weight vector of these attributes is $w = (0.15, 0.10, 0.30, 0.20, 0.15, 0.10)^T$. The characteristics of the ten new cars under the six attributes are represented by the IFSs, as shown in Table 2.2 (Xu et al. 2008).

We also use the simulated data set for the purpose of comparison, and assume that there are three classes in the simulated data set, denoted by $C_i (i = 1, 2, 3)$. The number of IFSs in each class is exactly the same: 300. The differences of the IFSs in different classes lie in the following aspects: (1) The IFSs in C_1 have relatively high and positive scores; (2) the IFSs in C_2 have relatively high and negative scores; and (3) the IFSs in C_3 have relatively high and uncertain scores. Along this line, we generate the simulated data set as follows: (1) $\mu(x) \sim U(0.7,1)$ and $v(x) + \pi(x) \sim U(0,1-\mu(x))$, for any $x \in C_1$; (2) $v(x) \sim U(0.7,1)$ and $\mu(x)+\pi(x) \sim U(0,1-v(x))$, for any $x \in C_2$; and (3) $\pi(x) \sim U(0.7,1)$, $\mu(x) + v(x) \sim U(0,1 - \pi(x))$, for any $x \in C_3$, where $U(a, b)$ means the uniform distribution on the interval $[a, b]$. By doing so, we generate a simulated data set which consists of 900 IFSs from 3 classes.

Now we utilize Algorithm 2.2 to cluster the ten new cars y_i ($i = 1, 2, \ldots, 10$), which involves the following steps (Xu et al. 2008):

Table 2.2 The car data set

	G_1		G_2		G_3		G_4		G_5		G_6	
	$\mu_{y_i}(G_1)$	$v_{y_i}(G_1)$	$\mu_{y_i}(G_2)$	$v_{y_i}(G_2)$	$\mu_{y_i}(G_3)$	$v_{y_i}(G_3)$	$\mu_{y_i}(G_4)$	$v_{y_i}(G_4)$	$\mu_{y_i}(G_5)$	$v_{y_i}(G_5)$	$\mu_{y_i}(G_6)$	$v_{y_i}(G_6)$
y_1	0.30	0.40	0.20	0.70	0.40	0.50	0.80	0.10	0.40	0.50	0.20	0.70
y_2	0.40	0.30	0.50	0.10	0.60	0.20	0.20	0.70	0.30	0.60	0.70	0.20
y_3	0.40	0.20	0.60	0.10	0.80	0.10	0.20	0.60	0.30	0.70	0.50	0.20
y_4	0.30	0.40	0.90	0.00	0.80	0.10	0.70	0.10	0.10	0.80	0.20	0.80
y_5	0.80	0.10	0.70	0.20	0.70	0.00	0.40	0.10	0.80	0.20	0.40	0.60
y_6	0.40	0.30	0.30	0.50	0.20	0.60	0.70	0.10	0.50	0.40	0.30	0.60
y_7	0.60	0.40	0.40	0.20	0.70	0.20	0.30	0.60	0.30	0.70	0.60	0.10
y_8	0.90	0.10	0.70	0.20	0.70	0.10	0.40	0.50	0.40	0.50	0.80	0.00
y_9	0.40	0.40	1.00	0.00	0.90	0.10	0.60	0.20	0.20	0.70	0.10	0.80
y_{10}	0.90	0.10	0.80	0.00	0.60	0.30	0.50	0.20	0.80	0.10	0.60	0.40

Step 1 Utilize

$$c(y_i, y_j) = \frac{\sum_{k=1}^{n} w_k \left(\mu_{y_i}(G_k) \cdot \mu_{y_j}(G_k) + v_{y_i}(G_k) \cdot v_{y_j}(G_k) + \pi_{y_i}(G_k) \cdot \pi_{y_j}(G_k)\right)}{\max\left(\sum_{k=1}^{n} w_k \left(\mu_{y_i}^2(G_k) + v_{y_i}^2(G_k) + \pi_{y_i}^2(G_k)\right),\ \sum_{k=1}^{n} w_k \left(\mu_{y_j}^2(G_k) + v_{y_j}^2(G_k) + \pi_{y_j}^2(G_k)\right)\right)} \tag{2.101}$$

to calculate the association coefficients of y_i ($i = 1, 2, \ldots, 10$), and then construct an association matrix:

$$C = \begin{pmatrix} 1.000 & 0.667 & 0.645 & 0.709 & 0.633 & 0.919 & 0.696 & 0.609 & 0.666 & 0.611 \\ 0.667 & 1.000 & 0.909 & 0.661 & 0.666 & 0.665 & 0.913 & 0.820 & 0.665 & 0.640 \\ 0.645 & 0.909 & 1.000 & 0.768 & 0.740 & 0.576 & 0.937 & 0.862 & 0.771 & 0.670 \\ 0.709 & 0.661 & 0.768 & 1.000 & 0.755 & 0.610 & 0.717 & 0.728 & 0.968 & 0.711 \\ 0.633 & 0.666 & 0.740 & 0.755 & 1.000 & 0.623 & 0.713 & 0.476 & 0.764 & 0.861 \\ 0.919 & 0.665 & 0.576 & 0.610 & 0.623 & 1.000 & 0.634 & 0.579 & 0.566 & 0.622 \\ 0.696 & 0.913 & 0.937 & 0.717 & 0.713 & 0.634 & 1.000 & 0.889 & 0.722 & 0.692 \\ 0.609 & 0.820 & 0.862 & 0.728 & 0.476 & 0.579 & 0.889 & 1.000 & 0.740 & 0.811 \\ 0.666 & 0.665 & 0.771 & 0.968 & 0.764 & 0.566 & 0.722 & 0.740 & 1.000 & 0.732 \\ 0.611 & 0.640 & 0.670 & 0.711 & 0.861 & 0.622 & 0.692 & 0.811 & 0.732 & 1.000 \end{pmatrix}$$

Step 2 Calculate

$$C^2 = C \circ C$$

$$= \begin{pmatrix} 1.000 & 0.696 & 0.709 & 0.709 & 0.709 & 0.919 & 0.709 & 0.709 & 0.709 & 0.709 \\ 0.696 & 1.000 & 0.913 & 0.768 & 0.740 & 0.667 & 0.913 & 0.889 & 0.771 & 0.811 \\ 0.709 & 0.913 & 1.000 & 0.771 & 0.764 & 0.665 & 0.937 & 0.889 & 0.771 & 0.811 \\ 0.709 & 0.768 & 0.771 & 1.000 & 0.764 & 0.709 & 0.768 & 0.768 & 0.968 & 0.755 \\ 0.709 & 0.740 & 0.764 & 0.764 & 1.000 & 0.665 & 0.740 & 0.811 & 0.764 & 0.861 \\ 0.919 & 0.667 & 0.665 & 0.709 & 0.665 & 1.000 & 0.696 & 0.665 & 0.666 & 0.640 \\ 0.709 & 0.913 & 0.937 & 0.768 & 0.740 & 0.696 & 1.000 & 0.889 & 0.771 & 0.811 \\ 0.709 & 0.889 & 0.889 & 0.768 & 0.811 & 0.665 & 0.889 & 1.000 & 0.771 & 0.811 \\ 0.709 & 0.771 & 0.771 & 0.968 & 0.764 & 0.666 & 0.771 & 0.771 & 1.000 & 0.740 \\ 0.709 & 0.811 & 0.811 & 0.755 & 0.861 & 0.640 & 0.811 & 0.811 & 0.740 & 1.000 \end{pmatrix}$$

then $C^2 \subseteq C$ does not hold, i.e., the association matrix C is not an equivalent association matrix. Thus, by Eq. (2.86), we further calculate

$$C^4 = C^2 \circ C^2$$

$$= \begin{pmatrix} 1.000 & 0.709 & 0.709 & 0.709 & 0.709 & 0.919 & 0.709 & 0.709 & 0.709 & 0.709 \\ 0.709 & 1.000 & 0.913 & 0.771 & 0.811 & 0.709 & 0.913 & 0.889 & 0.771 & 0.811 \\ 0.709 & 0.913 & 1.000 & 0.771 & 0.811 & 0.709 & 0.937 & 0.889 & 0.771 & 0.811 \\ 0.709 & 0.771 & 0.771 & 1.000 & 0.768 & 0.709 & 0.771 & 0.771 & 0.968 & 0.771 \\ 0.709 & 0.811 & 0.811 & 0.768 & 1.000 & 0.709 & 0.811 & 0.811 & 0.771 & 0.861 \\ 0.919 & 0.709 & 0.709 & 0.709 & 0.709 & 1.000 & 0.709 & 0.709 & 0.709 & 0.709 \\ 0.709 & 0.913 & 0.937 & 0.771 & 0.811 & 0.709 & 1.000 & 0.889 & 0.771 & 0.811 \\ 0.709 & 0.889 & 0.889 & 0.771 & 0.811 & 0.709 & 0.889 & 1.000 & 0.771 & 0.811 \\ 0.709 & 0.771 & 0.771 & 0.968 & 0.771 & 0.709 & 0.771 & 0.771 & 1.000 & 0.771 \\ 0.709 & 0.811 & 0.811 & 0.771 & 0.861 & 0.709 & 0.811 & 0.811 & 0.771 & 1.000 \end{pmatrix}$$

$$C^8 = C^4 \circ C^4$$

$$= \begin{pmatrix} 1.000 & 0.709 & 0.709 & 0.709 & 0.709 & 0.919 & 0.709 & 0.709 & 0.709 & 0.709 \\ 0.709 & 1.000 & 0.913 & 0.771 & 0.811 & 0.709 & 0.913 & 0.771 & 0.771 & 0.811 \\ 0.709 & 0.913 & 1.000 & 0.771 & 0.811 & 0.709 & 0.937 & 0.889 & 0.771 & 0.811 \\ 0.709 & 0.771 & 0.771 & 1.000 & 0.771 & 0.709 & 0.771 & 0.771 & 0.968 & 0.771 \\ 0.709 & 0.811 & 0.811 & 0.771 & 1.000 & 0.709 & 0.811 & 0.811 & 0.771 & 0.861 \\ 0.919 & 0.709 & 0.709 & 0.709 & 0.709 & 1.000 & 0.709 & 0.709 & 0.709 & 0.709 \\ 0.709 & 0.913 & 0.937 & 0.771 & 0.811 & 0.709 & 1.000 & 0.889 & 0.771 & 0.811 \\ 0.709 & 0.771 & 0.889 & 0.771 & 0.811 & 0.709 & 0.889 & 1.000 & 0.771 & 0.811 \\ 0.709 & 0.771 & 0.771 & 0.968 & 0.771 & 0.709 & 0.771 & 0.771 & 1.000 & 0.771 \\ 0.709 & 0.811 & 0.811 & 0.771 & 0.861 & 0.709 & 0.811 & 0.811 & 0.771 & 1.000 \end{pmatrix}$$

$$C^{16} = C^8 \circ C^8$$

$$= \begin{pmatrix} 1.000 & 0.709 & 0.709 & 0.709 & 0.709 & 0.919 & 0.709 & 0.709 & 0.709 & 0.709 \\ 0.709 & 1.000 & 0.913 & 0.771 & 0.811 & 0.709 & 0.913 & 0.771 & 0.771 & 0.811 \\ 0.709 & 0.913 & 1.000 & 0.771 & 0.811 & 0.709 & 0.937 & 0.889 & 0.771 & 0.811 \\ 0.709 & 0.771 & 0.771 & 1.000 & 0.771 & 0.709 & 0.771 & 0.771 & 0.968 & 0.771 \\ 0.709 & 0.811 & 0.811 & 0.771 & 1.000 & 0.709 & 0.811 & 0.811 & 0.771 & 0.861 \\ 0.919 & 0.709 & 0.709 & 0.709 & 0.709 & 1.000 & 0.709 & 0.709 & 0.709 & 0.709 \\ 0.709 & 0.913 & 0.937 & 0.771 & 0.811 & 0.709 & 1.000 & 0.889 & 0.771 & 0.811 \\ 0.709 & 0.771 & 0.889 & 0.771 & 0.811 & 0.709 & 0.889 & 1.000 & 0.771 & 0.811 \\ 0.709 & 0.771 & 0.771 & 0.968 & 0.771 & 0.709 & 0.771 & 0.771 & 1.000 & 0.771 \\ 0.709 & 0.811 & 0.811 & 0.771 & 0.861 & 0.709 & 0.811 & 0.811 & 0.771 & 1.000 \end{pmatrix}$$

hence, $C^{16} = C^8$, i.e., C^8 is an equivalent association matrix.

Step 3 Since the confidence level λ has a close relationship with the elements of the equivalent association matrix C^8, in the following, we give a detailed sensitivity analysis with respect to the confidence level λ, and by Eq. (2.87), we get all the possible classifications of the ten new cars y_i $(i = 1, 2, \ldots, 10)$:

(1) If $0 \le \lambda \le 0.709$, then y_i $(i = 1, 2, \ldots, 10)$ are of the same type:

$$\{y_1, y_2, y_3, y_4, y_5, y_6, y_7, y_8, y_9, y_{10}\}$$

(2) If $0.709 < \lambda \le 0.771$, then y_i $(i = 1, 2, \ldots, 10)$ are classified into the following two types:

$$\{y_1, y_6\}, \{y_2, y_3, y_4, y_5, y_7, y_8, y_9, y_{10}\}$$

(3) If $0.771 < \lambda \le 0.811$, then y_i $(i = 1, 2, \ldots, 10)$ are classified into the following five types:

$$\{y_1, y_6\}, \{y_2\}, \{y_3, y_5, y_7, y_{10}\}, \{y_8\}, \{y_4, y_9\}$$

(4) If $0.811 < \lambda \le 0.861$, then y_i $(i = 1, 2, \ldots, 10)$ are classified into the following six types:

$$\{y_1, y_6\}, \{y_2\}, \{y_3, y_7\}, \{y_8\}, \{y_4, y_9\}, \{y_5, y_{10}\}$$

(5) If $0.861 < \lambda \le 0.889$, then y_i $(i = 1, 2, \ldots, 10)$ are classified into the following seven types:

$$\{y_1, y_6\}, \{y_2\}, \{y_3, y_7\}, \{y_4, y_9\}, \{y_5\}, \{y_8\}, \{y_{10}\}$$

(6) If $0.889 < \lambda \le 0.913$, then y_i $(i = 1, 2, \ldots, 10)$ are classified into the following six types:

$$\{y_1, y_6\}, \{y_2, y_3, y_7\}, \{y_4, y_9\}, \{y_5\}, \{y_8\}, \{y_{10}\}$$

(7) If $0.913 < \lambda \le 0.919$, then y_i $(i = 1, 2, \ldots, 10)$ are classified the following into seven types:

$$\{y_1, y_6\}, \{y_2\}, \{y_3, y_7\}, \{y_4, y_9\}, \{y_5\}, \{y_8\}, \{y_{10}\}$$

(8) If $0.919 < \lambda \leq 0.937$, then y_i $(i = 1, 2, \ldots, 10)$ are classified into the following eight types:

$$\{y_1\}, \{y_2\}, \{y_5\}, \{y_6\}, \{y_3, y_7\}, \{y_4, y_9\}, \{y_8\}, \{y_{10}\}$$

(9) If $0.937 < \lambda \leq 0.968$, then y_i $(i = 1, 2, \ldots, 10)$ are classified into the following nine types:

$$\{y_1\}, \{y_2\}, \{y_3\}, \{y_5\}, \{y_6\}, \{y_7\}, \{y_8\}, \{y_4, y_9\}, \{y_{10}\}$$

(10) If $0.968 < \lambda \leq 1$, then y_i $(i = 1, 2, \ldots, 10)$ are classified into the following ten types:

$$\{y_1\}, \{y_2\}, \{y_3\}, \{y_4\}, \{y_5\}, \{y_6\}, \{y_7\}, \{y_8\}, \{y_9\}, \{y_{10}\}$$

If we utilize Algorithm 2.1 to cluster the ten new cars y_i $(i = 1, 2, \ldots, 10)$, then we first need to transform all the given IFSs (see Table 2.2) into the interval-valued fuzzy sets, listed in Table 2.3 (Xu et al. 2008).

After that, we utilize Eq. (2.11) (without loss of generality, here we let $\lambda = 2$, $\beta_1 = \beta_2 = \beta_3 = 1/3$) to calculate the intuitionistic fuzzy similarity degrees of y_i $(i = 1, 2, \ldots, 10)$, and then construct the intuitionistic fuzzy similarity matrix $\tilde{R} = (\tilde{r}_{ij})_{10 \times 10}$:

Table 2.3 The transformed car data set

	G_1	G_2	G_3	G_4	G_5	G_6
	$[\mu_{y_i}(G_1), 1 - v_{y_i}(G_1)]$	$[\mu_{y_i}(G_2), 1 - v_{y_i}(G_2)]$	$[\mu_{y_i}(G_3), 1 - v_{y_i}(G_3)]$	$[\mu_{y_i}(G_4), 1 - v_{y_i}(G_4)]$	$[\mu_{y_i}(G_5), 1 - v_{y_i}(G_5)]$	$[\mu_{y_i}(G_6), 1 - v_{y_i}(G_6)]$
y_1	[0.30, 0.60]	[0.20, 0.30]	[0.40, 0.50]	[0.80, 0.90]	[0.40, 0.50]	[0.20, 0.30]
y_2	[0.40, 0.70]	[0.50, 0.90]	[0.60, 0.80]	[0.20, 0.30]	[0.30, 0.40]	[0.70, 0.80]
y_3	[0.40, 0.80]	[0.60, 0.90]	[0.80, 0.90]	[0.20, 0.40]	[0.30, 0.30]	[0.50, 0.80]
y_4	[0.30, 0.60]	[0.90, 1.00]	[0.80, 0.90]	[0.70, 0.90]	[0.10, 0.20]	[0.20, 0.20]
y_5	[0.80, 0.90]	[0.70, 0.80]	[0.70, 1.00]	[0.40, 0.90]	[0.80, 0.80]	[0.40, 0.40]
y_6	[0.40, 0.70]	[0.30, 0.50]	[0.20, 0.40]	[0.70, 0.90]	[0.50, 0.60]	[0.30, 0.40]
y_7	[0.60, 0.60]	[0.40, 0.80]	[0.70, 0.80]	[0.30, 0.40]	[0.30, 0.30]	[0.60, 0.90]
y_8	[0.90, 0.90]	[0.70, 0.80]	[0.70, 0.90]	[0.40, 0.50]	[0.40, 0.50]	[0.80, 1.00]
y_9	[0.40, 0.60]	[1.00, 1.00]	[0.90, 0.90]	[0.60, 0.80]	[0.20, 0.30]	[0.10, 0.20]
y_{10}	[0.90, 0.90]	[0.80, 1.00]	[0.60, 0.70]	[0.50, 0.80]	[0.80, 0.90]	[0.60, 0.60]

$$\tilde{R} = \begin{pmatrix} [1,1] & [0.507,0.918] & [0.545,0.859] & [0.428,1.000] & [0.592,0.859] & [0.859,0.918] & [0.568,0.859] & [0.465,1.000] & [0.384,0.918] & [0.465,0.837] \\ [0.507,0.918] & [1,1] & [0.837,0.918] & [0.545,0.918] & [0.568,0.859] & [0.545,1.000] & [0.784,0.918] & [0.644,0.918] & [0.510,0.918] & [0.592,0.918] \\ [0.545,0.859] & [0.837,0.918] & [1,1] & [0.576,1.000] & [0.592,0.859] & [0.545,0.918] & [0.717,1.000] & [0.626,0.918] & [0.568,0.918] & [0.545,0.859] \\ [0.428,1.000] & [0.545,0.918] & [0.576,1.000] & [1,1] & [0.465,0.859] & [0.545,1.000] & [0.503,0.918] & [0.411,0.918] & [0.918,0.918] & [0.428,0.918] \\ [0.592,0.859] & [0.568,0.859] & [0.592,0.859] & [0.465,0.859] & [1,1] & [0.545,0.918] & [0.592,0.837] & [0.568,1.000] & [0.545,0.784] & [0.784,0.918] \\ [0.859,0.918] & [0.545,1.000] & [0.545,0.918] & [0.545,1.000] & [0.545,0.918] & [1,1] & [0.626,0.784] & [0.545,0.918] & [0.490,0.918] & [0.592,0.859] \\ [0.568,0.859] & [0.784,0.918] & [0.717,1.000] & [0.503,0.918] & [0.592,0.837] & [0.626,0.784] & [1,1] & [0.755,0.918] & [0.490,0.918] & [0.545,0.918] \\ [0.465,1.000] & [0.644,0.918] & [0.626,0.918] & [0.411,0.918] & [0.568,1.000] & [0.545,0.918] & [0.755,0.918] & [1,1] & [0.384,0.837] & [0.673,1.000] \\ [0.384,0.918] & [0.510,0.918] & [0.568,0.918] & [0.918,0.918] & [0.545,0.784] & [0.490,0.918] & [0.490,0.918] & [0.384,0.837] & [1,1] & [0.510,0.918] \\ [0.465,0.837] & [0.592,0.918] & [0.545,0.859] & [0.428,0.918] & [0.784,0.918] & [0.592,0.859] & [0.545,0.918] & [0.673,1.000] & [0.510,0.918] & [1,1] \end{pmatrix}$$

By the composition operation of interval-valued matrices, we have

$$\tilde{R}^2 = \tilde{R} \circ \tilde{R} = \begin{pmatrix} [1,1] & [0.568,0.918] & [0.592,1.000] & [0.545,1.000] & [0.592,1.000] & [0.859,1.000] & [0.592,0.918] & [0.568,1.000] & [0.545,0.918] & [0.592,1.000] \\ [0.568,0.918] & [1,1] & [0.837,0.918] & [0.576,0.918] & [0.592,0.918] & [0.626,1.000] & [0.784,0.918] & [0.755,0.918] & [0.568,0.918] & [0.592,0.918] \\ [0.592,1.000] & [0.837,0.918] & [1,1] & [0.576,1.000] & [0.592,1.000] & [0.626,1.000] & [0.784,1.000] & [0.717,0.918] & [0.576,0.918] & [0.626,0.918] \\ [0.545,1.000] & [0.576,0.918] & [0.576,1.000] & [1,1] & [0.576,0.918] & [0.545,1.000] & [0.576,1.000] & [0.576,1.000] & [0.918,0.918] & [0.545,0.918] \\ [0.592,1.000] & [0.592,0.918] & [0.592,1.000] & [0.576,0.918] & [1,1] & [0.592,0.918] & [0.592,0.918] & [0.592,1.000] & [0.568,0.918] & [0.784,1.000] \\ [0.859,1.000] & [0.626,1.000] & [0.626,1.000] & [0.545,1.000] & [0.592,0.918] & [1,1] & [0.626,0.918] & [0.626,0.918] & [0.545,0.918] & [0.592,0.918] \\ [0.592,0.918] & [0.784,0.918] & [0.784,1.000] & [0.576,1.000] & [0.592,0.918] & [0.626,0.918] & [1,1] & [0.755,0.918] & [0.568,0.918] & [0.673,0.918] \\ [0.568,1.000] & [0.755,0.918] & [0.717,0.918] & [0.576,1.000] & [0.592,1.000] & [0.626,0.918] & [0.755,0.918] & [1,1] & [0.568,0.918] & [0.673,1.000] \\ [0.545,0.918] & [0.568,0.918] & [0.576,0.918] & [0.918,0.918] & [0.568,0.918] & [0.545,0.918] & [0.568,0.918] & [0.568,0.918] & [1,1] & [0.545,0.918] \\ [0.592,1.000] & [0.592,0.918] & [0.626,0.918] & [0.545,0.918] & [0.784,1.000] & [0.592,0.918] & [0.673,0.918] & [0.673,1.000] & [0.545,0.918] & [1,1] \end{pmatrix}$$

$$\tilde{R}^4 = \tilde{R}^2 \circ \tilde{R}^2 = \left(\begin{matrix}
[1, 1] & [0.626, 0.918] & [0.626, 1.000] & [0.576, 1.000] & [0.592, 1.000] \\
[0.626, 0.918] & [1, 1] & [0.837, 1.000] & [0.576, 1.000] & [0.592, 0.918] \\
[0.626, 1.000] & [0.837, 1.000] & [1, 1] & [0.576, 1.000] & [0.626, 1.000] \\
[0.576, 1.000] & [0.576, 1.000] & [0.576, 1.000] & [1, 1] & [0.576, 1.000] \\
[0.592, 1.000] & [0.592, 0.918] & [0.626, 1.000] & [0.576, 1.000] & [1, 1] \\
[0.859, 1.000] & [0.626, 1.000] & [0.626, 1.000] & [0.576, 1.000] & [0.592, 1.000] \\
[0.626, 1.000] & [0.784, 0.918] & [0.784, 1.000] & [0.576, 1.000] & [0.673, 1.000] \\
[0.626, 1.000] & [0.755, 0.918] & [0.755, 1.000] & [0.576, 1.000] & [0.673, 1.000] \\
[0.576, 0.918] & [0.576, 0.918] & [0.576, 0.918] & [0.918, 0.918] & [0.576, 0.918] \\
[0.592, 1.000] & [0.673, 0.918] & [0.673, 1.000] & [0.576, 1.000] & [0.784, 1.000]
\end{matrix} \right.$$

$$\left. \begin{matrix}
[0.859, 1.000] & [0.626, 1.000] & [0.626, 1.000] & [0.576, 0.918] & [0.592, 1.000] \\
[0.626, 1.000] & [0.784, 0.918] & [0.755, 0.918] & [0.576, 0.918] & [0.673, 0.918] \\
[0.626, 1.000] & [0.784, 1.000] & [0.755, 1.000] & [0.576, 0.918] & [0.673, 1.000] \\
[0.576, 1.000] & [0.576, 1.000] & [0.576, 1.000] & [0.918, 0.918] & [0.576, 1.000] \\
[0.592, 1.000] & [0.673, 1.000] & [0.673, 1.000] & [0.576, 0.918] & [0.784, 1.000] \\
[1, 1] & [0.626, 1.000] & [0.626, 1.000] & [0.576, 0.918] & [0.626, 1.000] \\
[0.626, 1.000] & [1, 1] & [0.755, 1.000] & [0.568, 0.918] & [0.673, 0.918] \\
[0.626, 1.000] & [0.755, 1.000] & [1, 1] & [0.576, 0.918] & [0.673, 1.000] \\
[0.576, 0.918] & [0.568, 0.918] & [0.576, 0.918] & [1, 1] & [0.576, 0.918] \\
[0.626, 1.000] & [0.673, 0.918] & [0.673, 1.000] & [0.576, 0.918] & [1, 1]
\end{matrix} \right)$$

$$\tilde{R}^8 = \tilde{R}^4 \circ \tilde{R}^4 = \left(\begin{matrix}
[1, 1] & [0.626, 1.000] & [0.626, 1.000] & [0.576, 1.000] & [0.626, 1.000] \\
[0.626, 1.000] & [1, 1] & [0.837, 1.000] & [0.576, 1.000] & [0.673, 1.000] \\
[0.626, 1.000] & [0.837, 1.000] & [1, 1] & [0.576, 1.000] & [0.673, 1.000] \\
[0.576, 1.000] & [0.576, 1.000] & [0.576, 1.000] & [1, 1] & [0.576, 1.000] \\
[0.626, 1.000] & [0.673, 1.000] & [0.673, 1.000] & [0.576, 1.000] & [1, 1] \\
[0.859, 1.000] & [0.626, 1.000] & [0.626, 1.000] & [0.576, 1.000] & [0.626, 1.000] \\
[0.626, 1.000] & [0.784, 1.000] & [0.784, 1.000] & [0.576, 1.000] & [0.673, 1.000] \\
[0.626, 1.000] & [0.755, 1.000] & [0.755, 1.000] & [0.576, 1.000] & [0.673, 1.000] \\
[0.576, 0.918] & [0.576, 0.918] & [0.576, 0.918] & [0.918, 0.918] & [0.576, 0.918] \\
[0.626, 1.000] & [0.673, 1.000] & [0.673, 1.000] & [0.576, 1.000] & [0.784, 1.000]
\end{matrix} \right.$$

$$\left. \begin{matrix}
[0.859, 1.000] & [0.626, 1.000] & [0.626, 1.000] & [0.576, 0.918] & [0.626, 1.000] \\
[0.626, 1.000] & [0.784, 1.000] & [0.755, 1.000] & [0.576, 0.918] & [0.673, 1.000] \\
[0.626, 1.000] & [0.784, 1.000] & [0.755, 1.000] & [0.576, 0.918] & [0.673, 1.000] \\
[0.576, 1.000] & [0.576, 1.000] & [0.576, 1.000] & [0.918, 0.918] & [0.576, 1.000] \\
[0.626, 1.000] & [0.673, 1.000] & [0.673, 1.000] & [0.576, 0.918] & [0.784, 1.000] \\
[1, 1] & [0.626, 1.000] & [0.626, 1.000] & [0.576, 0.918] & [0.626, 1.000] \\
[0.626, 1.000] & [1, 1] & [0.755, 1.000] & [0.576, 0.918] & [0.673, 0.918] \\
[0.626, 1.000] & [0.755, 1.000] & [1, 1] & [0.576, 0.918] & [0.673, 1.000] \\
[0.576, 0.918] & [0.576, 0.918] & [0.576, 0.918] & [1, 1] & [0.576, 0.918] \\
[0.626, 1.000] & [0.673, 0.918] & [0.673, 1.000] & [0.576, 0.918] & [1, 1]
\end{matrix} \right)$$

$$\tilde{R}^{16} = \tilde{R}^{8} \circ \tilde{R}^{8} = \left(\begin{array}{ccccc} [1, 1] & [0.626, 1.000] & [0.626, 1.000] & [0.576, 1.000] & [0.626, 1.000] \\ [0.626, 1.000] & [1, 1] & [0.837, 1.000] & [0.576, 1.000] & [0.673, 1.000] \\ [0.626, 1.000] & [0.837, 1.000] & [1, 1] & [0.576, 1.000] & [0.673, 1.000] \\ [0.576, 1.000] & [0.576, 1.000] & [0.576, 1.000] & [1, 1] & [0.576, 1.000] \\ [0.626, 1.000] & [0.673, 1.000] & [0.673, 1.000] & [0.576, 1.000] & [1, 1] \\ [0.859, 1.000] & [0.626, 1.000] & [0.626, 1.000] & [0.576, 1.000] & [0.626, 1.000] \\ [0.626, 1.000] & [0.784, 1.000] & [0.784, 1.000] & [0.576, 1.000] & [0.673, 1.000] \\ [0.626, 1.000] & [0.755, 1.000] & [0.755, 1.000] & [0.576, 1.000] & [0.673, 1.000] \\ [0.576, 0.918] & [0.576, 0.918] & [0.576, 0.918] & [0.918, 0.918] & [0.576, 0.918] \\ [0.626, 1.000] & [0.673, 1.000] & [0.673, 1.000] & [0.576, 1.000] & [0.784, 1.000] \end{array} \right.$$

$$\left. \begin{array}{ccccc} [0.859, 1.000] & [0.626, 1.000] & [0.626, 1.000] & [0.576, 0.918] & [0.626, 1.000] \\ [0.626, 1.000] & [0.784, 1.000] & [0.755, 1.000] & [0.576, 0.918] & [0.673, 1.000] \\ [0.626, 1.000] & [0.784, 1.000] & [0.755, 1.000] & [0.576, 0.918] & [0.673, 1.000] \\ [0.576, 1.000] & [0.576, 1.000] & [0.576, 1.000] & [0.918, 0.918] & [0.576, 1.000] \\ [0.626, 1.000] & [0.673, 1.000] & [0.673, 1.000] & [0.576, 0.918] & [0.784, 1.000] \\ [1, 1] & [0.626, 1.000] & [0.626, 1.000] & [0.576, 0.918] & [0.626, 1.000] \\ [0.626, 1.000] & [1, 1] & [0.755, 1.000] & [0.576, 0.918] & [0.673, 0.918] \\ [0.626, 1.000] & [0.755, 1.000] & [1, 1] & [0.576, 0.918] & [0.673, 1.000] \\ [0.576, 0.918] & [0.576, 0.918] & [0.576, 0.918] & [1, 1] & [0.576, 0.918] \\ [0.626, 1.000] & [0.673, 0.918] & [0.673, 1.000] & [0.576, 0.918] & [1, 1] \end{array} \right)$$

Thus, $\tilde{R}^{16} = \tilde{R}^{8}$. Let $\tilde{R}^{8} = \tilde{R}^{*} = (\tilde{r}_{ij}^{*})_{10\times 10}$, where $\tilde{r}_{ij}^{*} = [\mu_{ij}^{*}, 1 - v_{ij}^{*}]$, $i, j = 1, 2, \ldots, 10$, then the λ-cutting matrix of $\tilde{R}^{*}$ can be constructed as $\tilde{R}_{\lambda}^{*} = ({}_{\lambda}\tilde{r}_{ij}^{*})_{10\times 10}$, where

$$ {}_{\lambda}\tilde{r}_{ij}^{*} = \begin{cases} 0, & \textit{if } 1 - v_{ij}^{*} < \lambda, \\ \dfrac{1}{2}, & \textit{if } \mu_{ij}^{*} < \lambda \leq 1 - v_{ij}^{*}, \quad i, j = 1, 2, \ldots, 10, \ \lambda \in [0, 1] \\ 1, & \textit{if } \mu_{ij}^{*} \geq \lambda. \end{cases} \tag{2.102}$$

Considering that the confidence level λ is directly related to the lower and upper limits of each $\tilde{r}_{ij}^{*}$ in the interval-valued matrix $\tilde{R}^{*}$, we get, based on $\tilde{R}_{\lambda}^{*}$, all the possible classifications of the ten new cars y_i $(i = 1, 2, \ldots, 10)$:

(1) If $0 \leq \lambda \leq 0.576$, then

$$\{y_1, y_2, y_3, y_4, y_5, y_6, y_7, y_8, y_9, y_{10}\}$$

(2) If $0.576 < \lambda \leq 0.626$, then

$$\{y_1, y_2, y_3, y_5, y_6, y_7, y_8, y_{10}\}, \{y_4, y_9\}$$

(3) If $0.626 < \lambda \leq 0.673$, then

$$\{y_1, y_6\}, \{y_2, y_3, y_5, y_7, y_8, y_{10}\}, \{y_4, y_9\}$$

(4) If $0.673 < \lambda \leq 0.755$, then

$$\{y_1, y_6\}, \{y_2, y_3, y_7, y_8\}, \{y_4, y_9\}, \{y_5, y_{10}\}$$

(5) If $0.755 < \lambda \leq 0.784$, then

$$\{y_1, y_6\}, \{y_2, y_3, y_7\}, \{y_8\}, \{y_4, y_9\}, \{y_5, y_{10}\}$$

(6) If $0.784 < \lambda \leq 0.837$, then

$$\{y_1, y_6\}, \{y_2, y_3\}, \{y_5\}, \{y_7\}, \{y_8\}, \{y_{10}\}, \{y_4, y_9\}$$

(7) If $0.837 < \lambda \leq 0.859$, then

$$\{y_1, y_6\}, \{y_2\}, \{y_3\}, \{y_5\}, \{y_7\}, \{y_8\}, \{y_{10}\}, \{y_4, y_9\}$$

(8) If $0.859 < \lambda \leq 0.918$, then

$$\{y_1\}, \{y_2\}, \{y_3\}, \{y_5\}, \{y_6\}, \{y_7\}, \{y_8\}, \{y_{10}\}, \{y_4, y_9\}$$

(9) If $0.918 < \lambda \leq 1$, then

$$\{y_1\}, \{y_2\}, \{y_3\}, \{y_4\}, \{y_5\}, \{y_6\}, \{y_7\}, \{y_8\}, \{y_9\}, \{y_{10}\}$$

From the above numerical analysis, we know that Algorithm 2.1 only takes into account the maximal and minimal deviation information, and ignores all the other deviation information, more importantly, it cannot take into account any information on attribute weights, and thus produces the loss of too much information, while Algorithm 2.2 can not only avoid losing the given information, but also require less computational effort and is more convenient in practical applications.

Now we further compare Algorithm 2.2 with Algorithm-FSC on the simulated data set:

We first exploit Algorithm 2.2 on the simulated data set. In the experiment, we set a series of λ values ranging from 0.6 to 1.0, and compute the values of the SI measure for each clustering result. The results can be found in Table 2.4 (Xu et al. 2008):

Table 2.4 The results derived by Algorithm 2.2 with different λ levels on the simulated data set

λ	0.60	0.65	0.70	0.75	0.80	0.85	0.90	0.95	1.00
SI	0.437	0.437	0.437	0.437	0.437	0.437	0.437	0.437	0.995
K	3	3	3	3	3	3	3	3	900

Note: (1) K is the number of clusters found by Algorithm 2.2.
(2) Since $C^{2^7} = C^{2^6}$, we get the equivalent associate matrix C^{2^6} after six iterations.

Table 2.5 The results derived by Algorithm-FSC with different λ levels on the modified data sets

Modified data set I									
λ	0.60	0.65	0.70	0.75	0.80	0.85	0.90	0.95	1.00
SI	0.466	0.466	0.466	0.466	0.466	0.466	0.466	0.466	0.999
K	2	2	2	2	2	2	2	2	2
Modified data set II									
λ	0.60	0.65	0.70	0.75	0.80	0.85	0.90	0.95	1.00
SI	0.474	0.474	0.474	0.474	0.474	0.474	0.474	0.474	0.999
K	2	2	2	2	2	2	2	2	2

As can be seen from Table 2.4, for most of the λ levels, Algorithm 2.2 produces three clusters, and the smallest SI values are exactly the same as 0.437. In fact, if we take a closer look at the assigned cluster label of each IFS, then we can find that Algorithm 2.2 recognizes the cluster structure perfectly under these λ levels. Clearly, by incorporating the uncertainty degree into the correlation computation of IFSs, Algorithm 2.2 has the ability to identify all the three classes. However, this is not the case for traditional clustering algorithms for fuzzy sets. To illustrate this, we also exploit Algorithm-FSC on the simulated data set. As mentioned above, Algorithm-FSC does not take into account the uncertain information. Therefore, to make sure $\mu(x) + v(x) = 1$ for any x in the simulated data set, we should modify the data set by adding $\pi(x)$ to either $v(x)$ or $\mu(x)$. We produce the two modified data sets and then exploit Algorithm-FSC on them. The results can be found in Table 2.5 (Xu et al. 2008).

As can be seen in Table 2.5, the clustering results of Algorithm-FSC on the two modified data sets are poor, since it cannot identify all the three classes precisely. This further justifies the importance of the uncertain information in IFSs.

In summary, by comparing the performance of Algorithm-IFSC with that of Algorithm-FSC on the simulated data set, we know that (1) Algorithm-IFSC is capable to cluster large scale IFSs; and (2) the uncertain information captured by IFSs is crucial for the success of some clustering tasks.

2.3 Intuitionistic Fuzzy Hierarchical Clustering Algorithms

Xu (2009) introduced an intuitionistic fuzzy hierarchical algorithm for clustering IFSs, which is based on the traditional hierarchical clustering procedure, the intuitionistic fuzzy aggregation operator, and the basic distance measures between IFSs. Then, the algorithm was extended for clustering IVIFSs. The algorithm and its extended form were applied to the classifications of building materials and enterprises respectively. In this section, we shall give a detailed introduction to the intuitionistic fuzzy hierarchical algorithms.

We first introduce some basic operations and distance measures for IFSs and IVIFSs:

Let $X = \{x_1, x_2, \ldots, x_n\}$ be a discrete universe of discourse, $A_j = \{\langle x_i, \mu_{A_j}(x_i), \nu_{A_j}(x_i)\rangle | x_i \in X\}$ $(j = 1, 2, \ldots, m)$ a collection of m IFSs. Then based on the operations of IFSs, Xu (2009) defined the average of m IFSs A_j $(j = 1, 2, \ldots, m)$ as:

$$f(A_1, A_2, \ldots, A_m) = \frac{1}{m}(A_1 \oplus A_2 \oplus \cdots \oplus A_m) \tag{2.103}$$

which can be further transformed into the following:

$$f(A_1, A_2, \ldots, A_m) = \left\{ \langle x_i, 1 - \prod_{j=1}^{m} (1 - \mu_{A_j}(x_i))^{\frac{1}{m}}, \prod_{j=1}^{m} (\nu_{A_j}(x_i))^{\frac{1}{m}} \rangle | x_i \in X \right\} \tag{2.104}$$

Xu (2009) defined the weighted Hamming distance, the normalized Hamming distance, the weighted Euclidean distance, and the normalized Euclidean distance for measuring IVIFSs:

Let $\tilde{A}_j = \{\langle x_i, \tilde{\mu}_{\tilde{A}_j}(x_i), \tilde{\nu}_{\tilde{A}_j}(x_i)\rangle | x_i \in X\}$ $(j = 1, 2)$ be two IVIFSs in X, where $\tilde{\mu}_{\tilde{A}_j}(x_i) = [\mu^-_{\tilde{A}_j}(x_i), \mu^+_{\tilde{A}_j}(x_i)] \subset [0, 1]$ and $\tilde{\nu}_{\tilde{A}_j}(x_i) = [\nu^-_{\tilde{A}_j}(x_i), \nu^+_{\tilde{A}_j}(x_i)] \subset [0, 1]$ $(j = 1, 2)$. Then

(1) The weighted Hamming distance:

$$\begin{aligned} d_{wH}(\tilde{A}_1, \tilde{A}_2) &= \frac{1}{4}\sum_{i=1}^{n} w_i(|\mu^-_{\tilde{A}_1}(x_i) - \mu^-_{\tilde{A}_2}(x_i)| + |\mu^+_{\tilde{A}_1}(x_i) - \mu^+_{\tilde{A}_2}(x_i)| + |\nu^-_{\tilde{A}_1}(x_i) - \nu^-_{\tilde{A}_2}(x_i)| \\ &\quad + |\nu^+_{\tilde{A}_1}(x_i) - \nu^+_{\tilde{A}_2}(x_i)| + |\pi^-_{\tilde{A}_1}(x_i) - \pi^-_{\tilde{A}_2}(x_i)| + |\pi^+_{\tilde{A}_1}(x_i) - \pi^+_{\tilde{A}_2}(x_i)|) \end{aligned} \tag{2.105}$$

Especially, if $w = (1/n, 1/n, \ldots, 1/n)^T$, then Eq. (2.105) reduces to the normalized Hamming distance:

$$\begin{aligned} d_{NH}(\tilde{A}_1, \tilde{A}_2) &= \frac{1}{4n}\sum_{i=1}^{n} (|\mu^-_{\tilde{A}_1}(x_i) - \mu^-_{\tilde{A}_2}(x_i)| + |\mu^+_{\tilde{A}_1}(x_i) - \mu^+_{\tilde{A}_2}(x_i)| + |\nu^-_{\tilde{A}_1}(x_i) - \nu^-_{\tilde{A}_2}(x_i)| \\ &\quad + |\nu^+_{\tilde{A}_1}(x_i) - \nu^+_{\tilde{A}_2}(x_i)| + |\pi^-_{\tilde{A}_1}(x_i) - \pi^-_{\tilde{A}_2}(x_i)| + |\pi^+_{\tilde{A}_1}(x_i) - \pi^+_{\tilde{A}_2}(x_i)|) \end{aligned} \tag{2.106}$$

(2) The weighted Euclidean distance:

$$d_{wE}(\tilde{A}_1, \tilde{A}_2) = \left(\frac{1}{4} \sum_{i=1}^{n} w_i ((\mu_{\tilde{A}_1}^-(x_i) - \mu_{\tilde{A}_2}^-(x_i))^2 + (\mu_{\tilde{A}_1}^+(x_i) - \mu_{\tilde{A}_2}^+(x_i))^2 + (v_{\tilde{A}_1}^-(x_i) - v_{\tilde{A}_2}^-(x_i))^2 + (v_{\tilde{A}_1}^+(x_i) - v_{\tilde{A}_2}^+(x_i))^2 + (\pi_{\tilde{A}_1}^-(x_i) - \pi_{\tilde{A}_2}^-(x_i))^2 + (\pi_{\tilde{A}_1}^+(x_i) - \pi_{\tilde{A}_2}^+(x_i))^2) \right)^{\frac{1}{2}} \quad (2.107)$$

Especially, if $w = (1/n, 1/n, \ldots, 1/n)^T$, then Eq. (2.107) reduces to the normalized Euclidean distance:

$$d_{NE}(\tilde{A}_1, \tilde{A}_2) = \left(\frac{1}{4n} \sum_{i=1}^{n} ((\mu_{\tilde{A}_1}^-(x_i) - \mu_{\tilde{A}_2}^-(x_i))^2 + (\mu_{\tilde{A}_1}^+(x_i) - \mu_{\tilde{A}_2}^+(x_i))^2 + (v_{\tilde{A}_1}^-(x_i) - v_{\tilde{A}_2}^-(x_i))^2 + (v_{\tilde{A}_1}^+(x_i) - v_{\tilde{A}_2}^+(x_i))^2 + (\pi_{\tilde{A}_1}^-(x_i) - \pi_{\tilde{A}_2}^-(x_i))^2 + (\pi_{\tilde{A}_1}^+(x_i) - \pi_{\tilde{A}_2}^+(x_i))^2) \right)^{\frac{1}{2}} \quad (2.108)$$

Moreover, let $\tilde{A}_j = \{\langle x_i, \tilde{\mu}_{\tilde{A}_j}(x_i), \tilde{v}_{\tilde{A}_j}(x_i)\rangle | x_i \in X\}$, where $\tilde{\mu}_{\tilde{A}_j}(x_i) = [\mu_{\tilde{A}_j}^-(x_i), \mu_{\tilde{A}_j}^+(x_i)] \subset [0, 1]$ and $\tilde{v}_{\tilde{A}_j}(x_i) = [v_{\tilde{A}_j}^-(x_i), v_{\tilde{A}_j}^+(x_i)] \subset [0, 1]$ $(j = 1, 2, \ldots, m)$. Then, based on the operations of IVIFSs, Xu (2009) defined the average of a collection of m IVIFSs $\tilde{A}_j$ $(j = 1, 2, \ldots, m)$ as:

$$f(\tilde{A}_1, \tilde{A}_2, \ldots, \tilde{A}_m) = \frac{1}{m}(\tilde{A}_1 \oplus \tilde{A}_2 \oplus \cdots \oplus \tilde{A}_m) \quad (2.109)$$

which can be further transformed into the following:

$$f(\tilde{A}_1, \tilde{A}_2, \ldots, \tilde{A}_m) = \left\{ \langle x_i, \left[1 - \prod_{j=1}^{m} (1 - \mu_{\tilde{A}_j}^-(x_i))^{\frac{1}{m}}, 1 - \prod_{j=1}^{m} (1 - \mu_{\tilde{A}_j}^+(x_i))^{\frac{1}{m}} \right], \left[\prod_{j=1}^{m} (v_{\tilde{A}_j}^-(x_i))^{\frac{1}{m}}, \prod_{j=1}^{m} (v_{\tilde{A}_j}^+(x_i))^{\frac{1}{m}} \right] \rangle | x_i \in X \right\} \quad (2.110)$$

The traditional hierarchical clustering algorithm (Anderberg 1972) is generally used to cluster numerical information. However, in many fields including medical informatics, information retrieval and bio-informatics, where the data information sometimes may be imprecise or uncertain, and is suitable to be expressed in IFSs or IVIFSs, the traditional hierarchical clustering algorithm fails in dealing with these situations. Based on the distance measures (2.105) and (2.106), and the intuitionistic fuzzy aggregation operator (2.103), Xu (2009) extended the traditional hierarchical clustering algorithm to the IFS theory:

Algorithm 2.4

Given a collection of m IFSs A_j $(j = 1, 2, \ldots, m)$, in the first stage each of the m IFSs A_j $(j = 1, 2, \ldots, m)$ is considered as a unique cluster. The IFSs A_j $(j = 1, 2, \ldots, m)$ are then compared among themselves by using the weighted Hamming distance:

$$d_{wH}(A_1, A_2) = \frac{1}{2}\sum_{i=1}^{n} w_i(|\mu_{A_i}(x_i) - \mu_{A_j}(x_i)| + |\nu_{A_i}(x_i) - \nu_{A_j}(x_i)| + |\pi_{A_i}(x_i) - \pi_{A_j}(x_i)|) \tag{2.111}$$

or the weighted Euclidean distance:

$$d_{wE}(A_1, A_2) = \left(\frac{1}{2}\sum_{i=1}^{n} w_i((\mu_{A_i}(x_i) - \mu_{A_j}(x_i))^2 + (\nu_{A_i}(x_i) - \nu_{A_j}(x_i))^2 + (\pi_{A_i}(x_i) - \pi_{A_j}(x_i))^2)\right)^{1/2} \tag{2.112}$$

The two clusters with smaller distance are jointed. The procedure is then repeated time after time until the desirable number of clusters is achieved. Only two clusters can be jointed in each stage and they cannot be separated after they are jointed. In each stage the center of each cluster is recalculated by using the average (derived from Eq. (2.103)) of the IFSs assigned to the cluster, and the distance between two clusters is defined as the distance between the centers of each clusters.

If the collected data information is expressed as IVIFSs, then based on the distance measures (2.105) and (2.107), and the interval-valued intuitionistic fuzzy aggregation operator (2.110), Xu (2009) gave an interval-valued intuitionistic fuzzy hierarchical algorithm for clustering IVIFSs:

Algorithm 2.5

Given a collection of m IVIFSs $\tilde{A}_j$ $(j = 1, 2, \ldots, m)$, in the first stage each of the m IVIFSs $\tilde{A}_j$ $(j = 1, 2, \ldots, m)$ is considered as a unique cluster. The IVIFSs $\tilde{A}_j(j = 1, 2, \ldots, m)$ are then compared among themselves by using the weighted Hamming distance (2.105) or the weighted Euclidean distance (2.107). The two clusters with smaller distance are jointed. The procedure is then repeated time after time until the desirable number of clusters is achieved. Only two clusters can be jointed in each stage and they cannot be separated after they are jointed. In each stage the center of each cluster is recalculated by using the average (derived by the interval-valued intuitionistic fuzzy aggregation operator (2.110)) of the IVIFSs assigned to the cluster, and the distance between two clusters is defined as the distance between the centers of each clusters.

Example 2.3 (Xu 2009) Given five building materials: sealant, floor varnish, wall paint, carpet, and polyvinyl chloride flooring, which are represented by the IFSs A_j $(j = 1, 2, 3, 4, 5)$ in the feature space $X = \{x_1, x_2, \ldots, x_8\}$. $w = (0.15, 0.10, 0.12, 0.15, 0.10, 0.13, 0.14, 0.11)^T$ is the weight vector of x_i $(i = 1, 2, \ldots, 8)$, and the given data are listed as follows:

$$\begin{aligned}
A_1 =&\{\langle x_1, 0.20, 0.50\rangle, \langle x_2, 0.10, 0.80\rangle, \langle x_3, 0.50, 0.30\rangle, \langle x_4, 0.90, 0.00\rangle,\\
&\langle x_5, 0.40, 0.35\rangle, \langle x_6, 0.10, 0.90\rangle, \langle x_7, 0.30, 0.50\rangle, \langle x_8, 1.00, 0.00\rangle\}\\
A_2 =&\{\langle x_1, 0.50, 0.40\rangle, \langle x_2, 0.60, 0.15\rangle, \langle x_3, 1.00, 0.00\rangle, \langle x_4, 0.15, 0.65\rangle,\\
&\langle x_5, 0.00, 0.80\rangle, \langle x_6, 0.70, 0.15\rangle, \langle x_7, 0.50, 0.30\rangle, \langle x_8, 0.65, 0.20\rangle\}\\
A_3 =&\{\langle x_1, 0.45, 0.35\rangle, \langle x_2, 0.60, 0.30\rangle, \langle x_3, 0.90, 0.00\rangle, \langle x_4, 0.10, 0.80\rangle,\\
&\langle x_5, 0.20, 0.70\rangle, \langle x_6, 0.60, 0.20\rangle, \langle x_7, 0.15, 0.80\rangle, \langle x_8, 0.20, 0.65\rangle\}\\
A_4 =&\{\langle x_1, 1.00, 0.00\rangle, \langle x_2, 1.00, 0.00\rangle, \langle x_3, 0.85, 0.10\rangle, \langle x_4, 0.75, 0.15\rangle,\\
&\langle x_5, 0.20, 0.80\rangle, \langle x_6, 0.15, 0.85\rangle, \langle x_7, 0.10, 0.70\rangle, \langle x_8, 0.30, 0.70\rangle\}\\
A_5 =&\{\langle x_1, 0.90, 0.00\rangle, \langle x_2, 0.90, 0.10\rangle, \langle x_3, 0.80, 0.10\rangle, \langle x_4, 0.70, 0.20\rangle,\\
&\langle x_5, 0.50, 0.15\rangle, \langle x_6, 0.30, 0.65\rangle, \langle x_7, 0.15, 0.75\rangle, \langle x_8, 0.40, 0.30\rangle\}
\end{aligned}$$

Now we utilize Algorithm 2.3 to classify the building materials A_j $(j = 1, 2, 3, 4, 5)$:

Step 1 In the first stage, each of the IFSs A_j $(j = 1, 2, 3, 4, 5)$ is considered as a unique cluster:

$$\{A_1\}, \{A_2\}, \{A_3\}, \{A_4\}, \{A_5\}$$

Step 2 Compare each IFS A_i with all the other four IFSs by using the weighted Hamming distance (2.110):

$$\begin{aligned}
&d_{wH}(A_1, A_2) = d_{wH}(A_2, A_1) = 0.4915, d_{wH}(A_1, A_3) = d_{wH}(A_3, A_1) = 0.5115\\
&d_{wH}(A_1, A_4) = d_{wH}(A_4, A_1) = 0.4310, d_{wH}(A_1, A_5) = d_{wH}(A_5, A_1) = 0.4045\\
&d_{wH}(A_2, A_3) = d_{wH}(A_3, A_2) = 0.2170, d_{wH}(A_2, A_4) = d_{wH}(A_4, A_2) = 0.4515\\
&d_{wH}(A_2, A_5) = d_{wH}(A_5, A_2) = 0.4545, d_{wH}(A_3, A_4) = d_{wH}(A_4, A_3) = 0.4480\\
&d_{wH}(A_3, A_5) = d_7(A_5, A_3) = 0.3735, d_{wH}(A_4, A_5) = d_{wH}(A_5, A_4) = 0.1875
\end{aligned}$$

Since

$$\begin{aligned}
d_{wH}(A_1, A_5) &= \min\{d_{wH}(A_1, A_2), d_{wH}(A_1, A_3), d_{wH}(A_1, A_4), d_{wH}(A_1, A_5)\} = 0.4045\\
d_{wH}(A_2, A_3) &= \min\{d_{wH}(A_2, A_1), d_{wH}(A_2, A_3), d_{wH}(A_2, A_4), d_{wH}(A_2, A_5)\} = 0.2170\\
d_{wH}(A_4, A_5) &= \min\{d_{wH}(A_4, A_1), d_{wH}(A_4, A_2), d_{wH}(A_4, A_3), d_{wH}(A_4, A_5)\} = 0.1875
\end{aligned}$$

and considering only two clusters can be jointed in each stage, the IFSs A_j $(j = 1, 2, 3, 4, 5)$ can be clustered into the following three clusters at the second stage:

$$\{A_1\}, \{A_2, A_3\}, \{A_4, A_5\}$$

Step 3 Calculate the center of each cluster by using Eq. (2.103):

$$\begin{aligned} c\{A_1\} &= A_1 \\ c\{A_2, A_3\} &= f(A_2, A_3) \\ &= \{\langle x_1, 0.48, 0.37\rangle, \langle x_2, 0.60, 0.21\rangle, \langle x_3, 1.00, 0.00\rangle, \langle x_4, 0.13, 0.72\rangle, \\ &\quad \langle x_5, 0.11, 0.75\rangle, \langle x_6, 0.65, 0.17\rangle, \langle x_7, 0.35, 0.49\rangle, \langle x_8, 0.47, 0.36\rangle\} \\ c\{A_4, A_5\} &= f(A_4, A_5) \\ &= \{\langle x_1, 1.00, 0.00\rangle, \langle x_2, 1.00, 0.00\rangle, \langle x_3, 0.83, 0.10\rangle, \langle x_4, 0.73, 0.17\rangle, \\ &\quad \langle x_5, 0.37, 0.35\rangle, \langle x_6, 0.23, 0.74\rangle, \langle x_7, 0.13, 0.72\rangle, \langle x_8, 0.35, 0.46\rangle\} \end{aligned}$$

and then compare each cluster with all the other two clusters by using the weighted Hamming distance (2.111):

$$\begin{aligned} d_{wH}(c\{A_1\}, c\{A_2, A_3\}) &= d_{wH}(c\{A_2, A_3\}, c\{A_1\}) = 0.4921 \\ d_{wH}(c\{A_1\}, c\{A_4, A_5\}) &= d_{wH}(c\{A_4, A_5\}, c\{A_1\}) = 0.4007 \\ d_{wH}(c\{A_2, A_3\}, c\{A_4, A_5\}) &= d_{wH}(c\{A_4, A_5\}, c\{A_2, A_3\}) = 0.3879 \end{aligned}$$

Hence, the IFSs A_j $(j = 1, 2, 3, 4, 5)$ can be clustered into the following two clusters at the third stage:

$$\{A_1\}, \{A_2, A_3, A_4, A_5\}$$

Finally, the above two clusters can be further clustered into a unique cluster:

$$\{A_1, A_2, A_3, A_4, A_5\}$$

All the above processes can be shown as in Fig. 2.1 (Xu 2009).

In the process of clustering, the number of clusters can be determined according to practical applications.

Example 2.4 (Xu 2009) Given four enterprises, represented by the IVIFSs $\tilde{A}_j$ $(j = 1, 2, 3, 4)$ in the attribute set $X = \{x_1, x_2, \ldots, x_6\}$, where (1) x_1: The ability of sale; (2) x_2: The ability of management; (3) x_3: The ability of production; (4) x_4: The ability of technology; (5) x_5: The ability of financing; and (6) x_6: The ability of risk bearing (the weight vector of x_i $(i = 1, 2, \ldots, 6)$ is $w = (0.25, 0.20, 0.15, 0.10, 0.15, 0.15)^T$. The given data are listed as follows:

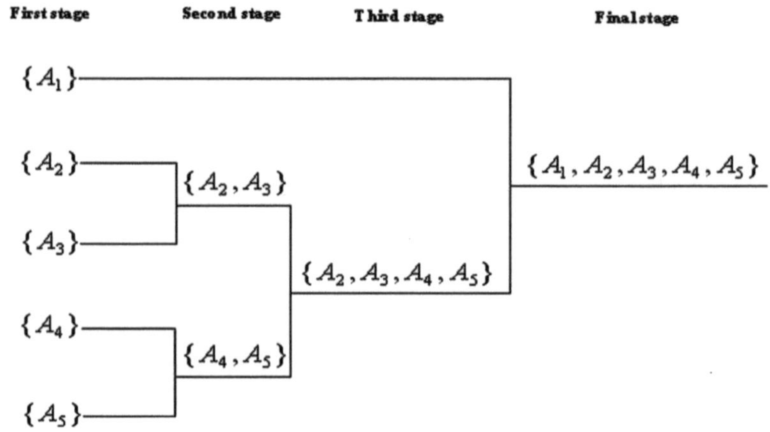

Fig. 2.1 Classification of the building materials A_j $(j = 1, 2, 3, 4, 5)$

$$\begin{aligned}
\tilde{A}_1 =&\{\langle x_1, [0.70, 0.75], [0.10, 0.15]\rangle, \langle x_2, [0.00, 0.10], [0.80, 0.90]\rangle,\\
&\langle x_3, [0.15, 0.20], [0.60, 0.65]\rangle, \langle x_4, [0.50, 0.55], [0.30, 0.35]\rangle,\\
&\langle x_5, [0.10, 0.15], [0.50, 0.60]\rangle, \langle x_6, [0.70, 0.75], [0.10, 0.15]\rangle\}\\
\tilde{A}_2 =&\{\langle x_1, [0.40, 0.45], [0.30, 0.35]\rangle, \langle x_2, [0.60, 0.65], [0.20, 0.30]\rangle,\\
&\langle x_3, [0.80, 1.00], [0.00, 0.00]\rangle, \langle x_4, [0.70, 0.90], [0.00, 0.10]\rangle,\\
&\langle x_5, [0.70, 0.75], [0.10, 0.20]\rangle, \langle x_6, [0.90, 1.00], [0.00, 0.00]\rangle\}\\
\tilde{A}_3 =&\{\langle x_1, [0.20, 0.30], [0.40, 0.45]\rangle, \langle x_2, [0.80, 0.90], [0.00, 0.10]\rangle,\\
&\langle x_3, [0.10, 0.20], [0.70, 0.80]\rangle, \langle x_4, [0.15, 0.20], [0.70, 0.75]\rangle,\\
&\langle x_5, [0.00, 0.10], [0.80, 0.90]\rangle, \langle x_6, [0.60, 0.70], [0.20, 0.30]\rangle\}\\
\tilde{A}_4 =&\{\langle x_1, [0.60, 0.65], [0.30, 0.35]\rangle, \langle x_2, [0.45, 0.50], [0.30, 0.40]\rangle,\\
&\langle x_3, [0.20, 0.25], [0.65, 0.70]\rangle, \langle x_4, [0.20, 0.30], [0.50, 0.60]\rangle,\\
&\langle x_5, [0.00, 0.10], [0.75, 0.80]\rangle, \langle x_6, [0.50, 0.60], [0.20, 0.25]\rangle\}
\end{aligned}$$

Here we can use Algorithm 2.4 to classify the enterprises $\tilde{A}_j$ $(j = 1, 2, 3, 4)$:

Step 1 In the first stage, each of the IVIFSs $\tilde{A}_j$ $(j = 1, 2, 3, 4)$ is considered as a unique cluster:

$$\{\tilde{A}_1\}, \{\tilde{A}_2\}, \{\tilde{A}_3\}, \{\tilde{A}_4\}$$

Step 2 Compare each IVIFS A_i with all the other three IVIFSs by using the weighted Hamming distance (2.111):

$$d_{wH}(\tilde{A}_1, \tilde{A}_2) = d_{wH}(\tilde{A}_2, \tilde{A}_1) = 0.4600,\ d_{wH}(\tilde{A}_1, \tilde{A}_3) = d_{wH}(\tilde{A}_3, \tilde{A}_1) = 0.4012$$
$$d_{wH}(\tilde{A}_1, \tilde{A}_4) = d_{wH}(\tilde{A}_4, \tilde{A}_1) = 0.2525,\ d_{wH}(\tilde{A}_2, \tilde{A}_3) = d_{wH}(\tilde{A}_3, \tilde{A}_2) = 0.4237$$

$$d_{wH}(\tilde{A}_2, \tilde{A}_4) = d_{wH}(\tilde{A}_4, \tilde{A}_2) = 0.4237, d_{wH}(\tilde{A}_3, \tilde{A}_4) = d_{wH}(\tilde{A}_4, \tilde{A}_3) = 0.2288$$

then the IVIFSs $\tilde{A}_j$ ($j = 1, 2, 3, 4$) can be clustered into the following three clusters at the second stage:

$$\{\tilde{A}_1\}, \quad \{\tilde{A}_2\}, \quad \{\tilde{A}_3, \tilde{A}_4\}$$

Step 3 Calculate the center of each cluster by using Eq. (2.109):

$$\begin{aligned} c\{\tilde{A}_1\} &= A_1, \quad c\{\tilde{A}_2\} = \tilde{A}_2 \\ c\{\tilde{A}_3, \tilde{A}_4\} &= f(\tilde{A}_3, \tilde{A}_4) \\ &= \{\langle x_1, [0.43, 0.51], [0.35, 0.40]\rangle, \langle x_2, [0.67, 0.78], [0.00, 0.20]\rangle, \\ &\quad \langle x_3, [0.15, 0.23], [0.67, 0.75]\rangle, \langle x_4, [0.18, 0.25], [0.59, 0.67]\rangle, \\ &\quad \langle x_5, [0.00, 0.10], [0.77, 0.85]\rangle, \langle x_6, [0.55, 0.65], [0.20, 0.27]\rangle\} \end{aligned}$$

and then compare each cluster with all the other two clusters by using the weighted Hamming distance (2.111):

$$\begin{aligned} d_{wH}(c\{\tilde{A}_1\}, c\{\tilde{A}_2\}) &= d_{wH}(c\{\tilde{A}_2\}, c\{\tilde{A}_1\}) = 0.4600 \\ d_{wH}(c\{\tilde{A}_1\}, c\{\tilde{A}_3, \tilde{A}_4\}) &= d_{wH}(c\{\tilde{A}_3, \tilde{A}_4\}, c\{\tilde{A}_1\}) = 0.3211 \\ d_{wH}(c\{\tilde{A}_2\}, c\{\tilde{A}_3, \tilde{A}_4\}) &= d_{wH}(c\{\tilde{A}_3, \tilde{A}_4\}, c\{\tilde{A}_2\}) = 0.3871 \end{aligned}$$

As a result, the IVIFSs $\tilde{A}_j$ ($j = 1, 2, 3, 4$) can be clustered into the following two clusters at the third stage:

$$\{\tilde{A}_2\}, \{\tilde{A}_1, \tilde{A}_3, \tilde{A}_4\}$$

In the final stage, the above clusters can be further clustered into a unique cluster:

$$\{\tilde{A}_1, \tilde{A}_2, \tilde{A}_3, \tilde{A}_4\}$$

All the above processes can be shown as in Fig. 2.2 (Xu 2009).

2.4 Intuitionistic Fuzzy Orthogonal Clustering Algorithm

We first introduce some basic concepts:

Definition 2.16 (Bustince 2000) Let X and Y be two non-empty sets. Then

$$R = \{\langle (x, y), \mu_R(x, y), v_R(x, y)\rangle | x \in X, y \in Y\} \tag{2.113}$$

is called an intuitionistic fuzzy relation, where

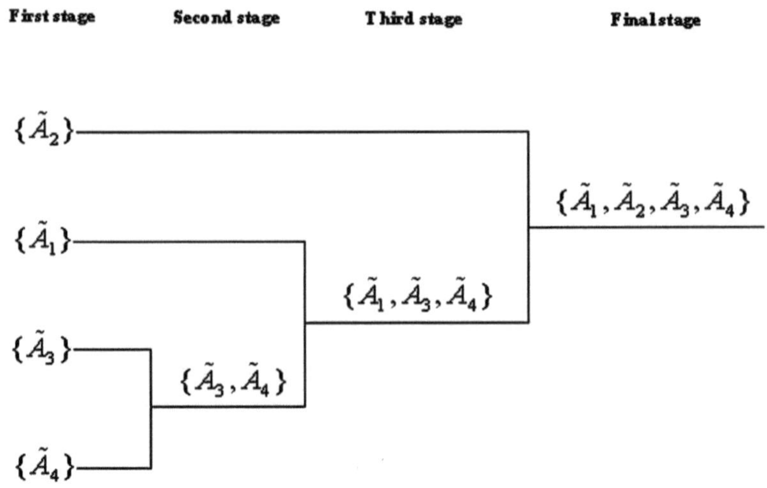

Fig. 2.2 Classification of the enterprises $\tilde{A}_j$ $(j = 1, 2, 3, 4)$

$$\mu_R: X \times Y \to [0, 1], v_R : X \times Y \to [0, 1] \tag{2.114}$$

and

$$0 \le \mu_R(x, y) + v_R(x, y) \le 1, \text{ for any } (x, y) \in X \times Y \tag{2.115}$$

Definition 2.17 (Bustince 2000) Let R be an intuitionistic fuzzy relation. If

(1) (**Reflexivity**). $\mu_R(x, x) = 1$, $v_R(x, x) = 0$, for any $x \in X$.
(2) (**Symmetry**). $\mu_R(x, y) = \mu_R(y, x)$, $v_R(x, y) = v_R(y, x)$, for any $(x, y) \in X \times Y$, then R is called an intuitionistic fuzzy similarity relation.

Definition 2.18 (Xu et al. 2011) Let $\alpha = (\alpha_1, \alpha_2, \ldots, \alpha_n)$ be a vector. If all $\alpha_i = (\mu_{\alpha_i}, v_{\alpha_i})$ $(i = 1, 2, \ldots, n)$ are IFVs, then we call α an intuitionistic fuzzy vector, and denote α^T as the transpose of α, where α^T is a n-dimensional column vector.

Definition 2.19 (Xu et al. 2011) Let $\alpha, \beta \in X_{1\times n}$, where $X_{1\times n}$ denotes the set of intuitionistic fuzzy vectors. Then

$$\begin{aligned} \alpha \cdot \beta &= (\max\{\min\{\mu_{\alpha_i}, \mu_{\beta_i}\}\}, \min\{\max\{v_{\alpha_i}, v_{\beta_j}\}\}) \\ &= (\mathop{\vee}_{i=1}^{n} (\mu_{\alpha_i} \wedge \mu_{\beta_i}), \mathop{\wedge}_{i=1}^{n} (v_{\alpha_i} \vee v_{\beta_j})) \end{aligned} \tag{2.116}$$

is called the inner product of α and β, where $\vee$ and $\wedge$ denote the max and min operations respectively.

Definition 2.20 (Xu et al. 2011) Let $\alpha, \beta \in X_{1\times n}$, if $\alpha \cdot \beta = (0, 1)$ or $(0, 0)$. Then we call that α is orthogonal to β.

Definition 2.21 (Xu et al. 2011) Let $\alpha, \beta \in X_{1\times n}$. Then

$$\begin{aligned}\alpha \circ \beta &= (\min\{\max\{\mu_{\alpha_i}, \mu_{\beta_i}\}\}, \max\{\min\{v_{\alpha_i}, v_{\beta_j}\}\}) \\ &= (\mathop{\wedge}_{i=1}^{n}(\mu_{\alpha_i} \vee \mu_{\beta_i}), \mathop{\vee}_{i=1}^{n}(v_{\alpha_i} \wedge v_{\beta_j}))\end{aligned} \tag{2.117}$$

is called the outer product of α and β.

Theorem 2.11 (Xu et al. 2011) Let $\alpha, \beta \in X_{1\times n}$. Then

$$(\alpha \cdot \beta)^c = \alpha^c \circ \beta^c, (\alpha \circ \beta)^c = \alpha^c \cdot \beta^c \tag{2.118}$$

where $\alpha^c = (\alpha_1^c, \alpha_2^c, \ldots, \alpha_n^c)$ and $\beta^c = (\beta_1^c, \beta_2^c, \ldots, \beta_n^c)$, $\alpha_i^c = (v_{\alpha_i}, \mu_{\alpha_i})$ and $\beta_i^c = (v_{\beta_i}, \mu_{\beta_i})$, $i = 1, 2, \ldots, n$.

Proof By Definitions 2.19 and 2.21, we have

$$(\alpha \cdot \beta)^c = (\mathop{\wedge}_{i=1}^{n}(v_{\alpha_i} \vee v_{\beta_j}), \mathop{\vee}_{i=1}^{n}(\mu_{\alpha_i} \wedge \mu_{\beta_i})) = a^c \circ \beta^c \tag{2.119}$$

$$(\alpha \circ \beta)^c = (\mathop{\vee}_{i=1}^{n}(v_{\alpha_i} \wedge v_{\beta_j}), \mathop{\wedge}_{i=1}^{n}(\mu_{\alpha_i} \vee \mu_{\beta_i})) = \alpha^c \cdot \beta^c \tag{2.120}$$

Similarly, we can easily prove the following properties:

Theorem 2.12 (Xu et al. 2011) Let $\alpha, \beta \in X_{1\times n}$. Then

$$\alpha \cdot \beta = \beta \cdot \alpha, \quad \alpha \circ \beta = \beta \circ \alpha \tag{2.121}$$

Theorem 2.13 (Xu et al. 2011) Let $\alpha, \beta, \gamma \in X_{1\times n}$. Then

$$\alpha \cdot (\beta \cdot \gamma) = (\alpha \cdot \beta) \cdot \gamma, \quad \alpha \circ (\beta \circ \gamma) = (\alpha \circ \beta) \circ \gamma \tag{2.122}$$

Theorem 2.14 (Xu et al. 2011) Let $\alpha, \beta \in X_{1\times n}$. Then $\alpha \cdot \beta$ and $\alpha \circ \beta$ are also IFVs.

Definition 2.22 (Xu et al. 2011) Let A and B be two IFSs on X. Then

$$A \cdot B = \{x, \langle \mathop{\vee}_{X}(\mu_A(x) \wedge \mu_B(x)), \mathop{\wedge}_{X}(v_A(x) \vee v_B(x))\rangle, x \in X\} \tag{2.123}$$

$$A \circ B = \{x, \langle \mathop{\wedge}_{X}(\mu_A(x) \vee \mu_B(x)), \mathop{\vee}_{X}(v_A(x) \wedge v_B(x))\rangle, x \in X\} \tag{2.124}$$

are called the inner and outer products of A and B respectively.

Definition 2.23 (Xu et al. 2011) Let A and B be two IFSs on X, $R(A, B)$ is a binary relation on $X \times X$. If

$$R(A, B) = \begin{cases} (1, 0), A = B, \\ (A \cdot B) \cap (A \circ B)^c, A \neq B, \end{cases} \tag{2.125}$$

then $R(A, B)$ is called the closeness degree of A and B.

By Eq. (2.125), we have

Theorem 2.15 (Xu et al. 2011) The closeness degree $R(A, B)$ of A and B is an intuitionistic fuzzy similarity relation.

Proof (1) We first prove that $R(A, B)$ is an IFV, since A and B are two IFSs on X, we have

(a) If $A = B$, then $R(A, B) = (1, 0)$;
(b) If $A \neq B$, then

$$0 \leq \mu_A(x), v_A(x) \leq 1, \ 0 \leq \mu_A(x) + v_A(x) \leq 1 \tag{2.126}$$

$$0 \leq \mu_B(x), v_B(x) \leq 1, 0 \leq \mu_B(x) + v_B(x) \leq 1 \tag{2.127}$$

$$(A \circ B)^c = \{\bigvee_X (v_A(x) \wedge v_B(x)), \bigwedge_X (\mu_A(x) \vee \mu_B(x))\} \tag{2.128}$$

$$\begin{aligned} R(A, B) = (&\min\{\bigwedge_X (\mu_A(x) \vee \mu_B(x)), \bigvee_X (v_A(x) \wedge v_B(x))\}, \\ &\min\{\bigwedge_X (v_A(x) \vee v_B(x)), \bigwedge_X (\mu_A(x) \vee \mu_B(x))\}) \end{aligned} \tag{2.129}$$

Thus, $R(A, B)$ is an IFV.
(2) Since $R(A, A) = (1, 0)$, then R is reflexive.
(3) Since $R(A, B) = (A \cdot B) \wedge (A \circ B)^c = (B \cdot A) \wedge (B \circ A)^c = R(B, A)$, then R is symmetrical. Thus, $R(A, B)$ is an intuitionistic fuzzy similarity relation.

Definition 2.24 (Xu et al. 2011) Let $R = (r_{ij})_{n\times n}$ be an intuitionistic fuzzy similarity matrix, where $r_{ij} = (\mu_{ij}, v_{ij}), i, j = 1, 2, \ldots, n$. Then ${}_{(\lambda,\delta)}R = ({}_{(\lambda,\delta)}r_{ij})_{n\times n} = ({}_{\lambda}\mu_{ij}, {}_{\delta}v_{ij})_{n\times n}$ is called a (λ, δ)-cutting matrix of R, where (λ, δ) is the confidence level, $0 \leq \lambda, \delta \leq 1, \ 0 \leq \lambda + \delta \leq 1$, and

$${}_{(\lambda,\delta)}r_{ij} = ({}_{\lambda}\mu_{ij}, {}_{\delta}v_{ij}) = \begin{cases} (1,0), \ if \ \mu_{ij} \geq \lambda, v_{ij} \leq \delta, \\ (0,1), \ if \ \mu_{ij} < \lambda, v_{ij} > \delta. \end{cases} \tag{2.130}$$

Theorem 2.16 (Xu et al. 2011) $R = (r_{ij})_{n\times n}$ is an intuitionistic fuzzy similarity matrix if and only if its (λ, δ)-cutting matrix ${}_{(\lambda,\delta)}R = ({}_{(\lambda,\delta)}r_{ij})_{n\times n}$ is an intuitionistic fuzzy similarity matrix.

Proof (Necessity) If $R = (r_{ij})_{n\times n}$ is an intuitionistic fuzzy similarity matrix, then

(1) (Reflexivity) Since $r_{ii} = (1,0), 0 \leq \lambda, \delta \leq 1, \ 0 \leq \lambda + \delta \leq 1$, then ${}_{(\lambda,\delta)}r_{ij} = (1,0)$.

(2) (Symmetry) Since $r_{ij} = r_{ji}$, i.e., $\mu_{ij} = \mu_{ji}$, $v_{ij} = v_{ji}$, from Eq. (2.130), it follows that ${}_{(\lambda,\delta)}r_{ij} = {}_{(\lambda,\delta)}r_{ji}$.

(Sufficiency) If ${}_{(\lambda,\delta)}R = ({}_{(\lambda,\delta)}r_{ij})_{n\times n}$ is an intuitionistic fuzzy similarity matrix, then

(1) (Reflexivity) Since ${}_{(\lambda,\delta)}r_{ii} = (1, 0)$, for any $0 \le \lambda, \delta \le 1,\ 0 \le \lambda + \delta \le 1$, $\mu_{ii} \ge \lambda,\ v_{ii} \le \delta$, we have $\mu_{ii} = 1,\ v_{ii} = 0$, i.e., $r_{ii} = (1, 0)$.

(2) (Symmetry) If there exists $r_{ij} \ne r_{ji}$, i.e., $\mu_{ij} \ne \mu_{ji}$ or $v_{ij} \ne v_{ji}$, in this case, without loss of generality, suppose that $\mu_{ij} < \mu_{ji}$, and let $\lambda = (\mu_{ij} + \mu_{ji})/2$. Then $\mu_{ij} < \lambda < \mu_{ji}$, ${}_{\lambda}\mu_{ij} = 0$, ${}_{\lambda}\mu_{ji} = 1$, and thus, ${}_{(\lambda,\delta)}r_{ij} \ne {}_{(\lambda,\delta)}r_{ji}$, which contradicts the condition that ${}_{(\lambda,\delta)}r_{ij} = {}_{(\lambda,\delta)}r_{ji}$, for any i, j. Therefore, $R = (r_{ij})_{n\times n}$ is symmetrical.

In what follows, we introduce the orthogonal principle of intuitionistic fuzzy cluster analysis:

Let $Y = \{y_1, y_2, \ldots, y_n\}$ be a collection of n objects, and $G = \{G_1, G_2, \ldots, G_m\}$ the set of attributes related to the considered objects. Assume that the characteristics of the objects $y_i (i = 1, 2, \ldots, n)$ with respect to the attributes G_j $(j = 1, 2, \ldots, m)$ are represented by the IFSs, shown as follows:

$$y_i = \left\{\langle G_j, \mu_{y_i}(G_j), v_{y_i}(G_j)\rangle | G_j \in G\right\}, i = 1, 2, \ldots, n; \quad j = 1, 2, \ldots, m \quad (2.131)$$

where $\mu_{y_i}(G_j)$ denotes the degree that the object y_i should satisfy the attribute G_j, $v_{y_i}(G_j)$ indicates the degree that the object y_i should not satisfy the attribute G_j, $\pi_{y_i}(G_j) = 1 - \mu_{y_i}(G_j) - v_{y_i}(G_j)$ indicates the indeterminacy degree of the object y_i to the attribute G_j. By Eqs. (2.125) and (2.131), we construct the intuitionistic fuzzy similarity matrix $R = (r_{ij})_{n\times n}$, where r_{ij} is an IFV, and $r_{ij} = (u_{ij}, v_{ij}) = R(y_i, y_j), i = 1, 2, \ldots, n; j = 1, 2, \ldots, m$. After that, the (λ, δ)-cutting matrix ${}_{(\lambda,\delta)}R = ({}_{(\lambda,\delta)}r_{ij})_{n\times n}$ can be determined under the confidence level (λ, δ). If we denote ${}_{(\lambda,\delta)}\overrightarrow{r_j} = ({}_{(\lambda,\delta)}r_{1j}, {}_{(\lambda,\delta)}r_{2j}, \ldots, {}_{(\lambda,\delta)}r_{nj})^T$ as the vector of the jth column of ${}_{(\lambda,\delta)}R$, then ${}_{(\lambda,\delta)}R = ({}_{(\lambda,\delta)}\overrightarrow{r_1}, {}_{(\lambda,\delta)}\overrightarrow{r_2}, \ldots, {}_{(\lambda,\delta)}\overrightarrow{r_n})$.

The orthogonal principle of intuitionistic fuzzy cluster analysis is to determine the orthogonality of the column vectors of (λ, δ)-cutting matrix ${}_{(\lambda,\delta)}R$. Let ${}_{(\lambda,\delta)}\overrightarrow{r_k}$, ${}_{(\lambda,\delta)}\overrightarrow{r_t}$ and ${}_{(\lambda,\delta)}\overrightarrow{r_j}$ $(k, t, j = 1, 2, \ldots, n)$ denote the kth, tth and jth column vectors of ${}_{(\lambda,\delta)}R$ respectively. Then the orthogonal principles for clustering intuitionistic fuzzy information can be classified into the following three categories:

(1) (Direct clustering principle) If

$${}_{(\lambda,\delta)}\overrightarrow{r_k} \cdot {}_{(\lambda,\delta)}\overrightarrow{r_j} = \begin{cases} (1, 1); \\ (1, 0), \end{cases} \quad (2.132)$$

then ${}_{(\lambda,\delta)}\overrightarrow{r_k}$ and ${}_{(\lambda,\delta)}\overrightarrow{r_j}$ are non-orthogonal. In this case, y_k and y_j are clustered into one class.

(2) (Indirect clustering principle) If ${}_{(\lambda,\delta)}\vec{r_k}$ and ${}_{(\lambda,\delta)}\vec{r_j}$ are non-orthogonal, ${}_{(\lambda,\delta)}\vec{r_t}$ and ${}_{(\lambda,\delta)}\vec{r_j}$ are non-orthogonal, then ${}_{(\lambda,\delta)}\vec{r_k}$ and ${}_{(\lambda,\delta)}\vec{r_j}$ are non-orthogonal. In this case, y_k and y_j are clustered into one class.

(3) (Heterogeneous principle) If

$$
{}_{(\lambda,\delta)}\vec{r_k} \cdot {}_{(\lambda,\delta)}\vec{r_j} = \begin{cases} (0, 1); \\ (0, 0), \end{cases} \tag{2.133}
$$

then ${}_{(\lambda,\delta)}\vec{r_k}$ is orthogonal to ${}_{(\lambda,\delta)}\vec{r_j}$. In this case, y_k and y_j do not belong to one class.

Theorem 2.17 (Xu et al. 2011) (Dynamic clustering theorem) If the objects y_k and y_j are clustered into one class by the orthogonal principle under the confidence level (λ_1, δ_1), then when $\lambda_2 < \lambda_1, \delta_2 > \delta_1$, y_k and y_j are still clustered into one class under the confidence level (λ_2, δ_2).

Proof Since the objects y_k and y_j are clustered into one class by the orthogonal principle under the confidence level (λ_1, δ_1), then two column vectors ${}_{(\lambda_1,\delta_1)}\vec{r_k}$ and ${}_{(\lambda_1,\delta_1)}\vec{r_j}$ of (λ_1, δ_1)-cutting matrix ${}_{(\lambda,\delta)}R$ are non-orthogonal, i.e., the inner product of ${}_{(\lambda_1,\delta_1)}\vec{r_k}$ and ${}_{(\lambda_1,\delta_1)}\vec{r_j}$ is equal to $(1, 0)$ or $(1, 1)$. Suppose that in the ith line, there exist $\mu_{ik} > \lambda_1$ and $\mu_{ij} > \lambda_1$. Then ${}_{\lambda_1}\mu_{ik} = 1$ and ${}_{\lambda_1}\mu_{ij} = 1$, and if $\lambda_2 < \lambda_1, \delta_2 > \delta_1$, $\mu_{ik} > \lambda_2$ and $\mu_{ij} > \lambda_2$, then ${}_{\lambda_2}\mu_{ik} = 1$ and ${}_{\lambda_2}\mu_{ij} = 1$ under the confidence level (λ_2, δ_2). Thus, two column vectors ${}_{(\lambda_2,\delta_2)}\vec{r_k}$ and ${}_{(\lambda_2,\delta_2)}\vec{r_j}$ are also non-orthogonal, i.e., y_k and y_j are clustered into one class.

Based on the orthogonal principle, Xu et al. (2011) presented an orthogonal algorithm for clustering intuitionistic fuzzy information:

Algorithm 2.6

Step 1 Let $Y = \{y_1, y_2, \ldots, y_n\}$ and $G = \{G_1, G_2, \ldots, G_m\}$ be defined as in Sect. 2.1, and assume that the characteristics of the objects y_i $(i = 1, 2, \ldots, n)$ with respect to the attributes $G_j (j = 1, 2, \ldots, m)$ are represented as in Eq. (2.131).

Step 2 Construct the intuitionistic fuzzy similarity matrix $R = (r_{ij})_{n\times n}$ by using Eqs. (2.125) and (2.131), where r_{ij} is an IFV, and $r_{ij} = (u_{ij}, v_{ij}) = R(y_i, y_j)$, $i = 1, 2, \ldots, n; j = 1, 2, \ldots, m$.

Step 3 Determine the (λ, δ)-cutting matrix ${}_{(\lambda,\delta)}R = ({}_{(\lambda,\delta)}r_{ij})_{n\times n}$ of $R = (r_{ij})_{n\times n}$ by using Eq. (2.130) under the confidence level (λ, δ).

Step 4 Calculate the inner products of the column vectors of the (λ, δ)-cutting matrix ${}_{(\lambda,\delta)}R$, and then check whether each pair of the column vectors are orthogonal or not.

Step 5 Cluster the objects $y_i (i = 1, 2, \ldots, n)$ by the orthogonal principles.

Example 2.5 (Xu et al. 2011) In the supply chain management, supplier strategies are to formulate the different levels of strategies considering the relationships among the suppliers. From the procurement point of view, the supplier classification is to

Table 2.6 The characteristics of the suppliers

	G_1	G_2	G_3	G_4	G_5	G_6
y_1	(0.61,0.32)	(0.24,0.53)	(0.14,0.76)	(0.77,0.18)	(0.36,0.62)	(0.54,0.42)
y_2	(0.18,0.65)	(0.81,0.17)	(0.12,0.84)	(0.62,0.24)	(0.21,0.68)	(0.43,0.37)
y_3	(0.62,0.11)	(0.26,0.62)	(0.33,0.25)	(0.91,0.08)	(0.22,0.75)	(0.12,0.86)
y_4	(0.45,0.35)	(0.62,0.24)	(0.74,0.15)	(0.41,0.52)	(0.18,0.81)	(0.32,0.65)
y_5	(0.13,0.76)	(0.26,0.75)	(0.24,0.68)	(0.81,0.12)	(0.74,0.13)	(0.55,0.36)
y_6	(0.32,0.45)	(0.45,0.25)	(0.73,0.24)	(0.62,0.36)	(0.12,0.82)	(0.22,0.75)
y_7	(0.55,0.35)	(0.24,0.75)	(0.03,0.84)	(0.39,0.61)	(0.49,0.28)	(0.85,0.14)
y_8	(0.65,0.25)	(0.38,0.45)	(0.92,0.06)	(0.24,0.57)	(0.82,0.17)	(0.04,0.92)

divide the suppliers into several groups in the supply markets, which is based on a variety of different factors. It aims at implementing the different supplier strategies according to the different types of suppliers.

A purchasing company wants to classify its eight suppliers y_i $(i = 1, 2, \ldots, 8)$, The six factors which are considered here in assessing the suppliers are: (1) G_1: Prices; (2) G_2: Product quality; (3) G_3: The degree of market impacting; (4) G_4: After-sales service; (5) G_5: Current assets efficiency; and (6) G_6: Deliveries. Assume that the characteristics of the suppliers y_i $(i = 1, 2, \ldots, 8)$ with respect to the factors G_j $(j = 1, 2, \ldots, 6)$ are represented by the IFSs, shown as in Table 2.6 (Xu et al. 2011).

In what follows, we utilize the intuitionistic fuzzy orthogonal clustering algorithm to classify the eight suppliers, which involves the following steps (Xu et al. 2011):

Step 1 By Eqs. (2.125) and (2.131), we first calculate $y_1 \cdot y_2 = (0.62, 0.24)$, $(y_1 \circ y_2)^c = (0.75, 0.14)$, $R(y_1, y_2) = (0.62, 0.24)$, and then calculate the others in a similar way. Consequently, we get the intuitionistic fuzzy similarity matrix:

$$R = \begin{pmatrix} (1,0) & (0.62,0.24) & (0.62,0.26) & (0.45,0.36) & (0.68,0.24) & (0.62,0.36) & (0.55,0.35) & (0.45,0.38) \\ (0.62,0.24) & (1,0) & (0.62,0.24) & (0.62,0.24) & (0.62,0.24) & (0.62,0.25) & (0.43,0.37) & (0.37,0.45) \\ (0.62,0.26) & (0.62,0.24) & (1,0) & (0.45,0.25) & (0.62,0.26) & (0.62,0.25) & (0.55,0.35) & (0.62,0.25) \\ (0.45,0.36) & (0.62,0.24) & (0.45,0.25) & (1,0) & (0.36,0.52) & (0.73,0.24) & (0.45,0.41) & (0.65,0.32) \\ (0.68,0.24) & (0.62,0.24) & (0.62,0.26) & (0.36,0.52) & (1,0) & (0.45,0.36) & (0.55,0.28) & (0.45,0.38) \\ (0.62,0.36) & (0.62,0.25) & (0.62,0.25) & (0.73,0.24) & (0.45,0.36) & (1,0) & (0.39,0.45) & (0.73,0.24) \\ (0.55,0.35) & (0.43,0.37) & (0.55,0.35) & (0.45,0.41) & (0.55,0.28) & (0.39,0.45) & (1,0) & (0.55,0.38) \\ (0.45,0.38) & (0.37,0.45) & (0.62,0.25) & (0.65,0.32) & (0.45,0.38) & (0.73,0.24) & (0.55,0.38) & (1,0) \end{pmatrix}$$

Step 2 Take the different values of the confidence level (λ, δ) from the elements of R, and determine the (λ, δ)-cutting matrix ${}_{(\lambda,\delta)}R = ({}_{(\lambda,\delta)}r_{ij})_{8\times 8}$ of R by using Eq. (2.130) under the different values of the confidence level (λ, δ).

Then we classify the suppliers y_i $(i = 1, 2, \ldots, 8)$ by the orthogonal principles. Concretely, we have

(1) If $(\lambda, \delta) = (1, 0)$, then each pair of the column vectors of the $(1, 0)$-cutting matrix ${}_{(1,0)}R$ are orthogonal. Thus the suppliers y_i $(i = 1, 2, \ldots, 8)$ are clustered into eight classes: $\{y_1\}, \{y_2\}, \{y_3\}, \{y_4\}, \{y_5\}, \{y_6\}, \{y_7\}, \{y_8\}$.

(2) If $(\lambda, \delta) = (0.73, 0.24)$, then we get the $(0.73, 0.24)$-cutting matrix:

$$
{}_{(0.73,0.24)}R = \begin{pmatrix}
(1,0) & (0,0) & (0,1) & (0,1) & (0,0) & (0,1) & (0,1) & (0,1) \\
(0,0) & (1,0) & (0,0) & (0,0) & (0,0) & (0,1) & (0,1) & (0,1) \\
(0,1) & (0,0) & (1,0) & (0,1) & (0,1) & (0,1) & (0,1) & (0,1) \\
(0,1) & (0,0) & (0,1) & (1,0) & (0,1) & (1,0) & (0,1) & (0,1) \\
(0,0) & (0,0) & (0,1) & (0,1) & (1,0) & (0,1) & (0,1) & (0,1) \\
(0,1) & (0,1) & (0,1) & (1,0) & (0,1) & (1,0) & (0,1) & (1,0) \\
(0,1) & (0,1) & (0,1) & (0,1) & (0,1) & (0,1) & (1,0) & (0,1) \\
(0,1) & (0,1) & (0,1) & (0,1) & (0,1) & (1.0) & (0,1) & (1,0)
\end{pmatrix}
$$

Calculating the inner products of all pairs of the column vectors of ${}_{(0.73,0.24)}R$, we know that ${}_{(0.73,0.24)}\vec{r}_1$, ${}_{(0.73,0.24)}\vec{r}_2$, ${}_{(0.73,0.24)}\vec{r}_3$, ${}_{(0.73,0.24)}\vec{r}_5$ and ${}_{(0.73,0.24)}\vec{r}_7$ are orthogonal to each other column of ${}_{(0.65,0.32)}R$; ${}_{(0.73,0.24)}\vec{r}_4$, ${}_{(0.73,0.24)}\vec{r}_6$ and ${}_{(0.73,0.24)}\vec{r}_8$ are non-orthogonal. Then the suppliers y_i $(i = 1, 2, \ldots, 8)$ are clustered into six classes: $\{y_1\}, \{y_2\}, \{y_3\}, \{y_5\}, \{y_7\}, \{y_4, y_6, y_8\}$.

(3) If $(\lambda, \delta) = (0.68, 0.24)$, then we get the $(0.68, 0.24)$-cutting matrix:

$$
{}_{(0.68,0.24)}R = \begin{pmatrix}
(1,0) & (0,0) & (0,1) & (0,1) & (1,0) & (0,1) & (0,1) & (0,1) \\
(0,0) & (1,0) & (0,0) & (0,0) & (0,0) & (0,1) & (0,1) & (0,1) \\
(0,1) & (0,0) & (1,0) & (0,1) & (0,1) & (0,1) & (0,1) & (0,1) \\
(0,1) & (0,0) & (0,1) & (1,0) & (0,1) & (1,0) & (0,1) & (0,1) \\
(1,0) & (0,0) & (0,1) & (0,1) & (1,0) & (0,1) & (0,1) & (0,1) \\
(0,1) & (0,0) & (0,1) & (1,0) & (0,1) & (1,0) & (0,1) & (1.0) \\
(0,1) & (0,1) & (0,1) & (0,1) & (0,1) & (0,1) & (1,0) & (0,1) \\
(0,1) & (0,1) & (0,1) & (0,1) & (0,1) & (1,0) & (0,1) & (1,0)
\end{pmatrix}
$$

Calculating the inner products of all pairs of the column vectors of ${}_{(0.68,0.24)}R$, we can see that ${}_{(0.68,0.24)}\vec{r}_1$ is non-orthogonal to both ${}_{(0.68,0.24)}\vec{r}_3$ and ${}_{(0.68,0.24)}\vec{r}_5$; ${}_{(0.68,0.24)}\vec{r}_4$ is non-orthogonal to both ${}_{(0.68,0.24)}\vec{r}_6$ and ${}_{(0.68,0.24)}\vec{r}_8$; ${}_{(0.68,0.24)}\vec{r}_3$, ${}_{(0.68,0.24)}\vec{r}_2$ and ${}_{(0.68,0.24)}\vec{r}_7$ are orthogonal to each other column of ${}_{(0.68,0.24)}R$. Then the suppliers y_i $(i = 1, 2, \ldots, 8)$ are clustered into four classes:

$$
\{y_1, y_5\}, \{y_2\}, \{y_3\}, \{y_7\}, \{y_4, y_6, y_8\}
$$

For the case where $(\lambda, \delta) = (0.65, 0.32)$, we can also get the above clustering result.

(4) If $(\lambda, \delta) = (0.62, 0.36)$, then we get the (0.62, 0.36)-cutting matrix:

$$
{}_{(0.62,0.36)}R = \begin{pmatrix}
(1,0) & (1,0) & (1,1) & (0,1) & (1,0) & (1,1) & (0,1) & (0,1) \\
(1,0) & (1,0) & (1,0) & (1,0) & (1,0) & (1,1) & (0,1) & (0,1) \\
(1,0) & (1,0) & (1,0) & (0,1) & (1,1) & (1,1) & (0,1) & (1,1) \\
(0,1) & (1,0) & (0,1) & (1,0) & (0,1) & (1,0) & (0,1) & (1,1) \\
(1,0) & (1,0) & (1,1) & (0,1) & (1,0) & (0,1) & (0,1) & (0,1) \\
(1,1) & (1,1) & (1,1) & (1,0) & (0,1) & (1,0) & (0,1) & (1,0) \\
(0,1) & (0,1) & (0,0) & (0,1) & (0,1) & (0,1) & (1,0) & (0,1) \\
(0,1) & (0,1) & (1,1) & (1,0) & (0,1) & (1,0) & (0,1) & (1,0)
\end{pmatrix}
$$

Since ${}_{(0.62,0.36)}\vec{r}_1$ is non-orthogonal to ${}_{(0.62,0.36)}\vec{r}_2$, ${}_{(0.62,0.36)}\vec{r}_3$, ${}_{(0.62,0.36)}\vec{r}_4$, ${}_{(0.62,0.36)}\vec{r}_5$, ${}_{(0.62,0.36)}\vec{r}_6$, ${}_{(0.62,0.36)}\vec{r}_8$, and ${}_{(0.62,0.36)}\vec{r}_1$ is orthogonal to ${}_{(0.62,0.36)}\vec{r}_7$, then the suppliers y_i $(i = 1, 2, \ldots, 8)$ are clustered into two classes: $\{y_1, y_2, y_3, y_4, y_5, y_6, y_8\}$, $\{y_7\}$.

For the cases where $(\lambda, \delta) = (0.62, 0.26), (0.62, 0.24)$, we can get the same clustering result as above.

(5) If $(\lambda, \delta) = (0.55, 0.38)$, then we get the (0.55, 0.38)-cutting matrix:

$$
{}_{(0.55,0.38)}R = \begin{pmatrix}
(1,0) & (1,0) & (1,0) & (0,0) & (1,0) & (1,0) & (1,0) & (0,0) \\
(1,0) & (1,0) & (1,0) & (1,0) & (1,0) & (1,0) & (0,0) & (0,1) \\
(1,0) & (1,0) & (1,0) & (0,0) & (1,0) & (1,0) & (1,0) & (1,0) \\
(0,0) & (1,0) & (0,0) & (1,0) & (0,1) & (1,0) & (0,1) & (1,0) \\
(1,0) & (1,0) & (1,0) & (0,1) & (1,0) & (0,0) & (1,0) & (0,0) \\
(1,0) & (1,0) & (1,0) & (1,0) & (0,0) & (1,0) & (0,1) & (1,0) \\
(1,0) & (0,0) & (1,0) & (0,1) & (1,0) & (0,1) & (1,0) & (1,0) \\
(0,0) & (0,1) & (1,0) & (1,0) & (0,0) & (1,0) & (1,0) & (1,0)
\end{pmatrix}
$$

Since the inner products of all pairs of the column vectors of ${}_{(0.55,0.38)}R$ are $(1, 0)$, i.e., all pairs of the column vectors of ${}_{(0.55,0.38)}R$ are non-orthogonal, the suppliers y_i $(i = 1, 2, \ldots, 8)$ are clustered into one class: $\{y_1, y_2, y_3, y_4, y_5, y_6, y_7, y_8\}$.

In the other cases where (λ, δ)=(0.55, 0.35), (0.55,0.28), (0.45,0.41), (0.45,0.38), (0.45,0.36), (0.43,0.37), (0.39,0.45), (0.37,0.45) or (0.36,0.52) or (0.36,0.52), all the suppliers y_i $(i = 1, 2, \ldots, 8)$ are also clustered into one class.

If we use the transitive closure clustering algorithm (Algorithm 2.1) to classify the suppliers, then we first derive the intuitionistic fuzzy equivalence matrix R^* after the finite times of compositions of R:

$$
R^* = \begin{pmatrix}
(1,0) & (0.62,0.24) & (0.62,0.24) & (0.62,0.24) & (0.68,0.24) & (0.62,0.24) & (0.55,0.28) & (0.62,0.24) \\
 & (1,0) & (0.62,0,24) & (0.62,0.24) & (0.62,0.24) & (0.62,0.24) & (0.55,0.28) & (0.62,0.24) \\
 & & (1,0) & (0.62,0.24) & (0.62,0.24) & (0.62,0.24) & (0.55,0.28) & (0.62,0.24) \\
 & & & (1,0) & (0.62,0.24) & (0.73,0.24) & (0.55,0.28) & (0.73,0.24) \\
 & & & & (1,0) & (0.62,0.24) & (0.55,0.28) & (0.62,0.24) \\
 & & & & & (1,0) & (0.55,0.28) & (0.73,0.24) \\
 & & & & & & (1,0) & (0.55,0.28) \\
 & & & & & & & (1,0)
\end{pmatrix}
$$

and then take the different values of the confidence level λ from the elements of R^*, by which we classify the suppliers y_i $(i = 1, 2, \ldots, 8)$. Concretely, we have

(1) If $0.73 < \lambda \leq 1$, then the suppliers $y_i (i = 1, 2, \ldots, 8)$ are clustered into eight classes:

$$\{y_1\}, \{y_2\}, \{y_3\}, \{y_4\}, \{y_5\}, \{y_6\}, \{y_7\}, \{y_8\}$$

(2) If $0.68 < \lambda \leq 0.73$, then the suppliers y_i $(i = 1, 2, \ldots, 8)$ are clustered into six classes:

$$\{y_1\}, \{y_2\}, \{y_3\}, \{y_5\}, \{y_7\}, \{y_4, y_6, y_8\}$$

(3) If $0.62 < \lambda \leq 0.68$, then the suppliers $y_i (i = 1, 2, \ldots, 8)$ are clustered into four classes:

$$\{y_1, y_5\}, \{y_2\}, \{y_3\}, \{y_7\}, \{y_4, y_6, y_8\}$$

(4) If $0.55 < \lambda \leq 0.62$, then the suppliers $y_i (i = 1, 2, \ldots, 8)$ are clustered into two classes:

$$\{y_1, y_2, y_3, y_4, y_5, y_6, y_8\}, \{y_7\}$$

(5) If $0 \leq \lambda \leq 0.55$, then the suppliers $y_i (i = 1, 2, \ldots, 8)$ are of the same class:

$$\{y_1, y_2, y_3, y_4, y_5, y_6, y_7, y_8\}$$

From the above numerical analysis, we can see that the intuitionistic fuzzy orthogonal clustering algorithm and the transitive closure clustering algorithm derive the same clustering results under the different confidence levels. Since the intuitionistic fuzzy similarity matrix generally does not has the transitivity property, and thus, the transitive closure clustering algorithm needs to derive the intuitionistic fuzzy equivalence matrix after the finite times of compositions of the intuitionistic fuzzy similarity matrix, and then get the λ-cutting matrix under the confidence level λ, by which the considered objects are clustered. However, the composition process of the transitive closure clustering algorithm is somewhat cumbersome, and is not easy to calculate; while the intuitionistic fuzzy orthogonal clustering algorithm only needs to derive the (λ, δ)-cutting matrix of the intuitionistic fuzzy similarity matrix according to the confidence level (λ, δ), and then directly clusters the considered objects by judging the orthogonality of the column vectors of the cutting matrix. The intuitionistic fuzzy orthogonal clustering algorithm does not need to take time to derive the intuitionistic fuzzy equivalence matrix, and is very easy to be implemented on a computer, and thus, it is more straightforward and convenient than the transitive closure clustering algorithm in practical applications.

2.5 Intuitionistic Fuzzy C-Means Clustering Algorithms

The algorithms presented previously are straightforward, but cannot provide the information about membership degrees of the objects to each cluster. To overcome this drawback, Xu and Wu (2010) developed an intuitionistic fuzzy C-means algorithm to cluster IFSs, which is based on the well-known fuzzy C-means clustering method (Bezdek 1981) and the basic distance measures between IFSs. Then, they extended the algorithm for clustering IVIFSs.

Here, we first introduce the intuitionistic fuzzy C-means (IFCM) algorithm for IFSs. We take the normalized Euclidean distance between the IFSs Z_i and Z_j:

$$d_{NE}(Z_i, Z_j) = \sqrt{\frac{1}{2n}\sum_{j=1}^{n}((\mu_{Z_i}(x_j) - \mu_{Z_j}(x_j))^2 + (v_{Z_i}(x_j) - v_{Z_j}(x_j))^2 + (\pi_{Z_i}(x_j) - \pi_{Z_j}(x_j))^2} \tag{2.134}$$

as the proximity function of the IFCM algorithm. Then the objective function of the IFCM algorithm can be formulated as follows:

$$\min J_m(U, V) = \sum_{j=1}^{p}\sum_{i=1}^{c} u_{ij}^m d_{NE}^2(A_j, V_i) \tag{2.135}$$

Subject to

$$\sum_{i=1}^{c} u_{ij} = 1,\ 1 \le j \le p$$
$$u_{ij} \ge 0,\ 1 \le i \le c,\ 1 \le j \le p$$
$$\sum_{j=1}^{p} u_{ij} > 0,\ 1 \le i \le c$$

where $\overline{A} = \{A_1, A_2, \ldots, A_p\}$ are p IFSs each with n elements, c is the number of clusters ($1 \le c \le p$), and $V = \{V_1, V_2, \ldots, V_c\}$ are the prototypical IFSs, i.e., the centroids, of the clusters. The parameter m is the fuzzy factor ($m > 1$), u_{ij} is the membership degree of the jth sample A_j to the ith cluster, $U = (u_{ij})_{c\times p}$ is a matrix of $c \times p$.

To solve the optimization problem in Eq. (2.135), we employ the Lagrange multiplier method (Ito and Kunisch 2008). Let

$$L = \sum_{j=1}^{p}\sum_{i=1}^{c} u_{ij}^m d_{NE}^2(A_j, V_i) - \sum_{j=1}^{p} \varsigma_j(\sum_{i=1}^{c} u_{ij} - 1) \tag{2.136}$$

where

$$d_{NE}^2(A_j, V_i) = \frac{1}{2n}\sum_{l=1}^{n}((\mu_{A_j}(x_l) - \mu_{V_i}(x_l))^2 + (v_{A_j}(x_l) - v_{V_i}(x_l))^2 + (\pi_{A_j}(x_l) - \pi_{V_i}(x_l))^2) \tag{2.137}$$

Furthermore, let

$$\begin{cases} \frac{\partial L}{\partial u_{ij}} = 0, 1 \le i \le c, 1 \le j \le p \\ \frac{\partial L}{\partial \varsigma_j} = 0, 1 \le j \le p \end{cases}$$

we have

$$u_{ij} = \frac{1}{\sum_{r=1}^{c}\left(\frac{d_{NE}(A_j, V_i)}{d_{NE}(A_j, V_r)}\right)^{\frac{2}{m-1}}}, 1 \le i \le c, 1 \le j \le p \tag{2.138}$$

Next we compute V, the prototypical IFSs. Let

$$\frac{\partial L}{\partial \mu_{V_i}(x_l)} = \frac{\partial L}{\partial v_{V_i}(x_l)} = \frac{\partial L}{\partial \pi_{V_i}(x_l)} = 0, 1 \le i \le c, 1 \le l \le n$$

We get

$$\mu_{V_i}(x_l) = \frac{\sum_{j=1}^{p} u_{ij}^m \mu_{A_j}(x_l)}{\sum_{j=1}^{p} u_{ij}^m}, 1 \le i \le c, 1 \le l \le n \tag{2.139}$$

$$v_{V_i}(x_l) = \frac{\sum_{j=1}^{p} u_{ij}^m v_{A_j}(x_l)}{\sum_{j=1}^{p} u_{ij}^m}, 1 \le i \le c, 1 \le l \le n \tag{2.140}$$

$$\pi_{V_i}(x_l) = \frac{\sum_{j=1}^{p} u_{ij}^m \pi_{A_j}(x_l)}{\sum_{j=1}^{p} u_{ij}^m}, 1 \le i \le c, 1 \le l \le n \tag{2.141}$$

For simplicity, we define a weighted average operator for IFSs as follows: Let $w = (w_1, w_2, \ldots, w_p)^T$ be a set of weights for the IFSs A_j $(j = 1, 2, \ldots, p)$, respectively, with $w_j \in [0, 1], j = 1, 2, \ldots, n$, and $\sum_{j=1}^{p} w_j = 1$. Then the weighted average operator f is defined as:

$$f(A, w) = \left\{ \langle x_l, \sum_{j=1}^{p} w_j \mu_{A_j}(x_l), \sum_{j=1}^{p} w_j v_{A_j}(x_l) \rangle \middle| 1 \le l \le n \right\} \tag{2.142}$$

According to Eqs. (2.139)–(2.142), if we let

$$w^{(i)} = \left\{ \frac{u_{i1}}{\sum_{j=1}^{p} u_{ij}}, \frac{u_{i2}}{\sum_{j=1}^{p} u_{ij}}, \ldots, \frac{u_{ip}}{\sum_{j=1}^{p} u_{ij}} \right\}, 1 \leq i \leq c \tag{2.143}$$

then the prototypical IFSs $V = \{V_1, V_2, \ldots, V_c\}$ of the IFCM algorithm can be computed as:

$$\begin{aligned} V_i &= f(\overline{A}, w^{(i)}) \\ &= \left\{ \left\langle x_s, \sum_{j=1}^{p} w_j^{(i)} \mu_{A_j}(x_s), \sum_{j=1}^{p} w_j^{(i)} v_{A_j}(x_s) \right\rangle \middle| 1 \leq s \leq n \right\}, 1 \leq i \leq c \end{aligned} \tag{2.144}$$

Since Eqs. (2.138) and (2.144) are computationally interdependent, we exploit an iterative procedure similar to the fuzzy C-means to solve these equations. The steps are as follows:

Algorithm 2.7 (IFCM algorithm)

Step 1 Initialize the seed $V(0)$, let $k = 0$, and set $\varepsilon > 0$.
Step 2 Calculate $U(k) = (u_{ij}(k))_{c \times p}$, where

(1) If for all j, r, $d_1(A_j, V_r(k)) > 0$, then

$$u_{ij}(k) = \frac{1}{\sum_{r=1}^{c} \left(\frac{d_{NE}(A_j, V_i(k))}{d_{NE}(A_j, V_r(k))} \right)^{\frac{2}{m-1}}}, 1 \leq i \leq c, 1 \leq j \leq p \tag{2.145}$$

(2) If there exist j and r such that $d_{NE}(A_j, V_r(k)) = 0$, then let $u_{rj}(k) = 1$ and $u_{ij}(k) = 0$, for all $i \neq r$.

Step 3 Calculate $V(k+1) = \{V_1(k+1), V_2(k+1), \ldots, V_c(k+1)\}$, where

$$V_i(k+1) = f(A, w^{(i)}(k+1)), 1 \leq i \leq c \tag{2.146}$$

where

$$w^{(i)}(k+1) = \left\{ \frac{u_{i1}(k)}{\sum_{j=1}^{p} u_{ij}(k)}, \frac{u_{i2}(k)}{\sum_{j=1}^{p} u_{ij}(k)}, \ldots, \frac{u_{ip}(k)}{\sum_{j=1}^{p} u_{ij}(k)} \right\}, 1 \leq i \leq c \tag{2.147}$$

Step 4 If $\sum_{i=1}^{c} \frac{d_1(V_i(k), V_i(k+1))}{c} < \varepsilon$, then end the algorithm; otherwise, let $k := k + 1$, and return to Step 2.

For cases where the collected data are expressed as IVIFSs, Xu and Wu (2010) extended Algorithm 2.7 to the interval-valued intuitionistic fuzzy C-means (IIFCM) algorithm. We take the basic distance measure (2.134) as the proximity function of the IIFCM algorithm, then the objective function of the IIFCM algorithm can be formulated as follows:

$$\min J_m(U,\tilde{V}) = \sum_{j=1}^{p}\sum_{i=1}^{c} u_{ij}^m d_{NE}^2(\tilde{A}_j,\tilde{V}_i) \tag{2.148}$$

Subject to

$$\sum_{i=1}^{c} u_{ij} = 1,\ 1 \le j \le p$$
$$u_{ij} \ge 0,\ 1 \le i \le c,\ 1 \le j \le p$$
$$\sum_{j=1}^{p} u_{ij} > 0,\ 1 \le i \le c$$

where $\tilde{A}_j$ $(j = 1, 2, \ldots, p)$ are p IVIFSs each with n elements, c is the number of clusters $(1 < c < p)$, and $\tilde{V}_i$ $(i = 1, 2, \ldots, c)$ are the prototypical IVIFSs of the clusters. The parameter m is the fuzzy factor $(m > 1)$, u_{ij} is the membership degree of the jth sample $\tilde{A}_j$ to the ith cluster, $U = (u_{ij})_{c\times p}$ is a matrix of $c \times p$.

To solve the optimization problem in Eq. (2.148), we also employ the Lagrange multiplier method. Let

$$L = \sum_{j=1}^{p}\sum_{i=1}^{c} u_{ij}^m d_{wE}^2(\tilde{A}_j,\tilde{V}_i) - \sum_{j=1}^{p} \varsigma_j\Big(\sum_{i=1}^{c} u_{ij} - 1\Big) \tag{2.149}$$

where

$$\begin{aligned} & d_{wE}^2(\tilde{A}_j,\tilde{V}_i) \\ & = \frac{1}{4}\sum_{l=1}^{n} w_l\Big(((\mu_{\tilde{A}_j}^-(x_l)) - \mu_{\tilde{V}_i}^-(x_l))^2 + (\mu_{\tilde{A}_j}^+(x_l) - \mu_{\tilde{V}_i}^+(x_l))^2 + (v_{\tilde{A}_j}^-(x_l) - v_{\tilde{V}_i}^-(x_l))^2 \\ & \quad + (v_{\tilde{A}_j}^+(x_l) - v_{\tilde{V}_i}^+(x_l))^2 + (\pi_{\tilde{A}_j}^-(x_l) - \pi_{\tilde{V}_i}^-(x_l))^2 + (\pi_{\tilde{A}_j}^+(x_l) - \pi_{\tilde{V}_i}^+(x_l))^2\Big) \end{aligned} \tag{2.150}$$

Similar to Algorithm 2.7, we can establish the system of partial differential functions of L as follows:

$$\begin{cases} \dfrac{\partial L}{\partial u_{ij}} = 0, 1 \le i \le c, 1 \le j \le p \\ \dfrac{\partial L}{\partial \lambda_j} = 0, 1 \le j \le p \\ \dfrac{\partial L}{\partial \mu^-_{\tilde{V}_i}(x_l)} = \dfrac{\partial L}{\partial v^-_{\tilde{V}_i}(x_l)} = \dfrac{\partial L}{\partial \pi^-_{\tilde{V}_i}(x_l)} = 0, 1 \le i \le c, 1 \le l \le n \\ \dfrac{\partial L}{\partial \mu^+_{\tilde{V}_i}(x_l)} = \dfrac{\partial L}{\partial v^+_{\tilde{V}_i}(x_l)} = \dfrac{\partial L}{\partial \pi^+_{\tilde{V}_i}(x_l)} = 0, 1 \le i \le c, 1 \le l \le n \end{cases}$$

The solution for the above equation system is:

$$u_{ij} = \frac{1}{\sum_{r=1}^{c} \left(\dfrac{d_{wE}(\tilde{A}_j, \tilde{V}_i)}{d_{wE}(\tilde{A}_j, \tilde{V}_r)} \right)^{\frac{2}{m-1}}} \tag{2.151}$$

$$\tilde{V}_i = \tilde{f}(\tilde{A}, w^{(i)}) = \left\{ \left\langle x_k, \left[\sum_{j=1}^{p} w_j^{(i)} \mu^-_{\tilde{A}_j}(x_l), \sum_{j=1}^{p} w_j^{(i)} \mu^+_{\tilde{A}_j}(x_l) \right], \left[\sum_{j=1}^{p} w_j^{(i)} v^-_{\tilde{A}_j}(x_l), \sum_{j=1}^{p} w_j^{(i)} v^+_{\tilde{A}_j}(x_l) \right] \right\rangle \middle| 1 \le l \le n \right\}, 1 \le i \le c \tag{2.152}$$

where

$$w^{(i)} = \left\{ \frac{u_{i1}}{\sum_{j=1}^{p} u_{ij}}, \frac{u_{i2}}{\sum_{j=1}^{p} u_{ij}}, \ldots, \frac{u_{ip}}{\sum_{j=1}^{p} u_{ij}} \right\}, 1 \le i \le c \tag{2.153}$$

Because Eqs. (2.152) and (2.153) are computationally interdependent, we also exploit an iteration procedure as follows:

Algorithm 2.8 (IIFCM algorithm)

Step 1 Initialize the seed $\tilde{V}(0)$, let $k = 0$, and set $\varepsilon > 0$.
Step 2 Calculate $U(k) = (u_{ij}(k))_{c \times p}$, where

(1) If for all j, r, $d_{wE}(\tilde{A}_j, \tilde{V}_r(k)) > 0$, then

$$u_{ij}(k) = \frac{1}{\sum_{r=1}^{c} \left(\frac{d_{wE}(\tilde{A}_j, \tilde{V}_i(k))}{d_{wE}(\tilde{A}_j, \tilde{V}_r(k))} \right)^{\frac{2}{m-1}}}, 1 \le i \le c, 1 \le j \le p \tag{2.154}$$

(2) If there exist j and r such that $d_{wE}(\tilde{A}_j, \tilde{V}_r(k)) = 0$, then let $u_{rj}(k) = 1$ and $u_{ij}(k) = 0$ for $i \neq r$.

Step 3 Calculate $\tilde{V}(k+1) = \left\{\tilde{V}_1(k+1), \tilde{V}_2(k+1), \ldots, \tilde{V}_c(k+1)\right\}$, where

$$\tilde{V}_i(k+1) = \tilde{f}(\tilde{A}, w^{(i)}(k+1)), 1 \leq i \leq c \tag{2.155}$$

$$w^{(i)}(k+1) = \left\{\frac{u_{i1}(k)}{\sum_{j=1}^{p} u_{ij}(k)}, \frac{u_{i2}(k)}{\sum_{j=1}^{p} u_{ij}(k)}, \ldots, \frac{u_{ip}(k)}{\sum_{j=1}^{p} u_{ij}(k)}\right\}, 1 \leq i \leq c \tag{2.156}$$

Step 4 If $\sum_{i=1}^{c} \frac{d_{wE}\left(\tilde{V}_i(k), \tilde{V}_i(k+1)\right)}{c} < \varepsilon$, then end the algorithm; otherwise, let $k := k + 1$, and return to Step 2.

Example 2.6 (Xu and Wu 2010) We conduct experiments on both the real-world and simulated data sets (Xu et al. 2008) in order to demonstrate the effectiveness of Algorithm 2.7 for IFSs.

Below we first introduce the experimental tool, the experimental data sets, and the cluster validity measures, respectively:

(1) Experimental tool. In the experiments, we use Algorithm 2.7 implemented by ourselves in C language. The parameters that can be set in Algorithm 2.7 are shown in Table 2.7 (Xu and Wu 2010).

Note that if we let $\pi(x) = 0$ for any $x \in X$, then Algorithm 2.7 reduces to the traditional fuzzy C-means (FCM) algorithm. Therefore, we can use the IFCM tool to compare the performance of both Algorithm 2.7 and the FCM algorithm.

(2) Experimental data sets. We use two kinds of data in our experiments. The car data set contains the information of ten new cars to be classified in the Guangzhou car market in Guangdong, China. We also use the simulated data set for the purpose of comparison. All these data are shown as in Example 2.2 (Table 2.2).

(3) Cluster validity measure. One of the unavoidable problems for Algorithm 2.7 is the setting of the parameter c, i.e., the number of the clusters. To meet this challenge, here we use two relative measures for fuzzy cluster validity given by Nasibov and Ulutagay (2007): Partition Coefficient (PC) and Classification Entropy (CE). The descriptions of these two measures are shown in Table 2.8 (Xu and Wu 2010).

Now we utilize Algorithm 2.7 to cluster the ten new cars y_i $(i = 1, 2, \ldots, 10)$, which involves the following steps (Xu and Wu 2010):

Step 1 Let $c = 3$ and $\varepsilon = 0.005$. Randomly select the initial centroid $V(0)$ from the data set, say for instance,

$$V(0) = \begin{bmatrix} y_9 \\ y_{10} \\ y_8 \end{bmatrix}$$

Table 2.7 IFCM parameters

Parameters	Explanation
f	The input file name
c	The number of clusters, the default value is 3
m	The fuzzy factor, the default value is 2
w	The type of the sample weights, 0-equal (default), 1-user specified
s	The type of the initial centroids, 0-random (default), 1-user specified
i	The maximal number of iterations until convergence, the default value is 100
t	The threshold for stopping the iterations, the default value is 0.001

Table 2.8 Descriptions of two cluster validity criteria

Validity criteria	Functional description	Optimal cluster number
Partition coefficient	$V_{PC} = \frac{1}{p}\sum\limits_{i=1}^{c}\sum\limits_{j=1}^{p} u_{ij}^2$	$\arg\max_c(V_{PC}, U, c)$
Classification entropy	$V_{CE} = -\frac{1}{p}\sum\limits_{i=1}^{c}\sum\limits_{j=1}^{p} u_{ij}\log u_{ij}$	$\arg\min_c(V_{CE}, U, c)$

where p is the number of samples in the data set, and c is the number of clusters

Step 2 Calculate the membership degrees and the centroids iteratively. First, according to Eq. (2.154), we have

$$U(0) = \begin{bmatrix} 0.401 & 0.317 & 0.281 \\ 0.215 & 0.252 & 0.533 \\ 0.289 & 0.231 & 0.480 \\ 0.896 & 0.054 & 0.051 \\ 0.166 & 0.631 & 0.203 \\ 0.319 & 0.390 & 0.291 \\ 0.179 & 0.213 & 0.607 \\ 0.000 & 0.000 & 1.000 \\ 1.000 & 0.000 & 0.000 \\ 0.000 & 1.000 & 0.000 \end{bmatrix}$$

Step 3 According to Eq. (2.155), update the centroids as follows:

$$V(1) = \left[\begin{matrix} \langle 0.365, 0.382\rangle & \langle 0.838, 0.084\rangle & \langle 0.782, 0.153\rangle \\ \langle 0.762, 0.151\rangle & \langle 0.677, 0.136\rangle & \langle 0.586, 0.258\rangle \\ \langle 0.678, 0.211\rangle & \langle 0.574, 0.206\rangle & \langle 0.666, 0.165\rangle \end{matrix}\right.$$
$$\left.\begin{matrix} \langle 0.625, 0.182\rangle & \langle 0.207, 0.700\rangle & \langle 0.190, 0.737\rangle \\ \langle 0.488, 0.203\rangle & \langle 0.707, 0.221\rangle & \langle 0.509, 0.457\rangle \\ \langle 0.361, 0.516\rangle & \langle 0.369, 0.561\rangle & \langle 0.667, 0.130\rangle \end{matrix}\right]$$

Step 4 Check whether we should stop the iterations:

$$\sum_{i=1}^{3} d_{wE}\left(V_i(0), V_i(1)\right)/3 = 0.088 > 0.005$$

Since this value is not small enough, we continue the iterations as follows:

K = 1:

$$U(1) = \begin{bmatrix} 0.399 & 0.326 & 0.275 \\ 0.138 & 0.169 & 0.693 \\ 0.202 & 0.176 & 0.622 \\ 0.919 & 0.042 & 0.039 \\ 0.128 & 0.724 & 0.148 \\ 0.309 & 0.410 & 0.280 \\ 0.101 & 0.127 & 0.772 \\ 0.071 & 0.164 & 0.766 \\ 0.899 & 0.054 & 0.048 \\ 0.057 & 0.840 & 0.102 \end{bmatrix}$$

$$V(2) = \begin{bmatrix} \langle 0.356, 0.387\rangle & \langle 0.841, 0.086\rangle & \langle 0.776, 0.157\rangle & \langle 0.647, 0.160\rangle & \langle 0.198, 0.705\rangle & \langle 0.181, 0.757\rangle \\ \langle 0.753, 0.150\rangle & \langle 0.661, 0.172\rangle & \langle 0.585, 0.236\rangle & \langle 0.494, 0.176\rangle & \langle 0.710, 0.225\rangle & \langle 0.479, 0.490\rangle \\ \langle 0.587, 0.258\rangle & \langle 0.530, 0.187\rangle & \langle 0.668, 0.179\rangle & \langle 0.321, 0.553\rangle & \langle 0.344, 0.601\rangle & \langle 0.630, 0.158\rangle \end{bmatrix}$$

$$\sum_{i=1}^{3} \frac{d_{wE}\left(V_i(1), V_i(2)\right)}{3} = 0.024 > 0.005$$

K = 2:

$$U(2) = \begin{bmatrix} 0.388 & 0.335 & 0.277 \\ 0.086 & 0.105 & 0.809 \\ 0.140 & 0.127 & 0.733 \\ 0.932 & 0.035 & 0.034 \\ 0.104 & 0.785 & 0.111 \\ 0.298 & 0.422 & 0.280 \\ 0.064 & 0.082 & 0.854 \\ 0.110 & 0.245 & 0.645 \\ 0.894 & 0.056 & 0.050 \\ 0.074 & 0.813 & 0.113 \end{bmatrix}$$

$$V(3) = \begin{bmatrix} \langle 0.355, 0.389\rangle & \langle 0.852, 0.080\rangle & \langle 0.780, 0.154\rangle & \langle 0.655, 0.152\rangle & \langle 0.193, 0.709\rangle & \langle 0.176, 0.766\rangle \\ \langle 0.759, 0.146\rangle & \langle 0.661, 0.184\rangle & \langle 0.587, 0.224\rangle & \langle 0.496, 0.165\rangle & \langle 0.715, 0.224\rangle & \langle 0.473, 0.498\rangle \\ \langle 0.542, 0.276\rangle & \langle 0.513, 0.176\rangle & \langle 0.670, 0.183\rangle & \langle 0.299, 0.574\rangle & \langle 0.331, 0.620\rangle & \langle 0.614, 0.170\rangle \end{bmatrix}$$

$$\sum_{i=1}^{3} \frac{d_{wE}\left(V_i(2), V_i(3)\right)}{3} = 0.011 > 0.005$$

K = 3:

$$U(3) = \begin{bmatrix} 0.383 & 0.337 & 0.280 \\ 0.0645 & 0.079 & 0.856 \\ 0.114 & 0.105 & 0.782 \\ 0.939 & 0.030 & 0.030 \\ 0.094 & 0.811 & 0.095 \\ 0.295 & 0.423 & 0.282 \\ 0.058 & 0.073 & 0.869 \\ 0.127 & 0.283 & 0.590 \\ 0.901 & 0.052 & 0.047 \\ 0.077 & 0.813 & 0.110 \end{bmatrix}$$

$$V(4) = \begin{bmatrix} \langle 0.356, 0.389\rangle & \langle 0.856, 0.077\rangle & \langle 0.783, 0.152\rangle & \langle 0.657, 0.150\rangle & \langle 0.190, 0.711\rangle & \langle 0.174, 0.769\rangle \\ \langle 0.763, 0.144\rangle & \langle 0.662, 0.186\rangle & \langle 0.590, 0.218\rangle & \langle 0.494, 0.164\rangle & \langle 0.716, 0.223\rangle & \langle 0.474, 0.497\rangle \\ \langle 0.524, 0.280\rangle & \langle 0.509, 0.172\rangle & \langle 0.671, 0.184\rangle & \langle 0.291, 0.581\rangle & \langle 0.326, 0.626\rangle & \langle 0.609, 0.175\rangle \end{bmatrix}$$

$$\sum_{i=1}^{3} \frac{d_{wE}\left(V_i(3), V_i(4)\right)}{3} = 0.004 < 0.005$$

So we stop the iterations, and finally have

Table 2.9 The clustering result of the car data set by IFCM

Instance	Cluster ID
y_4, y_9	1
y_5, y_{10}	2
y_2, y_3, y_7	3
y_1, y_6, y_8	No significant membership of any cluster

K = 4:

$$U(4) = \begin{bmatrix} 0.381 & 0.336 & 0.283 \\ 0.085 & 0.071 & 0.871 \\ 0.105 & 0.097 & 0.798 \\ 0.942 & 0.029 & 0.029 \\ 0.090 & 0.819 & 0.090 \\ 0.294 & 0.422 & 0.284 \\ 0.059 & 0.075 & 0.867 \\ 0.132 & 0.298 & 0.569 \\ 0.905 & 0.050 & 0.045 \\ 0.077 & 0.817 & 0.106 \end{bmatrix}$$

According to $U(4)$, we get the cluster validation measures V_{PC} and V_{CE}:

$$V_{PC} = \frac{1}{3}\sum_{i=1}^{3}\sum_{j=1}^{10} u_{ij}^2 = 0.638, \quad V_{CE} = -\frac{1}{10}\sum_{i=1}^{3}\sum_{j=1}^{10} u_{ij}\log u_{ij} = 0.947$$

If we further assume that $u_{ij} \geq 0.75 \Rightarrow A_j \in C_i$ $(1 \leq j \leq 10, 1 \leq i \leq 3)$, where C_i denotes Cluster i, then we have the clusters as follows (see Table 2.9) (Xu and Wu 2010).

Next, we pay special attention to the convergence of Algorithm 2.7 on the car data set. Figure 2.3 (Xu and Wu 2010) shows the movements of the objective function values $J_m(U, V)$ along the iterations:

As can be seen in Fig. 2.3, Algorithm 2.7 indeed can decrease the objective function value continuously by iterating the two phases—updating the membership degrees in Eq. (2.154) and updating the prototypical IFSs in Eq. (2.156).

If we utilize Algorithm 2.2 to cluster this car data set, the results are shown in Table 2.10 (Xu and Wu 2010).

By comparing the above result by Algorithm 2.2 with the result by Algorithm 2.7, we know that Algorithm 2.2 can only produce "crisp" clusters. That is, each instance of the car data set can only be assigned to one cluster if Algorithm-IFSC is used. For Algorithm 2.7, however, things are different. By using the membership degree matrix U, Algorithm 2.7 can produce "overlapped" clusters in which the instances have different membership degrees. This is noteworthy, since in many real-world applications, it makes sense that one instance shares some common grounds of

Table 2.10 The clustering results of the car data set by Algorithm-IFSC in different λ levels

λ level	Clustering results
$0 \le \lambda \le 0.709$	$\{y_1, y_2, y_3, y_4, y_5, y_6, y_7, y_8, y_9, y_{10}\}$
$0.709 < \lambda \le 0.771$	$\{y_1, y_6\}, \{y_2, y_3, y_4, y_5, y_7, y_8, y_9, y_{10}\}$
$0.771 < \lambda \le 0.811$	$\{y_1, y_6\}, \{y_2\}, \{y_3, y_5, y_7, y_{10}\}, \{y_8\}, \{y_4, y_9\}$
$0.811 < \lambda \le 0.861$	$\{y_1, y_6\}, \{y_2\}, \{y_3, y_7\}, \{y_8\}, \{y_4, y_9\}, \{y_5, y_{10}\}$
$0.861 < \lambda \le 0.889$	$\{y_1, y_6\}, \{y_2\}, \{y_3, y_7\}, \{y_4, y_9\}, \{y_5\}, \{y_8\}, \{y_{10}\}$
$0.889 < \lambda \le 0.913$	$\{y_1, y_6\}, \{y_2, y_3, y_7\}, \{y_4, y_9\}, \{y_5\}, \{y_8\}, \{y_{10}\}$
$0.913 < \lambda \le 0.919$	$\{y_1, y_6\}, \{y_2\}, \{y_3, y_7\}, \{y_4, y_9\}, \{y_5\}, \{y_8\}, \{y_{10}\}$
$0.919 < \lambda \le 0.937$	$\{y_1\}, \{y_2\}, \{y_5\}, \{y_6\}, \{y_3, y_7\}, \{y_4, y_9\}, \{y_8\}, \{y_{10}\}$
$0.937 < \lambda \le 0.968$	$\{y_1\}, \{y_2\}, \{y_3\}, \{y_5\}, \{y_6\}, \{y_7\}, \{y_8\}, \{y_4, y_9\}, \{y_{10}\}$
$0.968 < \lambda \le 1$	$\{y_1\}, \{y_2\}, \{y_3\}, \{y_4\}, \{y_5\}, \{y_6\}, \{y_7\}, \{y_8\}, \{y_9\}, \{y_{10}\}$

Note: (1) λ is used to cut the association matrix of Algorithm 2.2 to produce the clusters

several clusters. For instance, a VOLVO car is often famous for its safety equipment. On the other hand, it is also a luxury car with a relatively high price. So a VOLVO car can naturally be grouped into the safe car cluster and the luxury car cluster simultaneously. Viewing from this angle, Algorithm 2.7 indeed can generate more valuable information than Algorithm 2.2.

Furthermore, compared with Algorithm 2.2, Algorithm 2.7 has lower computational complexity. Roughly speaking, the storage required by Algorithm 2.7 is $O\ (p(n+c)+cn)$, where p is the number of samples in the data, n is the number of IFSs in a sample, and c is the number of clusters. The time requirement for Algorithm 2.7 is $O\ (\dot{I}cpn)$, where $\dot{I}$ is the maximum number of iterations preset for the optimal value searching process. Since in most cases n and c are much smaller than p, we can view Algorithm 2.7 as a linear algorithm in the sample size p. As to Algorithm-IFSC, it must compute and store the association matrix for each pair of samples, so the computational complexity of Algorithm-IFSC is roughly $O\ (p^2)$. Therefore, for

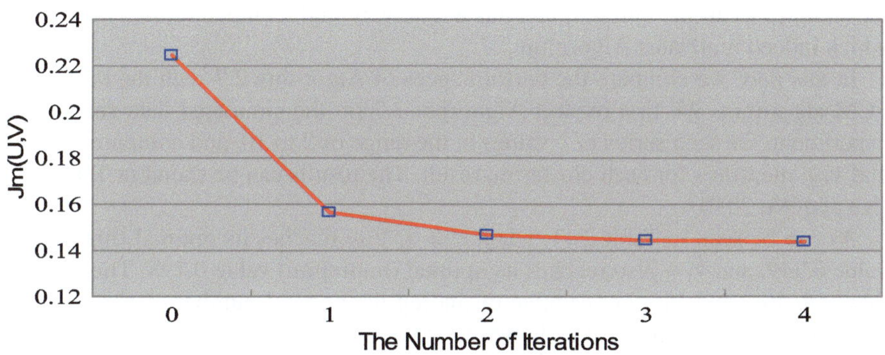

Fig. 2.3 Illustration of the convergence of IFCM on the car data set

Table 2.11 The results derived by Algorithm 2.7 with different cluster numbers on the simulated data set

c	2	3	4	5	6	7	8	9	10
Obj	76.760	7.087	5.853	5.389	3.543	3.138	2.743	2.536	**2.161**
V_{PC}	0.744	**0.949**	0.779	0.710	0.475	0.420	0.367	0.338	0.289
V_{CE}	0.582	**0.198**	0.563	0.809	1.198	1.404	1.598	1.749	1.927

Note: (1) "*Obj*" is the objective function value after the convergence of Algorithm 2.7
(2) The optimal values of the measures are highlighted in bold and italic fonts

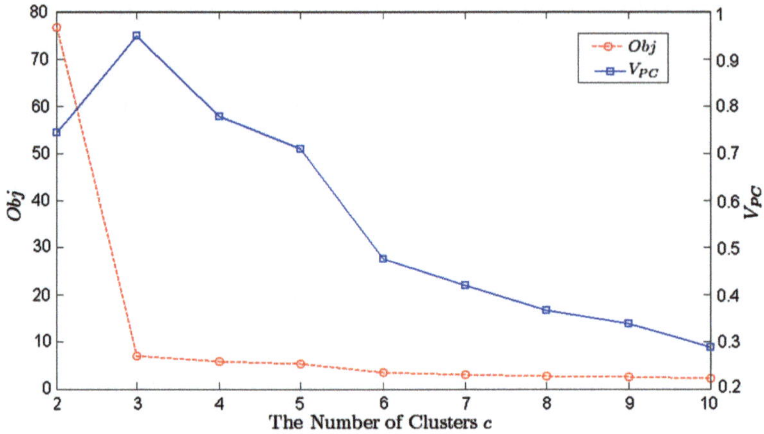

Fig. 2.4 Comparison of *Obj* and V_{PC} given different c values

a data set with a large sample size, say, 1,000,000, Algorithm-IFSC may encounter some computational troubles.

In summary, while Algorithm 2.2 has some unique merits such as simplicity and flexibility, it cannot provide the information about the membership degree of the samples to all the clusters, and has a relatively high computational complexity, which indeed motivates Algorithm 2.7.

In this part, we compare the performances of Algorithm 2.7 with the traditional FCM algorithm. We first exploit Algorithm 2.7 on the simulated data set. In this experiment, we set a series of c values in the range of 2 to 10, and compute the V_{PC} and V_{CE} measures for each clustering result. The results can be found in Table 2.11 (Xu and Wu 2010).

As can be seen in Table 2.11, when $c = 3$, V_{PC} reaches its optimal (maximum) value 0.949, and V_{CE} also reaches its optimal (minimum) value 0.198. This implies that both V_{PC} and V_{CE} are capable of finding the optimal number of clusters, i.e., c. The objective function value, however, is not the case. Let us look at Fig. 2.4 (Xu and Wu 2010).

As the increase of the number of clusters, *Obj* decreases continuously and finally reaches 2.161 when $c = 10$. This just illustrates why we employ V_{PC} and V_{CE} to evaluate the clustering results produced by Algorithm 2.7.

Table 2.12 The results derived by Algorithm 2.7 with different cluster numbers on the simulated data set

Modified data set I									
c	2	3	4	5	6	7	8	9	10
V_{PC}	**0.982**	0.648	0.531	0.469	0.324	0.289	0.239	0.216	0.196
V_{CE}	**0.073**	0.750	1.163	1.465	1.750	1.975	2.153	2.335	2.395
Modified data set II									
c	2	3	4	5	6	7	8	9	10
V_{PC}	**0.982**	0.648	0.531	0.381	0.324	0.289	0.266	0.248	0.235
V_{CE}	**0.072**	0.750	1.164	1.465	1.750	1.976	2.163	2.325	2.463

Note: (1) The optimal values of the measures are highlighted in bold and italic fonts

Next, we exploit the traditional FCM algorithm on the simulated data set for the comparison purpose. As mentioned above, the FCM algorithm does not take into account the uncertain information. Therefore, to make sure $\mu(x) + v(x) = 1$ for any x in the simulated data set, we should modify the data set by adding $\pi(x)$ to either $\mu(x)$ or $v(x)$. We produce the two modified data sets and then exploit Algorithm 2.7 on them. The results can be found in Table 2.12 (Xu and Wu 2010).

As indicated by the V_{PC} and V_{CE} measures in Table 2.12, Algorithm 2.7 prefers to cluster the modified simulated data sets into two clusters, which is actually away from the three "true" clusters in the data. In other words, the FCM algorithm cannot identify all the three classes precisely. This further justifies the importance of the uncertain information in IFSs.

2.6 Intuitionistic Fuzzy MST Clustering Algorithm

Zhao et al. (2012a) developed an intuitionistic fuzzy minimum spanning tree (MST) clustering algorithm to deal with intuitionistic fuzzy information. To do so, they first introduced some concepts related to the graph theory.

A graph is composed of a set of points called nodes and a set of node pairs called edges, which can be denoted by $(\dot{V}, \overline{E})$, where $\dot{V}$ is the set of nodes and $\overline{E}$ is the set of edges. In fact, the set $\overline{E}$ in a normal graph is a crisp relation over $\dot{V} \times \dot{V}$. That is to say, if there exists an edge between x and y, then the membership degree $\mu_{\overline{E}}(x, y) = 1$; otherwise $\mu_{\overline{E}}(x, y) = 0$, where $(x, y) \in \left(\dot{V} \times \dot{V}\right)$. If we define a fuzzy relation R over $\dot{V} \times \dot{V}$, then the membership function $\mu_R(x, y)$ takes various values from 0 to 1, and such a graph is called a fuzzy graph.

Definition 2.25 (Chen et al. 2007) Let $\dot{V} = \left\{\dot{V}_1, \dot{V}_2, \ldots, \dot{V}_n\right\}$ be a collection of n nodes, and $R = (r_{ij})_{n \times n}$ a fuzzy relation over the set $\dot{V}$. Then $\left(\dot{V}, R\right)$ is called a fuzzy graph. If $\overline{E} = \left\{\overline{E}_k = \dot{V}_i\dot{V}_j | \forall \dot{V}_i, \dot{V}_j \in \dot{V}\right\}$, then $\left(\dot{V}, \overline{E}\right)$ is called a basic graph of $\left(\dot{V}, R\right)$.

Definition 2.26 (Zhao et al. 2012a) Let $\dot{V} = \{\dot{V}_1, \dot{V}_2, \ldots, \dot{V}_n\}$ be a collection of n nodes, and $R = (r_{ij})_{n \times n}$ an intuitionistic fuzzy relation over $\dot{V} \times \dot{V}$. Then $\overline{G} = (\dot{V}, R)$ is called an intuitionistic fuzzy graph. If $\overline{E} = \{\overline{E}_k = \dot{V}_i\dot{V}_j | \forall \dot{V}_i, \dot{V}_j \in \dot{V}\}$, then $(\dot{V}, \overline{E})$ is called a basic graph of $(\dot{V}, R)$.

A path in a graph is a sequence of edges joining two nodes as $(ABCD)$. A circuit is a closed path as $(ABCA)$. A connected graph has paths between any pair of nodes. A tree is a connected graph with no circuits and a spanning tree of a connected graph is a tree in graph $(\dot{V}, R)$ which contains all nodes of $(\dot{V}, R)$ (Zahn 1971).

If we add every edge a weight and define the weight of a tree to be the sum of the weights of its constituent edges, then

Definition 2.27 (Zahn 1971) A minimum (maximum) spanning tree of a graph $(\dot{V}, R)$ is a spanning tree whose weight is minimum (maximum) among all spanning trees of the graph $(\dot{V}, R)$.

We usually compute the minimum (maximum) spanning tree of a graph $(\dot{V}, R)$ by Kruskal method (Kruskal 1956) or Prim method (Prim 1957). Because of the complexity of the objective world and the fuzziness of the human perception, the data information needed to be clustered is often imprecise or uncertain and sometimes is given by IFSs. In such situations, some effective and convenient intuitionistic clustering algorithms are needed. The MST (minimum spanning tree) clustering algorithm was first proposed by Zahn (1971), whose basic idea is that: a multi-attribute sample point can be considered as a point of a multi-dimensional space. If the density of the sample points in some regions in the multi-dimensional space is high, while in other regions is low or even blank, then the high-density regions can be separated from the blank or the low-density regions naturally, so that we get the clustering structure of the sample points which best embodies the distribution of the sample points. Based on the idea of Zahn (1971), Zhao et al. (2012a) introduced an intuitionistic fuzzy clustering method called intuitionistic fuzzy MST clustering algorithm based on the graph theoretic techniques and the intuitionistic fuzzy distance measure to cluster intuitionistic fuzzy information. In the following, we first introduce the concepts of intuitionistic fuzzy distance measure and intuitionistic fuzzy distance matrix:

Definition 2.28 (Zhao et al. 2012a) Let A_j $(j = 1, 2, \ldots, n)$ be n IFSs. Then $D = (d_{ij})_{n \times n}$ is called an intuitionistic fuzzy distance matrix, where $d_{ij} = d(A_i, A_j) = 1 - \hat{\vartheta}(A_1, A_2)$ is the intuitionistic fuzzy distance between A_i and A_j, which has the following properties:

(1) $d_{ij} (i, j = 1, 2, \ldots, n)$ are IFVs.
(2) $d_{ij} = (0, 1)$ if and only if $A_i = A_j$.
(3) $d_{ij} = d_{ji}$, for all $i, j = 1, 2, \ldots, n$,

where $\hat{\vartheta}(A_1, A_2)$ is defined in Theorem 2.2.

Based on the idea of the traditional MST clustering algorithm and the intuitionistic fuzzy distance matrix above, Zhao et al. (2012a) proposed an intuitionistic fuzzy MST clustering algorithm:

Algorithm 2.9

Step 1 Construct the intuitionistic fuzzy distance matrix and the intuitionistic fuzzy graph:

(1) Calculate the distance $d_{ij} = d\left(A_i, A_j\right)$, then we get the intuitionistic fuzzy distance matrix $D = \left(d_{ij}\right)_{n\times n}$.

(2) Construct the intuitionistic fuzzy graph $\left(\dot{V}, D\right)$ with n nodes associated to the samples $A_i (i = 1, 2, \ldots, n)$ to be clustered which are expressed by IFSs and every edge between A_i and A_j having the weight d_{ij}, which is an element (expressed by IFV) of the intuitionistic fuzzy distance matrix $D = (d_{ij})_{n\times n}$ and denotes the dissimilarity degree between the samples A_i and A_j.

Step 2 Compute the MST of the intuitionistic fuzzy graph (V, D) by Kruskal method (Kruskal 1956) or Prim method (Prim 1957):

(1) Arrange the edges of $\left(\dot{V}, D\right)$ in order from the smallest weight to the largest one. Because the weight of each edge is an IFV, we can firstly compute the score and the accuracy degree of each IFV, and then we use Definition 2.27 to sort all the intuitionistic fuzzy weights.

(2) Select the edge with the smallest weight.

(3) Select the edge with the smallest weight from the rest edges which do not form a circuit with those already chosen.

(4) Repeat the process (3) until $(n - 1)$ edges have been selected where n is the number of the nodes in $\left(\dot{V}, D\right)$. Thus we get the MST of the intuitionistic fuzzy graph $\left(\dot{V}, D\right)$.

Step 3 Group the nodes (sample points) into clusters by cutting down all the edges of the MST with weights greater than a threshold λ (where λ is an IFV), we can get a certain number of sub-trees (clusters) automatically. The clustering results induced by the sub-trees do not depend on some particular MST (Gaertler 2002).

Moreover, Zhao et al. (2012a) improved Algorithm 2.9 by changing the intuitionistic fuzzy distance measure by Eq. (2.111) or (2.112) so as to lessen the computational effort. They first defined another intuitionistic fuzzy distance matrix:

Definition 2.29 (Zhao et al. 2012a) Let A_j $(j = 1, 2, \ldots, n)$ be n IFSs. Then $D = \left(d_{ij}\right)_{n\times n}$ is called an intuitionistic fuzzy distance matrix, where $d_{ij} = d\left(A_i, A_j\right)$ is the distance between A_i and A_j, which has the following properties:

(1) $0 \leq d_{ij} \leq 1$, for all $i, j = 1, 2, \ldots, n$.
(2) $d_{ij} = 0$ if and only if $A_i = A_j$.
(3) $d_{ij} = d_{ji}$, for all $i, j = 1, 2, \ldots, n$.

Based on Definition 2.29, Zhao et al. (2012a) developed another intuitionistic fuzzy MST clustering algorithm:

Algorithm 2.10

Step 1 Compute the intuitionistic fuzzy distance matrix and draw the fuzzy graph:

(1) Calculate the distance $d_{ij} = d\left(A_i, A_j\right)$ by Eq. (2.111) or (2.112) and get the intuitionistic fuzzy distance matrix $D = \left(d_{ij}\right)_{n\times n}$ which is actually a fuzzy similarity relation.

(2) Draw the fuzzy graph $\left(\dot{V}, D\right)$. Although the n nodes associated to the samples $A_i (i = 1, 2, \ldots, n)$ to be clustered are still expressed by IFSs, the weight d_{ij} of every edge between A_i and A_j changes into a real number which comes from the second kind of intuitionistic fuzzy distance matrix $D = (d_{ij})_{n\times n}$ (the graph here is really a fuzzy graph and is quite different from the one in Algorithm 2.9).

Step 2 Compute the minimum spanning tree (MST) of the fuzzy graph $\left(\dot{V}, D\right)$, which is similar to Step 2 of Algorithm 2.9.

Step 3 See Step 3 of Algorithm 2.9.

In the following, we use an example to illustrate Algorithms 2.9 and 2.10:

Example 2.7 In an operational mission (adapted from Zhang et al. (2007), there are six operational plans y_i $(i = 1, 2, \ldots, 6)$. In order to group these operational plans with respect to their comprehensive functions, a military committee has been set up to provide assessment information on the operational plans. The attributes which are considered here in assessment of y_i $(i = 1, 2, \ldots, 6)$ are: (1) G_1: The effectiveness of operational organization; and (2) G_2: The effectiveness of operational command. The military committee evaluates the performance of all the operational plans according to the attributes G_j $(j = 1, 2)$, and gives the data as follows:

$$y_1 = \{\langle G_1, 0.70, 0.15\rangle, \langle G_2, 0.60, 0.20\rangle\}$$
$$y_2 = \{\langle G_1, 0.40, 0.35\rangle, \langle G_2, 0.80, 0.10\rangle\}$$
$$y_3 = \{\langle G_1, 0.55, 0.25\rangle, \langle G_2, 0.70, 0.15\rangle\}$$
$$y_4 = \{\langle G_1, 0.44, 0.35\rangle, \langle G_2, 0.60, 0.20\rangle\}$$
$$y_5 = \{\langle G_1, 0.50, 0.35\rangle, \langle G_2, 0.75, 0.20\rangle\}$$
$$y_6 = \{\langle G_1, 0.55, 0.25\rangle, \langle G_2, 0.57, 0.15\rangle\}$$

Let the weight vector of the attributes G_j $(j = 1, 2)$ be $w = (0.45, 0.55)^T$. We first utilize Algorithm 2.9 to group these operational plans y_j $(j = 1, 2, \ldots, 6)$:

Step 1 Construct the intuitionistic fuzzy distance matrix and the intuitionistic fuzzy graph:

(1) Calculate the distance $d_{ij} = d\left(y_i, y_j\right)$ (see Definition 2.28), and let $\lambda = 2$, $\alpha = \beta = \gamma = 1/3$. Then

$$
\begin{aligned}
&d(y_1, y_2) = d(y_2, y_1) = (0.141, 0.784), && d(y_1, y_3) = d(y_3, y_1) = (0.059, 0.892)\\
&d_1(y_1, y_4) = d_1(y_4, y_1) = (0, 0.808), && d(y_1, y_5) = d(y_5, y_1) = (0.123, 0.837)\\
&d(y_1, y_6) = d(y_6, y_1) = (0.057, 0.892), && d(y_2, y_3) = d(y_3, y_2) = (0.059, 0.892)\\
&d(y_2, y_4) = d(y_4, y_2) = (0.033, 0.859), && d(y_2, y_5) = d(y_5, y_2) = (0.071, 0.918)\\
&d(y_2, y_6) = d(y_6, y_2) = (0.108, 0.829), && d(y_3, y_4) = d(y_4, y_3) = (0.071, 0.914)\\
&d(y_3, y_5) = d(y_5, y_3) = (0.071, 0.929), && d(y_3, y_6) = d(y_6, y_3) = (0, 0.894)\\
&d(y_4, y_5) = d_1(y_5, y_4) = (0.049, 0.878), && d(y_4, y_6) = d(y_6, y_4) = (0.057, 0.914)\\
&d(y_5, y_6) = d(y_6, y_5) = (0.071, 0.829)
\end{aligned}
$$

Accordingly, we get the intuitionistic fuzzy distance matrix as follows:

$$
D = \begin{pmatrix}
(0,1) & (0.141,0.784) & (0.059,0.892) & (0,0.808) & (0.123,0.837) & (0.057,0.892)\\
(0.141,0.784) & (0,1) & (0.059,0.892) & (0.033,0.859) & (0.071,0.918) & (0.108,0.829)\\
(0.059,0.892) & (0.059.0.892) & (0,1) & (0.071,0.914) & (0.071,0.929) & (0,0.894)\\
(0,0.808) & (0.033,0.859) & (0.071,0.914) & (0,1) & (0.049,0.878) & (0.057,0.914)\\
(0.123,0.837) & (0.071,0.918) & (0.071,0.929) & (0.049,0.878) & (0,1) & (0.071,0.829)\\
(0.057,0.892) & (0.108,0.829) & (0,0.894) & (0.057,0.914) & (0.071,0.829) & (0,1)
\end{pmatrix}
$$

(2) Draw the intuitionistic fuzzy graph $(\dot{V}, D)$ with 6 nodes associated to the samples y_i $(i = 1, 2, ..., 6)$ to be clustered and every edge $\overline{E}_{ij}$ between y_i and y_j having the weight d_{ij}, which is an element of the intuitionistic fuzzy distance matrix $D = (d_{ij})_{6\times 6}$ and denotes the dissimilarity degree between the samples y_i and y_j (see Fig. 2.5) (Zhao et al. 2012a).

Step 2 Compute the intuitionistic fuzzy MST of the intuitionistic fuzzy graph by Kruskal method (Kruskal 1956):

(1) Arrange the edges of $(\dot{V}, D)$ in order from the smallest weight to the largest one. Because the weight of each edge is an IFV, we can first use the scores and the accuracy degrees of each IFV in the intuitionistic fuzzy distance matrix to sort all the intuitionistic fuzzy weights (based on Definition 2.28) as follows:

$$
\begin{aligned}
&S(d_{12}) = 0.141 - 0.784 = -0.643, && S(d_{13}) = 0.059 - 0.892 = -0.833\\
&S(d_{14}) = 0 - 0.808 = -0.808, && S(d_{15}) = 0.123 - 0.837 = -0.714\\
&S(d_{16}) = 0.057 - 0.892 = -0.835, && S(d_{23}) = 0.059 - 0.892 = -0.833\\
&S(d_{24}) = 0.033 - 0.859 = -0.826, && S(d_{25}) = 0.071 - 0.918 = -0.847\\
&S(d_{26}) = 0.108 - 0.829 = -0.721, && S(d_{34}) = 0.071 - 0.914 = -0.843\\
&S(d_{35}) = 0.071 - 0.929 = -0.858, && S(d_{36}) = 0 - 0.894 = -0.894\\
&S(d_{36}) = 0.049 - 0.878 = -0.829, && S(d_{46}) = 0.057 - 0.914 = -0.857\\
&S(d_{56}) = 0.071 - 0.829 = -0.758
\end{aligned}
$$

Thus

$$
\begin{aligned}
d_{36} &< d_{35} < d_{46} < d_{25} < d_{34} < d_{16} < d_{13}\\
&= d_{23} < d_{45} < d_{24} < d_{14} < d_{56} < d_{26} < d_{15} < d_{12}
\end{aligned}
$$

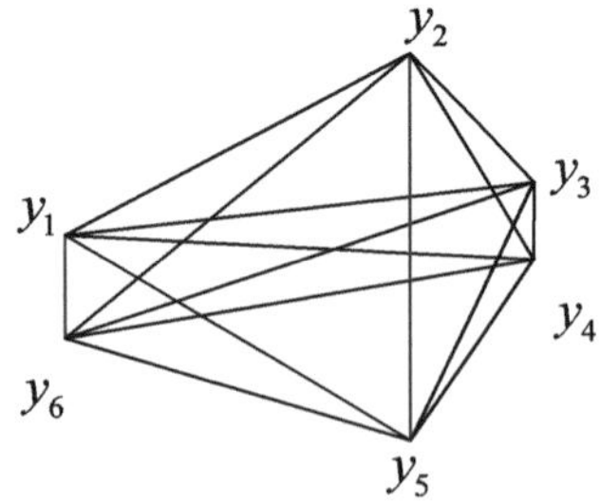

Fig. 2.5 The intuitionistic fuzzy graph

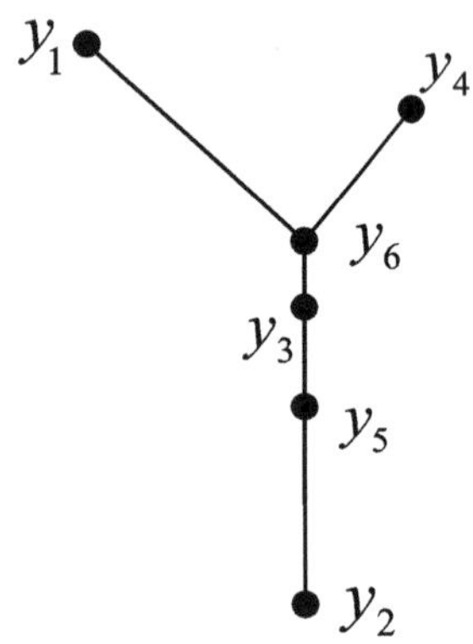

Fig. 2.6 The MST of the intuitionistic fuzzy graph

and then we sort all the intuitionistic fuzzy weights as follows:

(2) Select the edge with the smallest weight, that is the edge $\overline{E}_{36}$ between y_3 and y_6.

(3) Select the edge with the smallest weight from the rest edges, that is the edge $\overline{E}_{35}$ between y_3 and y_5.

(4) Select the edge with the smallest from the rest edges which do not form a circuit with those already chosen (we can choose the edge $\overline{E}_{46}$ between y_4 and y_6). Repeat (4) until five edges have been selected. Thus we get the MST of the intuitionistic fuzzy graph $\left(\dot{V}, D\right)$ (see Fig. 2.6) (Zhao et al. 2012a).

Step 3 Group the nodes (sample points) into clusters: by choosing a threshold λ and cutting down all the edges of the MST with the weights greater than λ, we can get a certain number of sub-trees (clusters).

(1) If $\lambda = d_{16} = (0.057, 0.892)$, then we get $\{y_1, y_2, y_3, y_4, y_5, y_6\}$.
(2) If $\lambda = d_{25} = (0.071, 0.918)$, then we get $\{y_1\}, \{y_2, y_3, y_4, y_5, y_6\}$.
(3) If $\lambda = d_{46} = (0.057, 0.914)$, then we get $\{y_1\}, \{y_2\}, \{y_3, y_4, y_5, y_6\}$.
(4) If $\lambda = d_{35} = (0.071, 0.929)$, then we get $\{y_1\}, \{y_2\}, \{y_4\}, \{y_3, y_5, y_6\}$.
(5) If $\lambda = d_{36} = (0, 0.894)$, then we get $\{y_1\}, \{y_2\}, \{y_4\}, \{y_5\}, \{y_3, y_6\}$.
(6) If $\lambda = (0, 1)$, then we get $\{y_1\}, \{y_2\}, \{y_3\}, \{y_4\}, \{y_5\}, \{y_6\}$.

Furthermore, we use Algorithm 2.10 to cluster these battle projects y_j $(j = 1, 2, \ldots, 6)$ as follows:

Step 1 Construct the intuitionistic fuzzy distance matrix and the fuzzy graph where each node is associated to a sample to be clustered which is expressed by IFS:

(1) Calculate the distances $d_{ij} = d\left(y_i, y_j\right)$ $(i, j = 1, 2, \ldots, 6)$ by Eq. (2.111):

$$\begin{array}{ll}
d(y_1, y_3) = d(y_3, y_1) = 0.1225, & d(y_1, y_4) = d(y_4, y_1) = 0.117 \\
d(y_1, y_5) = d(y_5, y_1) = 0.1725, & d(y_1, y_6) = d(y_6, y_1) = 0.1115 \\
d(y_2, y_3) = d(y_3, y_2) = 0.1225, & d(y_2, y_4) = d(y_4, y_2) = 0.128 \\
d(y_2, y_5) = d_7(y_5, y_2) = 0.1, & d(y_2, y_6) = d_7(y_6, y_2) = 0.194 \\
d(y_3, y_4) = d(y_4, y_3) = 0.1045, & d(y_3, y_5) = d(y_5, y_3) = 0.1 \\
d(y_3, y_6) = d(y_6, y_3) = 0.0715, & d(y_4, y_5) = d(y_5, y_4) = 0.1095 \\
d(y_4, y_6) = d(y_6, y_4) = 0.088, & d(y_5, y_6) = d(y_6, y_5) = 0.1715
\end{array}$$

then we get the intuitionistic fuzzy distance matrix as follows:

$$D = \begin{pmatrix}
0 & 0.245 & 0.1225 & 0.117 & 0.1725 & 0.1115 \\
0.245 & 0 & 0.1225 & 0.128 & 0.1 & 0.194 \\
0.1225 & 0.1225 & 0 & 0.1045 & 0.1 & 0.0715 \\
0.117 & 0.128 & 0.1045 & 0 & 0.1095 & 0.088 \\
0.1725 & 0.1 & 0.1 & 0.1095 & 0 & 0.1715 \\
0.1115 & 0.194 & 0.0715 & 0.088 & 0.1715 & 0
\end{pmatrix}$$

(2) Draw the fuzzy graph $\overline{G} = \left(\dot{V}, D\right)$ with 6 nodes associated to the samples y_i $(i = 1, 2, \ldots, 6)$ to be clustered and every edge between y_i and y_j having the weight d_{ij}, which is an element of the intuitionistic fuzzy distance matrix $D = (d_{ij})_{6\times6}$ and denotes the dissimilarity degree between the samples y_i and y_j (see Fig. 2.7) (Zhao et al. 2012a).

Step 2 Compute the MST of the fuzzy graph $\overline{G} = \left(\dot{V}, D\right)$ by Kruskal method (Kruskal 1956):

(1) Arrange the edges of $\overline{G}$ in order from the smallest weight to the largest one:

$$\begin{aligned}
&d_{36} < d_{46} < d_{35} \\
&\quad = d_{25} < d_{34} < d_{45} < d_{16} < d_{14} < d_{13} = d_{23} < d_{24} < d_{56} < d_{15} < d_{26} < d_{52}
\end{aligned}$$

(2) Select the edge with the smallest weight, that is the edge $\overline{E}_{36}$ between y_3 and y_6.

(3) Select the edge with the smallest weight from the rest edges, that is the edge $\overline{E}_{46}$ between y_4 and y_6.

(4) Select the edge with the smallest weight from the rest edges which do not form a circuit with those already chosen, we can choose the edge $\overline{E}_{35}$ between y_3 and y_5.

(5) Repeat the process (4) until five edges have been selected. Thus we get the MST of the fuzzy graph $\overline{G} = \left(\dot{V}, D\right)$ (see Fig. 2.8) (Zhao et al. 2012a).

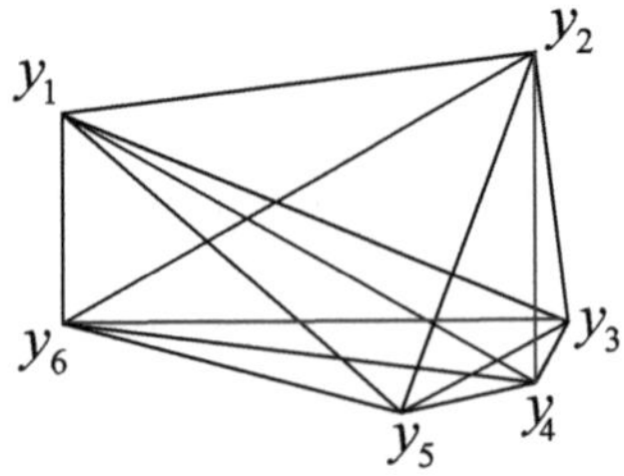

Fig. 2.7 The fuzzy graph

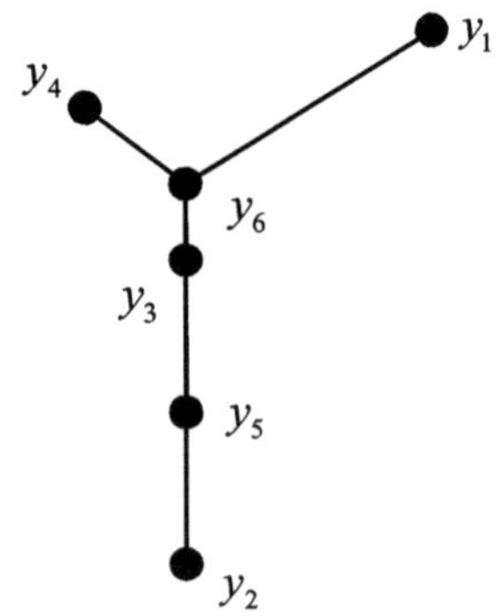

Fig. 2.8 The MST of the fuzzy graph

Step 3 Choose a threshold λ and cut down all the edges of the MST with weights greater than λ so that we could arrive at a certain number of sub-trees (clusters) automatically.

(1) If $\lambda = d_{16} = 0.1115$, then we get $\{y_1, y_2, y_3, y_4, y_5, y_6\}$.
(2) If $\lambda = d_{25} = d_{35} = 0.1$, then we get $\{y_1\}, \{y_2, y_3, y_4, y_5, y_6\}$.
(3) If $\lambda = d_{46} = 0.088$, then we get $\{y_1\}, \{y_2\}, \{y_5\}, \{y_3, y_4, y_6\}$.
(4) If $\lambda = d_{36} = 0.0715$, then we get $\{y_1\}, \{y_2\}, \{y_4\}, \{y_5\}, \{y_3, y_6\}$.
(5) If $\lambda = 0$, then we get $\{y_1\}, \{y_2\}, \{y_3\}, \{y_4\}, \{y_5\}, \{y_6\}$.

From the results of Algorithms 2.9 and 2.10, we have found that they coincide with each other on the whole.

Sometimes, it is not suitable to assume that the membership degrees and the non-membership degrees for certain elements are exactly real numbers, but fuzzy ranges can be given. As a result, Zhao et al. (2012a) defined the concept of interval-valued intuitionistic fuzzy distance matrix:

Definition 2.30 (Zhao et al. 2012a) Let y_j $(j = 1, 2, \ldots, n)$ be m IVIFSs. Then $D = \left(d_{ij}\right)_{n \times n}$ is called an interval-valued intuitionistic fuzzy distance matrix, where $d_{ij} = d\left(y_i, y_j\right)$ is the distance between y_i and y_j, which has the following properties:

(1) $0 \leq d_{ij} \leq 1$, for all $i, j = 1, 2, \ldots, n$.
(2) $d_{ij} = 0$ if and only if $y_i = y_j$.
(3) $d_{ij} = d_{ji}$, for all $i, j = 1, 2, \ldots, n$.

Drawing support from the interval-valued intuitionistic fuzzy distance matrix, we can extend Algorithm 2.10 to the interval-valued intuitionistic fuzzy environment and raise the interval-valued intuitionistic fuzzy MST clustering algorithm:

Algorithm 2.11

Step 1 Construct the interval-valued intuitionistic fuzzy distance matrix and the fuzzy graph:

In this step, we first calculate the distance $d_{ij} = d\left(y_i, y_j\right)$ by Eq. (2.105) or (2.107) to get the interval-valued intuitionistic fuzzy distance matrix $D = \left(d_{ij}\right)_{n\times n}$, and then draw the fuzzy graph $\left(\dot{V}, D\right)$ with n nodes associated to the samples y_i $(i = 1, 2, \ldots, n)$ which are expressed by IVIFSs and every edge between y_i and y_j having the weight d_{ij}, which is a real number coming from the interval-valued intuitionistic fuzzy distance matrix $D = (d_{ij})_{n\times n}$.

Step 2 Compute the minimum spanning tree (MST) of the fuzzy graph $\left(\dot{V}, D\right)$ by Kruskal method (Kruskal 1956) or Prim method (Prim 1957).

Step 3 Cluster through the minimum spanning tree (see to Step 3 of Algorithm 2.10).

Example 2.9 can also be used to illustrate Algorithm 2.11 when the evaluation information is expressed in IVIFSs (here omitted for brevity).

2.7 Intuitionistic Fuzzy Clustering Algorithm Based on Boole Matrix and Association Measure

2.7.1 Intuitionistic Fuzzy Association Measures

Since clustering is the grouping of similar objects, we usually need to find some sort of measure that can determine the degree of the relationship between two objects.

Generally, there are three main types of measures which can estimate this relation: distance measures, similarity measures and association measures. The choice of a good measure will directly influence the clustering effect. Next we shall seek for some association measures to be prepared for cluster analysis.

An association measure is an important tool for determining the degree of the relationship between two objects. Many scholars have given various association measures (see Xu and Chen 2008 for a review). For example, Xu et al. (2008) introduced the associate measures (2.89) and (2.100). Gerstenkorn and Mafiko (1991) proposed a method to calculate the association coefficient of IFSs, which was formulated in the following way:

$$c_1(A, B) = \frac{\sum_{j=1}^{n} \mu_A(x_j) \cdot \mu_B(x_j) + v_A(x_j) \cdot v_B(x_j)}{\sqrt{\sum_{j=1}^{n} \left(\mu_A^2(x_j) + v_A^2(x_j)\right) \cdot \sum_{j=1}^{n} \left(\mu_B^2(x_j) + v_B^2(x_j)\right)}} \tag{2.157}$$

Hong and Hwang (1995) further considered the case where the set X is infinite and defined another association coefficient of A-IFSs as follows:

$$c_2(A,B) = \frac{\int_X (\mu_A(x)\cdot\mu_B(x) + \nu_A(x)\cdot\nu_B(x))\,dx}{\sqrt{\int_X \left(\mu_A^2(x) + \nu_A^2(x)\right)dx \cdot \int_X \left(\mu_B^2(x) + \nu_B^2(x)\right)dx}} \tag{2.158}$$

where $c_1(A,B)$ and $c_2(A,B)$ satisfy the three conditions: (1) $0 \le c(A,B) \le 1$; (2) $c(A,B) = 1$ if $A = B$; and (3) $c(A,B) = c(B,A)$. But they cannot guarantee the necessity in the condition (2). Hong and Hwang (1995) and Mitchell (2004) pointed out that if association coefficients don't guarantee the necessity in the condition (2), then some situations where the obtained results are counter-intuitive will appear, although in most cases the association coefficient may give reasonable result. For this reason, Xu et al. (2008) proposed an axiomatic definition for the association measure of IFSs, which is an improved version of Gerstenkorn and Mafiko (1991) and Hong and Hwang (1995):

Definition 2.31 (Xu et al. 2008) Let c be a mapping c: $(\text{IFS}(X))^2 \to [0,1]$, then the association coefficient between two IFSs A and B is defined as $c(A,B)$, which has the following properties: (1) $0 \le c(A,B) \le 1$; (2) $c(A,B) = 1$ if and only if $A = B$; and (3) $c(A,B) = c(B,A)$.

Furthermore, Szmidt and Kacprzyk (2000) pointed out that omitting any one of the three parameters may lead to incorrect results, and therefore, we should take the three parameters into account when computing the association coefficients between IFSs.

Based on the two ideas above when constructing an association coefficient between IFSs, Zhao et al. (2012b) improved Eq. (2.155) to a new form, satisfying all the conditions proposed by Hong and Hwang (1995), Mitchell (2004) and Szmidt and Kacprzyk (2000):

$$c_3(A,B) = \frac{\sum_{j=1}^{n}\left(\mu_A(x_j)\cdot\mu_B(x_j) + \nu_A(x_j)\cdot\nu_B(x_j) + \pi_A(x_j)\cdot\pi_B(x_j)\right)}{\sqrt{\sum_{j=1}^{n}\left(\mu_A^2(x_j) + \nu_A^2(x_j) + \pi_A^2(x_j)\right)\cdot\sum_{j=1}^{n}\left(\mu_B^2(x_j) + \nu_B^2(x_j) + \pi_B^2(x_j)\right)}} \tag{2.159}$$

It is clear that $c_3(A,B)$ takes the third parameter of an IFS (the hesitancy degree) into consideration, moreover, we will prove that it also satisfies all the three conditions of Definition 2.31:

Proof Because $A, B \in \text{IFS}(X)$, then from the concept of IFS and Eq. (2.159), we know that $c_3(A,B) \ge 0$. To prove the inequality $c_3(A,B) \le 1$, we can use the famous Cauchy-Schwarz inequality:

$$\sum_{i=1}^{n} a_i b_i \leq \sqrt{\left(\sum_{i=1}^{n} a_i^2\right)\left(\sum_{i=1}^{n} b_i^2\right)} \tag{2.160}$$

with equality if and only if the two vectors $a = (a_1, a_2, \ldots, a_n)^T$ and $b = (b_1, b_2, \ldots, b_n)^T$ are linearly dependent, that is, there is a nonzero real number λ such that $a = \lambda b$. From Eq. (2.160), we know that $c_3(A, B) \leq 1$ with equality if and only if there is a nonzero real number λ such that

$$\mu_A(x_i) = \lambda \mu_B(x_i),\ \nu_A(x_i) = \lambda \nu_B(x_i),\ \pi_A(x_i) = \lambda \pi_B(x_i), \quad \text{for all } x_i \in X \tag{2.161}$$

while because

$$\pi_A(x_i) = 1 - \mu_A(x_i) - \nu_A(x_i),\ \ \pi_B(x_i) = 1 - \mu_B(x_i) - \nu_B(x_i), \quad \text{for all } x_i \in X \tag{2.162}$$

then by Eq. (2.161), we know that $\lambda = 1$, and thus, $c_3(A, B) = 1$ if and only if $A = B$. Hence we complete the proof of the conditions (1) and (2) in Definition 2.31.

In addition, by Eq. (2.159) we know that

$$\begin{aligned} c_3(A, B) &= \frac{\sum_{j=1}^{n} \left(\mu_A(x_j) \cdot \mu_B(x_j) + \nu_A(x_j) \cdot \nu_B(x_j) + \pi_A(x_j) \cdot \pi_B(x_j)\right)}{\sqrt{\sum_{j=1}^{n} \left(\mu_A^2(x_j) + \nu_A^2(x_j) + \pi_A^2(x_j)\right) \cdot \sum_{j=1}^{n} \left(\mu_B^2(x_j) + \nu_B^2(x_j) + \pi_B^2(x_j)\right)}} \\ &= \frac{\sum_{j=1}^{n} \left(\mu_B(x_j) \cdot \mu_A(x_j) + \nu_B(x_j) \cdot \nu_A(x_j) + \pi_B(x_j) \cdot \pi_A(x_j)\right)}{\sqrt{\sum_{j=1}^{n} \left(\mu_B^2(x_j) + \nu_B^2(x_j) + \pi_B^2(x_j)\right) \cdot \sum_{j=1}^{n} \left(\mu_A^2(x_j) + \nu_A^2(x_j) + \pi_A^2(x_j)\right)}} \\ &= c_3(B, A) \end{aligned} \tag{2.163}$$

Thus, the condition (3) in Definition 2.31 also holds.

It's very interesting that when we add the third parameter, i.e., the indeterminacy degree of IFSs, to $c_1(A, B)$, we get a good association coefficient $c_3(A, B)$, which not only takes the third parameter of IFS (the hesitancy degree) into consideration, but also satisfies all the three conditions of Definition 2.31.

In many cases, for instance, in cluster analysis, the weights of the attributes are always different, so we should take them into account, and thus extend $c_3(A, B)$ to the following form:

$$c_4(A,B) = \frac{\sum_{j=1}^{n} w_j \left(\mu_A(x_j)\cdot\mu_B(x_j) + \nu_A(x_j)\cdot\nu_B(x_j) + \pi_A(x_j)\cdot\pi_B(x_j)\right)}{\sqrt{\sum_{j=1}^{n} w_j \left(\mu_A^2(x_j) + \nu_A^2(x_j) + \pi_A^2(x_j)\right)\cdot\sum_{j=1}^{n} w_j \left(\mu_B^2(x_j) + \nu_B^2(x_j) + \pi_B^2(x_j)\right)}} \tag{2.164}$$

where $w = (w_1, w_2, \ldots, w_n)^T$ is the weight vector of x_j $(j = 1, 2, \ldots, n)$ with $w_j \geq 0, j = 1, 2, \ldots, n$ and $\sum_{j=1}^{n} w_j = 1$. Similar to Eq. (2.159), Eq. (2.164) also satisfies all the conditions of Definition 2.31.

If the universe of discourse, X, is continuous and the weight of the element $x \in X = [a, b]$ is $w(x)$, where $w(x) \geq 0$ and $\int_a^b w(x)dx = 1$, then Eq. (2.164) is transformed into the following form:

$$c_5(A,B) = \frac{\int_a^b w(x)\left(\mu_A(x)\mu_B(x) + \nu_A(x)\nu_B(x) + \pi_A(x)\pi_B(x)\right)dx}{\sqrt{\int_a^b w(x)\left(\mu_A^2(x) + \nu_A^2(x) + \pi_A^2(x)\right)dx \cdot \int_a^b w(x)\left(\mu_B^2(x) + \nu_B^2(x) + \pi_B^2(x)\right)dx}} \tag{2.165}$$

If all the elements have the same importance, i.e., $w(x) = \frac{1}{b-a} \in [0, 1]$ (in this case, $(b - a) \geq 1$), for any $x \in [a, b]$, then Eq. (2.165) is replaced by

$$c_6(A,B) = \frac{\int_a^b \left(\mu_A(x)\mu_B(x) + \nu_A(x)\nu_B(x) + \pi_A(x)\pi_B(x)\right)dx}{\sqrt{\int_a^b \left(\mu_A^2(x) + \nu_A^2(x) + \pi_A^2(x)\right)dx \cdot \int_a^b \left(\mu_B^2(x) + \nu_B^2(x) + \pi_B^2(x)\right)dx}} \tag{2.166}$$

2.7.2 Intuitionistic Fuzzy Clustering Algorithm

Let $C = (c_{ij})_{m\times m}$ be an association matrix, where $c_{ij} = c(A_i, A_j)$ is the association coefficient of A_i and A_j, which is derived by one of the intuitionistic fuzzy association measures (2.157) and (2.162)–(2.164). Then by Definition 2.12, we can directly derive the following result:

Theorem 2.18 (Zhao et al. 2012b) Let $C_\lambda = \left({}_\lambda c_{ij}\right)_{m\times m}$ be a λ-cutting matrix of the association matrix $C = (c_{ij})_{m\times m}$. Then C is an equivalent association matrix if and only if C_λ is an equivalent Boole matrix, for all $\lambda \in [0, 1]$, that is,

(1) C is reflexive, i.e., $I \subseteq C$ if and only if $I_\lambda \subseteq C_\lambda$, i.e., $I \subseteq C_\lambda$.
(2) C is symmetric, i.e., $C^T = C$ if and only if $\left(C^T\right)_\lambda = C_\lambda$, i.e., $(C_\lambda)^T = C_\lambda$.
(3) C is transitive, i.e., $C^2 \subseteq C$ if and only if $C_\lambda \circ C_\lambda \subseteq C_\lambda$.

From Theorem 2.18, we can see that if the association matrix is equivalent, then its λ-cutting matrix is an equivalent Boole matrix, and then we can use the equivalent Boole matrix to do clustering directly. But if the association matrix doesn't satisfy the transitivity, then we know that the λ-cutting matrix of C is just only a similar Boole matrix, and thus, we cannot do clustering. In this situation, we can transform the similar Boole matrix into an equivalent matrix for clustering. Let's see the following theorem:

Theorem 2.19 (Lei 1979) Let Bo be a similar Boole matrix over a discrete universe of discourse $X = \{x_1, x_2, \ldots, x_n\}$, then Bo is transitive if and only if Bo has not the following special sub-matrices:

$$\begin{pmatrix} 1 & 1 \\ 1 & 0 \end{pmatrix}, \begin{pmatrix} 1 & 1 \\ 0 & 1 \end{pmatrix}, \begin{pmatrix} 1 & 0 \\ 1 & 1 \end{pmatrix}, \begin{pmatrix} 0 & 1 \\ 1 & 1 \end{pmatrix} \tag{2.167}$$

no matter how the matrix Bo is arranged.

We can judge from Theorem 2.19 whether or not a similar Boole matrix is an equivalent one.

Based on Theorems 2.18 and 2.19, Zhao et al. (2012b) developed an intuitionistic fuzzy clustering algorithm based on Boole matrix and association measure as follows:

Algorithm 2.12

Step 1 Use Eq. (2.159) or (2.164) (if the weights of the attributes are the same, we use Eq. (2.159); otherwise, we use Eq. (2.164)) to compute the association coefficients of the IFSs A_j $(j = 1, 2, \ldots, m)$, and then construct an association matrix $C = (c_{ij})_{m\times m}$, where $c_{ij} = c_3(A_i, A_j)$ or $c_{ij} = c_4(A_i, A_j)$, $i, j = 1, 2, \ldots, m$.

Step 2 Construct a λ-cutting matrix $C_\lambda = \left({}_\lambda c_{ij}\right)_{m\times m}$ of C by using Eq. (2.87).

Step 3 If C_λ is an equivalent Boole matrix, then we can cluster the m samples as follows: If all the elements of the ith column are the same as the corresponding elements of the jth column in C_λ, then the IFSs A_i and A_j are in the same cluster. By this principle, we can cluster all these m samples A_j $(j = 1, 2, \ldots, m)$.

If C_λ is not an equivalent Boole matrix, then by Theorem 2.19, we know that no matter how the matrix C_λ is arranged, it must have some of the special sub-matrixes in Eq. (2.167). In such cases, we can transform the elements 0 into 1 in such special sub-matrices until C_λ has not any special sub-matrix, and thus, we get a new equivalent matrix C_λ^*.

Step 4 Employ the equivalent matrix C_λ^* to classify all the given IFSs A_j $(j = 1, 2, \ldots, m)$ by the procedure in Step 3.

Step 5 End.

The principal of choosing λ: Based on the idea of constructing the association matrix whose elements are association coefficients between every two alternatives (samples) in this paper, we balance the similarity degree between two alternatives mainly through the association coefficient (that is, the confidence level) of them. We choose the confidence level λ from the biggest one to the smallest one in the association matrix. After that, in terms of the chosen confidence level λ, we construct the corresponding λ-cutting matrix. With this principle, the clustering results come into being, the smaller the confidence level λ is, the more detailed the clustering will be.

2.7.3 Numerical Example

Example 2.8 (Zhao et al. 2012b) A military equipment development team needs to cluster five combat aircrafts according to their operational effectiveness. In order to group these combat aircrafts y_i $(i = 1, 2, \ldots, 5)$ with respect to their comprehensive functions, a team of military experts have been set up to provide their assessment information on y_i $(i = 1, 2, \ldots, 5)$. The attributes which are considered here in assessment of y_i $(i = 1, 2, \ldots, 5)$ are: (1) G_1 is the aircraft power; (2) G_2 is the fire power (a military capability to direct force at an enemy); (3) G_3 is the capacity for target detection; (4) G_4 is the controlling ability; (5) G_5 is the survivability; (6) G_6 is the range of voyage; and (7) G_7 is the electronic countermeasure effect. The military experts evaluate the performances of the combat aircrafts y_i $(i = 1, 2, \ldots, 5)$ according to the attributes G_j $(j = 1, 2, \ldots, 7)$, and gives the data as follows:

$$
\begin{aligned}
y_1 = \{&\langle G_1, 0.5, 0.3\rangle, \langle G_2, 0.6, 0.3\rangle, \langle G_3, 0.4, 0.3\rangle,\\
&\langle G_4, 0.8, 0.1\rangle, \langle G_5, 0.7, 0.2\rangle, \langle G_6, 0.5, 0.2\rangle, \langle G_7, 0.4, 0.3\rangle\}\\
y_2 = \{&\langle G_1, 0.6, 0.2\rangle, \langle G_2, 0.5, 0.3\rangle, \langle G_3, 0.5, 0.2\rangle,\\
&\langle G_4, 0.6, 0.2\rangle, \langle G_5, 0.6, 0.3\rangle, \langle G_6, 0.6, 0.3\rangle, \langle G_7, 0.5, 0.2\rangle\}\\
y_3 = \{&\langle G_1, 0.7, 0.1\rangle, \langle G_2, 0.6, 0.3\rangle, \langle G_3, 0.7, 0.2\rangle,\\
&\langle G_4, 0.5, 0.3\rangle, \langle G_5, 0.5, 0.2\rangle, \langle G_6, 0.5, 0.2\rangle, \langle G_7, 0.6, 0.3\rangle\}\\
y_4 = \{&\langle G_1, 0.4, 0.3\rangle, \langle G_2, 0.7, 0.2\rangle, \langle G_3, 0.5, 0.3\rangle,\\
&\langle G_4, 0.6, 0.2\rangle, \langle G_5, 0.7, 0.1\rangle, \langle G_6, 0.4, 0.3\rangle, \langle G_7, 0.7, 0.2\rangle\}\\
y_5 = \{&\langle G_1, 0.6, 0.2\rangle, \langle G_2, 0.6, 0.3\rangle, \langle G_3, 0.6, 0.2\rangle,\\
&\langle G_4, 0.5, 0.3\rangle, \langle G_5, 0.8, 0.1\rangle, \langle G_6, 0.6, 0.1\rangle, \langle G_7, 0.6, 0.1\rangle\}
\end{aligned}
$$

Suppose that the weights of the attributes G_j $(j = 1, 2, \ldots, 7)$ are equal, now we utilize Algorithm 2.12 to group these combat aircrafts y_i $(i = 1, 2, \ldots, 5)$:

Step 1 Use Eq. (2.160) to compute the association coefficients of the IFSs y_i $(i = 1, 2, \ldots, 5)$, and then construct an association matrix $C = (c_{ij})_{5\times 5}$, where $c_{ij} = c_3(y_i, y_j)$, $i, j = 1, 2, \ldots, 5$:

$$
C = \begin{pmatrix}
1.000 & 0.964 & 0.917 & 0.952 & 0.947\\
0.964 & 1.000 & 0.948 & 0.941 & 0.963\\
0.917 & 0.948 & 1.000 & 0.946 & 0.957\\
0.952 & 0.941 & 0.946 & 1.000 & 0.957\\
0.947 & 0.963 & 0.957 & 0.957 & 1.000
\end{pmatrix}
$$

Step 2 By Eq. (2.87), we give a detailed analysis with respect to the threshold λ, and then we get all the possible clusters of the combat aircrafts y_i $(i = 1, 2, \ldots, 5)$:

(1) If $\lambda = 1$, then y_i $(i = 1, 2, \ldots, 5)$ are grouped into the following nine types:

$$\{y_1\}, \{y_2\}, \{y_3\}, \{y_4\}, \{y_5\}$$

(2) If $\lambda = 0.964$, then by Eq. (2.87), the λ-cutting matrix $C_\lambda = \left({}_\lambda c_{ij}\right)_{5\times 5}$ of C is:

$$C_\lambda = \begin{pmatrix} 1 & 1 & 0 & 0 & 0 \\ 1 & 1 & 0 & 0 & 0 \\ 0 & 0 & 1 & 0 & 0 \\ 0 & 0 & 0 & 1 & 0 \\ 0 & 0 & 0 & 0 & 1 \end{pmatrix}$$

According to Theorem 2.19, we know that C_λ is an equivalent Boole matrix, we can use C_λ to cluster the combat aircrafts y_i $(i = 1, 2, \ldots, 5)$ directly, and then y_i $(i = 1, 2, \ldots, 5)$ are grouped into the following four types:

$$\{y_1, y_2\}, \{y_3\}, \{y_4\}, \{y_5\}$$

(3) If $\lambda = 0.963$, then the λ-cutting matrix $C_\lambda = \left({}_\lambda c_{ij}\right)_{5\times 5}$ of C is:

$$C_\lambda = \begin{pmatrix} 1 & 1 & 0 & 0 & 0 \\ 1 & 1 & 0 & 0 & 1 \\ 0 & 0 & 1 & 0 & 0 \\ 0 & 0 & 0 & 1 & 0 \\ 0 & 1 & 0 & 0 & 1 \end{pmatrix}$$

From Theorem 2.19, we know that C_λ is not an equivalent Boole matrix, we should first transform C_λ into an equivalent Boole matrix by changing the element "0" in the special sub-matrices into "1" and get

$$C_\lambda^* = \begin{pmatrix} 1 & 1 & 0 & 0 & 1 \\ 1 & 1 & 0 & 0 & 1 \\ 0 & 0 & 1 & 0 & 0 \\ 0 & 0 & 0 & 1 & 0 \\ 1 & 1 & 0 & 0 & 1 \end{pmatrix}$$

and thus, y_i $(i = 1, 2, \ldots, 5)$ are grouped into the following three types:

$$\{y_1, y_2, y_5\}, \{y_3\}, \{y_4\}$$

Table 2.13 Comparisons of the derived results

Types	The results derived by Zhao et al. (2012b)'s method	The results developed by Xu et al. (2008)'s method	The results developed by Pelekis et al. (2008)'s method
5	$\{y_1\}, \{y_2\}, \{y_3\}, \{y_4\}, \{y_5\}$	$\{y_1\}, \{y_2\}, \{y_3\}, \{y_4\}, \{y_5\}$	$\{y_1\}, \{y_2\}, \{y_3\}, \{y_4\}, \{y_5\}$
4	$\{y_1, y_2\}, \{y_3\}, \{y_4\}, \{y_5\}$	$\{y_1, y_2\}, \{y_3\}, \{y_4\}, \{y_5\}$	$\{y_2, y_5\}, \{y_1\}, \{y_3\}, \{y_4\}$
3	$\{y_1, y_2, y_5\}, \{y_3\}, \{y_4\}$	$\{y_1, y_2, y_5\}, \{y_3\}, \{y_4\}$	$\{y_2, y_4, y_5\}, \{y_1\}, \{y_3\}$
2			$\{y_1, y_2\}, \{y_3, y_4, y_5\}$
1	$\{y_1, y_2, y_3, y_4, y_5\}$	$\{y_1, y_2, y_3, y_4, y_5\}$	$\{y_1, y_2, y_3, y_4, y_5\}$

(4) If $\lambda = 0.957$, then the λ-cutting matrix $C_\lambda = \left({}_\lambda c_{ij}\right)_{5\times5}$ of C is:

$$C_\lambda = \begin{pmatrix} 1 & 1 & 0 & 0 & 0 \\ 1 & 1 & 0 & 0 & 1 \\ 0 & 0 & 1 & 0 & 1 \\ 0 & 0 & 0 & 1 & 1 \\ 0 & 1 & 1 & 1 & 1 \end{pmatrix}$$

Similarly, C_λ is not an equivalent Boole matrix, we should first transform C_λ into an equivalent Boole matrix by changing the element "0" in the special sub-matrices into "1" and get

$$C_\lambda^* = \begin{pmatrix} 1 & 1 & 1 & 1 & 1 \\ 1 & 1 & 1 & 1 & 1 \\ 1 & 1 & 1 & 1 & 1 \\ 1 & 1 & 1 & 1 & 1 \\ 1 & 1 & 1 & 1 & 1 \end{pmatrix}$$

and thus, y_i $(i = 1, 2, \ldots, 5)$ are grouped into the following one type:

$$\{y_1, y_2, y_3, y_4, y_5\}.$$

In the following, some simple comparisons are made among Zhao et al. (2012b)'s method, Xu et al. (2008)'s method which may be regarded as a generalization of Yang and Shih (2001)'s method and Pelekis et al. (2008)'s method in Table 2.13 (Zhao et al. 2012b).

Through Table 2.13, we know that Zhao et al. (2012b)'s method has the same clustering results with those of Xu et al. (2008)'s method, and Pelekis et al. (2008)'s method can make more detailed clustering results.

In order to demonstrate the effectiveness of the intuitionistic fuzzy Boole clustering method, we further conduct an experiment with more samples to compare these methods:

Example 2.9 (Zhao et al. 2012b) Below we first introduce the experimental data sets, and then make a comparison among these methods:

Experimental data sets: Suppose that the military experts evaluate the performance of another group of combat aircrafts y_i ($i = 1, 2, \ldots, 10$) according to the attributes G_j ($j = 1, 2, \ldots, 7$), and give the data as:

$$\begin{aligned}
y_1 = \{&\langle G_1, 0.5, 0.3\rangle, \langle G_2, 0.6, 0.3\rangle, \langle G_3, 0.4, 0.3\rangle,\\
&\langle G_4, 0.8, 0.1\rangle, \langle G_5, 0.7, 0.2\rangle, \langle G_6, 0.5, 0.2\rangle, \langle G_7, 0.4, 0.3\rangle\}\\
y_2 = \{&\langle G_1, 0.6, 0.2\rangle, \langle G_2, 0.5, 0.3\rangle, \langle G_3, 0.5, 0.2\rangle,\\
&\langle G_4, 0.6, 0.2\rangle, \langle G_5, 0.6, 0.3\rangle, \langle G_6, 0.6, 0.3\rangle, \langle G_7, 0.5, 0.2\rangle\}\\
y_3 = \{&\langle G_1, 0.7, 0.1\rangle, \langle G_2, 0.6, 0.3\rangle, \langle G_3, 0.7, 0.2\rangle,\\
&\langle G_4, 0.5, 0.3\rangle, \langle G_5, 0.5, 0.2\rangle, \langle G, 0.5, 0.2\rangle, \langle G_7, 0.6, 0.3\rangle \}\\
y_4 = \{&\langle G_1, 0.4, 0.3\rangle, \langle G_2, 0.7, 0.2\rangle, \langle G_3, 0.5, 0.3\rangle,\\
&\langle G_4, 0.6, 0.2\rangle, \langle G_5, 0.7, 0.1\rangle, \langle G_6, 0.4, 0.3\rangle, \langle G_7, 0.7, 0.2\rangle\}\\
y_5 = \{&\langle G_1, 0.6, 0.2\rangle, \langle G_2, 0.6, 0.3\rangle, \langle G_3, 0.6, 0.2\rangle,\\
&\langle G_4, 0.5, 0.3\rangle, \langle G_5, 0.8, 0.1\rangle, \langle G_6, 0.6, 0.1\rangle, \langle G_7, 0.6, 0.1\rangle\}\\
y_6 = \{&\langle G_1, 0.8, 0.1\rangle, \langle G_2, 0.5, 0.2\rangle, \langle G_3, 0.7, 0.1\rangle,\\
&\langle G_4, 0.7, 0.1\rangle, \langle G_5, 0.7, 0.2\rangle, \langle G_6, 0.8, 0.1\rangle, \langle G_7, 0.7, 0.2\rangle\}\\
y_7 = \{&\langle G_1, 0.7, 0.2\rangle, \langle G_2, 0.6, 0.3\rangle, \langle G_3, 0.8, 0.1\rangle,\\
&\langle G_4, 0.8, 0.1\rangle, \langle G_5, 0.6, 0.3\rangle, \langle G_6, 0.5, 0.4\rangle, \langle G_7, 0.8, 0.1\rangle\}\\
y_8 = \{&\langle G_1, 0.5, 0.2\rangle, \langle G_2, 0.7, 0.2\rangle, \langle G_3, 0.7, 0.2\rangle,\\
&\langle G_4, 0.6, 0.2\rangle, \langle G_5, 0.5, 0.3\rangle, \langle G_6, 0.7, 0.1\rangle, \langle G_7, 0.6, 0.2\rangle\}\\
y_9 = \{&\langle G_1, 0.6, 0.2\rangle, \langle G_2, 0.5, 0.3\rangle, \langle G_3, 0.6, 0.3\rangle,\\
&\langle G_4, 0.5, 0.2\rangle, \langle G_5, 0.8, 0.1\rangle, \langle G_6, 0.8, 0.1\rangle, \langle G_7, 0.5, 0.2\rangle\}\\
y_{10} = \{&\langle G_1, 0.9, 0.0\rangle, \langle G_2, 0.9, 0.1\rangle, \langle G_3, 0.8, 0.1\rangle,\\
&\langle G_4, 0.7, 0.2\rangle, \langle G_5, 0.5, 0.15\rangle, \langle G_6, 0.3, 0.65\rangle, \langle G_7, 0.15, 0.75\rangle\}
\end{aligned}$$

Comparison results among these methods are listed in Table 2.14 (Zhao et al. 2012b).

Again we can see from Table 2.14 that Zhao et al. (2012b)'s method has the same clustering results with those of Xu et al. (2008)'s method, and Pelekis et al. (2008)'s method can make more detailed clustering results. It is worthy of pointing out that the clustering results of Zhao et al. (2012b)'s method are exactly the same with those of Xu et al. (2008)'s method, but Zhao et al. (2012b)'s method does not need to use the transitive closure technique to calculate the equivalent matrix of the association matrix, and thus requires much less computational effort than Xu et al. (2008)'s method. Let's examine into the computing process of the two methods: whether in Xu et al. (2008)'s method or Zhao et al. (2012b)'s method, the clustering processes are all based on λ-cutting matrix. Before getting the λ-cutting matrix, Xu et al. (2008) first transformed the intuitionistic fuzzy association matrix into

Table 2.14 Comparisons of the clustering results

Types	The results derived by Zhao et al. (2012b)'s method	The results developed by Xu et al. (2008)'s method	The results developed by Pelekis et al. (2008)'s method
10	$\{y_1\}, \{y_2\}, \{y_3\}, \{y_4\}, \{y_5\}, \{y_6\}, \{y_7\}, \{y_8\}, \{y_9\}, \{y_{10}\}$	$\{y_1\}, \{y_2\}, \{y_3\}, \{y_4\}, \{y_5\}, \{y_6\}, \{y_7\}, \{y_8\}, \{y_9\}, \{y_{10}\}$	$\{y_1\}, \{y_2\}, \{y_3\}, \{y_4\}, \{y_5\}, \{y_6\}, \{y_7\}, \{y_8\}, \{y_9\}, \{y_{10}\}$
9	$\{y_5, y_9\}, \{y_1\}, \{y_2\}, \{y_3\}, \{y_4\}, \{y_6\}, \{y_7\}, \{y_8\}, \{y_{10}\}$	$\{y_5, y_9\}, \{y_1\}, \{y_2\}, \{y_3\}, \{y_4\}, \{y_6\}, \{y_7\}, \{y_8\}, \{y_{10}\}$	$\{y_5, y_9\}, \{y_1\}, \{y_2\}, \{y_3\}, \{y_4\}, \{y_6\}, \{y_7\}, \{y_8\}, \{y_{10}\}$
8	$\{y_3, y_8\}, \{y_5, y_9\}, \{y_1\}, \{y_2\}, \{y_4\}, \{y_6\}, \{y_7\}, \{y_{10}\}$	$\{y_3, y_8\}, \{y_5, y_9\}, \{y_1\}, \{y_2\}, \{y_4\}, \{y_6\}, \{y_7\}, \{y_{10}\}$	$\{y_1, y_4\}, \{y_5, y_9\}, \{y_2\}, \{y_3\}, \{y_6\}, \{y_7\}, \{y_8\}, \{y_{10}\}$
7			$\{y_1, y_4\}, \{y_2, y_8\}, \{y_5, y_9\}, \{y_3\}, \{y_6\}, \{y_7\}, \{y_{10}\}$
6	$\{y_1, y_2, y_5, y_9\}, \{y_3, y_8\}, \{y_4\}, \{y_6\}, \{y_7\}, \{y_{10}\}$	$\{y_1, y_2, y_5, y_9\}, \{y_3, y_8\}, \{y_4\}, \{y_6\}, \{y_7\}, \{y_{10}\}$	$\{y_1, y_4\}, \{y_3, y_8\}, \{y_5, y_6, y_9\}, \{y_2\}, \{y_7\}, \{y_{10}\}$
5	$\{y_1, y_2, y_5, y_6, y_9\}, \{y_3, y_8\}, \{y_4\}, \{y_7\}, \{y_{10}\}$	$\{y_1, y_2, y_5, y_6, y_9\}, \{y_3, y_8\}, \{y_4\}, \{y_7\}, \{y_{10}\}$	$\{y_1, y_4\}, \{y_2, y_3, y_8\}, \{y_5, y_6, y_9\}, \{y_7\}, \{y_{10}\}$
4	$\{y_1, y_2, y_3, y_5, y_6, y_8, y_9\}, \{y_4\}, \{y_7\}, \{y_{10}\}$	$\{y_1, y_2, y_3, y_5, y_6, y_8, y_9\}, \{y_4\}, \{y_7\}, \{y_{10}\}$	$\{y_1, y_4\}, \{y_3, y_7, y_8\}, \{y_2, y_5, y_6, y_9\}, \{y_{10}\}$
3	$\{y_1, y_2, y_3, y_4, y_5, y_6, y_8, y_9\}, \{y_7\}, \{y_{10}\}$	$\{y_1, y_2, y_3, y_4, y_5, y_6, y_8, y_9\}, \{y_7\}, \{y_{10}\}$	$\{y_1, y_2, y_5, y_6, y_9\}, \{y_3, y_4, y_7, y_8\}, \{y_{10}\}$
2	$\{y_1, y_2, y_3, y_4, y_5, y_6, y_7, y_8, y_9\}, \{y_{10}\}$	$\{y_1, y_2, y_3, y_4, y_5, y_6, y_7, y_8, y_9\}, \{y_{10}\}$	$\{y_1, y_2, y_3, y_4, y_5, y_6, y_7, y_8, y_9\}, \{y_{10}\}$
1	$\{y_1, y_2, y_3, y_4, y_5, y_6, y_7, y_8, y_9, y_{10}\}$	$\{y_1, y_2, y_3, y_4, y_5, y_6, y_7, y_8, y_9, y_{10}\}$	$\{y_1, y_2, y_3, y_4, y_5, y_6, y_7, y_8, y_9, y_{10}\}$

an intuitionistic fuzzy equivalent association matrix by transitive closure technique, which needs lots of computational effort. In Zhao et al. (2012b)'s method, we get the λ-cutting matrix directly from the intuitionistic fuzzy association matrix.

Furthermore, Let m and n represent the amount of alternatives and attributes respectively. Then the computational complexity of our method is $O\ (nm^2)$, Xu et al. (2008)'s method is $O\ ((1+k)nm^2)$ where k (usually, $k \geq 2$) represents the transfer times until we get the equivalent matrix, and Pelekis et al. (2008)'s method is $O\ (nm^2 + jcm)$ where c is the number of the clusters, j is the times of judgment if $\left\| U^{j+1} - U^j \right\|_F > \varepsilon$ is valid.

In summary, Xu et al. (2008)'s method and Pelekis et al. (2008)'s method have relatively high computational complexity, which indeed motivates the intuitionistic fuzzy Boole clustering method given by Zhao et al. (2012b).

Furthermore, from Examples 2.8 and 2.9, we can see that the clustering results have much to do with the threshold λ, the smaller the confidence level λ is, the more detailed the clustering will be.

Either in Example 2.8 or in Example 2.9, we all use the association coefficient Eq. (2.159) but not Eq. (2.157), the reason is that Eq. (2.157) cannot guarantee the necessity in the condition (2) of Definition 2.31 and omits the hesitation degree, which may lead to the incorrect results. The following example shows these ideas:

Example 2.10 (Zhao et al. 2012b) Suppose that the military experts evaluate the performance of another group of combat aircrafts y_i $(i = 1, 2, \ldots, 9)$ according to the attributes G_j $(j = 1, 2, \ldots, 7)$, and give the data as:

$$\begin{aligned}
y_1 = \{&\langle G_1, 0.5, 0.3\rangle, \langle G_2, 0.6, 0.3\rangle, \langle G_3, 0.4, 0.3\rangle,\\
&\langle G_4, 0.8, 0.1\rangle, \langle G_5, 0.7, 0.2\rangle, \langle G_6, 0.5, 0.2\rangle, \langle G_7, 0.4, 0.3\rangle\}\\
y_2 = \{&\langle G_1, 0.6, 0.2\rangle, \langle G_2, 0.5, 0.3\rangle, \langle G_3, 0.5, 0.2\rangle,\\
&\langle G_4, 0.6, 0.2\rangle, \langle G_5, 0.6, 0.3\rangle, \langle G_6, 0.6, 0.3\rangle, \langle G_7, 0.5, 0.2\rangle\}\\
y_3 = \{&\langle G_1, 0.7, 0.1\rangle, \langle G_2, 0.6, 0.3\rangle, \langle G_3, 0.7, 0.2\rangle,\\
&\langle G_4, 0.5, 0.3\rangle, \langle G_5, 0.5, 0.2\rangle, \langle G_6, 0.5, 0.2\rangle, \langle G_7, 0.6, 0.3\rangle\}\\
y_4 = \{&\langle G_1, 0.4, 0.3\rangle, \langle G_2, 0.7, 0.2\rangle, \langle G_3, 0.5, 0.3\rangle,\\
&\langle G_4, 0.6, 0.2\rangle, \langle G_5, 0.7, 0.1\rangle, \langle G_6, 0.4, 0.3\rangle, \langle G_7, 0.7, 0.2\rangle\}\\
y_5 = \{&\langle G_1, 0.6, 0.2\rangle, \langle G_2, 0.6, 0.3\rangle, \langle G_3, 0.6, 0.2\rangle,\\
&\langle G_4, 0.5, 0.3\rangle, \langle G_5, 0.8, 0.1\rangle, \langle G_6, 0.6, 0.1\rangle, \langle G_7, 0.6, 0.1\rangle\}\\
y_6 = \{&\langle G_1, 0.8, 0.1\rangle, \langle G_2, 0.5, 0.2\rangle, \langle G_3, 0.7, 0.1\rangle,\\
&\langle G_4, 0.7, 0.1\rangle, \langle G_5, 0.7, 0.2\rangle, \langle G_6, 0.8, 0.1\rangle, \langle G_7, 0.7, 0.2\rangle\}\\
y_7 = \{&\langle G_1, 0.7, 0.2\rangle, \langle G_2, 0.6, 0.3\rangle, \langle G_3, 0.8, 0.1\rangle,\\
&\langle G_4, 0.8, 0.1\rangle, \langle G_5, 0.6, 0.3\rangle, \langle G_6, 0.5, 0.4\rangle, \langle G_7, 0.8, 0.1\rangle\}\\
y_8 = \{&\langle G_1, 0.5, 0.2\rangle, \langle G_2, 0.7, 0.2\rangle, \langle G_3, 0.7, 0.2\rangle,\\
&\langle G_4, 0.6, 0.2\rangle, \langle G_5, 0.5, 0.3\rangle, \langle G_6, 0.7, 0.1\rangle, \langle G_7, 0.6, 0.2\rangle\}\\
y_9 = \{&\langle G_1, 0.6, 0.2\rangle, \langle G_2, 0.5, 0.3\rangle, \langle G_3, 0.6, 0.3\rangle,\\
&\langle G_4, 0.5, 0.2\rangle, \langle G_5, 0.8, 0.1\rangle, \langle G_6, 0.8, 0.1\rangle, \langle G_7, 0.5, 0.2\rangle\}
\end{aligned}$$

If we use Eq. (2.157) to compute the association coefficients of the IFSs y_i $(i = 1, 2, \ldots, 9)$, then the association matrix $C = (c_{ij})_{6\times 6}$, where $c_{ij} = c_1(y_i, y_j)$, $i, j = 1, 2, \ldots, 9$ will be:

$$C = \begin{pmatrix} 1.000 & 0.971 & 0.931 & 0.960 & 0.945 & 0.933 & 0.934 & 0.943 & 0.948 \\ 0.971 & 1.000 & 0.973 & 0.956 & 0.970 & 0.970 & 0.971 & 0.972 & 0.970 \\ 0.931 & 0.973 & 1.000 & 0.945 & 0.968 & 0.964 & 0.965 & 0.973 & 0.953 \\ 0.960 & 0.956 & 0.945 & 1.000 & 0.962 & 0.923 & 0.952 & 0.950 & 0.938 \\ 0.945 & 0.970 & 0.968 & 0.962 & 1.000 & 0.967 & 0.946 & 0.965 & 0.985 \\ 0.933 & 0.970 & 0.964 & 0.923 & 0.967 & 1.000 & 0.963 & 0.969 & 0.971 \\ 0.934 & 0.971 & 0.965 & 0.952 & 0.946 & 0.963 & 1.000 & 0.960 & 0.923 \\ 0.943 & 0.972 & 0.973 & 0.950 & 0.965 & 0.969 & 0.960 & 1.000 & 0.960 \\ 0.948 & 0.970 & 0.953 & 0.938 & 0.985 & 0.971 & 0.923 & 0.960 & 1.000 \end{pmatrix}$$

If we use Eq. (2.159) to compute the association coefficients of the IFSs y_i $(i = 1, 2, \ldots, 9)$, then the association matrix $C = (c_{ij})_{m\times m}$, where $c_{ij} = c_3(y_i, y_j)$, $i, j = 1, 2, \ldots, 9$ will be:

$$C = \begin{pmatrix} 1.000 & 0.964 & 0.917 & 0.952 & 0.947 & 0.914 & 0.914 & 0.934 & 0.933 \\ 0.964 & 1.000 & 0.948 & 0.941 & 0.963 & 0.959 & 0.950 & 0.959 & 0.964 \\ 0.917 & 0.948 & 1.000 & 0.946 & 0.957 & 0.945 & 0.948 & 0.969 & 0.936 \\ 0.952 & 0.941 & 0.946 & 1.000 & 0.957 & 0.908 & 0.934 & 0.950 & 0.923 \\ 0.947 & 0.963 & 0.957 & 0.957 & 1.000 & 0.950 & 0.930 & 0.960 & 0.976 \\ 0.914 & 0.959 & 0.945 & 0.908 & 0.950 & 1.000 & 0.956 & 0.953 & 0.961 \\ 0.914 & 0.950 & 0.948 & 0.934 & 0.930 & 0.956 & 1.000 & 0.947 & 0.911 \\ 0.934 & 0.959 & 0.969 & 0.950 & 0.960 & 0.953 & 0.947 & 1.000 & 0.955 \\ 0.933 & 0.964 & 0.936 & 0.923 & 0.976 & 0.961 & 0.911 & 0.955 & 1.000 \end{pmatrix}$$

Based on the above two association matrices, using the intuitionistic fuzzy Boole clustering method, we can make comparisons between the clustering results of the two association coefficients (See Table 2.15) (Zhao et al. 2012b).

We can see from Table 2.15 that Eq. (2.159) can derive more detailed clustering results than Eq. (2.157). Since Eq. (2.157) cannot guarantee the necessity in the condition (2) of Definition 2.31, and omits the hesitation degree, some information may be missing. Namely, Eq. (2.157) cannot reflect all the information that the intuitionistic fuzzy data contains. Considering the stated reasons above, it is not hard for us to comprehend why Eq. (2.159) can get more detailed types than Eq. (2.157). Therefore, Compared to Eq. (2.157), Eq. (2.159) has much more potential for practical applications.

Table 2.15 Comparisons of the clustering results of Eqs. (2.157) and (2.159)

Types	The clustering result using Eq. (2.157)	The clustering result using Eq. (2.159)
9	$\{y_1\}, \{y_2\}, \{y_3\}, \{y_4\}, \{y_5\}, \{y_6\}, \{y_7\}, \{y_8\}, \{y_9\}$	$\{y_1\}, \{y_2\}, \{y_3\}, \{y_4\}, \{y_5\}, \{y_6\}, \{y_7\}, \{y_8\}, \{y_9\}$
8	$\{y_5, y_9\}, \{y_1\}, \{y_2\}, \{y_3\}, \{y_4\}, \{y_6\}, \{y_7\}, \{y_8\}$	$\{y_5, y_9\}, \{y_1\}, \{y_2\}, \{y_3\}, \{y_4\}, \{y_6\}, \{y_7\}, \{y_8\}$
7		$\{y_3, y_8\}, \{y_5, y_9\}, \{y_1\}, \{y_2\}, \{y_4\}, \{y_6\}, \{y_7\}$
6	$\{y_1\}, \{y_2, y_3, y_8\}, \{y_5, y_9\}, \{y_4\}, \{y_6\}, \{y_7\}$	
5		$\{y_1, y_2, y_5, y_9\}, \{y_3, y_8\}, \{y_4\}, \{y_6\}, \{y_7\}$
4		$\{y_1, y_2, y_5, y_6, y_9\}, \{y_3, y_8\}, \{y_4\}, \{y_7\}$
3	$\{y_1, y_2, y_3, y_7, y_8\}, \{y_5, y_6, y_9\}, \{y_4\}$	$\{y_1, y_2, y_3, y_5, y_6, y_8, y_9\}, \{y_4\}, \{y_7\}$
2	$\{y_1, y_2, y_3, y_5, y_6, y_7, y_8, y_9\}, \{y_4\}$	$\{y_1, y_2, y_3, y_4, y_5, y_6, y_8, y_9\}, \{y_7\}$
1	$\{y_1, y_2, y_3, y_4, y_5, y_6, y_7, y_8, y_9\}$	$\{y_1, y_2, y_3, y_4, y_5, y_6, y_7, y_8, y_9\}$

2.7.4 Interval-Valued Intuitionistic Fuzzy Clustering Algorithm

Let IVIFS(X) be the set of all IVIFSs over X, Xu et al. (2008) defined the concept of association coefficient between two IVIFS as follows:

Definition 2.32 (Xu et al. 2008) Let $\dot{c}$ be a mapping $\dot{c}$: $(\text{IVIFS}(X))^2 \rightarrow [0, 1]$, then the association coefficient between two IVIFSs $\tilde{A}$ and $\tilde{B}$ is defined as $\dot{c}(\tilde{A}, \tilde{B})$, which satisfies the following conditions: (1) $0 \leq \dot{c}(\tilde{A}, \tilde{B}) \leq 1$; (2) $\dot{c}(\tilde{A}, \tilde{B}) = 1$ if and only if $\tilde{A} = \tilde{B}$; and (3) $\dot{c}(\tilde{A}, \tilde{B}) = \dot{c}(\tilde{B}, \tilde{A})$.

In the case where $X = \{x_1, x_2, \ldots, x_n\}$ is a discrete universe of discourse, we extend $c_3(A, B)$ to IVIFSs to calculate the association coefficient between two IVIFSs $\tilde{A}$ and $\tilde{B}$ as below:

$$\dot{c}_7(\tilde{A}, \tilde{B}) = \frac{\sum_{j=1}^{n} f_{\tilde{A},\tilde{B}}(x_j)}{\sqrt{\sum_{j=1}^{n} g_{\tilde{A}}(x_j) \cdot \sum_{j=1}^{n} g_{\tilde{B}}(x_j)}} \tag{2.168}$$

where

$$g_{\tilde{A}}(x_j) = \left(\mu_{\tilde{A}}^{-}(x_j)\right)^2 + \left(v_{\tilde{A}}^{-}(x_j)\right)^2 + \left(\pi_{\tilde{A}}^{-}(x_j)\right)^2 + \left(\mu_{\tilde{A}}^{+}(x_j)\right)^2 + \left(v_{\tilde{A}}^{+}(x_j)\right)^2 + \left(\pi_{\tilde{A}}^{+}(x_j)\right)^2 \tag{2.169}$$

$$g_{\tilde{B}}\left(x_j\right) = \left(\mu_{\tilde{B}}^-\left(x_j\right)\right)^2 + \left(v_{\tilde{B}}^-\left(x_j\right)\right)^2 + \left(\pi_{\tilde{B}}^-\left(x_j\right)\right)^2 + \left(\mu_{\tilde{B}}^+\left(x_j\right)\right)^2 + \left(v_{\tilde{B}}^+\left(x_j\right)\right)^2 + \left(\pi_{\tilde{B}}^+\left(x_j\right)\right)^2 \tag{2.170}$$

$$f_{\tilde{A},\tilde{B}}\left(x_j\right) = \mu_{\tilde{A}}^-\left(x_j\right)\mu_{\tilde{B}}^-\left(x_j\right) + v_{\tilde{A}}^-\left(x_j\right)v_{\tilde{B}}^-\left(x_j\right) + \pi_{\tilde{A}}^-\left(x_j\right)\pi_{\tilde{B}}^-\left(x_j\right) + \mu_{\tilde{A}}^+\left(x_j\right)\mu_{\tilde{B}}^+\left(x_j\right) + v_{\tilde{A}}^+\left(x_j\right)v_{\tilde{B}}^+\left(x_j\right) + \pi_{\tilde{A}}^+\left(x_j\right)\pi_{\tilde{B}}^+\left(x_j\right) \tag{2.171}$$

If we need to consider the weights of the element $x_i \in X$, then Eq. (2.166) can be extended to its weighted counterpart:

$$\dot{c}_8(\tilde{A}, \tilde{B}) = \frac{\sum_{j=1}^n w_j f_{\tilde{A},\tilde{B}}\left(x_j\right)}{\sqrt{\sum_{j=1}^n w_j g_{\tilde{A}}\left(x_j\right) \cdot \sum_{j=1}^n w_j g_{\tilde{B}}\left(x_j\right)}} \tag{2.172}$$

where $w = (w_1, w_2, \ldots, w_n)^T$ is the weight vector of x_i $(i = 1, 2, \ldots, n)$, with $w_j \geq 0, i = 1, 2, \ldots, n$ and $\sum_{j=1}^n w_j = 1$. If $w_1 = w_2 = \cdots = w_n = 1/n$, then Eq. (2.172) reduces to Eq. (2.168).

In the following, we prove that Eq. (2.172) satisfies all the conditions of Definition 2.32:

Proof Since $\tilde{A}, \tilde{B} \in \text{IVIFS}(X)$, then

$$0 \leq \mu_{\tilde{A}}^-(x_j) \leq \mu_{\tilde{A}}^+(x_j) \leq 1, 0 \leq v_{\tilde{A}}^-(x_j) \leq v_{\tilde{A}}^+(x_j) \leq 1,\ 0 \leq \pi_{\tilde{A}}^-(x_j) \leq \pi_{\tilde{A}}^+(x_j) \leq 1, \quad \text{for all } x_j \in X \tag{2.173}$$

$$0 \leq \mu_{\tilde{B}}^-(x_j) \leq \mu_{\tilde{B}}^+(x_j) \leq 1, 0 \leq v_{\tilde{B}}^-(x_j) \leq v_{\tilde{B}}^+(x_j) \leq 1,\ 0 \leq \pi_{\tilde{B}}^-(x_j) \leq \pi_{\tilde{B}}^+(x_j) \leq 1, \quad \text{for all } x_j \in X \tag{2.174}$$

and thus, by Eq. (2.172), we get $\dot{c}_8(\tilde{A}, \tilde{B}) \geq 0$. According to the famous Cauchy-Schwarz inequality Eq. (2.160), we have

$$\sum_{j=1}^n w_j f_{\tilde{A},\tilde{B}} \leq \sqrt{\left(\sum_{j=1}^n w_j g_{\tilde{A}}\left(x_j\right)\right)\left(\sum_{j=1}^n w_j g_{\tilde{B}}\left(x_j\right)\right)} \tag{2.175}$$

and thus, $\dot{c}_8(\tilde{A}, \tilde{B}) \leq 1$ with equality if and only if there exists a nonzero real number λ, such that

$$\mu_{\tilde{A}}^{-}(x_j) = \lambda\mu_{\tilde{B}}^{-}(x_j),\ \mu_{\tilde{A}}^{+}(x_j) = \lambda\mu_{\tilde{B}}^{+}(x_j),\ v_{\tilde{A}}^{-}(x_j) = \lambda v_{\tilde{B}}^{-}(x_j)$$
$$v_{\tilde{A}}^{+}(x_j) = \lambda v_{\tilde{B}}^{+}(x_j),\ \pi_{\tilde{A}}^{-}(x_j) = \lambda\pi_{\tilde{B}}^{-}(x_j),\ \pi_{\tilde{A}}^{+}(x_j) = \lambda\pi_{\tilde{B}}^{+}(x_j)$$
$$\text{for all } x_j \in X \tag{2.176}$$

while because

$$\pi_{\tilde{A}}^{-}(x_j) = 1 - \mu_{\tilde{A}}^{+}(x_j) - v_{\tilde{A}}^{+}(x_j),\ \pi_{\tilde{A}}^{+}(x_j) = 1 - \mu_{\tilde{A}}^{-}(x_j) - v_{\tilde{A}}^{-}(x_j), \text{ for all } x_j \in X \tag{2.177}$$
$$\pi_{\tilde{B}}^{-}(x_j) = 1 - \mu_{\tilde{B}}^{+}(x_j) - v_{\tilde{B}}^{+}(x_j),\ \pi_{\tilde{B}}^{+}(x_j) = 1 - \mu_{\tilde{B}}^{-}(x_j) - v_{\tilde{B}}^{-}(x_j), \text{ for all } x_j \in X \tag{2.178}$$

Then by Eq. (2.178), we have $\lambda = 1$, i.e., $\tilde{A} = \tilde{B}$, which completes the proofs of the conditions (1) and (2) in Definition 2.32. Furthermore, by Eq. (2.172), we have

$$\dot{c}_8(\tilde{A}, \tilde{B}) = \frac{\sum_{j=1}^{n} w_j f_{\tilde{A},\tilde{B}}(x_j)}{\sqrt{\sum_{j=1}^{n} w_j g_{\tilde{A}}(x_j) \cdot \sum_{j=1}^{n} w_j g_{\tilde{B}}(x_j)}} = \frac{\sum_{j=1}^{n} w_j f_{\tilde{B},\tilde{A}}(x_j)}{\sqrt{\sum_{j=1}^{n} w_j g_{\tilde{B}}(x_j) \cdot \sum_{j=1}^{n} w_j g_{\tilde{A}}(x_j)}} = \dot{c}_8(\tilde{B}, \tilde{A}) \tag{2.179}$$

Thus, we can prove that $\dot{c}_8(\tilde{A}, \tilde{B})$ also satisfies the condition (3) of Definition 2.32.

If the universe of discourse, X, is continuous and the weight of the element $x \in X = [a, b]$ is $w(x)$, where $w(x) \geq 0$ and $\int_a^b w(x)dx = 1$, then we get the continuous form of Eq. (2.172):

$$\dot{c}_9(\tilde{A}, \tilde{B}) = \frac{\int_a^b w(x) f_{\tilde{A},\tilde{B}}(x)\,dx}{\sqrt{\int_a^b w(x) g_{\tilde{A}}(x)\,dx \cdot \int_a^b w(x) g_{\tilde{B}}(x)\,dx}} \tag{2.180}$$

where

$$g_{\tilde{A}}(x) = \left(\mu_{\tilde{A}}^{-}(x)\right)^2 + \left(v_{\tilde{A}}^{-}(x)\right)^2 + \left(\pi_{\tilde{A}}^{-}(x)\right)^2 + \left(\mu_{\tilde{A}}^{+}(x)\right)^2 + \left(v_{\tilde{A}}^{+}(x)\right)^2 + \left(\pi_{\tilde{A}}^{+}(x)\right)^2 \tag{2.181}$$
$$g_{\tilde{B}}(x) = \left(\mu_{\tilde{B}}^{-}(x)\right)^2 + \left(v_{\tilde{B}}^{-}(x)\right)^2 + \left(\pi_{\tilde{B}}^{-}(x)\right)^2 + \left(\mu_{\tilde{B}}^{+}(x)\right)^2 + \left(v_{\tilde{B}}^{+}(x)\right)^2 + \left(\pi_{\tilde{B}}^{+}(x)\right)^2 \tag{2.182}$$

$$f_{\tilde{A},\tilde{B}}(x_j) = \mu_{\tilde{A}}^{-}(x)\,\mu_{\tilde{B}}^{-}(x) + v_{\tilde{A}}^{-}(x)\,v_{\tilde{B}}^{-}(x) + \pi_{\tilde{A}}^{-}(x)\,\pi_{\tilde{B}}^{-}(x) + \mu_{\tilde{A}}^{+}(x)\,\mu_{\tilde{B}}^{+}(x) + v_{\tilde{A}}^{+}(x)\,v_{\tilde{B}}^{+}(x) + \pi_{\tilde{A}}^{+}(x)\,\pi_{\tilde{B}}^{+}(x) \tag{2.183}$$

If all the elements have the same importance, then Eq. (2.181) reduces to

$$\dot{c}_{10}(\tilde{A}, \tilde{B}) = \frac{\int_a^b f_{\tilde{A},\tilde{B}}(x)\, dx}{\sqrt{\int_a^b g_{\tilde{A}}(x)\, dx \cdot \int_a^b g_{\tilde{B}}(x)\, dx}} \tag{2.184}$$

For convenience, we introduce the concept of interval-valued intuitionistic fuzzy association matrix:

Definition 2.33 (Xu et al. 2008) Let $\tilde{A}_j$ $(j = 1, 2, \ldots, m)$ be m IVIFSs, then $\dot{C} = (\dot{c}_{ij})_{m\times m}$ is called an association matrix, where $\dot{c}_{ij} = \dot{c}(\tilde{A}_i, \tilde{A}_j)$ is the interval-valued intuitionistic fuzzy association coefficient of $\tilde{A}_i$ and $\tilde{A}_j$, which has the following properties: (1) $0 \leq \dot{c}_{ij} \leq 1$ for all $i, j = 1, 2, \ldots, m$; (2) $\dot{c}_{ij} = 1$ if and only if $\tilde{A}_i = \tilde{A}_j$; and (3) $\dot{c}_{ij} = \dot{c}_{ji}$, for all $i, j = 1, 2, \ldots, m$.

Based on the definition above, in what follows, we introduce an algorithm for clustering IVIFSs (Zhao et al. 2012b):

Algorithm 2.13

Step 1 Use Eqs. (2.168) or (2.172) (if the weights of the attributes are the same, we use Eq. (2.168); otherwise, we use Eq. (2.172)) to calculate the association coefficients of the IVIFSs $\tilde{A}_j$ $(j = 1, 2, \ldots, m)$, and then construct an association matrix $\dot{C} = (\dot{c}_{ij})_{m\times m}$, where $\dot{c}_{ij} = \dot{c}_7(\tilde{A}_i, \tilde{A}_j)$ or $\dot{c}_{ij} = \dot{c}_8(\tilde{A}_i, \tilde{A}_j)$, $i, j = 1, 2, \ldots, m$.

Step 2 Construct a λ-cutting matrix $\dot{C}_\lambda = \left({}_\lambda\dot{c}_{ij}\right)_{m\times m}$ of $\dot{C}$ by using Eq. (2.87).

Step 3 See Algorithm 2.12.

Step 4 See Algorithm 2.12.

Step 5 End.

Example 2.11 (Zhao et al. 2012b) Suppose that there are six samples y_i $(i = 1, 2, \ldots, 6)$ to be classified. According to the attributes G_i $(i = 1, 2)$, their attribute values are expressed by IVIFSs as follows:

$$y_1 = \{\langle G_1, [0.60, 0.80], [0.10, 0.20]\rangle, \langle G_2, [0.50, 0.70], [0.10, 0.30]\rangle\}$$
$$y_2 = \{\langle G_1, [0.30, 0.50], [0.25, 0.45]\rangle, \langle G_2, [0.70, 0.85], [0.00, 0.15]\rangle\}$$
$$y_3 = \{\langle G_1, [0.45, 0.65], [0.15, 0.35]\rangle, \langle G_2, [0.60, 0.80], [0.05, 0.20]\rangle\}$$
$$y_4 = \{\langle G_1, [0.34, 0.54], [0.25, 0.45]\rangle, \langle G_2, [0.50, 0.70], [0.10, 0.30]\rangle\}$$
$$y_5 = \{\langle G_1, [0.40, 0.60], [0.25, 0.40]\rangle, \langle G_2, [0.65, 0.80], [0.10, 0.20]\rangle\}$$
$$y_6 = \{\langle G_1, [0.45, 0.65], [0.15, 0.35]\rangle, \langle G_2, [0.47, 0.67], [0.05, 0.25]\rangle\}$$

Suppose that the weights of the attributes G_j $(j = 1, 2)$ are equal, now we utilize Algorithm 2.13 to group these samples y_i $(i = 1, 2, \ldots, 6)$:

Step 1 Use Eq. (2.168) to compute the association coefficients of the IFSs y_i $(i = 1, 2, \ldots, 6)$, and then construct an association matrix $C = (c_{ij})_{6\times 6}$, where $c_{ij} = \dot{c}_7(y_i, y_j)$, $i, j = 1, 2, \ldots, 6$:

$$C = \begin{pmatrix} 1.000 & 0.908 & 0.973 & 0.944 & 0.950 & 0.977 \\ 0.908 & 1.000 & 0.979 & 0.975 & 0.987 & 0.950 \\ 0.973 & 0.979 & 1.000 & 0.982 & 0.992 & 0.986 \\ 0.944 & 0.975 & 0.982 & 1.000 & 0.981 & 0.983 \\ 0.950 & 0.987 & 0.992 & 0.981 & 1.000 & 0.967 \\ 0.977 & 0.950 & 0.986 & 0.983 & 0.967 & 1.000 \end{pmatrix}$$

Step 2 By Eq. (2.87) we give a detailed analysis with respect to the threshold λ, and then we get all the possible clusters of the samples y_i $(i = 1, 2, \ldots, 6)$:

(1) If $\lambda = 1$, then y_i $(i = 1, 2, \ldots, 6)$ are grouped into the following six types:

$$\{y_1\}, \{y_2\}, \{y_3\}, \{y_4\}, \{y_5\}, \{y_6\}$$

(2) If $\lambda = 0.992$, then by Eq. (2.87), the λ-cutting matrix $C_\lambda = \left({}_\lambda c_{ij}\right)_{m\times m}$ of C is:

$$C_\lambda = \begin{pmatrix} 1 & 0 & 0 & 0 & 0 & 0 \\ 0 & 1 & 0 & 0 & 0 & 0 \\ 0 & 0 & 1 & 0 & 1 & 0 \\ 0 & 0 & 0 & 1 & 0 & 0 \\ 0 & 0 & 1 & 0 & 1 & 0 \\ 0 & 0 & 0 & 0 & 0 & 1 \end{pmatrix}$$

According to Theorem 2.19, we know that C_λ is an equivalent Boole matrix, we can use C_λ to cluster the samples y_i $(i = 1, 2, \ldots, 6)$ directly, and then y_i $(i = 1, 2, \ldots, 6)$ are grouped into the following five types:

$$\{y_1\}, \{y_2\}, \{y_3, y_5\}, \{y_4\}, \{y_6\}$$

(3) If $\lambda = 0.987$, then the λ-cutting matrix $C_\lambda = \left({}_\lambda c_{ij}\right)_{m\times m}$ of C is:

$$C_\lambda = \begin{pmatrix} 1 & 0 & 0 & 0 & 0 & 0 \\ 0 & 1 & 0 & 0 & 1 & 0 \\ 0 & 0 & 1 & 0 & 1 & 0 \\ 0 & 0 & 0 & 1 & 0 & 0 \\ 0 & 1 & 1 & 0 & 1 & 0 \\ 0 & 0 & 0 & 0 & 0 & 1 \end{pmatrix}$$

Similar to (2), y_i $(i = 1, 2, \ldots, 6)$ are grouped into the following four types:

$$\{y_1\}, \{y_2, y_3, y_5\}, \{y_4\}, \{y_6\}$$

(4) If $\lambda = 0.986$, then the λ-cutting matrix $C_\lambda = \left({}_\lambda c_{ij}\right)_{m \times m}$ of C is:

$$C_\lambda = \begin{pmatrix} 1 & 0 & 0 & 0 & 0 & 0 \\ 0 & 1 & 0 & 0 & 1 & 0 \\ 0 & 0 & 1 & 0 & 1 & 1 \\ 0 & 0 & 0 & 1 & 0 & 0 \\ 0 & 1 & 1 & 0 & 1 & 0 \\ 0 & 0 & 1 & 0 & 0 & 1 \end{pmatrix}$$

By Theorem 2.19, we know that C_λ is not an equivalent Boole matrix, to transform C_λ into an equivalent Boole matrix, we should change the element "0" in the special sub-matrices into "1" and then we get

$$C_\lambda^* = \begin{pmatrix} 1 & 0 & 0 & 0 & 0 & 0 \\ 0 & 1 & 1 & 0 & 1 & 1 \\ 0 & 1 & 1 & 0 & 1 & 1 \\ 0 & 0 & 0 & 1 & 0 & 0 \\ 0 & 1 & 1 & 0 & 1 & 1 \\ 0 & 1 & 1 & 0 & 1 & 1 \end{pmatrix}$$

Obviously, C_λ^* is an equivalent Boole matrix, by which we can group y_i $(i = 1, 2, \ldots, 6)$ into the following three types:

$$\{y_1\}, \{y_2, y_3, y_5, y_6\}, \{y_4\}$$

(5) If $\lambda = 0.982$, then the λ-cutting matrix $C_\lambda = \left({}_\lambda c_{ij}\right)_{6 \times 6}$ of C is:

$$C_\lambda = \begin{pmatrix} 1 & 0 & 0 & 0 & 0 & 0 \\ 0 & 1 & 0 & 0 & 1 & 1 \\ 0 & 0 & 1 & 1 & 1 & 1 \\ 0 & 0 & 1 & 1 & 0 & 0 \\ 0 & 1 & 1 & 0 & 1 & 0 \\ 0 & 1 & 1 & 0 & 0 & 1 \end{pmatrix}$$

Similar to (4), y_i $(i = 1, 2, \ldots, 6)$ are grouped into the following two types:

$$\{y_1\}, \{y_2, y_3, y_4, y_5, y_6\}$$

(6) If $\lambda = 0.977$, then the λ-cutting matrix $C_\lambda = \left({}_\lambda c_{ij}\right)_{6\times 6}$ of C is:

$$C_\lambda = \begin{pmatrix} 1 & 0 & 0 & 0 & 0 & 1 \\ 0 & 1 & 1 & 1 & 1 & 1 \\ 0 & 1 & 1 & 1 & 1 & 1 \\ 0 & 1 & 1 & 1 & 1 & 1 \\ 0 & 1 & 1 & 1 & 1 & 1 \\ 1 & 1 & 1 & 1 & 1 & 1 \end{pmatrix}$$

Similar to (4), y_i $(i = 1, 2, \ldots, 6)$ are grouped into the following one types:

$$\{y_1, y_2, y_3, y_4, y_5, y_6\}$$

2.8 A Netting Method for Clustering Intuitionistic Fuzzy Information

2.8.1 An Approach to Constructing Intuitionistic Fuzzy Similarity Matrix

Now we consider a multi-attribute decision making problem, let Y and G be as defined previously. The characteristic of each alternative y_i under all the attributes G_j $(j = 1, 2, \ldots, n)$ is represented as an IFS:

$$y_i = \{\langle G_j, \mu_{y_i}(G_j), v_{y_i}(G_j)\rangle | G_j \in G\}, i = 1, 2, \ldots, m; j = 1, 2, \ldots, n \tag{2.185}$$

where $\mu_{y_i}(G_j)$ denotes the membership degree of y_i to G_j, and $v_{y_i}(G_j)$ denotes the non-membership degree of y_i to G_j. Obviously, $\pi_{y_i}(G_j) = 1 - \mu_{y_i}(G_j) - v_{y_i}(G_j)$ is the uncertainty (or hesitation) degree of y_i to G_j. If let $r_{ij} = (\mu_{ij}, v_{ij}) = (\mu_{y_i}(G_j), v_{y_i}(G_j))$, which is an IFV, then based on these IFVs r_{ij} $(i = 1, 2, \ldots, m;$ $j = 1, 2, \ldots, n)$, we can construct an $m \times n$ intuitionistic fuzzy matrix $R = (r_{ij})_{m\times n}$.

Next, we shall introduce an approach to constructing an intuitionistic fuzzy similarity matrix based on the intuitionistic fuzzy matrix $R = (r_{ij})_{m\times n}$.

For any two alternatives y_i and y_k, we first use the normalized Hamming distance to get the average value of the absolute deviations of the non-membership degrees v_{ij} and v_{kj}, for all $j = 1, 2, \ldots, n$:

$$\dot{d}_{NH}(y_i, y_k) = \frac{1}{n}\sum_{j=1}^{n} |v_{ij} - v_{kj}|, i, k = 1, 2, \ldots, m \tag{2.186}$$

Analogously, we get the average value of the absolute deviations of the membership degrees μ_{ij} and μ_{kj}, for all $j = 1, 2, \ldots, n$:

$$d_{NH}(y_i, y_k) = \frac{1}{n}\sum_{j=1}^{n} |\mu_{ij} - \mu_{kj}|, i, k = 1, 2, \ldots, m \tag{2.187}$$

Obviously, the distances (2.186) and (2.187) show the closeness degrees of the characteristics of each two alternatives y_i and y_k. The smaller the values of $\dot{d}_{NH}(y_i, y_k)$ and $d_{NH}(y_i, y_k)$ are, the more similar the two alternatives y_i and y_k.

In an intuitionistic fuzzy similarity matrix, each of its elements is an IFV. To get an intuitionistic fuzzy closeness degrees of y_i and y_k, we may consider the value of $\dot{d}_{NH}(y_i, y_k)$ as a non-membership degree $\dot{v}_{ik}$, and then it may be hopeful to define

$$\dot{\mu}_{ik} = 1 - \frac{1}{n}\sum_{j=1}^{n} |\mu_{ij} - \mu_{kj}|, i, k = 1, 2, \ldots, m \tag{2.188}$$

as a membership degree. Now we need to check whether $0 \leq \dot{\mu}_{ik} + \dot{v}_{ik} \leq 1$ holds or not. However,

$$\dot{\mu}_{ik} + \dot{v}_{ik} = 1 - \frac{1}{n}\sum_{j=1}^{n} |\mu_{ij} - \mu_{kj}| + \frac{1}{n}\sum_{j=1}^{n} |v_{ij} - v_{kj}| \geq 0 \tag{2.189}$$

$$\begin{aligned}\dot{\mu}_{ik} + \dot{v}_{ik} &= 1 - \frac{1}{n}\sum_{j=1}^{n} |\mu_{ij} - \mu_{kj}| + \frac{1}{n}\sum_{j=1}^{n} |v_{ij} - v_{kj}| \\ &= 1 - \frac{1}{n}\sum_{j=1}^{n} |(1 - \mu_{ij}) - (1 - \mu_{kj})| + \frac{1}{n}\sum_{j=1}^{n} |v_{ij} - v_{kj}| \end{aligned} \tag{2.190}$$

$$\begin{aligned} &= 1 - \frac{1}{n}\sum_{j=1}^{n} |(v_{ij} + \pi_{ij}) - (v_{kj} + \pi_{kj})| + \frac{1}{n}\sum_{j=1}^{n} |v_{ij} - v_{kj}| \\ &= 1 - \frac{1}{n}\sum_{j=1}^{n} |(v_{ij} - v_{kj}) + (\pi_{ij} - \pi_{kj})| + \frac{1}{n}\sum_{j=1}^{n} |v_{ij} - v_{kj}| \\ &\geq 1 - \frac{1}{n}\sum_{j=1}^{n} |v_{ij} - v_{kj}| - \frac{1}{n}\sum_{j=1}^{n} |\pi_{ij} - \pi_{kj}| + \frac{1}{n}\sum_{j=1}^{n} |v_{ij} - v_{kj}| \\ &= 1 - \frac{1}{n}\sum_{j=1}^{n} |\pi_{ij} - \pi_{kj}|, i, k = 1, 2, \ldots, m \end{aligned} \tag{2.191}$$

where $\dot{\pi}_{ij} = 1 - \dot{\mu}_{ij} - \dot{v}_{ij}$. Thus, $0 \leq \dot{\mu}_{ik} + \dot{v}_{ik} \leq 1$ cannot be guaranteed.

In the numerical analysis above, we can see that in an IFV, the membership degree is closely related to both the non-membership and the uncertainty degree. Motivated by this idea, we may modify Eq. (2.188) as:

$$\dot{\mu}_{ik} = 1 - \frac{1}{n}\sum_{j=1}^{n} |v_{ij} - v_{kj}| - \frac{1}{n}\sum_{j=1}^{n} |\pi_{ij} - \pi_{kj}|, \; i, k = 1, 2, \ldots, m \tag{2.192}$$

with $\mu_{ik} = 1$ if and only if $\dot{v}_{ij} = \dot{v}_{kj}$ and $\dot{\pi}_{ij} = \dot{\pi}_{kj}$, for all $j = 1, 2, \ldots, n$.

Based on Eqs. (2.186) and (2.192), we have the following concept:

Definition 2.34 (Wang et al. 2011) Let y_i and y_k be two IFSs on X, and $Z(y_i, y_k)$ a binary relation on $X \times X$, if

$$Z(y_i, y_k) = \begin{cases} (1, 0), \; y_i = y_k, \\ \left(1 - \frac{1}{n}\sum\limits_{j=1}^{n} \left|v_{ij} - v_{kj}\right| - \frac{1}{n}\sum\limits_{j=1}^{n} \left|\pi_{ij} - \pi_{kj}\right|, \; \frac{1}{n}\sum\limits_{j=1}^{n} \left|v_{ij} - v_{kj}\right|\right), \\ y_i \neq y_k, \end{cases} \tag{2.193}$$

then $Z(y_i, y_k)$ is called a closeness degree of y_i and y_k.

By Eq. (2.193), we have

Theorem 2.20 (Wang et al. 2011) The closeness degree $Z(y_i, y_k)$ of y_i and y_k is an intuitionistic fuzzy similarity relation.

Proof (1) Let's first prove that $Z(y_i, y_k)$ is an IFV:

(a) If $y_i = y_k$, then $Z(y_i, y_k) = (1, 0)$;
(b) If $y_i \neq y_k$, then

$$\begin{aligned} \dot{\mu}_{ik} &= 1 - \frac{1}{n}\sum_{j=1}^{n} |v_{ij} - v_{kj}| - \frac{1}{n}\sum_{j=1}^{n} |\pi_{ij} - \pi_{kj}| \\ &\leq 1 - \frac{1}{n}\sum_{j=1}^{n} |v_{ij} - v_{kj} + \pi_{ij} - \pi_{kj}| \\ &= 1 - \frac{1}{n}\sum_{j=1}^{n} |\mu_{ij} - \mu_{kj}| \end{aligned} \tag{2.194}$$

Obviously, we have $0 \leq \dot{\mu}_{ik} \leq 1$, with $\dot{\mu}_{ik} = 1$ if and only if $\mu_{ij} = \mu_{kj}$, for all $j = 1, 2, \ldots, n$, and with $\dot{\mu}_{ik} = 0$ if and only if $\mu_{ij} = 1$ and $\mu_{kj} = 0$, for all $j = 1, 2, \ldots, n$, or $\mu_{ij} = 0$ and $\mu_{kj} = 1$, for all $j = 1, 2, \ldots, n$.

Similarly, we have $0 \leq \dot{v}_{ik} = \sum_{j=1}^{n} |v_{ij} - v_{kj}|/n \leq 1$, with $\dot{v}_{ik} = 1$ if and only if $v_{ij} = v_{kj}$, for all $j = 1, 2, \ldots, n$, and with $\dot{v}_{ik} = 0$ if and only if $v_{ij} = 1$ and $v_{kj} = 0$, for all $j = 1, 2, \ldots, n$, or $v_{ij} = 0$ and $v_{kj} = 1$, for all $j = 1, 2, \ldots, n$.

Also since

$$\begin{aligned}\dot{\mu}_{ik}+\dot{v}_{ik}&=1-\frac{1}{n}\sum_{j=1}^{n}|v_{ij}-v_{kj}|-\frac{1}{n}\sum_{j=1}^{n}|\pi_{ij}-\pi_{kj}|+\frac{1}{n}\sum_{j=1}^{n}|v_{ij}-v_{kj}|\\&=1-\frac{1}{n}\sum_{j=1}^{n}|\pi_{ij}-\pi_{kj}|\leq 1\end{aligned} \tag{2.195}$$

then we have $0\leq\dot{\mu}_{ij}+\dot{v}_{kj}\leq 1$, with $\dot{\mu}_{ik}+\dot{v}_{ik}=1$ if and only if $\pi_{ij}=\pi_{kj}$, for all $j=1,2,\ldots,n$, and $\dot{\mu}_{ik}+\dot{v}_{ik}=0$, if and only if $\pi_{ij}=1$ and $\pi_{kj}=0$, for all $j=1,2,\ldots,n$, or $\pi_{ij}=0$ and $\pi_{kj}=1$, for all $j=1,2,\ldots,n$.

(2) Since $Z(y_i,y_i)=(1,0)$, then Z is reflexive.

(3) Since $|v_{ij}-v_{kj}|=|v_{kj}-v_{ij}|$ and $|\pi_{ij}-\pi_{kj}|=|\pi_{kj}-\pi_{ij}|$, then $Z(y_i,y_k)=Z(y_k,y_i)$, i.e., Z is symmetrical. Thus, $Z(A,B)$ is an intuitionistic fuzzy similarity relation.

From Eq. (2.193), we can see that if all the differences of the non-membership degrees and the differences of the uncertainty degrees of two alternatives y_i and y_k with respect to the attributes G_j $(j=1,2,\ldots,n)$ get smaller, then the two alternatives are more similar to each other.

In the following section, we shall use Eq. (2.193) to introduce a clustering method.

2.8.2 A Netting Clustering Method

The so called netting means a simple process: Firstly, for an intuitionistic fuzzy similarity matrix Z, we should choose a confidence level $\lambda\in[0,1]$, and then get a λ-cutting matrix Z_λ and change the elements on the diagonal of Z_λ with the symbol of the alternatives. Under the diagonal, we replace '1' with the nodal point '*' and ignore all the '0' in Z_λ. From the node '*', we draw the vertical line and the horizontal line to the diagonal and the corresponding alternatives on the diagonal will be clustered into one type (He 1983).

Netting method was first used to cluster data in the field of fuzzy mathematics (He 1983). With this method, we can get the clustering results by 'netting' the elements of similarity matrix directly. Wang et al. (2011) proposed a netting method for clustering the objects with intuitionistic fuzzy information:

Step 1 For a multi-attribute decision making problem, Let $Y=\{y_1,y_2,\ldots,y_m\}$ and $G=\{G_1,G_2,\ldots,G_n\}$ be defined previously, and assume that the characteristics of the alternatives y_i $(i=1,2,\ldots,m)$ with respect to the attributes G_j $(j=1,2,\ldots,n)$ are represented as in Eq. (2.185).

Step 2 Construct the intuitionistic fuzzy similarity matrix $Z=(z_{ij})_{m\times m}$ by using Eq. (2.193), where z_{ij} is an IFV, and $z_{ij}=(\mu_{ij},v_{ij})=Z(y_i,y_j)$, $i,j=1,2,\ldots,m$.

Step 3 Delete all the elements above the diagonal and replace the elements on the diagonal with the symbol of the alternatives.

Table 2.16 The characteristics information of the cars

	G_1	G_2	G_3	G_4	G_5	G_6
y_1	(0.3,0.5)	(0.6,0.1)	(0.4,0.3)	(0.8,0.1)	(0.1,0.6)	(0.5,0.4)
y_2	(0.6,0.3)	(0.5,0.2)	(0.6,0.1)	(0.7,0.1)	(0.3,0.6)	(0.4,0.3)
y_3	(0.4,0.4)	(0.8,0.1)	(0.5,0.1)	(0.6,0.2)	(0.4,0.5)	(0.3,0.2)
y_4	(0.2,0.4)	(0.4,0.1)	(0.9,0.0)	(0.8,0.1)	(0.2.0.5)	(0.7,0.1)
y_5	(0.5,0.2)	(0.3,0.6)	(0.6.0.3)	(0.7,0.1)	(0.6,0.2)	(0.5,0.3)

Step 4 Choose the confidence level λ and construct the corresponding λ-cutting matrix. Replace '1' with '*' and delete all the '0' in the matrix before drawing the vertical and horizontal line to the symbol of alternatives on the diagonal from '*'. Corresponding to each '*', we have a type which contains two elements. Unit the types together which have the common elements, and then we get the types corresponding to the selected λ. Update the values of λ before all the alternatives are clustered into one type.

The principal to choose λ: Based on the idea of constructing the similarity degree matrix, we balance the similarity degree of two alternatives mainly through the membership degree of the corresponding IFV. We choose the confidence level λ from the biggest one to the smallest one. When we encounter that two membership degrees are equal, we firstly choose the one with the smaller non-membership degree. If both of them are equal, they are clustered into the same type. After that, in terms of the chosen λ, we construct the corresponding λ-cutting matrix. With this principle, the clustering results will be more detailed.

2.8.3 Illustrative Examples

Example 2.12 (Wang et al. 2011) An auto market wants to classify five different cars y_i $(i = 1, 2, 3, 4, 5)$ into several kinds (Liang and Shi 2003). Each car has six evaluation factors: (1) G_1: Oil consumption; (2) G_2: Coefficient of friction; (3) G_3: Price; (4) G_4: Comfortable degree; (5) G_5: Design; (6) G_6: Safety coefficient. The evaluation results of each car with respect to the factors G_j $(j = 1, 2, \ldots, 6)$ are represented by the IFSs, shown as in Table 2.16 (Wang et al. 2011).

In the following, we utilize the intuitionistic fuzzy netting method to classify the five cars, which involves the following steps (Wang et al. 2011):

Step 1 By Eq. (2.192), we calculate

$$\dot{\mu}_{12} = 1 - \frac{1}{6}\sum_{j=1}^{6} |\nu_{1j} - \nu_{2j}| - \frac{1}{6}\sum_{j=1}^{6} |\pi_{1j} - \pi_{2j}|$$

$$
\begin{aligned}
&= 1 - \frac{1}{6}(0.2 + 0.1 + 0.2 + 0.0 + 0.0 + 0.1) \\
&\quad - \frac{1}{6}(0.1 + 0.0 + 0.0 + 0.1 + 0.2 + 0.2) \\
&= 0.8 \\
\dot{v}_{12} &= \frac{1}{6}(0.2 + 0.1 + 0.2 + 0.0 + 0.0 + 0.1) = 0.1
\end{aligned}
$$

and then calculate the others in a similar way. Consequently, we get the intuitionistic fuzzy similarity matrix:

$$
Z = \begin{pmatrix}
(1,0) & (0.8,0.1) & (0.72,0.12) & (0.75,0.13) & (0.65,0.22) \\
(0.8,0.1) & (1,0) & (0.82,0.08) & (0.72,0.1) & (0.68,0.18) \\
(0.72,0.12) & (0.82,0.08) & (1,0) & (0.7,0.05) & (0.63,0.23) \\
(0.75,0.13) & (0.72,0.1) & (0.7,0.05) & (1,0) & (0.63,0.25) \\
(0.65,0.22) & (0.68,0.18) & (0.63,0.23) & (0.63,0.25) & (1,0)
\end{pmatrix}
$$

Step 2 Delete all the elements above the diagonal and replace the elements on the diagonal in Z with the symbol of the alternatives y_i $(i = 1, 2, 3, 4, 5)$:

$$
Z' = \begin{pmatrix}
y_1 & & & & \\
(0.8,0.1) & y_2 & & & \\
(0.72,0.12) & (0.82,0.08) & y_3 & & \\
(0.75,0.13) & (0.72,0.1) & (0.7,0.05) & y_4 & \\
(0.65,0.22) & (0.68,0.18) & (0.63,0.23) & (0.63,0.25) & y_5
\end{pmatrix}
$$

Step 3 Choose the confidence level λ properly, and get the corresponding clustering results with intuitionistic fuzzy netting method:

(1) When $0.82 < \lambda \leq 1.0$, we have

$$
Z'' = \begin{pmatrix}
y_1 & & & & \\
 & y_2 & & & \\
 & & y_3 & & \\
 & & & y_4 & \\
 & & & & y_5
\end{pmatrix}
$$

and then each car is clustered into a type: $\{y_1\}$, $\{y_2\}$, $\{y_3\}$, $\{y_4\}$, $\{y_5\}$.

(2) When $0.8 < \lambda \leq 0.82$, we have

$Z'' =$

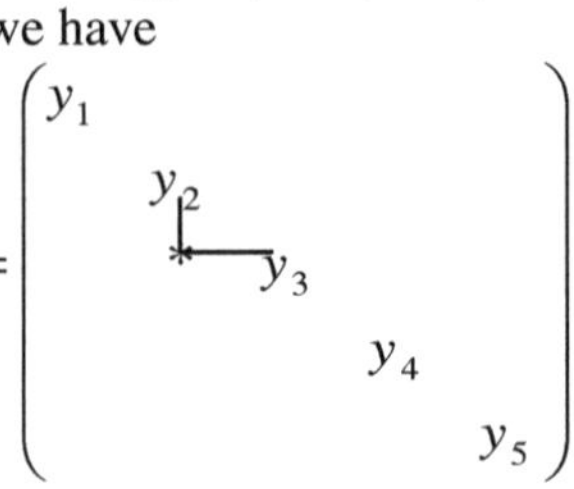

and then the cars y_i $(i = 1, 2, 3, 4, 5)$ are clustered into following four types: $\{y_1\}, \{y_2, y_3\}, \{y_4\}, \{y_5\}$.

(3) When $0.75 < \lambda \leq 0.8$, we have

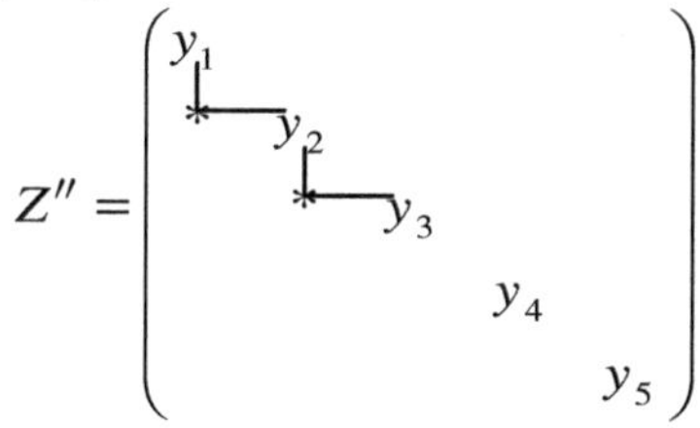

and then the cars y_i $(i = 1, 2, 3, 4, 5)$ are clustered into three types: $\{y_1, y_2, y_3\}$, $\{y_4\}, \{y_5\}$.

(4) When $0.72 < \lambda \leq 0.75$, we have

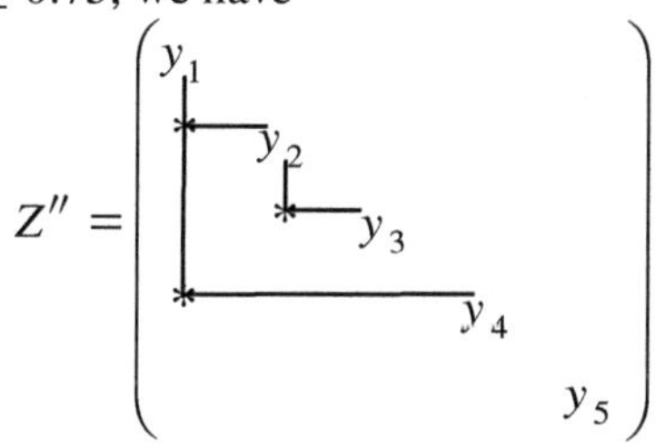

then the cars y_i $(i = 1, 2, 3, 4, 5)$ are clustered into two types: $\{y_1, y_2, y_3, y_4\}, \{y_5\}$.

(5) When $0.68 < \lambda \leq 0.72$, we have the following two cases:

(a)

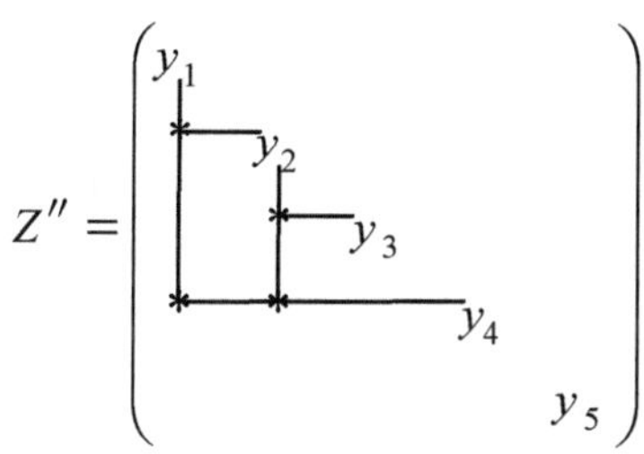

In this case, the cars y_i $(i = 1, 2, 3, 4, 5)$ are clustered into two types: $\{y_1, y_2, y_3, y_4\}, \{y_5\}$;

(b)

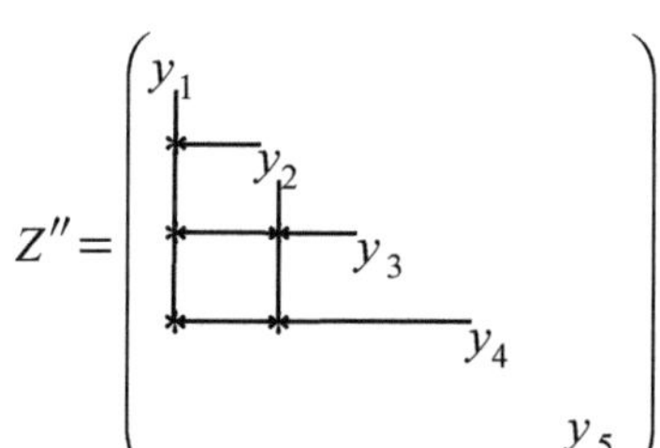

Table 2.17 Comparisons of the derived results

Types	The result derived by intuitionistic fuzzy netting method	The result developed by Zhang et al.'s method (2007)
5	$\{y_1\}, \{y_2\}, \{y_3\}, \{y_4\}, \{y_5\}$	$\{y_1\}, \{y_2\}, \{y_3\}, \{y_4\}, \{y_5\}$
4	$\{y_1\}, \{y_2, y_3\}, \{y_4\}, \{y_5\}$	
3	$\{y_1, y_2, y_3\}, \{y_4\}, \{y_5\}$	$\{y_1, y_2, y_3\}, \{y_4\}, \{y_5\}$
2	$\{y_1, y_2, y_3, y_4\}, \{y_5\}$	
1	$\{y_1, y_2, y_3, y_4, y_5\}$	$\{y_1, y_2, y_3, y_4, y_5\}$

In this case, the cars y_i $(i = 1, 2, 3, 4, 5)$ are also clustered into two types: $\{y_1, y_2, y_3, y_4\}, \{y_5\}$.

(6) When $0.65 < \lambda \leq 0.68$, we have

$Z'' =$

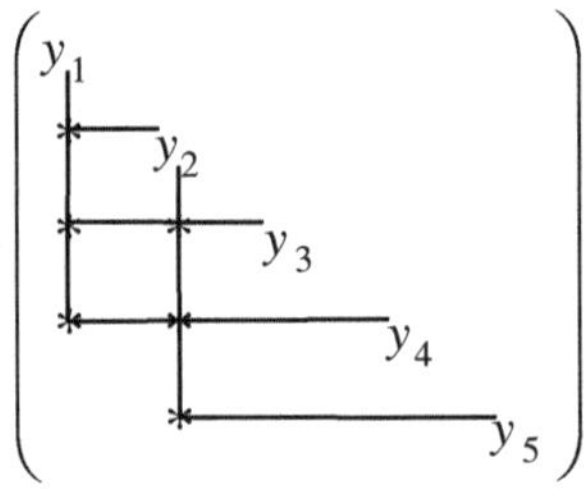

and then the cars y_i $(i = 1, 2, 3, 4, 5)$ are clustered into one type: $\{y_1, y_2, y_3, y_4, y_5\}$.

In the following, let's make simple comparisons between the intuitionistic fuzzy netting method and Zhang et al.'s method (2007) in Table 2.17 (Wang et al. 2011).

Through Table 2.17, we know that the intuitionistic fuzzy netting method has some desirable advantages over Zhang et al.'s method (2007): (1) It does not need to calculate the equivalent matrix, and thus requires much less computational efforts; (2) It can derive more detailed clustering results. Therefore, Compared to Zhang et al. (2007)'s method, the intuitionistic fuzzy netting method has more prospects for practical applications.

Why the intuitionistic fuzzy netting method has these characteristics? For one thing, the proposed netting method can rely on similarity relation instead of equivalent relation as in fuzzy environment. For another, whether in Zhang et al. (2007) method or in Wang et al. (2011)'s work, the type stander are all based on λ-cutting matrix, so λ is an important parameter to decide the type scalar. Before getting the λ-cutting matrix, Zhang et al. (2007) first transformed the intuitionistic fuzzy matrix into an intuitionistic fuzzy similarity matrix, and then calculated its equivalent matrix which needs lots of computational efforts. Wang et al. (2011) not only got the λ-cutting matrix directly from the intuitionistic fuzzy similarity matrix, but also improved the principle of choosing λ. Since Zhang et al. (2007)'s work needs to transform the intuitionistic fuzzy similarity matrix into an intuitionistic fuzzy equivalent matrix, and some information may be missing during this process. Namely, the intuitionistic fuzzy equivalent matrix cannot reflect all the information that the intuitionistic fuzzy

Table 2.18 The characteristics of the cars

	G_1	G_2	G_3	G_4	G_5	G_6
y_1	(0.8,0.1)	(0.4,0.1)	(0.6,0.1)	(0.7,0.3)	(0.6,0.2)	(0.5,0.0)
y_2	(0.0,0.3)	(0.1,0.3)	(0.0,0.6)	(0.0,0.5)	(0.5,0.3)	(0.4,0.2)
y_3	(0.2,0.0)	(0.9,0.1)	(0.0,0.7)	(0.0,0.1)	(0.3,0.2)	(0.8,0.2)
y_4	(0.0,0.5)	(0.3,0.0)	(0.7,0.1)	(0.6,0.1)	(0.0.0.7)	(0.7,0.2)
y_5	(0.4,0.6)	(0.2,0.4)	(0.9.0.1)	(0.6,0.1)	(0.7,0.2)	(0.7,0.3)
y_6	(0.0,0.2)	(0.0,0.0)	(0.5.0.4)	(0.5,0.4)	(0.3,0.6)	(0.0,0.0)
y_7	(0.8,0.1)	(0.2,0.1)	(0.1.0.0)	(0.7,0.0)	(0.6,0.4)	(0.0,0.6)
y_8	(0.1,0.7)	(0.0,0.5)	(0.8.0.1)	(0.7,0.1)	(0.7,0.1)	(0.0,0.0)
y_9	(0.0,0.1)	(0.5,0.1)	(0.3.0.1)	(0.7,0.3)	(0.1,0.3)	(0.7,0.2)
y_{10}	(0.3,0.2)	(0.7,0.1)	(0.2.0.2)	(0.2,0.0)	(0.1,0.9)	(0.9,0.1)

similarity matrix contains. Considering the stated reasons above, it is not hard for us to comprehend why the intuitionistic fuzzy netting method can get more detailed types than Zhang et al. (2007).

Here we only make a comparison with that of Zhang et al. (2007), because that the method in Zhang et al. (2007) is a representation of solving this class of problems, some closely-related results can be found in Xu et al. (2008) and Cai et al. (2009).

In order to demonstrate the effectiveness of the proposed clustering algorithm, we further conduct experiments with the simulated data through comparing these two methods:

Example 2.13 (Wang et al. 2011) As we have explained above, the computational complexity is mainly related with the computations of intuitionistic fuzzy similarity matrix and intuitionistic fuzzy equivalent matrix. Next, we shall illustrate this with simulated experiments. Below we first introduce the experimental tool, the experimental data sets, and then make a comparison with other method (Zhang et al. 2007):

(1) Experimental tool. In the experiments, we use the netting algorithm implemented by MATLAB. Note that if we let $\pi(x) = 0$ for any $x \in X$, then the netting algorithm reduces to the traditional fuzzy netting algorithm. Therefore, we can use this process to compare the performances of both the netting algorithm under intuitionistic fuzzy environment and the netting algorithm under fuzzy environment.

(2) Experimental data sets. The car data set contains the information of ten new cars to be classified in an auto market. Let y_i $(i = 1, 2, \ldots, 10)$ be the cars, each of which is described by six attributes: (1) G_1: Oil consumption; (2) G_2: Coefficient of friction; (3) G_3: Price; (4) G_4: Comfortable degree; (5) G_5: Design; and (6) G_6: Safety coefficient, as in Example 2.12 (For convenience, here we do not consider the weights of these attributes). The characteristics of the ten new cars under the six attributes, generated at random by MATLAB, are represented by the IFSs, as shown in Table 2.18 (Wang et al. 2011).

In order to express the validity of the netting method, we shall make a comparison with Zhang et al. (2007)'s method:

With the netting method, we have the following clustering results (Wang et al. 2011):

Using Zhang et al. (2007)'s method, we first construct the intuitionistic fuzzy similarity matrix based on the data in Table 2.18.

$$Z = \left(\begin{array}{ccccc}
(1,0) & (0.41,0.08) & (0.33,0.24) & (0.43,0.08) & (0.63,0.08) \\
(0.41,0.08) & (1,0) & (0.41,0.08) & (0.49,0.16) & (0.36,0.14) \\
(0.33,0.24) & (0.41,0.08) & (1,0) & (0.46,0.08) & (0.35,0.08) \\
(0.43,0.08) & (0.49,0.16) & (0.46,0.08) & (1,0) & (0.49,0.00) \\
(0.63,0.08) & (0.36,0.14) & (0.35,0.08) & (0.49,0.00) & (1,0) \\
(0.38,0.14) & (0.57,0.08) & (0.22,0.16) & (0.33,0.22) & (0.27,0.22) \\
(0.55,0.0) & (0.41,0.14) & (0.43,0.36) & (0.43,0.08) & (0.30,0.08) \\
(0.46,0.08) & (0.43,0.14) & (0.25,0.29) & (0.33,0.08) & (0.27,0.08) \\
(0.35,0.0) & (0.49,0.16) & (0.33,0.08) & (0.67,0.00) & (0.36,0.08) \\
(0.43,0.24) & (0.57,0.22) & (0.49,0.08) & (0.63,0.14) & (0.46,0.16)
\end{array} \right.$$

$$\left. \begin{array}{ccccc}
(0.38,0.14) & (0.55,0.00) & (0.46,0.08) & (0.35,0.00) & (0.43,0.24) \\
(0.57,0.08) & (0.41,0.14) & (0.43,0.14) & (0.49,0.16) & (0.57,0.22) \\
(0.22,0.16) & (0.43,0.36) & (0.25,0.29) & (0.33,0.08) & (0.49,0.08) \\
(0.33,0.22) & (0.43,0.08) & (0.33,0.08) & (0.67,0.00) & (0.63,0.14) \\
(0.27,0.22) & (0.30,0.08) & (0.27,0.08) & (0.36,0.08) & (0.46,0.16) \\
(1,0) & (0.38,0.22) & (0.55,0.00) & (0.33,0.08) & (0.22,0.22) \\
(0.38,0.22) & (1,0) & (0.38,0.08) & (0.34,0.21) & (0.36,0.22) \\
(0.55,0.00) & (0.38,0.08) & (1,0) & (0.33,0.16) & (0.22,0.36) \\
(0.33,0.08) & (0.35,0.22) & (0.33,0.16) & (1,0) & (0.43,0.08) \\
(0.22,0.22) & (0.36,0.22) & (0.22,0.36) & (0.43,0.08) & (1,0)
\end{array} \right)$$

In order to get the clustering result with Zhang et al. (2007)'s method, we should get the equivalent matrix. By the composition operations of similarity matrices, we have

$$Z^2 = Z \circ Z = \left(\begin{array}{ccccc}
(1,0) & (0.43,0.08) & (0.43,0.08) & (0.49,0.00) & (0.63,0.08) \\
(0.43,0.08) & (1,0) & (0.49,0.08) & (0.57,0.08) & (0.49,0.08) \\
(0.43,0.08) & (0.49,0.08) & (1,0) & (0.49,0.08) & (0.46,0.08) \\
(0.49,0.00) & (0.57,0.08) & (0.49,0.08) & (1,0) & (0.49,0.00) \\
(0.63,0.08) & (0.49,0.08) & (0.46,0.08) & (0.49,0.00) & (1,0) \\
(0.46,0.08) & (0.57,0.08) & (0.41,0.08) & (0.49,0.08) & (0.38,0.08) \\
(0.55,0.0) & (0.43,0.08) & (0.43,0.08) & (0.43,0.08) & (0.55,0.08) \\
(0.46,0.08) & (0.55,0.08) & (0.41,0.08) & (0.43,0.08) & (0.46,0.08) \\
(0.43,0.0) & (0.49,0.08) & (0.46,0.08) & (0.67,0.00) & (0.49,0.00) \\
(0.46,0.08) & (0.57,0.08) & (0.49,0.08) & (0.63,0.08) & (0.49,0.08)
\end{array} \right.$$

$$\left.\begin{matrix}
(0.46,0.08) & (0.55,0.00) & (0.46,0.08) & (0.43,0.00) & (0.46,0.08) \\
(0.57,0.08) & (0.43,0.08) & (0.55,0.08) & (0.49,0.08) & (0.57,0.08) \\
(0.41,0.08) & (0.43,0.08) & (0.41,0.08) & (0.46,0.08) & (0.49,0.08) \\
(0.49,0.08) & (0.43,0.08) & (0.43,0.08) & (0.67,0.00) & (0.63,0.08) \\
(0.38,0.08) & (0.55,0.08) & (0.46,0.08) & (0.49,0.00) & (0.49,0.08) \\
(1,0) & (0.41,0.08) & (0.55,0.00) & (0.49,0.08) & (0.57,0.08) \\
(0.41,0.08) & (1,0) & (0.46,0.08) & (0.43,0.00) & (0.43,0.14) \\
(0.55,0.00) & (0.46,0.08) & (1,0) & (0.43,0.08) & (0.43,0.14) \\
(0.49,0.08) & (0.43,0.00) & (0.43,0.08) & (1,0) & (0.63,0.08) \\
(0.57,0.08) & (0.43,0.14) & (0.43,0.14) & (0.63,0.08) & (1,0)
\end{matrix}\right)$$

$$Z^4 = Z^2 \circ Z^2 = \left(\begin{matrix}
(1,0) & (0.49,0.08) & (0.49,0.08) & (0.49,0.00) & (0.63,0.00) \\
(0.49,0.08) & (1,0) & (0.49,0.08) & (0.57,0.08) & (0.49,0.08) \\
(0.49,0.08) & (0.49,0.08) & (1,0) & (0.49,0.08) & (0.49,0.08) \\
(0.49,0.00) & (0.57,0.08) & (0.49,0.08) & (1,0) & (0.49,0.00) \\
(0.63,0.00) & (0.49,0.08) & (0.49,0.08) & (0.49,0.00) & (1,0) \\
(0.49,0.08) & (0.57,0.08) & (0.49,0.08) & (0.57,0.08) & (0.49,0.08) \\
(0.55,0.00) & (0.49,0.08) & (0.46,0.08) & (0.49,0.00) & (0.55,0.00) \\
(0.46,0.08) & (0.55,0.08) & (0.49,0.08) & (0.55,0.08) & (0.49,0.08) \\
(0.49,0.0) & (0.57,0.08) & (0.49,0.08) & (0.67,0.00) & (0.49,0.00) \\
(0.49,0.08) & (0.57,0.08) & (0.49,0.08) & (0.63,0.08) & (0.49,0.08)
\end{matrix}\right.$$

$$\left.\begin{matrix}
(0.49,0.08) & (0.55,0.00) & (0.46,0.08) & (0.49,0.00) & (0.49,0.08) \\
(0.57,0.08) & (0.49,0.08) & (0.55,0.08) & (0.57,0.08) & (0.57,0.08) \\
(0.49,0.08) & (0.46,0.08) & (0.49,0.08) & (0.49,0.08) & (0.49,0.08) \\
(0.57,0.08) & (0.49,0.00) & (0.55,0.08) & (0.67,0.00) & (0.63,0.08) \\
(0.49,0.08) & (0.55,0.00) & (0.49,0.08) & (0.49,0.00) & (0.49,0.08) \\
(1,0) & (0.46,0.08) & (0.55,0.00) & (0.57,0.08) & (0.57,0.08) \\
(0.46,0.08) & (1,0) & (0.46,0.08) & (0.49,0.00) & (0.49,0.08) \\
(0.55,0.00) & (0.46,0.08) & (1,0) & (0.49,0.08) & (0.55,0.08) \\
(0.57,0.08) & (0.49,0.00) & (0.49,0.08) & (1,0) & (0.63,0.08) \\
(0.57,0.08) & (0.49,0.08) & (0.55,0.08) & (0.63,0.08) & (1,0)
\end{matrix}\right)$$

After computation, we have $Z^8 = Z^4$, thus we can make cluster analysis with Zhang et al. (2007)'s method. The clustering results are shown in Table 2.20 (Wang et al. 2011).

We can see from Tables 2.19 and 2.20 that the netting method can make more detailed clustering results than Zhang et al. (2007)'s method.

In order to illustrate the computation complexity, we generate an amount of IFVs at random by MATLAB. Then we measure the computation time before we get the corresponding matrix that can make cluster analysis for the two methods respectively. The results are shown in Table 2.21 (Wang et al. 2011).

Table 2.19 The clustering results with the netting method

λ_{level}	Clustering results
$0.67 < \lambda \leq 1$	$\{y_1\}, \{y_2\}, \{y_3\}, \{y_4\}, \{y_5\}, \{y_6\}, \{y_7\}, \{y_8\}, \{y_9\}, \{y_{10}\}$
$0.63 < \lambda \leq 0.67$	$\{y_4, y_9\}, \{y_1\}, \{y_2\}, \{y_3\}, \{y_5\}, \{y_6\}, \{y_7\}, \{y_8\}, \{y_{10}\}$
$(0.63,0.14) < \lambda \leq (0.63,0.08)$	$\{y_1, y_5\}, \{y_4, y_9\}, \{y_2\}, \{y_3\}, \{y_6\}, \{y_7\}, \{y_8\}, \{y_{10}\}$
$0.57 < \lambda \leq 0.63$	$\{y_1, y_5\}, \{y_4, y_9, y_{10}\}, \{y_2\}, \{y_3\}, \{y_6\}, \{y_7\}, \{y_8\}$
$(0.57,0.22) < \lambda \leq (0.57,0.08)$	$\{y_1, y_5\}, \{y_4, y_9, y_{10}\}, \{y_2, y_6\}, \{y_3\}, \{y_7\}, \{y_8\}$
$0.55 < \lambda \leq 0.57$	$\{y_1, y_5\}, \{y_2, y_4, y_6, y_9, y_{10}\}, \{y_3\}, \{y_7\}, \{y_8\}$
$0.49 < \lambda \leq 0.55$	$\{y_1, y_5, y_7\}, \{y_2, y_4, y_6, y_8, y_9, y_{10}\}, \{y_3\}$
$(0.49,0.16) < \lambda \leq (0.49,0.08)$	$\{y_1, y_5, y_7\}, \{y_2, y_3, y_4, y_6, y_8, y_9, y_{10}\}$
$0 < \lambda \leq 0.49$	$\{y_1, y_2, y_3, y_4, y_5, y_6, y_7, y_8, y_9, y_{10}\}$

Table 2.20 The clustering results with Zhang et al. (2007)'s method

λ_{level}	Clustering results
$0.67 < \lambda \leq 1$	$\{y_1\}, \{y_2\}, \{y_3\}, \{y_4\}, \{y_5\}, \{y_6\}, \{y_7\}, \{y_8\}, \{y_9\}, \{y_{10}\}$
$0.63 < \lambda \leq 0.67$	$\{y_4, y_9\}, \{y_1\}, \{y_2\}, \{y_3\}, \{y_5\}, \{y_6\}, \{y_7\}, \{y_8\}, \{y_{10}\}$
$0.57 < \lambda \leq 0.63$	$\{y_1, y_5\}, \{y_4, y_9, y_{10}\}, \{y_2\}, \{y_3\}, \{y_6\}, \{y_7\}, \{y_8\}$
$0.55 < \lambda \leq 0.57$	$\{y_1, y_5\}, \{y_2, y_4, y_6, y_9, y_{10}\}, \{y_3\}, \{y_7\}, \{y_8\}$
$0.49 < \lambda \leq 0.55$	$\{y_1, y_5, y_7\}, \{y_2, y_3, y_4, y_6, y_8, y_9, y_{10}\}$
$0 < \lambda \leq 0.49$	$\{y_1, y_2, y_3, y_4, y_5, y_6, y_7, y_8, y_9, y_{10}\}$

Table 2.21 Elapsed time for each method

Alternatives Time(Seconds) Methods	10	50	100	500	1000	2000
Netting method	0.000174	0.004637	0.013933	1.585204	11.721117	102.472592
Zhang et al. (2007)'s method	0.002361	0.035407	0.167295	10.636214	78.620455	691.554396

Let n and m represent the amount of alternatives and attributes, respectively. Then the computational complexities of our method and Zhang et al. (2007)'s method are $O(mn + 12n^2)$ and $O(mn + 12n^2 + kn^2)$ respectively, where $k(k \geq 2)$ represents the transfer times until we get the equivalent matrix. The elapsed time may become closed as n increases. Considering the practical application, we think the netting method can save much more time and computational efforts.

2.9 Direct Cluster Analysis Based on Intuitionistic Fuzzy Implication

2.9.1 The Intuitionistic Fuzzy Implication Operator and Intuitionistic Fuzzy Products

Definition 2.35 (Kohout and Bandler 1980, 1984) Let $U_i(i = 1, 2)$ be two ordinary subsets, and $L \subset U_1 \times U_2$ an ordinary relation. Then for any $a, b \in U_2, Lb = \{a|aLb\}$ and $aL = \{b|aLb\}$ are respectively called a former set and a latter set.

Definition 2.36 (Kohout and Bandler 1980, 1984) Let $U_i(i = 1, 2, 3)$ be ordinary subsets, $L_1 \subset U_1 \times U_2$ and $L_2 \subset U_2 \times U_3$, then a triangle product $L_1 \lhd L_2 \subset U_1 \times U_3$ of L_1 and L_2 can be defined as:

$$aL_1 \lhd L_2c \Leftrightarrow aL_1 \subset L_2c, \text{ for any } (a, c) \in U_1 \times U_2 \tag{2.196}$$

Similarly, a square product $L_1 \square L_2$ is defined as:

$$aL_1 \square L_2c \Leftrightarrow aL_1 = L_2c, \text{ for any } (a, c) \in U \times W \tag{2.197}$$

where $aL_1 = L_2c$ if and only if $aL_1 \subset L_2c$ and $aL_1 \supset L_2c$.

Wang and Liu (1999) introduced a fuzzy implication operator as follows:

Definition 2.37 (Wang and Liu 1999) Let I_1 be a binary operation on [0, 1], if

$$I_1(0, 0) = I_1(0, 1) = I_1(1, 1) = 1 \text{ and } I(1, 0) = 0 \tag{2.198}$$

then I_1 is called a fuzzy implication operator.

For any $a, b \in [0, 1]$, $I_1(a, b)$ is a fuzzy implication operator, which can also be denoted as $a \to b$. Especially, the well-known Lukasiewicz implication operator is given as $\varphi(a, b) = \min(1 - a + b, 1)$, which means that the result of "a imply b" is $\min(1 - a + b, 1)$.

Motivated by the idea of Definition 2.37, Wang et al. (2012) defined the concept of intuitionistic fuzzy implication operator:

Definition 2.38 (Wang et al. 2012) Let I_1 be a binary operation on the set of all IFVs, V, if

$$\begin{aligned} I_1((0, 1), (0, 1)) &= I_1((0, 1), (1, 0)) = I_1((1, 0), (1, 0)) \\ &= (1, 0), \quad I_1((1, 0), (0, 1)) = (0, 1) \end{aligned}$$

then I_1 is called an intuitionistic fuzzy implication operator.

Now we extend Lukasiewicz implication operator to intuitionistic fuzzy environment. For any two IFVs $\alpha = (\mu_\alpha, v_\alpha)$ and $\beta = (\mu_\beta, v_\beta)$, if we only consider the membership degrees μ_α and μ_β of α and β, then $\min\{1-\mu_\alpha+\mu_\beta, 1\}$ cannot reflect the superiority of IFVs, so we should consider the non-memberships v_α and v_β as well. Then based on the components of IFVs and the form of Lukasiewicz implication operator, Wang et al. (2012) defined an intuitionistic fuzzy Lukasiewicz implication operator $\varphi(\alpha, \beta)$, whose membership degree and non-membership degree are expressed as:

$$\min\{1, \min\{1-\mu_\alpha+\mu_\beta, 1-v_\beta+v_\alpha\}\} = \min\{1, 1-\mu_\alpha+\mu_\beta, 1-v_\beta+v_\alpha\}$$

and

$$\max\{0, \min\{1-(1-\mu_\alpha+\mu_\beta), 1-(1-v_\beta+v_\alpha)\}\} = \max\{0, \min\{\mu_\alpha-\mu_\beta, v_\beta-v_\alpha\}\}$$

respectively, i.e.,

$$\varphi(\alpha, \beta) = \left(\min\{1, 1-\mu_\alpha+\mu_\beta, 1-v_\beta+v_\alpha\}, \max\{0, \min\{\mu_\alpha-\mu_\beta, v_\beta-v_\alpha\}\}\right) \tag{2.199}$$

Clearly, we need to prove that the value of $\varphi(\alpha, \beta)$ should satisfy all the conditions of an IFV. In fact, from Eq. (2.199), we have

$$\min\{1, 1-\mu_\alpha+\mu_\beta, 1-v_\beta+v_\alpha\} \geq 0, \max\{0, \min\{\mu_\alpha-\mu_\beta, v_\beta-v_\alpha\}\} \geq 0 \tag{2.200}$$

and since

$$\max\{0, \min\{\mu_\alpha-\mu_\beta, v_\beta-v_\alpha\}\} = 1-\min\{1, \max\{1-\mu_\alpha+\mu_\beta, 1-v_\beta+v_\alpha\}\} \tag{2.201}$$

$$\min\{1, \max\{1-\mu_\alpha+\mu_\beta, 1-v_\beta+v_\alpha\}\} \geq \min\{1, 1-\mu_\alpha+\mu_\beta, 1-v_\beta+v_\alpha\} \tag{2.202}$$

then

$$1-\min\{1, \max\{1-\mu_\alpha+\mu_\beta, 1-v_\beta+v_\alpha\}\}+\min\{1, 1-\mu_\alpha+\mu_\beta, 1-v_\beta+v_\alpha\} \leq 1$$

which indicates that the value of $\varphi(\alpha, \beta)$ derived by Eq. (2.201) is an IFV.

Example 2.14 (Wang et al. 2012) Let $\alpha = (0, 1)$ and $\beta = (1, 0)$, then by Eq. (2.198), we have

$$\varphi(\alpha, \alpha) = (\min\{1, 1-0+0, 1-1+1\}, \max\{0, \min\{0-0, 1-1\}\}) = (1, 0)$$

$$\varphi(\beta, \beta) = (\min\{1, 1-1+1, 1-0+0\}, \max\{0, \min\{1-1, 0-0\}\}) = (1, 0)$$

$$\varphi(\alpha, \beta) = (\min\{1, 1-0+1, 1-0+1\}, \max\{0, \min\{0-1, 0-1\}\}) = (1, 0)$$

$$\varphi(\beta, \alpha) = (\min\{1, 1 - 1 + 0, 1 - 1 + 0\}, \max\{0, \min\{1 - 0, 1 - 0\}\}) = (0, 1)$$

With the intuitionistic fuzzy Lukasiewicz implication, the traditional triangle product and the square product (Kohout and Bandler 1980), below we further introduce an intuitionistic fuzzy triangle product and an intuitionistic fuzzy square product respectively:

Definition 2.39 (Wang et al. 2012) Let $\alpha = \{\alpha_1, \alpha_2, \ldots, \alpha_l\}$, $\gamma = \{\gamma_1, \gamma_2, \ldots, \gamma_m\}$ and $\beta = \{\beta_1, \beta_2, \ldots, \beta_n\}$ be three sets of IFVs, $Z_1 \in F(\alpha \times \gamma)$ and $Z_2 \in F(\gamma \times \beta)$ two intuitionistic fuzzy relations, then an intuitionistic fuzzy triangle product $Z_1 \triangleleft Z_2 \in F(\alpha \times \beta)$ of Z_1 and Z_2 can be defined as:

$$(Z_1 \triangleleft Z_2)\ (\alpha_i, \beta_j) = \left(\frac{1}{m}\sum_{k=1}^{m} \mu_{Z_1(\alpha_i,\gamma_k)\to Z_2(\gamma_k,\beta_j)}, \frac{1}{m}\sum_{k=1}^{m} v_{Z_1(\alpha_i,\gamma_k)\to Z_2(\gamma_k,\beta_j)}\right),$$
$$\text{for any } (\alpha_i, \beta_j) \in (\alpha, \beta), i = 1, 2, \ldots, l;\ j = 1, 2, \ldots, n \tag{2.203}$$

where "→" represents the intuitionistic fuzzy Lukasiewicz implication.

Similarly, Wang et al. (2012) defined an intuitionistic fuzzy square product $Z_1 \square Z_2 \in F(\alpha \times \beta)$ of Z_1 and Z_2 as:

$$(Z_1 \square Z_2)\ (\alpha_i, \beta_j) = \min_{1 \le k \le m} \big(\mu_{\min(Z_1(\alpha_i,\gamma_k)\to Z_2(\gamma_k,\beta_j), Z_2(\gamma_k,\beta_j)\to Z_1(\alpha_i,\gamma_k))},$$
$$v_{\min(Z_1(\alpha_i,\gamma_k)\to Z_2(\gamma_k,\beta_j), Z_2(\gamma_k,\beta_j)\to Z_1(\alpha_i,\gamma_k))}\big)$$
$$\text{for any } (\alpha_i, \beta_j) \in (\alpha, \beta), i = 1, 2, \ldots, l; j = 1, 2, \ldots, n \tag{2.204}$$

For convenience, we denote z_{ik} as $Z(\alpha_i, \gamma_k)$ for short, and the same with others. As a result, Eqs. (2.203) and (2.204) can be respectively simplified as:

$$(Z_1 \triangleleft Z_2)\ (\alpha_i, \beta_j) = \left(\frac{1}{m}\sum_{j=1}^{m} \mu_{z_{ik}\to z_{kj}}, \frac{1}{m}\sum_{j=1}^{m} v_{z_{ik}\to z_{kj}}\right) \tag{2.205}$$

$$(Z_1 \square Z_2)\ (\alpha_i, \beta_j) = \min_{1 \le k \le m} \big(\mu_{\min(z_{ik}\to z_{kj}, z_{kj}\to z_{ik})}, v_{\min(z_{ik}\to z_{kj}, z_{kj}\to z_{ik})}\big) \tag{2.206}$$

Indeed, the intuitionistic fuzzy triangle product and the intuitionistic fuzzy square product are very closely-related with each other. That is, the former is the basis of the latter, due to that $(Z_1 \square Z_2)(\alpha_i, \beta_j)$ is directly derived from $(Z_1 \triangleleft Z_2)(\alpha_i, \beta_j)$ and $(Z_2 \triangleleft Z_1)(\alpha_i, \beta_j)$.

2.9.2 The Applications of Two Intuitionistic Fuzzy Products

In this subsection, we shall apply the intuitionistic fuzzy triangle product to compare any two alternatives in multi-attribute decision making with intuitionistic fuzzy information, and then use the intuitionistic fuzzy square product to construct an intuitionistic fuzzy similarity matrix which is used as a basis for further investigating intuitionistic fuzzy clustering technique.

Consider a multi-attribute decision making problem, let Y and G be as defined previously. The characteristic (or called attribute value) of each alternative y_i under all the attributes $G_j (j = 1, 2, \ldots, m)$ is represented as an IFS:

$$y_i = \{\langle G_j, \mu_{y_i}(G_j), v_{y_i}(G_j)\rangle | G_j \in G\}, i = 1, 2, \ldots, n; j = 1, 2, \ldots, m \quad (2.207)$$

where $\mu_{y_i}(G_j)$ denotes the membership degree of y_i to G_j and $v_{y_i}(G_j)$ denotes the non-membership degree of y_i to G_j. Obviously, $\pi_{y_i}(G_j) = 1 - \mu_{y_i}(G_j) - v_{y_i}(G_j)$ is the uncertainty (or hesitation) degree of y_i to G_j. If we let $z_{ij} = (\mu_{ij}, v_{ij}) = (\mu_{y_i}(G_j), v_{y_i}(G_j))$, which is an IFV, then based on these IFVs z_{ij} $(i = 1, 2, \ldots, n; j = 1, 2, \ldots, m)$, we can construct an $n \times m$ intuitionistic fuzzy decision matrix $Z = (z_{ij})_{n\times m}$.

2.9.3 The Application of the Intuitionistic Fuzzy Triangle Product

For the above problem, the characteristic vectors of any two alternatives y_i and y_j are expressed as $Z_i = (z_{i1}, z_{i2}, \ldots, z_{im})$ and $Z_j = (z_{j1}, z_{j2}, \ldots, z_{jm})$ respectively. The implication degree of the alternatives y_i and y_j can be calculated with the following intuitionistic fuzzy triangle product:

$$(Z_i \lhd Z_j^{-1})_{ij} = \left(\frac{1}{m}\sum_{k=1}^{m} \mu_{z_{ik}\to z_{jk}}, \frac{1}{m}\sum_{k=1}^{m} v_{z_{ik}\to z_{jk}}\right) \quad (2.208)$$

which shows the degree that how much the alternative y_j is preferred to the alternative y_i, where Z_j^{-1} denotes the inverse of Z_j, which is defined as $(Z_j^{-1})_{kj} = (Z_j)_{jk} = z_{jk}$, $\mu_{z_{ik}\to z_{jk}}$ and $v_{z_{ik}\to z_{jk}}$ are respectively as shown in Eq. (2.199) for any k.

Similarly, we can calculate

$$(Z_j \lhd Z_i^{-1})_{ji} = \left(\frac{1}{m}\sum_{k=1}^{m} \mu_{z_{jk}\to z_{ik}}, \frac{1}{m}\sum_{k=1}^{m} v_{z_{jk}\to z_{ik}}\right) \quad (2.209)$$

which shows the degree that how much the alternative y_i is preferred to the alternative y_j.

From Eqs. (2.208), (2.209) and Xu and Yager (2006)'s ranking method, we can get an ordering of the alternatives y_i and y_j. Concretely speaking, (1) if $(Z_i \lhd Z_j^{-1})_{ij} > (Z_j \lhd Z_i^{-1})_{ji}$, then the alternative y_j is preferred to the alternative y_i; (2) if $(Z_i \lhd Z_j^{-1})_{ij} = (Z_j \lhd Z_i^{-1})_{ji}$, then there is no difference between the alternatives y_i and y_j; and (3) if $(Z_i \lhd Z_j^{-1})_{ij} < (Z_j \lhd Z_i^{-1})_{ji}$, then the alternative y_i is preferred to the alternative y_j.

Example 2.15 (Wang et al. 2012) We express the evaluation results of the cars y_i $(i = 1, 2, 3, 4, 5)$ in Table 2.16 as the vectors $Z_i = (z_{i1}, z_{i2}, \ldots, z_{i6})$ $(i = 1, 2, 3, 4, 5)$, respectively, where $z_{ij} = (\mu_{ij}, v_{ij})$ $(i = 1, 2, 3, 4, 5;\ j = 1, 2, 3, 4, 5, 6)$:

$$
\begin{aligned}
Z_1 &= ((0.3,0.5),(0.6,0.1),(0.4,0.3),(0.8,0.1),(0.1,0.6),(0.5,0.4))\\
Z_2 &= ((0.5,0.3),(0.5,0.2),(0.6,0.1),(0.7,0.1),(0.3,0.6),(0.4,0.3))\\
Z_3 &= ((0.4,0.4),(0.8,0.1),(0.5,0.1),(0.6,0.2),(0.4,0.5),(0.3,0.2))\\
Z_4 &= ((0.2,0.4),(0.4,0.1),(0.9,0.0),(0.8,0.1),(0.2,0.5),(0.7,0.1))\\
Z_5 &= ((0.5,0.2),(0.3,0.6),(0.6.0.3),(0.7,0.1),(0.6,0.2),(0.5,0.3))
\end{aligned}
$$

Then we utilize the intuitionistic fuzzy triangle products Eqs. (2.208) and (2.209) to calculate the implication degrees $(Z_i \lhd Z_j^{-1})_{ij}$ and $(Z_j \lhd Z_i^{-1})_{ji}$ $(i = 1, 2, 3, 4, 5;$ $j = 1, 2, \ldots, 6)$ respectively:

$$
\begin{aligned}
(Z_1 \lhd Z_2^{-1})_{12} &= \left(\frac{1}{6}\sum_{k=1}^{6} \mu_{z_{1k}\to z_{2k}},\ \frac{1}{6}\sum_{k=1}^{6} v_{z_{1k}\to z_{2k}}\right)\\
&= \left(\frac{1}{6}\sum_{k=1}^{6} \min\{1, 1-\mu_{1k}+\mu_{2k}, 1-v_{2k}+v_{1k}\},\right.\\
&\qquad \left.\frac{1}{6}\sum_{k=1}^{6} \max\{0, \min\{\mu_{1k}-\mu_{2k}, v_{2k}-v_{1k}\}\}\right)\\
&= (0.9500, 0.0167)
\end{aligned}
$$

$$
\begin{aligned}
(Z_2 \lhd Z_1^{-1})_{21} &= \left(\frac{1}{6}\sum_{k=1}^{6} \mu_{z_{2k}\to z_{1k}},\ \frac{1}{6}\sum_{k=1}^{6} v_{z_{2k}\to z_{1k}}\right)\\
&= \left(\frac{1}{6}\sum_{k=1}^{6} \min\{1, 1-\mu_{2k}+\mu_{1k}, 1-v_{1k}+v_{2k}\},\right.\\
&\qquad \left.\frac{1}{6}\sum_{k=1}^{6} \max\{0, \min\{\mu_{2k}-\mu_{1k}, v_{1k}-v_{2k}\}\}\right)\\
&= (0.8833, 0.0667)
\end{aligned}
$$

Similarly, we have

$$(Z_1 \lhd Z_3^{-1})_{13} = (0.9333, 0.0167), (Z_3 \lhd Z_1^{-1})_{31} = (0.8333, 0.0500)$$
$$(Z_1 \lhd Z_4^{-1})_{14} = (0.9500, 0.000), (Z_4 \lhd Z_1^{-1})_{41} = (0.8333, 0.1000)$$
$$(Z_1 \lhd Z_5^{-1})_{15} = (0.9000, 0.0500), (Z_5 \lhd Z_1^{-1})_{51} = (0.8167, 0.1000)$$
$$(Z_2 \lhd Z_3^{-1})_{23} = (0.9333, 0.0333), (Z_3 \lhd Z_2^{-1})_{32} = (0.9167, 0.0333)$$
$$(Z_2 \lhd Z_4^{-1})_{24} = (0.9167, 0.0167), (Z_4 \lhd Z_2^{-1})_{42} = (0.8833, 0.0500)$$
$$(Z_2 \lhd Z_5^{-1})_{25} = (0.9000, 0.0333), (Z_5 \lhd Z_2^{-1})_{52} = (0.9000, 0.0500)$$
$$(Z_3 \lhd Z_4^{-1})_{34} = (0.8667, 0.0000), (Z_4 \lhd Z_3^{-1})_{43} = (0.8333, 0.0500)$$
$$(Z_3 \lhd Z_5^{-1})_{35} = (0.8667, 0.0833), (Z_5 \lhd Z_3^{-1})_{53} = (0.8500, 0.0667)$$
$$(Z_4 \lhd Z_5^{-1})_{45} = (0.8167, 0.1000), (Z_5 \lhd Z_4^{-1})_{54} = (0.8833, 0.0833)$$

According to Xu and Yager (2006)'s ranking method, we know that

$$(Z_1 \lhd Z_2^{-1})_{12} > (Z_2 \lhd Z_1^{-1})_{21}, (Z_1 \lhd Z_3^{-1})_{13} > (Z_3 \lhd Z_1^{-1})_{31}$$
$$(Z_1 \lhd Z_4^{-1})_{14} > (Z_4 \lhd Z_1^{-1})_{41}, (Z_1 \lhd Z_5^{-1})_{15} > (Z_5 \lhd Z_1^{-1})_{51}$$
$$(Z_2 \lhd Z_3^{-1})_{23} > (Z_3 \lhd Z_2^{-1})_{32}, (Z_2 \lhd Z_4^{-1})_{24} > (Z_4 \lhd Z_2^{-1})_{42}$$
$$(Z_2 \lhd Z_5^{-1})_{25} > (Z_5 \lhd Z_2^{-1})_{52}, (Z_3 \lhd Z_4^{-1})_{34} > (Z_4 \lhd Z_3^{-1})_{43}$$
$$(Z_3 \lhd Z_5^{-1})_{35} > (Z_5 \lhd Z_3^{-1})_{53}, (Z_4 \lhd Z_5^{-1})_{45} < (Z_5 \lhd Z_4^{-1})_{54}$$

from which we get $y_4 \succ y_5 \succ y_3 \succ y_2 \succ y_1$.

From the above process, we can see that the intuitionistic fuzzy triangle product can be used to compare the alternatives in multi-attribute decision making with intuitionistic fuzzy information, but the computational complexity increases rapidly as the numbers of the alternatives and attributes increase.

2.9.4 The Application of the Intuitionistic Fuzzy Square Product

From Eq. (2.204), we know that the intuitionistic fuzzy square product $(Z_1 \Box Z_2)_{ij}$ can be interpreted as: it measures the similarity degree of the ith row of an intuitionistic fuzzy matrix Z_1 and the jth row of an intuitionistic fuzzy matrix R_2 mathematically. Therefore, considering the problem stated at the beginning of Sect. 2.9.2, $(Z_i \Box Z_j^{-1})_{ij}$ reflects the similarity of the alternatives y_i and y_j. We can use the following formula to construct an intuitionistic fuzzy similarity matrix for the alternatives y_i $(i = 1, 2, \ldots, n)$:

$$sim(y_i, y_j) = (Z_i \,\square\, Z_j^{-1})_{ij} = \min_{1\leq k\leq n} \left(\mu_{\min(z_{ik}\rightarrow z_{jk}, z_{jk}\rightarrow z_{ik})}, \nu_{\min(z_{ik}\rightarrow z_{jk}, z_{jk}\rightarrow z_{ik})}\right) \tag{2.210}$$

Equation (2.210) has the following desirable properties (Wang et al. 2012):

(1) $sim(y_i, y_j)$ is an IFV.
(2) $sim(y_i, y_i) = (1, 0)$ $(i = 1, 2, \ldots, n)$.
(3) $sim(y_i, y_j) = sim(y_j, y_i)$ $(i, j = 1, 2, \ldots, n)$.

Proof (1) Let's prove that $sim(y_i, y_j)$ is an IFV:

Since the results of $z_{ik} \rightarrow z_{jk}$ and $z_{jk} \rightarrow z_{ik}$ are all IFVs as proven previously, then $\left(\mu_{\min(z_{ik}\rightarrow z_{jk}, z_{jk}\rightarrow z_{ik})}, \nu_{\min(z_{ik}\rightarrow z_{jk}, z_{jk}\rightarrow z_{ik})}\right)$ is an IFV, for any k.

(2) Since

$$sim(y_i, y_i) = (Z_i \,\square\, Z_i^{-1})_{ii} = \min_{1\leq k\leq n} \left(\mu_{\min(z_{ik}\rightarrow z_{ik}, z_{ik}\rightarrow z_{ik})}, \nu_{\min(z_{ik}\rightarrow z_{ik}, z_{ik}\rightarrow z_{ik})}\right)$$

and with Definition 2.4, we can easily know that $sim(y_i, y_i) = (1, 0)$.

(3) Since

$$\begin{aligned} sim(y_i, y_j) &= (Z_i \,\square\, Z_j^{-1})_{ij} = \min_{1\leq k\leq n} \left(\mu_{\min(z_{ik}\rightarrow z_{jk}, z_{jk}\rightarrow z_{ik})}, \nu_{\min(z_{ik}\rightarrow z_{jk}, z_{jk}\rightarrow z_{ik})}\right) \\ &= \min_{1\leq k\leq n} \left(\mu_{\min(z_{jk}\rightarrow z_{ik}, z_{ik}\rightarrow z_{jk})}, \nu_{\min(z_{jk}\rightarrow z_{ik}, z_{ik}\rightarrow z_{jk})}\right) \\ &= (Z_j \,\square\, Z_i^{-1})_{ji} = sim(y_j, y_i) \end{aligned}$$

then $sim(y_i, y_j) = sim(y_j, y_i)$ $(i, j = 1, 2, \ldots, n)$.

From the analysis above, we can know that Eq. (2.210) satisfies the conditions of intuitionistic fuzzy similarity relation, and thus, we can use it to construct an intuitionistic fuzzy similarity matrix.

2.9.5 A Direct Intuitionistic Fuzzy Cluster Analysis Method

After we have gotten an intuitionistic fuzzy similarity matrix R, with this method, there is no need to seek for its equivalent matrix before doing cluster analysis. Starting with an intuitionistic fuzzy similarity matrix, we may get the wanted cluster analysis results as with an intuitionistic fuzzy equivalent matrix, which has been proven strictly (Luo 1989). Luo (1989) introduced a direct method for clustering fuzzy sets which can only consider the membership degrees of fuzzy sets. In this section, we shall introduce a direct intuitionistic fuzzy cluster analysis method, which can take into account both the membership degrees and the non-membership degrees of IFVs under intuitionistic fuzzy environments. The method involves the following steps (Wang et al. 2012):

Step 1 Let $Z = (z_{ij})_{n\times n}$ be an intuitionistic fuzzy similarity matrix, where $z_{ij} = (\mu_{ij}, v_{ij})$ $(i,j = 1,2,\ldots,n)$ are IFVs, then we select one of the elements of Z to determine the confidence level λ_1, which obeys the following principles:

(1) Rank the membership degrees of r_{ij} $(i,j = 1,2,\ldots,n)$ in descending order, and then take $\lambda_1 = (\mu_{\lambda_1}, v_{\lambda_1}) = (\mu_{i_1j_1}, v_{i_1j_1})$, where $\mu_{i_1j_1} = \max\limits_{i,j}\{\mu_{ij}\}$.

(2) If there exist two IFVs $(\mu_{i_1j_1}, v_{i_1j_1})$ and $(\mu_{i_1j_1}, \overline{v}_{i_1j_1})$ in (1), such that $v_{i_1j_1} \neq \overline{v}_{i_1j_1}$ (without loss of generality, let $v_{i_1j_1} < \overline{v}_{i_1j_1}$), then we choose the first one as λ_1, i.e., $\lambda_1 = (\mu_{i_1j_1}, v_{i_1j_1})$.

Then, for each alternative y_i, we let

$$[y_i]_Z^{(1)} = \{y_j | z_{ij} = \lambda_1\} \tag{2.211}$$

In this case, y_i and all of the alternatives in $[y_i]_Z^{(1)}$ are clustered into one type, and each of the other alternatives is clustered into one type.

Step 2 Choose the confidence level λ_2 such that $\lambda_2 = (\mu_{\lambda_2}, v_{\lambda_2}) = (\mu_{i_2j_2}, v_{i_2j_2})$, with $\mu_{i_2j_2} = \max\limits_{(i,j)\neq(i_1,j_1)}\{\mu_{ij}\}$ (in particular, if there exist two or more IFVs whose membership degrees have the same value $\mu_{i_2j_2}$, then we can follow the policy in (2) of Step 1. Then, we let $[y_i]_Z^{(2)} = \{y_j | z_{ij} = \lambda_2\}$, in this case, y_i and all of alternatives in $[y_i]_Z^{(2)}$ are clustered into one type, and each of the other alternatives is clustered into one type. Merging $[y_i]_Z^{(1)}$ and $[y_i]_Z^{(2)}$, we get $[y_i]_Z^{(1,2)} = \{y_j | z_{ij} \in \{\lambda_1, \lambda_2\}\}$, and thus, y_i and all of the alternatives in $[y_i]_Z^{(1,2)}$ are clustered into one type, and the types of the other alternatives keep unchanged.

Step 3 Take the other confidence levels and do cluster analysis following the procedure of Step 2 until all the alternatives are clustered into one type.

From the above processes, we can see that the direct method can realize the cluster analysis just based on the subscripts of alternatives, and there is even no need to get the λ-cutting matrix, which is a notable advantage of the direct method. In practical applications, after choosing some proper confidence levels, we just need to confirm their locations in the intuitionistic fuzzy similarity matrix, and then we can get the types of the considered objects on the basis of their location subscripts.

Example 2.16 (Wang et al. 2012) We use the same example as Example 2.15, and utilize the direct method developed above to classify the five cars, which involves the following steps:

Step 1 By Eq. (2.208), we calculate

$$sim(y_1, y_2) = (Z_1 \square Z_2^{-1})_{12} = \min_{1\leq k\leq 6}\left(\mu_{\min(z_{1k}\to z_{2k}, z_{2k}\to z_{1k})}, v_{\min(z_{1k}\to z_{2k}, z_{2k}\to z_{1k})}\right)$$

and get $sim(y_1, y_2) = (0.7, 0.2)$.

Then we calculate the others in a similar way. Consequently, we get the intuitionistic fuzzy similarity matrix:

$$Z = \begin{pmatrix} (1,0) & (0.7,0.2) & (0.7,0.1) & (0.5,0.3) & (0.5,0.4) \\ (0.7,0.2) & (1,0) & (0.7,0.1) & (0.6,0.1) & (0.6,0.3) \\ (0.7,0.1) & (0.7,0.1) & (1,0) & (0.6,0.1) & (0.5,0.5) \\ (0.5,0.3) & (0.6,0.1) & (0.6,0.1) & (1,0) & (0.6,0.3) \\ (0.5,0.4) & (0.6,0.3) & (0.5,0.5) & (0.6,0.3) & (1,0) \end{pmatrix}$$

Step 2 Choose the confidence levels properly, and get the corresponding clustering results with the direct method:

(1) When $0.7 < \mu_{\lambda_1} \leq 1.0$, by Eq. (2.210), we know that there is no value z_{ij} in R such that $z_{ij} = \lambda_1$, i.e., $[y_i]_Z^{(1)} = \phi$. Thus, each car is clustered into one type: $\{y_1\}$, $\{y_2\}$, $\{y_3\}$, $\{y_4\}$ and $\{y_5\}$.

(2) When $0.6 < \mu_{\lambda_2} \leq 0.7$, we have the following two cases:

(i) $z_{13} = z_{23} = (0.7,0.1)$: In this case, by Eq. (2.209), we know that y_1, y_2 and y_3 can be clustered into one type: $\{y_1, y_2, y_3\}$. Then, by Step 2 of the clustering method, we get that the cars y_i $(i = 1, 2, 3, 4, 5)$ are clustered into three types: $\{y_1, y_2, y_3\}$, $\{y_4\}$ and $\{y_5\}$.

(ii) $z_{12} = (0.7,0.2)$: In this case, y_1 and y_2 can be clustered into one type. Thus, by Step 2 of the clustering method, we know that the cars y_i $(i = 1, 2, 3, 4, 5)$ are also clustered into three types: $\{y_1, y_2, y_3\}$, $\{y_4\}$ and $\{y_5\}$.

(3) When $0.5 < \mu_{\lambda_3} \leq 0.6$, we have the following two cases:

(i) $z_{24} = z_{34} = (0.6,0.1)$: In this case, y_2, y_3 and y_4 can be clustered into one type. Then, merging the clustering results of (1) and (2), we can see that the cars $y_i (i = 1, 2, 3, 4, 5)$ are clustered into two types: $\{y_1, y_2, y_3, y_4\}$ and $\{y_5\}$.

(ii) $z_{25} = (0.6,0.3)$: In this case, y_2 and y_5 can be clustered into one type. Then, merging the clustering results above, it can be obtained that the cars y_i $(i = 1, 2, 3, 4, 5)$ are clustered into one type: $\{y_1, y_2, y_3, y_4, y_5\}$.

Compared with Zhang et al. (2007)'s method, we can know that the direct method with less calculation amount can have better clustering results.

References

Anderberg MR (1972) Cluster analysis for applications. Academic Press, New York

Atanassov K (1983) Intuitionistic fuzzy sets. In: Sgurev V (ed) VII ITKR's session. Central Sci and Technology Library of the Bulgarian Academy of Sci, Sofia

Atanassov K (1986) Intuitionistic fuzzy sets. Fuzzy Sets Syst 20:87–96

Atanassov K (1995) Remark on the intuitionistic fuzzy sets-III. Fuzzy Sets Syst 75:401–402

Atanassov K (1999) Intuitionistic fuzzy sets: theory and applications. Springer, Heidelberg

Atanassov K, Gargov G (1989) Interval-valued intuitionistic fuzzy sets. Fuzzy Sets Syst 31:343–349

Beliakov G, Bustince H, Goswami DP, Mukherjee UK, Pal NR (2011) On averaging operators for Atanassov's intuitionistic fuzzy sets. Inf Sci 181:1116–1124

Beliakov G, James S, Mordelová J, Rückschlossová T, Yager RR (2010) Generalized Bonferroni mean operators in multi-criteria aggregation. Fuzzy Sets Syst 161:2227–2242

Beliakov G, Pradera A, Calvo T (2007) Aggregation functions: a guide for practitioners. Springer, Heidelberg, Berlin, New York

Bezdek JC (1981) Pattern recognition with fuzzy objective function algorithms. Plenum, New York

Bonferroni C (1950) Sulle medie multiple di potenze. Bolletino Matematica Italiana 5:267–270

Boran FE, Genç S, Kurt M, Akay D (2009) A multi-criteria intuitionistic fuzzy group decision making for supplier selection with TOPSIS method. Expert Syst Appl 36:11363–11368

Burillo P, Bustince H (1996) Construction theorems of intuitionistic fuzzy sets. Fuzzy Sets Syst 84:271–281

Bustince H (2000) Construction of intuitionistic fuzzy relations with predetermined properties. Fuzzy Sets Syst 109:379–403

Bustince H, Burillo P (1995) Correlation of interval-valued intuitionistic fuzzy sets. Fuzzy Sets Syst 74:237–244

Cai R, Lei YJ, Zhao XJ (2009) Clustering method based on intuitionistic fuzzy equivalent dissimilarity matrix. J Comput Appl 29:123–126

Chen DS, Li KX, Zhao LB (2007) Fuzzy graph maximal tree clustering method and its application. Oper Res Manag Sci 16:69–73

Chen SM, Tan JM (1994) Handing multicriteria fuzzy decision-making problems based on vague set theory. Fuzzy Sets Syst 67:221–236

Chen TY (2011) Bivariate models of optimism and pessimism in multi-criteria decision-making based on intuitionistic fuzzy sets. Inf Sci 181:2139–2165

Christopher J, Burges C (1998) A tutorial on support vector machines for pattern recognition. Data Min Knowl Discov 2:121–167

Z. Xu, *Intuitionistic Fuzzy Aggregation and Clustering*, Studies in Fuzziness and Soft Computing 279, DOI: 10.1007/978-3-642-28406-9,

Dyckhoff H, Pedrycz H (1984) Generalized means as model of compensative connectives. Fuzzy Sets Syst 14:143–154

Fan ZP, Yu CH, You TH (2004) An FCM clustering algorithm for multiple attribute information with triangular fuzzy numbers. Control Decis 19:1407–1411

Gaertler M (2002) Clustering with spectral methods. Master's thesis, Universitat Konstanz

Gerstenkorn T, Mafiko J (1991) Correlation of intuitionistic fuzzy sets. Fuzzy Sets Syst 44:39–43

Harsanyi JC (1955) Cardinal welfare, individualistic ethics, and interpersonal comparisons of utility. J Political Econ 63:309–321

He ZX (1983) Fuzzy mathematics and its application. Tianjin Science and Technology Press, Tianjing

Hong DH, Choi CH (2000) Multicriteria fuzzy decision making problems based on vague set theory. Fuzzy Sets Syst 114:103–113

Hong DH, Hwang SY (1995) Correlation of intuitionistic fuzzy sets in probability spaces. Fuzzy Sets Syst 75:77–81

Hwang CL, Yoon K (1981) Multiple attribute decision making: methods and applications. Springer, Berlin

Ito K, Kunisch K (2008) Lagrange multiplier approach to variational problems and applications. Society for Industrial and Applied Mathematics, Philadelphia

Klement EP, Mesiar R (2005) Logical, algebraic, analytic, and probabilistic aspects of triangular norms. Elsevier, New York

Klir G, Yuan B (1995) Fuzzy sets and fuzzy logic: theory and applications. Prentice Hall, Upper Saddle River, p 1995

Kohout LJ, Bandler W (1980) Fuzzy relation product as a tool for analysis and synthesis of the behaviour of complex natural and artificial systems. In: Wang SK, Chang PP (eds) Fuzzy sets: theory and application to policy analysis and information systems. Plenum Press, New York, pp 341–367

Kohout LJ, Bandler W (1984) Automatic documentary information retrieval by means of fuzzy relational products. TMS/Stud Manag Sci 20:343–383

Kruskal JB (1956) On the shortest spanning subtree of a graph and the traveling salesman problem. Proc Am Math Soc 7:48–50

Lei TD (1979) Matrix discriminance for equivalence relation. J Shaanxi Normal University (Natural Sci Edition) 1:33–36

Li DF, Chen GH, Huang ZG (2010) Linear programming method for multiattribute group decision making using IF sets. Inf Sci 180:1591–609

Li F, Rao Y (2001) Weighted methods of multi-criteria fuzzy decision making based on vague sets. Comput Sci 28:60–65

Liang ZZ, Shi PF (2003) Similarity measures on intuitionistic fuzzy sets. 2003. Pattern Recognit Lett 24:2687–2693

Liu HW (2005) New similarity measures between intuitionistic fuzzy sets and between elements. Math Comput Model 42:61–70

Liu HW, Wang GJ (2007) Multi-criteria decision making methods based on intuitionistic fuzzy sets. Eur J Oper Res 179:220–233

Luo CZ (1989) An introduction to fuzzy sets. Beijing Normal University Press, Beijing

Mitchell HB (2004) A correlation coefficient for intuitionistic fuzzy sets. Int J Intell Syst 19:483–490

Narukawa Y, Torra V (2006) Non-monotonic fuzzy measure and intuitionistic fuzzy set. Lect Notes Artif Intell 3885:150–160

Nasibov EN, Ulutagay G (2007) A new unsupervised approach for fuzzy clustering. Fuzzy Sets Syst 158:2118–2133

Pelekis N, Iakovidis DK, Kotsifakos EE, Kopanakis I (2008) Fuzzy clustering of intuitionistic fuzzy data. Int J Bus Intell Data Min 3:45–65

Prim RC (1957) Shortest connection networks and some generalizations. Bell Syst Technol J 36:1389–1401

Szmidt E, Kacprzyk J (2000) Distances between intuitionistic fuzzy sets. Fuzzy Sets Syst 114:505–518
Szmidt E, Kacprzyk J (2004) A similarity measure for intuitionistic fuzzy sets and its application in supporting medical diagnostic reasoning. Lect Notes Artif Intell 3070:388–393
Szmidt E, Kacprzyk J (2009a) Amount of information and its reliability in the ranking of Atanassov's intuitionistic fuzzy alternatives. In: Rakus-Andersson E, Yager RR, Ichalkaranje N, Jain LC (eds) Recent advances in decision making. Springer, Berlin, pp 7–19
Szmidt E, Kacprzyk J (2009b) Ranking of intuitionistic fuzzy alternatives in a multi-criteria decision making problem. The 28th North American fuzzy information processing society annual conference (NAFIPS2009), Cincinnati, Ohio, USA, 14–17 June 2009
Szmidt E, Kacprzyk J (2010) On an enhanced method for a more meaningful ranking of intuitionistic fuzzy alternatives. In: Proceedings of the 10th international conference on artificial intelligence and soft computing (ICAISC 2010). Part I, Lecture Notes in Artificial Intelligence, vol 6113. Springer, Berlin, pp 232–239
Tan CQ, Chen XH (2010) Intuitionistic fuzzy Choquet integral operator for multi-criteria decision making. Expert Syst Appl 37:149–157
Torra V (1997) The weighted OWA operator. Int J Intell Syst 12:153–166
Wang PZ (1983) Fuzzy set fuzzy sets theory and applications. Shanghai Scientific and Technical Publishers, Shanghai
Wang TC, Lee HD (2009) Developing a fuzzy TOPSIS approach based on subjective weights and objective weights. Expert Syst Appl 36:8980–8985
Wang XZ, Liu JS (1999) Application of fuzzy relation products in group decision making. Fuzzy Syst Math 13:40–44
Wang WZ, Liu XW (2011) Intuitionistic fuzzy geometric aggregation operators based on Einstein operations. Int J Intell Syst 26:1049–1075
Wang ZJ, Li KW, Wang WZ (2009) An approach to multiattribute decision making with interval-valued intuitionistic fuzzy assessments and incomplete weights. Inf Sci 179:3026–3040
Wang Z, Xu ZS, Liu SS, Tang J (2011) A netting clustering analysis method under intuitionistic fuzzy environment. Appl Soft Comput 11:5558–5564
Wang Z, Xu ZS, Liu SS, Yao ZQ (2012) Direct clustering analysis based on intuitionistic fuzzy implication. Appl Soft Comput, submitted
Wu MC, Chen TY (2011) The ELECTRE multicriteria analysis approach based on Atanassov's intuitionistic fuzzy sets. Expert Syst Appl 38:12318–12327
Xia MM, Xu ZS (2010) Generalized point operators for aggregating intuitionistic fuzzy information. Int J Intell Syst 25:1061–1080
Xia MM, Xu ZS (2011) Generalized intuitionistic fuzzy aggregation based on Hamacher t-conorm and t-norm. Technical report
Xia MM, Xu ZS, Zhu B (2012a) Geometric Bonferroni means with their application in multi-criteria decision making. Knowledge-Based Systems, in press
Xia MM, Xu ZS, Zhu B (2012b) Generalized intuitionistic fuzzy Bonferroni means. Int J Intell Sys 27:23–47
Xia MM, Xu ZS, Zhu B (2012c) Some issues on intuitionistic fuzzy aggregation operators based on Archimedean t-conorm and t-norm. Knowl-Based Syst 31:78–88
Xu ZS (2006) Multiple attribute group decision making with multiplicative preference information on alternatives. In: Proceedings of 2006 international conference on management science and engineering. South-Central University for Nationalities, China, pp 1383–1388
Xu ZS (2007) Intuitionistic fuzzy aggregation operators. IEEE Trans Fuzzy Syst 15:1179–1187
Xu ZS (2009) Intuitionistic fuzzy hierarchical clustering algorithms. J Syst Eng Electron 20:90–97
Xu ZS (2010) Choquet integrals of weighted intuitionistic fuzzy information. Inf Sci 180:726–736
Xu ZS (2011) Approaches to multiple attribute group decision making based on intuitionistic fuzzy power aggregation operators. Knowl-Based Syst 24:749–760

Xu ZS, Cai XQ (2009) Incomplete interval-valued intuitionistic fuzzy preference relations. Int J Gen Syst 38:871–886

Xu ZS, Cai XQ (2010a) Nonlinear optimization models for multiple attribute group decision making with intuitionistic fuzzy information. Int J Intell Syst 25:489–513

Xu ZS, Cai XQ (2010b) Recent advances in intuitionistic fuzzy information aggregation. Fuzzy Optim Decis Mak 9:359–381

Xu ZS, Cai XQ (2012) Intuitionistic fuzzy information aggregation: theory and application. Science Press, Beijing; Springer-Verlag, Berlin

Xu ZS, Chen J (2007a) Approach to group decision making based on interval-valued intuitionistic judgment matrices. Syst Eng-Theory Pract 27:126–133

Xu ZS, Chen J (2007b) On geometric aggregation over interval-valued intuitionistic fuzzy information. The 4th international conference on fuzzy systems and knowledge discovery (FSKD'07). Haikou, China, vol 2, pp 466–471

Xu ZS, Chen J (2008) An overview of distance and similarity measures of intuitionistic fuzzy sets. Int J Uncertain Fuzziness Knowl-Based Syst 16:529–555

Xu ZS, Chen J, Wu JJ (2008) Clustering algorithm for intuitionistic fuzzy sets. Inf Sci 178:3775–3790

Xu ZS, Da QL (2003) An overview of operators for aggregating information. Int J Intell Syst 18:953–969

Xu ZS, Hu H (2010) Projection models for intuitionistic fuzzy multiple attribute decision making. Int J Inf Technol Decis Mak 9:267–280

Xu ZS, Tang J, Liu SS (2011) An orthogonal algorithm for clustering intuitionistic fuzzy information. Inf Int Interdiscip J 14:65–78

Xu ZS, Wu JJ (2010) Intuitionistic fuzzy c-means clustering algorithms. J Syst Eng Electron 21:580–590

Xu ZS, Xia MM (2011) Induced generalized intuitionistic fuzzy operators. Knowl-Based Syst 24:197–209

Xu ZS, Yager RR (2006) Some geometric aggregation operators based on intuitionistic fuzzy sets. Int J General Syst 35:417–433

Xu ZS, Yager RR (2008) Dynamic intuitionistic fuzzy multi-attribute decision making. Int J Approx Reason 48:246–262

Xu ZS, Yager RR (2009) Intuitionistic and interval-valued intuitionistic fuzzy preference relations and their measures of similarity for the evaluation of agreement within a group. Fuzzy Optim Dec Mak 8:123–139

Xu ZS, Yager RR (2010) Power geometric operators and their use in group decision making. IEEE Trans Fuzzy Syst 18:94–105

Xu ZS, Yager RR (2011) Intuitionistic fuzzy Bonferroni means. IEEE Trans Syst Man Cybern-Part B 41:568–578

Yager RR (1988) On ordered weighted averaging aggregation operators in multi-criteria decision making. IEEE Trans Syst Man Cybern 18:183–190

Yager RR (2001) The power average operator. IEEE Trans Syst Man Cybern-Part A 31:724–731

Yager RR (2004) Generalized OWA aggregation operators. Fuzzy Optimization and Decision Making 3:93–107

Yager RR (2009) On generalized Bonferroni mean operators for multi-criteria aggregation. Int J Approx Reason 59:1279–1286

Yang MS, Shih HM (2001) Cluster analysis based on fuzzy relations. Fuzzy Sets Syst 120:197–212

Yoon K (1989) The propagation of errors in multiple-attribute decision analysis: a practical approach. J Oper Res Soc 40:681–686

Zadeh LA (1965) Fuzzy sets. Inf Control 8:338–353

Zahn CT (1971) Graph-theoretical methods for detecting and describing gestalt clusters. IEEE Trans Comput 20:68–86

Zhang HM, Xu ZS, Chen Q (2007) On clustering approach to intuitionistic fuzzy sets. Control Decis 22:882–888

Zhang XM, Xu ZS (2012) A new method for ranking intuitionistic fuzzy values and its application in multi-attribute decision making. Fuzzy Optim Decis Mak 12:135–146

Zhao H, Xu ZS, Ni MF, Liu SS (2010) Generalized aggregation operators for intuitionistic fuzzy sets. Int J Intell Syst 25:1–30

Zhao H, Xu ZS, Liu SS, Wang Z (2012a) Intuitionistic fuzzy MST clustering algorithms. Comput Ind Eng 62:1130–1140

Zhao H, Xu ZS, Wang Z (2012b) Intuitionistic fuzzy clustering algorithm based on Boole matrix and association measure. Int J Inf Technol Decis Mak in press

Index

Z. Xu, *Intuitionistic Fuzzy Aggregation and Clustering*, Studies in Fuzziness and Soft Computing 279, DOI: 10.1007/978-3-642-28406-9,

MIX
Papier aus verantwortungsvollen Quellen
Paper from responsible sources
FSC® C105338

If you have any concerns about our products,
you can contact us on
ProductSafety@springernature.com

In case Publisher is established outside the EU,
the EU authorized representative is:
Springer Nature Customer Service Center GmbH
Europaplatz 3, 69115 Heidelberg, Germany

Printed by Libri Plureos GmbH
in Hamburg, Germany